# Lecture Notes in Computer Science 15380

Founding Editors

Gerhard Goos
Juris Hartmanis

AF148027

The series Lecture Notes in Computer Science (LNCS), including its subseries Lecture Notes in Artificial Intelligence (LNAI) and Lecture Notes in Bioinformatics (LNBI), has established itself as a medium for the publication of new developments in computer science and information technology research, teaching, and education.

LNCS enjoys close cooperation with the computer science R & D community, the series counts many renowned academics among its volume editors and paper authors, and collaborates with prestigious societies. Its mission is to serve this international community by providing an invaluable service, mainly focused on the publication of conference and workshop proceedings and postproceedings. LNCS commenced publication in 1973.

Aaron Marcus · Elizabeth Rosenzweig ·
Marcelo M. Soares · Pei-Luen Patrick Rau ·
Abbas Moallem
Editors

# HCI International 2024 – Late Breaking Papers

26th International Conference on
Human-Computer Interaction, HCII 2024
Washington, DC, USA, June 29 – July 4, 2024
Proceedings, Part VII

 Springer

*Editors*
Aaron Marcus
Aaron Marcus and Associates
Berkeley, CA, USA

Marcelo M. Soares
Federal University of Pernambuco
Recife, Pernambuco, Brazil

Abbas Moallem
San Jose State University
San Jose, CA, USA

Elizabeth Rosenzweig
World Usability Day and Bubble Mountain
Consulting
Newton Center, MA, USA

Pei-Luen Patrick Rau
Tsinghua University
Beijing, China

ISSN 0302-9743          ISSN 1611-3349 (electronic)
Lecture Notes in Computer Science
ISBN 978-3-031-76820-0          ISBN 978-3-031-76821-7 (eBook)
https://doi.org/10.1007/978-3-031-76821-7

This Springer imprint is published by the registered company Springer Nature Switzerland AG
The registered company address is: Gewerbestrasse 11, 6330 Cham, Switzerland

If disposing of this product, please recycle the paper.

# Foreword

This year we celebrate 40 years since the establishment of the HCI International (HCII) Conference, which has been a hub for presenting groundbreaking research and novel ideas and collaboration for people from all over the world.

The HCII conference was founded in 1984 by Prof. Gavriel Salvendy (Purdue University, USA, Tsinghua University, P.R. China, and University of Central Florida, USA) and the first event of the series, "1st USA-Japan Conference on Human-Computer Interaction", was held in Honolulu, Hawaii, USA, 18–20 August. Since then, HCI International is held jointly with several Thematic Areas and Affiliated Conferences, with each one under the auspices of a distinguished international Program Board and under one management and one registration. Twenty-six HCI International Conferences have been organized so far (every two years until 2013, and annually thereafter).

Over the years, this conference has served as a platform for scholars, researchers, industry experts and students to exchange ideas, connect, and address challenges in the ever-evolving HCI field. Throughout these 40 years, the conference has evolved itself, adapting to new technologies and emerging trends, while staying committed to its core mission of advancing knowledge and driving change.

As we celebrate this milestone anniversary, we reflect on the contributions of its founding members and appreciate the commitment of its current and past Affiliated Conference Program Board Chairs and members. We are also thankful to all past conference attendees who have shaped this community into what it is today.

The 26th International Conference on Human-Computer Interaction, HCI International 2024 (HCII 2024), was held as a 'hybrid' event at the Washington Hilton Hotel, Washington, DC, USA, during 29 June – 4 July 2024. It incorporated the 21 thematic areas and affiliated conferences listed below.

A total of 5108 individuals from academia, research institutes, industry, and government agencies from 85 countries submitted contributions, and 1271 papers and 309 posters were included in the volumes of the proceedings that were published just before the start of the conference. Additionally, 222 papers and 104 posters were included in the volumes of the proceedings published after the conference, as "Late Breaking Work". The contributions thoroughly cover the entire field of human-computer interaction, addressing major advances in knowledge and effective use of computers in a variety of application areas. These papers provide academics, researchers, engineers, scientists, practitioners and students with state-of-the-art information on the most recent advances in HCI. The volumes constituting the full set of the HCII 2024 conference proceedings are listed on the following pages.

I would like to thank the Program Board Chairs and the members of the Program Boards of all thematic areas and affiliated conferences for their contribution towards the high scientific quality and overall success of the HCI International 2024 conference. Their manifold support in terms of paper reviewing (single-blind review process, with a minimum of two reviews per submission), session organization and their willingness to act as goodwill ambassadors for the conference is most highly appreciated.

This conference would not have been possible without the continuous and unwavering support and advice of Gavriel Salvendy, founder, General Chair Emeritus, and Scientific Advisor. For his outstanding efforts, I would like to express my sincere appreciation to Abbas Moallem, Communications Chair and Editor of HCI International News.

September 2024                                                    Constantine Stephanidis

# HCI International 2024 Thematic Areas
## and Affiliated Conferences

- HCI: Human-Computer Interaction Thematic Area
- HIMI: Human Interface and the Management of Information Thematic Area
- EPCE: 21st International Conference on Engineering Psychology and Cognitive Ergonomics
- AC: 18th International Conference on Augmented Cognition
- UAHCI: 18th International Conference on Universal Access in Human-Computer Interaction
- CCD: 16th International Conference on Cross-Cultural Design
- SCSM: 16th International Conference on Social Computing and Social Media
- VAMR: 16th International Conference on Virtual, Augmented and Mixed Reality
- DHM: 15th International Conference on Digital Human Modeling & Applications in Health, Safety, Ergonomics & Risk Management
- DUXU: 13th International Conference on Design, User Experience and Usability
- C&C: 12th International Conference on Culture and Computing
- DAPI: 12th International Conference on Distributed, Ambient and Pervasive Interactions
- HCIBGO: 11th International Conference on HCI in Business, Government and Organizations
- LCT: 11th International Conference on Learning and Collaboration Technologies
- ITAP: 10th International Conference on Human Aspects of IT for the Aged Population
- AIS: 6th International Conference on Adaptive Instructional Systems
- HCI-CPT: 6th International Conference on HCI for Cybersecurity, Privacy and Trust
- HCI-Games: 6th International Conference on HCI in Games
- MobiTAS: 6th International Conference on HCI in Mobility, Transport and Automotive Systems
- AI-HCI: 5th International Conference on Artificial Intelligence in HCI
- MOBILE: 5th International Conference on Human-Centered Design, Operation and Evaluation of Mobile Communications

# Conference Proceedings – Full List of Volumes

**https://2024.hci.international/proceedings**

# 26th International Conference on Human-Computer Interaction (HCII 2024)

The full list with the Program Board Chairs and the members of the Program Boards of all thematic areas and affiliated conferences of HCII2024 is available online at:

**http://www.hci.international/board-members-2024.php**

# HCI International 2025 Conference

The 27th International Conference on Human-Computer Interaction, HCI International 2025, will be held jointly with the affiliated conferences at the Swedish Exhibition & Congress Centre and Gothia Towers Hotel, Gothenburg, Sweden, June 22–27, 2025. It will cover a broad spectrum of themes related to Human-Computer Interaction, including theoretical issues, methods, tools, processes, and case studies in HCI design, as well as novel interaction techniques, interfaces, and applications. The proceedings will be published by Springer. More information is available on the conference website: https://2025.hci.international/.

General Chair
Prof. Constantine Stephanidis
University of Crete and ICS-FORTH
Heraklion, Crete, Greece
Email: general_chair@2025.hci.international

**https://2025.hci.international/**

# Contents – Part VII

## Safety, Security and Privacy

# User Experience Design and Evaluation: Novel Approaches and Case Studies

# Toward Individual Displays, the Role of Color Vision

David Alleysson$^{(\boxtimes)}$ and David Meary

Laboratoire de Psychologie et NeuroCognition, CNRS/UGA UMR 5105,
Grenoble, France
david.alleysson@univ-grenoble-alpes.fr

**Abstract.** In order to reduce fatigue and pain caused by prolonged use
of a computer screen, visual displays can be adapted to the individual.
According to the ecological theory of vision, human bodies have adapted
to natural circumstances for vision. Tiredness is the consequence of the
unnatural viewing that the visual system is optimized for. Through the
prism of human color vision, we examined this question. What does the
knowledge of color vision tell us about the inadequacy of displays to
reproduce natural viewing conditions? To argue, we will discuss some
recent results on human color vision geometry obtained by the authors
a few months ago. In a preceding experiment we show that the human
visual system operates a decomposition of the display color space into
a stack of hyperboloid sheets of different photometrical levels. We will
discuss the consequences of this hyperbolic geometry in color vision for
the human computer interface.

**Keywords:** Individual displays · Color Vision · Photometry

## 1 Introduction

Nowadays, most people spend several hours watching a computer screen for
work or for entertainment. Prolonged use of a computer display is not without
consequence on health and tiredness. Increased prevalence of myopia in the young
generation is suspected to correlates with the use of computer displays [1–4],
specifically for children and young adults. But a direct evidence for computer
use as a cause for myopia has not been found, and rather this is the lack of
outdoor activities that is favor to explain the increase of prevalence for children
and young adult [2,4]. However, tiredness and a loose of cognitive abilities is
implied by cognitive load induced by watching a display for long specially for
learning [5,6].

The main researches on individual displays are done from the point of view
of spatial vision. The flatness of the display may induce a lot of optometrical
problems because the eye is not longer train for accommodation and vergence
over objects placed at different depth [7–9]. Color vision is not involved when
one talk about ergonomy of the visual displays. One supposes that color in

display reproduction is good enough to not perturbed the physiology of the visual system. For us, however, this question remains crucial because the way color reproduction quality is estimated do not take into account the variability of color metric induced by the local and global context. Objectives of the present study is to describe the different step in modeling the way a human observer capture light from the display and interpret it as a colored image.

There are three domains to consider. At first, it is the physical capabilities of light produced by a display that depends on the technology used but are often based on additive color mixture of three primary colors. Then there is the physiology of the retina and visual pathways to the brain. This is for sure a complex system that allows the regularization of light, its encoding and its interpretation. The third one is the appearance or sensation of colorfulness. It is construct by the physiology but not necessary directly derived from physiology activity. There are clear evidences that our conscious perception of colors is constructed from the neural activities but not in a trivial way (Think for example of the blind spot [10] or the lack of S-cone photoreceptors [11] in the center of the fovea - those behaviors are not visible in our conscious vision). Therefore, there is a real difference in light acquisition by the visual system and color perception by our consciousness.

In a previous paper [12], we presented a novel method for measuring the color space of an observer using stimuli produced by a computer screen. The advantage of the method is to perform the measurement in-situ, directly on the display system the user will used. Another advantage is the easiness of the experiment that allow to perform on a large population. What we found in that study is (1) that the photometry function in human depends on the resting adaptation making a hyperbolic color space for the steady state space of color vision (2) the geometry shows a large variability between observers. This is these results that we discuss in depth here.

## 2  Geometry of Color Spaces

### 2.1  Space of Light's Spectrum

Usual spectra are emission spectra or the spectral power density of the light source. Alternatively spectra are the reflection of a light source over an object called reflectance spectra. Those two kinds of spectra are called physical because they are positive functions of wavelength, the value of the function being the rate of photon emetted by the light source or reflected by the object. In general here we adopt the position of Schrödinger concerning spectra [13–15]. At any moment of time one can consider a light C as defined by the spectral function $C(\xi)$ in the visible domain. The energy element is given by $C(\xi)d\xi$ neglecting the other term $d\omega$, $d\sigma$, $dt$. Whatever are the solid angle of view $d\omega$, the surface area $d\sigma$ and the measurement time $dt$ they are consider normalized to 1.

To formalize the notion of spectra let's defined some mathematical objects. We consider that a spectra is a function of wavelength rather then frequency. We consider that the visible range of wavelength $\lambda$ is between 380nm to 780nm that is reparameterized into a variable $\xi = \frac{\lambda-380}{780} - 1/2 \in [-1/2, 1/2]$ (See Fig. 1(a)). A light that produce a color C is defined by its spectrum $C(\xi)$ as follow:

$$C: [-1/2, 1/2] \to \mathbb{R}^+ \tag{1}$$
$$\xi \mapsto C(\xi)$$

The variable $\xi$ is either a continuous variable or a discrete variable if the spectrum is measured with a spectrophotometer for instance. To account for both these alternatives we define the spectra of a color C as a ket vector as follow:

$$C(\xi) = |C\rangle = [C(-1/2) \ldots C(1/2)]^t \tag{2}$$

This vector is either infinite if the variable $\xi$ is continuous or finite is the variable is discrete. The rule that belong on such mathematical object is described in Dirac's book [16].

A spectrum can be decomposed over a basis. In the case of $\xi$ is a continuous variable the basis in made on Dirac delta distribution $\delta(\xi)$ and the spectrum vector writes $|C\rangle = [C(\xi)] = [\int_{\xi_i} C(\xi_i)\delta(\xi - \xi_i)d\xi_i]$. If the variable $\xi$ is discrete the integral is replaced by a sum, and the Dirac delta distribution by an indexing vector having a 1 at the position $\xi_i$ and 0 elsewhere. The decomposition of the spectrum into the $\delta$ basis has a physical interpretation, it corresponds to what is called a monochromatic light. Every light can be decomposed into a sum (finite or infinite) of monochromatic lights (Fig. 1(a)).

The space of light spectra can favorably be constructed with the vector notation representing a spectrum. If two lights are added together, say $C_1$ and $C_2$, the resulting spectrum is the sum of their corresponding spectra, $|C_1\rangle + |C_2\rangle = |C_1 + C_2\rangle$. A physical increase of the power of the light source by a positive factor say $k \in \mathbb{R}^+$, corresponds to a multiplication of a specrum by the factor $k|C\rangle = |kC\rangle$. The space of light's spectra is also endowed with an identity element, $|0\rangle$ and associativity, commutativity and distributivity are easily verifiable. But this does not confer to the space of light's spectra the nature of a vector space because the substraction (the inverse of addition) is not defined. It does not exist a light spectrum that could be added to another in order to obtained the zero spectra. Or at least no one knows how to construct such a light couple. But has it is described in [21] the space of positive spectra distribution generate the whole vector space.

## 2.2 Space of Absorption's Spectrum

The main hypothesis for color vision is that there exists neurons that capture light and able to transfer the count of absorbed photons into electrical and chemical power along the visual pathways [17, 18]. Moreover, these neurons can be characterized through their absorption spectra in the visible domain. Absorption spectra are of a different kind because they can take negative values and have not necessarily a physical meaning but rather a physiological meaning.

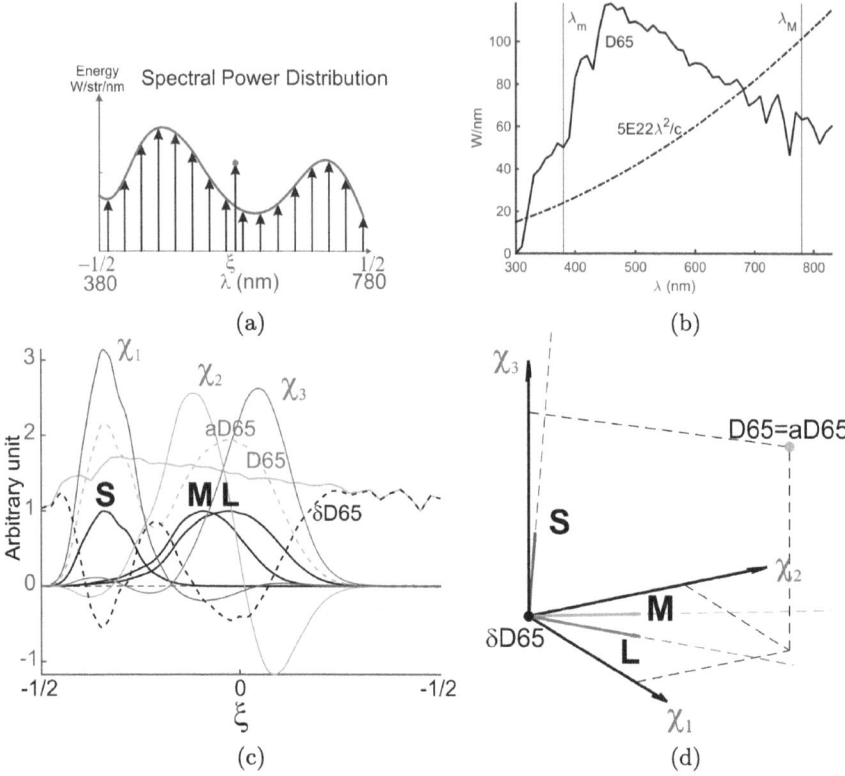

**Fig. 1. Metamerism space.** Metamerism produce by the set of virtual spectra given for the visual system. (a) The continuous spectrum or the spectral power distribution of a light can be decomposed on a succession of vectors for each value of the hue variable $\xi$ corresponding to the wavelength $\lambda$. (b) The daylight illuminant correspond to the radiance of the sun by a clear day and is the closest to the black body at 6500K. (c) Simulation of the measurement of the daylight illuminant with the LMS cone fundamentals. Function aD65 is the approximation of the function D65 when represented by the LMS fundamentals (d) Representation of the geometry described by the mathematics of figure (c). See text for explanation.

At the early stage of vision, neurons compare there activity and the retina first layers can be considered as a comparator. As a consequence the signal carried by neurons in the retina is bipolar having positive or negative values. Bipolarity is illustrated by the so-called ON and OFF pathway inside the retina [19]. Because synapses cannot change there properties with the incoming light (they are either excitatory or inhibitory but cannot change along time of with the incoming signal) the retina system had doubling the pathways. The ON pathway carried the positive part of the signal wherever the OFF pathway carried the negative part of the signal. The flexibility imposed by the retina coding may confer to the space of encoded light the nature of a vector space.

A precise mechanism of encoding of positive spectrum of light into bipolar spectrum carried by neuron in the retina is not possible because it involves the spatial, temporal description of the scene seen. But for our purpose here one has to consider that physical light are confined into a positive part of a vector space. The whole vector space may be covered by virtual spectra that correspond to efficiency functions in the visual system.

## 2.3   Color Space

Adding with several rules the notion of color space can be derived from the vector space described above. Recall it is the space of spectra function or distribution along the visible spectrum that represents the spectral power distribution to the light under study.

The first rule is to add to the vector space of light's spectra the vector space of the observer. In this system a color is a triplet of values being the orthogonal projection from the space of light's spectra to the three-dimensional space of metamer. This expressed as:

$$c \colon \mathcal{L} \times \mathcal{L} \to \mathbb{R}^3 \tag{3}$$

$$(|\psi\rangle, |C\rangle) \mapsto c = \langle\psi|C\rangle = \int_\xi \psi(\xi)C(\xi)d\xi$$

A color, that is to say, the triplet of value that characterized the color in the space, whatever it is a perceptual space or a bio-physical space, it is a three-dimensional object that corresponds to the coordinates of the light C onto the visual system $\psi$ of the observer. Its coordinates depend on both the physical property of the light and the adaptation state of the observer represented by the functions $\psi$ [22].

## 3   Maxwell Triangle

The first color space in that sense is the so-called Maxwell space that index color by their proportion in an additive color mixing [24]. Maxwell even proposed what is called the Maxwell's triangle (Fig. 2) that is a two-dimensional color space, or a chromaticity diagram, that can serve as an map of the different perceived colors induced by the three primaries. He concluded that three primary colors are necessary and sufficient to provide the whole shade of perceived colors. So from a point of view of color synthesis by mixing, the perceived color space is a vector space of dimension three. A two dimensional chromaticity diagram enable the identification of a color by its proportion on the mixed color.

Because three primaries are sufficient and necessary for producing the whole shade of colors, this defined the perceived color space as a three-dimensional vector space. To each color produce by the mixing of three primaries (or the maxwell disk one) we write:

$$[C] \hat{=} r[R] + g[G] + b[B], \tag{4}$$

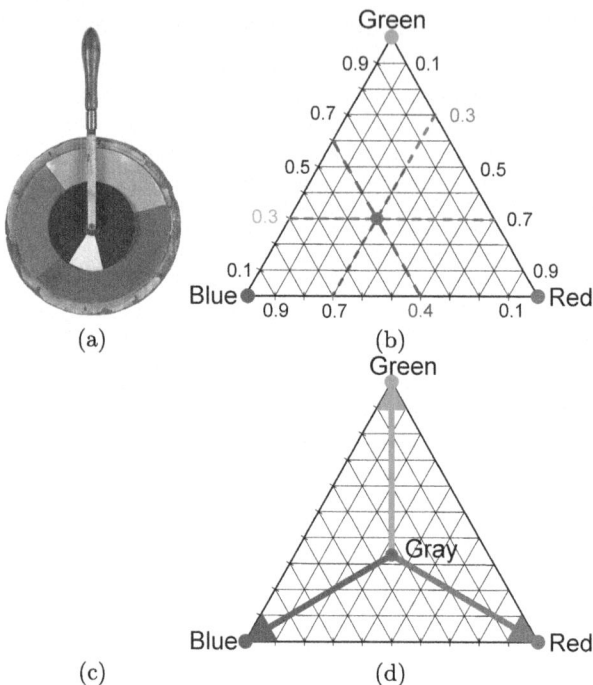

**Fig. 2. Maxwell's triangle.** (a) Maxwell disk. This simple apparatus can be used to simply assessed trichromacy in color vision. The three primaries (external disk) are arranged in a proportion that is used to match a color in the center disk (in black/white here). (b) Maxwell triangle that index of color by its coordinates as a proportion in the mixing. (c) The relationship with spectra is that the primary spectra is represented with a unit vector from the origin. Whatever is the real length of the vectors corresponding to a spectra, the projection of the mixing onto the plane $R + G + B = 1$ made the projective point to follow the law of proportions. (Color figure online)

with $r$, $g$ and $b$ are the proportion of the three primary colors $[R]$, $[G]$ and $[B]$. Thus $(r, g, b) \in [0, 1]^3$ are the coordinates of the color in the color triangle because in the triangle they are constraint by the rule $r + g + b = 1$ thus they are relative proportion. It is not necessary to account for the intensity of $[C]$ because we will represented it in the projective plane. In the three-dimensional space this representation works if the vector for red, green and blue form an orthogonal basis. It is not enough that the basis is unitary or orthogonal it should be both to rely vectors from the three-dimensional vector space to proportions in the triangle. So if:

$$[R] = \begin{bmatrix} 1 \\ 0 \\ 0 \end{bmatrix}, \quad [G] = \begin{bmatrix} 0 \\ 1 \\ 0 \end{bmatrix}, \quad [B] = \begin{bmatrix} 0 \\ 0 \\ 1 \end{bmatrix}, \tag{5}$$

then

$$[C] = r[R] + g[G] + b[B] \tag{6}$$
$$= ((r + g + b)/3) [R + G + B] \tag{7}$$
$$-(r/3)[R - (G + B)/2]$$
$$-(g/3)[G - (R + B)/2]$$
$$-(b/3)[B - (R + G)/2]$$

$$= \begin{bmatrix} R & G & B \end{bmatrix} \begin{bmatrix} r \\ g \\ b \end{bmatrix}$$

$$= \begin{bmatrix} R & G & B \end{bmatrix} \left( \ell + \begin{bmatrix} r - \ell \\ g - \ell \\ b - \ell \end{bmatrix} \right) \tag{8}$$

If the value $r$, $g$ and $b$ are such that they are relative proportions of the primary such that $r + b + b = 1$, then the decomposition into luminance $[L] = [R + G + B]$ and chrominance $[R - L]$, $[G - L]$, $[B - L]$ provides directly the coordinates of the point in the triangle.

In the case where $r + g + b \neq 1$, there is a transformation that normalized the values to sum to one. Writing $[W] = [R] + [G] + [B]$ is equivalent to $w = r + g + b = 3$ with $r = 1$, $g = 1$ and $b = 1$. Let's now called $r' = r/w$, $g' = g/w$, $b' = b/w$. The projection onto the plane orthogonal to $[W]$ defined $[W'] = [W]/3$. So this transformation enable to transform any proportion of the primaries into one that sum to unity. In turn those coordinates are the coordinates in the triangle.

In some sense, the Maxwell triangle has the property that its coordinates express its position on the triangle as well as the normalized intensity of light that composed the stimulus. This property is given by the central projection itself. The measurement is done by $\ell = v^t x$ with $v = [111]^t$, then the locus of constant measure equal one is the plane $v^t x = r + g + b = 1$.

## 4 Projective Hyperbolic Color Space

There is a way to write this in term of spectra directly. Simply replace a color vector $[C]$ by its spectral vector $|C\rangle$. The definition of the observer space is given through the absorption spectrum matrix called $\langle \varphi |$ represented as a vector of bra spectrum, through the following definition:

$$c = \langle \varphi | C \rangle = \begin{bmatrix} \int_\xi \varphi_1(\xi) C(\xi) d\xi \\ \int_\xi \varphi_2(\xi) C(\xi) d\xi \\ \int_\xi \varphi_3(\xi) C(\xi) d\xi \end{bmatrix}, \tag{9}$$

where $\varphi_1$, $\varphi_2$ and $\varphi_3$ are the absorption spectra of the three visual color mechanisms that samples the visual light's spectrum. Because they are absorption spectra they remain positive (or null). But has explained above, they will be treated as bipolar signal at the next step of visual processing. Because of the positive constrained they can not be orthogonal. Imagine a set of three distributions that is mutually orthogonal and positive. They must be separated otherwise there exist some wavelength that integrates by the two mechanisms and this *positive* correlation cannot be compensated by a *negative* correlation because the function are positives.

The only manner to allowed for orthogonality of color mechanisms is to relax the positive constraint, considering the visual system to function with a bipolar signal (ON and OFF pathways for instance). Generalized spectra are spectral function having positive and negative values. Among them some are constraints in a positive domain, the real spectra of light source and object reflectance.

## 4.1 Metamer Orthogonal Projection

The first projection to consider is the projection of spectral power distribution onto a vector on the three-dimensional space of metamerism. Let's defines an operator æ that is a linear application from the space of spectrum into a three-dimensional vector space belonging to $\mathbb{R}^3$.

$$æ: \mathcal{L} \to \mathbb{R}^3 \tag{10}$$
$$|C\rangle \mapsto c = æ(|C\rangle) = \langle \varphi | C \rangle$$

There is however two cases to consider for this operator. Either $\varphi$ is an orthogonal set of function or not. In the first case, we have $æ(|\varphi\rangle) = \langle \varphi | \varphi \rangle = \mathcal{I}$ where $\mathcal{I}$ is the identity matrix of $\mathbb{R}^3$. But if $\varphi$ is not made on orthogonal vectors there is a need to render them orthogonal. The change of space can be given by the following rule. Consider a transformation $\langle \chi | = \langle \varphi | T$. It can be shown that $T = (\langle \varphi | \varphi \rangle)^{-\frac{1}{2}}$ is a symmetric solution $T^t = T$. In that case $\langle \chi | \chi \rangle = \langle \varphi | TT | \varphi \rangle = \langle \varphi | (\langle \varphi | \varphi \rangle)^{-1} | \varphi \rangle = (\langle \varphi | \varphi \rangle)^{-1} \langle \varphi | \varphi \rangle = \mathcal{I}$. Thus $\langle \chi |$ is an orthogonal set of function.

This calculation is illustrated on Fig. 1. In Fig. 1(b) the spectral power distribution of the daylight illuminant D65 [20] is shown along the wavelength variable. Figure 1(c) shows the LMS absorption spectra taken from [25] and now adopted as a standard by the CIE. They are not orthogonal functions based on the scalar product defined above. Let $\langle \varphi_{LMS} |$ be the matrix composed by the three absorption spectra. The intercorrelation $\Gamma$ between cone signals is given by:

$$\Gamma = \langle \varphi_{LMS} | \varphi_{LMS} \rangle / N \tag{11}$$
$$= \begin{bmatrix} 0.2132 & 0.1717 & 0.0107 \\ 0.1717 & 0.1647 & 0.0171 \\ 0.0107 & 0.0171 & 0.1027 \end{bmatrix},$$

$N = 401$ being the number of sample of the discrete absorption spectrum given for a range of 380nm to 780nm, 1nm step. This normalisation by the number of sample point is arbitrary but arrange the curves for having almost same maximum. This gives a transformation $T = \Gamma^{-\frac{1}{2}}$ which is a symetric matrix.

$$T = \Gamma^{-\frac{1}{2}} \tag{12}$$

$$= \begin{bmatrix} 4.4192 & -3.1860 & 0.1393 \\ -3.1860 & 5.3528 & -0.3286 \\ 0.1393 & -0.3286 & 3.1520 \end{bmatrix}$$

The functions $\langle\chi| = \langle\varphi|T$ are represented on Fig. 1(c) as $\langle\chi_1|$, $\langle\chi_2|$ and $\langle\chi_3|$. The figure also show the spectra of daylight illuminant D65 as well its approximation aD65 by the visual system based on the LMS absorption spectra and the residual $\delta D65 = D65 - aD65$. Figure 1d) shows the corresponding color space drawn as a three dimensional space by applying the operator æ on the spectral functions. Because absorption spectra $\langle\varphi|$ are render orthonormal when transformed into $\langle\chi|$, one can represent the basis formed by $\langle\chi|$ as the orthonormal basis of $\mathbb{R}^3$.

The visual system did an approximation if using only three different absorption spectra. This is illustrated on the Fig. 1(c)(d) where D65 is the spectrum of daylight illuminant D65, aD65 its approximation, and $\delta D65$ the residual. In the color space $D65$ and $aD65$ match, they are represented by the same point, whereas $\delta D65$ project onto 0 even if it is not a null function. This spectrum belong to the kernel of the application æ.

From the representation of Fig. 1 it is quite clear that the correlation between L and M axis gives to the space of physical stimulus as regarded by the visual system as a flattened rectangle parallelepiped. But, this is also because we defined the scalar product as a uniform integration along the wavelength variable. This can be discuss and a way to integrate different strength in the wavelength contribution is to integrate a weighting function in the integral as follow:

$$\langle\varphi|C\rangle_\ell = \int_\xi \ell(\xi)\varphi(\xi)C(\xi)d\xi \tag{13}$$

where $\ell(\xi)$ can be chosen as the illuminant [22,23]. Notice that in this case it is equivalent to define a new coordinate system $\langle\varphi'| = \langle\ell\varphi|$. This is a source of ambiguity when considering the estimation of reflectance of object, because the problem of mixing between reflectance and illuminance is multiplicative, its estimation is not trivial. But as we will see on the next paragraph a central projection governed by a Minkowski's quadratic form can help solving the problem by providing a multiplicative decomposition between intensity and color.

## 4.2   Central Projection

A way to extend the properties of the maxwell triangle to the spectral domain is to change the way a measure is defined. It is straight forward to consider a quadratic measure such as $r^2 + g^2 + b^2 = 1$ or in the more general manner:

$$x = [r, b, g] \in \mathbb{R}^3, x^t G x = 1 \tag{14}$$

The metric $G$ can be used for defining a distance $dist(x, y) = \|x - y\| = \sqrt{(x - y)^t G(x - y)}$ if the metric is definite positive. But more interestingly it can provide a pseudo-distance for the case the metric is a Minkowski metric. Moreover, the projection provided by using that metric has the same flavor than the Maxwell triangle. It is oriented and we show above how important is the orientation in the case of the Maxwell disk. From physics to appearance the conversion must account for the placement of the illuminant in the three dimensional space of stimuli.

Using this decomposition the color vector is equal to [26]:

$$c = k(\sqrt{2}(\sinh s)u(\xi) + (\cosh s)\mathbb{1}) \tag{15}$$

where $k$ is the strength of the color, its intensity, $u(\xi) = [\cos 2\pi\xi, \sin 2\pi\xi, 0]^t$ is the hue position, parametrized by the hue angle $\xi$, $\mathbb{1} = [0,0,1]^t$ is the white point, the position of the illuminant in the vector space. Variable $s$ is the saturability calculated as $s = \operatorname{arctanh} \sigma/\Sigma$ where $\sigma$ is the saturation and $\Sigma = \sqrt{2}$ the maximal saturation. It could be shown that at color defined as such follow the metrical property of the Minkowski form:

$$c^t \mathcal{J}c = k^2, \quad \mathcal{J} = \tfrac{1}{2} \begin{bmatrix} -1 & 0 & 0 \\ 0 & -1 & 0 \\ 0 & 0 & 2 \end{bmatrix} \tag{16}$$

which is the equation of an hyperboloid of radius $k$ inscribed into a cone defined by its envelop $x^t \mathcal{J}x = 0$. But those two later equations are not expressed in the basis $\langle\varphi|$ nor the basis $\langle\chi|$. It is expressed in the basis called $\langle\psi|$ that writes:

$$\langle\psi| = P\langle\chi| = PT^{-1}\langle\varphi|, \quad P = \frac{1}{\sqrt{3}} \begin{bmatrix} -\frac{1}{\sqrt{2}} & \sqrt{2} & -\frac{1}{\sqrt{2}} \\ -\frac{\sqrt{6}}{2} & 0 & \frac{\sqrt{6}}{2} \\ 1 & 1 & 1 \end{bmatrix} \tag{17}$$

From a color vector $c$, the parameters $k$, $s$ and $\xi$ can be expressed as $k = \sqrt{c^t \mathcal{J}c}$, $s = \operatorname{arctanh} \sqrt{c_1^2 + c_2^2}/(\sqrt{2}c_3)$, $\xi = \arctan c_2/c_1$.

Notice that with the parameter $\Sigma = \sqrt{2}$ we have a canonical transformation between the linear central projection of the Maxwell disk and the central hyperbolic projection. Canonical in the sense that both $\langle\chi|$ and $\langle\psi|$ are orthogonal and normed basis which are canonical basis of $\mathbb{R}^3$ making the transformation between them as a rotation $P$. Moreover, canonical because the expression of linear projective geometry in $\langle\chi|$ is made canonically (i.e. the denominator of the projector is $r+g+b$) as well as the expression of hyperbolic projective geometry in $\langle\psi|$ (matrix $\mathcal{J}$ is a diagonal matrix).

The two representations (linear and hyperbolic) are illustrated in Fig. 3. Linear projective geometry with the maxwell triangle defined two planes. $P_1$ is the projection plane and $P\infty$ is the plane to infinity. Any point $p$ corresponding to a color stimulus is include into the cone formed by its envelop $\delta C$ and the plane $P_1$. This is because any reflected light is the product between the illuminant $OW$ and a function restricted to the domain $[01]$ and is limited in saturation by the envelopp of the cone. Instead of defining linear geometry one can defined a hyperbolic geometry, given by the cone and the unitary hyperboloid $H_1$.

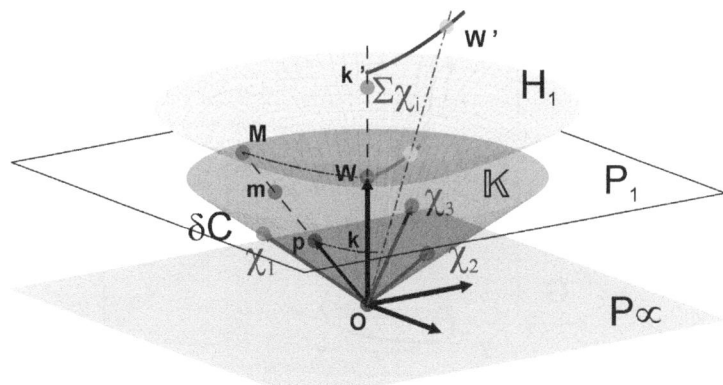

**Fig. 3. Yilmaz Color Solid.** Comparison between linear projective geometry and hyperbolic projective geometry. Linear projective geometry defined two planes $P_1$ and $P_\infty$. A point $p$ corresponding to a color stimulus is projected into the chromaticity diagram or projective plane $P_1$ onto the point m. Alternatively it is projected onto the point M in the unitary hyperboloid $H_1$ of the hyperbolic model.

The change of model from the linear projective geometry and hyperbolic projective geometry is not a big gap because the position of the symmetry axis, the white, in the hyperbolic projective geometry is similar to that of linear geometry. Only the distance between colored stimulus is changed over the two geometries. In projective terms, this is the surface of projection which provide an isoluminant surface that change from a plane in linear geometry to a hyperboloid in hyperbolic geometry.

## 5    Conclusion and Discussion

For considering color vision aspect in human computer interaction one have to consider three steps instead than two. The two classical steps are biophysics and neurosciences that fill the gap between physics and physiology for the former and the gap between physiology and conscience for the later. Here we show the need for a decomposition into three steps (Fig. 4). The physical composition of lights generates a vector space on which the geometry is linear, because spectra add together in a mixing. The physiological space which corresponds to the measurement by the visual system rather interprets as hyperbolic geometry to account for the circularity of the spectrum locus. It is likely that the perceptual space is circular but even more, perfectly circular, to allowed for a constancy of perception whatever is the orientation of the white.

This is the view entertained by Yilmaz and its predecessor working on the geometry of color. But this state of fact can be considered the steady-state of the color vision space. The steady state can only be obtained when the observer see a unique color. When two colors are involved in the stimulus, the adaptation

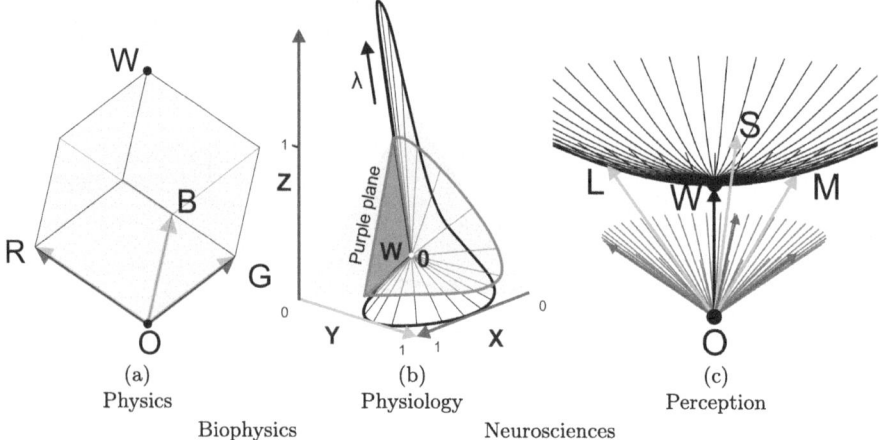

**Fig. 4. The wishing conversion between spaces** (a) Physical space is design from the additive synthesis of colors that stipulate a vector addition rule. Notice that this is realistic from the rule of spectra operation because spectra add in a mixing. (b) Physiological space and (c) Perceptual space. Those spaces shared some common components but the relationship between them is still unknown. From physics point of view the decomposition with disciplines is about biophysics of vision and neurosciences of vision. But from a mathematical psychophysics, the decomposition is rather between physical space of light, physiological space of light and perceptual space of light. Those different space can be linked together through transformation on projective space of dimension three.

state of the observer can navigate in between them [27]. In the experiment we did [12] for measuring the color space of an individual watching a computer screen, we used a fixed color point $p$ that cover the whole pixels of the display. Around that point we perform two sessions of minimum motion in a central visual area (approx. 4°), minimizing the strength of the modulation. Because adaptation state is maintain as fixed as possible, the direction of the luminous vector (estimated as the direction for which their is no motion with the minimum motion experiment, i.e. the photometric direction) can be measured precisely. Those vectors form a vector field that is sightly convergent showing a hyperbolic metric for the whole steady color space. This hyperbolic space is the multi-adapted steady space that represent the global extend of the color space of the observer when steadily adapted to each and every point of the color space. But from one point to the other, the adaptation may have changed and for sure have changed. Again this is the only way to have a fixed adaptation state of the observer and a corresponding multi-adapted global steady color space of the observer.

What happens when the observer leaves the steady state is the future question for a color vision science that may predict or explain how spectra are transformed into colors by the visual system. What is evident from the analysis here is that there is a kind of transformation of geometry from linear to hyperbolic.

Adaptation can be seen as a homomorphism between hyperbolic spaces having different luminous axis and/or different basis and/or different origins [23]. Using projective geometry of dimension three those transformations should be set up as homographies that change from linear to hyperbolic geometries and from hyperbolic to hyperbolic geometry for accounting adaptation.

There is still a long route for enabling the correspondence between spectra and colors. Displays have been design on technological constraint and good compromise have been found to render the image perceptually similar to the real scene. But physiological space is different than perceptual space and the best color rendering is not a guarantee of the best safety in using. There is probably a room to modify images content in order to follow the geometry of physiology without perturbing much the appearance of the image.

# References

1. Enthoven, C.A., Tideman, J.W.L., Polling, J.R., Yang-Huang, J., Raat, H., Klaver, C.C.: The impact of computer use on myopia development in childhood: the generation R study. Prev. Med. **132**, 105988 (2020)
2. Mutti, D.O., Zadnik, K.: Is computer use a risk factor for myopia? J. Am. Optom. Assoc. **67**(9), 521–530 (1996)
3. Fernández-Montero, A., et al.: The impact of computer use in myopia progression: a cohort study in Spain. Prev. Med. **71**, 67–71 (2015)
4. Lanca, C., Saw, S.M.: The association between digital screen time and myopia: a systematic review. Ophthalmic Physiol. Opt. **40**(2), 216–229 (2020)
5. Hollender, N., Hofmann, C., Deneke, M., Schmitz, B.: Integrating cognitive load theory and concepts of human-computer interaction. Comput. Hum. Behav. **26**(6), 1278–1288 (2010)
6. Ayres, P., Van Gog, T.: State of the art research into cognitive load theory. Comput. Hum. Behav. **25**(2), 253–257 (2009)
7. Jaiswal, S., Asper, L., Long, J., Lee, A., Harrison, K., Golebiowski, B.: Ocular and visual discomfort associated with smartphones, tablets and computers: what we do and do not know. Clin. Exp. Optom. **102**(5), 463–477 (2019)
8. Hayes, J.R., Sheedy, J.E., Stelmack, J.A., Heaney, C.A.: Computer use, symptoms, and quality of life. Optom. Vis. Sci. **84**(8), E738–E755 (2007)
9. Collier, J.D., Rosenfield, M.: Accommodation and convergence during sustained computer work. Optometry-J. Am. Optom. Assoc. **82**(7), 434–440 (2011)
10. Ramachandran, V.S.: Blind spots. Sci. Am. **266**(5), 86–91 (1992)
11. Calkins, D.J.: Seeing with S cones. Prog. Retin. Eye Res. **20**(3), 255–287 (2001)
12. Alleysson, D., Méary, D.: Measurement of individual color space using a luminous vector field. JOSA A **40**(3), A199–A207 (2023)
13. Schrödinger, E.: Grundlinien einer theorie der farbenmetrik im tagessehen. Ann. Phys. **368**(21), 427–456 (1920)
14. MacAdam, D.L.: Sources of Color Science. MIT Press, Cambridge (1970)
15. Niall, K.K.: Erwin Schrödinger's Color Theory. Translated with Modern Comentary. Springer, Cham (2017)
16. Dirac, P.A.: The mathematical foundations of quantum theory. In: Mathematical Foundations of Quantum Theory. Academic Press (1978)

17. Van De Grind, W.A., Koenderink, J.J., Bouman, M.A.: Models of the processing of quantum signals by the human peripheral retina. Kybernetik **6**, 213–227 (1970)
18. Koenderink, J.J., Van de Grind, W.A., Bouman, M.A.: Models of retinal signal processing at high luminances. Kybernetik **6**(6), 227–237 (1970)
19. Nelson, R., Kolb, H.: ON and OFF pathways in the vertebrate retina and visual system. Vis. Neurosci. **1**, 260–278 (2004)
20. Commission Internationale de l'Éclairage. CIE 15.2-1986: Colorimetry (1986)
21. Benzécri, J.P.: La vision des couleurs. I. Structure physique des stimuli et axiomes de l'équivalence sensorielle. Les cahiers de l'analyse des données **6**(1), 59–85 (1981)
22. Benzécri, J.P.: La vision des couleurs. II. Qualités physiologiques des stimuli colorés: la photométrie. Les cahiers de l'analyse des données **6**(2), 145–155 (1981)
23. Yilmaz, H.: On color perception. Bull. Math. Biophys. **24**, 5–29 (1962)
24. Koenderink, J.J.: Color for the Sciences. MIT Press, Cambridge (2010)
25. Stockman, A., Sharpe, L.T.: The spectral sensitivities of the middle-and long-wavelength-sensitive cones derived from measurements in observers of known genotype. Vision. Res. **40**(13), 1711–1737 (2000)
26. Alleysson, D., Meary, D.: Hyperbolic models for color vision (2019). https://hal.science/hal-03515596/
27. Alleysson, D., Méary, D.: Neurogeometry of color vision. J. Physiol.-Paris **106**(5–6), 284–296 (2012)

# Improving the Understandability and Actionability of Clinical Notes to Support Self-care in Patients with a Chronic Disease: A Pilot Study Applies Survey and Eye-Tracking Approach

Tseng-Ping Chiu[1] [ID], Tripura Vithala[2], Shu-Ching Li[1], Ling-Wen Huang[1], Somya Pandey[2], Hexuan Liu[3], and Danny T. Y. Wu[2(✉)]

[1] Industrial Design Department, National Cheng Kung University, Tainan, Taiwan 701, People's Republic of China
[2] College of Medicine, University of Cincinnati, Cincinnati, OH 45221, USA
mattchiu@gs.ncku.edu.tw
[3] School of Criminal Justice, University of Cincinnati, Cincinnati, OH 45221, USA

**Abstract.** The OpenNotes movement, advocating for healthcare transparency, has positively impacted over 50 million patients by sharing clinical notes. Although note sharing has many positive benefits, such as enhancing medication adherence and communication, patients, particularly with low health literacy, may not be able to understand the notes written by physicians due to medical jargon and complex terminology. To address this, we propose an informatics-based approach to help simplify clinic notes in order to help improve understandability and actionability. This paper outlines the pilot study conducted with clinical notes from diabetic patients in a academic teaching hospital. These de-identified notes were revised using a semi-automated pipeline. Nine pre-medical undergraduate students evaluated the understandability and actionability of the original and revised notes. The results showed significant improvements in both aspects. Eye-tracking data indicated increased focus on the revised notes, especially on sections explaining diabetic terms, despite their smaller size compared to the main text. This study suggests the potential for improvements in clinic notes for diabetic patients using informatics and form a solid basis for large scale research and development to help promote shared decision making with patients.

**Keywords:** Understandability and Actionability of Clinical Notes · Diabetes Patients · User-Center Design · Visual Attention · Eye-Tracking Studies

## 1 Introduction

In recent decades, medical providers, health systems, and legislators have prioritized increasing patient's access to their health information by sharing clinical notes. Clinical notes are written from a clinician's perspective for care team communication and handoff.

© The Author(s), under exclusive license to Springer Nature Switzerland AG 2025
A. Marcus et al. (Eds.): HCII 2024, LNCS 15380, pp. 17–29, 2025.
https://doi.org/10.1007/978-3-031-76821-7_2

These notes capture chief complaints, review of systems, physical exam findings, vital signs, diagnosis, and treatment plans by following the Subjective-Objective-Assessment-Plan (SOAP) structure. Increasing transparency and accessibility of these notes can bridge enhanced communication within patient-provider relationships.

Specifically, the initial OpenNotes study, conducted in 2010 [1], surveyed both patients and physicians in a variety of rural and urban healthcare settings on the impact of clinical note-sharing via online portals [2]. The study participants highlighted common concerns such as patient privacy, note comprehensibility, increased workload burden, and the possibility of reduced patient-provider collaboration. However, they also perceived significant benefits including increased treatment adherence, improved trust and communication between patients and providers, and better overall health outcomes, particularly for chronic condition management [3]. In the past few decades, other Open-Notes studies generated empirical evidence for the potential benefits of note-sharing, such as patient autonomy, transparency, and stronger patient-physician relationships [4]. Additionally, a study conducted on patients in urban, underserved areas found that the subjects believed that online note-sharing would improve their confidence in managing their health, increase their medical knowledge and awareness, and help their relationship with their medical provider(s) [5]. Those who access and utilize doctor's notes through the portal become better equipped to manage their conditions. The primary aim of note-sharing is to empower patients, improve treatment adherence, and foster effective communication with their family, friends, and healthcare team, the notes are written for those with higher health literacy (HL) and numeric literacy [5].

HL is the ability to understand, contextualize, and make well-informed decisions based on health information. A subpopulation of patients with chronic conditions, particularly those with low HL, encounter additional obstacles that hinder their ability to access quality care. These individuals are usually 65 and older, with limited education, income below $15,000, are non-native English speakers [6], and face challenges in understanding written and oral instructions given by healthcare professionals. Specifically, they have more difficulty following directions such as managing prescriptions, scheduling appointments, and navigating the healthcare system effectively [7]. The 2003 National Adult Assessment of Literacy found that approximately 36% of Americans (77 million) have basic or below basic health literacy skills, leading to poor long-term health outcomes, limited understanding of their medical condition, and decreased medical access overall [5]. Non-native English speakers are even more susceptible to misinterpretation of instructions due to the ambiguity of clinical notes. For example, trauma referring to the brain due to a "physical blow" can also suggest psychological trauma, making it challenging for patients to fully comprehend notes to act. Consequently, a high HL is correlated to having higher levels of shared decision-making between patients and physicians and promotes positive health outcomes. Therefore, understanding HL's nature and role in interactions with social determinants of health (SDoH) can indicate how to best design low HL-targeting interventions for patients who struggle to understand health information.

One such intervention can be restructuring the clinic notes and summarizing and simplifying the language used in them to be more readable and understandable to patients. For example, studies conducted in 2015 suggested the use of the Universal Medication

Schedule to improve understanding of medication use instructions for patients taking multiple medications [8]. This is particularly important for people with chronic conditions since these conditions such as diabetes are often associated with comorbidities like obesity, cardiovascular disease, kidney disease, neuropathy, and mental health issues. Treatment and prevention strategies to mitigate the deterioration of these conditions involve strict medication adherence. Additionally, studies found that summarization of information, larger font sizes, and elimination of medical jargon helped create inclusive patient-centered notes [9, 10]. Despite these potential benefits, it is impractical for clinicians to spend addition time in modifying existing notes or creating separate patient-centered notes in their busy clinical routines [11, 12]. To address this gap, the present study focused on diabetic patients and proposes a preliminary informatics method to automatically revise clinical notes and generate a revised version that has higher understandability and actionability. It is hypothesized that 1) the revised notes have higher understandability and actionability than the original notes, and 2) the revised notes have more focused attention than the original notes.

## 2   Literature Review

### 2.1   Clinic Notes

In order to further contextualize this research, a literature review was conducted. In particular, we looked into the effect that low health literacy (HL) might have on the shared decision-making abilities of patients. Adequate HL has been shown to help patients better manage their health and understand their treatment. Moreover, they are better able to communicate with healthcare providers and participate in the decision-making process [13–16]. On the contrary, low HL can have adverse effects, such as a poor understanding of a treatment plan. Additionally, patients may not be able to interpret results correctly, or understand the advantages and disadvantages of a particular treatment. Low HL can also lead to a poorer quality of life, as those with low HL may not be able to adopt a healthy lifestyle [5, 16]. HL is also heavily related to Social Determinants of Health (SDoH), as shown by a literature search conducted in-house [17]. Low HL may severely decrease a patient's ability to understand their clinic notes and follow doctor's orders, making the benefits from note sharing almost null.

### 2.2   Eye-Tracking Basic Theory and Applications

Eye-tracking has the potential to offer insights into problem solving, reasoning, mental imagery and search strategies. The use of eye-tracking technology has a long history in the fields of marketing and psychology. For example, eye-tracking has been used in measuring how the degree of attention to a given brand on a shelf is correlated with subsequent purchasing decisions [18, 19]. The eye-tracking technique is a method used for observing and recording the movement of the human eye, which can be used to identify eye movement patterns and behavior among consumers receiving visual stimuli or viewing products. Information about consumers' eye-fixation behavior is collected in an objective, rapid, and non-invasive way [20]. Through recording the duration of a consumer's fixation and the areas of the product where consumers fixate when viewing packaging, eye-tracking technology can help in determining how packaging design attracts consumer attention. Eye movements are typically categorized into saccades and fixations, with the latter describing the eye in a relatively fixed state in which focus remains on an area the consumer is interested in for more than 60 ms (ms), while the former describes rapid eye movements between parts of the visual field, with the focus of the eye moving between two areas of the visual field in order to locate "Areas of Interest" (AOI) and obtain more visual information [21]. Past research has also pointed out more characters on the display would distract users' attention and then influence search behaviors [22].

## 3   Methods

### 3.1   Study 1 of Survey Design

The development and evaluation of a proof-of-concept note revision pipeline encompasses five key stages. Initially, clinical notes from diabetic patients were collected from the EHR system. Subsequently, a small set of clinic notes were randomly sampled, and eligibility criteria were determined. These notes were then revised using a semi-automated method, involving reorganization, summarization, simplification, and visualization steps, with input from clinician collaborators. After revision, a pilot evaluation was conducted using the PEMAT-P survey. Each participant assessed five revised notes, and data were analyzed using t-test to compare understandability and actionability scores between the original and revised notes. Additionally, short exit interviews were conducted to gather feedback on the strengths and weaknesses of the revised notes.

**Note Selection.** The process to develop and evaluate a proof-of-concept note revision pipeline was divided into five stages: 1) extraction, 2) sampling, 3) exclusion, 4) revision, and 5) evaluation. First, clinical notes of the diabetic patient population were collected from our institution's EHR system, resulting in 268,697 notes for 31,547 patients (UC IRB #2021-0659). Second, 100 clinic notes were randomly sampled. Third, two members (reviewers) of the research team reviewed each of them to determine eligibility. The first criterion is whether a note contains all the following subjects: Subjective, Objective, Assessment, and Plan. Additionally, an eligible note must have lab data that can be visualized, terminology, and details that can be summarized. Any discrepancy was resolved by a third reviewer. Fifteen notes (N = 15) were determined to be eligible for the pilot evaluation. The reasons for exclusion for the clinic notes include: One lined note (N = 18); Not contain all 4 sections of SOAP (N = 44), No lab data (N = 18), Not diabetes-related (N = 5). In the fourth (revision) stage, these notes were revised using a semi-automated method developed by the research team. Before revision, these 15 notes were de-identified.

**Note Revision.** The revision (fourth) stage was divided into four steps: 1) reorganization, 2) summarization, 3) simplification, and 4) visualization. Two researchers reorganized the 15 notes from the existing SOAP (Subjective, Objective, Assessment, and Plan) format into the new SAPO format, which was reviewed and agreed by the clinician collaborators (Drs. Michael Binder and Hillary Liebler). Next, a validated algorithm

(Python library SUMY27), was used to summarize each individual section. To reduce clutter, within the objective section, the Review of Systems (ROS) section was omitted, as the relevant results were summarized within the Assessment section. The lab values from the test were retained. In the third step, text simplification was accomplished using frequently used diabetes-related terms from the American Diabetes Association's (ADA28). Since the revised notes were presented in a Microsoft Word document, terms definitions were left as comments to simulate an interactive user interface. In the fourth step, relevant lab data in each note were visualized in graphs. Lab data visualization was restricted to the metrics deemed important by the ADA (e.g., A1C, weight, Creatinine), and the rest was omitted (e.g., LDLs, Bilirubin). Figure 1 shows an example of the revised notes, where the highlighted terms (T2DM, Trulicity, and Hypoglycemia) have an explanation as a comment in the Word document.

**Participant.** Once the notes were all revised following the process described above, the research team conducted a pilot evaluation, where 9 pre-med undergraduate students with above average health literacy were recruited as a proxy of patients to score the deidentified original clinic note and the revised clinic note using the Agency for Healthcare for Research and Quality (AHRQ)'s Patient Education Materials Assessment Tool for Printable Materials (PEMAT-P). Prior to scoring, participants completed the AHRQ's SAHL-E survey to score their English health literacy levels.

**Procedure.** Each participant was randomly assigned to five revised notes, and each note was assessed by three participants. After viewing the original and the revised notes, each participant filled out the PEMAT-P survey to assess the understandability and actionability of each version of notes. The AHRQ's PEMAT-P was used to score and measure the change in understandability and actionability between the deidentified original clinical note and the revised clinical note. The PEMAT-P is categorized into Content, Word Choice & Style, Use of Numbers, Organization, Layout & Design, Use of Visual Aids, and Actionability. Each statement had 3 possible responses: Disagree = 0, Agree = 1, or N/A. Following completion of the PEMAT-P, a short exit interview was conducted to identify strengths and weaknesses of the revised notes. In terms of data analysis, the understandability and actionability scores of the original and the revised notes were compared using a t-test.

**Measurement.** The exit interview consisted of three questions: "What worked best in the revised note?", "What did not work well in the revised note?", and "Do you have any specific suggestions for the revised note?" These questions were collected in the free-text format, and the participants were allowed five to ten minutes to type in answers to the questions. The understandability and actionability scores of the original and the revised notes were compared using a t-test. This analysis was required to address our first hypothesis, that the revised notes would have a greater understandability and actionability score than the original notes. On the other hand, the interview responses were analyzed thematically following the 6 steps of a best practice [23]. One independent researcher reviewed all the responses for each question, generated codes, and identified themes for the data.

## 3.2   Study 2 of Eye-Tracking Experiment

**Participant.** As mentioned above, 9 undergraduate medical students with above-average health literacy were recruited as patient proxies, and none of them had eye diseases or wore pupil-dilating lenses that may affect the accuracy of the eye tracking activities in the present study.

**Material.** The experimental stimuli, as mentioned earlier, consists of two versions: the Original Note and the Revised Note. Each document contains one original note paired with its revised version. A total of 14 sets of "documents" were randomly assigned to nine participants, with each participant reviewing five sets of notes. Each "documents" were named with an "N" followed by a number in the following text. During the experiment, the selected presentation screens primarily focused on "text", during the data analysis process, experimental data was selected from three groups, they are Group 1-N04, Group 2-N14, and Group 3-N03. When analyzing data, Area of Interest (AOI) delineation was done with a focus on the "Main Document Area" and the "Note Area" for comparison purposes.

**Procedure.** This study conducted experiments with participants in a natural and comfortable posture, with their eyes approximately 60 cm away from the screen. The eye-tracking system used in this experiment was Tobii Pro, with a sampling rate of 60 Hz, meaning it sampled eye movements every $1/60^{th}$ of a second. This software calculates the vector of the participant's eye movements to correspond to the coordinates on the screen. In this study, if a participant's gaze remained at a certain position on the screen for more than 60 ms, it was defined as a fixation; if it was less than 60 ms, it was defined as a saccade. Eye movement data were captured, recorded, and analyzed using analysis software. Tobii Pro's eye-tracking equipment consists of a high-speed processing personal computer (PC) coupled with an eye-tracking recording device (Tobii Pro nano Eye-tracker), mainly used to record a large amount of eye movement data. Another PC served as the display screen for experimental stimuli (Display PC). When the Tobii nano is connected to the PC, eye-tracking experiments can be performed using Tobii Pro Lab software, enabling the integration of stimulus graphics data with eye movement data. Tobii Pro's eye-tracking equipment records eye positions using cameras to measure eye movement and pupil dilation. The eye tracker (Tobii Pro nano) is shaped like a rectangular bar and can be directly attached to the bottom of a laptop screen or a multifunctional display screen. It is equipped with two cameras to record the positions of the left and right eyes and the size of the pupils. Eye movement is calculated based on the movement of the pupils and iris reflections. At the front end of this eye tracker, there is a camera corresponding to four sensors on the screen to calibrate the position of the head (as Fig. 1.).

The experimental procedure for this stage of the research is as follows:

1. *Preparatory Setup*: Participants undergo familiarization with the equipment and procedures, including complete routine calibration training.
2. *Eye Data Calibration*: Following the eye calibration test, the eye movement data of the participants are recorded and documented using Tobii Pro Lab software. Participants were asked to carefully observe the calibration target when it appeared and

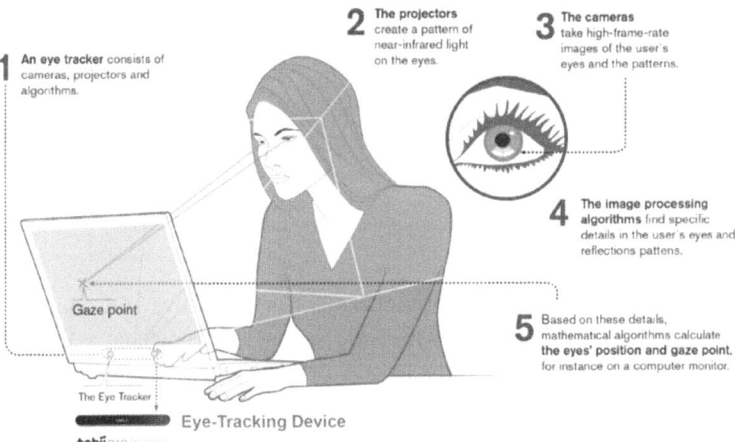

**Fig. 1.** Eye-tracking Equipment and Techniques Used in this Study

then calibrate it using an automatic calibration method. The calibration targets were displayed sequentially, one at a time. After the calibration was completed, all calibration targets were displayed simultaneously, allowing the operator to visually inspect the calibration results while the participants viewed the targets and determine if the calibration quality was satisfactory.

3. *Practice Session*: Participants practice viewing several experimental samples to avoid any potential psychological factors due to unfamiliarity with the stimuli, thus minimizing interference with the experiment.

4. *Formal Experiment:* The main experiment begins, where participants browse through the word documents assigned to their group without any time or length restrictions and scanning through eye-tracking equipment. The experiment concludes once the participant has finished viewing all assigned documents. The collected data were then transferred back to the Display PC for storage.

**Measurement.** The fixation structure can reflect the method by which participants perceive information encoded within graphics (considered as an AOI). In addition, visit (the duration of time spent visiting an AOI) reflects the method by which participants compare information between images. Participants will enter an AOI multiple times before making a decision, or, in more complex circumstances, after entering other AOIs multiple times. Therefore, the duration and count of fixations and visits are very important aspects of our experimental analysis. See Fig. 2 for further explanation. In this figure, "AOI 1" has three visits and four fixations (the 4 circles numbered).

*Total Fixation Duration.* The total duration of each individual fixation within one AOI is measured. To calculate the descriptive statistics (e.g. mean and standard deviation).

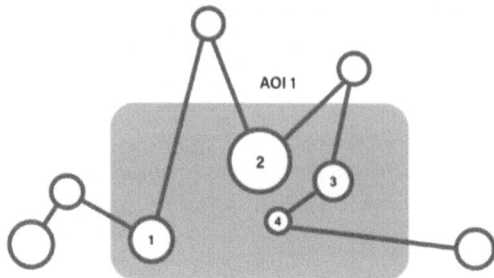

**Fig. 2.** Illustration demonstrating AOI

*Visit Count.* This approach counts the number of visits to an active AOI, which represents the number of times the participants viewed the AOI. A visit is defined as the time period between the primary fixation point on a specific AOI and the end of the last fixation point, while no fixations have occurred outside this specific AOI. Note that a visit is simply a glance that does not include the initial saccade into an AOI. A visit may also include blinks.

*Attention Ratio.* The proportion of total gaze duration on the AOI relative to the overall stimulus. A higher value indicates a higher level of attention and attractiveness to the participants. This value, obtained through categorizing and aggregating AOIs, provides users with insights into the distribution of attention across page content.

*Effective Attention Ratio.* The actual proportion of effective attention generated during navigation within a specific AOI. A higher value indicates that participants are more focused on navigating through that content.

## 4  Results

### 4.1  Data Analysis for Study 1: Survey Design

**Survey Data Analysis.** As shown in Table 1, a significance was shown between the original clinic notes and the revised clinic notes in the overall PEMAT-P score ($P < 0.01$). Furthermore, the revised notes improved the understandability more than the actionability of the documents. Analysis at the document level showed that Document 2 achieved the greatest improvement with details about a check-up appointment. The free-text feedback indicates the original notes contained abundant undefined medical abbreviations, disorganized spacing and formatting, and inconsistent narrating. The revised notes, on the other hand, could be improved by implementing subheadings and indentations, providing more visual aids about the condition, and indicating action items for the patient at the beginning of the note.

**Interview Data Analysis.** After interview data was collected, an independent researcher reviewed all the response and identified a few key responses through a thematic analysis. The results of this analysis, supplemented by a few quotes, can be found below:

**Table 1.** Score Comparisons

| Score | Original Notes | Revised Notes | P-Value |
|---|---|---|---|
| Understandability (U) | 4.20 | 12.97 | <0.01 |
| Actionability (A) | 1.13 | 3.67 | <0.01 |
| Overall (U+A) | 5.33 | 16.63 | <0.01 |

*Question 1: "What Worked Best in the Revised Note?".* The responses for this question involved the themes of Reorganization, Summarization, and Text Simplification. Data Visualization was also heavily represented in the responses, but less frequently than the other three themes. Under reorganization, the most common point brought across by the participants was the reorganization of the notes to include the Plan before the Objective section, as per the SAPO format. Under summarization, the reduced text and omission of unnecessary details was often mentioned. Under Text Simplification, participants highlighted the definitions on the side of the note and noted their purpose in reducing clutter in the page. Additionally, the use of a medication table (to track medication, dosage, and refill dates) and graphs was appreciated by the participants. P01 stated "Cutting down in the information, making it less overwhelming, having headers to see what information related to what, having a medication table with dosage and refills, and graphs were all visually appealing, and helped with the flow of the note."

*Question 2: "What Did Not Work Well in the Revised Note?".* The participants of the study primary highlighted two main concerns: the potential for lost information during the summarization and the fact that the next steps were not clearly outlined in the plan section of the revised note. P03 mentioned, "There was a loss of certain pieces of information, which may or may not be vital." Additionally, P06 mentioned that "Later parts of the notes require actionable items. It would be best to clearly establish what the next steps are."

*Question 3: "Do You Have Any Specific Suggestions for the Revised Note?".* For this question, the majority of the responses revolved around the implementation of a "Next Steps" section and that the Assessment and Plan section needs to be summarized more. For example, P06 said "Later parts of the notes require actionable items. It would be best to clearly establish what the next steps are." Almost all participants echoed similar sentiments.

### 4.2 Data Analysis for Study 2: Eye-Tracking Experiment

**Heat Map Data Analysis.** From the heatmap analysis (see Fig. 3.), this study observed that, in most cases, the revised versions have more "red spots" compared to the original versions. The "red spots" represent areas where the gaze duration is longer and more concentrated, indicating higher and more focused points of attention by the readers. The revised versions achieve this by modularizing information, distinguishing between primary content (main text) and supplementary information (annotations). This modular approach helps readers categorize information more easily and locate key messages.

## N02_Original Note    N02_Revised Note

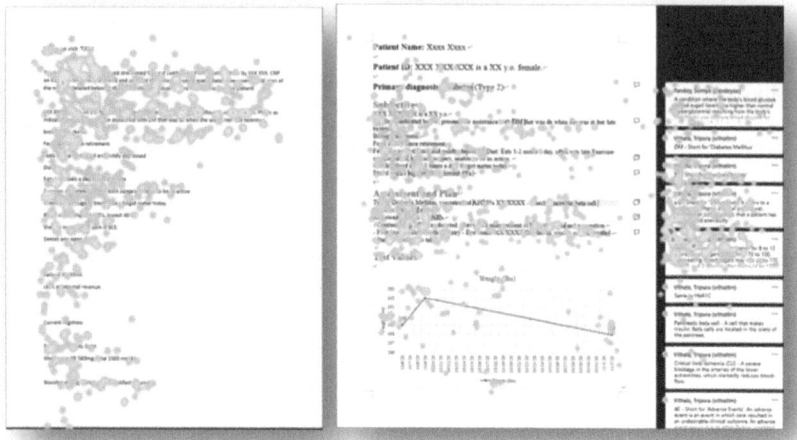

**Fig. 3.** The revised version of the document exhibits a higher concentrated for heat map

**Attention Ration and Effective Attention Ratio Data Analysis**

In general, the main content of the text is the primary reading material, with annotations serving as supplementary information. Consequently, the focus on the main text area is naturally greater than that on the annotation area. This is evident in the charts, in the documents N04, N03, and N14, a similar trend is observed. The attention given to the Original Note in documents N04, N03, and N14 is 79.78%, 72.50%, and 81.34%, while the attention given to the Revised Notes is 20.22%, 27.50%, and 18.66%. Due to the smaller size of the notes section and the fact that it is not the primary focus of reading, participants typically do not spend much time reading the notes. However, the situation is quite different when considering the effective attention ratio. The effective attention ratios for the Original Note in documents N04, N03, and N14 are 80.92%, 78.78%, and 81.81%, while effective attention ratios for the Revised Notes are 79.38%, 89.01%, and 82.66%. These results exceed the attention given to the main text, indicating a high level of interest and attraction to the smaller notes section. These data suggest that participants show a high degree of focus and a desire to acquire information when viewing the notes, highlighting the significant importance of the notes content (See as Fig. 4.).

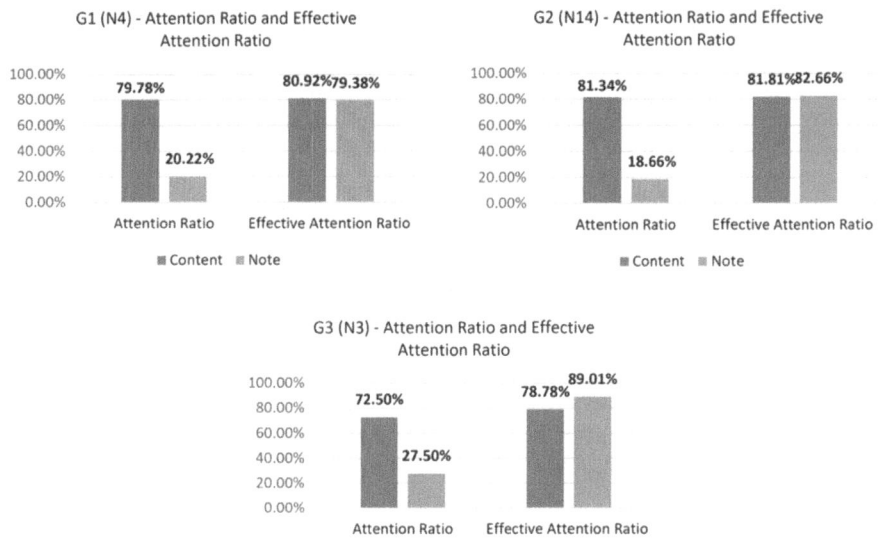

**Fig. 4.** Note exhibits high level of interest and attractiveness towards annotations

## 5  Conclusion and Discussion

### 5.1  Research Contributions

This study had two specific aims. The first was to show that the revised notes would have higher understandability and actionability scores. The results of this study indicate that the revised notes had significantly higher understandability and actionability scores, both individually and together. The second aim was tested using a qualitative exit interview. Analysis of the exit interview responses indicated that participants derived a greater understanding from the revised notes.

This paper highlights an important gap in the current note-sharing system. It is apparent that in order to help remedy the effects of low HL, some form of intervention is necessary. Informatics based solutions could potentially help streamline and automate the process of helping to increase actionability and understandability of clinic notes, without creating a new burden for physicians. The results of this study indicate that there was quantitative improvement in the readability and actionability scores for the revised notes, as compared to the originals. This can help patients better monitor their health, have a better understanding of their condition, and be able to follow physician instructions better. Furthermore, the eye-tracking analysis shows a qualitative improvement in the revised notes.

The results of the eye-tracking study can be interpreted from the perspective of visual psychology. According to the study results, although the Note section is small, it has a high effective attention ratio. This indicates that the Note is useful in UI design. This is also highly related to Gestalt psychology. According to the Gestalt psychology principle of Proximity, the human brain tends to perceive objects that are closer as a single entity, while objects that are farther away are classified as separate blocks. Therefore, in situations with multiple blocks of information, the reading sequence or process is inevitably fragmented or interrupted. This leads readers to require more time for repeated viewing and re-focusing on information content. This study also delves into the physiological feedback of visual perception in human-computer interaction.

### 5.2 Limitations and Future Research

This paper highlights an important gap in the current note-sharing system. It is apparent that in order to help remedy the effects of low HL, some form of intervention is necessary. Informatics based solutions could potentially help streamline and automate the process of helping to increase actionability and understandability of clinic notes, without creating a new burden for physicians. The results of this study indicate that there was quantitative improvement in the readability and actionability scores for the revised notes, as compared to the originals. This can help patients better monitor their health, have a better understanding of their condition, and be able to follow physician instructions better. Furthermore, the eye-tracking analysis shows a qualitative improvement in the revised notes.

# References

1. Our History: Fifty Years In the Making. https://www.opennotes.org/history/. Accessed 1 Oct 2023
2. Strategy 6C: OpenNotes. https://www.ahrq.gov/cahps/quality-improvement/improvement-guide/6-strategies-for-improving/access/strategy6c-opennotes.html. Accessed 1 Oct 2023
3. Delbanco, Y., et al.: Inviting patients to read their doctors' notes: a quasi-experimental study and a look ahead. Ann. Intern. Med. **157**(7), 461 (2012). https://doi.org/10.7326/0003-4819-157-7-201210020-00002
4. Sharing Notes with Patients: The Basics. https://www.opennotes.org/implementation/. Accessed 22 Mar 2024
5. America's Health Literacy: Why We Need Accessible Health Information. https://www.ahrq.gov/sites/default/files/wysiwyg/health-literacy/dhhs-2008-issue-brief.pdf. Accessed 1 Oct 2023
6. Nouri, S.S., et al.: Use and usefulness of after-visit summaries by language and health literacy among latinx and chinese primary care patients. J. Health Commun. **25**(8), 632–639 (2020). https://doi.org/10.1080/10810730.2020.1833385
7. Hickey, K.T., et al.: Low health literacy: Implications for managing cardiac patients in practice. Nurse Practice **43**(8), 49–55 (2018). https://doi.org/10.1097/01.NPR.0000541468.54290.49
8. Kenning, C., Protheroe, J., Gray, N., Ashcroft, D., Bower, P.: The potential for using a Universal Medication Schedule (UMS) to improve adherence in patients taking multiple medications in the UK: a qualitative evaluation. BMC Health Serv. Res. **15**(1), 94 (2015). https://doi.org/10.1186/s12913-015-0749-8
9. Federman, A., et al.: Challenges optimizing the after-visit summary. Int. J. Med. Inf. **120**, 14–19 (2018). https://doi.org/10.1016/j.ijmedinf.2018.09.009
10. Federman, A.D., Sanchez-Munoz, A., Jandorf, L., Salmon, C., Wolf, M.S., Kannry, J.: Patient and clinician perspectives on the outpatient after-visit summary: a qualitative study to inform improvements in visit summary design. J. Am. Med. Inform. Assoc. **24**(e1), e61–e68 (2017). https://doi.org/10.1093/jamia/ocw106

11. Sinsky, C.A., Willard-Grace, R., Schutzbank, A.M., Sinsky, T.A., Margolius, D., Boden-heimer, T.: In search of joy in practice: a report of 23 high-functioning primary care practices. Ann. Fam. Med. **11**(3), 272–278 (2013). https://doi.org/10.1370/afm.1531

12. Day, J., et al.: Quality, satisfaction, and financial efficiency associated with elements of primary care practice transformation: preliminary findings. Ann. Fam. Med. **11**(Suppl_1), S50–S59 (2013). https://doi.org/10.1370/afm.1475

13. Edwards, M., Wood, F., Davies, M., Edwards, A.: The development of health literacy in patients with a long-term health condition: the health literacy pathway model. BMC Public Health **12**(1), 30 (2012). https://doi.org/10.1186/1471-2458-12-130

14. Sørensen, K., et al.: The call for a strategic framework to improve cancer literacy in Europe. Arch. Public Health **78**(1), 60 (2020). https://doi.org/10.1186/s13690-020-00441-y

15. Levin-Zamir, D., Bertschi, I.: Media health literacy, ehealth literacy, and the role of the social environment in context. Int. J. Environ. Res. Public. Health **15**(8), Art. no. 8 (2018). https://doi.org/10.3390/ijerph15081643

16. Hasannejadasl, H., Roumen, C., Smit, Y., Dekker, A., Fijten, R.: Health literacy and eHealth: challenges and strategies. JCO Clin. Cancer Inform. **6**, e2200005 (2022). https://doi.org/10.1200/CCI.22.00005

17. Bindhu, S., et al.: Roles of health literacy in relation to social determinants of health and recommendations for informatics-based interventions: systematic review. Online J. Public Health Inform. **16**, e50898 (2024). https://doi.org/10.2196/50898

18. Aribarg, A., Pieters, R., Wedel, M.: Raising the BAR: bias adjustment of recognition tests in advertising. J. Mark. Res. **47**(3), 387–400 (2010). https://doi.org/10.1509/jmkr.47.3.387

19. Bialkova, S., Grunert, K.G., van Trijp, H.: From desktop to supermarket shelf: Eye-tracking exploration on consumer attention and choice. Food Qual. Preferen. **81** (2020). https://doi.org/10.1016/j.foodqual.2019.103839

20. Graham, D.J., Orquin, J.L., Visschers, V.H.: Eye tracking and nutrition label use: a review of the literature and recommendations for label enhancement. Food Policy **37**(4), 378–382 (2012). https://doi.org/10.1016/j.foodpol.2012.03.004

21. Balcombe, K., Fraser, I., McSorley, E.: Visual attention and attribute attendance in multi-attribute choice experiments. J. Appl. Economet. **30**(3), 447–467 (2015). https://doi.org/10.1002/jae.2383

22. Janiszewski, C.: The influence of display characteristics on visual exploratory search behavior. J. Consum. Res. **25**(3), 290–301 (1998). https://doi.org/10.1086/209540

# User Participatory In-Vehicle Gesture Interaction Design Based on Electric Vehicles

Yuncheng Ge[ORCID], Chengxi Xie, Dian Jin, Zhe Cheng, Yu Zhang[✉], and Meng Li[✉]

Xi'an Jiaotong University, No.28 Xianning West Road, Xi'an, Shaanxi 710049,
People's Republic of China
zhang.yu@xjtu.edu.cn, limeng.81@mail.xjtu.edu.cn

**Abstract.** Gesture interaction is an important topic in the field of human-computer interaction of electric vehicles, which can reduce the driver's cognitive load and distraction, and improve the safety and experience of driving. However, the current gesture design lacks norms and guidelines, and different people in different regions or backgrounds have different gesture cognition for the same function. Therefore, this paper puts forward usability evaluation index, introduces user participatory design method, combined with gesture recognition technology, and finally defines a group of car gestures with high usability and high user satisfaction. The study also emphasis that it is important to involve users in the design process.

**Keywords:** Gesture Interaction · In-Vehicle Interaction · User Participation · Usability Evaluation · Gesture Recognition

## 1 Introduction

In the era of rapid technological development, gesture interaction has been playing an important role in human-machine interaction (HMI, human-computer interaction) nowadays by virtue of its smooth, natural and efficient features. According to Saffer [1], gesture-based HMI can be divided into two categories: touchscreen gestures and free-form gestures or in-air gestures. Comparing to the touchscreen gestures, in-air gesture interaction combined with gesture recognition technology overcomes the previous interaction restrictions based on "touch", which makes the user's interaction experience more excellent. In this paper, "gesture interaction" and "gesture" refer to in-air gestures.

In-air gestures are increasingly included in in-vehicle interaction systems (IVIS). The gesture interaction for IVIS provides innovative interaction technology in terms of user experience. In a usability study by Geiger et al. [2], gesture-based control concepts for in-car devices were accepted by the users and were rated as intuitive and less distracting. However, Laack et al. [3] have suggested that gestural interaction is better suited for performing tasks with low relevance to driving (e.g., informational or entertaining functions (infotainment)) comparing tasks with high relevance to driving (e.g., activating turn signals).

© The Author(s), under exclusive license to Springer Nature Switzerland AG 2025
A. Marcus et al. (Eds.): HCII 2024, LNCS 15380, pp. 30–40, 2025.
https://doi.org/10.1007/978-3-031-76821-7_3

With the intelligent development of new energy vehicles, more and more intelligent automation functions are added to the vehicle system, and the elimination of traditional buttons and other functions triggers people to innovate the design of human-machine interaction, and gesture interaction [4]. As an innate interaction mode, gestural inter-activity can greatly reduce the cognitive load and reduce the driver's distraction [5–7]. Moreover, with the application of autonomous driving, the driver is more and more like a "passenger", which raises the demand for interaction and amusement [8, 9]. Therefore, the study of gesture interaction design of electric vehicles is conducive to avoiding the overload of a single interaction channel, and is crucial to improving driving safety, user experience and interaction efficiency.

This paper aims to propose the design method and usability evaluation index of car gestures, and, combined with gesture recognition technology, carry out user participatory gesture design to define a set of car gestures with high usability and user satisfaction. Specifically, the paper first summarizes the usability evaluation index of in-vehicle gesture design. Then, in order to clarify the design content, the paper define the core function set through interviews with people with driving experience. Finally, the user participative gesture design is carried out to define a set of car gestures with high usability and user satisfaction.

Innovation: (1) This paper puts forward the usability evaluation indexes to guide the in-vehicle gesture design.

(2) User participatory gesture design is introduced to avoid the cognitive load caused by the different mental models of professional designers and ordinary users, which proposed a reference design method for the future user-centred design process.

## 2 Method

### 2.1 Participants

A total of 40 subjects (18 females, mean age = 22.6 years, ranging from 19 to 32 years) participated in the experiment. All subjects were qualified to drive a car and were right-handed. The participants were divided into two groups. In the first group, there are 20 subjects (9 females, mean age = 24.1 years, ranging from 22 to 32 years) who had more than 3 years of driving experience participating in the first experiment, which is called experienced group. In the second group, there are 20 subjects (9 females, mean age = 21.1 years, ranging from 19 to 24 years) who had no actual driving experience participating in the second experiment, so as to eliminate the influence of mind-set, which is called learning group. It should be emphasized that there were individuals from Asia, Africa and Europe in both groups to overcome the non-universality brought about by single regional and cultural backgrounds. All participants received financial or other compensation.

### 2.2 Measurement

**Usability Evaluation Index.** The international standard ISO 9241-11 defines the standards of product usability in terms of universal design and product usability evaluation from three aspects: effectiveness, efficiency and satisfaction. J. Nielsen [10] summarized the factors that affect usability into five factors: learnability, efficiency, memorability, error rate, and subjective user satisfaction. In terms of gesture design principles and evaluation indicators, M. Nielsen [11] suggested using benchmark tests to compare the usability of different gesture sets, including easiness to learn, efficiency and metaphor, that is, the matching degree of gesture and function, the memory of gesture and the fatigue degree of gesture operation. Norman [12] believes that gesture design should be natural, easy to learn and remember, and provide necessary guidance and feedback. He pointed out that the disunity of the platform system makes gesture design lack of consistent design standards.

Based on the occurrence frequency of the main indexes in the above research, according to the characteristics of electric vehicles, the usability evaluation indexes of vehicle gesture design can be summarized as follows:

1. Affinity, that is, the design of gestures should conform to people's habits and cognition.
2. Easiness, that is, gestures should be easy to use, without too much learning costs.
3. Memorability, that is, the actions and processes of the design should be simple to reduce the memory load of the user.
4. Comfort, that is, there should be a good experience in the operation process, not easy to fatigue.
5. Satisfaction, that is, users are subjectively satisfied with gesture design and the entire interaction system.

**Self-Evaluation of Gesture Design by Users.** In the following paragraphs, the participants rated partners' designs, which excluded theirs, after participatory design. Each group of tasks corresponded to 5 indexes, namely, affinity, easiness of learning, memorability, comfort and satisfaction. The subjects were asked to evaluate each dimension with a score of 1 to 5 points, which were assessed on a 5-point Likert scale (1 = "not at all" to 5 = "extremely").

### 2.3  Procedure: User Participatory Design

**Preliminary Experiment: Definition of Core Function Set.** Starting from the existing study of vehicle gesture interaction [13–15], this paper sorts out the functional gestures that have been applied, collects the car gestures mentioned in previous studies, groups and merges them with existing gestures, and gets a total of 65 sub-tasks. In order to further clarify the design content, this paper invited the experienced group, who had more than 3 years of driving experience, to participate in the first experiment and conduct a simple interview to determine the core function set.

After the interview, considering the excessive number of gestures will cause memory load and increase learning cost, the number of car gesture design is set to 7 categories, and then only the existing car gesture test and gesture design are carried out according to the user's core gesture function set, as shown in the Table 1 for details.

**Main Experiment: User Participatory Gesture Interaction Design.** The characteristic of user participatory gesture interaction design is user-centred, and more favourable

**Table 1.** User's core gesture function set.

| Task category | | Number | Core gesture function |
|---|---|---|---|
| Activate/ deactivate | Activate/confirm | 0-1 | Play music/answer phone calls |
| | Deactivate/cancel | 0-2 | Pause the music/hang up the phone |
| Switch | Previous one | 0-3 | Previous song/Previous page |
| | Next one | 0-4 | Next song/Next page |
| Adjust | Turn up | 0-5 | Increase the volume/air volume |
| | Turn down | 0-6 | Reduce the volume/air volume |
| Custom task | | 0-7 | Custom gesture function |

information can be obtained through user participation. The general design process of this paper is shown in Fig. 1.

**Fig. 1.** General design process.

In terms of specific experimental design, the learning group, who had no actual driving experience, were invited to participate in the second experiment, so as to eliminate the influence of mind-set. The whole process can be divided into the following stages, and the complete process would take about 20–30 min:

*1. Basic introduction of the experiment and collection of basic information.*

Before the formal start of the experiment, it was explained to the subjects that the purpose of the experiment was to allow users to participate in the process of car gesture design, and then informed the subjects of the basic process of the complete experiment. The experimenter also asked them to fill in the personal information related to the experiment and informed that it was only for the study of this paper.

*2. The user designs gestures to achieve the target function.*

Based on Kinect V2, participants were asked to design corresponding gestures for the following on-board tasks, as shown in Table 2. The tasks can be divided into 6 groups. Groups 1–5 require participants to design a gesture for each task, and group 6 requires participants to design the same gesture for the 3 tasks listed, so that users can customize the settings. The subjects can design gestures according to personal preferences, and at the same time need to consider the design principles summarized above, namely: affinity, easiness, memorability, comfort and satisfaction. During the whole process, the subjects were asked to describe their views on the task, and act accordingly. The original reactions of the subjects were recorded as much as possible.

**Table 2.** The target task of car gesture design.

| Group | Category | Function |
|-------|----------|----------|
| 1 | Play/pause | Play music Pause the music |
| 2 | Switch songs/pages | Previous song/page Next song/page |
| 3 | Volume adjustment | Increase the volume Reduce the volume |
| 4 | Answer/hang up | Answer the phone Hang up the phone |
| 5 | Air conditioning volume adjustment | Increase the air volume Reduce the air volume |
| 6 | Custom task | Quickly navigate to preset points, call up the main menu, mute on/off |

*3. Users conduct self-evaluation of gesture design.*
After conducting designs, the participants were asked to rated their partners' designs, which excluded theirs. Each group of tasks corresponded to 5 indexes, namely, affinity, easiness of learning, memorability, comfort and satisfaction. The subjects were asked to score each question with a score of 1 to 5 points, which were assessed on a 5-point Likert scale (1 = "not at all" to 5 = "extremely").

## 3   Result

According to the arrangement of user design, the gesture most recognized by experienced users corresponding to the above functions is shown in Fig. 2.

The gestures most recognized by users are combined with existing representative gestures, and then the usability score of these gestures is analysed. In order to facilitate the result statistics, gestures are grouped, as shown in Table 3.

According to the feedback of the participants, the score of each gesture is shown in Fig. 3.

In terms of reliability and validity analysis, factor analysis was used in this paper to test the definition of availability indicators and the structural validity of evaluation methods. IBM SPSS Statistics 26.0 software was used to perform KMO and Bartlett tests on data results. The total $\alpha$ value is 0.824, which is greater than 0.7, indicating good reliability.

Similarly, software was used to analyse the validity of the scale data, and the KMO value was 0.702, ranging from 0.7 to 0.8. The degree of freedom of Bartlett test was 10, and the significance was 0.002, indicating good validity.

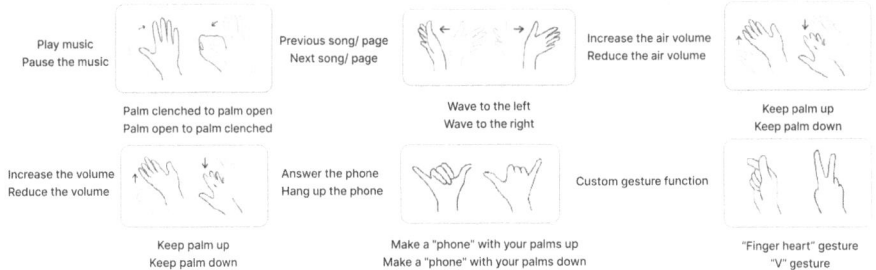

**Fig. 2.** Final user gesture set.

**Table 3.** Group task and gesture numbers.

| Group | Function | Number | Gesture description |
|---|---|---|---|
| 1 | Play music<br>Pause the music | 1-1 | "V" gesture |
| | | 1-2 | Palm clenched to palm open,<br>palm open to palm clenched |
| 2 | Previous song/ page<br>Next song/ page | 2-1 | Thumb slide left,<br>thumb slide right |
| | | 2-2 | Wave to the left,<br>wave to the right |
| 3 | Increase the volume<br>Reduce the volume | 3-1 | Circle Index finger clockwise,<br>Circle index finger counterclockwise |
| | | 3-2 | Palm up,<br>palm down |
| 4 | Answer the phone<br>Hang up the phone | 4-1 | Point finger,<br>wave to the right |
| | | 4-2 | Make a "phone" with your palms up,<br>make a "phone" with your palms down |
| 5 | Increase the air volume<br>Reduce the air volume | 5-1 | Thumb right,<br>thumb left |
| | | 5-2 | Keep palm up,<br>keep palm down |
| 6 | Custom gesture function | 6-1 | "V" gesture |
| | | 6-2 | "Finger heart" gesture |

According to the data obtained through the design method mentioned above, this paper defined the final in-vehicle gesture set.

For the functions of "play/pause music", the average scores of 1-1 and 1-2 were 4.32 and 4.28 respectively. 1-1 was more comfortable than 1-2, but its satisfaction was lower than 1-2. Users explained that the play and pause functions would be more interesting and experienced if operated by 1-2's dynamic gestures. The scores of the other three

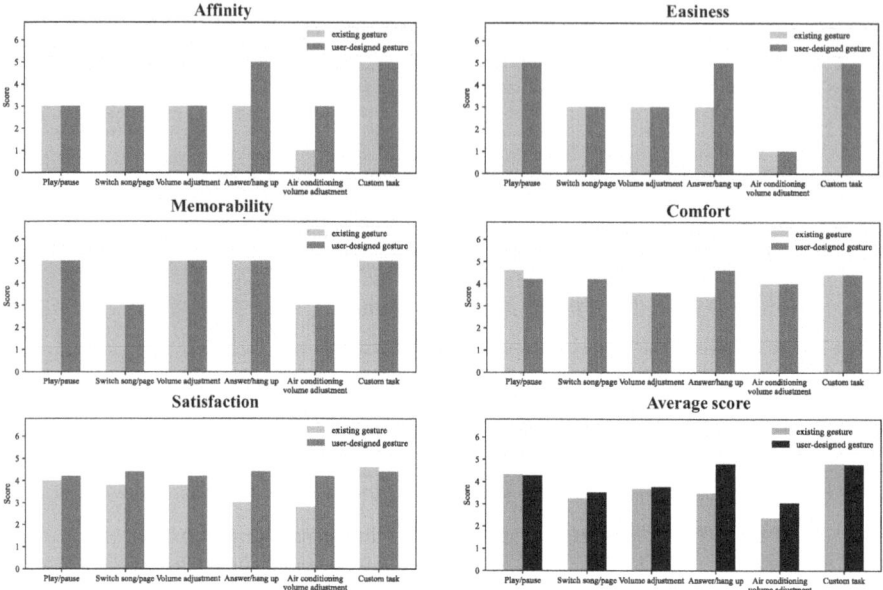

**Fig. 3.** Score by each gesture.

indicators were the same, so the gesture combination of 1-2 "palm clenched to open, palm open to clenched" was finally selected in the two groups.

For the group of functions of " previous song/page, next song/page", the average scores of 2-2 and 2-1 were 3.52 and 3.24 respectively, and the scores of comforts and satisfaction of 2-2 were higher than 2-1, and the scores of the other three indicators were consistent. Therefore, the gesture combination of 2-2 "wave to the left, wave to the right" was finally selected in the two groups of gestures.

For the function group of "increase/reduce the volume", the average score of 3-2 and 3-1 was 3.76 and 3.68 respectively, and the scores of the first four indicators of 3-1 and 3-2 were consistent, while the overall satisfaction of 3-2 was higher than that of 3–1. Therefore, the gesture combination of 3-2 "palm up, palm down" was finally selected in the two groups.

For the group of functions of "Answer/hang up the phone", the average scores of 4-1 and 4-2 are 3.48 and 4.8 respectively. Except for the memorability scores of 4-1 and 4-2, the other four indicators of 4-2 are better than 4-1. Therefore, In the two groups of gestures, the final choice is 4-2" make a "phone" with your palms up/down".

For the group of functions of "increase/decrease air volume", the average scores of 5-1 and 5-2 are 2.36 and 3.04 respectively. The scores of easiness, memorability and comfort of 5-1 and 5-2 are the same, and affinity and satisfaction index 5-2 are better than 5-1. In the two groups of gestures, the combination of hand gestures of 5-2 "palm up, palm down" is finally selected, which is consistent with the gesture of the third group "increase/reduce volume", which is also conducive to reducing the user's memory load.

For the custom gesture function, the average score of 6-1 and 6-2 is 4.8 and 4.76 respectively, and there is no significant difference in the scores of each indicator of the two gestures. Considering the small movement range of 6-2, the gesture effect of different people is also quite different, which is not easy to identify. Therefore, the 6-1 "V" shape of the two gestures is finally chosen. Based on the above research, the final definition of the vehicle gesture set is shown in Figure (Fig. 4).

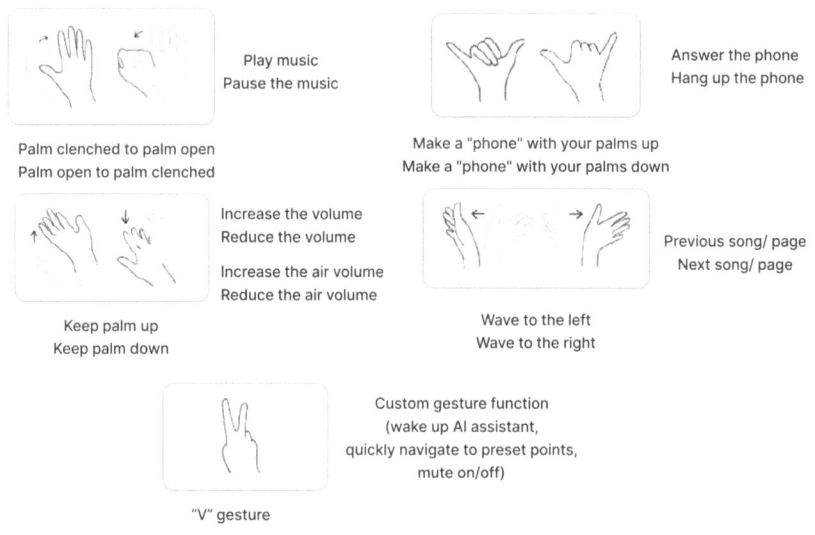

Fig. 4. Final in-vehicle gesture set.

## 4   Discussion

This study proposes to design interactive gestures in the car by means of user participation design, and obtains a set of gestures with higher usability than the existing gestures. The theory behind this is that there are certain differences in the mental models of users and professional designers. As a functional design, compared with other design fields, interaction design needs to adhere to the user-centred concept. However, most of the existing car gesture sets are produced entirely by professional designers, and do not take into account the cognitive characteristics and mental models of ordinary users.

A key point of this study is the selection of subjects. In order to overcome the problem that gesture design of professional designers will bring cognitive load to ordinary users due to different mental models, all subjects in this study major in non-design fields. The first group, which had actual driving experience, was asked to select the core gesture function. The second group of subjects without actual driving experience was asked to conduct gesture design and evaluation on the core function set selected by the first group of subjects.

Following the trend of electric vehicles, in order to weaken the interaction logic based on physical keys or touch controls, this paper first analyses the existing cases of in-vehicle gesture interaction, and summarizes their main features. Moreover, this paper put forward usability indexes to better evaluate the feasibility of the specific gesture set. After the user participatory design, we finally defined an in-vehicle gesture set with high usability and user satisfaction.

The result of the work represented the advantages of user participatory design, which is specifically reflected in that the gestures obtained by user participatory design show better characteristics than the existing gestures under the evaluation system of ordinary users in the evaluation stage. However, to some functions, the specific indexes of the two gestures are both low. For example, the affinity and the easiness of the function of increase/decrease the air volume are low, which may be caused by the characteristic of the function and the entire gesture set. In future research, it may be one of the most critical problems about how to coordinate the logic of the whole gesture set to reduce the adverse effects between gestures and improve the usability of the whole set.

The present work reveals new insights into UX of in-vehicle gesture interaction. The main research results of this paper are as follows:

1. Analyse electric vehicles and their human-computer interaction interfaces through literature research and user interviews, and propose the characteristics and advantages of gesture interactivity based on multi-channel interaction. Based on previous studies, the design principles of car gestures and 5 usability indicators including affinity, easiness, memorability, comfort and satisfaction are summarized and used to evaluate the usability of gesture design.
2. The core gesture function set expected by users is summarized through user interviews, which provides a research object for the determination of the final gesture set.
3. Combined with the user participatory design method, the design method and process of the vehicle gesture are proposed, which mainly includes the definition of the core function set of the vehicle gesture, the design of the user participatory vehicle gesture, the usability evaluation of the gesture set, and the definition of the final gesture set which is suitable for the EVs, providing a reference method for the user-centred design process.

Limited by the level and conditions of the team, there are many shortcomings in this paper, which still need further research:

1. In the process of user participatory gesture design, the emphasis is on the selection of samples. The number of samples involved in this paper is not large enough, and there may be accidental errors.
2. In the usability evaluation process, only the usability of a single gesture was evaluated in isolation, and the usability between gestures and the whole system was not studied.

## 5  Conclusion

The popularity of smart electric vehicles gradually diminishes the importance of the driver, which provides the possibility of more integration of in-vehicle functions. It is an important topic about how to improve the efficiency of human-computer interaction while increasing the interactive function in the field of in-vehicle interaction at present. The key to solve the problem is to design a set of interactive paradigms with excellent logic and practicability by combining multi-channel interaction and user-centred design ideas. In this study, we take gesture interaction as an example, introduce the idea of user participatory design, and through unique experimental ideas, overcome the problem of different mental models of designers and target subject user groups, which are prone to occur in the conventional design path. Through the introduction of user participatory design method, a set of in-vehicle gestures is defined with high usability and user satisfaction. Following the trend of electric vehicles, the presented work provides a new perspective on the improvement of usability and user experience of in-vehicle gesture interaction. Furthermore, the study also emphasis it is of great importance to involving users in the design process, rather than just having professional designers complete the design. This design concept is not limited to gesture design, but applies to a variety of user experience-centred design fields.

# References

1. Saffer, D.: Designing gestural interfaces (2008)
2. Geiger, M., Nieschulz, R., Zobl, M., Lang, M.: Gesture-based control concept for in-car devices; Bedienkonzept zur Gestenbasierten Interaktion mit Geraeten im Automobil (2002)
3. Laack, D.A. van, Kirsch, O., Tuzar, G.-D., Judy, blessing: consumer insights about gesture interaction in vehicles (2016)
4. Harvey, C., Stanton, N.A., Pickering, C.A., McDonald, M., Zheng, P.: In-vehicle information systems to meet the needs of drivers. Int. J. Hum.-Comput. Interact. **27**, 505–522 (2011). https://doi.org/10.1080/10447318.2011.555296
5. Zöller, I., Bechmann, R., Abendroth, B.: Possible applications for gestures while driving. Automot. Engine Technol. **3**, 11–20 (2018). https://doi.org/10.1007/s41104-017-0023-7
6. Graichen, L., Graichen, M., Krems, J.F.: Evaluation of gesture-based in-vehicle interaction: user experience and the potential to reduce driver distraction. Hum. Factors **61**, 774–792 (2019). https://doi.org/10.1177/0018720818824253
7. Graichen, L., Graichen, M., Krems, J.F.: Effects of gesture-based interaction on driving behavior: a driving simulator study using the projection-based vehicle-in-the-loop. Hum. Factors **64**, 324–342 (2022). https://doi.org/10.1177/0018720820943284
8. Bengler, K., Rettenmaier, M., Fritz, N., Feierle, A.: From HMI to HMIs: towards an HMI framework for automated driving. Information **11**, 61 (2020). https://doi.org/10.3390/info11 020061
9. Detjen, H., Faltaous, S., Geisler, S., Schneegass, S.: User-defined voice and mid-air gesture commands for maneuver-based interventions in automated vehicles. In: Proceedings of Mensch und Computer 2019, pp. 341–348. ACM, Hamburg Germany (2019)
10. Nielsen, J.: The usability engineering life cycle. Computer **25**, 12–22 (1992). https://doi.org/ 10.1109/2.121503
11. Nielsen, M., Störring, M., Moeslund, T.B., Granum, E.: A procedure for developing intuitive and ergonomic gesture interfaces for HCI. In: Camurri, A., Volpe, G. (eds.) Gesture-Based Communication in Human-Computer Interaction, pp. 409–420. Springer, Berlin, Heidelberg (2004)
12. Norman, D.A.: Natural user interfaces are not natural. Interactions **17**, 6–10 (2010). https:// doi.org/10.1145/1744161.1744163
13. May, K.R., Gable, T.M., Walker, B.N.: A multimodal air gesture interface for in vehicle menu navigation. In: Adjunct Proceedings of the 6th International Conference on Automotive User Interfaces and Interactive Vehicular Applications, pp. 1–6. ACM, Seattle WA USA (2014)

14. März, P., Schwahlen, D., Geisler, S., Kopinski, T.: User expectations on touchless gestures in vehicles (2016)
15. Pickering, C.A., Burnhamt, K.J., Richardson, M.J.: A research study of hand gesture recognition technologies and applications for human vehicle interaction (2007)

# Optimized User Experience for Labeling Systems for Predictive Maintenance Applications

Michelle Hallmann[1]([✉])(ID), Michael Stern[1](ID), Francesco Vona[1](ID), Ute Franke[2](ID), Thomas Ostertag[3](ID), Benjamin Schlüter[4](ID), and Jan-Niklas Voigt-Antons[1](ID)

[1] Hamm-Lippstadt University of Applied Sciences, 59557 Lippstadt, Germany
`michelle.hallmann@hshl.de`
[2] 5micron GmbH, Rudower Ch 29, 12489 Berlin, Germany
[3] OSTAKON GmbH, Forster Str. 54, 10999 Berlin, Germany
[4] Deutsche Eisenbahn Service AG, Pritzwalker Str. 8, 16949 Putlitz, Germany

**Abstract.** This paper presents the design and implementation of a graphical labeling user interface for a monitoring and predictive maintenance system for trains and rail infrastructure in a rural area of Germany. Aiming to enhance rail transportation's economic viability and operational efficiency, our project utilizes cost-effective wireless monitoring systems that combine affordable sensors and machine learning algorithms. Given that a successful labeling phase is indispensable for training a supervised machine learning system, we emphasize the importance of a user-friendly labeling user interface, which can be optimally integrated into the daily work routines of annotators. The labeling system has been designed based on best practices in usability heuristics and will be validated for usability and user experience through a study, the protocol for which is presented here. The value of this work lies in its potential to reduce maintenance costs and improve service reliability in rail transportation, contributing to the academic literature and offering practical insights for research on effective labeling user interfaces, as well as for the development of labeling systems in the industry. Upon completion of the study, we will share the results, refine the system as necessary, and explore its scalability in other areas of infrastructure maintenance.

**Keywords:** usability · predictive maintenance · labeling system · user interface design

## 1 Introduction

The economic success of rail transportation is heavily dependent on infrastructure and vehicle maintenance costs [12]. Insufficient maintenance of rail infrastructure and vehicles provokes train delays and malfunctions [9], leading to heightened public discontentment with the public transportation system [6,21]. Therefore, cost-efficient solutions must be found to enhance transport capacity

© The Author(s), under exclusive license to Springer Nature Switzerland AG 2025
A. Marcus et al. (Eds.): HCII 2024, LNCS 15380, pp. 41–53, 2025.
https://doi.org/10.1007/978-3-031-76821-7_4

in rural areas and increase the attractiveness of rail transportation. A promising solution involves deploying cost-effective wireless monitoring systems for rail infrastructure and vehicles [7], combining affordable sensors and machine learning algorithms for data analysis and predictive maintenance. These systems must be designed with low-threshold retrofit solutions to allow seamless integration into existing infrastructure. To build a reliable predictive maintenance system based on machine learning algorithms, a high-quality labeling process must be ensured, as the capabilities of a machine learning system are heavily dependent on the quality of the training data [11]. The labeling, which is needed for a machine learning system to be deployed, is often seen as a tedious task [25], which can when the annotator is using a system with low usability and user experience can lead to frustration [8], and thus lower performance results and lower label quality. Thus, ensuring that the user of the labeling system inputs high-quality data necessitates a user interface with a high usability and user experience, making the labeling activity pleasant instead of exhausting or annoying. Despite the importance of high usability and user experience in labeling systems, few guidelines exist for designing labeling user interfaces for predictive maintenance, with even fewer specific examples presented for software solutions [19]. This paper presents the design of a graphical labeling user interface for integrating a monitoring and predictive maintenance system for trains and rail infrastructure in a rural area of Germany. It is part of a research project where we assess the effectiveness of structure-borne noise measurement methods for monitoring and maintenance investigations on rails and vehicles. For this purpose, two train cars and one rail section are equipped with structure-borne noise measurement sensor systems for data collection from 5micron, which are general-purpose, cost-effective, and highly scalable. Acoustics' special characteristic of deriving specific findings from non-specific signals is used to detect the condition and material properties of vehicles and infrastructure. The two sensors in the train cars monitor the state of the rails, while the sensor on the rail section monitors the state of the train cars as they enter and leave the railway workshop. The train drivers label events occurring during the train rides, while the workshop foreman labels faults and repairs to the vehicles. A distributed ledger network (DLT) is implemented, which lifts the infrastructure to the web3 standard and makes the essential use cases cross-company-wide available. The DLT network realizes the decentralized data exchange and transfers the labeling data to a data analysis server, where machine learning algorithms process the labels and training data to generate recommended measures for the workshop foreman. With the presentation of the processes and the design implementation in our project, we aim to provide suggestions for the design of labeling systems in the area of Industry 4.0, specifically focusing on the integration of predictive maintenance systems in the rail transportation industry. Our design decisions are based on the best practices in usability heuristics [18]. Further, the study protocol we plan to conduct as a next step for evaluating our labeling user interface's usability and user experience is also presented.

## 2   Related Work

### 2.1   Supervised Machine Learning for Predictive Maintenance

If machines are not serviced promptly in the event of imminent defects, this can result in major damage and, therefore, higher repair costs, which are detrimental to the company. However, if systems are serviced too regularly and without need, time and economic resources are used that are not yet required [23]. With machine learning for predictive maintenance, developers can build monitoring systems out of sensors, which detect anomalies in usage and predict future damage and repair measures to improve the maintenance of machinery [5]. To develop predictive maintenance systems in this field, usually supervised learning is required to train the machine learning system, where in addition to the sensor data, experts from the field assign labels to the data [24]. The success of the machine learning system depends on the accuracy and quality of the data and labels, which is why the acquisition of data and labels in the training phase is an important part of the process [14].

### 2.2   Usability and User Experience for Labeling Quality

In the conception, design, and development of user interfaces, two concepts are of great importance and must be considered by designers and developers throughout: Usability and User Experience. Usability focuses on making the system simple, intuitive, and user-friendly, ensuring users can achieve their goals with the system [10]. As early as 1994, Nielson [18] developed 10 heuristics to help systems achieve better usability. These heuristics include, for example, making the system status visible to the user when designing the system, maintaining consistency and adhering to standards, and displaying only necessary elements through aesthetic and minimal design. User Experience, as described by Jacobsen and Meyer [10], encompasses the comprehensive overall experience that the user has before, during, and after using the system. Ideally, this experience should leave the user happy or enthusiastic, encouraging them to return to the system [10]. User experience considers the user's perception and emotional experience during use, as well as their needs and the degree to which these needs are fulfilled [13,20]. A system's degree of usability and user experience indicates how much users like and enjoy interacting with this system [10,22]. The labeling task can be very tedious [25], but as this part of the process and the label quality are very important, we aim for a high Usability and User Experience of the Labeling User Interface to ensure efficient and high-quality labeling by the expert.

### 2.3   Heuristics and Guidelines for Labeling User Interfaces

To our knowledge, there are few guidelines in the literature on designing user interfaces for labeling systems. The only guideline we found specifically for this kind of system was the one from Passos developed in 2021 [19], where the guidelines were derived from the usability heuristics from Nielson [18]. As the guidelines were not scientifically validated yet, we decided to base our design decisions on the usability heuristics from Nielson, which serve as general guidance for the design of user interfaces [10,13,18,20]. Thus, we will explain our design decisions based on Nielson's usability heuristics when we present the Labeling User Interface.

## 3   Software Design

### 3.1   Conceptualization of the Labeling Process

To develop an effective integrable labeling system, we conceptualized the labeling processes in collaboration with the railroad company, sensor system developers, and data exchange companies. To this end, we held several meetings involving employees from the train company. Rail infrastructure experts informed us about the previous maintenance processes and common messages during journeys. During a visit to the workshop, we consulted with the workshop foreman about the previous maintenance processes for the train cars and collaboratively discussed the design of the labeling processes. The labeling processes were designed closely with the train company employees and the entire project consortium. As recommended in Guideline 1, "Identification of the labeling task," the labeling requirements were identified during the discussions with the sensor company. Even if the data type "structure-borne sound recording" to be labeled is not listed among the data types in the guideline, we could determine the multi-label text classification as the labeling task since descriptions should be assigned to the fault.

### 3.2   Labeling Environment

We have decided to assign the task of labeling rail faults to the train drivers and faults on train cars to the workshop foreman, who possesses the necessary technical expertise. To ensure that these employees' involvement in the research project does not disrupt their daily work, the user interface (UI) for labeling must be seamlessly integrated into their work processes. The workshop foreman handles maintenance orders on the computer in his office within the workshop. Therefore, we selected the computer as the medium for labeling in collaboration with him. He confirmed he could keep a website open alongside the maintenance system, allowing him to perform labeling tasks between assignments. Each driver is equipped with a company cell phone and a company tablet. The drivers' supervisor assured us that they could dedicate a few minutes at the end of their shifts to label events that occurred during their routes. Since the service tablet's larger size can accommodate more information than the service cell phone, we selected the service tablet as the medium for labeling infrastructure events. To create a simple system, we used a website as the UI. After logging in, users are directed to either the train drivers' labeling interface web page or the workshop foreman's labeling interface web page.

### 3.3   Labeling Sequence

To label faults on the rails, the train driver is instructed to press a button integrated with the sensor while driving if they observe an anomaly in the rail infrastructure. The sensor data for the corresponding route section is marked and transmitted to the data-analysis server, where it is stored in a database. After completing the train ride, the train driver is prompted to access the labeling user interface on their tablet, where the unlabeled events are listed. When a train car enters the workshop, the data from the sensor is forwarded to the server system and embedded as an event on the website. The workshop foreman is instructed to label the found and repaired defects of the inspection by selecting fault categories from predefined lists or creating new ones. Once verified and submitted, the selected labels from the train drivers and the workshop foreman are sent to the server, and the system is trained with the newest acquired data. After recording the labeling system requirements, we created, iterated, and tested initial design approaches. Ultimately, we developed a labeling system that can label faults on the rails and train cars, facilitating the collection of the necessary data for data analysis.

### 3.4   Design Methodology

The design of the labeling system followed a codesign approach, resulting in the formalization of all functional and non-functional requirements for the UI. Following discussions with the entire project team, the design and development team established all functional and non-functional requirements for the user interface intended for the annotators, coordinating these requirements with all stakeholders. Wireframes were used to determine how the elements and functions of the labeling system should be arranged on the screen. Once agreement was reached on the structure of the user interfaces, an initial digital design prototype for the user flows for both the train drivers and the workshop foreman was created. The labeling system was to be implemented using Vue.js, focusing on developing a minimalist design to ensure the interface was easy to understand and use for the annotators [17]. The Vue.js framework Vuetify [4] was utilized for this minimalist design. After the first iteration and discussions on the prototype with university experts, additional design iterations were made, leading to the development of the website's final design.

## 4   Labeling User Interface

The labeling system is divided into a log-in page for all annotators and one dashboard for each labeling use case. For a minimalist design, as recommended in the heuristic "Aesthetic and Minimalist Design" [18], we used white- and gray-colored backgrounds, black font color and the font-family "Roboto". The muted blue tone from the project logo is reused for highlighting and some buttons so that the user recognizes the project when opening the labeling system, aligning with the heuristic "Recognition Rather Than Recall" [18]. Our conversations with the railroad employees gave us an impression of their language. As described in the heuristic "Match Between The System And The Real World" [18], we were able to adapt the system to the user and thus simplify its use.

## 4.1   Labeling of Train Cars

The user interface for the train car labeling Fig. 1 is divided into 3 parts: a bar at the top with the logo and a logout button, a list of events on the left which shows the identification numbers of the train cars which entered and left the workshop and a main view for the labeling. The currently selected event is highlighted in the events list so the user can always see which train car is being labeled. This aligns with the heuristic "Visibility of System Status" [18]. The upper part of the main view provides only the necessary information about the train car, including the train identification number, entrance time, and exit time, keeping the interface minimalist.

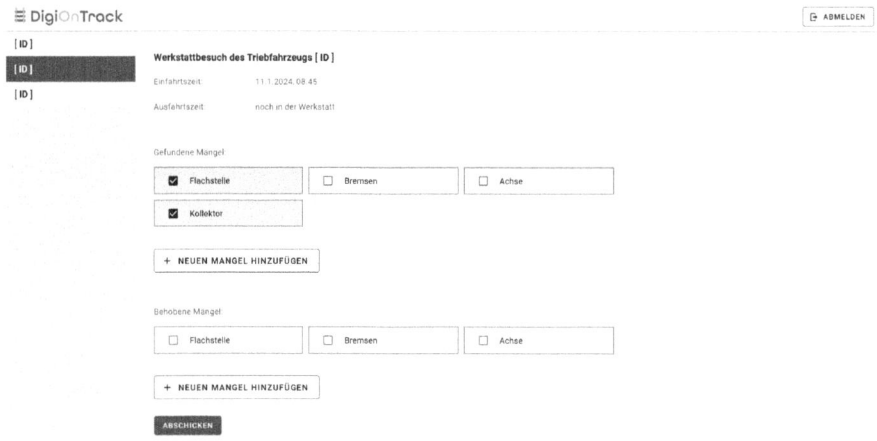

**Fig. 1.** Dashboard for the Labeling of Train Cars for the Workshop Foreman: List with Train Vehicles on the Left, Entry and Exit Time at the Top, Lists with Labels for Labeling of Faults and Repairs in the Center

A hierarchical structure for the labels was deemed unnecessary, as there were only three labels at the beginning of the labeling phase, and the workshop foreman expected that not many labels would be added in the future. This decision helps avoid long interaction sequences with the system and keeps the interface minimalist. However, since annotators may need to create new labels, an option to create labels through a button below the list of labels was implemented. As multiple faults can be found or repaired on train cars, the system allows for the selection and creation of multiple labels. When the workshop foreman clicks on the button "create new label," a small and simple overlay appears, where he is asked which label he wants to create and can create it through an input field Fig. 2. Above the input field, all already selectable labels of the labeling type are listed, so the workshop foreman has an overview of the system while editing it. This might prevent creating a label from the annotator, which already exists in the system and aligns with the heuristic "Error Prevention" [18]. The workshop foreman can close the overview through the close button, go back with the back button, or confirm the label to be created by the confirm button. Not only does the close button align with the heuristic "Consistency and Standards," but it also gives the user two easy ways to go back to the labeling if they clicked on the button by mistake, aligning with the heuristic "User Control and Freedom."

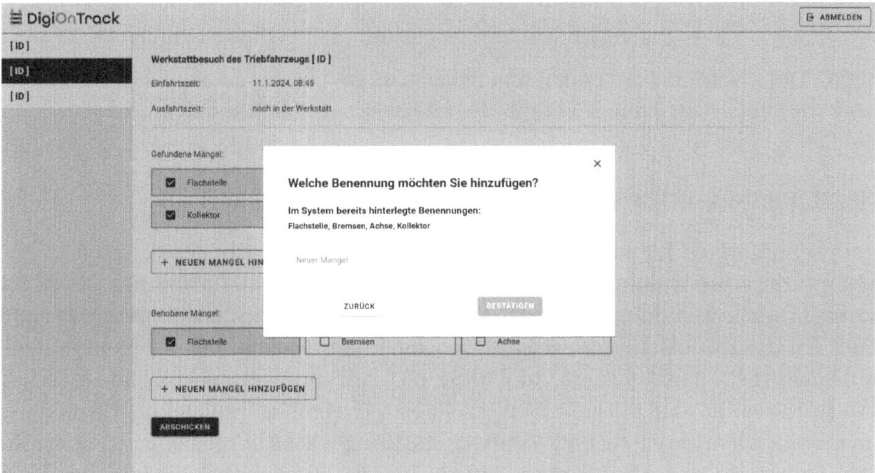

**Fig. 2.** Overlay for Creating a new Label: User is asked for the new Label, List with already available Labels and Input Field for Entering new Label

When the workshop foreman selects the labels and clicks on the blue send button at the bottom of the page, an overlay appears, where the workshop foreman can check the data that he is submitting Fig. 3. This provides another opportunity to correct any mistakes and makes the system status visible by showing which data has been saved and will be sent upon submission [18]. The overlay is designed to be simple and apportioned to maintain a minimalist approach. The workshop foreman can close the overlay with a close button, return to the labeling UI with the back button, or submit the data to the server with the confirm button. This again gives the user full control and freedom over what to do next [18].

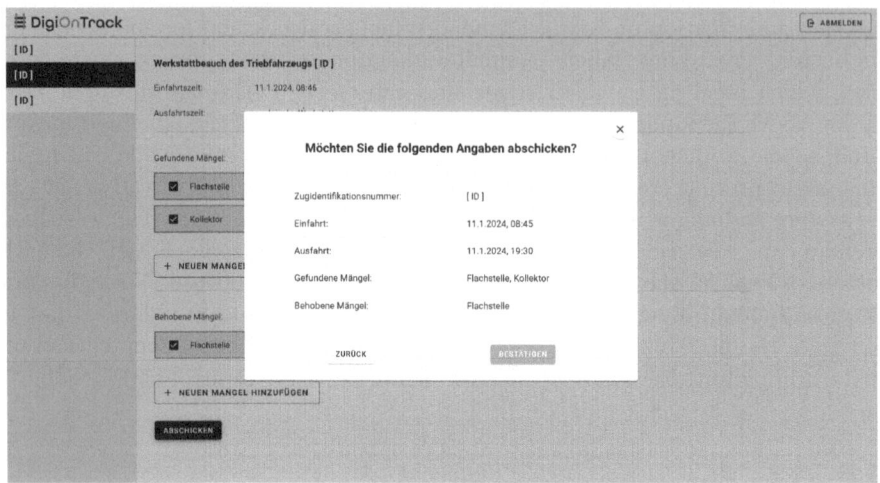

**Fig. 3.** Data Verification before submitting Labels: User is asked if following Data should be submitted, Train Vehicle Data with selected Labels is listed

## 4.2    Labeling of Rail Infrastructure

The user interface for labeling the rails (Fig. 4) is similarly constructed to the user interface for train car labeling but is designed for the tablet used by train drivers. On the left side of the screen, events are listed with their event date and time. At the top of the screen is a logo for identification and a logout button to return to the main system, providing recognition, user control, and freedom [18]. In the main part of the screen, the selected event is displayed with its date, time, train identification, and location, ensuring visibility of the system status [18]. The location is shown via a pin on a map, implemented using the open-source framework OpenStreetMap [2]. The pin indicates where the train driver pressed the button to tag an event during the journey. The train driver can zoom in and out and navigate the map by touch to better orient themselves with the location. Initially, the labels are implemented with a flat hierarchy similar to those in the train car labeling interface. However, if numerous new labels are created, resulting in an overly large list, a hierarchical structure for the labels will be considered for better organization and overview.

## 5    Usability and User Experience Study

In the following, we present the study protocol for a planned usability and user experience study for our developed labeling system to verify these user interface aspects and provide a validated example of labeling the user interface for predictive maintenance for other researchers and developers. Further, we aim to investigate the correlation between the participants' affinity for technological interaction and gender and the application's usability and user experience.

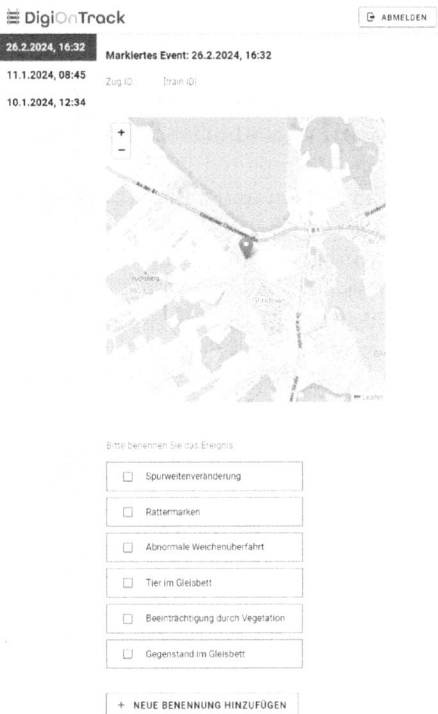

**Fig. 4.** User Interface for Labeling of the Rails for the Train Drivers: On the Left is the List of Events, at the Top Date, Time, Train Identification and Event Location are shown, Below the Map the List with eligible Labels is positioned

## 5.1   Participants

Due to the challenges of recruiting sufficient specialists for a robust study, we will initially conduct a preliminary study involving academic staff and students from our university. We aim to recruit 40 participants, ensuring diversity in age and gender. To maintain a controlled environment and facilitate observation of the participants, we will use the university's usability lab to conduct the study.

## 5.2   Study Design

The study will begin with an explanation of a labeling system, its development purpose, and the objectives of the experimental study. This information will be provided orally, allowing for questions and answers. The experiment will be divided into two rounds: one for labeling rail faults by the train drivers and the other for labeling train vehicle faults by the workshop foremen. At the beginning of each round, participants will be given a text explanation outlining the goals and motivations behind the annotator user group. Following this, participants will be assigned tasks to complete on their own. As suggested by Nielsen [18], we have designed the test tasks to be as representative as possible. Tasks for the labeling of the train vehicles by the workshop foremen:

- A train vehicle with the ID 918061439587DDB visited the workshop. You found a defect in the axle and repaired it. Now, you need to label the found and repaired defect in the system and submit the data to DigiOnTrack.
- Another train vehicle with the ID 918544650040CHBLS visited the workshop yesterday. You found two defects during maintenance, categorized as a flat spot and a commutator issue. Now, you must label the found and repaired defects in the labeling system and submit the data to DigiOnTrack.

Tasks for the labeling of the rails by the train drivers:

- Two events occurred during today's journey. The machine was very loud at around 1 pm near the Meyenburg train station, likely due to chatter marks. Later, at 4 pm, just before arriving at Putlitz station, you had to brake sharply because a deer was on the rails. Now, you must label these events and submit the data to DigiOnTrack.
- During your journey today, shortly after leaving Putlitz station, a loud bang indicated a rail breakage. You recall this event occurred around 8 pm. Now, you must label the event and submit the data to DigiOnTrack.

To eliminate any potential carryover effects, participants will be divided into two groups: one will start with the tasks designated for the workshop foreman, and the other will begin with the tasks assigned to the train drivers. The experiment is estimated to take 30 min. The next round will start either when participants have finished their tasks or when 10 min have passed. Participants will perform the round for labeling train vehicles by the workshop foremen on a desktop computer and the round for labeling rails by the train drivers on a tablet.

### 5.3    Data Collection and Analysis

In addition to collecting demographic information such as age, gender, and occupation, we will use the Affinity for Technological Interaction scale [1] to assess participants' affinity for technological interaction. After each round, usability will be measured using the System Usability Scale [16], and user experience will be measured using the User Experience Questionnaire [3]. The System Usability Scale is a proven tool for measuring participants' perceived usability [16], while the User Experience Questionnaire evaluates attractiveness, perspicuity, efficiency, dependability, stimulation, and novelty [15]. In addition to the questionnaires, participants' performance will be measured by the time taken to complete tasks and the ratio of successful interactions to errors. After completing the questionnaires in the second round, participants will undergo a debriefing session with the experimenter, during which they can comment on the system and suggest improvements. Finally, the Spearmen-Correlation Test will be used to investigate whether there are correlations between age, affinity for technological interaction, and system usability or User Experience.

# 6 Conclusion

In this paper, we presented the design and implementation of a graphical labeling user interface integrated into a monitoring and predictive maintenance system for trains and rail infrastructure in a rural area of Germany. Our project aims to enhance rail transportation's economic viability and operational efficiency by utilizing cost-effective wireless monitoring systems, which combine affordable sensors and machine learning algorithms for predictive maintenance. By ensuring a high-quality labeling process through a user interface with high usability and user experience, we strive to integrate a successful and reliable predictive maintenance system. The design of our labeling user interface was grounded in best practices of usability heuristics, specifically addressing the unique requirements in the field. By engaging closely with stakeholders, including railroad company employees, sensor system developers, and data exchange experts, we ensured that the labeling process was seamlessly integrated into the existing workflows of train drivers and workshop foremen.

Currently, our project is at the stage where the labeling system has been technically implemented and is ready for usability and user experience testing. We have outlined a comprehensive study protocol to evaluate the system, aiming to validate our design approach and provide a useful reference for other researchers and developers working on labeling user interfaces for predictive maintenance systems in the rail transportation industry. Additionally, we aim to explore the scalability of our approach to other areas of infrastructure maintenance and extend the application of our system to broader contexts within the transportation industry. The value of our work lies in its potential to significantly reduce maintenance costs and improve service reliability in rail transportation through a successfully integrated labeling system. By addressing the critical aspects of usability and user experience, we aim to ensure high-quality data labeling, which is essential for successfully deploying machine learning algorithms in predictive maintenance. Our approach not only contributes to the academic literature but also offers practical insights and solutions for the rail transportation sector, advancing the integration of Industry 4.0 technologies in this field.

**Acknowledgment.** We gratefully acknowledge financial support through the TÜV Rheinland Consulting GmbH with funds provided by the Federal Ministry for Digital and Transport (BMDV) under Grant No. 19F2265 (DigiOnTrack). We also want to thank the reviewers for their thoughtful feedback. In this paper, we used Overleaf's built-in spell checker, the current version of ChatGPT (GPT 3.5), and Grammarly. These tools helped us fix spelling mistakes and get suggestions to improve our writing. If not noted otherwise in a specific section, these tools were not used in other forms.

**Disclosure of Interests.** The authors have no competing interests to declare relevant to this article's content.

# References

1. Affinity for technological interaction scale homepage. https://ati-scale.org/. Accessed 22 May 2024

2. Openstreetmap homepage. https://www.openstreetmap.org/. Accessed 18 May 2024

3. User experience questionnaire homepage. https://www.ueq-online.org/. Accessed 22 May 2024

4. Vuetify homepage. https://vuetifyjs.com/. Accessed 17 May 2024

5. Barlow, M.: Predictive Maintenance, 1st edn. O'Reilly Media, Inc. (2015)

6. Bates, J., Polak, J., Jones, P., Cook, A.: The valuation of reliability for personal travel. Transp. Res. Part E Logist. Transp. Rev. **37**(2), 191–229 (2001). https://doi.org/10.1016/S1366-5545(00)00011-9

7. Elkhoury, N., Hitihamillage, L., Moridpour, S., Robert, D.J.: Degradation prediction of rail tracks: a review of the existing literature. Open Transp. J. **12**(1), 88–104 (2018). https://doi.org/10.2174/1874447801812010088

8. Garrett, J.J.: The elements of user experience user-centered design for the web and beyond, 2nd edn. New Riders, Berkeley, Calif (2010)

9. Ivina, D., Palmqvist, C.W., Olsson, N., Winslott Hiselius, L.: Train delays due to trackwork in Sweden. In: 9th International Conference on Railway Operations Modelling and Analysis (ICROMA) - RailBeijing, Beijing, China (2021)

10. Jacobsen, J., Meyer, L.: Praxisbuch Usability und UX, 2nd edn. Rheinwerk Computing, Bonn (2019)

11. Jain, A., et al.: Overview and importance of data quality for machine learning tasks. In: Proceedings of the 26th ACM SIGKDD International Conference on Knowledge Discovery & Data Mining (KDD 2020), pp. 3561–3562. Association for Computing Machinery, New York (2020). https://doi.org/10.1145/3394486.3406477

12. Kans, M., Galar, D., Thaduri, A.: Maintenance 4.0 in railway transportation industry. In: Koskinen, K.T., et al. (eds.) Proceedings of the 10th World Congress on Engineering Asset Management (WCEAM 2015). LNME, pp. 317–331. Springer, Cham (2016). https://doi.org/10.1007/978-3-319-27064-7_30

13. Kauer-Franz, M., Franz, B.: Usability und User Experience Design: Das umfassende Handbuch, 1st edn. Rheinwerk Computing, Bonn (2022)

14. Kusumaningrum, D., Kurniati, N., Santosa, B.: Machine learning for predictive maintenance. In: Proceedings of the International Conference on Industrial Engineering and Operations Management, IEOM 2021, pp. 2348–2356. IEOM Society (2021)

15. Laugwitz, B., Held, T., Schrepp, M.: Construction and evaluation of a user experience questionnaire. In: Holzinger, A. (ed.) USAB 2008. LNCS, vol. 5298, pp. 63–76. Springer, Heidelberg (2008). https://doi.org/10.1007/978-3-540-89350-9_6

16. Lewis, J.R.: The system usability scale: past, present, and future. Int. J. Hum.-Comput. Interact. **34**(7), 577–590 (2018). https://doi.org/10.1080/10447318.2018.1455307

17. Li, Y., Fu, K.: Research on minimalism in interface design based on gestalt psychology. In: Proceedings of the 2022 International Conference on Science Education and Art Appreciation (SEAA 2022), pp. 825–837. Atlantis Press (2022). https://doi.org/10.2991/978-2-494069-05-3_101

18. Nielsen, J.: Usability Engineering. Morgan Kaufmann (1993)

19. Passos, L.C., Viana, L., Oliveira, E., Conte, T.: Labelux! guidelines to support software engineers to design data labeling systems. In: Proceedings of the XX Brazilian

Symposium on Software Quality (SBQS 2021), pp. 1–10. Association for Computing Machinery, New York (2021). https://doi.org/10.1145/3493244.3493252

20. Preim, B., Dachselt, R.: Interaktive Systeme: Band 1: Grundlagen, Graphical User Interfaces, Informationsvisualisierung, 2nd edn. Springer, Heidelberg (2010). https://doi.org/10.1007/978-3-642-05402-0

21. Rietveld, P., Bruinsma, F.R., van Vuuren, D.J.: Coping with unreliability in public transport chains: a case study for Netherlands. Transp. Res. Part A Policy Pract. **35**(6), 539–559 (2001). https://doi.org/10.1016/S0965-8564(00)00006-9

22. Rogers, Y., Sharp, H., Preece, J.: INTERACTION DESIGN: Beyond Human-Computer Interaction, 3rd edn. Wiley, Chichester (2011)

23. Selcuk, S.: Predictive maintenance, its implementation and latest trends. In: Proceedings of the Institution of Mechanical Engineers, Part B: Journal of Engineering Manufacture, vol. 231, pp. 1670–1679 (2017). https://doi.org/10.1177/0954405415601640

24. Singh, C.D., Kaur, H.: Factories of the Future: Technological Advancements in the Manufacturing Industry. Wiley and Scrivener Publishing LLC, Hoboken (2023). https://doi.org/10.1002/9781119865216

25. Sun, Y., Lank, E., Terry, M.: Label-and-learn: visualizing the likelihood of machine learning classifier's success during data labeling. In: Proceedings of the 22nd International Conference on Intelligent User Interfaces (IUI 2017), pp. 523–534. Association for Computing Machinery, New York (2017). https://doi.org/10.1145/3025171.3025208

# A Quantitative Study of the Impact of Icon Complexity on Users' Sense of Control

Yuke Hu[✉]

Nanjing University of Science and Technology, No. 200 Xiaolingwei Street, Xuanwu District, Nanjing, Jiangsu, China
1215662847@qq.com

**Abstract.** In recent years, the development of information technology is rapidly changing, electronic products have become the most important human-computer interaction carriers and platforms to meet the needs of daily life, and icons have become an indispensable part of people's daily work. In order to explore the association between icon complexity and user's sense of control, we take the attribute of icon visual complexity as the entry point, and from the perspective of visual search, we combine E-prime3 psychological experimental research with subjective evaluation methods to determine the subjects' visual perception of icon stimuli with different levels of complexity, and then analyze the perception evaluation data through statistical methods using SPSS27.0. In order to explore the design strategies to effectively improve the user's sense of control when using electronic products, reduce the user's cognitive load and optimize the icon design. The results show that icons of different levels of complexity have a significant impact on users' sense of control, and the integration of iconic colors enhances users' sense of control.

**Keywords:** Icon complexity · user sense of control · operational efficiency · cognitive load

## 1 Introduction

With the advent of the big data era, all kinds of electronic products have become indispensable items in people's daily life and work, and huge and complex information is spilling out. As a visual symbol, icon is an important human-computer interaction tool in the interactive interface. It is closely related to human perception, cognition, memory and other processes. The complexity of icons affects the efficiency of users' operation, i.e., icons with a large amount of information may lead to cognitive overload, and icons with a small amount of information may affect their recognizability and lead to unrecognizable by users. Therefore, how to control icon complexity in design is particularly important in the pursuit of efficient society. Studying the relationship between icon complexity and user's sense of control, in order to construct a semantic system of icon complexity and user's sense of control and rationalize the design of icons in line with the laws of user cognition, can deepen people's understanding of the human information processing and cognitive process, reduce the user's cognitive load, enhance the efficiency of information interaction, and improve the user's sense of control [1].

© The Author(s), under exclusive license to Springer Nature Switzerland AG 2025
A. Marcus et al. (Eds.): HCII 2024, LNCS 15380, pp. 54–67, 2025.
https://doi.org/10.1007/978-3-031-76821-7_5

## 2   Research Status

### 2.1   Icon Complexity

Icons not only have aesthetic value, as a visual language, but also have the ability of cross-cultural communication. Excellent icon design has the advantages of reducing the complexity of interactive interface, minimizing cognitive load and enhancing work efficiency. Unique and attractive icon design can increase the recognition and memorability of a brand or APP. A unique and creative icon design can help a brand stand out in the market and create a deep emotional connection with the target audience. By using icons with clear meanings, users can quickly understand and recognize the function or category they represent, helping to shorten the time users spend in the search process and improve search efficiency.

Scholars and experts at home and abroad have made numerous achievements in icon design research. But there are few studies on the complexity of icons. To explore the complexity of icons, we must first find out from which dimensions to analyze icons. McDougall et al. [2] proposed five classification criteria for computer icons: specificity, semantic distance, familiarity, complexity and aesthetic attractiveness. Complexity refers to the number of basic shapes that make up the icon pattern. Compared to other classification criteria, the study of complexity of icons is more difficult. Because it is not only related to the objective amount of graphic information, but also related to the subjective aesthetics, the abstraction of the object shown in the icon [3]. Foreign research on icons has formed three major systems, although based on different experiments, theories, but they are in a common standard and form a complete branch [4]. Foreign icon classification method is mainly developed from three aspects: physical appearance, user cognition and representation strategy. The classification based on physical appearance of icons has been widely accepted for a long time. Lodding, one of the representative characters, categorizes icons into representational, abstract and arbitrary. Representational icons are defined as examples of general representation objects. Abstract icons are those that express concepts rather than show the objects themselves. Arbitrary icons are defined as icons that are created and designed according to specific conventions [5].Gittins [6] analyzed icons based on form, type and color, focusing mainly on the form of the icon.

Related scholars have carried out research on the effect of icon complexity and visual search performance. Some scholars believe that icon information should be as simple as possible, e.g., Byrne [7] argues that icons with simple structure have higher recognition performance than complex icons. While the other part of scholars asked for more icon details, such as Zifan Xu et al. [8] argued that icons with complex information can provide more clues than simple icons, and the meanings are easier to use as they can easily match each other with the assumptions in the user's mind. Many studies have taken the number of basic graphic units appearing in an icon as a direct indicator for estimating complexity. McDougall et al. [9] disassembled icons into constituent elements at both the content (graphic characters, indicators, line characters, etc.) and attribute (color shape, size, etc.) levels. Gordon et al. [10] scholars defined icon complexity as the number of constituent elements contained within a unit of space. The authors of Garcia et al. [11] constructed quantitative metrics based on icon complexity in terms of the number of icon elements. Cardaci et al. [12] evaluated the complexity of images with the method commonly used by computer experts to analyze spatial dimensions in order to deal with automated visualization problems, i.e., fuzzy methods, and classified them into high, medium, and low grades. In addition, the basis for judging the complexity of the icon structure includes the number of contained objects, the foreground and background images in between the objects, and so on.

## 2.2  Sense of Control

In the field of user experience design, the sense of control is often used to describe the phenomenon of people's positive or negative feelings towards a product, and this feeling is often affected by the advantages and disadvantages of product design, and maintaining the sense of control can provide users with a good experience and cognitive security [13].

Synthesizing the psychological discourse, Maslow divided the basic human needs into five levels, and at the same time defined the order of precedence, which are physiological needs, safety needs, the need for belonging and love, the need for respect, and the need for self-actualization. In the subsequent argumentation he further found that the safety needs are of a fairly high hierarchy of needs in the human living environment. Security needs can be categorized into 3 levels from low to high, which are, in order, sense of certainty, sense of security, and sense of control [14]. Sense of control is the subjective feeling that individuals have the ability to participate in decision-making to change events, the sense of control and competence that arises from achieving the user's expectations through the operation, and the sense of security during the operation. American psychologist J.B. Rotter [15] proposed the control point theory, which refers to the process of pursuing goals, based on the experience of facing many problematic situations, individuals will develop a classified anticipation or attitude of how to make the best constructs of the situation, and the classified anticipation of internal and external control is called the control point. This theory has since evolved into a universal psychological definition of a sense of control.

Xiao Jiang [16] proposed design principles to enhance the sense of control from five aspects: behavior and feedback, expression-mediated scenarios, physical buttons, and learned helplessness. Hai Chang [17] proposed that personal sense of control can be combined with job performance in an organization to study the relationship between the three using influencing factors as the independent variable, sense of control as the mediating variable, and job performance as the dependent variable. Weijuan Gao [18] found that an individual's sense of control over a stressful event directly affects an individual's motivation, and the stronger the sense of control the higher the motivation of the individual to improve the individual's sense of control to stimulate the engine to increase the benefits. Dongqing Chen [19] combined the two main goals of interaction design usability and emotional experience, to study some methods and principles that should be noted and followed in the process of smartphone application interaction design from the point of view of the sense of control, to help users create a good user experience.

# 3 Experimental

## 3.1 Experimental Design

This experiment explores the effect of icon complexity on user's sense of control, guided by quantitative visual experimental research methodology, to explore the differences in user's sense of control between icon complexity under different task situations, to summarize the perceptual problems and further find icon design specifications, and to output strategic guidance for icon design practice. E-prime3 was used to write the experimental procedure, recruit subjects, and conduct within-subject experiments, including practice experiments and formal experiments. The formal experiment used a 9 (9 icons) X5 (5 complexity) X2 (loop twice) within-subject design to quantify the sense of user control by recording the reaction time of receiving and responding to commands as well as two behavioral indicators: correctness or incorrectness.

The independent variable in this experiment was icon complexity. Icon complexity is objectively categorized by the number of icon design elements, which is categorized into five levels in this experiment, and is a multi-category independent variable. The dependent variable is the user's sense of control. In this experiment, based on the exploration of icons, the user's sense of control was limited to being able to quickly recognize, perceive, and understand icons, and the user's reaction time (i.e., rt) from listening to the instruction to making the instruction and the correctness rate (i.e., acc) were used to objectively measure the user's sense of control. Both dependent variables are continuous dependent variables.

## 3.2 Purpose of the Experiment

In order to investigate the differences in users' sense of control over icons, under random operation instructions, behavioral data indicators such as the subjects' response time, correctness or not for icons of different complexity levels are obtained to determine the influence of icon complexity levels on users' sense of control. According to the previous theoretical analysis, it is assumed that the icon complexity will affect the user's sense of control, and the user's sense of control is different under different levels of complexity, and this experiment is conducted to verify that the user's sense of control is expected to have a significant difference under five levels of complexity. The relationship between icon complexity and users' sense of control is explored in order to construct a semantic system of icon complexity and users' sense of control to guide the optimization of icon design.

## 3.3 Experimental Material Construction

**Icon Drawing.** Combined with the analysis of icon complexity in the preliminary literature reading, the construction of icon experimental materials under different task situations is carried out. Before the experiment, 9 commonly used APP icons are redrawn, and each icon is divided into 5 levels according to how many kinds of icon design elements, as shown in Fig. 1, level 1: only line elements; level 2: black and white gray block elements; level 3: color elements; level 4: add shadows, gradient and other effects; and level 5: add text elements underneath.

**Fig. 1.** Level 5 complexity icon

**Preparation of the Experimental Program.** The preparation of the experimental hardware equipment included a 14.5-inch monitor with a resolution of 1920 * 1080 pixels as a task environment simulation device. The psychology experiment E-prime3 software was used to prepare the experimental program (see Fig. 2), the experimental stimuli (see Fig. 3) were presented on the computer and the behavioral data (rt as well as correctness acc) were recorded, and the subjects participated in the task as responders, a total of 98 experiments were required (including 8 practice experiments and 90 formal experiments), and the experimental materials were presented randomly.

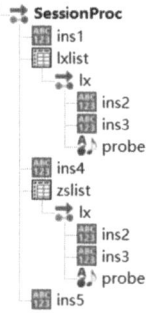

**Fig. 2.** Flow of the experimental program

**Relevant Questionnaire Design.** The research questionnaire consists of the basic information part and the evaluation part of the user's sense of control. A Likert 5-level scale was used to evaluate and analyze the icon users' sense of control. The grades are $-2$, $-1$, $0$, $1$, $2$, which represent the five evaluation degrees of "very strong sense of control, strong, general, weak, and very weak: respectively (Fig. 4).

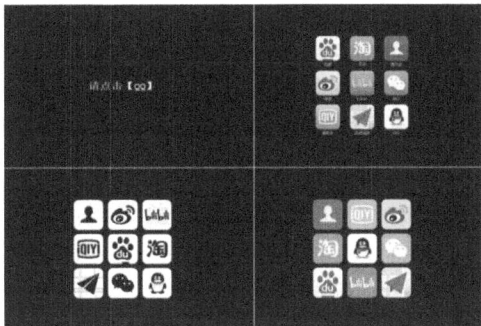

**Fig. 3.** Experiment running interface

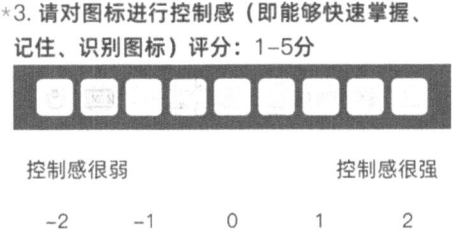

**Fig. 4.** Questionnaire Sense of Control Rating Scale

### 3.4 Experimental Material Construction

**Recruit Subjects.** 60 people, including 30 males and 30 females, invited subjects with normal naked eye or corrected vision, and no color blindness, color weakness, strabismus and other eye diseases, and no bad hobbies or psychological diseases, easy to focus, age 19–28 years old. Before the start of the formal experience, the equipment used in the experiment and the basic operation, as well as the main process of this experiment, need to be introduced to the subjects, and participants need to give informed consent to the experimental process.

**Confirmation of Experimental Location.** Dormitories, classrooms, and conference rooms, controlling light, noise, and other factors to ensure that subjects can be in a state of concentration to ensure that the experimental data are not interfered with by external factors.

**Entry of Subject's Personal Information.** Subjects were registered with basic information such as name, gender, and age, and the experimenter confirmed the subject's experiment number.

**Practice Experiment.** The procedure and content of this experiment in the practice phase are exactly the same as that of the formal experiment. First, the subjects were introduced to the requirements, procedures, and operation methods of the whole experiment. The subjects were given 8 practice experiments of 1 min duration to ensure that they were fully familiar with the experimental procedure and content before entering the formal experiment.

**Formal Experiment.** This experiment was a one-factor, five-level within-subjects design in which each subject received the same experimental treatment, i.e., experienced five different experimental materials. Due to the incomplete within-subjects design, counterbalancing was required through the all-possible-order method, where experimental stimulus materials of different complexity levels appeared randomly to minimize the influence of order effects. In the formal experiment, in order to exclude the influence of the distribution of icon positions on subjects' behavioral data measurements learned by subjects through multiple experiments during the course of the experiment, the icons appeared randomly in their positions in the screen. First, subjects were reminded to focus their attention, and a red "+" plus sign was presented on the screen for 1000 ms, i.e., to provide a central focus point. Next, the screen presented 1000ms of clicking instructions, such as "Please click on Bilibili\QQ/iqiyi\Baidu\Amap\Taobao\Address Book\Weibo\WeChat", and similarly, the instructions were given randomly, with each one appearing randomly 10 times. And then the icon positions were presented for an unlimited duration until the subject responded by clicking on the corresponding icon position. In order to minimize the interference of other external factors on the subjects' reaction time and correctness, the icon positions appeared randomly and each complexity level was randomly cycled for 2 rounds. Each subject had to go through 9 icons * 5 levels of complexity * 2 rounds, totaling 90 formal experiments. The length of the experiment was 10 min (Fig. 5).

**Fig. 5.** Some photos of the experimental process

**Poll.** After completing the experiment, subjects were reminded to complete the Sense of Control Measurement Questionnaire.

## 4 Experimental Results and Discussion

After the experiment, the response duration, correct or incorrect judgment of 98 experiments of 60 subjects were obtained. First, the experimental data were preprocessed. The valid data of 60 groups of subjects were integrated using E-Merge3. Since the data of practice experiments were not included in the data analysis, the data measured in the practice experiments were excluded, and the data of 9 icons under the same complexity level were merged to obtain the average of reaction time as well as the correct rate.

## 4.1 Response Time

SPSS27.0 software was utilized to process the experimental data for One-way Repeated Measures Anova with five levels of icon complexity as the independent variable and the length of subjects' responses as the dependent variable.

After descriptive statistics, the average value rt1 > rt2 > rt4 > rt5 > rt3(see Table 1), i.e., in terms of response time, the icon of complexity level 3 color elements has the shortest projection time and the strongest sense of user control. Judged by the box-and-line diagram, the data conformed to no outliers; after the Shapiro-Wilk test, as shown in Table 2, the data of each group obeyed the normal distribution (P > 0.05) (Table 3).

**Table 1.** Reaction time descriptive statistics

|      | Average    | Standard deviation | Number of cases |
|------|------------|--------------------|-----------------|
| rt1  | 1821.2998  | 318.40645          | 60              |
| rt2  | 1560.1843  | 249.93740          | 60              |
| rt3  | 1125.9688  | 243.64601          | 60              |
| rt4  | 1185.4260  | 275.51648          | 60              |
| rt5  | 1183.5802  | 276.92221          | 60              |

**Table 2.** Reaction time normality statistics

| Kolmogorov–Smirnov (a) | | | | Shapiro Wilke | | |
|------|--------------|-----|-------|--------------|-----|-------|
|      | statisticians | df  | sig   | statisticians | df  | sig   |
| rt1  | 0.113        | 60  | 0.056 | 0.971        | 60  | 0.157 |
| rt2  | 0.074        | 60  | .200* | 0.986        | 60  | 0.712 |
| rt3  | 0.108        | 60  | 0.076 | 0.932        | 60  | 0.002 |
| rt4  | 0.101        | 60  | .200* | 0.957        | 60  | 0.033 |
| rt5  | 0.108        | 60  | 0.076 | 0.944        | 60  | 0.008 |

After Mauchly's test of sphericity, the above table shows that: the study data did not pass the test of sphericity (p = 0.00 < 0.035), implying that a correction process is needed. Combined with the sphericity W-value, it can be seen that W = 0.58 < 0.75, implying that the Greenhouse-Geisser correction results should be used, as described in the table below (Table 4).

**Table 3.** Mokhirai sphericity test[a]

| Within-subjects effect | Mogilai-W | Approximate chi-square | df | sig | Epsilonb | | |
|---|---|---|---|---|---|---|---|
| | | | | | Greenhouse-Geisser | Sin Feddert | Lower limit |
| rt | 0.58 | 30.95 | 9.00 | 0.00 | 0.79 | 0.84 | 0.25 |

**Table 4.** Tests for within-subjects' effects

| Clauses | Adjusted | III -square sum | df | MS | F | sig |
|---|---|---|---|---|---|---|
| rt | Satisfies the spherical test | 22084363.73 | 4.00 | 5521090.93 | 297.37 | 0.00 |
| | GG Correction | 22084363.73 | 3.16 | 6990176.39 | 297.37 | 0.00 |
| | HF Correction | 22084363.73 | 3.36 | 6574971.39 | 297.37 | 0.00 |
| | Lower limit | 22084363.73 | 1.00 | 22084363.73 | 297.37 | 0.00 |

The sphericity test shows that eventually the GG correction should be used. For the icons to see, it shows a significance at the 0.1 level ($p = 0.000 < 0.1$), i.e., it shows that there is a significant variability in the reaction time to recognize different icons (Table 5).

From the table below, it can be concluded that among the 5 levels of complexity, there is no significant difference ($p = 1$) between only between level 4 adding effects such as shadows and level 5 adding text elements below. All other levels of complexity have significant differences with $p < 0.05$.

## 4.2 Correct Rate

Next, a One-way Repeated Measures Anova was conducted with five levels of icon complexity as the independent variable and subject correctness as the dependent variable.

After descriptive statistics, acc1, acc2 average is lower, level 1 only line elements, level 2 black and white gray block elements are easy to make subjects make wrong response after instruction. Acc3, acc4, acc5 average is higher than 0.95 (see Table 6), it can be judged that level 3 color elements, level 4 add shadow gradient and other effects, level 5 add text elements for subjects to have a stronger sense of control. The box-and-line plot judged that the data conformed to no outliers (Table 7).

In one-way repeated measures ANOVA, the first thing that needs to be done is the test of sphericity, as can be seen in the table above: the study data did not pass the test of sphericity ($p = 0.01 < 0.035$), implying that the correction process needs to be done. Combined with the value of sphericity W, it can be seen that $W = 0.68 < 0.75$, implying that GG should be used to correct the results, as described in the Table 8.

The sphericity test shows that eventually the GG correction results should be used. For the correctness rate, it shows a significance at the 0.1 level ($p = 0.000 < 0.1$), i.e., it

**Table 5.** Pairwise comparison

| (I) rt | (J) rt | Mean difference (I-J) | Standard error | sig[b] | 95% confidence interval of the difference | |
|---|---|---|---|---|---|---|
| | | | | | Lower limit | Upper limit |
| 1 | 2 | 261.115* | 32.485 | 0.001 | 166.374 | 355.857 |
| | 3 | 695.331* | 24.234 | 0.001 | 624.653 | 766.009 |
| | 4 | 635.874* | 25.954 | 0.001 | 560.179 | 711.569 |
| | 5 | 637.720* | 24.799 | 0.001 | 565.394 | 710.046 |
| 2 | 1 | −261.115* | 32.485 | 0.001 | −355.857 | −166.374 |
| | 3 | 434.216* | 26.169 | 0.001 | 357.894 | 510.537 |
| | 4 | 374.758* | 25.86 | 0.001 | 299.338 | 450.179 |
| | 5 | 376.604* | 29.332 | 0.001 | 291.059 | 462.149 |
| 3 | 1 | −695.331* | 24.234 | 0.001 | −766.009 | −624.653 |
| | 2 | −434.216* | 26.169 | 0.001 | −510.537 | −357.894 |
| | 4 | −59.457* | 17.947 | 0.016 | −111.797 | −7.117 |
| | 5 | −57.611* | 19.341 | 0.042 | −114.019 | −1.203 |
| 4 | 1 | −635.874* | 25.954 | 0.001 | −711.569 | −560.179 |
| | 2 | −374.758* | 25.86 | 0.001 | −450.179 | −299.338 |
| | 3 | 59.457* | 17.947 | 0.016 | 7.117 | 111.797 |
| | 5 | 1.846 | 18.638 | 1 | −52.512 | 56.203 |
| 5 | 1 | −637.720* | 24.799 | 0.001 | −710.046 | −565.394 |
| | 2 | −376.604* | 29.332 | 0.001 | −462.149 | −291.059 |
| | 3 | 57.611* | 19.341 | 0.042 | 1.203 | 114.019 |
| | 4 | −1.846 | 18.638 | 1 | −56.203 | 52.512 |

**Table 6.** Correct rate descriptive statistics

| | Average | Standard deviation | Number of cases |
|---|---|---|---|
| acc1 | 0.8733 | 0.07113 | 60 |
| acc2 | 0.9008 | 0.06184 | 60 |
| acc3 | 0.9663 | 0.04815 | 60 |
| acc4 | 0.9632 | 0.04394 | 60 |
| acc5 | 0.9677 | 0.04545 | 60 |

**Table 7.** Mokhirai sphericity test[a]

| Within-subjects effect | Mogilai-W | Approximate chi-square | df | sig | Epsilonb | | |
|---|---|---|---|---|---|---|---|
| | | | | | Greenhouse-Geisser | Sin Feddert | Lower limit |
| correct rate | 0.68 | 22.54 | 9.00 | 0.01 | 0.836 | 0.892 | 0.25 |

**Table 8.** Tests for within-subjects' effects

| Clauses | Adjusted | III -square sum | df | MS | F | sig |
|---|---|---|---|---|---|---|
| Correct rate | Satisfies the spherical test | 0.47 | 4.00 | 0.12 | 44.763 | 0.00 |
| | GG Correction | 0.47 | 3.34 | 0.14 | 44.763 | 0.00 |
| | HF Correction | 0.47 | 3.57 | 0.13 | 44.763 | 0.00 |
| | Lower limit | 0.47 | 1.00 | 0.47 | 44.763 | 0.00 |

shows that there is a significant variability in the correctness rate of recognizing different icons.

From the Table 9, it can be concluded that among the 5 levels of complexity, there is no significant difference between level 1-line elements only, level 2 black-white-gray block elements $p = 0.188 > 0.05$. There is no significant difference between level 3 colored elements, level 4 added shadows gradient and other effects, and level 5 added text elements. All other levels of complexity are significantly different from each other with $p < 0.05$.

## 4.3 Poll

Descriptive statistical analysis of the results of the questionnaire shows that in the subjective ratings of the subjects, there is a weak sense of control of the line only elements at level 1, an average sense of control of the black-white-gray block elements at level 2, and a strong sense of control of the colored elements at level 3, the addition of effects such as shadows and gradients at level 4, and the addition of text elements at level 5. (see Tables 10 and 11).

The results of users' ratings on the sense of control scale in the questionnaire were similar to the experimental results, which verified the rationality of the experimental design to objectively measure users' sense of control by reaction time and correctness.

To sum up, this experiment classifies the icon complexity by the type of icon design elements and divides the experimental materials into five levels: level 1 only line elements, level 2 black-white-gray block elements, level 3 color elements, level 4 adding shadows, gradients and other effects, and level 5 adding text elements. Through the experiment of icon complexity and user control, we get the behavioral data of the time

**Table 9.** Pairwise comparison

| (I) acc | (J) acc | Mean difference (I-J) | Standard error | sig[b] | 95% confidence interval of the difference[b] | |
|---------|---------|-----------------------|----------------|--------|---------|---------|
| | | | | | Lower limit | Upper limit |
| 1 | 2 | −0.028 | 0.011 | 0.188 | −0.061 | 0.006 |
| | 3 | −.093* | 0.010 | 0.001 | −0.123 | −0.063 |
| | 4 | −.090* | 0.010 | 0.001 | −0.12 | −0.059 |
| | 5 | −.094* | 0.011 | 0.001 | −0.126 | −0.062 |
| 2 | 1 | 0.028 | 0.011 | 0.188 | −0.006 | 0.061 |
| | 3 | −.065* | 0.009 | 0.001 | −0.091 | −0.04 |
| | 4 | −.062* | 0.008 | 0.001 | −0.086 | −0.039 |
| | 5 | −.067* | 0.009 | 0.001 | −0.094 | −0.039 |
| 3 | 1 | .093* | 0.010 | 0.001 | 0.063 | 0.123 |
| | 2 | .066* | 0.009 | 0.001 | 0.04 | 0.091 |
| | 4 | 0.003 | 0.008 | 1 | −0.02 | 0.027 |
| | 5 | −0.001 | 0.007 | 1 | −0.022 | 0.019 |
| 4 | 1 | .090* | 0.010 | 0.001 | 0.059 | 0.12 |
| | 2 | .062* | 0.008 | 0.001 | 0.039 | 0.086 |
| | 3 | −0.003 | 0.008 | 1 | −0.027 | 0.02 |
| | 5 | −0.004 | 0.008 | 1 | −0.028 | 0.019 |
| 5 | 1 | .094* | 0.011 | 0.001 | 0.062 | 0.126 |
| | 2 | .067* | 0.009 | 0.001 | 0.039 | 0.094 |
| | 3 | 0.001 | 0.007 | 1 | −0.019 | 0.022 |
| | 4 | 0.004 | 0.008 | 1 | −0.019 | 0.028 |

**Table 10.** Sense of Control Scale Results Statistics

| | Level1 | Level2 | Level3 | Level4 | Level5 |
|---|--------|--------|--------|--------|--------|
| Very weak sense of control | 53.33% | 1.67% | 0% | 0% | 0% |
| Weak sense of control | 20% | 38% | 0% | 1.67% | 1.67% |
| General | 15% | 25% | 30% | 8.33% | 1.67% |
| Strong sense of control | 8.33% | 25.00% | 28.33% | 46.67% | 16.67% |
| Very strong sense of control | 3.33% | 10% | 41.67% | 43.33% | 80% |

**Table 11.** Descriptive Statistics for the Sense of Control Scale

|        | Average | Standard deviation |
|--------|---------|--------------------|
| Level1 | −1.12   | 1.15               |
| Level2 | 0.03    | 1.06               |
| Level3 | 1.12    | 0.85               |
| Level4 | 1.32    | 0.7                |
| Level5 | 1.75    | 0.57               |

and correct rate of users' capturing and reacting to the information under different levels of complexity of the icons and analyze the data to conclude that the complexity of the icons affects the user's sense of control. 1 level of line elements only has a weaker sense of control, 2 level of black-white-gray block elements has a general sense of control. There is less variability in the sense of control between level 3 colored elements, level 4 adding shadows gradients and other effects, and level 5 adding text elements, all of which have a strong sense of user control.

After adding color to the icon, the user's sense of control is greatly enhanced, which shows the significance of color in icon design. Color is an important element of visual communication, which can arouse the audience's emotion, attract attention and convey specific information. Color enhances the recognition and identifiability of the icon, which can help the icon to be more eye-catching and prominent visually, thus improving the user's sense of control. By using bright, vibrant colors, designers can make icons easier to notice in a variety of environments and leave a lasting impression on users. Designers can choose specific colors to communicate the characteristics and values of the brand, product or concept that the icon represents. Iconic colors can help icons establish a unique brand identity in the marketplace. By choosing specific colors, companies can create a lasting impression in the minds of users and differentiate themselves from competitors. For example, WeChat's green color and Bilibili's pink color can help users quickly access information and complete instructions, reducing the cognitive load on users and improving operational efficiency.

**Acknowledgments.** The writing has finally ended here. A new song is about to be played and the title page is written in this chapter. This essay is a coursework for the Data Analytics course and the Product Semantics course. There are so many people to thank along the way. First of all, thanks to my friends. In the experimental phase, 60 subjects were needed, and my friends gave me a lot of help and helped me pull a lot of subjects. Second, to thank my teachers for their guidance. I benefited a lot from the teachers' wise teachings. Take the dream as a horse, not to be ashamed of it. It's time to say thank you to yourself. I would like to thank myself for teaching myself Eprime software and learning how to analyze data. Although I have a lot of minor problems on the way of research, such as late-stage procrastination, I barely managed to finish the mini-paper at the right time. Thank you to the self that doesn't give up and thank you to the self that becomes brave and independent little by little. I hope to continue to work hard on the road ahead, and the future is promising.

**Disclosure of Interests.** The authors have no competing interests.

# References

1. Bao, G.Y.: Quantitative study on the impact of icon complexity on search performance in construction machinery. Mech. Electric. Prod. Develop. Innov. **36**(03), 197–202 (2023)
2. McDougall, S.J., De Bruijn, O., Curry, M.B.: Exploring the effects of icon characteristics on user performance: the role of icon concreteness, complexity, and distinctiveness. J. Exp. Psychol. Appl. **6**(4), 291 (2000)
3. Kim, S., Lee, S.: Smash the dichotomy of Skeuomorphism and flat design: designing an affordable interface to correspond with the human perceptuomotor process. Int. J. Hum Comput Stud. **141**, 102435 (2020)
4. Zhang, X.F., Xue, C.Q., Shen, Z.F.: An analysis of icon complexity in digital interfaces for human-computer interaction. Design **19**, 119–120 (2017)
5. Zhang, X.F: Research on icon complexity of interactive interfaces based on user experience. Southeast University (2018)
6. Gittins, D.: Icon-based human-computer interaction. Int. J. Man Mach. Stud. **24**(6), 519–543 (1986)
7. Byrne, M.D.: Using icons to find documents: simplicity is critical. In: Proceedings of the INTERACT'93 and CHI'93 Conference on Human Factors in Computing Systems, pp. 446–453 (1993)
8. Hsu, T.F.: Recognition efficiency and pattern of graphical symbols based on information loads and cognitive styles: a study of ALGA symbols. J. Des. Sci. **11**(1), 87–105 (2008)
9. McDougall, S.J., Curry, M.B., De Bruijn, O.: Measuring symbol and icon characteristics: norms for concreteness, complexity, meaningfulness, familiarity, and semantic distance for 239 symbols. Behav. Res. Methods Instrum. Comput. **31**(3), 487–519 (1999)
10. Gordon, I.E.: Theories of visual perception. Psychology press, London (2004)
11. García, M., Badre, A.N., Stasko, J.T.: Development and validation of icons varying in their abstractness. Interact. Comput. **6**(2), 191–211 (1994)
12. Cardaci, M., Di Gesù, V., Petrou, M., Tabacchi, M.E.: A fuzzy approach to the evaluation of image complexity. Fuzzy Sets Syst. **160**(10), 1474–1484 (2009)
13. Zhang, X.: Research on localization of interaction design based on sense of control. Beijing University of Posts and Telecommunications (2018)
14. Xia, F., Tao, J.: Exploration of user's sense of control in service design. Indust. Des. Res. **00**, 185–190 (2018)
15. Zhang, Y.Y.: Research on the sense of control in HTML5 web interaction design. Art Technol. **30**(05), 82 (2017)
16. Jiang, X., Wang, Y.M., Wang, Y.H.: Research on user's sense of control in the design of urban smart travel help service - taking Hangzhou as an example. Design **32**(24), 118–120 (2019)
17. Chang, H.: Research on the sense of control in interaction design. Jiangnan University (2010)
18. Gao, W.J.: A psychological understanding of the sense of control. Jilin University (2005)
19. Chen, D.Q: Research on the sense of control in smartphone application interaction design. Beijing University of Posts and Telecommunications (2014)

# A Computational Aesthetic Design Science Study on Online Video Based on Triple-Dimensional Multimodal Analysis

Zhangguang Kang[1] , Fiona Fui-Hoon Nah[2] , and Keng Leng Siau[2]($\boxtimes$) 

[1] City University of Hong Kong, Kowloon Tong, Kowloon, Hong Kong SAR
zhangkang2-c@my.cityu.edu.hk
[2] Singapore Management University, Singapore, Singapore
{fionanah,klsiau}@smu.edu.sg

**Abstract.** Computational video aesthetic prediction refers to using models that automatically evaluate the features of videos to produce their aesthetic scores. Current video aesthetic prediction models are designed based on bimodal frameworks. To address their limitations, we developed the Triple-Dimensional Multimodal Temporal Video Aesthetic neural network (TMTVA-net) model. The Long Short-Term Memory (LSTM) forms the conceptual foundation for the design framework. In the multimodal transformer layer, we employed two distinct transformers: the multimodal transformer and the feature transformer, enabling the acquisition of modality-specific patterns and representational features uniquely adapted to each modality. The fusion layer has also been redesigned to compute both pairwise interactions and overall interactions among the features. This study contributes to the video aesthetic prediction literature by considering the synergistic effects of textual, audio, and video features. This research presents a novel design framework that considers the combined effects of multimodal features.

**Keywords:** Computational Video Aesthetic · Multimodal Analysis · Neural Network · Design Science

## 1 Introduction

Video is a medium used on many social media platforms to disseminate information. Sora, a Generative Artificial Intelligence (AI) application, brings video creation to the forefront (Wang et al. 2024). "Aesthetics" refers to the enjoyment and beauty that people derive from their senses (Adorno 1997). Computational video aesthetic prediction refers to using models and algorithms that automatically evaluate the features of videos to produce their aesthetic scores (Murray & Gordo 2017). It can be used for content quality assessment, ranking and recommending videos, understanding subjective human preferences, and automatic video generation (Hernández-García et al. 2016). In the context of AI video generation, video aesthetic prediction is an important matrix in guiding video generation (Liu & Yu 2023). The multimodal features of videos provide a rich and engaging viewing experience by incorporating various forms of sensory input (Pandeya & Lee

© The Author(s), under exclusive license to Springer Nature Switzerland AG 2025
A. Marcus et al. (Eds.): HCII 2024, LNCS 15380, pp. 68–79, 2025.
https://doi.org/10.1007/978-3-031-76821-7_6

2020). In the context of video, "multimodal" refers to the utilization of multiple features of communication or information presentation within the video content (Knight 2013). These features could include visual (e.g., color, spatial properties), auditory (e.g., sound effects, music), and textual (e.g., font type and size) features.

Despite numerous methods proposed to predict video aesthetics, there are two problems in the existing designs. The first problem is that video aesthetic prediction models are bimodal in design, and hence, they do not align with the viewing patterns of videos. Most videos consist of three or more modalities. The second problem is the inadequacy of past design models for assessing the intra-element interactions in multidimensional video aesthetic analysis with three or more aesthetic features.

In our research, we designed a Triple-Dimensional Multimodal Temporal Video Aesthetic neural network (TMTVA-net) model to address the two problems mentioned above. Our prediction research is based on sequential video data, so we use Long Short-Term Memory (LSTM) as the conceptual foundation. The main advantage of the LSTM network lies in its ability to selectively remember or forget information over long periods (Y. Yu et al. 2019a, b).

The fundamental concept underlying this new design is that it considers the effect of adding a third aesthetic feature to the interaction effect of the first two aesthetic features. By altering the order of the aesthetic features, we consider all the combinations of features of the three-dimensional multimodal model. Based on the LSTM model structure, we first extract the combined features of two aesthetic modalities (e.g., video and audio). We then add a hidden layer to represent the combined effect of the two aesthetic modalities. Building upon the combined feature of these two aesthetic modalities, we introduced the third modality (e.g., text) and used the last hidden layer to represent its combined effect with the interaction effect of the first two aesthetic modalities. This design implements the triple-feature interaction in video aesthetic prediction. The combination of modalities in different orders represents the influence of a third modality on the joint effect of the first two modalities. We then determine the average combined effect of the three-dimensional multimodal interaction by pivoting the hierarchical sequence of the triple aesthetic features of the model and averaging the triple-dimensional multimodal analysis results. Finally, we utilize features derived from both the bivariate and trivariate combined models to predict the aesthetic value of the video content.

This study makes two contributions. The first contribution is the use of the tripartite synergy of text, audio, and video in the analysis of video aesthetics. This research lays the conceptual groundwork for future multimodal analyses. Future research can build on the design concept proposed in this study. The second research contribution is that this study analyzes the synergistic effects of three information features and identifies the combined effects from both the bivariate and trivariate multimodal model aesthetic modalities. Building upon the previous design that measures the synergistic effect of bivariate aesthetic modalities, the new design introduces a novel multimodal prediction model for video aesthetic prediction. This model considers the combined effect of features involving bivariate and triple modalities. This design not only enhances prediction accuracy but also contributes to the design of multimodal prediction models.

Following the introduction, the paper proceeds to present the literature review, research design, results, and discussion.

## 2  Literature Review

The literature review consists of two parts. The first part introduces visual, sound, and textual aesthetic features from past video aesthetic prediction studies. The second part summarizes the research methods and models for multimodal aesthetic prediction studies of videos in previous studies.

### 2.1  Multimodal Aesthetic Features

Photo-based aesthetic features have been widely used in previous video prediction studies to assess visual aesthetic features. Photo-based aesthetic features consist of 'Low-level' (i.e., bottom-up) features and 'High-level' (i.e., top-down) features (Iigaya et al. 2021). Low-level visual features are elemental attributes or characteristics of visual stimuli, typically found in images or videos. Low-level visual features (e.g., color properties, spatial properties, and mood) are extracted directly from raw pixel data and usually do not involve high-level cognitive aesthetic interpretation (Berman et al. 2014). 'High-level' aesthetic features (e.g., golden ratio and rule of three) reflect subjective judgment about an image and contribute to the overall perception of appeal, beauty, or artistic quality (Palmer et al. 2013).

In this research, we also focus on perceptual sound features that are related to how humans perceive sound, including intensity, luminosity, rhythm, timbre, and loudness (Pols et al. 1969; Yang et al. 2023). There are two forms of perceptual sound features: the first involves sounds emitted by humans and the second pertains to background music produced by humans using musical instruments (Alías et al. 2016). Perceptual sound features can affect people's emotions (Sezgin et al. 2012) and transmit a particular semantic message or aesthetic feeling to humans (Alías et al. 2016).

Textual features are used in previous image aesthetic prediction (Liu et al. 2017; Zhang et al. 2021) or video aesthetic prediction in multimodal research (Schindler 2020). Textual features refer to any textual information included in video, and the text content can include dialogue, narration, scene descriptions, or other relevant information to the viewers (Phatak & Asarkar 2019; Yin 2020). The textual features can shape the video's overall aesthetic perception by shaping the video's visual style, narrative coherence, emotional resonance, and theme (Hoogland 2004; Ma et al. 2018; Prinz 2011). Textual features are essential expression features that impact the aesthetic perceptions of video (Hoogland 2004).

### 2.2  Multimodal Video Aesthetic Prediction

Video aesthetic prediction tasks involve evaluating the aesthetic quality and appeal of videos through their various modalities (Lemarchand 2017). To organize past research findings, we reviewed previous research findings based on the steps of video aesthetic prediction.

Combining multimodal information effectively within a deep neural network framework is fundamental in video aesthetic prediction research. Video aesthetic prediction tasks require integrating data from multiple sources, such as visual, sound, and textual content, and creating a unified representation for aesthetic prediction tasks (Knight

2013). Some researchers designed a residual-aided intermediate fusion (RAIF) deep learning-based architecture by combining audio and visual aesthetic features based on Convolutional Neural Network (CNN) (Iffath & Gavrilova 2023). Other researchers proposed a brain-inspired multimodal interaction network (BMI-Net) to leverage image and text features. The BMI-Net approach employs the LSTM method to effectively learn the combined effects of images and text based on time series data (Nie et al. 2023).

Researchers have implemented various models or designed new deep-learning structures to measure cross-modal relationships. One method involves utilizing multimodal canonical correlation analysis to identify linear inter-modality relationships and cross-modality generalization information (Gao et al. 2020). Moreover, researchers have employed probabilistic graphical models to learn crucial cross-modal correlations by integrating modalities in a shared latent space (Guo et al. 2019). This method facilitates the exploration of correlations between different modalities, thereby enhancing understanding of relationships across diverse data sources. Additionally, deep learning architectures like EmbraceNet have been specifically designed to capture cross-modal correlations of data acquired from the same target but through different sensors (Choi & Lee 2019). This architecture aids in identifying correlations and relationships between modalities, thereby contributing to a comprehensive understanding of multimodal data. Some researchers effectively integrate information from multiple sources of modalities by developing a data fusion layer that involves creating a component within a neural network architecture (Durrant-Whyte & Henderson 2016).

When dealing with continuous data (videos), the video aesthetic prediction task should simultaneously consider multimodal analysis and continuous prediction. When designing the data fusion layer, researchers use different methods to predict the video aesthetic based on the time-interval continuous data. Positional embeddings are techniques to provide the model with information about the position of tokens within the sequence (Gupta et al. 2022). Positional embeddings should be added to the input embeddings before passing them into the neural network architecture (Bucur et al. 2023). The design of the data fusion layer should aggregate multimodal representations that can aid in generating conditional probabilities for aesthetic predictions over varying time intervals (Vale-Silva & Rohr 2021). This design allows for a comprehensive analysis of multimodal data streams, leading to more accurate and dynamic aesthetic predictions. Researchers also argue that dimensionality reduction techniques can help extract essential features for multimodal analysis based on time series data (Ashraf et al. 2023).

The literature emphasizes the significance of multimodal data fusion techniques in generating effective model explanations. The interpretability of multimodal deep learning models is crucial for understanding how different modalities contribute to the aesthetic prediction process (Joshi et al. 2021). Multimodal deep autoencoders (MDA) capture the fusion relationship between images and text. The MDA model can provide valuable insights and explanations for generating conditional probabilities based on multimodal inputs (Gao et al. 2020). Researchers also discussed feature fusion layers, such as the "concat layer" and "eltwise layer", which are crucial in combining features from different modalities. Integrating these fusion layers can aid in explaining the aesthetic analysis results by elucidating how information from diverse modalities is integrated (Li et al. 2020).

To summarize, past studies have reviewed video, audio, and textual features utilized in multimodal analysis. To conduct aesthetic prediction based on multimodal deep learning, researchers can draw on methodologies combining multimodal information, leveraging time-series deep representation learning, incorporating data fusion layers, and ensuring model interpretability. By integrating these approaches, it is possible to develop robust and accurate aesthetic prediction models that consider diverse modalities for video aesthetic prediction.

However, there are still two research gaps. First, video aesthetic prediction models are bimodal models that only consider two aesthetic features. In past research, some scholars have examined the combined effect of textual content and video, while others have explored the combined effect of audio and video. From the literature, we argue that these three features are all crucial in multimodal analysis, and we should consider all three factors simultaneously in model design.

The second research gap pertains to the design of previous research models. The architectures of these models are constrained in achieving multimodal integration analysis, as the structure of a single fusion layer proves insufficient in capturing the interactions among multiple features within the model. The literature review shows that the models proposed in previous studies can compute the general synergistic effects of multimodalities but fail to assess the interactions among internal features. When the model features exceed two, the design of a single fusion layer cannot achieve the extraction of the internal multi-element interaction features within the model.

## 3   Research Design

A public dataset, CERTH-ITI-VAQ700, was used in this research (Xu et al. 2015). This dataset contains 700 YouTube videos spanning diverse categories. Twelve annotators were tasked to assess the aesthetic value of these videos by assigning binary aesthetic quality ratings: 1 denoting videos of high aesthetic quality and 0 representing videos of low aesthetic quality. Each video underwent evaluation by five annotators. The overall aesthetic score for each annotated video was derived as the median score from the individual annotators. Following the annotation process, 350 videos were rated as exhibiting high aesthetic quality, while another 350 were deemed to have low aesthetic quality. The duration of each of these videos ranges from 1 to 6 min.

For each sequential video frame, we generated 128 high-level and 256 low-level photo-based aesthetic features, as recommended in previous research (Rao et al. 2019). The deep-learning real-time visual simultaneous localization and mapping (RT-SLAM) method extracts visual features based on multi-task feature extraction networks and self-supervised features (Li et al. 2021). These visual features are fed into a fully connected layer with 64 units.

We used Audio Event Net Feature (AENet) (Takahashi et al. 2018) to extract features directly from the time series raw audio data. The pooling layer was adjusted to $2 \times 64$ based on the time frame and the frequency of the signals. We used six $3 \times 3$ kernels convolutional layers and three fully connected layers to calculate the audio feature based on the time serious data.

The Bidirectional Encoder Representations for Transformers (BERT) method (Devlin et al. 2018) was used for positive and negative sentiment analysis. We used the mapping convergence algorithm (Ganguly et al. 2014) to generate text aesthetic features based on the content of the video. We extracted negative, positive, and neutral sentiments from sentiment analysis and extracted seven features from text aesthetic features according to predetermined rules. All of the features are shown in Table 1.

**Table 1.** Text aesthetic features

| Abbreviation | Feature | Rule of Calculation |
|---|---|---|
| T1 | Topic Diversity | Variety of different themes covered within a specific context |
| SENT | Sentiment | Emotion of text expression (positive, negative, or neutral) |
| W1 | Word repetition | Recurrence of the same word or phrase within a text or speech |
| SD1 | First-order semantic distance | Similarity or dissimilarity between two concepts or entities based on their semantic meaning at a basic grammar level |
| T2 | Topic abstractness | Degree of conceptual distance between a topic and concrete, tangible entities or ideas |

All hidden layers are enhanced with the Rectified Linear Unit (ReLU) non-linearity, except for the final fully connected layer. The final fully connected layer was designed for the fusion structure of three features in the multimodal analysis.

We designed a TMTVA-net to solve two problems mentioned in the previous section. The model is shown in Fig. 1. The model is based on LSTM networks (Greff et al. 2017). LSTM networks are suitable for multimodal analysis because they can handle sequential data, capture temporal dependencies, and model complex relationships involving multiple modalities (Xu et al. 2017).

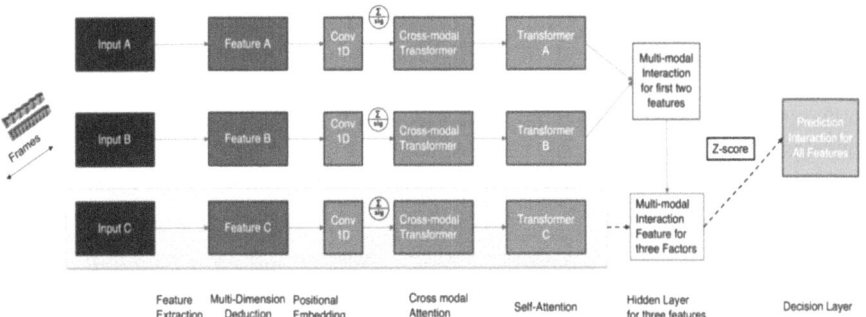

**Fig. 1.** Model design

The first step of the model involves extracting features from video, audio, and text separately using modality-specific neural network architectures based on the feature extraction methodologies. The multi-dimensional reduction method, t-distributed Stochastic Neighbor Embedding (t-SNE) (Belkina et al. 2019), was used to reduce the number of input variables or features in a dataset while preserving important information.

Positional embeddings were computed separately for video, audio, and textual features based on the position of each token in the sequence. We applied multiple one-dimensional convolutional layers (Conv1D) in our study considering the task complexity. The number of Conv1D layers depends on the complexity of the three features. We repeat the positional embeddings along the temporal dimension to match each feature's sequence length of the Conv1D layer output.

The output of a Conv1D layer may contain high-dimensional feature representations. As our research is a binary classification task, we applied a sigmoid activation function that compresses these features into a bounded range between 0 and 1, which can benefit certain tasks such as binary classification.

A cross-modular transformer is a type of transformer architecture designed to efficiently process and integrate information from multiple modalities (e.g., text, image, and audio). Unlike traditional transformers that primarily focus on sequential or spatial data within a single modality, cross-modal transformers are tailored to handle diverse data types and their interactions (Yan et al. 2023).

Conv1D layers effectively extract local patterns and features from sequential data (Nguyen et al. 2021). The output of the Conv1D layers was fed into a multimodal transformer after the sigmoid transformation. By passing the Conv1D output through a multimodal transformer, the model further processes and integrates extracted features with information from other modalities.

We use an additional hidden layer to enhance the explanation and representation of the interaction features. Hidden layers can facilitate information fusion from different modalities by combining representations from individual transformers and encoding their interactions (Ma et al. 2016). By measuring the interaction between modalities in hidden layers, the model can learn to combine complementary information from different modalities effectively.

By utilizing the cosine similarity function, we initially computed the interaction between the first two features, followed by the similarity computation between the third element and the interaction term of the first two features. The triple-dimensional multimodal vector is calculated by the interaction of the third feature with that of the first two features. By altering the order of the three features, we can generate all the triple-dimensional multimodal vectors. The calculation of cosine similarity is shown in the formula below. One example of a triple-dimensional multimodal vector representation of three features is depicted in Fig. 2.

$$cos\theta = \frac{\overrightarrow{FeatureA} * \overrightarrow{FeatureB}}{\left[\left[\overrightarrow{FeatureA}\right]\right] * \left[\left[\overrightarrow{FeatureB}\right]\right]} = \frac{\sum_{i=1}^{n} FeatureA_i * FeatureB_i}{\sqrt{\sum_{i=1}^{n} FeatureA_i^2} * \sqrt{\sum_{i=1}^{n} FeatureB_i^2}}$$

$$(1)$$

While a multimodal transformer can integrate information from multiple modalities, it may not effectively capture all modality-specific details or nuances (J. Yu et al.

2019a, b). The multimodal transformer learns modality-specific patterns and relationship features representation specific to each modality.

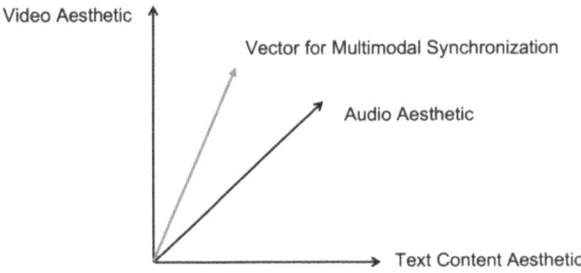

**Fig. 2.** Triple-dimensional multimodal vector representation

## 4  Research Results

By training, tuning parameters, and making predictions using the model we have constructed, we compared the prediction outcomes with those of the currently proposed research methods to demonstrate our study's effectiveness. We compared our results with previous benchmark results (Lemarchand 2017; Li et al. 2022) using F-Score, Accuracy, and Area under the ROC Curve (AUC), and the comparison is shown in Table 2. Compared to the previous results, our proposed method outperforms the earlier methods in all three metrics.

**Table 2.**  Comparison of prediction results

| Model | Matrix | Results |
|---|---|---|
| MVVA-Net | F-Score | 64.7399% |
| ResNet V2 + LSTM | | 80% |
| **TMTVA-net (Proposed)** | | **82.7%** |
| MVVA-Net | Accuracy | 65.1429% |
| ResNet V2 + LSTM | | 77.31% |
| **TMTVA-net (Proposed)** | | **79.6%** |
| MVVA-Net | AUC | 70.109% |
| ResNet V2 + LSTM | | 86% |
| **TMTVA-net (Proposed)** | | **87.2%** |

## 5  Conclusion

In this research, we designed a TMTVA-net model by incorporating textual content, audio, and video features. Our findings demonstrate that integrating these diverse modalities allows for a more comprehensive prediction of video aesthetics, which outperforms unimodal approaches.

This study presents two research contributions. First, it designed a novel model by considering the three-dimensional interaction of textual content, audio, and visual features in video aesthetic prediction. This study creates a more comprehensive model that better reflects real-world multimodal environments, laying a new conceptual foundation for future video aesthetic multimodal analyses by incorporating three modalities. This design enhances the authenticity and applicability of multimodal analyses, paving the way for a more nuanced understanding of complex phenomena. Second, the study examines the interactions of three distinct information modalities, elucidating the intricate interplay between bivariate and trivariate multimodal model aesthetic features. Departing from the conventional approach of assessing the combined effects of all aesthetic features, this research proposes an innovative multimodal design model tailored specifically for video aesthetic prediction. This model accounts for the dynamic interactions among the factors and discerns the interactions between pairwise elements. This model not only elevates prediction but also lays the groundwork for advancing video multimodal aesthetic prediction models.

Despite the promising results obtained from our study on computational video aesthetic design using an LSTM model incorporating textual, audio, and video features, several limitations must be acknowledged. First, the dataset used for training and evaluation, although extensive, may not encompass the full diversity of video content types, which could affect the generalizability of our findings. Future research should expand the dataset to include a broader range of video genres and incorporate user feedback to provide deeper insights into the aesthetic preferences across different audiences. Expanding the dataset to include a broader range of video genres and cultural contexts could improve the robustness of our models. Second, the complexity of the LSTM model, combined with the triple-dimensional multimodal inputs, results in substantial computational resource requirements, potentially limiting its scalability and real-time application. Future research can incorporate computational load reduction and principal component extraction techniques into the process of calculating the interactions among the three elements.

## References

Adorno, T.W.: Aesthetic theory. A&C Black (1997)

Alías, F., Socoró, J.C., Sevillano, X.: A review of physical and perceptual feature extraction techniques for speech, music and environmental sounds. Appl. Sci. 6(5), 143 (2016). https://doi.org/10.3390/app6050143

Ashraf, M., et al.: A survey on dimensionality reduction techniques for time-series data. IEEE Access 11, 42909–42923 (2023). https://doi.org/10.1109/ACCESS.2023.3269693

Belkina, A.C., Ciccolella, C.O., Anno, R., Halpert, R., Spidlen, J., Snyder-Cappione, J.E.: Automated optimized parameters for T-distributed stochastic neighbor embedding improve visualization and analysis of large datasets. Nat. Commun. **10**(1), 5415 (2019). https://doi.org/10.1038/s41467-019-13055-y

Berman, M.G., et al.: The perception of naturalness correlates with low-level visual features of environmental scenes. PLoS ONE **9**(12), e114572 (2014). https://doi.org/10.1371/journal.pone.0114572

Bucur, A.-M., Cosma, A., Rosso, P., Dinu, L. P.: It's just a matter of time: detecting depression with time-enriched multimodal transformers. In: European Conference on Information Retrieval, Lecture Notes in Computer Science, vol. 13980, pp. 200–215 (2023). https://doi.org/10.1007/978-3-031-28244-7_13

Choi, J.-H., Lee, J.-S.: EmbraceNet: a robust deep learning architecture for multimodal classification. Inform. Fus. **51**, 259–270 (2019). https://doi.org/10.1016/j.inffus.2019.02.010

Devlin, J., Chang, M.-W., Lee, K., Toutanova, K.: Bert: pre-training of deep bidirectional transformers for language understanding. arXiv preprint arXiv:1810.04805 (2018)

Durrant-Whyte, H., Henderson, T.C.: Multisensor data fusion. In: Siciliano, B., Khatib, O. (eds.) Springer Handbook of Robotics. Springer, Berlin, Heidelberg (2016). https://doi.org/10.1007/978-3-540-30301-5_26

Ganguly, D., Leveling, J., Jones, G.J.F.: Automatic prediction of text aesthetics and interestingness. In: Proceedings of the 25th International Conference on Computational Linguistics: Technical Papers, pp. 905–916. Dublin City University and Association for Computational Linguistics, Dublin, Ireland (2014)

Gao, J., Li, P., Chen, Z., Zhang, J.: A survey on deep learning for multimodal data fusion. Neural Comput. **32**(5), 829–864 (2020). https://doi.org/10.1162/neco_a_01273

Greff, K., Srivastava, R.K., Koutnik, J., Steunebrink, B.R., Schmidhuber, J.: LSTM: a search space odyssey. IEEE Trans. Neural Networks Learn. Syst. **28**(10), 2222–2232 (2017). https://doi.org/10.1109/tnnls.2016.2582924

Guo, W., Wang, J., Wang, S.: Deep multimodal representation learning: a survey. IEEE Access **7**, 63373–63394 (2019). https://doi.org/10.1109/access.2019.2916887

Gupta, A., Tian, S., Zhang, Y., Wu, J., Martín-Martín, R., Li, F.-F.: Maskvit: masked visual pre-training for video prediction. arXiv preprint arXiv:2206.11894 (2022). https://doi.org/10.48550/arXiv.2206.11894

Hernández-García, A., Fernández-Martínez, F., Díaz-de-María, F.: Comparing visual descriptors and automatic rating strategies for video aesthetics prediction. Signal Process. Image Commun. **47**, 280–288 (2016). https://doi.org/10.1016/j.image.2016.07.004

Hoogland, C.: An aesthetics of language. J. Can. Assoc. Curricul. Stud. **2**(2), 42–59 (2004)

Iffath, F., Gavrilova, M.: RAIF: a deep learning-based architecture for multi-modal aesthetic biometric system. Comput. Anim. Virtual Worlds **34**(3–4), e2163 (2023). https://doi.org/10.1002/cav.2163

Iigaya, K., Yi, S., Wahle, I.A., Tanwisuth, K., O'Doherty, J.P.: Aesthetic preference for art can be predicted from a mixture of low-and high-level visual features. Nat. Hum. Behav. **5**(6), 743–755 (2021). https://doi.org/10.1038/s41562-021-01124-6

Joshi, R.S., et al.: Discovery of potential multi-target-directed ligands by targeting host-specific SARS-CoV-2 structurally conserved main protease. J. Biomol. Struct. Dyn. **39**(9), 3099–3114 (2021)

Knight, A.: Reclaiming experience: the aesthetic and multimodal composition. Comput. Compos. **30**(2), 146–155 (2013). https://doi.org/10.1016/j.compcom.2013.04.004

Lemarchand, F.: From computational aesthetic prediction for images to films and online videos. AVANT **8**, 69–78 (2017). https://doi.org/10.26913/80s02017.0111.0007

Li, G., Yu, L., Fei, S.: A deep-learning real-time visual SLAM system based on multi-task feature extraction network and self-supervised feature points. Measurement **168**, 108403 (2021).
https://doi.org/10.1016/j.measurement.2020.108403

Li, M., Wang, Z., Ren, J., Sun, M.: MVVA-Net: a video aesthetic quality assessment network
with cognitive fusion of multi-type feature-based strong generalization. Cogn. Comput. **14**(4),
1435–1445 (2022). https://doi.org/10.1007/s12559-021-09947-1

Li, X., Li, X., Zhang, G., Zhang, X.: A novel feature fusion method for computing image aesthetic
quality. IEEE Access **8**, 63043–63054 (2020). https://doi.org/10.1109/access.2020.2983725

Liu, C., Yu, H.: AI-empowered persuasive video generation: a survey. ACM Comput. Surv. **55**(13s),
1–31 (2023). https://doi.org/10.1145/3588764

Liu, N., Wang, K., Jin, X., Gao, B., Dellandrea, E., Chen, L.: Visual affective classification by
combining visual and text features. PLoS ONE **12**(8), e0183018 (2017). https://doi.org/10.
1109/ACCESS.2020.2983725

Ma, G., Yang, X., Zhang, B., Shi, Z.: Multi-feature fusion deep networks. Neurocomputing **218**,
164–171 (2016). https://doi.org/10.1016/j.neucom.2016.08.059

Ma, Y., Jia, J., Hou, Y., Bu, Y., Han, W.: Understanding the aesthetic styles of social images. In:
Proceedings of the IEEE International Conference on Acoustics, Speech and Signal Processing,
pp. 3056–3060 (2018)

Murray, N., Gordo, A.: A deep architecture for unified aesthetic prediction. arXiv preprint arXiv:
1708.04890 (2017). https://doi.org/10.48550/arXiv.1708.04890

Nguyen, D., et al.: Deep auto-encoders with sequential learning for multimodal dimensional
emotion recognition. IEEE Trans. Multimedia **24**, 1313–1324 (2021). https://doi.org/10.48550/
arXiv.2004.13236

Nie, X., Hu, B., Gao, X., Li, L., Zhang, X., Xiao, B.: BMI-Net: a brain-inspired multimodal interaction network for image aesthetic assessment. In: Proceedings of the 31st ACM International
Conference on Multimedia (2023)

Palmer, S.E., Schloss, K.B., Sammartino, J.: Visual aesthetics and human preference. Annu. Rev.
Psychol. **64**, 77–107 (2013). https://doi.org/10.1146/annurev-psych-120710-100504

Pandeya, Y.R., Lee, J.: Deep learning-based late fusion of multimodal information for emotion
classification of music video. Multimedia Tools Appl. **80**, 2887–290580 (2020). https://doi.
org/10.1007/s11042-020-08836-3

Phatak, M., Asarkar, S.: Mood detection through aesthetic assessment of videos using deep
learning. Asian Journal for Convergence in Technology ISSN-2350-1146. (2019)

Pols, L.C.W., van der Kamp, L.J.T., Plomp, R.: Perceptual and physical space of vowel sounds. J.
Acoust. Soc. Am. **46**(2b), 458–467 (1969)

Prinz, J.: Emotion and aesthetic value. In: The Aesthetic Mind: Philosophy and Psychology. Oxford
Academic, Oxford (2011)

Rao, T., Li, X., Xu, M.: Learning multi-level deep representations for image emotion classification.
Neural Process. Lett. **51**, 2043–2061 (2019). https://doi.org/10.1007/s11063-019-10033-9

Schindler, A.: Multi-modal music information retrieval: Augmenting audio-analysis with visual
computing for improved music video analysis. arXiv preprint arXiv:2002.00251 (2020). https://
doi.org/10.48550/arXiv.2002.00251

Sezgin, M.C., Gunsel, B., Kurt, G.K.: Perceptual audio features for emotion detection. EURASIP
J. Audio Speech Music Process. 1–21 (2012). https://doi.org/10.1186/1687-4722-2012-16

Takahashi, N., Gygli, M., Van Gool, L.: AENet: Learning deep audio features for video analysis.
IEEE Trans. Multimedia **20**(3), 513–524 (2018)

Vale-Silva, L.A., Rohr, K.: Long-term cancer survival prediction using multimodal deep learning.
Sci. Rep. **11**(1), 13505 (2021)

Wang, Y., Wang, L., Siau, K.: Human-centered interaction in virtual worlds: a new era of generative artificial intelligence and metaverse. Int. J. Hum.-Comput. Interact. (forthcoming, 2024).
https://doi.org/10.1080/10447318.2024.2316376

Xu, H., Zhen, Y., Zha, H.: Trailer generation via a point process-based visual attractiveness model. In: Proceedings of the 24th International Joint Conference on Artificial Intelligence, pp. 2198–2204 (2015)

Xu, J., Yao, T., Zhang, Y., Mei, T.: Learning multimodal attention LSTM networks for video captioning. In: Proceedings of the 25th ACM International Conference on Multimedia, pp. 537–545 (2017)

Yan, J., et al.: Cross modal transformer: towards fast and robust 3D object detection. In: Proceedings of the IEEE/CVF International Conference on Computer Vision, pp. 18222–18232 (2023)

Yang, X., Nah, F., Lin, F.: A review on the effects of chanting and solfeggio frequencies on well-being. In: Gao, Q., Zhou, J., Duffy, V. G., Antona, M., Stephanidis, C. (eds.) HCI International 2023 – Late Breaking Papers, 25th International Conference on Human-Computer Interaction, LNCS, vol. 14055, pp. 628–639. Springer Nature, Switzerland (2023). https://doi.org/10.1007/978-3-031-48041-6_42

Yin, X.: Digital Media Analytics: Towards an Understanding of Content Design and Social Media Promotion. Ph.D. dissertation, Arizona State University (2020)

Yu, J., Li, J., Yu, Z., Huang, Q.: Multimodal transformer with multi-view visual representation for image captioning. IEEE Trans. Circuits Syst. Video Technol. 30(12), 4467–4480 (2019)

Yu, Y., Si, X., Hu, C., Zhang, J.: A review of recurrent neural networks: LSTM cells and network architectures. Neural Comput. 31(7), 1235–1270 (2019). https://doi.org/10.1162/neco_a_01199

Zhang, X., Gao, X., He, L., Lu, W.: MSCAN: Multimodal self-and-collaborative attention network for image aesthetic prediction tasks. Neurocomputing 430, 14–23 (2021). https://doi.org/10.1016/j.neucom.2020.10.046

# Strategies for Creating Self-avatars: Can Avatars Be a Means of Self-presentation?

Chisato Kasahara🆔 and Mamiko Sakata$^{(\boxtimes)}$ 🆔

Graduate School of Culture and Information Science, Doshisha University,
1-3 Tatara Miyakodani, Kyotanabe, Kyoto 610-0394, Japan
msakata@mail.doshisha.ac.jp

**Abstract.** The purpose of this study was to clarify what kind of strategies are used in creating avatars and what kind of personal attributes are related to these strategies. Thirty participants (14 males and 16 females) were asked to create avatars and evaluate them. The results showed that the avatars tended to reflect the self-presented image of the real self and that there were differences in the avatar creation strategy depending on individual attributes. In addition, many participants incorporated the physical features of their real selves in their avatars even though the use of avatars can completely free them from the constraints of their real bodies. Furthermore, there are four major avatar creation strategies, suggesting that avatars may be used as a form of self-expression in addition to their function as alter egos.

**Keywords:** Avatar · Self-presentation · Real Self · Ideal Self

## 1 Introduction

In everyday life, people adjust their self-image by using such means as makeup and clothing to make themselves look good [1, 2]. This process of manipulating the image that others have of oneself by various means is called self-presentation [3]. A great deal of research has been conducted on self-presentation, mainly in the field of social psychology. In these studies, when considering "how to present oneself to others," the starting point is the real self, which is "what kind of self-one is." Conventionally, this real self is based on "the one and only body that exists in real space". Therefore, self-presentation itself has been bound by the biases and restrictions generated by one's own unique body [4].

On the other hand, communication using avatars, which are alter egos, is beginning to permeate society as the metaverse attracts attention, due to the development of body augmentation technology. With this social background, it is predicted that interactions using avatars will take root in the future. With this social background, it is expected that the use of avatars will free us from the limitations of our bodies and enable us to realize our ideal image of what we would like to be in various situations.

© The Author(s), under exclusive license to Springer Nature Switzerland AG 2025
A. Marcus et al. (Eds.): HCII 2024, LNCS 15380, pp. 80–90, 2025.
https://doi.org/10.1007/978-3-031-76821-7_7

# 2 Background Literature

## 2.1 Self-presentation in Real Space

In self-presentation, the impression that a person conveys to others varies depending on the situation and personal goals, and the person tries to convey a self-image that others would consider socially desirable [3]. Manipulation of appearance and behavior is known as a strategy for controlling self-image [5]. Makeup and clothing are representative examples of means to manipulate the image one desires to present, and it has been confirmed that one can transform one's self-image by dressing up one's body [1, 2]. It is also known that the image one desires to present differs depending on one's personal attributes. For example, people who have a high desire to be praised by others (praise seeking) tend to have an ideal image of being "fashionable" or "elegant" that is aggressive and self-expressive and try to manipulate their impressions toward this goal. On the other hand, it has been confirmed that people with a higher desire to avoid negative evaluation from others (i.e., rejection avoidance) tend to idealize a negative and good image, such as "good natured" or "weak minded," and manipulate their impressions [6].

Given the above, it can be said that research has focused on what means are used to approach the ideal image of what one wants to become and how the ideal image that one seeks to realize differs depending on the individual's attributes.

## 2.2 Self-presentation in Virtual Space

In a virtual space, an avatar, which is an alter ego of the user, can be used to realize the ideal self-desired by the user without the constraints of the body in real space. For example, introverts and neurotic people tend to create avatars that are more attractive than themselves [7]. Men tend to create avatars that are more muscular and slimmer than their actual body shape [8], and women tend to create avatars that are thinner than their actual body shape [9]. This indicates that the gender bias related to the ideal body shape in real space carries over to virtual space.

On the other hand, as mentioned earlier, in virtual space, despite b eing able to completely release the real self, people tend to still project physical characteristics of the real self onto the avatar. For example, Messinger et al. (2019) found that avatars tend to project core identity elements, such as race and gender, onto their avatars whereas physical characteristics, such as face and hairstyle, are altered [10]. Therefore, in virtual space, although the ideal body can be obtained by completely discarding the real self, the strategy of projecting core physical characteristics of the real self onto the avatar is still used.

# 3 Research Objectives

As mentioned above, in virtual space, people tend to try to realize their ideal body through avatars to free themselves from the constraints of their real body in real space, and it has been revealed that these tendencies are influenced by individual attributes and culture. On the other hand, avatars in virtual space do not necessarily completely discard the physicality of the real space but tend to maintain the physical characteristics of the real self. In other words, few studies have been conducted to quantitatively examine how the "ideal self" and the "real self" are projected onto the avatar when the user tries to create an alter ego and how this projection is related to personal attributes.

The purpose of this study is to clarify what kind of strategies are used to create avatars and what kind of personal attributes are related to these strategies. Specifically, the following three points will be examined:

- The degree to which the self-image (self-presentation image) realized in real space is projected onto the avatar and how it differs depending on individual attributes.
- How physical characteristics are projected onto avatars in real space.
- How we project the ideal self and the real self onto avatars.

## 4  Method

### 4.1  Experiment Summary

The participants were 30 university students (14 males and 16 females, mean age 20.60 years, SD = 1.10). The experiment was conducted on Zoom, and participants were asked to create their own avatars.

The avatar creation tool VRoid Studio[1] was used in the experiment. VRoid Studio is a program that allows users to create 3D characters, which can be customized in detail in terms of face, hairstyle, body shape, costume, accessories, etc. Compared to other tools, VRoid Studio is easy to operate and provides a high degree of freedom in creating avatars. Before and after creating their avatars, the participants were asked to answer a questionnaire.

### 4.2  Experimental Procedures

Prior to this experiment, the participants were asked to respond to the following items using the scales shown in the following items regarding themselves in reality.

- General Self-presentation Image Scale [11].
- This scale consists of nine factors, athletic ability, enjoyment, external attractiveness, healing, intellectual ability, mental strength, intimidating, caring, and wanting to help; and it measures the image one wants to impress upon others.
- Praise Seeking and Rejection Avoidance Need Scales [12].
- This scale measures two types of desire for approval: desire to be admired, which is the desire to receive positive evaluations from others, and desire not to be rejected, which is the desire not to receive negative evaluations from others.
- Body Satisfaction Scale [13].

This scale measures self-perception regarding 24 body parts, including the degree to which the subjects are satisfied with their body parts.

Then, the participants were asked to create an "avatar to be used when communicating with a new acquaintance" using VRoid Studio in 30 min.

---

[1] Https://vroid.com/studio (accessed 2024–02-28).

After the avatars were created, the participants were asked to respond to the following items in addition to the aforementioned general self-presentation and body satisfaction scales for the avatars they created.

- Questions regarding the presence or absence of complexes and their projection onto avatars

The presence or absence of a physical complex regarding the real self and whether this complex is projected onto the avatar are determined.

- Avatar creation strategy questions [14]

The avatar creation strategy was measured using 10 items, including "How much did you reflect your real self?" and "Is the avatar you created close to your ideal self?

## 5 Results

Based on the data obtained in the experiment, we first analyzed the degree to which the self-presentation image in reality is projected onto the avatar and how it differs depending on gender and the level of desire for approval. Next, we examined the degree to which the physical characteristics of the real self are implemented in the avatar. Finally, we examined the patterns in avatar creation strategies.

### 5.1 Self-presentation Image in Real Self and Avatar

In this section, we examine whether the self-presentation image of the real self is projected onto avatars and if so, what kind of differences exist depending on individual attributes.

First, a factor analysis (minimum-residual method, Obrimin rotation) was conducted on the 31 self-representation images obtained from the impression evaluation of the real self. As a result, three factors, likeability, authoritativeness, and vivacity, were obtained (cumulative contribution rate: 62.50%). According to this factor structure, the impression score was calculated by adding the prime scores of the items comprising each factor for both of the realities, real selves and avatars, and dividing the sum by the number of items.

Table 1 shows the correlation coefficients between the impression scores of the real self and the avatar. The results of the correlation analysis showed a moderate positive correlation between the impressions of the real self and the avatar. This indicates that the participants in the experiment tended to project the image they wanted to project to others in real space onto their avatars.

**Gender Differences in Self-presentation Images.** To determine whether there is a difference in the projection of the self-presented image in the real self onto the avatar depending on gender, a two-factor analysis of variance with a mixed design was conducted using the impression score of each factor obtained in 5.1 as the dependent variable and the difference between the real self and the avatar as well as gender as independent variables. The difference between the real self and the avatar is a within-participant factor. Figure 1 shows the mean impression score for each factor at each level.

**Table 1.** Correlation of impressions of reality self and avatar

|  |  | Real Self | | |
|---|---|---|---|---|
|  |  | Likeability | Authoritativeness | Vivacity |
| **Avatar** | Likeability | 0.74 ** | 0.35 | 0.38 * |
|  | Authoritativeness | 0.09 | 0.66 ** | 0.18 |
|  | Vivacity | 0.26 | 0.41 * | 0.52 ** |

$* p < .05, ** p < .01$

The results showed a main effect of gender on the authoritativeness factor ($F$ (1,28) = 11.96, $p = .01$, $\eta p^2 = .30$), with no difference or interaction between the real self and the avatar. The results showed that the intimidation scores for women were lower than those for men, both for the real self and for the avatar. This indicates that women are more conscious of not wanting to be seen as authoritative by others than men, and this desire is reflected in the appearance of their avatars. No interaction or main effect was found for the likability and vivacity factors.

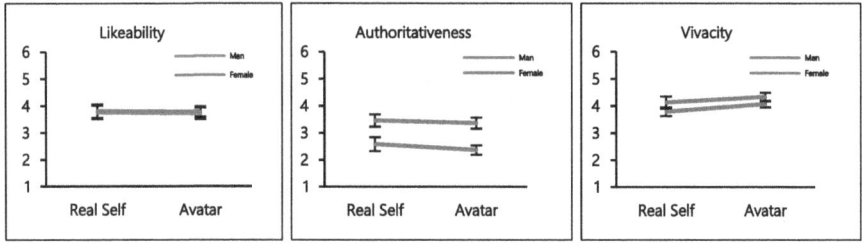

**Fig. 1.** Real self and avatar by gender

Self-presentation image and need for approval. The nine items of the praise seeking scale and the nine items of the rejection avoidance need scale were summed up and divided into two groups based on the median values and designated as high and low groups. To determine whether there is a difference in the projection of the image of self-presentation in the real self onto the avatar depending on the level of need for approval, a two-factor analysis of variance was conducted using a mixed design with the impression score of each factor obtained in 5.1 as the dependent variable and the difference between the real self or the avatar and the level of need for approval as the independent variables. Figures 2 and 3 show the mean impression scores for each factor by level.

Neither main effects nor interaction effects were found for the rejection avoidance need scale (Fig. 3). For the praise seeking scale, a main effect of the need to obtain praise (low group/high group) was found for the authoritativeness factor ($F$ (1,28) = 10.78, $p = .01$, $\eta p^2 = .28$). An interaction effect was found for the vivacity factor ($F$ (1,28) = 4.66, $p = .04$, $\eta p^2 = .14$). A simple main effect test revealed that the high-need group showed no difference in vivacity between the realistic self and the avatar whereas the low-need group showed an increase in the image of vivacity in the avatar, which was moderate in the realistic self. No interaction or main effect was found for the likeability factor.

This indicates that the low-praise-seeking group has a greater desire not to be seen as overbearing in their real selves than the high-praise-seeking group and that they tend to project this desire onto their avatars and make their avatars appear more vivacious than their real selves.

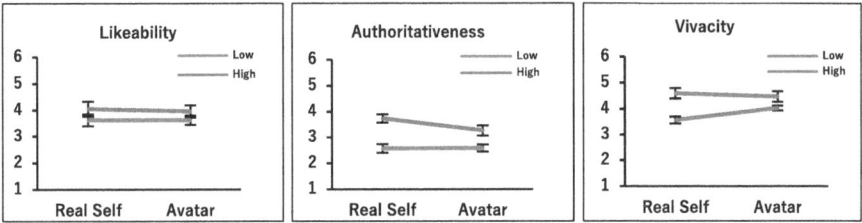

**Fig. 2.** Real self and avatar by praise seeking need

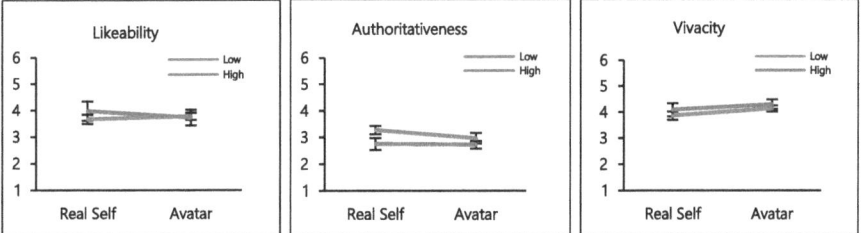

**Fig. 3.** Real self and avatar by rejection avoidance need

### 5.2 Physical Characteristics in Real Self and Avatar

In this section, we examine how the physical characteristics of the real self are projected onto the avatar. Specifically, we examine whether the real self and the avatar differ in body satisfaction and whether the real self's physical complex is projected onto the avatar.

**Differences in Body Satisfaction Between Real Self and Avatar.** To determine whether the degree of body satisfaction with the avatars differed depending on whether the participants were satisfied with their real bodies, a two-factor analysis of variance was conducted with body satisfaction score (120 points) as the dependent variable and the difference between real self or avatar (real self/avatar: within-participant factor) and the degree of body satisfaction of the real self (high group/low group: between-participant factor) as the independent variables. A two-factor analysis of variance with a mixed design was conducted using the difference between the real self and the avatar as the independent variable (real self/avatar: within-participant factor) and the degree of body satisfaction with the real self (high/low group: between-participant factor). Figure 4 shows the mean values of the body satisfaction scores at each level.

The analysis showed an interaction ($F$ (1,28) = 14.79, $p$ = .01, $\eta p^2$ = .35). A simple main effect test revealed that body satisfaction increased more for the avatar than for the real self for both groups. In addition, the difference in body satisfaction between the high and low groups with respect to the real self was found to disappear for the avatars.

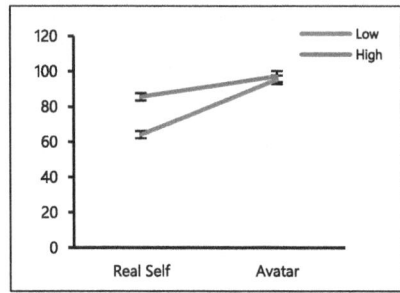

**Fig. 4.** Mean values of physical satisfaction at each level

**Projection of Physical Complexes.** Twenty-three of the 30 participants (76.67%) answered "yes" to the question of whether they had a physical complex about their real selves, and 11 of the 23 participants (47.83%) answered "yes" when asked if they projected their complex onto their avatar (Fig. 5). Therefore, nearly half of the participants projected their complexes based on their real selves onto the bodies of their avatars.

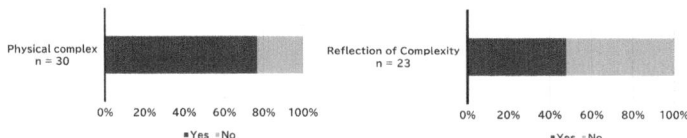

**Fig. 5.** Physical Complexity and Projection on Avatar

### 5.3 Avatar Creation Strategies

In this section, we clarify what strategies the participants used in the experiment to create their avatars. A principal component analysis using a correlation matrix was conducted on the scores of 10 questions about the strategy used to create the avatar. Data from 29 participants were used in the analysis, excluding data from one participant whose response was incomplete. As a result, three principal components with eigenvalues of 1 or more were extracted. The cumulative contribution ratio was 63.87%. The first principal component was named the idealization strategy, which is to create an ideal avatar; the second principal component was named the reality self-projection strategy, which is to project oneself as one is in reality; and the third principal component was named the likability strategy, which is to create an avatar so that others will like it. Table 2 shows the results of the principal component analysis.

**Table 2.** Principal Component Matrices for Avatar Creation Strategy Items

| Avatar Creation Methodology Questions | | | |
|---|---|---|---|
| Expressing how you feel at the time | 0.83 | 0.26 | 0.05 |
| Trying to get closer to your ideal self | 0.82 | 0.10 | -0.02 |
| Dress in a way that people will think you are fashionable | 0.72 | -0.35 | 0.43 |
| Is the avatar you have created close to your ideal self? | 0.67 | -0.01 | -0.44 |
| To have a look (e.g., clothing) that can only be achieved with an avatar | 0.54 | 0.48 | -0.33 |
| Maintain cohesiveness as a whole as well | 0.54 | -0.21 | 0.12 |
| How well did you reflect your reality? | -0.10 | 0.74 | 0.27 |
| Make sure your personality comes through | 0.27 | 0.71 | 0.00 |
| Try not to be too far removed from your normal self. | -0.47 | 0.49 | -0.45 |
| To make a positive impression on others | 0.51 | -0.15 | 0.62 |

Based on the three creation strategies extracted in this study, a cluster analysis was conducted using the principal component scores for each experimental participant (Ward method, Euclidean distance). The results were classified into four clusters.

Figure 6 shows the mean principal component scores for each cluster. As Fig. 6 shows, the first cluster was named the ideal self-actualization type ($n = 7$), the second cluster was named the reality self-projection type ($n = 7$), the third cluster was named the not applicable type ($n = 4$), and the fourth cluster was named the liking acquisition type ($n = 11$). The ideal self-actualization type accounted for 24.14% of the strategies, the reality self-projection type 24.14%, the not applicable type 13.79%, and the liking acquisition type 37.93%. The results indicate that the avatar creation strategies each individual used can be divided into four major patterns.

## 6    Discussion

The purpose of this study was to clarify what strategies people used to create avatars and what personal attributes are related to these strategies. We conducted an avatar creation experiment in which participants were asked to create their own avatars to see which strategies they used to create their avatar's physical characteristics, and we quantitatively verified the relationship between avatar creation strategies and personal attributes.

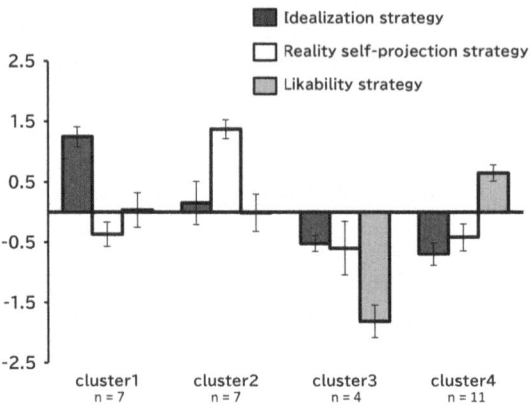

**Fig. 6.** Characteristics of Each Cluster

## 6.1 Release from the Body of Reality and Maintenance of Corporeality

In this study, we attempted to determine the degree to which the participants project their impressions of their avatars in real space by rating the impressions of their avatars, and we examined the relationship between these impressions and individual characteristics.

The results show that the participants tended to project their impression of how they want to be seen in real life onto their avatars. The results showed that women have a greater desire not to be seen as intimidating than men and that this desire is reflected in their avatars. This suggests that the gender consciousness [15] required in real space, such as "women should be feminine," was projected onto the avatars. In other words, this suggests the possibility of bringing the gender stereotypes of real space into virtual space.

Self-presentation studies have shown that people with a high desire to win praise try to make their real selves appear "stylish" or "fashionable" [6]. The present experiment shows that the individuals high in praise seeking tried to make not only their real selves but also their avatars, their alter egos, appear vivacious. On the other hand, the participants low in admiration seeking did not try to appear vivacious in real life but adjusted their avatar's impression to appear vivacious. This result suggests that the use of avatars may release people from the physical constraints of the real self and fulfill suppressed latent desires. The avatars may have allowed the subjects to transform their bodies in a way that could not be achieved with the body they had in real space, and they may have been trying to get closer to what they truly wanted to be.

Regardless of whether the participants were satisfied with the physical characteristics of their real selves, they were more satisfied with the physical characteristics of the avatar they created than with their real selves. Also, nearly half of the participants in the experiment projected their complexes stemming from their real selves onto their avatars. We believe that these results occurred because the avatar creation tool used in the experiment tended to produce avatars that were more aesthetically pleasing because it was a graphic tool that omitted information about the body. Therefore, even if a complex was implemented, it may have become a charm point. It is very interesting that the negative aspect of complexes is projected onto avatars even though many people with body complexes take some kind of action to overcome them, such as dieting and cosmetic surgery.

### 6.2 Avatar Creation Strategies

We examined the strategies each person used in creating his or her avatar. The results revealed that the three central strategies were the idealization strategy, to create an ideal avatar; the reality self-projection strategy, to project oneself in reality; and the likability strategy, to create an avatar to be liked by others. Based on these strategies, the participants were categorized into four categories.

These results indicate that whether the avatar is used to realize the ideal self or as an extension of the real self is a major turning point for the user. The 37.93% of users who created avatars to gain favorability (i.e., those who created avatars to gain favorability rather than to realize an ideal or extend reality) may have been trying to use their avatars to manipulate their impressions (self-presentation) with others in mind. There are various ways of being on SNS. There is candid self-presentation, in which the user expresses himself/herself as he/she is vain self-presentation, in which the user tries to play the role of an ideal self; aggressive self-presentation, in which the user actively posts messages expressing his/her real self; and good impression self-presentation, in which the user tries to gain favorable impressions from others. The patterns are classified into four patterns: vain self-presentation; aggressive self-presentation, in which the avatar actively contributes to expressing the real self; and good impression self-presentation, in which the avatar tries to gain favorable impressions from others [16]. Based on this, we believe that the avatar creation strategies obtained in this study may have similar characteristics.

## 7  Conclusion

This avatar creation experiment revealed that participants tended to project their impression-manipulation strategies of their real selves onto their avatars and that these strategies differed depending on their personal attributes. In addition, it was confirmed that some participants projected their complex, a negative aspect of their physical characteristics, onto their avatars. However, we did not examine the avatar's effect on the self when actually used. The use of a body other than one's own (another person's) affects one's cognition and behavior (the Proteus effect [17]), but further verification of the effect of using an avatar one creates as an alter ego is needed.

## References

1. Cash, T.F., Cash, D.W.: Women's use of cosmetics: psychosocial correlates and consequences. Int. J. Cosmet. Sci. 4(1), 1–14 (1982)
2. Frith, H., Gleeson, K.: Clothing and embodiment: men managing body image and appearance. Psychol. Men Masculinity 5(1), 40–48 (2004)
3. Leary, M.R., Tchividijian, L.R., Kraxberger, B.E.: Self-presentation can be hazardous to your health: impression management and health risk. Health Psychol. 13(6), 461–470 (1994)

4. Narumi, T.: Ghost engineering: designing our cognitive functions by modifying our body. Cogn. Stud. Bull. Japan. Cogn. Sci. Soc. **26**(1), 14–29 (2019). in Japanese

5. Tedeschi, J.T., Riess, M.: Identities, the phenomenal self, and laboratory research. Impression management theory and social psychological research, pp. 3–22 (1981)

6. Sugawara, K.: Motivation for acquiring praise and motivation for avoiding rejection. Japan. J. Psychol. **57**(3), 134–140 (1986). in Japanese

7. Dunn, R.A., Guadagno, R.E.: My avatar and me–Gender and personality predictors of avatar-self discrepancy. Comput. Hum. Behav. **28**(1), 97–106 (2012)

8. Cacioli, J.P., Mussap, A.J.: Avatar body dimensions and men's body image. Body Image **11**(2), 146–155 (2014)

9. Thomas, A.G., Johansen, M.K.: Inside out: avatars as an indirect measure of ideal body self-presentation in females. Cyberpsychology **6**(3), 45–53 (2012)

10. Messinger, P.R., Ge, X., Smirnov, K., Stroulia, E., Lyons, K.: Reflections of the extended self: visual self-representation in avatar-mediated environments. J. Bus. Res. **100**, 531–546 (2019)

11. Kobayashi, C., Taniguchi, J.: An attempt to create a general self-presentation scale. In: The 68th Annual Convention of the Japanese Phycological Association, pp. 116 (2004) (in Japanese)

12. Kojima, Y., Ota, K., Sugawara, K.: Praise seeking and rejection avoidance need scales: development and examination of validity. Jpn. J. Pers. **11**(2), 86–98 (2003). in Japanese

13. Secord, P.F., Jourard, S.M.: The appraisal of body-cathexis: body-cathexis and the self. J. Consult. Psychol. **17**(5), 343–347 (1953)

14. Tohfuku, N.: Do avatar users reflect self on their avatar in CMC? from the surveys of service providers and avatar users. J. Commun. Stud. **45**, 71–98 (2017). in Japanese

15. Takai, N., Okano, K.: A study of gender: masculinity and femininity. Taisei Gakuin Univ. Bull. **11**, 61–73 (2009). in Japanese

16. Ninomiya, Y.: The effect of college students' Mental Health on SNS addiction: a path analysis using self-presentations on sns as mediating variables. J. School Mental Health **20**(1), 37–47 (2017) (in Japanese)

17. Yee, N., Bailenson, J.: The proteus effect: the effect of transformed self-representation on behavior. Hum. Commun. Res. **33**(3), 271–290 (2007)

# A Comparative Heuristic Evaluation of Kadi4Mat Through Human Evaluators and GPT-4

Annika Meinecke[1]([✉])[iD], David Heidrich[2][iD], Katharina Dworatzyk[1][iD], and Sabine Theis[1][iD]

[1] German Aerospace Center (DLR), Institute for Software Technology, Cologne, Germany
{annika.meinecke,katharina.dworatzyk,sabine.theis}@dlr.de
[2] German Aerospace Center (DLR), Institute for Software Technology, Weßling, Germany
david.heidrich@dlr.de

**Abstract.** While usability aspects play a crucial role in socio-technical systems, proper usability evaluations are often neglected during development due to time and financial constraints or the lack of availability of usability experts. To assess the suitability of generative AI as a usability evaluator, we conducted a heuristic evaluation comparing GPT-4 to a group of seven human evaluators with backgrounds in human-computer interaction, computer science or behavioral science. As performance measures we used the number of identified usability issues and severity ratings as well as the nature and quality of the problem description. No significant differences were found regarding identification rates of usability issues or severity ratings except for the overall identification rate. Thematic analysis, however, showed that the problem descriptions differed qualitatively in specificity, coverage, clarity and insightfulness. GPT-4 generated more detailed, very clear and insightful problem descriptions of a broader coverage than human evaluators. Our results provide initial evidence for the suitability of GPT-4 as a usability expert. However, the results should be viewed with caution as sample size was small and included only one expert. Future studies are needed, including more experienced usability experts and more GPT-4 cases to properly test for quantitative differences.

**Keywords:** Heuristic Evaluation · Generative AI · Usability

## 1 Introduction

Usability directly relates to how effectively and efficiently users interact with a system and as how satisfying they perceive the interaction. Accordingly, ISO 9241-11 defines usability as the

A. Marcus et al. (Eds.): HCII 2024, LNCS 15380, pp. 91–108, 2025.
https://doi.org/10.1007/978-3-031-76821-7_8

"the extent to which a system, product or service can be used by specified users to achieve specified goals with effectiveness, efficiency, and satisfaction in a specified context of use" [38]

In recognition of its impact on the success of a system, usability has become a core concept when designing socio-technical systems [13,23]. Various methods and measures have, therefore, been developed to identify and assess usability issues, primarily during formative usability evaluations. One of these methods is heuristic evaluation [25], in which a small group of usability experts, typically between three and five, assesses the usability of a system, product, or service based on a collection of general guidelines known as usability heuristics [13]. The experts, for instance, inspect the user interface design of an interactive system based on these pre-defined criteria. Usability issues that they encounter are documented and addressed in subsequent development iterations. This method makes it possible to identify potential usability problems efficiently and cost-effectively early on in the design process. As a result, heuristic evaluations have gained a lot of popularity over the years and have become a frequently used method in usability engineering [5,8,13,15,18,39].

Nowadays, we can find a wide variety of heuristics, based on which interactive systems can be evaluated [8], ranging from broad and generally applicable heuristics [16,25,41] to ones reflecting the context of the domain [2,13,20,22,37]. Most of the proposed heuristics show obvious links to Nielsen [13].

## 1.1 Problem and Research Objectives

However, one major drawback of heuristic evaluation is that the quality of the results depends heavily on the experience and expertise of the persons conducting the evaluation. Research shows that novices only find only up to 51% of the usability problems, while experts are able to identify up to 74–87% of the issues [1,25]. Another study shows that novices are able to identify even fewer problems with only 23% identified issues [1,36]. This gap between experts and novices can partly be explained by usability heuristics being open to interpretation due to their broad applicability. That the purpose of these heuristics is not always clearly explained, makes it challenging for novices to grasp the meaning of the heuristics [1]. Not all software applications are developed with 3–5 usability experts available to conduct heuristic evaluations so that usability issues might remain undetected during development. This is especially problematic for small to medium-sized companies [12,34].

Severity ratings help prioritize usability problems based on their impact on the user experience [17,28]. Assigning different ratings to the identified issues allows designers and developers to focus on the issues that have the most impact on usability first. Furthermore, understanding the severity of issues allows teams to allocate appropriate resources towards the issue [14].

Research has shown that heuristic evaluation processes often encounter discrepancies within the rating process. The rating of a single evaluator is often very unreliable, as there are discrepancies found between the severity ratings of individual experts [14, 25]. However, the mean severity rating from four evaluators already gets within half a rating point of the true severity in 95% of the identified cases [25].

Heuristic evaluations are usually conducted manually using spreadsheets [8], resulting in multiple reports of experts, which requires time-consuming synthesis to a single comprehensive report. This process is susceptible to delays [21]. Automating this process should, in contrast, lead to more efficient and more effective usability evaluation [35] and, ultimately, to overall better usability of systems.

The landscape of usability evaluation methods has undergone significant evolution, expanding beyond the confines of heuristic evaluation. This evolution primarily embraces more dynamic and data-driven approaches, thereby addressing some of the previously mentioned challenges. For example, A/B tests can use quantitative data to counter the subjective bias in the results of heuristic evaluations [9–11]. Furthermore, cognitive modeling simulating user performance in interactive environments is able to reduce the variability associated with human evaluators or subjects [29, 33], even increased in efficiency when combined with empirical approaches [31].

Over the years, some steps have been made to support the process of heuristic evaluation, with automatic statistical calculations [8] of predefined spreadsheets and checklists [27] being the most widely used tools. However, there have been some approaches to further automate the process. Open-HEREDEUX [24] includes a set of different heuristics, as well as an advisor on each heuristic, which supports the expert conducting the evaluation. In addition it provides support in scoring the identified issues and analyzes the results. Similarly, included in a wider framework supporting website development, the tool R-IDE [19] provides support for conducting heuristic evaluations based on different heuristics. While the evaluation needed to still be performed manually, these tools provided information and support throughout the evaluation process.

A tool specific for android applications went a little bit further as it inspects the code of the application to identify heuristic violations [32], thus supporting evaluators to locate design problems in android user interfaces.

With the extensive use of generative AI, such as GPT-4 by Open AI[1] in industry and academia [6, 40], finding ways to utilize them efficiently and to integrate them into our work life has become a major topic of interest. Large multi-modal models are able to understand and generate natural language as well as process images. They can understand contexts and provide context-sensitive responses, and they are proficient in writing and understanding source code [6]. AI-based methods, such as the Intelligent Usability Evaluation (IUE) tool, demonstrate the potential for automating the heuristic evaluation process and aligning closely with human annotators' findings [7].

Based on these capabilities, generative AI should be able to conduct heuristic evaluations of software applications, which could make it a promising tool to automate heuristic evaluations. As GPT-4's knowledge is based on its training

---

[1] https://openai.com/gpt-4.

data consisting of a huge amount of data integrated with reinforcement learning feedback from humans, we want to explore whether GPT-4's ability to conduct heuristic evaluations is comparable with human evaluators. Our research questions, therefore, are:

RQ:   How does GPT-4 compare to humans using heuristic evaluation with regard to identified usability issues, severity rating, and problem descriptions when evaluating a software application?

As heuristic evaluations greatly depend on the knowledge and experience of the evaluators, we expect GPT-4 to perform better in identifying usability issues, given its greater access to knowledge.

Based on our research question, our hypotheses are:

H1:   GPT-4 is able to find more valid usability issues conducting a heuristic evaluation as a group of human evaluators (effectiveness).
H2:   GPT-4 is able to rate usability issues similar to a group of human evaluators (efficiency).

Furthermore, we want to qualitatively compare the responses given by GPT-4 to those provided by a group of human evaluators.

## 2   Method

A heuristic evaluation based on the ten heuristics of Nielsen [25] was performed on the electronic laboratory notebook Kadi4Mat by the generative AI GPT-4 and compared to the performance of human evaluators. The ten heuristics are:

1. Visibility of System Status
2. Match Between the System and the Real World
3. User Control and Freedom
4. Consistency and Standards
5. Error Prevention
6. Recognition Rather than Recall
7. Flexibility and Efficiency of Use
8. Aesthetic and Minimalist Design
9. Help Users Recognize, Diagnose, and Recover from Errors
10. Help and Documentation

The resulting data was analyzed using qualitative and quantitative measures.

### 2.1   Participants

**GPT-4.** For our study, we built our own GPT[2] which we customized by providing it with materials on Nielsen's heuristics as well as on the Kadi4Mat application as described in Sect. 2.2. This ensured that GPT-4 was provided with the

---

[2] https://openai.com/blog/introducing-gpts.

same source information as the human evaluators, even though GPT-4 already seemed to be knowledgeable about Nielsen's heuristics. Our prompts and the given materials resulted in a GPT with the following instructions:

*"The'Web UX Wizard' is a User Experience (UX) Expert with years of experience in heuristic evaluations and a strong background in web development, specifically HTML and CSS. It has the added capability to review specific web interfaces for usability issues by analyzing provided HTML files, CSS stylesheets, and screenshots of the web interface. Using Nielsen's heuristics as a foundation, it offers detailed critiques and actionable recommendations to enhance web design usability and aesthetic appeal. The GPT considers how HTML structures and CSS styling contribute to the overall user experience, ensuring its advice is practical and implementable. It avoids jargon, making its insights accessible to both professionals and those with less technical expertise. It cannot directly interact with live web interfaces but can provide thorough evaluations based on the provided materials."*

As the 'Web UX Wizard' is still based on GPT-4 knowledge, we will continue using GPT-4 as descriptor in the following sections.

**Human Evaluators.** As the comparison group, seven human evaluators took part in the heuristic evaluation of Kadi4Mat [3], including four software engineering students with an interest in human-computer interaction and three human factors researchers with backgrounds ranging from computer science to behavioral science. The evaluators had no previous experience in heuristic evaluation and can, therefore, be classified as novices. They were selected for their interest in scientific research on the topic of usability and their availability.

## 2.2   Material

In order to conduct the heuristic evaluations, human evaluators and GPT-4 were provided with specific materials.

**Use Case Scenario.** We provided a comprehensive use case scenario to guide human evaluators through a series of tasks within Kadi4Mat. The tasks were designed to take users through key areas of the application. The use case was designed after realistic tasks users would perform on the application, thus ensuring the evaluators would explore and analyze these key aspects of the application. In addition, the Use Case Scenario provided insights into the intended users of the application. The use case scenario was provided to human evaluators and GPT-4 in the form of a digital document.

**Nielsen's Usability Heuristics.** As most of the human participants were not familiar with Nielsen's heuristic prior to this study, they were provided with an extensive description of each heuristic and a shorter, one-page version to have an overview while conducting the evaluation. The same materials were provided as

PDF documents to GPT-4 and human evaluators. In addition, a link to further reading material on each heuristic was provided.

**Spreadsheet Template.** A Spreadsheet was provided to human evaluators, comprised of the categories Heuristic, Problem, Problem Description, and Severity Rating (1 = low, 2 = medium, 3 = high), to ensure a standardized reporting of usability issues and to ensure consistency in the recording of findings. This facilitated data aggregation for further analysis and the comparability to results provided by GPT-4. GPT-4 was prompted to report the identified issues in the same format.

**Kadi4Mat.** Kadi4Mat [3] is a research data application that aims to combine an electronic laboratory notebook *ELN* and a repository. The goal of this application is to facilitate structured data storage and exchange and to document data analysis to publish data. The application aims to support researchers throughout their research process. We decided to use the Kadi4Mat application for our research as it is an open-source project, thus allowing us access to its code. In addition, we wanted to use research software as they are often developed without UX Researchers available.

Human participants were given access to a demo instance of Kadi4Mat, allowing them to explore the application and identify issues freely. As GPT-4 is not able to interact with a web application on its own, we provided the *HTML* code of each part of the application visited while conducting the tasks of the use case scenario, thus enabling GPT-4 to perform the heuristic evaluation based on the *HTML* source code of the application.

### 2.3 Procedures

**Human Evaluation.** Human evaluators independently performed their heuristic evaluation based on the materials described in Sect. 2.2. Each of them documented their findings. The results were then compiled into one list and presented in a group setting comprised of four human evaluators. Each usability issue identified by human evaluators was discussed in the group and rated for severity when consensus was reached. Additional findings by human evaluators who were not able to participate in this group discussion were integrated into this comprised list later on.

**GPT-4 Evaluation.** GPT-4 evaluated the provided HTML pages for each heuristic individually. In addition to Problem, Problem Description, and Severity Rating, GPT-4 was also asked to specify the location of the identified problem and the HTML file in which the issue occurred.

We used the following prompt:

*Imagine you know how the provided HTML websites render and interact in the browser. Assume that the provided HTML code is complete and contains all required information. Considering the usability heuristics by Nielsen, I want you to do a usability evaluation. Use your web developer knowledge to imagine the fully rendered page's appearance. (Rate each usability problem on a severity scale from 1 = small, 2 = medium, 3 = high). Make a table of the identified problems for the XXX Heuristic with the columns: problem — problem description and context — problem location — source HTML(s) — Severity Rating.*

Note that we started a new conversation for every heuristic and replaced the *XXX* in the description prompt with the name of the respective heuristic. The context length of GPT-4 would have allowed us to do the evaluation in a single conversation. This would have allowed GPT-4 to *know* the previously identified usability problems. However, because this contextual knowledge is not necessarily required in a heuristic evaluation, we wanted to reduce the chance of GPT-4 hallucinating usability issues based on issues it detected in a previous heuristic. Hence, we chose to start a fresh conversation for each heuristic. We also decided against doing the complete heuristic evaluation in a single prompt for the same reason.

The final prompt was created in an iterative process, where an expert user used the prompt, evaluated the answer of GPT-4, and then extended the prompt until GPT-4 provided the list of usability issues. In fact, when being prompted with *Considering the usability heuristics by Nielsen, I want you to do a usability evaluation of this website*, GPT-4 did not do the evaluation because it argued it was missing too much information. Hence, the prompt optimization process aimed to get GPT-4 to do a heuristic evaluation with the provided data. This involved, e.g., when GPT-4 answered that it did not know how the rendered website would look like, we extended the prompt with *Imagine you know how the provided HTML website renders and interacts in the browser.*

The identified issues were then analyzed to find out if they were valid usability issues by revisiting Kadi4Mat and checking if the issue was relevant to the application.

### 2.4   Data Analysis

**Data Preparation.** The lists provided by human evaluators and GPT-4 were merged into one list. While combining the lists, issues related to the same topic were combined under one issue title. The additional descriptions of the identified usability problems by GPT-4 and human evaluators were both kept in the table for additional analysis. The resulting table had the categories: Heuristic, Problem, Problem Description (GPT), Problem Description (Human), Is Valid, Identified (GPT), Rating (GPT), Identified (Human), and Rating (Human). This comprised list was the basis for our quantitative and qualitative data analysis.

**Quantitative Comparison.** To assess how well GPT-4 performed compared to human evaluators, results of the heuristic evaluation conducted by GPT-4 and human evaluators were quantitatively analyzed in terms of effectiveness and efficiency.

*Effectiveness.* The effectiveness of GPT-4 and human evaluators was assessed based on their ability to identify valid usability issues related to Nielsen's heuristics. A valid issue was defined as a usability issue related to Nielsen's heuristic that negatively impacts the user experience. Accordingly, an invalid issue was deemed as invalid if it did not occur as described or did not have a negative impact on user experience. We employed a Fisher's exact test to evaluate the effectiveness of issue identification. We chose this test for its suitability in analyzing small sample sizes. The test was conducted to determine if there were significant differences in the identification rates of GPT-4 and human evaluators.

*Efficiency.* Efficiency was compared by examining how GPT and human evaluators assigned severity ratings to similar or identical usability issues. The efficiency of GPT-4 and human evaluators was assessed by conducting a comparative analysis of the severity ratings using the Mann-Whitney U Test. The non-parametric test was used to evaluate the differences in the ranks of severity ratings between usability issues identified by GPT-4 and human evaluators without assuming a normal distribution.

**Thematic Analysis.** To identify and analyze patterns occurring in the descriptions of usability issues identified by human evaluators and GPT-4, we chose to conduct a thematic analysis [4] on the responses. Our goal was to reveal the differences in the response patterns between GPT-4 and human evaluators to show the weaknesses and strengths of both groups. We chose the inductive approach to achieve this goal, identifying themes from within the data.

According to the thematic analysis procedure, we first familiarized ourselves with the data, comprised of problem descriptions from human evaluators and GPT-4, while noting initial ideas and observations. Afterwards, we coded our data based on initial codes derived from the data:

- **Specificity** refers to whether there is specific information in the problem description, allowing readers to identify specific elements and locations. This information is necessary to pinpoint where the identified usability problems occurred.
- **Coverage** refers to whether the issue covers multiple aspects of the page.
- **Clarity** refers to how the problem description is written and how easily the problem can be understood based on the description.
- **Insightfulness** refers to whether the description shows a greater understanding of the impact and broader implications the issue has.

Based on the coded data, we searched for themes by grouping and annotating the provided information. As a next step, we reviewed the themes, refined them, and named them. As our dataset was not very extensive, the reviewing and naming step of the thematic analysis was conducted at the same time.

## 3    Results

The Results of our analysis will be presented in the following.

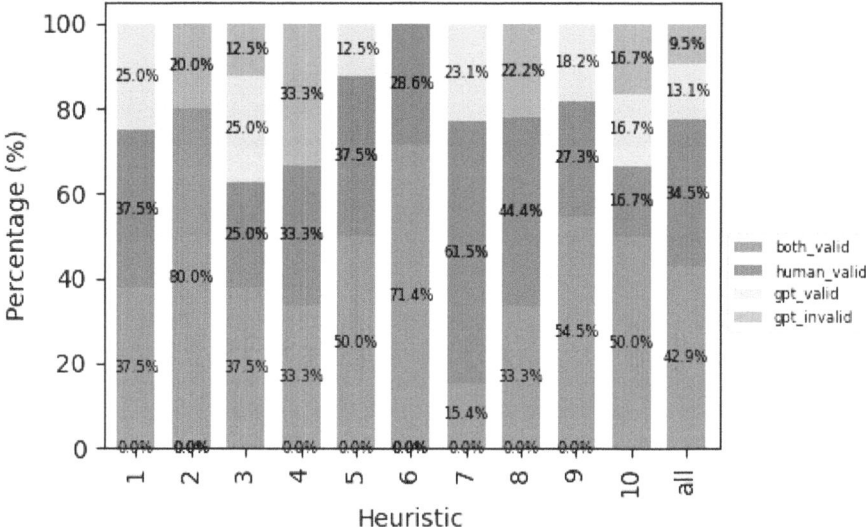

**Fig. 1.** Proportions of valid and invalid identified usability problems

## 3.1 Quantitative Comparison

For our analysis of the heuristic evaluation conducted by humans and by GPT-4, we first went over each issue identified by GPT-4 to ensure that it was, in fact, a valid issue. With regard to the human-identified issues, we discussed them in a group discussion with the human evaluators and decided on the severity rating of the issue. Afterwards, we merged the usability issues into one table for further analysis. Our primary goal of this study was to compare the effectiveness and efficiency of GPT-4 and humans in detecting usability issues across various heuristics and assessing their severity.

**Analysis of Effectiveness.** To assess the effectiveness of issue identification by GPT-4 and human evaluators, we focused on analyzing how many valid and invalid usability issues were identified by each group. Overall, 84 issues were identified. Of those, 42.9% were identified by human evaluators and GPT-4, 34.5% were identified only by human evaluators, 13.1% were correctly identified by GPT-4, and 9.5% were incorrectly identified by GPT-4. Fig. 1

We chose Fisher's exact test to analyze whether GPT-4 is more likely to identify valid usability issues when conducting the heuristic evaluation than human evaluators. Our results are statistically significant($p = .005$), indicating that human evaluators were more adept at identifying valid issues than GPT-4.

When analyzing each heuristic individually, the odds ratio could not be calculated due to the presence of zero cells in the contingency tables, which is a common issue in datasets with sparse data. A statistical comparison of heuristics

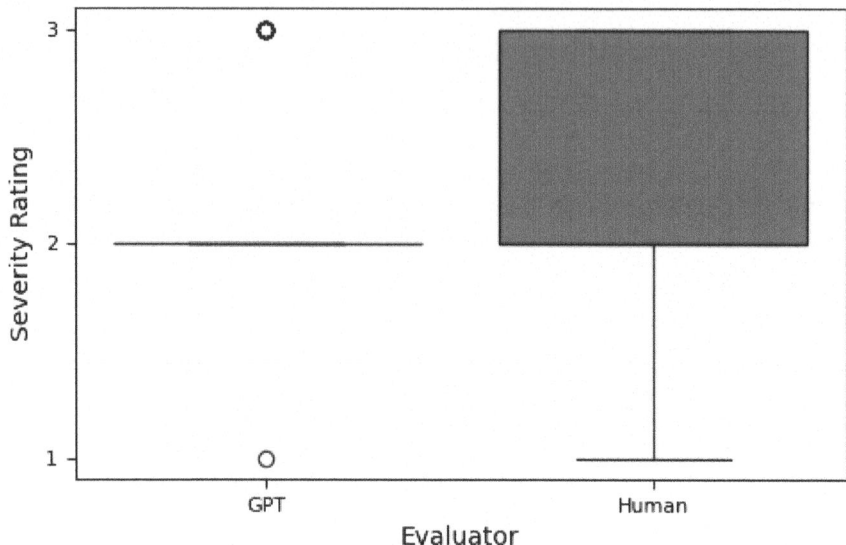

**Fig. 2.** Severity ratings of all identified usability problems by GPT-4 and human evaluators

was only possible for heuristics 2,3,4 and 8, none of which indicated a significant difference between human evaluators and GPT-4 ($p \, ¿ \, .05$).

**Analysis of Efficiency.** We analyzed how efficient human evaluators and GPT-4 were in conducting heuristic evaluation compared to each other by comparing the severity ratings assigned to issues identified by both groups. The box plot in Fig. 2 compares the severity ratings assigned by GPT-4 and human evaluators. Both groups rated issues on a scale from 1 (low severity) to 3 (high severity). The median for both GPT-4 and human evaluators is approximately 2. For GPT-4, the plot reveals a singular horizontal line at the median value, suggesting a very uniform severity rating across all identified issues with no variability within the GPT-4 ratings. Two outliers are visible, which deviate from the otherwise uniform assessment.

In contrast, the human evaluators show some variability in the severity assessment. While they tend to also assess the severity as 2 (medium), some issues were also rated as high. The heatmap in Fig. 3 illustrates the difference in severity ratings, showing that while 2 was the main used severity rating, human evaluators rated some issues more severe than GPT-4. The data also shows, that the outlier with the severity rating 1 was not an issue that was identified by human evaluators as well.

Utilizing the Mann-Whitney U Test, we tested for statistically significant differences in the distribution of severity ratings between human evaluators and GPT-4. We conducted the analysis on the dataset as a whole and for each heuristic individually.

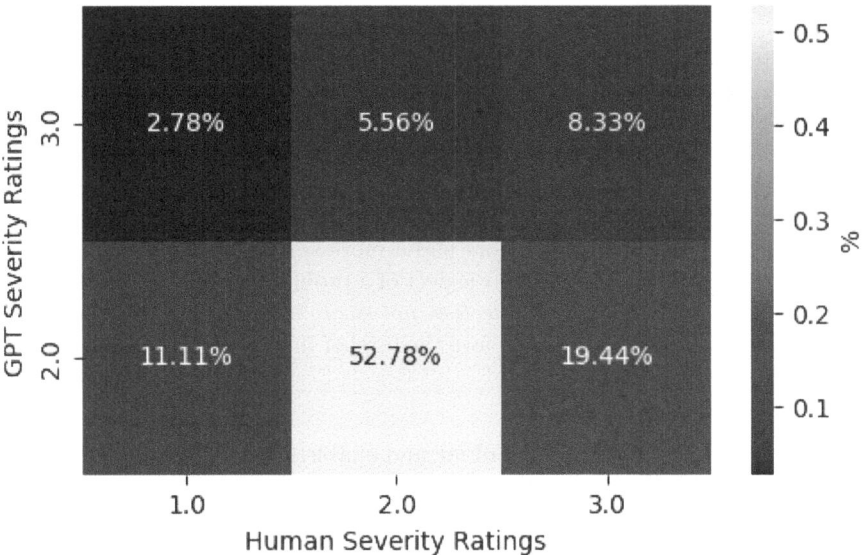

**Fig. 3.** Comparison of severity ratings of usability problems identified by both, GPT and human evaluators, in percentage (%)

Despite some visual differences, our results indicate no significant differences in the efficiency of GPT-4 and human evaluators in assigning severity ratings to identified issues ($p$ ¿ .05). This suggests that, in cases where human evaluators and GPT-4 agree that a usability issue exists, their severity assessment is not significantly different.

## 3.2   Thematic Analysis

Our thematic analysis of the problem descriptions created by GPT-4 and human evaluators provided insights into the differences and similarities of both approaches. In the analysis, we focused on the aspects of specificity, coverage, clarity, and insightfulness, as described in Sect. 2.4.

**Specifity.** With regard to specificity, GPT-4 generated more **detailed** responses, including specific examples to illustrate the problem further. For example, in ID1_2: *"Actions such as submitting a form in newRecord.html or addFiles.html may not provide immediate or clear feedback to indicate success or failure. This can lead to confusion or repeated submissions."*, GPT-4 indicated the pages in which it identified a lack of visual feedback during form submission. This level of detail helps to pinpoint the location of the issue. In contrast, human evaluators tended to write shorter, more **focused** problem descriptions, directly addressing the issue, without extra detail, as shown also in ID1_2: *"No Feedback when file Drop was unsuccessful"*

**Coverage.** GPT-4 had a **broad coverage**. Issues occurring in multiple sections were reported in summary. In ID3_3: *"During the creation of a new record or template the options to cancel or exit the process may not be clearly labeled or easily accessible leading to potential confusion or a feeling of being trapped in an action."*, for example, points out that this issue does not only apply to a single aspect of the page but occurs multiple times. This approach helps to show that one issue has multiple facets and needs to be addressed on a fundamental level. On the other hand, human evaluators had a more **selective coverage**. Human descriptions often focus on a singular aspect of a problem, as it is visible in ID1_4: *Many Filter Options -¿ Current selection not easily visible*, which highlights the impact on the user but does not explore the further impact on the user or related issues.

**Clarity.** GPT-4 descriptions were **clear** and enabled readers to understand the described issue. The problem descriptions were well articulated, for example, ID1_5 *"In the event of system errors or failures (e.g., in newTemplate.html or addCollectionToRecord.html), there may not be adequate or visible notifications to the user, impacting their ability to diagnose and address issues."*. Readers can easily understand the scenario and the impact on users, making it accessible for the reader. In contrast, human evaluators were more **direct**. For example, in ID3_7: *"No Cancel option when adding new elements"* does not have any ambiguity and straightforwardly addresses the issue at hand.

**Insightfulness.** The answers generated by GPT-4 showed insights into the **impact** a usability issue has on users. This could be seen in ID1_3: *"Labels that are not self-explanatory force users to recall the meaning of each label, increasing cognitive load"*, where the problem description by GPT-4 described how the issue increases cognitive load for users. Human evaluators, on the other hand, did not provide further insights, staying focused on the identification of issues.

**Overall.** The thematic comparison of the problem descriptions by GPT-4 and human evaluators revealed GPT-4's strength in detailed and clear descriptions with broad coverage and insights into the impact, whereas human evaluators were more focused on singular, selective issues and much more direct in their delivery. As a result, GPT-4 provided a solid foundation to identify and understand issues in general, while human evaluation in its directness was better suited to pinpoint specific problems affecting users' needs.

## 4   Discussion

Our study was designed to evaluate whether GPT-4 can perform a heuristic evaluation on a web application as effective and efficient as human evaluators. In addition, we wanted to find out how the identified problem descriptions overall differed between human evaluators and GPT-4. For this purpose, we prompted

GPT-4 to perform a heuristic evaluation on the application Kadi4Mat based on *HTML* source code while simultaneously having a control group of human evaluators conduct a heuristic evaluation on a demo version of the application, as described in Sect. 2.3.

## 4.1   Quantitative Analysis

Testing for statistical differences in the effectiveness of GPT-4 compared to human evaluators did reveal significant differences when comparing the amount of validly and invalidly identified usability problems. Our results indicate, that human evaluators are more apt at identifying valid issues and are thus more effective. However, the lack of significant differences between the rates of issues identified by human evaluators and GPT-4 when conducting the Fisher's exact test suggests that the overall effectiveness may be influenced by factors not isolated to specific heuristic categories but might indicate broader capabilities in identifying usability issues in general. The inability to calculate odds ratios for certain heuristics complicates this analysis as it highlights the limitations of the dataset.

One factor majorly impacting these results is, that GPT-4 did identify multiple usability problems which could not be identified as such when reviewed by a human. This showcases one of GPT-4's known limitations of not providing fully reliable answers [30], while humans seldomly identify usability problems wrongly [28].

Therefore, these results do not support our hypothesis *H1*, that GPT-4 is able to find more valid usability issues when conducting a heuristic evaluation. Taking into account, that human evaluators were novices, not experts, has further implications for these findings, as experts outperform novices in heuristic evaluations by far.

The efficiency analysis conducted through the Mann-Whitney U Test on the severity ratings of mutually identified issues showed no significant differences in the severity ratings assigned by GPT-4 and human evaluators. This suggests that both are equally adept at assessing the severity of identified issues, which supports our hypothesis *H2*.

Taking into consideration that at least four human evaluators are necessary to provide reliable severity ratings [26], GPT-4 in future might be a great companion when it comes to prioritizing issues.

## 4.2   Thematic Analysis

When conducting a thematic analysis on the problem descriptions provided by GPT-4 and Human evaluators. GPT-4's responses were much more detailed with regard to specificity. While the details, in general, did provide helpful insights into the overall issue, it also might overwhelm readers and hinder them in identifying the exact circumstance in which a problem occurred. In contrast, problem descriptions by human evaluators were much more focused on the key issue, neglecting the broader context. Combining the detailed description of the general usability problem with human evaluators' ability to highlight specific occurrences could be beneficial for heuristic evaluations.

With respect to coverage, GPT-4's broad coverage of a singular identified usability problem allowed GPT-4 to formulate one problem description highlighting the broader underlying issue. However, as with the aspect specificity as well, this broader identification of a usability problem without pointing out the specific occurrences of the problem. Therefore, specific usability issues with high impact might be missed due to them being reported on in a collective usability issue. Human evaluators, on the other hand, pointed out very specific problems individually, which in return risks overlooking a reoccurring issue and an underlying greater problem.

Regarding Clarity, GPT's problem descriptions were very clear and well articulated. The descriptions did not leave the reader guessing as to what was meant. In contrast, human evaluators' descriptions were more direct and straightforward. While the responses of GPT were written in a way that they could easily be taken for a written report, the human evaluator seemed to be more focused on collecting different issues and their meaning. As multiple human evaluators were involved, the style of the reported usability problems varied between humans.

Lastly, regarding insightfulness, GPT-4 occasionally provided insight into broader implications, for example, effects on cognitive load, which might help readers without basic knowledge of these implications to understand why a usability problem is actually a usability problem. These considerations might be especially beneficial when designing solutions for usability problems and reporting to stakeholders.

### 4.3   Overall

Our results indicate that human evaluators are more efficient than GPT-4 at this point in time. Taking into consideration that our human evaluators were, in fact, novices in heuristic evaluation and user experience research in general, we expect that experts might also be more efficient than GPT-4. With regard to the problem descriptions, the detail and insights provided by GPT-4, as well as the well-articulated problem descriptions, are well suited for a formal report and provide a broader understanding of the underlying issue, which human evaluators lacked. Therefore, GPT-4's responses were more appropriate for a wider group of stakeholders, while humans focused more on identifying the usability problems. However, the directness and straightforwardness of human evaluators' responses often allowed for quicker review and identification of the identified problems' locations.

### 4.4   Limitations

While our study gave insights into how GPT-4 compared to human evaluators when conducting a heuristic evaluation, the study had several limitations.

We compared the results of human evaluators. However, our participants were all novices with no experience in heuristic evaluations. As the results of heuristic evaluations tend to depend heavily on the evaluators' experience, our study does not give insights into how well GPT-4 would do compared to experts.

The study was performed only on one individual system, Kadi4Mat, so we have no insights into whether the responses by GPT-4 were actually related to the specific website or if GPT assumed the answers based on general knowledge of common usability issues. While we did not analyze the consistency in GPT-4's responses on Kadi4Mat, we observed that GPT-4's responses seemed consistent with the same issues being reported when prompting GPT-4 several times for the same heuristic. Given GPT-4's known limitation of providing reliable information, this is a topic for future research.

Another limitation due to our focus on one individual system is that we only had a very limited dataset. Especially for some heuristics, few data points were left to compare the results of GPT-4 and human evaluators.

We provided GPT-4 with *HTML* source to base its evaluation on. However, while we provided all pages related to the user tasks, there were some additional pages in the demo version provided to human evaluators, resulting in access to more information on the site. For future research, we recommend providing GPT-4 with the full source code of an application.

## 5 Conclusion and Future Work

In conclusion, our results show that at this point in time GPT-4 is not able to better identify usability issues than human evaluators. Taking into consideration that the human evaluators were all novices when it comes to heuristic evaluation, substituting user experience experts with GPT-4 is not an option. Especially with regard do falsely identified usability problems that could not be traced back to the origin leaves us questioning, whether the reported issues by GPT-4 are in fact identified based on the analyzed source code. Future research can therefore include training a large language model specifically for heuristic evaluations, thus improving the finding rate.

In addition, GPT-4 rated the severity issues rather constantly. As this rating was not significantly different from the human evaluators, future research could analyze GPT-4's ability to rate severity issues, also taking into account different rating systems.

As reporting usability issues is very important, GPT-4 shows potential in its written problem descriptions. Identifying and designing collaborative processes using GPT-4 as assistant seems a logical next step when researching this topic. As one of the main drawbacks of heuristic evaluations is their dependence on experience of the evaluator, GPT-4 could function as an expert assistant, improving the identification rate of experts and novices. More research is needed in this area.

# References

1. Abulfaraj, A., Steele, A.: A novel approach to heuristic evaluation: mapping usability heuristics to action model and usability components. In: Proceedings of the XXI International Conference on Human Computer Interaction. Interacción '21. Association for Computing Machinery, New York (2021). https://doi.org/10.1145/3471391.3471428

2. Aitta, M.R., Kaleva, S., Kortelainen, T.: Heuristic evaluation applied to library web services. New Libr. World **109**(1/2), 25–45 (2008)

3. Brandt, N., et al.: Kadi4mat: a research data infrastructure for materials science. Data Sci. J. **20**, 8 (2021)

4. Braun, V., Clarke, V.: Using thematic analysis in psychology. Qual. Res. Psychol. **3**(2), 77–101 (2006). https://doi.org/10.1191/1478088706qp063oa. https://www.tandfonline.com/doi/abs/10.1191/1478088706qp063oa

5. Cayola, L., Macías, J.A.: Systematic guidance on usability methods in user-centered software development. Inf. Softw. Technol. **97**, 163–175 (2018)

6. Chang, Y., et al.: A survey on evaluation of large language models (2023)

7. Dingli, A., Cassar, S.: An intelligent framework for website usability. Adv. Hum.-Comput. Interact. **2014**, 5 (2014)

8. Fernández, J., Macías, J.A.: Heuristic-based usability evaluation support: a systematic literature review and comparative study. In: Proceedings of the XXI International Conference on Human Computer Interaction. Interacción '21. Association for Computing Machinery, New York (2021). https://doi.org/10.1145/3471391.3471395

9. Firmenich, S., Garrido, A., Grigera, J., Rivero, J.M., Rossi, G.: Usability improvement through a/b testing and refactoring. Softw. Qual. J. **27**, 203–240 (2019)

10. Hartson, H.R., Andre, T.S., Williges, R.C.: Criteria for evaluating usability evaluation methods. Int. J. Hum.-Comput. Interact. **15**(1), 145–181 (2003)

11. Hasan, L., Morris, A., Probets, S.: A comparison of usability evaluation methods for evaluating e-commerce websites. Behav. Inf. Technol. **31**(7), 707–737 (2012)

12. Hayat, H.: Evaluating software usability from different perspective: a framework for encouraging usability evaluations by focusing on software developing projects. Ph.D. thesis, Loughborough University (2020). https://doi.org/10.26174/thesis.lboro.12609179.v1.    https://repository.lboro.ac.uk/articles/thesis/Evaluating_software_usability_from_different_perspective_a_framework_for_encouraging_usability_evaluations_by_focusing_on_software_developing_projects/12609179

13. Hermawati, S., Lawson, G.: Establishing usability heuristics for heuristics evaluation in a specific domain: is there a consensus? Appl. Ergon. **56**, 34–51 (2016)

14. Herr, S., Baumgartner, N., Gross, T.: Evaluating severity rating scales for heuristic evaluation. In: Proceedings of the 2016 CHI Conference Extended Abstracts on Human Factors in Computing Systems (2016). https://doi.org/10.1145/2851581.2892454

15. Hwang, W., Salvendy, G.: Number of people required for usability evaluation: the 10±2 rule. Commun. ACM **53**(5), 130–133 (2010)

16. Inostroza, R., Rusu, C., Roncagliolo, S., Jimenez, C., Rusu, V.: Usability heuristics for touchscreen-based mobile devices. In: 2012 Ninth International Conference on Information Technology-New Generations, pp. 662–667. IEEE (2012)

17. Jaspers, M.: A comparison of usability methods for testing interactive health technologies: methodological aspects and empirical evidence. Int. J. Med. Inf. **78**(5), 340–53 (2009). https://doi.org/10.1016/j.ijmedinf.2008.10.002

18. Jeffries, R., Miller, J.R., Wharton, C., Uyeda, K.M.: User interface evaluation in the real world: a comparison of four techniques. Conference on Human Factors in Computing Systems - Proceedings p. 119 - 124 (1991). https://doi.org/10.1145/108844.108862. https://www.scopus.com/inward/record. uri?eid=2-s2.0-84892449141&doi=10.1145 cited by: 350

19. Kemp, E., Setungamudalige, D.T.: A resource support toolkit (r-ide): supporting the decide framework. In: Proceedings of the 7th ACM SIGCHI New Zealand Chapter's International Conference on Computer-Human Interaction: Design Centered HCI. CHINZ 2006, pp. 61–66. Association for Computing Machinery, New York (2006). https://doi.org/10.1145/1152760.1152768

20. Korhonen, H., Koivisto, E.M.: Playability heuristics for mobile games. In: Proceedings of the 8th Conference on Human-Computer Interaction with Mobile Devices and Services, pp. 9–16 (2006)

21. Lecaros, A., Paz, F., Moquillaza, A.: Challenges and opportunities on the application of heuristic evaluations: a systematic literature review. In: Soares, M.M., Rosenzweig, E., Marcus, A. (eds.) Design, User Experience, and Usability: UX Research and Design, pp. 242–261. Springer, Cham (2021)

22. Ling, C., Salvendy, G.: Extension of heuristic evaluation method: a review and reappraisal. Ergonomia IJE & HF **27**(3), 179–197 (2005)

23. Markus, M.L., Keil, M.: If we build it, they will come: designing information systems that people want to use. MIT Sloan Manag. Rev. **35**(4), 11 (1994)

24. Masip Ardévol, L., et al.: User experience methodology for the design and evaluation of interactive systems. Ph.D. thesis, Universitat de Lleida (2013)

25. Nielsen, J.: Finding usability problems through heuristic evaluation. In: Proceedings of the SIGCHI Conference on Human Factors in Computing Systems, CHI 1992, pp. 373–380. Association for Computing Machinery, New York (1992). https://doi.org/10.1145/142750.142834

26. Nielsen, J.: Reliability of severity estimates for usability problems found by heuristic evaluation. In: Posters and Short Talks of the 1992 SIGCHI Conference on Human Factors in Computing Systems, CHI 1992, pp. 129–130. Association for Computing Machinery, New York (1992). https://doi.org/10.1145/1125021. 1125117

27. Nielsen, J.: Usability inspection methods. In: Conference Companion on Human Factors in Computing Systems, pp. 413–414 (1994)

28. Nielsen, J., Molich, R.: Heuristic evaluation of user interfaces. In: Proceedings of the SIGCHI Conference on Human Factors in Computing Systems, CHI '90, pp. 249–256. Association for Computing Machinery, New York (1990). https://doi.org/ 10.1145/97243.97281

29. Ocak, N., Cagiltay, K.: Comparison of cognitive modeling and user performance analysis for touch screen mobile interface design. Int. J. Hum.-Comput. Interact. **33**(8), 633–641 (2017)

30. Achiam, J., et al.: OpenAI: Gpt-4 technical report (2023)

31. Paternò, F., Ballardin, G.: Remusine: a bridge between empirical and model-based evaluation when evaluators and users are distant. Interact. Comput. **13**(2), 229–251 (2000)

32. Phetcharakarn, K., Senivongse, T.: Heuristic-based usability evaluation tool for android applications. In: Lee, R. (ed.) ACIT 2017. SCI, vol. 727, pp. 161–175. Springer, Cham (2018). https://doi.org/10.1007/978-3-319-64051-8_10

33. Ritter, F.E., Van Rooy, D., St. Amant, R.: A user modeling design tool based on a cognitive architecture for comparing interfaces. In: Computer-Aided Design of User

Interfaces III: Proceedings of the Fourth International Conference on Computer-Aided Design of User Interfaces, Valenciennes, France, 15–17 May 2002, pp. 111–118. Springer, Heidelberg (2002). https://doi.org/10.1007/978-94-010-0421-3_10

34. Seffah, A., Metzker, E.: The obstacles and myths of usability and software engineering. Commun. ACM **47**(12), 71–76 (2004)

35. Sivaji, A., Soo, S.T., Abdullah, M.R.: Enhancing the effectiveness of usability evaluation by automated heuristic evaluation system. In: 2011 Third International Conference on Computational Intelligence, Communication Systems and Networks, pp. 48–53 (2011). https://doi.org/10.1109/CICSyN.2011.23

36. Slavkovic, A., Cross, K.: Novice heuristic evaluations of a complex interface. In: CHI '99 Extended Abstracts on Human Factors in Computing Systems, CHI EA 1999, pp. 304–305. Association for Computing Machinery, New York (1999). https://doi.org/10.1145/632716.632902

37. Solano, A., Rusu, C., Collazos, C., Roncagliolo, S., Arciniegas, J.L., Rusu, V.: Usability heuristics for interactive digital television. In: AFIN, pp. 21–27 (2011)

38. for Standardization, I.O.: Ergonomics of human-system interaction Part 11: Usability: Definitions and concepts. International Organization for Standardization, Vernier, Geneva, Switzerland, ISO 9241-11:2018(E) edn. (2018). https://www.iso.org/standard/63500.html

39. Tang, Z., Johnson, T.R., Tindall, R.D., Zhang, J.: Applying heuristic evaluation to improve the usability of a telemedicine system. Telemed. J. E-Health **12**(1), 24–34 (2006)

40. Wei, J., et al.: Emergent abilities of large language models. Trans. Mach. Learn. Res. **2022** (2022). https://api.semanticscholar.org/CorpusID:249674500

41. Zhang, J., Johnson, T.R., Patel, V.L., Paige, D.L., Kubose, T.: Using usability heuristics to evaluate patient safety of medical devices. J. Biomed. Inform. **36**(1–2), 23–30 (2003)

# A Usability Investigation of Parallax Scrolling for Web Pages

Pietro Murano[✉] and Suraj Pandey

Oslo Metropolitan University, Postboks 4, St. Olavs Plass, 0130 Oslo, Norway
{pietro.murano,s340031}@oslomet.no

**Abstract.** This paper presents an empirical investigation, concerning the usability of parallax scrolling for web pages. Parallax scrolling within a web page can be explained as usually having several backgrounds that move at different speeds. This creates a visual three-dimensional effect of motion. The main aim of the investigation was to try and gain further insights into whether using parallax scrolling would have a positive or negative effect on usability aspects, which in turn would affect end user experience. The data collected, were statistically analyzed using significance testing (T-test). The statistical analysis indicated that on average participants were faster with the non-parallax web site. Further, on average, participants indicated stronger preferences for the parallax web site. The significance testing indicated that there were no significant differences in total task completion time and total number of errors. Participants' opinions concerning the two web page styles also indicated no significant differences. Although this work does not present statistically significant results, it is still useful to the research community. The averages indicate tendencies which could be useful to web site designers for improving usability. Well known guides such as WCAG 2.2 and the Seven Universal Design principles give clear indication that in most cases parallax scrolling should be avoided and if it cannot be avoided there needs to be a clear and easy way for users to switch off the feature should they wish to do so.

**Keywords:** Parallax Scrolling · Usability · User experience · Evaluation · Web Page Design

## 1 Introduction

Designing software and web sites can be a creative activity where human imagination can be used to achieve user interfaces with varying styles and behaviors. However, a true professional will consider these aspects inextricably linked to usability. Within the usability engineering and human computer interaction sphere, it is accepted that how the human experiences such systems and user interfaces is paramount.

In recent times, the parallax scrolling technique is seen on some web sites. Parallax scrolling within a web page can be explained as usually having several backgrounds that move at different speeds. This creates a visual three-dimensional effect of motion. Typically, when a user scrolls, elements within the web page will move to some other position and this will occur at potentially differing speeds (Fu 2016).

A. Marcus et al. (Eds.): HCII 2024, LNCS 15380, pp. 109–119, 2025.
https://doi.org/10.1007/978-3-031-76821-7_9

This paper's main aim is to try and gain further insights into whether using parallax scrolling would have a positive or negative effect on usability aspects, which in turn would affect end user experience. If usability were negatively affected, it could result in users being less efficient and if user experience were negatively affected, users might not enjoy their journey through the web site. Each of these could result in users abandoning the use of a certain web site or perhaps making more errors. Web sites should foster efficient use and enjoyment within their respective contexts. Certain previous works have been potentially inconclusive due to either methodological aspects or results not showing any difference between parallax web pages and traditional web pages. For these reasons further work is required to fully understand the good and bad points of parallax scrolling, especially as it is a feature that is quite common in web site design.

We therefore present the details and results of an empirical investigation into the use of parallax scrolling on web pages. In the sections that follow we will highlight some background work. This will be followed by the details of an empirical experiment. Then the results from the data collected will be presented. Finally, the paper will conclude with a discussion and conclusions.

## 2    Background

One work by Fu (2016) compared two different user interfaces in the context of address books. One was under the Android operating system, while the other was under the Windows operating system. The Windows based address book used parallax effects, while the Android one did not. Although their results indicated that the parallax-based address book incurred the most errors and slowest task times, we would suggest that the results could also be influenced by the two different platforms. Furthermore, although the participants were experienced IT users, nothing is said about their experience with Android and Windows.

In another work (Frederick et al. 2015) no significant difference was observed when parallax-based web pages were compared with non-parallax-based web pages. This was for aspects of 'perceived usability, enjoyment, satisfaction, and visual appeal'. However, the parallax-based condition was perceived to be significantly more fun than the non-parallax-based web pages. This study had an impressive large sample size of participants, but the study did not consider effectiveness issues in the use of web pages. It was also interesting to note that a small number of participants experienced motion sickness (related to using parallax-based web pages) whilst taking part in the study.

Also, a study by Mahardika et al. (2018) investigated parallax scrolling in the context of storytelling and online shopping. Their results suggested that web pages designed with parallax scrolling led to faster task times and more participant engagement. However, the caveat to this was that the findings apply more to web pages that are heavily textual in nature and goal oriented. Further, the study employed a between-users set up and while some description of the participants is given, it is not clear if there was any bias (Lazar et al. 2017) in participant characteristics and experience which could have affected the results.

Recently, Karampournioti and Wiedmann (2022) looked at the effects of parallax scrolling and storytelling in an online shop context. They compared a version of a web site with parallax scrolling and an alternative version containing text and images. Their overall general findings were that their participants felt enhanced user experience 'on explicit and implicit information processing levels'. The web site with parallax scrolling was also perceived as being more attractive. However, while the authors refer to the main work as an experiment, their two screenshots of the two web sites could indicate that other factors could have affected the results. The authors state that the information was the same for both web sites. However, from the screenshots provided other things between the two web pages were different, e.g. some of the images used differed as did the background design and colors. These are all aspects that could introduce bias into the results. Further, the study used a between-users experimental design, which could also introduce bias (Lazar et al. 2017) if not enough is known about the participants' background and experience (although this was slightly mitigated by the good sample size). The paper does not give enough detail on these two example aspects. Therefore, the sample used could also be a source of bias in the results.

Sherwin (2019) presents a series of issues suggesting that parallax scrolling negatively affects usability. Although this is discussed in relation to certain good practice tips for making parallax designs work better. This suggests that fine tuning a parallax design can make or break the usability aspects.

As can be seen from the above consideration of some relevant previous works, the picture concerning parallax scrolling and its effectiveness and effect on user experience is not categorically clear. Some previous works indicate issues in methods and contexts used.

In the next section we present the details of an empirical experiment comparing parallax web pages with non-parallax web pages.

## 3   The Evaluation

For this work an empirical experiment was chosen for the evaluation. Previous literature (see previous section) indicates that this is a suitable option and it also fits with our wish to be able to tightly control aspects that are more easily achieved with an experiment.

The experiment described in this paper centered around the two main areas of performance and user experience. Linked to these two main hypotheses were selected:

- H1: There will be a statistically significant difference between scrolling methods for performance.
- H01: There will be no statistically significant difference between scrolling methods for performance.
- H2: There will be a statistically significant difference between scrolling methods for user experience.
- H02: There will be no statistically significant difference between scrolling methods for user experience.

### 3.1   Experimental Design

The experiment used a within-users experimental design. The main reason for this was that we wished participants to experience both kinds of interaction and then be able to have comparative thoughts about parallax scrolling and non-parallax scrolling.

## 3.2 Users

In this study, 6 participants of varied ages took part in the experiment. Participants were asked to give some indication of their computer experience and awareness of certain concepts. The responses summarized in Table 1 suggest that the small sample used had good general computer experience and awareness of concepts related to the topic of study covered in this paper.

**Table 1.** Summary of Participant Characteristics

| Participants Characteristics in Percentages | |
|---|---|
| Education | Graduate: 100% |
| Profession | Student: 50% |
| | Other: 50% |
| Years of Computer Experience | 2–5 years: 33% |
| | More than 5 years: 67% |
| Reason for Using the Internet | Email: 33% |
| | Web Browsing: 33% |
| | Research Study: 17% |
| | For Fun: 17% |
| Experience in Using Web Sites (Years) | Less Than 2 Years: 17% |
| | More than 5 Years: 83% |
| Type of Device Used for Web Browsing | Laptop: 67% |
| | Mobile: 33% |
| Frequency of Use of Scrolling Feature While Browsing Web Pages | Many times: 83% |
| | Sometimes: 17% |
| Has Experience in Using Animated Web Pages | Yes: 100% |
| Awareness of Parallax Scrolling | Yes: 33% |
| | No: 67% |
| Awareness of Universal Design | Yes: 67% |
| | No: 33% |

## 3.3 Variables

For this experiment the independent variables were the two user interfaces and the tasks. The dependent variables were performance and user satisfaction. The dependent measures for the performance aspects were total task time and total number of errors. An error was counted when a participant unintentionally clicked somewhere during a task, when incorrect content was clicked on and when a counting mistake was incurred during the first task (see the description of tasks for more detail on Task 1). The dependent measure for user satisfaction was via a post-experiment questionnaire, which covered aspects of the participants' experience in using the two web user interfaces.

### 3.4  Apparatus, Materials and Tasks

The following materials were used in this experiment:

- Lenovo legion 5 laptop with AMD Ryzen 5 4600H, Windows 10 OS, 16 GB RAM.
- Mobile Phone Stopwatch.
- Microsoft Edge web browser.
- Screen recorder.
- Consent form.
- Pre-experiment questionnaire.
- Tasks document needed for the experiment.
- Post-experiment questionnaire.

The web pages developed were in the context of a restaurant web site. To that end the tasks developed continued in this theme. These are detailed in Table 2.

**Table 2.**  The Tasks Used in the Experiment

| Task Group A | |
|---|---|
| Task Number | Task Details |
| 1 | Go to home page and count the number of vegetable food items |
| 2 | Find the information about the Restaurant on the home page |
| 3 | Fill the form on the takeaway page and order two vegetable food items and one drink. Select the option of home delivery as well |
| Task Group B | |
| Task Number | Task Details |
| 1 | Go to home page and count the number of non-vegetable food items |
| 2 | Find the email address of the restaurant on the home page |
| 3 | Fill the form and order two non-vegetable items and one drink with the option of home delivery from the takeaway page |

Figures 1 and 2 show the main elements of the web site that was designed. Both versions were identical, however one used the parallax scrolling concept, while the other did not (Note: it is not possible to show statically via images the parallax effect).

**Fig. 1.** Homepage

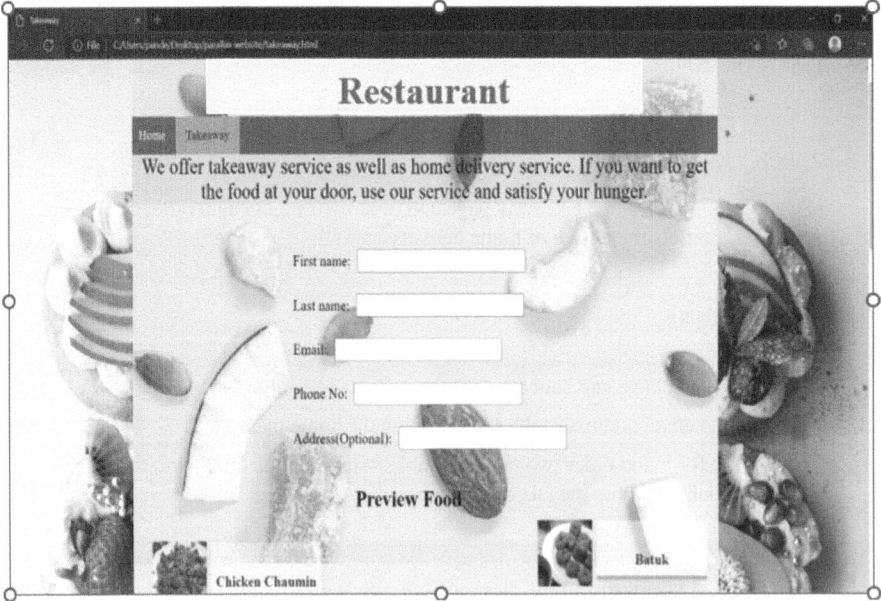

**Fig. 2.** Food Takeaway Page

### 3.5 Procedure

A procedure was designed for the experiment which was followed with all the participants. The first part of the experiment involved participants reading pre-prepared information about the experiment and process and then giving consent if they were in agreement. The whole experiment followed Norwegian requirements for ethics in research studies of this kind. Having completed the consent aspects, participants were then asked to complete a questionnaire that elicited a few aspects concerning their background experience.

When the questionnaire was completed, the participants were given information about the procedure that would be followed and the tasks they would carry out.

Then using the two prototype web sites the participants carried out the tasks detailed in Table 2. The usage of the tasks in relation to the parallax and non-parallax web pages was as detailed in Table 3.

**Table 3.** Tasks and Web Page Type Order of Execution

| Participant Number | Web Site | Task Group | Web Site | Task Group |
|---|---|---|---|---|
| 1 | Parallax | A | Non-Parallax | B |
| 2 | Non-Parallax | B | Parallax | A |
| 3 | Parallax | B | Non-Parallax | A |
| 4 | Parallax | A | Non-Parallax | B |
| 5 | Non-Parallax | B | Parallax | A |
| 6 | Parallax | B | Non-Parallax | A |

As the experiment proceeded, any questions asked by participants concerning the tasks, were dealt with by giving small hints to allow for progress through the experiment.

As a conclusion to the experiment, participants were subsequently asked to complete a post-experiment questionnaire. This concerned aspects of their experience with the two web user interfaces.

### 3.6 Results

The data collected was analyzed and the initial exploration showed the data to be parametric in nature (actual results for this aspect are not included for brevity). It was therefore decided to use a t-test for each pair of data.

For the total time to complete the tasks, the parallax scrolling incurred a Mean (M) time of 145.83 s with a Standard Deviation (SD) of 48.72. The non-parallax scrolling incurred a Mean time of 137.33 s with a Standard Deviation of 76.62. The paired t-test result is $t(5) = 0.276$, $p = .794$ (two-tailed). Therefore, the result suggests a lack of a significant difference. The means suggested that the non-parallax scrolling method was a little faster for task completion time.

For errors, we do not present significance testing as both scrolling methods incurred equal means in terms of amounts of errors (M = 1.167 for both). Further, for each condition, the standard deviations were comparably low (SD = 1.3292 Parallax Scrolling, SD = .7528 Non-Parallax Scrolling).

Each post-experiment question from the questionnaire was also analyzed. The questionnaire contained eight questions answered by participants using a 5-point Likert-type scale (Likert 1932). The scale ranged from 1 – Strongly Disagree to 5 – Strongly Agree. Four questions elicited opinions about the tasks and the web page designs used. These aimed to give some confidence that the whole context of the experiment in relation to the tasks and web page designs appeared acceptable to the participants. As can be seen in Fig. 3, these aspects were all rated very positively and consistently.

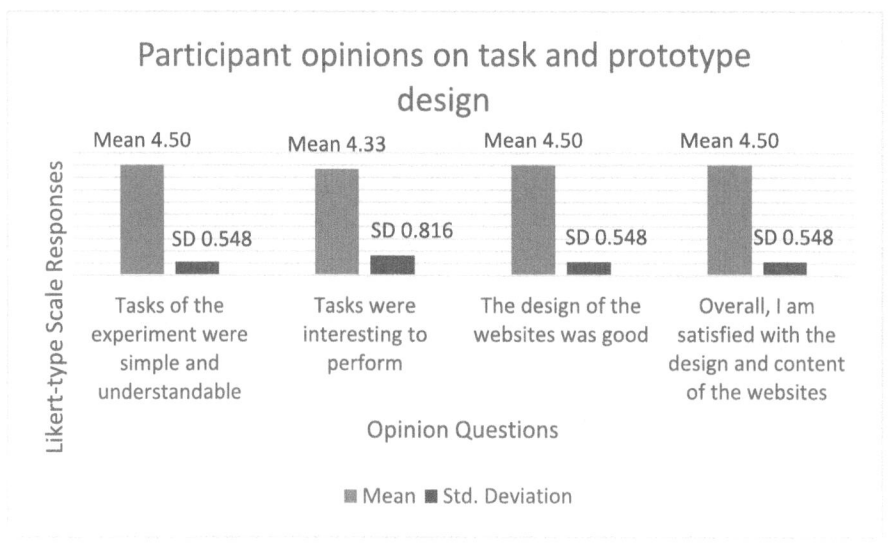

**Fig. 3.** Participant Opinions on Task and Prototype Design

The remaining four questions were more specifically about the comparison of parallax scrolling and non-parallax scrolling. Using the same scale as described, each question was answered two times. Once in relation to each scrolling method. Therefore, this allowed participants to select scores for each in a comparative manner.

For the question asking participants to rate their level of interest while scrolling through the content of the web site, the results were as follows: The parallax scrolling incurred a Mean (M) score of 3.67 with a Standard Deviation (SD) of 1.211. The non-parallax scrolling incurred a Mean score of 3.17 with a Standard Deviation of 1.169. The paired t-test result is t(5) = 0.808, p = .456 (two-tailed). Therefore, the result suggests a lack of a significant difference. The means suggested that the non-parallax scrolling method was rated slightly less interesting than the parallax design.

For the question asking participants to rate how pleasant it was to scroll through the content of the web site, the results were as follows: The parallax scrolling incurred a Mean (M) score of 3.83 with a Standard Deviation (SD) of 1.169. The non-parallax scrolling incurred a Mean score of 3.33 with a Standard Deviation of .816. The paired t-test result is t(5) = 0.745, p = .490 (two-tailed). Therefore, the result suggests a lack of a significant difference. The means suggested that the non-parallax scrolling method was rated to be slightly less pleasant than the parallax design.

For the question asking participants to rate how confident they felt whilst carrying out the tasks, the results were as follows: The parallax scrolling incurred a Mean (M) score of 4.00 with a Standard Deviation (SD) of .894. The non-parallax scrolling incurred a Mean score of 3.67 with a Standard Deviation of 1.033. The paired t-test result is t(5) = 1.00, p = .363 (two-tailed). Therefore, the result suggests a lack of a significant difference. The means suggested that the non-parallax scrolling method fostered potentially less confidence in the participants.

For the question asking participants to rate their level of preference of the scrolling methods, the results were as follows: The parallax scrolling incurred a Mean (M) score of 4.00 with a Standard Deviation (SD) of 1.26. The non-parallax scrolling incurred a Mean score of 3.33 with a Standard Deviation of .816. The paired t-test result is t(5) = .877, p = .421 (two-tailed). Therefore, the result suggests a lack of a significant difference. The means suggested that the parallax scrolling method was preferred slightly more over the non-parallax design.

Having presented the analysis of the results, the next section concludes this paper with a discussion and conclusion.

## 4   Discussion and Conclusions

The investigation aimed to explore aspects of performance and subjective preferences concerning parallax scrolling and non-parallax scrolling. Our data collection and subsequent analysis suggests that performance in terms of task time and errors is not significantly affected by the scrolling methods we implemented. Subjective opinions were also not significantly affected by the scrolling method. In terms of the experiment and the associated hypotheses presented in this paper, we accept the outcomes as being in line with the null hypotheses presented earlier.

However, the data showed slight trends in a certain direction. The task time data showed that the non-parallax version was quicker to use, although the small data set was not so consistent having high standard deviations. The four subjective comparative questions posed to the participants showed a slight overall preference for the parallax-based version of the web site we implemented. In these cases, all indicated a more consistent level of opinion, where each had low standard deviations.

Certain standard guidelines suggest that parallax scrolling should either be avoided or be implemented in such a manner that it can be controlled or switched off at will by a user. The Web Content Accessibility Guidelines (WCAG) 2.2 in section 2.3.3 (W3C, 2023) suggest implementations that allow 'motion animation triggered by interaction' to be switched off. The exception to this is if the animation itself is a complete requirement in terms of some functionality or that the information itself needs such an animation. Further, the WCAG 2.2 Understanding Docs, Understanding SC 2.3.3: Animation from Interactions (Level AAA) (W3C 2024), gives further information on the negative aspects of parallax scrolling. In line with the nausea observations made by Frederick et al.

(2015), mention is made that animations can cause nausea and migraine headaches. Parallax scrolling is specifically mentioned in (W3C 2024) as being a potential problem, particularly if there is no option to switch off the feature.

The aspect of parallax scrolling can also be looked into in light of the well-established principles of universal design (Story 1998). If a designer or developer implements parallax scrolling that cannot be switched off and for no particular reason other than it may be considered to be 'nice' or 'cool', then this approach may go against the universal design principles. For example, Principle 1 is about 'Equitable Use' and Principle 1b concerns avoiding 'segregating or stigmatizing any users' (Story 1998). If parallax scrolling causes nausea or headaches in some users, then it clearly stigmatizes some users and should not be used or at the very least should be easily turned off. Principle 2 is about 'Flexibility in Use' and Principle 2a says to 'Provide choice in methods of use (Story 1998).' Clearly if users are forced to use parallax scrolling that in many cases is unnecessary, then such an implementation does not provide a choice for end-users. Principle 6 is about 'Low Physical Effort' (Story 1998). It should be clear that an interaction method that can create in users' nausea and headaches is not fostering lower physical effort in using the web site.

Overall, our work did not present any categorical results. The results we did obtain, could be referred to as being a hint in a certain direction, where for performance aspects it might be better to have no parallax effects. However, participants tended to prefer the parallax effect in the web site.

Established guidelines suggest more strongly that parallax effects should not be used. If parallax effects are used, they should either be essential to something on the web site or in all or most cases there must be the option to switch off the feature in an easy and quick manner.

In future work it would be good to address the limitations of this research. We had two potential issues. The first was a rather small sample size. The second was that perhaps the web pages designed did not foster complex enough tasks to really bring out any potential differences in interacting with or without the parallax effects. Another aspect difficult to implement in this kind of research is the long-term use of a web site with parallax effects. It could be that participants' opinions change over time or become stronger towards a certain direction over time. Also, when the initial novelty feeling wears off, this can be a cause for a change in opinion.

# References

Frederick, D., Mohler, J., Vorvoreanu, M., Glotzbach, R.: The effects of parallax scrolling on user experience in web design. J. Usabil. Stud. **10**(2) (2015)

Fu, J.: Parallax Scrolling Interface research based on Fitts' law. Paper Presented at the 2016 IEEE Advanced Information Management, Communicates, Electronic and Automation Control Conference (IMCEC) (2016)

Karampournioti, E., Wiedmann, K.: Storytelling in online shops: the impacts on explicit and implicit user experience, brand perceptions and behavioral intention. Internet Res. **32**(7) (2022)

Lazar, J., Feng, J., Hochheiser, H.: Research methods in human-computer interaction, 2nd edn. Morgan Kaufmann, Cambridge (2017)

Likert, R.A.: Technique for the measurement of attitudes. Columbia University Press, NY (1932)

Mahardika, W., Wibirama, S., Ferdiana, R., Kusumawardani, S.S.: A novel user experience study of parallax scrolling using eye tracking and user experience questionnaire. Int. J. Adv. Sci. Eng. Inform. Technol. **8**(4)(2018)

Sherwin, K.: What Parallax Lacks, Nielsen Norman Group (2019). https://www.nngroup.com/articles/parallax-usability/ Accessed May 2024

Story, M.F.: Maximizing usability: the principles of universal design. Assist. Technol. Official J. RESNA **10**(1), 4–12 (1998)

W3C: Web Content Accessibility Guidelines (WCAG) 2.2 (2023). https://www.w3.org/TR/WCAG22/#animation-from-interactions. Accessed May 2024

W3C: WCAG 2.2 Understanding Docs, Understanding SC 2.3.3: Animation from Interactions (Level AAA) (2024). https://www.w3.org/WAI/WCAG22/Understanding/animation-from-interactions.html. Accessed May 2024

# Understanding and Enhancing the Usability of MCCD Forms: A Human-Centered Design Approach

Thummala Nomeshwari[✉]

National Institute of Design, Bengaluru, India
thummala_n@nid.edu

**Abstract.** This research addresses the challenges of conventional Medical Certificate for Cause of Death (MCCD) forms within the Indian healthcare system. Despite historical efforts to establish uniform registration systems, MCCD documentation still faces issues of transparency and accuracy. Drawing upon a human-centered design approach, this study proposes innovative solutions to enhance MCCD forms usability and effectiveness.

Key findings reveal significant gaps between reported deaths and medically certified causes, highlighting the need for improved documentation processes. Through iterative design informed by stakeholder feedback, the research introduces a novel framework prioritizing clarity, simplicity, and user-friendliness in MCCD forms. Case studies and pilot implementations demonstrate the feasibility and potential impact of these redesigned forms on healthcare outcomes.

This research underscores the transformative potential of rethinking MCCD forms as tools for transparent, empathetic, and collaborative mortality documentation. By leveraging user-centered design principles, the study aims to empower healthcare professionals and foster trust among stakeholders in the Indian healthcare context.

**Keywords:** Medical certificate for Cause of Death · MCCD · civil registration · mortality · vital events · Design/evaluation for cross-cultural users · Health and DUXU · Heuristics · Usability · User Experience (UX) · Design Excellence · Human-Centered Design · Innovation · User-Centric Solutions · Accessibility · Interaction Design · User Engagement · Empathy · Problem-Solving · User Feedback · Iterative Design · Impactful Design

## 1 Introduction

The demand for better health statistics is growing at a very rapid pace, including both empirical data and estimates on various aspects of health such as births, deaths, morbidity, risk factors, health systems, and health service coverage. These parameters are the basis for evidence-based decision-making about resource allocation, monitoring of indicators, identifying the priorities for programs and other related activities in public [1].

© The Author(s), under exclusive license to Springer Nature Switzerland AG 2025
A. Marcus et al. (Eds.): HCII 2024, LNCS 15380, pp. 120–140, 2025.
https://doi.org/10.1007/978-3-031-76821-7_10

The Civil Registration System (CRS) in India is generating these vital statistics [3]. The Medical Certificate for Cause of Death (MCCD) reports are the series of the publication presenting statistics on causes of death obtained through the Civil Registration System under the Registration of Births and Deaths Act, 1969 [2]. In many developing countries including India, the civil registration data are not following the data quality parameters of completeness and not available in time and therefore, compromising the usefulness of these data [4].

The non-availability of reliable and quality data of mortality, morbidity and cause specific deaths are a major concern as they result in countries incapable of tracking and safeguarding the well-being of their populations due to unavailability of the records of millions of deaths and births in the country [5].

During the nineteenth century, various provinces in India implemented civil registration systems (CRS), each established under different Acts. Consequently, in the post-independence era, the Parliament passed the Registration of Births and Deaths (RBD) Act in 1969 to enforce a consistent legal framework for registering and reporting births and deaths across all Indian states and union territories (UTs) [2].

The Office of the Registrar General of India (ORGI), under the Ministry of Home Affairs, Government of India (GOI), is tasked with several responsibilities:

(a) Issuing directives to chief registrars.
(b) Coordinating activities.
(c) Annually releasing vital statistics (VS) reports.

Chief registrars serve as the implementing authorities of the Registration of Births and Deaths (RBD) Act in states/UTs and are responsible for publishing the annual VS report for their respective areas. States/UTs appoint officials from various departments such as health, economics, statistics, planning, and local bodies as chief registrars, district registrars, and registrars at the state, district, and local levels, respectively.

Thus, the CRS (civil registration systems) necessitates extensive coordination among multiple departments for its functioning. Despite being in operation for over 50 years, the CRS (civil registration systems) still lacks the necessary political and administrative support, as well as financial resources, to be considered a reliable source of mortality statistics in India.

In 2019, 93% of estimated deaths were registered, and only 19% of estimated deaths had a Medical Certificate for Cause of Death (MCCD) [3, 6]. Mortality statistics have large state-wise variation. The level of death registration varies from 28% to 100% and MCCD varies from 3% to 100%. Although completeness of death registration has increased at about 4% per year from 2010 to 2019, rise in MCCD in this period has been slower (2.3%) [7].

As per the 2019 SRS report, medical attention was sought before death at government or private hospitals in 48.7% of cases. However, the MCCD report indicates that only 19% of estimated deaths were accompanied by an MCCD [3, 6].

In the aftermath of the COVID-19 pandemic, the urgency to understand the full magnitude of the crisis propelled my curiosity. News agencies globally echoed similar concerns, with headlines such as "Covid toll may never be known" from BBC. Alarming estimates suggested that the actual death toll in India could be significantly higher than reported (Fig. 1).

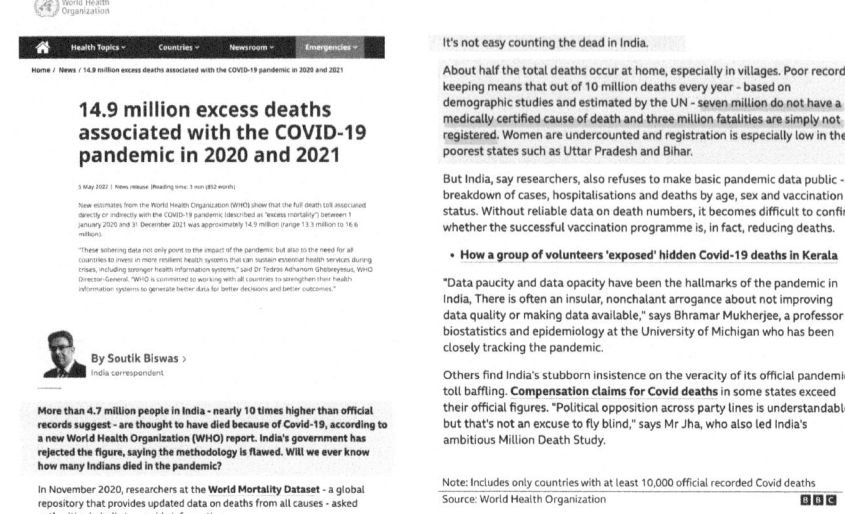

**Fig. 1.** Newspaper Clippings from WHO and BBC Highlighting Excess Deaths During the COVID-19 Pandemic in India.

### This Discrepancy Prompts the Question

Are our systems for recording deaths accurate? Why are MCCD Forms either not being completed or not proving to be highly useful?

These question became the catalyst for my exploration into mortality documentation practices.

In response to these challenges, this paper presents a comprehensive examination of the limitations associated with conventional MCCD forms and proposes innovative solutions aimed at enhancing transparency, accuracy, and collaboration in mortality documentation processes.

Grounded in the context of the Indian healthcare system, this research endeavors to revolutionize MCCD documentation practices through a human-centered design approach. Drawing upon principles of transparency, empathetic communication, and user-centric design, this research seeks to rethink and redesign MCCD forms to better meet the needs of healthcare professionals, administrators, and bereaved families.

Through an iterative design process informed by stakeholder feedback and empirical research, a novel approach to MCCD form design is introduced, prioritizing clarity, simplicity, and user-friendliness. The proposed framework integrates elements of human-centered design, usability principles, and collaborative documentation practices to foster a culture of transparency and accountability in mortality documentation.

Furthermore, this paper explores the potential impact of redesigned MCCD forms on healthcare outcomes, including improved data accuracy, enhanced communication among healthcare providers, and greater satisfaction among bereaved families. Case studies and pilot implementations of the redesigned MCCD forms in real-world healthcare settings are presented to illustrate their feasibility, effectiveness, and scalability.

## 2  Background

The realm of healthcare documentation, numerous initiatives have been undertaken to streamline the process of mortality documentation and enhance the accuracy of recorded data. Notable efforts include the implementation of standardized Medical Certificate for Cause of Death (MCCD) forms, improved data collection methods, and enhanced training programs for healthcare professionals. These initiatives have been driven by the recognition that accurate mortality data is crucial for informing public health policies, resource allocation, and disease surveillance.

### 2.1  Related Work in Mortality Documentation

Previous research has primarily focused on technical solutions to improve data accuracy. For example, studies have explored the use of electronic health records (EHRs) to automate the completion of MCCD forms, thereby reducing human error [8]. Other efforts have concentrated on enhancing the training of healthcare professionals, emphasizing the importance of accurate and complete documentation [9].

Despite these advancements, significant challenges remain, particularly within the context of the Indian healthcare system. The diversity of regional practices, coupled with varying levels of resource availability, has contributed to inconsistencies in mortality documentation. Furthermore, previous initiatives have often overlooked the user experience, leading to forms that are cumbersome and difficult to complete accurately.

### 2.2  Innovative Aspects of the Approach

This research introduces a novel approach that emphasizes human-centered design principles. Unlike previous initiatives that have predominantly focused on technical solutions, our approach prioritizes the needs and experiences of end-users, including healthcare professionals, administrators, and bereaved families. By integrating usability and user-friendliness into the design of MCCD forms, we aim to create documentation tools that are intuitive, easy to understand, and efficient to complete.

A key distinguishing factor of our work is its holistic impact on the healthcare system. Beyond enhancing data accuracy, our approach aims to foster greater trust and transparency within the healthcare system. By providing more accurate and transparent information about mortality trends, our work can inform public health policies and interventions, ultimately leading to better health outcomes for communities.

### 2.3  Significance of the Research

This research not only addresses the technical aspects of mortality documentation but also considers the broader societal implications. Successful implementation of our approach has the potential to bridge the gap between recorded data and actual occurrences of death, ensuring that mortality statistics reflect reality more accurately. This, in turn, can enhance the credibility of public health data and support more effective responses to health crises, as demonstrated during the COVID-19 pandemic.

# 3  Problem Statement

In contemporary mortality documentation practices, there exists a significant gap between the actual occurrence of deaths and their accurate recording, [3, 6, 7, 10] leading to potentially unreliable information and critical implications for public health. Despite the indispensable role of accurate mortality data in informing healthcare policies, resource allocation, and disease surveillance, the current systems for documenting deaths exhibit substantial deficiencies, fail to meet the needs of healthcare professionals, administrators, and bereaved families, hindering the accurate reporting and analysis of mortality statistics.

## 3.1  The Impact of Inaccurate Mortality Data

The consequences of inaccurate mortality data are further exacerbated during public health crises, as demonstrated during the COVID-19 pandemic. In India, a staggering number of deaths remain unaccounted for, with millions lacking a medically certified cause of death, and millions more fatalities going unregistered [10]. This discrepancy not only undermines the credibility of mortality statistics but also hampers efforts to assess the true burden of disease, allocate resources effectively, and devise timely interventions to mitigate public health emergencies.

# 4  Understanding the Process Flow Following a Death Event in Karnataka: An Overview

In Karnataka, the process following a death event involves a structured sequence of steps mandated by the Karnataka Registration of Births and Deaths Rules, 1970, and the Registration of Births & Deaths Act, 1969 [2, 9]. This section provides an in-depth exploration of the system architecture governing death records within the Karnataka State Government, elucidating the key stages and stakeholders involved in registering a death and maintaining accurate mortality data.

## 4.1  Process Analysis

By comprehensively analyzing this process flow, the aim is to gain insights into the intricacies of death record management and identify areas for potential improvement in data accuracy, efficiency, and transparency.

**The Process Flow Following a Death Event Can Be Divided into Several Key Stages:**

1. **Notification of Death:** The process begins with the notification of a death event to the appropriate authorities, typically by a medical practitioner or family member of the deceased.
2. **Medical Certification:** A medical certificate for cause of death (MCCD) is issued by a qualified medical practitioner, stating the cause of death based on clinical observations or post-mortem examination findings.

3. **Registration of Death:** The death event is registered with the local registrar of births and deaths, where relevant information such as the deceased individual's demographics, date and place of death, and cause of death are recorded.
4. **Verification and Compilation:** The registered death records are verified for accuracy and completeness, compiled into official reports, and transmitted to higher administrative authorities for consolidation and analysis (Fig. 2).

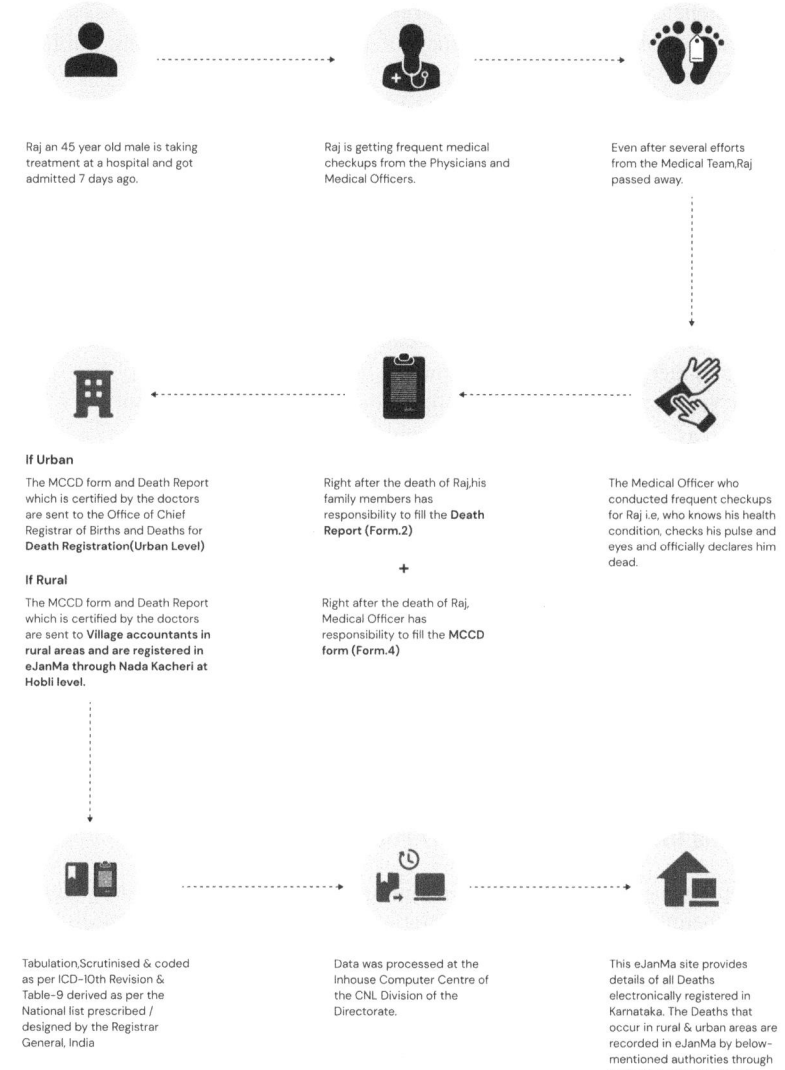

**Fig. 2.** Flowchart depicting the journey of information from the occurrence of a death event to its registration with the state government.

## 4.2    Challenges of Mortality Documentation

- Delays in notification and registration of death events, leading to under-reporting and inaccuracies in mortality data.
- It has been identified that if the MCCD (Medical Certificate for Cause of Death) form is filled out incorrectly by the physician, it can have significant implications for the accuracy and reliability of mortality data in India.
- Lack of standardized protocols for medical certification of cause of death, resulting in inconsistencies and discrepancies in reported causes of death.
- Limited accessibility and transparency of death records, hindering public health surveillance and policy formulation efforts.

# 5    Medical Certificate for Cause of Death (MCCD) Forms

Medical Certificate for Cause of Death (MCCD) forms are essential documents used to record the cause(s) and circumstances surrounding an individual's death. In Karnataka, India, there are various types of MCCD forms tailored to different scenarios and settings. Among them, Form No. 4 is a prominent variant utilized in specific contexts:

**1. Form No. 4:** Form No. 4 is designated for individuals who pass away in hospital settings while undergoing medical treatment.

**2. Form No. 4A:** Form No. 4A is utilized for individuals who die outside of hospital premises, such as at home, on roads, or in public places.

**3. Still Births:** Apart from deaths involving individuals, MCCD forms also cater to stillbirths, referring to infants who are born without signs of life after a certain period of gestation.

## 5.1    Focus of Study on MCCD Form No. 4

For this research endeavor, Form No. 4 emerges as the primary focus, given its relevance to deaths occurring within hospital settings. Understanding the intricacies of Form No. 4 and its utilization by healthcare professionals is paramount for enhancing the accuracy and reliability of mortality data recording in Karnataka, India (Fig. 3).

## 5.2    Exploring the Evolution of MCCD Forms

To gain comprehensive insights into the evolution of MCCD forms and their significance in mortality documentation, further exploration is warranted. A historical study delving into the development, modifications, and contextual nuances of MCCD forms throughout history can provide valuable perspectives. By tracing the evolution of these forms, researchers can identify trends, challenges, and innovations that have shaped mortality documentation practices over time (Figs. 4 and 5).

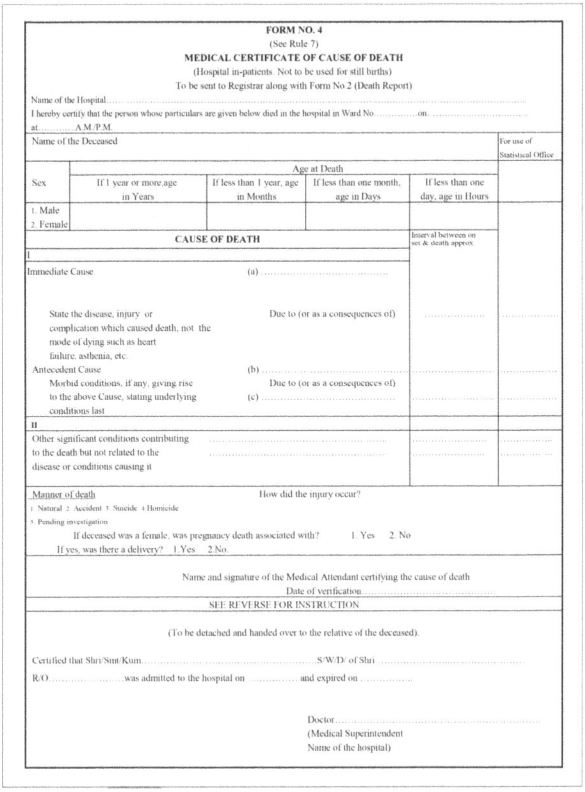

**FORM NO. 4**
(See Rule 7)
**MEDICAL CERTIFICATE OF CAUSE OF DEATH**
(Hospital in-patients. Not to be used for still births)
To be sent to Registrar along with Form No.2 (Death Report)

Name of the Hospital........
I hereby certify that the person whose particulars are given below died in the hospital in Ward No............on...........
at...........A.M./P.M.

Name of the Deceased | For use of Statistical Office

| Sex | Age at Death | | | |
|---|---|---|---|---|
| | If 1 year or more, age in Years | If less than 1 year, age in Months | If less than one month, age in Days | If less than one day, age in Hours |
| 1. Male<br>2. Female | | | | |

CAUSE OF DEATH | Interval between on set & death approx

I
Immediate Cause (a) ..........
State the disease, injury or complication which caused death, not the mode of dying such as heart failure, asthenia, etc.
Due to (or as a consequences of)
Antecedent Cause (b) ..........
Morbid conditions, if any, giving rise to the above Cause, stating underlying conditions last
Due to (or as a consequences of)
(c) ..........

II
Other significant conditions contributing to the death but not related to the disease or conditions causing it ..........

Manner of death
1. Natural 2. Accident 3. Suicide 4. Homicide
5. Pending investigation
How did the injury occur?
If deceased was a female, was pregnancy death associated with? 1. Yes 2. No
If yes, was there a delivery? 1.Yes 2.No.

Name and signature of the Medical Attendant certifying the cause of death
Date of verification..........

SEE REVERSE FOR INSTRUCTION

(To be detached and handed over to the relative of the deceased).

Certified that Shri/Smt/Kum..........S/W/D/ of Shri ..........
R/O..........was admitted to the hospital on ..........and expired on ..........

Doctor..........
(Medical Superintendent
Name of the hospital)

**Fig. 3.** Presenting the current MCCD Form No.4.

# 6 Primary Research

**Methodology:** To gain deeper insights into the utilization and challenges associated with MCCD Form 4, primary research was conducted involving structured interviews with 30 medical practitioners across various regions of India. The selection criteria included practitioners with a minimum of 3 years and a maximum of 20 years of experience in healthcare, ensuring a diverse representation of perspectives and experiences. Interviews were conducted using a semi-structured approach, allowing for open-ended discussions on MCCD form filling practices, challenges faced, and recommendations for improvement. Additionally, observation studies were conducted to supplement the interview findings, providing valuable insights into real-time MCCD form filling processes.

## 6.1 Challenges Faced by Medical Practitioners

This section outlines the challenges faced by medical practitioners in accurately filling out MCCD forms. These challenges include time constraints due to demanding schedules, lack of standardization leading to confusion, ambiguity in form design, and

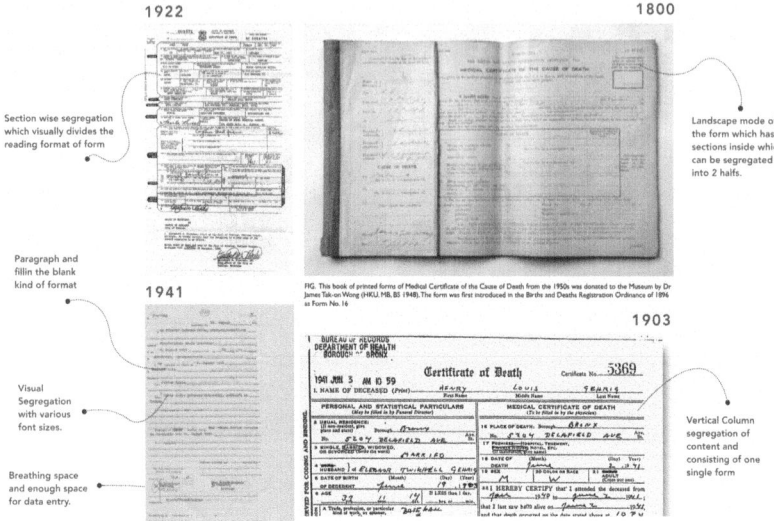

**Fig. 4.** Analysis of MCCD Forms over time and examination of their format

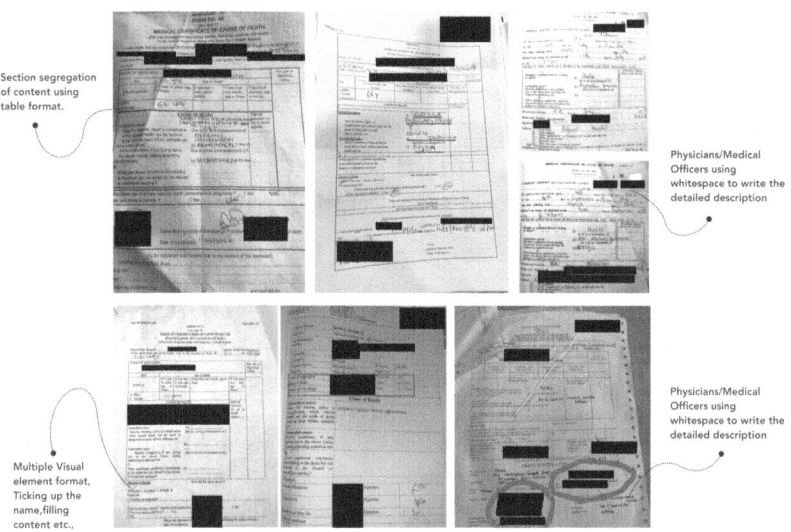

**Fig. 5.** Analysis of MCCD Forms completed by Physicians.

insufficient training, emphasizing the need for standardized formats and comprehensive training programs.

- **Time Constraints:** Practitioners often face time constraints in accurately filling out MCCD forms amidst their demanding work schedules, potentially compromising the quality and completeness of data.

- **Lack of Standardization:** Variations in MCCD forms across different regions and institutions contribute to confusion and inconsistencies in documentation practices, highlighting the need for standardized formats and protocols.
- **Ambiguity in Design:** Ambiguities in certain sections of MCCD forms pose challenges for practitioners, potentially leading to misinterpretation and inaccuracies in data recording.
- **Insufficient Training:** Many practitioners lack sufficient training in MCCD form filling, underscoring the importance of comprehensive training programs to enhance proficiency and adherence to standardized practices.

## 7 UX Audit of MCCD Form

In this section, we aimed to assess the usability and accessibility features of the Medical Certificate of Cause of Death (MCCD) form. Given the conventional nature of printed forms, the evaluation primarily focused on aspects such as layout, readability, and clarity, rather than interactive accessibility features typically associated with digital interfaces.

**Methodology**
The UX audit methodology involved a systematic assessment of the MCCD form's design and usability based on established UX evaluation criteria. The audit was conducted under the guidance of trained evaluators with expertise in human-computer interaction and usability testing.

**Key Aspects Evaluated Included:**

1. **Navigation and Layout:** Assessment of the form's organization and layout to ensure intuitive navigation and ease of information retrieval.
2. **Clarity and Readability:** Evaluation of the clarity of content presentation, including text legibility, language comprehensibility, and visual hierarchy.
3. **Input Fields and Data Entry:** Examination of input fields, validation prompts, and data entry mechanisms to facilitate accurate and efficient data input.
4. **Error Handling:** Analysis of error messages and feedback mechanisms to assist users in resolving input errors and ensuring data accuracy.
5. **Accessibility:** Assessment of the form's accessibility features to accommodate diverse user needs, including individuals with disabilities (Fig. 6).

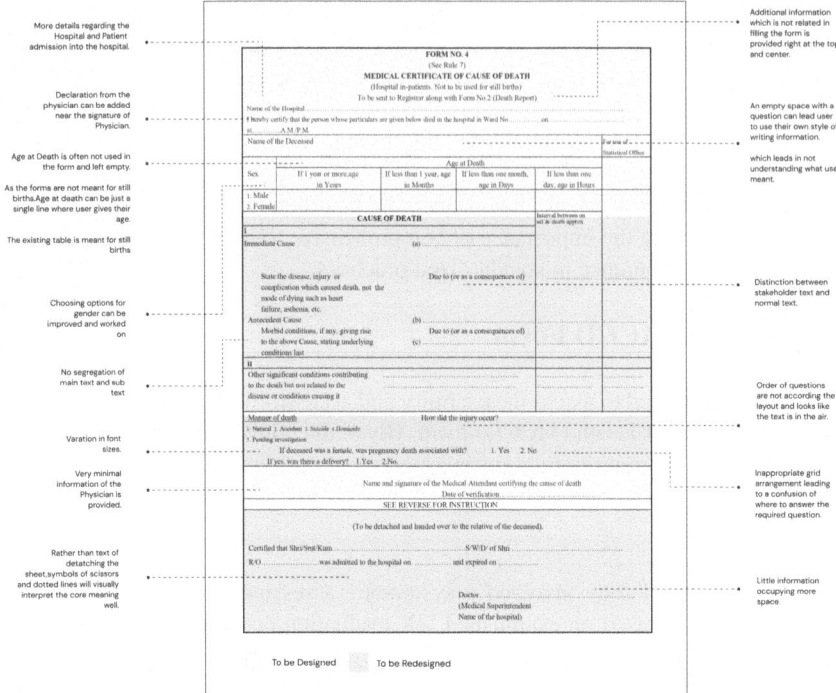

**Fig. 6.** The audit of MCCD Form No. 4 includes color-coded indicators to denote areas for design enhancement and redesign.

## 7.1 UX Audit Observations and Insights

1. **Additional Information Placement:** Extraneous details unrelated to form completion were prominently displayed at the top and centre, potentially distracting users from the primary task of filling out the form.
2. **Age at Death Field Usage:** The Age at Death field often remained unused, leading to inconsistencies in data recording. Considering the form's applicability to hospital inpatients, a streamlined approach to capturing age information is warranted.
3. **Layout and Content Arrangement:** The layout lacked uniformity and clarity, with variations in font sizes, text hierarchy, and content organization. This resulted in confusion and inefficiencies in form completion.
4. **Grid Arrangement and Segregation:** The form lacked clear visual segregation and sectioning, making it challenging for users to navigate and comprehend the information hierarchy. Improving grid arrangements and introducing visual cues for section differentiation could enhance user clarity.
5. **Layout Concerns:** Inadequate layout structure and organization hindered form completion efficiency and accuracy.
6. **Information Management:** Balancing the inclusion of necessary information while minimizing excess and irrelevant content is crucial for optimizing form usability.
7. **Hierarchy and Clarity:** Establishing a clear information hierarchy and visual segregation is imperative to enhance form comprehension and usability (Fig. 7).

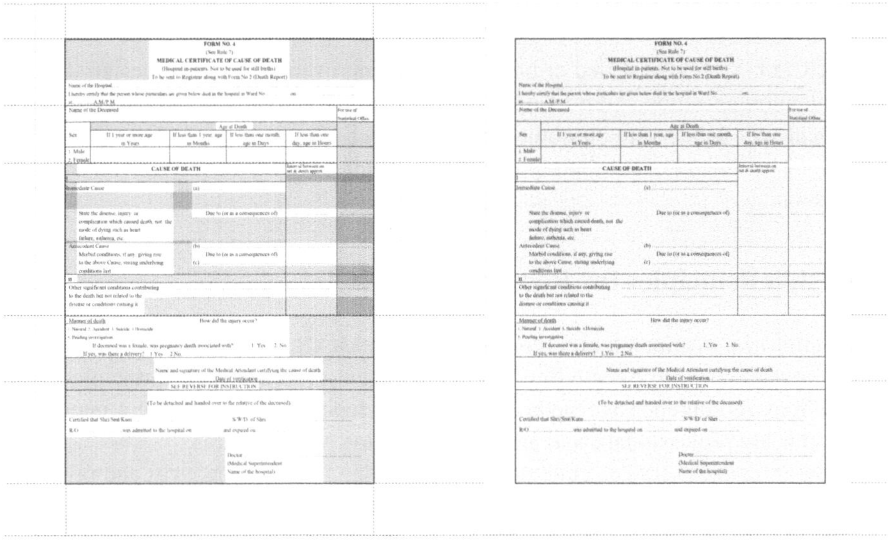

**Fig. 7.** a. Examination of White Space versus Content b. Evaluation of Horizontal Sections and their Spacing from Each Other

## 7.2   Recommendations for Improvement

- **Uniform Layout and Spacing:** The form layout should be standardized and aligned to centre, optimizing the use of white space and ensuring consistent borders throughout

- **Improved Hierarchy and Segmentation:** Enhancements in text hierarchy and content segmentation can facilitate ease of use and understanding for busy medical practitioners.

- **Information about the Deceased:** Key demographic details such as full name, parents' names, date of birth, and age, Date of Admission, Time of Admission, Date of Death, Time of Death are essential for accurate record-keeping.

- **Hospital Information:** Comprehensive hospital details including name, code, admission/registration number, and medical practitioner credentials are necessary for certification and documentation.

- **Autopsy Details:** Inclusion of autopsy details, if applicable, adds depth to the medical history section, contributing to a comprehensive record of the deceased's health status.

- **Certification by Physician/Doctor:** Complete certification by the attending physician or doctor, including signature, stamp, license number, and relevant credentials, ensures the authenticity and validity of the MCCD form.

### 7.3  Conclusion from the UX Audit1

The MCCD UX audit revealed critical areas for improvement in form design, layout, and content organization. Addressing these challenges through thoughtful redesign and refinement will enhance the usability, accuracy, and efficiency of mortality data documentation, ultimately contributing to improved public health surveillance and policy formulation.

## 8  Design Principles for Redesign of MCCD

Formulating design principles for the redesign of the MCCD Form is essential to provide a structured framework for guiding the improvement process. These principles were derived from a comprehensive methodology that included a literature review, interviews with healthcare professionals, and analysis of existing MCCD forms.

These principles serve as guiding tenets, outlining the key objectives and priorities for enhancing the usability, accuracy, and efficiency of the form. By establishing clear design principles, stakeholders gain a shared understanding of the goals and expectations for the redesigned form, facilitating collaboration and decision-making throughout the redesign process.

**1. Usability and User Experience:** Prioritizing user-centered design principles to enhance usability and optimize user experience throughout the MCCD Form interaction process.

**2. Efficiency & Time Saving:** Streamlining form completion workflows and minimize user effort through intuitive design elements and efficient data entry mechanisms.

**3. Data Consistency & Accessibility:** Ensuring data consistency and accessibility by standardizing form elements, providing clear instructions, and facilitating seamless data retrieval and sharing.

**4. Accuracy and Completeness:** Emphasizing data accuracy and completeness by implementing validation checks, error prompts, and quality assurance measures to minimize errors and omissions.

**5. Standardisation:** Establishing standardized design conventions and formatting guidelines to promote consistency, clarity, and interoperability across MCCD Forms used in different healthcare settings.

## 9  Redesigned MCCD Form (Iteration-1)

After formulating the design principles based on the identified challenges, a redesigned version of the Medical Certificate for Cause of Death (MCCD) Form was developed. The new design aimed to address the deficiencies identified during the UX Audit and Usability Studies, focusing on improving usability, efficiency, and data accuracy (Fig. 8).

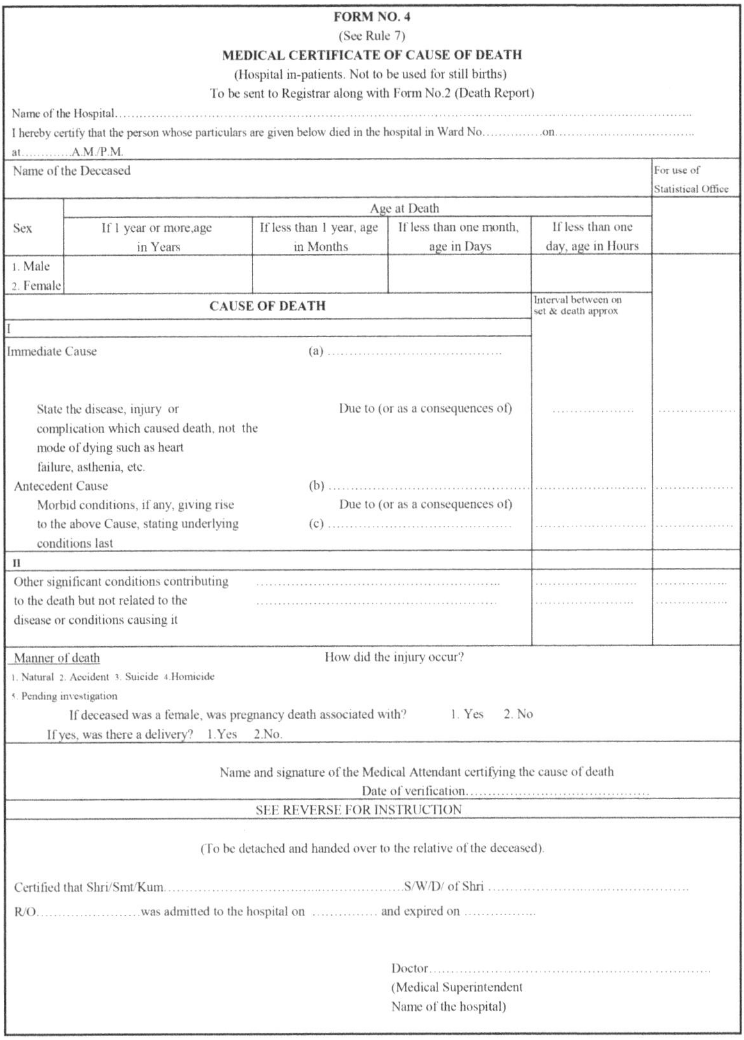

**FORM NO. 4**
(See Rule 7)
**MEDICAL CERTIFICATE OF CAUSE OF DEATH**
(Hospital in-patients. Not to be used for still births)
To be sent to Registrar along with Form No.2 (Death Report)

Name of the Hospital............................................................................................................
I hereby certify that the person whose particulars are given below died in the hospital in Ward No..............on...............................
at............A.M./P.M.

| Name of the Deceased | | | | | For use of Statistical Office |
|---|---|---|---|---|---|
| | Age at Death | | | | |
| Sex | If 1 year or more, age in Years | If less than 1 year, age in Months | If less than one month, age in Days | If less than one day, age in Hours | |
| 1. Male<br>2. Female | | | | | |

| CAUSE OF DEATH | | Interval between on set & death approx | |
|---|---|---|---|
| I | | | |
| Immediate Cause | (a) ..................................... | | |
| State the disease, injury or complication which caused death, not the mode of dying such as heart failure, asthenia, etc. | Due to (or as a consequences of) | .................. | ................ |
| Antecedent Cause<br>Morbid conditions, if any, giving rise to the above Cause, stating underlying conditions last | (b) ........................................<br>Due to (or as a consequences of)<br>(c) ........................................ | ....................<br><br>.................... | ................<br><br>................ |
| II | | | |
| Other significant conditions contributing to the death but not related to the disease or conditions causing it | ..................................................<br>.................................................. | ....................<br>.................... | ................<br>................ |

Manner of death — How did the injury occur?
1. Natural 2. Accident 3. Suicide 4. Homicide
5. Pending investigation
If deceased was a female, was pregnancy death associated with? 1. Yes 2. No
If yes, was there a delivery? 1. Yes 2. No.

Name and signature of the Medical Attendant certifying the cause of death
Date of verification.........................................

SEE REVERSE FOR INSTRUCTION

(To be detached and handed over to the relative of the deceased).

Certified that Shri/Smt/Kum.........................................S/W/D/ of Shri ..........................................
R/O........................was admitted to the hospital on .............. and expired on ...............

Doctor............................................................
(Medical Superintendent
Name of the hospital)

**Fig. 8.** . Redesigned MCCD Form Iteration-1

# 10 Usability Testing of Redesigned MCCD Form

The redesigned MCCD Form underwent extensive usability testing, involving physicians, doctors, and medical officers with varying levels of experience in mortality documentation. Participants were asked to fill out the form and provide feedback on its usability, clarity, and functionality.

## 10.1  Methodology for Usability Testing

The usability testing of the redesigned MCCD Form followed a structured methodology to gather comprehensive feedback from participants. The methodology included the following steps:

1. **Participant Selection:** A diverse group of participants, including physicians, doctors, and medical officers with varying levels of experience in mortality documentation, was selected for the usability testing. This ensured that feedback represented a range of perspectives and user scenarios.
2. **Test Environment:** The usability testing sessions were conducted in controlled environments, such as hospital settings or medical facilities, to simulate real-world usage scenarios. This allowed participants to interact with the form in a familiar context and provided researchers with valuable insights into practical challenges and considerations.
3. **Observation and Note-Taking:** Researchers observed participants as they interacted with the form, taking note of any difficulties, errors, or areas of confusion encountered during the testing process. This qualitative data provided valuable insights into user behaviour and preferences.
4. **Feedback Collection:** After completing the tasks, participants were asked to provide feedback on their overall experience with the form. Structured interviews or surveys were used to gather feedback on usability, clarity, functionality, and any suggestions for improvement.
5. **Analysis and Iteration:** The feedback collected during usability testing was analysed to identify common themes, patterns, and areas for improvement. Based on this analysis, Iteration 2 of the MCCD Form was developed, incorporating suggested enhancements and refinements to optimize usability and user satisfaction.

## 10.2  Objective

The objective of gathering user feedback on the redesigned MCCD form was to evaluate its usability and effectiveness in real-world medical practice. Feedback from healthcare professionals was crucial to ensure the form met the needs of its primary users and addressed previous issues.

## 10.3  User Feedback

- "The form seamlessly integrates clarity with functionality – a much-needed upgrade."- Dr. Neetu Singh - Chief Cardiologist.
- "The intuitive design drastically reduces the time I spend on documentation." - Dr. Rajesh Menon - Head of Neurology.
- "Every section feels thoughtfully crafted, addressing previous ambiguities." - Dr. Preetham Desai - Senior Pediatrician.
- "The redesigned form strikes a balance between comprehensive data capture and user-friendly design." - Dr. Arvind Ranganathan - Director of Orthopedics (Fig. 9).

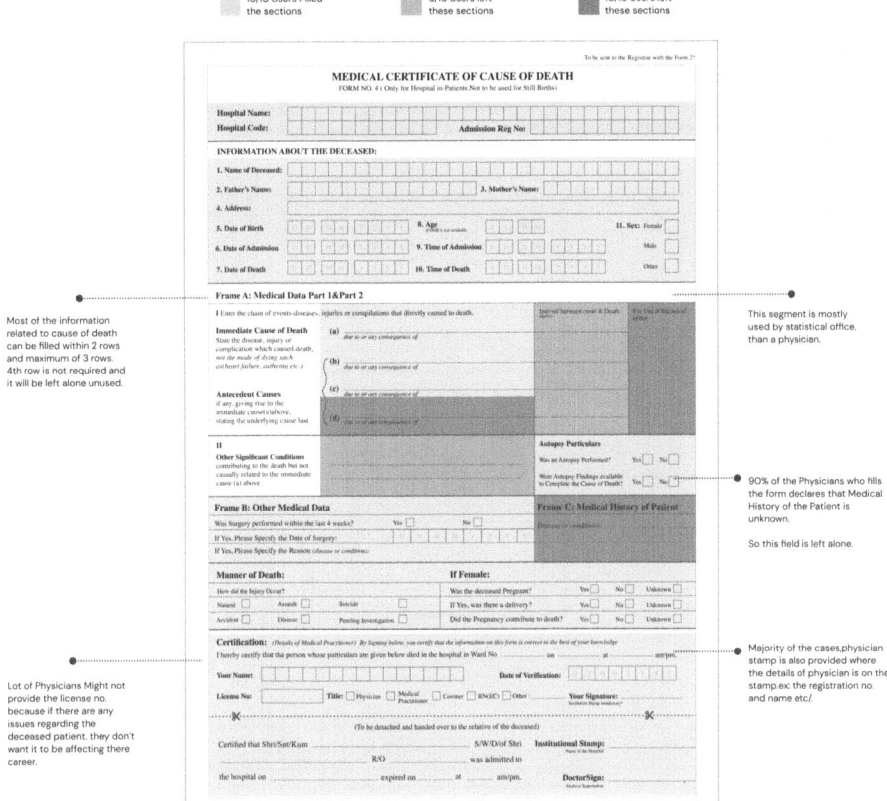

**Fig. 9.** In-depth Examination of User Interaction with the Form

## 11    Redesigned MCCD Form (Iteration-2)

Based on the insights gathered from usability testing, Iteration 2 of the MCCD Form was developed. This iteration incorporated the suggested enhancements and refinements, ensuring that the form effectively addressed the needs and preferences of its users while maintaining compliance with regulatory requirements (Figs. 10 and 11).

## 12    Before and After the Redesign of MCCD Forms

The evolution of the Medical Certificate for Cause of Death (MCCD) Form involved iterative improvements informed by practitioner feedback and usability testing.

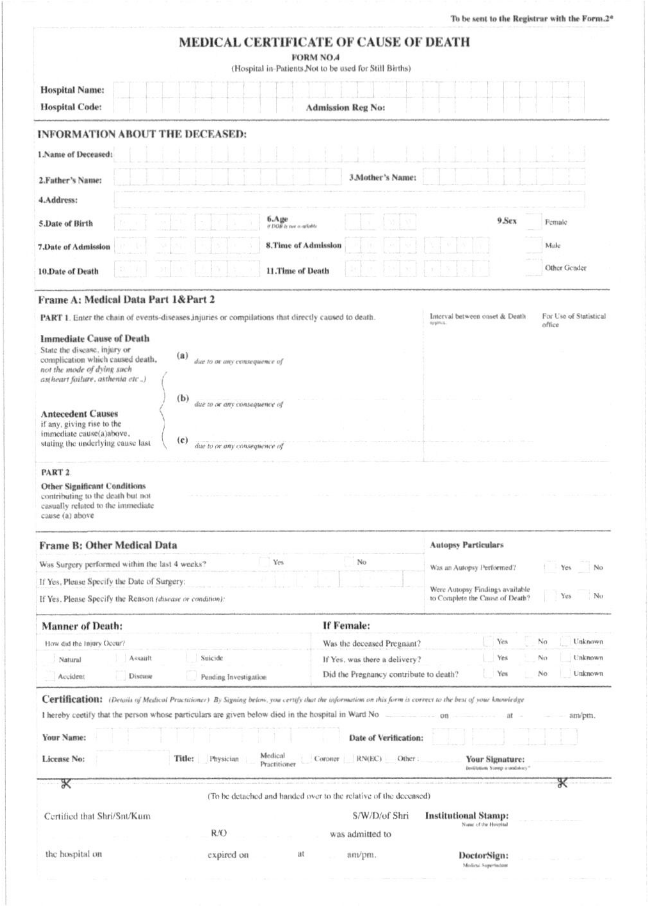

To be sent to the Registrar with the Form.2*

MEDICAL CERTIFICATE OF CAUSE OF DEATH
FORM NO.4
(Hospital in-Patients,Not to be used for Still Births)

Hospital Name:
Hospital Code: Admission Reg No:

INFORMATION ABOUT THE DECEASED:
1.Name of Deceased:
2.Father's Name: 3.Mother's Name:
4.Address:
5.Date of Birth 6.Age 9.Sex Female
7.Date of Admission 8.Time of Admission Male
10.Date of Death 11.Time of Death Other Gender

Frame A: Medical Data Part 1&Part 2
PART 1. Enter the chain of events-diseases,injuries or compilations that directly caused to death. Interval between onset & Death For Use of Statistical office

Immediate Cause of Death
State the disease, injury or complication which caused death, *not the mode of dying such as(heart failure, asthenia etc.,)* (a) *due to or any consequence of*

(b) *due to or any consequence of*

Antecedent Causes
if any, giving rise to the immediate cause(a)above, stating the underlying cause last (c) *due to or any consequence of*

PART 2.
Other Significant Conditions
contributing to the death but not casually related to the immediate cause (a) above

Frame B: Other Medical Data
Was Surgery performed within the last 4 weeks? Yes No
If Yes, Please Specify the Date of Surgery:
If Yes, Please Specify the Reason *(disease or condition)*:

Autopsy Particulars
Was an Autopsy Performed? Yes No
Were Autopsy Findings available to Complete the Cause of Death? Yes No

Manner of Death:
How did the Injury Occur?
Natural Assault Suicide
Accident Disease Pending Investigation

If Female:
Was the deceased Pregnant? Yes No Unknown
If Yes, was there a delivery? Yes No Unknown
Did the Pregnancy contribute to death? Yes No Unknown

Certification: *(Details of Medical Practitioner) By Signing below, you certify that the information on this form is correct to the best of your knowledge*
I hereby ceetify that the person whose particulars are given below died in the hospital in Ward No on at am/pm.
Your Name: Date of Verification:
License No: Title: Physician Medical Practitioner Coroner RN(EC) Other: Your Signature:

(To be detached and handed over to the relative of the deceased)
Certified that Shri/Smt/Kum S/W/D/of Shri Institutional Stamp:
R/O was admitted to
the hospital on expired on at am/pm. DoctorSign:

**Fig. 10.** Redesigned MCCD Form (Iteration-2)

Iteration 2 addressed usability issues, optimized space allocation, and streamlined the documentation process compared to both the existing form and Iteration one. Removal of the medical history section, refinement of layout and space allocation, and incorporation of user-friendly design elements were key enhancements. Physician feedback guided the iterative design process, resulting in a more efficient, user-friendly, and accurate MCCD Form conducive to improved mortality documentation.

EXISTING FORM                                    REDESIGNED FORM ITERATION-1                    REDESIGNED FORM ITERATION-2

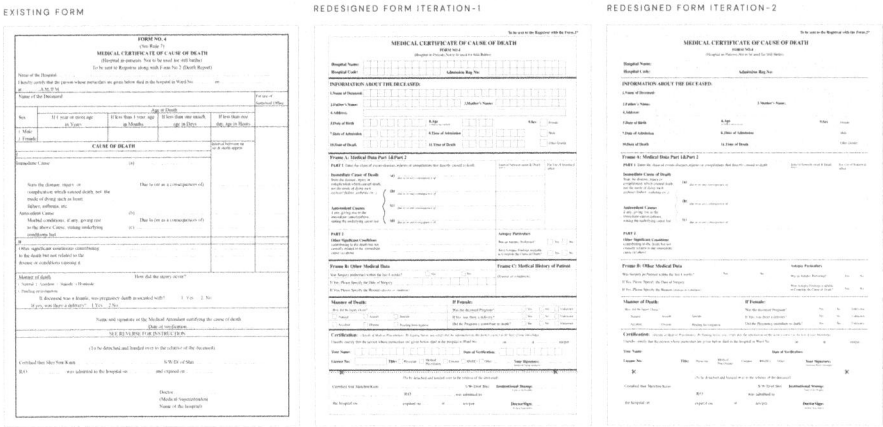

**Fig. 11.** Visual representation illustrating the Existing MCCD Form alongside the attempted Iterations (a. Current MCCD Form, b. Iteration-1, c. Iteration-2)

## 13   Conclusion

In this research paper, I have embarked on a comprehensive exploration of mortality documentation practices in India, focusing on the Medical Certificate for Cause of Death (MCCD) Form. The journey began with an analysis of the existing challenges in mortality data recording, emphasizing the critical role of accurate mortality statistics in informing public health policies and interventions. Through primary research and insights gathered from healthcare professionals, I've delved into the complexities of MCCD form filling, uncovering issues related to layout, information adequacy, and usability.

The subsequent phases of the study involved iterative design improvements and usability testing of the MCCD Form. Drawing upon user feedback and insights from practitioners, I've refined the form's layout, streamlined information fields, and optimized space allocation. Iteration 2 of the MCCD Form addressed key usability issues identified during testing, resulting in a more efficient, user-friendly, and standardized documentation process.

The research underscores significance of human-centered design principles in enhancing mortality documentation practices. By integrating insights from practitioners, leveraging iterative design methodologies, and prioritizing usability, I have laid the groundwork for a more effective and transparent MCCD documentation system in India. The iterative improvements made to the MCCD Form not only enhance data accuracy and completeness but also contribute to the overall reliability of mortality statistics.

Moving forward, it is imperative to continue refining and optimizing mortality documentation processes to meet the evolving needs of healthcare professionals and stakeholders. Future research endeavours should focus on longitudinal studies to assess the long-term impact of MCCD form redesign on mortality data accuracy and public health outcomes.

## 14   Lessons Learned from the Redesign of MCCD Forms

The redesign of the MCCD forms provided several key insights into usability and user-centered design principles that are broadly applicable to interactive systems.

1. **User-Centered Design**: Engaging with healthcare professionals throughout the design process emphasized the importance of understanding user needs and contexts. This approach ensures that the final product aligns closely with user requirements, leading to higher acceptance and usability.
2. **Efficiency and Time Management**: The feedback highlighted that streamlining workflows and minimizing user effort significantly enhances user satisfaction. This principle is crucial in designing any interactive system where efficiency is a priority.
3. **Data Consistency and Accuracy**: Incorporating features like validation checks and clear instructions helps maintain data integrity, which is essential for systems handling critical information.
4. **Standardization**: Establishing uniform design conventions facilitates easier adoption and interoperability across different platforms, a lesson applicable to various domains beyond healthcare.
5. **Training and Support**: The necessity of sufficient training for users to effectively utilize the new form underscores the broader need for comprehensive user support and training in interactive system design.

By integrating these lessons, designers can create more effective, user-friendly systems that meet the needs of their intended users, enhancing both usability and overall user experience.

## 15   Future Plans

As we move forward with the redesigned Medical Certificate for Cause of Death (MCCD) form, several next steps are envisioned to enhance its implementation, usability, and impact within the healthcare ecosystem.

**1. Introducing the Redesigned MCCD Form into the Healthcare Ecosystem:** The redesigned MCCD form will be introduced across healthcare institutions, ensuring its widespread adoption and usage by medical practitioners.

**2. Digital Integration**

a. **Digital Forms:** Develop a digital version of the MCCD, making it easier to fill, store, and retrieve. This digital format will streamline the documentation process and facilitate data management.
b. **Database Integration:** Link the digital MCCD form to national or regional health databases, ensuring real-time updates and facilitating trend analyses. By integrating with existing databases, the MCCD form becomes a valuable tool for health surveillance and policymaking.
c. **Smart Features:** Implement AI-driven prompts to assist medical practitioners in filling out causes of death. These prompts can suggest common causes based on symptoms or conditions, improving the accuracy and efficiency of form completion.

**3. Continuous Feedback Mechanism:** Establish a system for practitioners to provide continuous feedback on the form, ensuring it remains relevant and up-to-date. Periodically review the feedback and make necessary updates to the form to address emerging needs and challenges..

**4. Collaboration with Health Organizations:** Partner with regional, national, and international health organizations to advocate for the adoption of the redesigned MCCD form. Collaborate on initiatives to gather wider feedback and ensure the form meets international standards for mortality data recording. Work on integrating the MCCD data with other health data sources for comprehensive health analytics, enabling deeper insights into disease patterns and trends.

**5. Legal Endorsements:** Engage with legal bodies to ensure the redesigned form is recognized and endorsed for all requisite legal purposes, such as insurance claims and inheritance cases. Legal endorsement enhances the credibility and acceptance of the form within the legal and regulatory framework.

**6. Multilingual Versions:** Create multilingual versions of the MCCD to cater to diverse populations, ensuring that language is not a barrier to accurate recording. Multilingual versions enhance accessibility and inclusivity, empowering all communities to participate in mortality data reporting.

## 16   Limitations to the Project

**Despite the Comprehensive Approach Taken in Redesigning the Medical Certificate for Cause of Death (MCCD) Form and Conducting Usability Testing, Several Limitations Should be Acknowledged:**

While the redesign of the Medical Certificate for Cause of Death (MCCD) form and subsequent usability testing represent significant strides in improving mortality data recording practices, several limitations should be acknowledged. These include the scope of research primarily focused on Indian government's MCCD form, potentially limiting generalizability.

The sample size of medical practitioners engaged in usability testing, possibly restricting the breadth of insights.

Time constraints that may have curtailed the depth of research and testing; resource limitations, including availability of funding and expertise; potential technical challenges in digital integration.

Anticipated resistance to change within healthcare institutions; considerations of language and cultural diversity; and the need to ensure legal and regulatory compliance.

Addressing these limitations in future iterations of the project will be essential to maximize the effectiveness and impact of the redesigned MCCD form on mortality data recording and public health outcomes.

## 17   Ethical Considerations

This study involved human subjects, and ethical considerations were thoroughly addressed. Informed consent was obtained from all participants, ensuring they were aware of the study's purpose, procedures, and their right to withdraw at any time.

Data privacy and confidentiality were strictly maintained, with all personal information anonymized to protect participants' identities. Although my institute does not provide an IRB-approved research number, multiple mentors monitored and guided me on ethical considerations throughout the research, ensuring compliance with ethical standards for research involving human subjects.

**Acknowledgements.** I extend my deepest gratitude to all who contributed to this project's success. My sincere appreciation goes to Prof. Chakradhar Saswade for his invaluable guidance and support. Heartfelt thanks to the healthcare professionals whose insights were indispensable. Special acknowledgment to Elizabeth Rosenzweig for her mentorship in crafting the research paper. I am also grateful to Parag Gupta for his assistance in refining the MCCD Form. Lastly, I thank my parents (Ramanjineya Reddy and Saraswathi), friends, and the National Institute of Design for their unwavering support and resources.

# References

1. Shibuya, K., Scheele, S., Boerma, T.: Health statistics: time to get serious. Bull World Health Organ (2005) http://archive.today/1ExDF. Cited 2024 May 8
2. The Registration Births and Deaths Act. Act Number 18 of 1969, Government of India, New Delhi, 31 May 1969. http://archive.today/5B4xh
3. Vital Statistics of India Based on the Civil Registration System 2019. Office of the Registrar General of India, Vital Statistics Division, Civil Registration Section, Ministry of Home Affairs, Government of India, New Delhi. http://archive.today/PcrXr
4. Kumar, G.A., Dandona, L., Dandona, R.: Completeness of death registration in the Civil Registration System, India (2005 to 2015). Indian J. Med. Res. (2019). http://archive.today/y5yrX
5. Steel, P.W., Macfarlane, S.B., Streeter, S., Mikkelsen, L., Jha, P., Stout, S., et al.: A scandal of invisibility: making everyone count by counting everyone. The Lancet **370**(9598), 1569–1577 (2007). http://archive.today/Z2vtg
6. Report of the Medical Certification of Cause of Death. Office of the Registrar General of India, Vital Statistics Division, Ministry of Home Affairs, Government of India, New Delhi. http://censusindia.gov.in/census.website/data/mccdrep
7. Pandey, A.K., Gautam, D., Thomas, M.B., Kharakwal, Y.: Registration and medical certification of deaths in the Indian States: a comparative analysis of data of CRS and MCCD reports (2010–2019) medRxiv pre-print. 2021 https://doi.org/10.1101/2021.12.09.21267291. http://archive.today/jGPpI
8. Lawrence, J.E., Cundall-Curry, D., Stewart, M.E., Fountain, D.M., Gooding, C.R.: The use of an electronic health record system reduces errors in the National Hip Fracture Database. Age Ageing **48**(2), 285–290 (2019). https://doi.org/10.1093/ageing/afy177. PMID: 30395143. http://archive.today/LrVCB
9. Hart, J.D., Sorchik, R., Bo, K.S., et al.: Improving medical certification of cause of death: effective strategies and approaches based on experiences from the Data for Health Initiative. BMC Med. **18**, 74 (2020). https://doi.org/10.1186/s12916-020-01519-8. http://archive.today/7Lgf3
10. Biswa, S.: Why India's real Covid toll may never be known. http://archive.today/EkX9p
11. Karnataka Registration of Births & Deaths Rules: Directorate of Economics and Statistics, Govt. of Karnataka (1999). http://archive.today/h2Igj

# Serious Games Beyond Entertainment and Learning: An Evaluation Methodology for Assessing Awareness Raising, Empathy, and Social Change

Stavroula Ntoa[1]([✉]) [ID], Anastasia Ntagianta[1] [ID], Fernanda Flores[2], Lukáš Kolek[3,4,5] [ID], Alexandra Petrova[3], Konstantinos C. Apostolakis[1] [ID], Stefania Stamou[1] [ID], George Margetis[1] [ID], and Constantine Stephanidis[1,4,5] [ID]

[1] Institute of Computer Science, Foundation for Research and Technology—Hellas (FORTH), 70013 Heraklion, Crete, Greece
{stant,dagianta,kapostol,stefstamou,gmarget,cs}@ics.forth.gr
[2] War Childhood Museum, 71000 Sarajevo, Bosnia and Herzegovina
fernanda.flores@warchildhood.org
[3] Charles Games, 110 00 Prague, Czech Republic
{lukas.kolek,alex}@charlesgames.net, kolek@ksvi.mff.cuni.cz
[4] Faculty of Mathematics and Physics, Charles University, 121 16 Prague, Czech Republic
[5] University of Crete, Heraklion, Crete, Greece

**Abstract.** Serious games have emerged as a powerful tool for achieving targeted outcomes beyond entertainment, such as learning or raising awareness about a topic. Considering their pervasiveness and wide adoption in the educational domain, traditional assessment approaches of these games have predominantly focused on their entertainment value and achievement of learning objectives. This paper proposes a comprehensive evaluation framework that goes beyond traditional dimensions to include aspects relevant to empathy raising and attitude change. The proposed framework has been validated through three user studies, assessing entertainment, historical awareness, empathy raising, and attitude change for three games, involving in total 98 high school students. Results from the studies are presented, as well as implications and lessons learned regarding the overall methodological approach, the evaluation instruments used, and the procedures followed.

**Keywords:** serious games · video games · evaluation · methodology · entertainment · learning · historical awareness · empathy · attitude change · user study

## 1 Introduction

When designing a game, players' entertainment and satisfaction constitute key driving goals. However, the playful nature of games, which incorporates interactive and engaging elements, can be utilized further, such as in educational settings, to facilitate learning and

A. Marcus et al. (Eds.): HCII 2024, LNCS 15380, pp. 141–164, 2025.
https://doi.org/10.1007/978-3-031-76821-7_11

skills development. This notion has led to the creation of games beyond entertainment, namely serious games [1], which can reshape the traditional learning model into an engaging and interactive process. To do so, serious games provide gamification elements, such as challenges and rewards, to enhance learners' engagement and motivation.

Traditionally, serious games have been used in education, in fields such as mathematics and physics, and have proven to be successful in this endeavor [2]. However, the use of these games has been extended to include more diverse fields, hence the creation of serious games beyond education. These games include, but are not limited to, topics on raising awareness on climate change and sustainability [3] or history [4, 5], training children with disabilities [6], cultivating prosocial behaviors [7], popularizing cultural heritage [8, 9], or acting as vehicles for social change [10].

Aiming to verify if they are successful in their claims as entertaining educational tools, serious games have been repeatedly subjected to evaluation, adopting expert-based reviews and user-based studies [11, 12]. Although expert-based reviews are invaluable, user-based studies constitute the cornerstone of game evaluation approaches [13], ensuring a deep understanding of how players engage with a game, their preferences and the difficulties they encounter when playing it. Usually, such evaluations focus primarily on assessing the usability of the game, the level of entertainment provided, while remaining educational, or whether the game was successful in reaching its educational purpose [14]. While there are numerous examples of these evaluations, there is a lack of methodologies to assess serious games beyond entertainment and education [14, 15]. This work aims to provide a methodology for evaluating serious games as tools for remembrance and vehicles for social change, while also assessing their entertainment value.

To assess the proposed methodology, a series of user-based trials has been conducted. Typically, user-based studies include user feedback and preferences, as well as performance data, which offer helpful insights into the point of view and overall experience of users. In order to explore both implicit and explicit attitudes, user-based studies often utilize usability testing, user interviews, questionnaires and observational analysis. This process ensures that the final evaluation is not only a technical analysis, but also provides a thorough understanding of how players interact with and experience the game, encouraging the development of more entertaining and engaging game experiences. In this regard, a mixed-methods approach is employed in the context of the proposed methodology, aiming to provide a holistic framework for game evaluation.

Following a review of related work (Sect. 2), this paper addresses the methodology and procedures employed in the studies (Sect. 3). Following this, in Sect. 4, a thorough presentation of the trials, including participant details, results, and the lessons derived from the research is provided. Finally, a discussion is undertaken to analyze the results in Sect. 5, concluding with key insights drawn from the trials and how these can be helpful for the planning of future studies.

## 2 Related Work

Serious game design and development are mature topics in the academic and research community. Assessing their efficacy in the claim of enhancing motivation, engagement and learning across different domains has become a trending subject in recent years, fostering the emergence of various frameworks and methodologies that facilitate their assessment.

In the field of assessing serious games, various systematic literature reviews have been conducted. According to Calderón et al. [16], who researched and analyzed 119 papers to extract key characteristics of the methods followed to assess serious games, the primary goal of assessment was their educational effectiveness. The most followed procedure was regarded as 'simple', since it only selected questionnaires as the main method of assessment.

However, adding a comparison between pre- and post-test questionnaire results can further highlight the learning effect [17]. In this direction, Mayer et al. [18] proposed a methodology that supports the notion of dividing the evaluation of serious games into three parts: the 'pregame', 'in-game,' and 'postgame'. For each part, they propose a set of validated and reusable questions, i.e., 'pregame' includes questions about demographics, skills, previous experience and attitudes; 'in-game' focuses on game experience, performance and effort; and finally, 'postgame' addresses issues such as player satisfaction and learning outcomes. Steiner et al. [19] expanded this approach by introducing the notion of control groups – or baseline measurements – to perform a comparative approach to identify the effects of serious games.

Wilson et al. [11] and Yáñez-Gómez et al. [20] added that there is a lack of well-defined evaluation methodology that can be accepted as a standard for the scientific community and highlighted the need for more rigorous evaluations and support systems for game creators in developing serious games.

Towards creating a universal methodology for assessing serious games, several frameworks have been proposed. Such frameworks propose that serious games' evaluation should be conducted in a broader context to include the game system as a whole, instead of primarily focusing on assessing its learning outcomes [21], extending testing beyond laboratory settings into real world circumstances, which can reveal previously unknown issues. In addition, it has been suggested to consider several quality characteristics when evaluating the use of serious games, namely usability, understandability, motivation, engagement and user experience [22], since the absence of those characteristics in a serious game can result in failure to deliver its educational content successfully.

In the process of providing a robust methodology for assessing serious games, studies highlighted that the assessment should be integrated throughout the development process of the game and be present in all stages from conceptualization to deployment [23, 24].

Finally, a more recent work [3] expanded the evaluation context of serious games by highlighting that these games can be utilized beyond entertainment and formal education purposes. More specifically, the authors considered the potential of using serious games to raise awareness towards climate adaptation. One of the key insights from this research is the value of structured context when conducting an evaluation, as in utilizing debriefing sessions to ensure reflections of the participants after the game.

## 3   Methodology

The overall methodological approach proposed serves a threefold purpose, aiming to assess serious games as (a) entertainment products, (b) meaningful tools for shaping historical awareness and inducing empathy, and (c) vehicles for advocating social change, involving both subjective and objective measurements. The proposed method encompasses subjective and objective measurements, standardized and custom questionnaires when necessary, as well as questionnaires adapted from existing standardized methodologies. Figure 1 presents an overview of the proposed methodology.

**Fig. 1.** The proposed Serious Games Evaluation Framework

To validate the proposed methodology, three distinct user studies were carried out, each addressing one of the aforementioned objectives. At the same time, one of the objectives of these studies was to evaluate the research tools and questionnaires used. In this regard, the procedure followed in each one of the studies was sought to be as uniform as possible to streamline the study better and to ensure consistency of results. The procedure comprised four phases, namely planning, dry-runs, actual study, data collection and analysis. The first phase, planning, included selecting the appropriate participants, finding games relevant to the evaluation goals and preparation of the necessary evaluation instruments (i.e., informed consent documents and questionnaires). Once the planning phase concluded, a dry run phase followed, during which the overall setup of the methodology was tested and adapted accordingly based on the results. Following, each study was executed, the results were collected, and data was curated to ensure consistency and participants' anonymity. As a last step, the analysis and reporting of results followed.

### 3.1 Target School Selection

The target school selection was based on several key considerations. High schools with English-speaking programs and international high schools with adequate equipment to facilitate the studies were prioritized, since the questionnaires' base language is English. However, in the case of Study 1, involving participants from Belgium, a French translation of the evaluation documents was required. To ensure the validity of the translation, two independent translators synthesized a French version, which was subsequently translated by another independent translator back to English [25]. The understandability of the translated versions was tested by the target population during the user studies.

### 3.2 Target Game Selection

The main criterion for selecting the games that would be evaluated was that they are designed with dual objectives that align with the overarching goals of our study – incorporating both entertainment and educational elements. The evaluation objective of Study 1 is to assess the perceived quality of video games in terms of their capacity to achieve entertainment goals while still being educational. For this purpose, Beecarbonize[1] was selected, a strategy card game which thematizes climate change, outlines the processes behind it and its possible solutions. On the other hand, Study 2 centers on the 'educational' aspect of games, with a specific focus on games acting as tools for remembrance. Therefore, Train to Sachsenhausen[2], recounting Czechoslovakian anti-Nazi demonstrations of 1939, was selected as a video game suitable for assessing historical awareness and empathy. Study 3 addresses the impact of video games on players' attitudes towards social issues depicted in game narratives. In this regard, the topic of refugees and migration was chosen, and Path Out[3], a narrative game based on the real-life experiences of Abdullah Karam, offering insights into his challenging journey through war-torn Syria, was selected as the target game.

### 3.3 Evaluation Instruments

The evaluation methodology adopted a mixed-methods approach, pursuing both objective and subjective measurements, whereas data collected were sought to be both quantitative and qualitative.

Objective measurements involve quantifiable and tangible data, which in the case of the conducted studies, involve historical knowledge and the number of technical issues occurring during the procedure. On the other hand, subjective measurements take into account the user's individual experience, preferences and game satisfaction. These include components such as overall enjoyment, immersion and creative freedom, and

---

[1] https://charlesgames.net/beecarbonize/.

[2] https://charlesgames.net/train/.

[3] https://causacreations.net/presskit/path_out/index.html.

usually refer to users' perceptions of game attributes. Combining both methods can result in a thorough evaluation to produce a balanced analysis of the game, considering that each may lead to different conclusions and lead to a more complete picture [26].

To ensure obtaining reliable data and enhance the credibility of the study, a set of validated questionnaires were used. In particular, the Game Experience Questionnaire (GEQ) [27] and the Game User Experience Satisfaction Scale (GUESS) [28] were used to measure game experience and user satisfaction with the games studied. Furthermore, the Basic Empathy Scale [29] questionnaire was used to measure the players' affective and cognitive empathy.

In addition to the validated questionnaires, three custom questionnaires were developed, namely the "Historical Awareness Questionnaire", the "Empathy Vignettes" and the "General Beliefs Questionnaire", in alignment with the methodology described by Saleme et al. [30] (See Annex). In the scope of this study, which utilizes educational games, the first one aims to measure the learning outcomes or historical awareness, the second one highlights whether the game was successful in empathy raising, and the third one demonstrates any attitude changes in participants' general beliefs. These questionnaires were administered both before and after the test, in order to identify whether any changes in the pre and post-test answers could be attributed to the game.

When it comes to measuring attitudes, attitudes were conceptualized according to the Associative-Propositional Evaluation model - APE model [31–35]. The APE model understands attitudes as two complementary processes – associative and propositional, which are measured using implicit measurements (experimental measures derived from cognitive psychology) and explicit measurements (typically self-report questionnaires), respectively [33]. As the implicit measure, the Single Category Implicit Associations Test was used (SC-IAT - [36]). SC-IAT is a modification of the original Implicit Association Test (IAT) [37], which allows measuring implicit attitudes towards only one concept compared to the original IAT, which could only do it relative to two concepts. As the explicit measure, a version of the migration scale [38] was used, with two questions modified to make it more understandable to younger audiences. Both measures were administered in both pre-test and post-test to allow for measuring attitude change as a result of the game used in the intervention.

To facilitate the observation of participants and note-taking during the procedure, an observation sheet was provided, where, to begin with, facilitators were asked to provide information about the participants' IDs and indicate the starting and ending times of each phase of the experiment. The observation sheet also included fields to note irregularities identified, such as equipment malfunctions or software bugs and the fixes that were provided to resolve them, issues raised regarding the questionnaires' clarity, comments vocalized by the participants during gameplay, and any other issues of note, such as teacher or user behaviors and feedback or the experimental protocol.

Finally, a questionnaire for conducting semi-structured interviews at the end of the evaluation session was developed, as well as a questionnaire for collecting background information about participants, supporting a more thorough data analysis.

The questionnaires identified as the instruments to be used for the small-scale studies were uploaded to EUSurvey[4], which supports the creation and publishing of accessible and privacy-preserving online surveys, in order to be readily accessible to participants. The list of questionnaires and instruments per study can be seen in Table 1.

**Table 1.** List of questionnaires uploaded to EUSurvey

| Study | Questionnaires |
|---|---|
| Study 1 | • Background information questionnaire (pre-test)<br>• Game Experience Questionnaire (post-test)<br>• Game User Experience Satisfaction Scale Questionnaire (post-test) |
| Study 2 | • Background information questionnaire (pre-test)<br>• Basic Empathy Scale Questionnaire (pre and post-test)<br>• General Beliefs Questionnaire (pre and post-test)<br>• Historical Awareness Questionnaire (pre and post-test)<br>• Empathy Vignettes Questionnaire (pre and post-test)<br>• Game User Experience Satisfaction Scale Questionnaire (post-test) |
| Study 3 | • Background information questionnaire (pre-test)<br>• Explicit attitude questionnaire (pre and post-test)<br>• Single Category Implicit Associations Test (pre and post-test) |

For Study 1, French versions of all questionnaires were also devised in the EUSurvey platform.

## 4 Assessment of Serious Games in Terms of Enjoyment, Historical Awareness and Social Change

The three pilot studies conducted encompass a range of objectives outlined in their respective sections. A consistent procedure was followed for all the studies, with each study assessing at least one component of the overall evaluation methodology.

The first step, before a study, was to acquire the consent of all parents or legal guardians of the non-adult students, using consent forms distributed to teachers prior to the appointed session date, who in turn shared them with students and/or their legal guardians. All forms were collected before the sessions to ensure that every participant had explicit permission to partake in the study[5]. Additionally, representatives from the schools signed a consent form specifically designed for educational institutions.

After the collection of the consent forms, the study was divided into three main parts, the " "Pre-test", the "Main session" and the "Post-test" part.

During the first part, the facilitators of the experiment welcomed the students and provided information about the procedure. This included explaining that the students

---

[4] https://ec.europa.eu/eusurvey/home/welcome.

[5] This study has been approved by the Ethics Committee of Charles University on 30 January 2024.

would be asked to play a game and answer a collection of questionnaires, in order to assist in improving the game. After the short introduction, the students were presented with the first set of questionnaires, which included the background demographics questionnaire, being the same for all three studies, as well as the pre-test questionnaires, which were adapted to fit each study's purpose.

The "Main session" was divided into two parts, featuring a short break in the middle. During the first part, the students were observed as they freely progressed in the game, while during the second part, the facilitators encouraged the players to explore different aspects of the game to achieve different outcomes and access new information.

Finally, after the allocated gameplay time concluded, the students were required to answer a second set of questionnaires – forming the "Post-test" part, which included game experience and satisfaction questionnaires (Study 1 and Study 2), as well as study-specific questionnaires. As a final step to the "Post-test" part, the students were divided into small groups of five to attend the debriefing session. During this step, particular attention was paid to ensuring that all students within a group had the chance to express their own opinions and overall experience. This section offers a thorough presentation of each study, focusing on participant details and results. Additionally, it delves into the valuable insights derived from the trials, aiming to consolidate lessons learned from the methodological approach followed.

### 4.1 Study 1: Game Quality Assessment

The first study aimed to assess the perceived quality of video games concerning their ability to primarily achieve entertainment goals while also being educational. Twenty students participated in the testing session, where they played the game Beecarbonize.

Study 1 was conducted with a single group and used the background information questionnaire, Game Experience Questionnaire (GEQ), and the Game User Satisfaction Scale (GUESS) questionnaire. The total duration of the study was approximately one hour, with 10 min allocated to the pre-test part, 25 min to the main part (featuring also a short break), and 25 min to the post-test part.

**Participants.** All 20 participants involved in this study were students of the 5th year of high school (16–18 years old). Notably, all students were male students of an Information Technology (IT) class. Regarding technology expertise, most of the participants were experienced in using computers and smartphones or tablets[6]. Finally, concerning game expertise, most of the participants had prior experience in gaming, mostly on a computer or laptop and gaming consoles, playing mainly action games, adventure games, and simulation games (Table 2).

**Results.** Analysis of results entailed the study of game experience based on question-naires, interviews with participants and observers' notes.

Results from the GUESS questionnaire highlighted that the overall experience was positive (M:4.36, SD:1.64). The highest average score was achieved for personal grati-fication (M:5.60, SD:1.28), followed by usability/playability (M:5.37, SD:1.64), visual

---

[6] 50% use computers all the time, 45% often and 5% sometimes, whereas 95% use mobile devices all the time and 5% often.

**Table 2.** Gaming expertise of participants in Study 1

| Gaming frequency (per week) | | Game genres | |
| --- | --- | --- | --- |
| >than 30 h | 20% | action | 45% |
| between 15 and 30 h | 45% | adventure | 15% |
| between 5 and 15 h | 25% | simulation | 15% |
| less than 5 h | 10% | racing | 5% |
| **Gaming device** | | strategy | 5% |
| Computer or laptop | 60% | role-playing | 5% |
| Gaming console | 35% | war | 5% |
| Smartphone or tablet | 5% | sports | 5% |

aesthetics (M:4.92, SD:1.29), and narratives (M:4.25, SD:1.15). Game attributes that received scores lower than average include social connectivity (M:3.61, SD:1.52), audio aesthetics (M:3.80, SD:1.40), creative freedom (M:3.55, SD:1.41), enjoyment (M:3.82, SD:1.80), and play engrossment (M:3.85, SD:1.67). Nevertheless, it should be noted that the game did not support multiplayer roles or any other social features, therefore the score acquired for social connectivity is reasonable.

Results from the GEQ questionnaire yielded overall positive findings for all the scales studied. In particular, the game received its highest scores for challenge (M:2.63, SD:1.10) and positive affect (M:2.56, SD:0.90), followed by competence (M:2.15, SD:1.12), flow (M:1.95, SD:1.38) and immersion (M:1.88, SD:1.10). Negative affect (M:0.74, SD:1.09) and tension/annoyance (M:1.30, SD:1.42), received a low score, which is considered a good result indicating that players were generally not affected negatively or annoyed.

For the purposes of this study, three modules of the GEQ questionnaire were used, namely core, in-game, and post-game. Considering that the gameplay session was rather short, and in such cases, there may be no reason to administer separately two different versions of GEQ, a statistical analysis was conducted to explore any important differences between the two versions of the questionnaire. All scales, with the exception of positive affect and negative affect, did not exhibit any statistically important differences. For negative affect, there was a significant difference in the scores of the core module (MD:0.74, SD:1.09) against the in-game module (MD:1.22, SD:1.14); $t(118) = -2.27$, p $= 0.02$. A statistically significant difference was also noted for positive affect between the scores of the core module (MD:2.56, SD:0.90) and the in-game module (MD:2.10, SD:0.80); $t(138) = 2.80$, p $= 0.005$. Considering that the core module has been validated, future studies can consider using only this module, especially if there is no need to assess the game experience during gameplay.

Furthermore, results from the post-game module highlighted that, in general, players did not have difficulty returning to reality (MD:0.50, SD:0.83), did not experience tiredness (MD:0.33, SD:0.66) and did not have negative experience (MD:0.43, SD:0.83). However, positive experience (MD:1.15, SD:1.22) as perceived after the game was rather low compared to the positive affect reported in the core module (MD:2.56, SD:0.90). This difference has to do with the formulation of the specific questions asked and not the timing of the questionnaire, since the core module and post-game module were administered sequentially. In particular, questions in the positive experience section ask players to rate if they felt revived, like a victory, energized, and satisfied. All these statements are quite powerful and there may be some uncertainty about the extent to which these emotions can be replicated in an experimental setting, particularly considering that the students' participation was structured within their in-class activities rather than being entirely spontaneous.

In addition to questionnaires, a thematic analysis approach was applied for the analysis of participants' responses to the debriefing interview. Overall, while a group leading effect was identified, the participants indicated that the game was nice and simple in terms of graphics and mechanics. However, it was noted that the use of a smartphone for this game felt restrictive.

Feedback on the study itself pointed out that the 20 min allocated to gameplay were not enough, that the questionnaires were lengthy and that a gameplay tutorial would have been useful before the study.

**Lessons Learned.** The planning and execution of the session encountered certain challenges. Securing a school that was willing to allocate two consecutive time slots (each of 50 min) for the testing session proved to be challenging, considering that it was not easy for them to deviate from their schedule. In addition, ensuring that each student had a functioning smartphone added to the logistical complexities. Student comprehension of the game mechanics within a brief playtime sometimes presented a challenge, and researchers had to provide guidance while ensuring that it did not influence the results.

Analysis of the results produced valuable findings regarding the evaluation instruments employed. In particular, regarding the GUESS questionnaire, it became evident that some dimensions assessed (such as creativity and social connectivity) were not applicable for the studied game, and therefore although using a standardized questionnaire presents important benefits, in future evaluation studies questionnaire items that are not applicable should be excluded. Furthermore, the length of the GEQ questionnaire proved burdensome for some participants, whereas results highlighted that filling out both core and in-game modules is repetitive and does not provide added value in short play sessions. Furthermore, the post-game module may be superficial in experimental setups where participants do not engage with a game voluntarily. The lack of voluntariness as in the context of the current study setup, where students were asked to engage with the game in the context of a class activity, may also impact their overall attitude toward the game studied. Nevertheless, considering that serious games may be played beyond classroom activities, this is a workable practice that may be eligible for future studies.

Findings regarding the evaluation setup revealed that in a setting where children play all together, group dynamics can influence findings. Furthermore, in such multiuser setups particular care needs to be devoted to the preparation, ensuring that the setup does not interfere with the achieved user experience (e.g., ensuring that each student is equipped with headphones so that they can play the game with the sound on). Finally, the need for a balanced user sample (e.g. in terms of gender) was evident, highlighting that additional effort may be required to plan a study not bounded by the composition of a single class.

## 4.2   Study 2: Games as a Tool for Remembrance

The second pilot study aimed to evaluate games' ability to engage players with the theme of memorialization, serving as tools to enhance historical awareness and foster increased empathy towards past injustices and those affected by them. This study was conducted as a controlled experiment, aiming to investigate whether the game has an actual impact on participants' historical awareness and empathy toward repressed Czech students. In this respect, the sample of participants were randomly divided into two equivalent groups. In the experimental group, students played Train to Sachsenhausen, while the control group played Beecarbonize.

In the context of this study, the following instruments were used: background information questionnaire, basic empathy scale, questionnaire for the assessment of historical awareness, general beliefs questionnaire, and empathy assessment vignettes. Except for the background information questionnaire and the basic empathy scale, all other instruments were specifically designed and tailored to the evaluated game.

The total duration of the study was approximately one hour and a half, with 30 min for the pre-test part, followed by 20 min of gameplay, and after a short break, 30 min for the post-test part.

### Participants

*Experimental Group.* Although the experimental group was run with more than 20 participants, a total of 6 valid responses were eventually acquired due to difficulties encountered by students in filling out the online questionnaires. All participants were aged 15 or 16 years old and the majority of them were female (67%). All participants use mobile devices all the time and computers all the time or often[7], however, they do not play games for many hours on a daily basis, while some of them do not play games at all. When gaming, participants used smartphones most often and the most preferred genre of choice was 'adventure', with an equal number of students, however, indicating that they do not play games at all (Table 3).

*Control Group.* A total of 19 students, mostly female (72%), participated in the control group experiment, aged 17 or 18 years old. All responses acquired in this group were valid. The majority of students indicated using smartphones or tablets regularly, whereas half of them use computers regularly[8]. While smartphones and computers are mostly used as the gaming device of choice, with a preference for action games, a considerable number indicated that they do not play games at all (Table 3).

### Results

*Experimental Group.* Results from the GUESS questionnaire highlight a high user satisfaction towards visual aesthetics (M:5.50, SD:1.31), narratives (M:5.33, SD:0.77) and

---

[7] 83% use computers all the time and 17% often, whereas 100% use mobile devices all the time.

[8] 21% use computers all the time, 37% often, 37% sometimes and 5% rarely, whereas 100% use mobile devices all the time.

**Table 3.** Gaming expertise of participants in Study 2

| Gaming frequency (per week) | Exp. | Con. | Game genre | Exp. | Con. |
|---|---|---|---|---|---|
| >than 30 h | 0% | 0% | action | 0% | 37% |
| between 15 and 30 h | 0% | 5% | adventure | 33% | 5% |
| between 5 and 15 h | 17% | 21% | simulation | 0% | 5% |
| less than 5 h | 50% | 48% | Racing | 0% | 0% |
| Not at all | 33% | 26% | strategy | 17% | 5% |
| **Gaming device** | | | role-playing | 0% | 11% |
| Computer or laptop | 17% | 32% | war | 0% | 0% |
| Gaming console | 17% | 5% | sports | 0% | 0% |
| Smartphone or tablet | 33% | 37% | puzzle | 17% | 11% |
| None | 33% | 26% | none | 33% | 26% |

usability (M:5.50, SD:1.78) and a promising score for personal gratification (M:4.91, SD:1.24), creative freedom (M:4.83, SD:1.33), audio aesthetics (M:4.72, SD:1.19), enjoyment (M:4.41, SD:0.99) and play engrossment (M:4.00, SD:1.65). Regarding the social connectivity score, it should be noted that the game studied does not support any social features, such as multiplayer gaming. Therefore, the acquired score in the lower range is justified (M:2.45, SD:1.03).

Regarding empathy, the overall (MD:5.46, SD: 1.74), affective (MD:4.84, SD: 2.04), and cognitive (MD:6.22, SD: 0.79) scores were significantly high.

General beliefs were examined along two sides, one regarding real life events and behaviors and the second about gaming behaviors. Generally, the answers aligned more towards the 'being nice' behavior rather than the opposite. For example, in the first question about being wrong to hit other people, all responses aligned with the 'Agree' answer. In Table 4, general beliefs results are presented, along the different experiment sides, both before and after the game.

**Table 4.** General beliefs questionnaire results (experimental group)

| | Before the game | | | After the game | | |
|---|---|---|---|---|---|---|
| | Real life | Games | Overall | Real life | Games | Overall |
| Mean | 4.37 | 3.63 | 4.00 | 4.27 | 3.70 | 3.98 |
| SD | 1.88 | 1.75 | 1.84 | 1.74 | 1.44 | 1.61 |

It is notable that there was a significant difference between real life and in-game behaviors and beliefs, hence a further statistical analysis was required to identify any noteworthy differences. However, no statistically significant difference were identified in before the game responses between real-life (MD:4.37, SD:1.88) and in-game (MD:3.63,

SD:1.75) situations, t(29) = 2.04, p = 0.06, or for responses after the game, between real-life (MD:4.27, SD:1.74) and in-game (MD:3.70, SD:1.44) situations, t(29) = 2.04, p = 0.15.

A statistical analysis was also carried out to determine the effect of the game on attitudes against real-life and in-game events. No effect of the game was identified for real life situations, between pre-game (MD:4.37, SD:1.88) and post-game (MD:4.27, SD:1.74) responses, t(29) = 2.04, p = 0.74. Likewise, no effect of the game was identified for in-game situations, between pre-game (MD:3.63, SD:1.75) and post-game (MD:3.70, SD:1.44) responses, t(29) = 2.04, p = 0.84.

This leads to the conclusion that the game did not affect participants' empathy. Nevertheless, it should be acknowledged that a limitation of this study is the small user sample of participants. Moreover, future studies could consider a prolonged and more extended game experience, in order to study the impact of a game on player empathy.

Empathy was also assessed by exploring participants' responses to the empathy vignettes. For questions administered before the study, a rather negative score was obtained for questions 5 and 6, asking participants to indicate if they would advise a family person to join a protest against a political situation and if they would leave their country when at war. The remaining questions achieved a generally neutral score (close to 0), with responses including both empathic and indifferent attitudes. A differentiation in participants' responses was noted for the empathy vignettes questionnaire that was delivered after playing the game, with the majority of questions marking a slight increase in their overall average score. Results from the pre- and post-study questionnaires are presented in Table 5.

**Table 5.** Empathy vignettes results pre-study and post-study (experimental group)

|  | Q1 | Q2 | Q3 | Q4 | Q5 | Q6 | Overall |
|---|---|---|---|---|---|---|---|
| Mean (pre) | −0.67 | 0.67 | 0.17 | −0.33 | −0.83 | −1.00 | −0.33 |
| SD (pre) | 1.37 | 1.37 | 1.33 | 1.51 | 0.98 | 0.00 | 1.26 |
| Mean (post) | −0.17 | 1.17 | 0.17 | 0.83 | −0.83 | −0.67 | −0.08 |
| SD (post) | 1.33 | 1.17 | 1.33 | 0.98 | 0.98 | 1.37 | 1.34 |

A statistical analysis was carried out to identify possible attitude changes after playing the game, as indicated in participants' responses to the empathy vignettes questionnaire. However, the results do not confirm a statistically significant difference in participants' empathy for any of the hypothetical situations described in the vignettes. As a result, it cannot be implied that the game can influence and shape a player's behavior in the context of the explored game topic. This may be due to the limitation of the small number of participants, as well as due to the short exposure of participants to the game, or the game itself, which may have not being designed to increase empathy.

Finally, regarding historical awareness, participants' responses to the pre-test questionnaire achieved an overall high score (87.50%), and an overall above-average score for the post-test questionnaire (79.16%). The pre-test questionnaire focused more on general knowledge of the target population, whereas post-test questions were crafted based on the knowledge acquired after playing the game.

Considering the generally good scores achieved on the pre-test historical awareness questionnaire for both groups, it turns out that in order to observe the effect of the game with regard to learning, the questionnaires delivered should aim to elicit participants' knowledge regarding facts that are not generally known to the general public or learned by students through their school education; it should aim to assess historical facts that are conveyed through the game.

Participants' responses to the debriefing interview highlighted an overall good experience, with the visual style and game art being well liked. While they indicated that the storyline was interesting and the various options available enabled the player to create their own story, there were negative concerns about the simplicity of interaction and the excess amount of textual information. In addition, a few participants indicated that the questionnaires were long and that they were troubled by the game being available only in specific operating system versions.

*Control Group.* Results from the GUESS questionnaire reveal a high overall user satisfaction (M:4.95, SD:1.68), as well as high satisfaction regarding visual aesthetics (M:6.03, SD:0.79), personal gratification (M:6.03, SD:1.05), narratives (M:5.29, SD:1.43) and usability (M:5.55, SD:1.20).

Regarding empathy, although the aim of the control study was not to assess increased empathy towards past injustices and historical awareness, the overall (MD:4.89, SD:1.99), affective (MD:5.76, SD:1.44) and cognitive (MD:5.28, SD:1.81) empathy results were rather high.

In terms of general beliefs, results for all measures are presented in Table 6, with high scores observed along all dimensions. Nevertheless, considering that a difference was noted between real-life and in-game situations, a statistical analysis was carried out to identify any statistically important difference. For responses before the game, a statistically significant difference in general beliefs was identified between real-life (MD = 4.37, SD = 2.04) and in-game (MD = 3.63, SD = 1.91) situations, $t(94) = 2.59$, $p = 0.01$. Likewise, for responses after the game, a statistically significant difference in general beliefs was identified between real-life (MD = 4.49, SD = 2.01) and in-game (MD = 3.84, SD = 1.83) situations, $t(94) = 2.63$, $p = 0.009$. These results led to the preliminary conclusion that people who are in general empathetic, would sometimes adopt less nice behaviors in games, whereas they would not do this in real life.

**Table 6.** General beliefs questionnaire results (control group)

|  | Before the game | | | After the game | | |
|---|---|---|---|---|---|---|
|  | Real life | Games | Overall | Real life | Games | Overall |
| Mean | 4.37 | 3.63 | 4 | 4.49 | 3.84 | 4.17 |
| SD | 2.04 | 1.91 | 2.00 | 2.01 | 1.83 | 1.95 |

A statistical analysis was also carried out to determine the effect of the game on attitudes against real-life and in-game events. No effect of the game was identified for real life situations, between pre-game (MD = 4.36, SD = 2.04) and post-game (MD = 4.49, SD = 2.01) responses, t(94) = −0.58, p = 0.56, or for in-game situations, between pre-game (MD = 3.63, SD = 1.91) and post-game (MD = 3.84, SD = 1.95) responses, t(94) = −0.93, p = 0.35.

Analysis of the empathy vignettes revealed an overall neutral score both before the game and after the game (Table 7).

**Table 7.** Results of empathy vignettes pre-study and post-study (control group)

|  | Q1 | Q2 | Q3 | Q4 | Q5 | Q6 | Overall |
|---|---|---|---|---|---|---|---|
| Mean (pre) | −0.37 | 1.32 | 0.21 | −0.26 | −0.42 | −0.47 | 0.00 |
| SD (pre) | 1.61 | 1.11 | 1.36 | 1.41 | 1.43 | 1.47 | 1.51 |
| Mean (post) | −0.37 | 1.32 | 0.26 | −0.32 | −0.37 | −0.42 | −0.37 |
| SD (post) | 1.38 | 1.11 | 1.63 | 1.34 | 1.50 | 1.43 | 1.38 |

A statistical analysis was also carried out to explore the potential effect of the game on participants' responses to each question of the empathy vignettes. The results did not indicate any such effect, which is an expected finding considering that the game was not relevant to the particular topic of the vignettes, regarding dilemmas and personal choices in times of war. It is noted that analysis of the questionnaires identified the need for offering participants with a neutral response to the dilemmas posed, such as "I do not know", a component which was absent during the assessment.

Finally, regarding historical awareness, participants' responses to the pre-test questionnaire achieved an overall high score, as opposed to the overall score achieved for the post-test questionnaire. This was probably due to the fact the pre-test questionnaire inquired about facts that are generally known to the target population, whereas the post-test questionnaire was constructed to contain on purpose questions that can be answered only after playing the game, which however was not played by the control group. This highlights that games do in fact have the potential to add to the existing knowledge with specific knowledge of lesser known facts.

For data collected in the debriefing interview, the group leading effect was also evident in this study, leaving a deteriorated set of results for analysis. Overall, the game was well received and characterized as fast, easy to control, not so easy to master, had nice graphics and design, and offered the possibility to speed up the game. However, the simplicity of interaction and the complexity of the game were identified as the least liked characteristics.

*Comparative Analysis.* Statistical analysis was carried out to explore the effect of the game on participants' general beliefs, knowledge, and empathy, by comparing responses between the two groups (control and experimental). Results did not indicate any significant differences in general beliefs, before or after the game, between the two groups.

Likewise, no statistically important differences were found for knowledge of the specific game topic for the questions administered before the test, verifying that both groups had a similar understanding and knowledge of the topic at hand. Nevertheless, for the questions after the test, significant differences were identified for question 2, between the experimental group (MD:0.83, SD:0.41) and the control group (MD:0.16, SD:0,37); t(8) = 2.31, p = 0.006. The post-test results indicate that the game allowed participants to learn about topics that they might not have otherwise known about. For empathy, no statistical differences were identified in the general attitude of participants as explored through the empathy scale, and participants' responses to the vignettes before and after the game.

**Lessons Learned.** The impact of the game on learning outcomes, in this case historical awareness, was confirmed by observing a statistically significant difference in participants' scores after the game between the two groups (control and experimental), yet the results should be interpreted with caution due to the limited number of participants. In terms of general attitudes, empathetic character, and empathy toward the specific situations studied, no effect of the game was identified. Besides limitations referring to the sample size of the experimental group, this result signifies that additional studies are needed to explore whether empathy-related changes require long-term exposure the game.

After the conclusion of the sessions, certain key lessons emerged. Firstly, logistics challenges were encountered, including non-shows from students scheduled to participate in the study, or incomplete filling-out of online questionnaires. Print-versions of the questionnaires may also be considered as an alternative, if it they are easier for students to fill-in and for facilitators to monitor.

Data analysis revealed useful findings as well. At first, group interviews should be avoided, as they yield incomplete results. Moreover, comparisons between participants' attitudes before and after playing the game highlighted there was a lack of notable differences in opinions, at least in the context of their short exposure to the game. Future studies should explore whether longer exposure to a game could lead to such differences noted as an outcome of the game itself.

### 4.3  Study 3: Games as Vehicles for Social Change

The third study was designed to explore the impact of video games on players' attitudes toward human rights and social issues presented in game narratives, focusing on themes of refugees and migration. For the purpose of this study, the participants were randomly divided into an experimental and a control group.

The following instruments were used for Study 3: background demographics questionnaire, Single-Category Implicit Associations test (for implicit attitude measurement - SC-IAT) and a modified version of the migration scale (to measure explicit attitudes).

The duration of the study extended slightly beyond one hour, with 25 min devoted to the pre-test part, 30 min to the main gameplay, and 20 min to the post-test part.

**Participants**
*Experimental Group.* The experimental group consisted of 25 participants, the majority

of whom were male (60%), aged between 17–19 years old. Most of the participants indicated a high use of computer and smartphone or tablet devices[9], the latter of which were not used primarily for gaming. While participants' expertise with games varied, the most usual gaming device was indicated to be the computer, with action game genre the most commonly selected (Table 8).

**Table 8.** Gaming expertise of participants in Study 3

| Gaming frequency (per week) | Exp. | Con. | Game genre | Exp. | Con. |
|---|---|---|---|---|---|
| >than 30 h | 16% | 3% | action | 40% | 43% |
| between 15 and 30 h | 12% | 11% | adventure | 20% | 3% |
| between 5 and 15 h | 20% | 36% | simulation | 8% | 14% |
| less than 5 h | 32% | 39% | racing | 8% | 3% |
| Not at all | 20% | 11% | strategy | 4% | 4% |
| **Gaming device** | | | role-playing | 0% | 11% |
| Computer or laptop | 36% | | war | 0% | 0% |
| Gaming console | 10% | | sports | 0% | 0% |
| Smartphone or tablet | 43% | | puzzle | 0% | 11% |
| None | 11% | | none | 20% | 11% |

*Control Group.* The participants of the control group were almost equally divided into males (46%) and females (54%), with a total of 28 students aged 16 to 18 years old. The participants in the control group reported also varying expertise with games, as well as a high use of computer and smartphone devices[10], with the latter being the gaming platform of choice. Similarly to the experimental group, the gaming genre of choice was 'action' (Table 8).

## Results

*Implicit Attitudes.* Results from the analysis of the SC-IAT suggest that implicit attitudes in the experimental condition have not changed compared to those in the control condition (Table 9).

These results are in line with assumptions based on the APE model that frequent co-occurrences of the attitude object with another concept of positive or negative valence will cause changes in implicit attitudes. When taking into account this assumption, the chosen game, Path Out, is not designed in a way that would cause changes in implicit attitudes. Also, the latest meta-analytical evidence [39] indicated that even though video games in general can affect players' implicit attitudes, longer intervention durations

---

[9] 92% use computers and smartphones all the time and 8% often.

[10] 46% use computers all the time, 50% often and 4% sometimes, whereas 95% use smartphones all the time and 5% often.

**Table 9.** Implicit attitudes

| Group (n) | Pre-test M | Post-test M | Cohen's d |
|---|---|---|---|
| Experimental (25) | 0.026 | 0.045 | −0.055 |
| Control (28) | −0.013 | −0.008 | −0.011 |

resulted in larger implicit attitude changes. Our game intervention was relatively short for it to create frequent co-occurrences of the measured attitude object (refugees) with stimuli of positive or negative valence. Moreover, the game design of the game Path Out does not have persuasive game mechanics which were proven to have large effects on implicit attitudes (Stereotyping and Meaningful feedback - [39]). This suggests that longer interventions or the inclusion of a relevant persuasive game mechanics are needed to study implicit attitude change effectively.

*Explicit attitudes.* Both the experimental and the control group did not raise significant statistical pre-test-post-test changes in the experimental group nor in the control group (Table 10). However, the explicit attitude questionnaires have proven to be viable for our use, with our measured Cronbach alpha = 0.84 for pre-test and 0.817 for post-test.

**Table 10.** Explicit attitudes – Experimental group

| Group (n) | Pre-test M | Post-test M | Cohen's d |
|---|---|---|---|
| Experimental (25) | 3.393 | 3.48 | 0.072 |
| Control (28) | 3.077 | 3.142 | 0.057 |

*Interviews.* Two different sessions were conducted for the control group, with the first group exhibiting a positive rating of the game, and the second group mostly negative. The participants generally cited gameplay, concept and challenge of the game as what they liked most. In the experimental group sessions, the answers were better aligned, generally feeling positive towards the game, with a few frustrations towards the lack of explanations in-game.

**Lessons Learned.** Some general findings from the pilot interventions are that the questionnaires are viable and functional and that the software tools (both the SC-IAT application and the game) are stable. A group leading effect was noted during the sessions, thus creating the need for better monitoring and separating participants into individual or smaller-group sessions to ensure the validity of the data acquired.

During the planning and execution phases, certain technical difficulties arose, especially during the setting of the games on the school's equipment, making the preparation phase prior to the experiment an important step to ensure a smooth process. The influence of teachers on students' attitudes and discipline also highlighted the need to engage teachers effectively, especially for a large-scale testing. Facilitators also reported that having two researchers coordinating a group of 25 students is not sufficient, especially when children posed numerous questions simultaneously, making it challenging to manage time, address queries, and resolve other issues concurrently.

## 5   Discussion and Conclusion

Motivated by the impact that games can have beyond entertainment and education, toward raising historical awareness and empathy, as well as contributing to social change, but also the absence of a comprehensive methodology to assess game impact along these directions, this work has proposed a methodological approach for game evaluation. The proposed approach was validated through three individual studies that were carried out aimed to apply the individual components of the methodology, demonstrating that the approach proposed is modular and can be tailored to the evaluation needs of the research team depending on the scope of the game. In particular, the first study aimed to assess video game quality, primarily focusing on entertainment goals with an educational dimension. In the second study, run as a controlled experiment, the aim was to evaluate games' capacity to engage players with memorialization themes, functioning as tools to enhance historical awareness and foster enhanced empathy towards past injustices and those afflicted by them. The third study, also organized as a controlled experiment, explored the impact of video games on attitudes towards human rights and social issues, focusing on themes of refugees and migration. Lessons learned from these studies are related to the proposed methodological approach and the selected instruments, but also to the procedures applied.

Overall, the methodological approach was considered suitable for comprehensively evaluating games. It also highlighted that different component of the proposed approach can be employed individually, depending on the game being studied. Regarding the evaluation instruments, useful lessons were drawn. Regarding the instruments used, it is noted that standardized questionnaires may need to be adapted to the scope of the study, removing inapplicable questions. In addition, questionnaires measuring educational outcomes should be purposefully designed to avoid assessing general knowledge that may be well-known to students even without the playing game. Results of the controlled studies did not reveal an impact of the game to player's empathy and general beliefs, which may be attributed to the players' short exposure to the game or the lack of corresponding game mechanics.

In terms of the evaluation procedures applied several useful findings occurred for game evaluation in classroom settings. School and teacher engagement is a major concern. In particular, the session should be well-planned to fit one or two school hours, otherwise it will be difficult to find teachers willing to participate. Effective engagement with teachers and clear communication regarding their role and expectations during the testing sessions is also fundamental for a successful study delivery. Furthermore, children should be appropriately motivated by teachers to avoid perceiving their participation in the study as an obligatory mundane task, which may in turn affect their game experience. A thorough advance preparation is required to streamline the process, allowing the focus during testing sessions to be solely on the assessment itself. Indicative preparatory activities include the preparation of all questionnaires, acquisition of consent before the study, the assessment of the evaluation space and its available equipment, as well as compatibility checks and pre-installation of the games to the respective platforms. When planning the studies, the time required to complete the questionnaires should be appropriately estimated, especially when children are involved. Too lengthy questionnaires should be avoided, as they can be burdensome for children. During the study, group leading effects should be mitigated, to ensure that all participants express their own opinions and are not biased. Additionally, during the study, it is important to monitor in-person whether participants have handed in all questionnaires to avoid data loss, especially when online questionnaires are entailed. Considering that this may require additional resources in testing sessions with many children, printed versions of questionnaire may be preferrable when there is a scarcity of study facilitators. An important trade-off refers to the number of students partaking in the study simultaneously (e.g., an entire class) with regard to the drawbacks and difficulties entailed. Although from an organizational point of view having an entire class participate in the study may be beneficial – and in some cases the only viable solution – this resulted in practical challenges, such as the need for a large number of facilitators to appropriately monitor and guide the test, group leading effects in interviews, and a general fussier attitude of students during the testing session.

The lessons learned derived from the execution of the three pilot studies, collectively establish a strong foundation for the proposed methodology. Despite the identified limitations, the conceptual framework was proved to be valid and flexible to accommodate the needs of different assessment purposes across various games. Future work will focus on applying the improved methodology to additional game evaluation studies, aiming to produce guidelines for developing questionnaires to assess historical awareness, empathy, and social change.

**Acknowledgements.** This work has received funding from the European Union (Grant agreement no. 101061496). Views and opinions expressed are however those of the author(s) only and do not necessarily reflect those of the European Union or the Research Executive Agency. Neither the European Union nor the granting authority can be held responsible for them. The authors would like to thank all the study participants, their teachers and schools for their valuable contribution to this research. They would also like to thank all the facilitators of the three studies, They would also like to thank all the facilitators of the three studies, Ms. Christelle Dethy, Ms. Emilie Divoy, Ms. Laila Saaidi, Ms. Louise Wilmotte, Ms. Petra Černoušková, Mr. Štěpán Černoušek, Ms. Magdaléna Hájková, Ms. Viktorie Kovářová, Ms. Merima Ražanica, and Ms. Mia Babić, whose role in the successful delivery of the studies has been instrumental. Also, the authors thank Mr. Vangjel Gjorgjiev, from Trilateral Research, for his contributions and guidance in addressing the ethical issues of the study. Finally, we thank Charles Games (https://charlesgames.net/) and Causa Creations (https://causacreations.net/) for availing their games in the context of the three user studies.

# Annex

**Empathy Vignettes**

1. A fellow student confides in you their concern about the political situation in your country. Even though life seems to continue normally, and the people seem unbothered you agree that the situation is unacceptable. Your friend asks that you help them hand out fliers to raise awareness on the issues. You have a lot of homework to do and you generally dislike making public your political stance. Would you help your fellow student and do it?
2. Your country is at war, facing an invasion from a neighboring country. Trying to keep the moral high, schools remain open. You are studying hard to pass an important test at school. While you are studying, you hear shots being fired outside and people calling for help. You know that if you don't study, you may flunk the test. Would you go out and see if someone has got hurt?
3. You arrive at the cinema to see a movie with your date. They inform you that the movie will not be shown, because war has broken out in a neighboring country, and people are getting hurt. However, they will give you a refund and show the news. Would you do something else to entertain yourselves or call it a night?
4. A fellow student is seriously injured during a demonstration, and is taken to hospital. You do not know this student personally. Would you go visit your fellow student at the hospital?
5. Your country is at war. During these hard times some people stay and fight for their country, whereas others leave their country, families, and friends, and seek safety as refugees to other countries. You find that there is a friend who can help you flee to a neighboring country. Would you leave the country?
6. Your brother is a university student. Despite the gloomy situation in your country, he is determined to study hard and get his degree as soon as possible. One evening you hear his conversation with a friend asking him to stop studying and join a protest against the political situation in your country. You know his main concern is his studies. Also, there is a high risk of getting kicked out of school if he participates in the protest. However, as a person, he likes to freely express his opinion and he is certainly opposed to the current political situation. Do you advise your brother to keep studying and avoid being exposed to danger?

**General Beliefs Questionnaire**

1. In general, it is wrong to hit other people
2. In general, it is ok to hit other people if they hit you first
3. In general, it is wrong to be impolite, rude, and offensive to others
4. It is usually ok to lie if this helps you to achieve a goal
5. In times of distress, it is generally ok to mind your own business to protect yourself
6. In general, in video games, it is wrong to do bad things to harmless video characters
7. In general, in video games, it is ok to engage in violent or unlawful acts to achieve a game goal

8. In video games, it is wrong to opt for a mean or evil character or select mean and inappropriate responses when talking with other game characters
9. When playing games, it is ok to lie to achieve a game goal.
10. When playing a game, it is wrong to chat to get through the tougher areas

# References

1. Susi, T., Johannesson, M., Backlund, P.: Serious Games: An Overview. Institutionen för kommunikation och information (2007)
2. Connolly, T.M., Boyle, E.A., MacArthur, E., Hainey, T., Boyle, J.M.: A systematic literature review of empirical evidence on computer games and serious games. Comput. Educ. **59**, 661–686 (2012). https://doi.org/10.1016/j.compedu.2012.03.004
3. Neset, T.-S., Andersson, L., Uhrqvist, O., Navarra, C.: Serious gaming for climate adaptation—assessing the potential and challenges of a digital serious game for urban climate adaptation. Sustainability **12**, 1789 (2020). https://doi.org/10.3390/su12051789
4. Tegos, S., Kioumousidou, M., Vavami, M., Kioutsiouki, D., Gkoumas, D., Tsiatsos, T.: HistoryLand: a serious game for history learning in primary education. In: European Conference on Games Based Learning, p. 838. Academic Conferences International Limited (2014)
5. Selekos, P., et al.: A video game about gulag archaeology and the memoirs of women prisoners. In: 2024 IEEE Gaming, Entertainment, and Media Conference (GEM), Turin, Italy, pp. 1–6. IEEE (2024)
6. Papadaki, E., Ntoa, S., Adami, I., Stephanidis, C.: Let's cook: an augmented reality system towards developing cooking skills for children with cognitive impairments. In: Guidi, B., Ricci, L., Calafate, C., Gaggi, O., Marquez-Barja, J. (eds.) GOODTECHS 2017. LNICST, vol. 233, pp. 237–247. Springer, Cham (2018). https://doi.org/10.1007/978-3-319-76111-4_24
7. Stefanidis, K., Psaltis, A., Apostolakis, K.C., Dimitropoulos, K., Daras, P.: Learning prosocial skills through multiadaptive games: a case study. J. Comput. Educ. (2019). https://doi.org/10.1007/s40692-019-00134-8
8. Xhako, A., et al.: Gamified experiences using 360° photography: a methodology for creating gamified learning experiences in 360° virtual environments. In: Proceedings of the 16th International Conference on PErvasive Technologies Related to Assistive Environments, pp. 53–61. Association for Computing Machinery, New York (2023)
9. Partarakis, N., et al.: Enhancing the educational value of tangible and intangible dimensions of traditional crafts through role-play gaming. In: Brooks, A., Brooks, E.I., Jonathan, D. (eds.) ArtsIT 2020. LNICST, vol. 367, pp. 243–254. Springer, Cham (2021). https://doi.org/10.1007/978-3-030-73426-8_14
10. Stamou, S., Apostolakis, K.C., Ntoa, S., Margetis, G., Stephanidis, C.: Museum-inspired video games as a symbolic transitional justice policy: overview, concepts and research directions. ACM Games (2024). https://doi.org/10.1145/3651279
11. Petri, G., Gresse von Wangenheim, C.: How games for computing education are evaluated? A systematic literature review. Comput. Educ. **107**, 68–90 (2017). https://doi.org/10.1016/j.compedu.2017.01.004
12. Let players evaluate serious games. Design and validation of the Serious Games Evaluation Scale - IOS Press. https://content.iospress.com/articles/icga-journal/icg190111
13. Ntoa, S.: Usability and user experience evaluation in intelligent environments: a review and reappraisal. Int. J. Hum. Comput. Interact., 1–30 (2024). https://doi.org/10.1080/10447318.2024.2394724

14. Bellotti, F., Kapralos, B., Lee, K., Moreno-Ger, P., Berta, R.: Assessment in and of serious games: an overview. Adv. Hum. Comput. Interact. **2013**, e136864 (2013). https://doi.org/10.1155/2013/136864

15. Mayer, I., et al.: The research and evaluation of serious games: toward a comprehensive methodology. Br. J. Educ. Technol. **45**, 502–527 (2014). https://doi.org/10.1111/bjet.12067

16. Calderón, A., Ruiz, M.: A systematic literature review on serious games evaluation: an application to software project management. Comput. Educ. **87**, 396–422 (2015). https://doi.org/10.1016/j.compedu.2015.07.011

17. Design and evaluation of a Serious Game for immersive cultural training | IEEE Conference Publication | IEEE Xplore. https://ieeexplore.ieee.org/abstract/document/5665978

18. Mayer, I., et al.: The research and evaluation of serious games: toward a comprehensive methodology. Br. J. Edu. Technol. **45**, 502–527 (2014). https://doi.org/10.1111/bjet.12067

19. Steiner, C., et al.: Evaluation of serious games: a holistic approach: ICERI2015. In: ICERI 2015 Proceedings, pp. 4334–4342 (2015)

20. Yáñez-Gómez, R., Cascado-Caballero, D., Sevillano, J.-L.: Academic methods for usability evaluation of serious games: a systematic review. Multimedia Tools Appl. **76**, 5755–5784 (2017). https://doi.org/10.1007/s11042-016-3845-9

21. Wilson, D.W., et al.: Serious games: an evaluation framework and case study. In: 2016 49th Hawaii International Conference on System Sciences (HICSS), pp. 638–647 (2016)

22. Serious games: Quality characteristics evaluation framework and case study | IEEE Conference Publication | IEEE Xplore. https://ieeexplore.ieee.org/abstract/document/8340460

23. Mitgutsch, K., Alvarado, N.: Purposeful by design? A serious game design assessment framework. In: Proceedings of the International Conference on the Foundations of Digital Games, pp. 121–128. Association for Computing Machinery, New York (2012)

24. Emmerich, K., Bockholt, M.: Serious games evaluation: processes, models, and concepts. In: Dörner, R., Göbel, S., Kickmeier-Rust, M., Masuch, M., Zweig, K. (eds.) Entertainment Computing and Serious Games. LNCS, vol. 9970, pp. 265–283. Springer, Cham (2016). https://doi.org/10.1007/978-3-319-46152-6_11

25. Guidelines for the Process of Cross-Cultural Adaptation of S... : Spine. https://journals.lww.com/spinejournal/fulltext/2000/12150/Guidelines_for_the_Process_of_Cros_Cultural.14.aspx

26. Hornbæk, K.: Current practice in measuring usability: challenges to usability studies and research. Int. J. Hum. Comput. Stud. **64**, 79–102 (2006). https://doi.org/10.1016/j.ijhcs.2005.06.002

27. Systematic review and validation of the game experience questionnaire (GEQ) - implications for citation and reporting practice. In: Proceedings of the 2018 Annual Symposium on Computer-Human Interaction in Play (2018). https://dl.acm.org/doi/abs/10.1145/3242671.3242683

28. Keebler, J., Shelstad, W., Smith, D., Chaparro, B., Phan, M.: Validation of the GUESS-18: a short version of the game user experience satisfaction scale (GUESS). J. Usability Stud. **16**, 49–62 (2020)

29. Jolliffe, D., Farrington, D.P.: Development and validation of the basic empathy scale. J. Adolesc. **29**, 589–611 (2006). https://doi.org/10.1016/j.adolescence.2005.08.010

30. Saleme, P., Dietrich, T., Pang, B., Parkinson, J.: A gamified approach to promoting empathy in children. J. Soc. Mark. **10**, 321–337 (2020). https://doi.org/10.1108/JSOCM-11-2019-0204

31. Unraveling the processes underlying evaluation: attitudes from the perspective of the ape model. Soc. Cogn. https://guilfordjour-nals.com/doi/abs/10.1521/soco.2007.25.5.687

32. Gawronski, B., Bodenhausen, G.V.: Associative and propositional processes in evaluation: an integrative review of implicit and explicit attitude change. Psychol. Bull. **132**, 692–731 (2006). https://doi.org/10.1037/0033-2909.132.5.692

33. Gawronski, B., Brannon, S.M.: What is cognitive consistency, and why does it matter? In: Cognitive Dissonance: Reexamining a Pivotal Theory in Psychology, 2nd ed, pp. 91–116. American Psychological Association, Washington, DC (2019)
34. Hütter, M.: An integrative review of dual- and single-process accounts of evaluative conditioning. Nat. Rev. Psychol. **1**, 640–653 (2022). https://doi.org/10.1038/s44159-022-001 02-7
35. Implicit and Explicit Evaluation: A Brief Review of the Associative–Propositional Evaluation Model - Gawronski - 2014 - Social and Personality Psychology Compass - Wiley Online Library. https://compass.onlinelibrary.wiley.com/doi/full/10.1111/spc3.12124
36. Karpinski, A., Steinman, R.B.: The single category implicit association test as a measure of implicit social cognition. J. Pers. Soc. Psychol. **91**, 16–32 (2006). https://doi.org/10.1037/0022-3514.91.1.16
37. Greenwald, A.G., Banaji, M.R.: Implicit social cognition: attitudes, self-esteem, and stereotypes. Psychol. Rev. **102**, 4–27 (1995). https://doi.org/10.1037/0033-295X.102.1.4
38. Kotzur, P.F., Friehs, M.-T., Schmidt, P., Wagner, U., Pötzschke, S., Weiß, B.: Attitudes towards refugees: introducing a short three-dimensional scale. Br. J. Soc. Psychol. **61**, 1305–1331 (2022). https://doi.org/10.1111/bjso.12538
39. Kolek, L., Ropovik, I., Šisler, V., van Oostendorp, H., Brom, C.: Video games and attitude change: a meta-analysis. Contemp. Educ. Psychol. **75**, 102225 (2023). https://doi.org/10.1016/j.cedpsych.2023.102225

# Assessing the Usability of GIS and Emergency Management Software: A Meta-analysis of User Experience Methodologies Using Natural Language Processing

Maddalena Romano[1,2(✉)] and Jochen Albrecht[1,2]

[1] Department of Earth and Environmental Sciences, The Graduate Center, City University of New York, 365 Fifth Avenue, New York, NY 10016, USA
mromano@gradcenter.cuny.edu
[2] Department of Geography and Environmental Science, Hunter College, City University of New York, 695 Park Avenue, New York, NY 10065, USA

**Abstract.** Emergency Management Systems (EMS) are vital to communicating information between agencies, operations centers, and field personnel before, during, and after a disaster. However, when Emergency Management personnel sit down with software developers to gather requirements to create this bespoke software, they often overlook factors that would make the software more user-friendly and intuitive. Insufficient involvement of end-users in the design process and usability tests exacerbates these problems. Recent studies on user experience have identified recurring usability problems. Unlike past research, this study is a meta-analysis of usability methodologies using machine learning to determine the most common analytical approaches. The research compiles anonymized resource materials from published articles from the last five years, and uses machine learning to look for keywords, or tokens, that are common throughout the work.

To determine what the most common research methodology is employed, the authors created four tasks. The first task creates a Python script to search for a curated set of tokens, the second task uses the Gensim library to produce a token list, and the third task uses NVivo to create the list. The authors review the results of these tasks and use them to adjust the last task. The results reveal that the most used research methodology in recent years involves having conversations with users, while field research to directly observe user behavior not frequently employed. The study concludes with suggestion for improvements.

**Keywords:** Emergency Management · User Experience · User Interface · qualitative data analysis · communication · workflow transparency · Open-Source Solutions · Python · Machine Learning · Natural Language Processing (NLP) · spaCy · Genism · NVIVO · tokens · corpus · stemming · lemmatization · text frequency · document frequency · dictionary · Bag of Words (BoW) · test frequency · inverse document frequency · TF-IDF · Corpora · Model · Latent Dirichlet Allocation (LDA)

A. Marcus et al. (Eds.): HCII 2024, LNCS 15380, pp. 165–182, 2025.
https://doi.org/10.1007/978-3-031-76821-7_12

# 1  Introduction

Human Computer Interaction (HCI) in Geographic Information Systems (GeoHCI) and in Emergency Management Systems (EMS) play a crucial role in distributing information both within the Emergency Operations Center and in the field. The best systems provide a good user experience and an intuitive interface so that minimal training is needed. However, this is not usually the case with commercial or customized software products. Many times, software developers do not gather all the necessary business requirements needed to create a product that meets the needs of all emergency management professionals because either the right questions are not asked of those professionals, or the right professionals are not being interviewed for their needs. When developers neglect to include end users in the development phase, the results are usually a product that falls short.

There have been many studies over the years that study recurring usability problems to assess issues and suggest improvements, most notably by Jakob Nielsen (1994a, 1994b). The conclusions of these studies differ based on the type of software studied, which can make implementing suggested improvements a challenge. This study will examine the most recently published work of usability experts to determine the most common analytical methodologies used when assessing usability. This meta-analysis endeavors to reveal patterns in the types of methodologies used and to assess if the disparity of the conclusions lies in the analytical approaches employed.

To achieve this goal, this study will create bespoke machine learning code using Natural Language Processing (NLP) libraries available in Python. These language models can be useful for scanning a large body of primary (i.e., interviews) and secondary (i.e., published studies) sources, and can reduce the time needed for analysis. Tasks are designed to specifically answer the research question. The results demonstrate that the analytical methods most employed involve communicating with users.

# 2  Methods

This study is particularly interested in usability issues that affect the user interface (UI) or user experience (UX) of both Geographic Information Systems (GIS) applications and emergency management applications. These overlaps can reveal missed opportunities for communication between the stakeholders using an application, and the developers creating the application. The approach used in this study compiles systematic literature reviews in a similar fashion to the studies by Abraham (2021), Dias et al (2017), and Unrau and Kray (2019, 2021). Unlike Unrau and Kray (2019, 2021), whose focus was GIS Human-Computer Interaction (HCI), Abraham (2021) and Dias et al (2017) relied on HCI concepts, and their methodology is not specific to GIS HCI nor to how GIS is applied in Emergency Management. All studies used search engines and keywords to compile papers for their review. To compile published studies for this analysis, the search terms 'Usability in GIS applications,' and 'Usability in Emergency Management Applications,' were entered into the Google Scholar[1] database to retrieve papers. Papers

---

[1] Google scholar https://scholar.google.com/intl/en/scholar/about.html.

were selected based on title, abstract, and keywords to include studies related to the usability evaluation of GIS and Emergency Management applications. Unless a paper was a seminal study, only papers published within the last five years were analyzed (see References for a list of works analyzed).

Unlike the other studies, to analyze the documents for keywords and patterns, the authors created a natural language processing (NLP) script. Natural language processing (NLP) sits at the intersection of computer science and linguistics. Its primary focus is empowering computers to comprehend and work with human language. This field involves managing natural language data sets—like text or speech corpora—using rule-based or probability-based machine learning methods (including statistical and neural network approaches). The ultimate objective is enabling computers to understand document content, capturing the contextual intricacies of language. This technology allows for precise extraction of information and insights from documents while efficiently categorizing and organizing the documents themselves.

The Python scripting language has two libraries that are particularly useful for this flavor of machine learning—spaCy and Gensim. spaCy, an open-source Python library, offers advanced functionalities for performing high-speed natural language processing (NLP) on extensive text datasets. It supports the creation of models and operational applications crucial for document analysis, chatbot development, and various text analysis tasks. Meanwhile, Gensim, another open-source library, specializes in unsupervised topic modeling, document indexing, similarity-based retrieval, and other NLP functionalities, employing contemporary statistical machine learning techniques. Notably, Gensim includes robust implementations of Latent Dirichlet Allocation (LDA), a widely used algorithm for topic modeling. The authors employ the Corpora and Model modules of the Gensim library.

In the Corpora module, the primary function is doc2bow, which transforms a word collection into its bag-of-words representation: a sequence of (word_id, word_frequency) pairs. In Gensim, this corpus comprises word IDs alongside their frequencies within each document. Creating a Bag of Words (BoW) corpus involves converting a simple document list or text files. BoW represents a document as a list of words. The process involves passing a tokenized word list to a JSON object and associating each object with the corresponding JavaScript variable named Dictionary.doc2bow ().

The Model module facilitates LDA model estimation from a training corpus and inferring topic distribution for new, unseen documents. It also supports updating the model with new documents for online training. The Vector Model encodes records as lists, where the index signifies the token, and the value represents the text frequency. These lists are multidimensional vectors, with each column adding a new dimension. IDs and TFs are stored as tuples (ID, TF), minimizing storage by focusing only on non-zero tokens. TF-IDF (Term Frequency-Inverse Document Frequency) measures a token's commonness across all documents. A low TF-IDF suggests a common token, while a high value indicates a token specific to certain documents subsets.

To answer the research question, "How are researchers approaching usability analysis," we will need to answer the following research objectives:

1. What are the results of a selected token extraction using a predetermined list?
2. What are the results of automated token extraction?
3. What are the results of automated thematic extraction?

After the results of these three tasks are reviewed, we will answer the following research objective:

1. What are the results of a selected token extraction using a predetermined list augmented after quality control?

Each task described below is designed to provide an answer to one of these four research objectives. The results will be used to determine the most common approaches used to assess user experience (see our methodology workflow diagram in Fig. 1). Each task builds upon the other until we get a final result for Task 4.

To prepare for analysis, we chose forty-eight papers for our corpus[2] and converted them to lower-case text. Titles and authors were removed to anonymize the articles. Since some of these documents[3] were converted from PDF formats, the text was cleaned to remove any white spaces, special characters, and hidden carriage returns so that the script would return true paragraphs. The script first specifies the path to the folder containing the text documents, and the full path to the 'en_core_web_sm' model directory. This model is a general-purpose pipeline package (a network of interlinked elements that analyze and handle data as it moves within the system). Python's spaCy library is a toolkit that helps develop a Named Entity Recognition to scan text, identify and extract fundamental keywords, known as tokens[4], and machine learning algorithms help to continuously train the model. In this model, the sentences are divided into tokens, assigned a part of speech, and unimportant tokens (i.e., 'a,' 'an,' 'the') are removed. Instead of finding only the stem[5] of word, words are lemmatized[6] so that information would not be lost due to truncation (i.e., caring becomes care not car). The script then Initializes an empty list to store the corpus using the Corpora module.

The script then performs four tasks: 1) scrutinizing the corpus to look for tokens selected by the authors and their frequency[7] (pre-QA), 2) scrutinizing the corpus for tokens selected using Genism's LDA, 3) scrutinizing the corpus for tokens selected by NVIVO's automated thematic analysis and 4) scrutinizing the corpus to look for tokens using the new dictionary[8] complied with additional tokens added post-QA.

**Task 1 Description-Extracted Tokens (pre-QA).** Professionals specializing in usability and user-centered design (UCD) utilize diverse methods to gather user information,

---

[2] A corpus comprises multiple documents.

[3] Each document consists of various tokens.

[4] Tokens represent singular terms within a document.

[5] Stemming involves shortening words to uncover their roots.

[6] Lemmatization aims to determine a word's base form, minimizing differences due to tense, person, number, gender, mood, voice, and case.

[7] Document frequency quantifies how many documents contain a particular token.

[8] A dictionary encompasses the unique tokens found across all documents within the corpus.

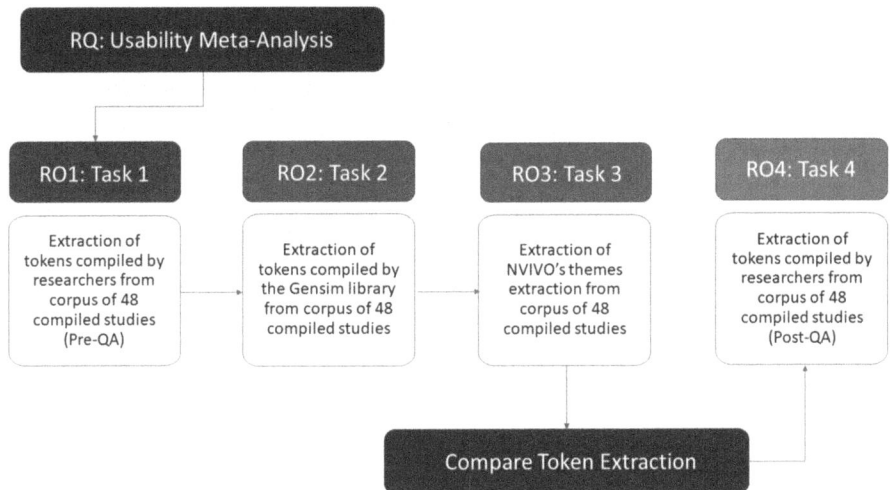

**Fig. 1.** Workflow for Task 1–4. Each task is designed to answer a research objective, the results of which will answer the overarching research question.

analyze needs, devise design solutions, refine designs through testing, assess efficiency, effectiveness, and gauge satisfaction. For Task 1, we created a function to extract specific tokens from the corpus, check if the selected token matches selected tokens in the list, extract the token and associated document filename, and add it to a dataframe for later export. The tokens for Task 1 were obtained from the concepts highlighted in an article written by Christian Rohrer for the Nielsen Norman Group[9] (2022. See Table 1). Rohrer describes the twenty usability frameworks most used by UX and UI researchers and categorizes them into Attitudinal (what is said), Behavioral (what is done upon observation), Qualitative (indirect measures), Quantitative (direct metrics), and their Context of Use (whether the study uses the product in its research). The dataframe is then exported to CSV file in a specified directory path.

**Task 2 Description-Gensim Extracted Tokens.** This function used Python's Gensim library to extract tokens using Gensim's LDA. Unlike Task 1, where the authors provide the keywords from the Rohrer (2022), Task 2 uses the Corpora and Model modules from Gensim's LDA to create a Bag-of-Words from the text. The tokens were stored in a matrix dataframe. The name of each document was used as a header label for the fields of the dataframe, and the tokens were used as row labels. The script then calculates the document frequency of each token and exports that matrix to a CSV file (Fig. 2).

**Task 3 Description-NVIVO Autocoded Themes.** In thematic analysis, the primary hurdle lies in pinpointing the essential themes embedded within your data. For Task 3, we used NVIVO's qualitative thematic analysis algorithms to detect themes. NVIVO's

---

[9] The Nielsen Norman Group was founded by Don Norman, who first used the term user experience when he worked for Apple and best known for his book The Design of Everyday Things, and Jakob Nielsen, who is widely known for his work on usability testing, most notably for his 10 Usability Heuristics checklist and his watershed book Usability Engineering.

**Table 1.** User Research Methods Matrix*

|  | Qualitative (Direct) | Quantitative (Indirect) |
|---|---|---|
| **Behavioral** | Field Studies, Eye Tracking, Usability Testing, Remote Moderated Testing | Clickstream/Analytics, A/B Testing, Usability Benchmarking, Unmoderated Testing |
| **Attitudinal** | Focus Groups, Interviews, Contextual Inquiry, Diary Studies, Customer Feedback, Participatory Design, Concept Testing, Card Sorting/Tree Testing, Desirability Studies | Surveys |

*Based on A Landscape of User Research Method by Christian Rohrer, Nielsen Norman Group (2022). This chart creates a matrix of twenty usability research frameworks for easy visualization. The context of use is Green: Natural Use of Product, Red: Scripted Use of Product, Orange: Decontextualized (no use of product), Blue: Limited (limited use of product).

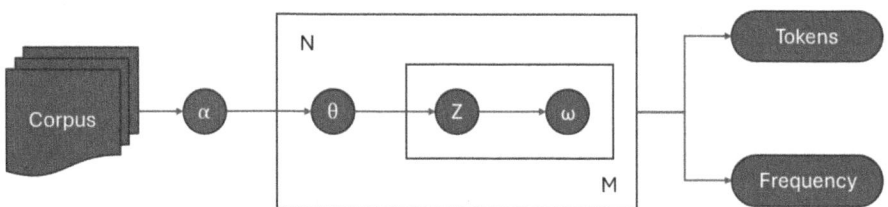

**Fig. 2.** Gensim LDA Model Diagram, where α represents the Dirichlet parameter, θ represents the document-topic distribution, z represents the word-topic assignment, ω represents the observed word, N represents the number of words in a document, and M represents the number of documents in the corpus.

autocoding text analysis tool scrutinized the corpus utilizing an installed language pack. This tool discerns themes by identifying noun phrases, organizing them into groups, and tagging each idea, prioritizing certain themes based on the frequency of appearance of each noun phrase. It then clusters these noun phrases under overarching themes and assigns codes to each theme, with additional child codes for the noun phrases falling within each theme. For this task, no additional editing of the encoding was performed by the authors (Fig. 3).

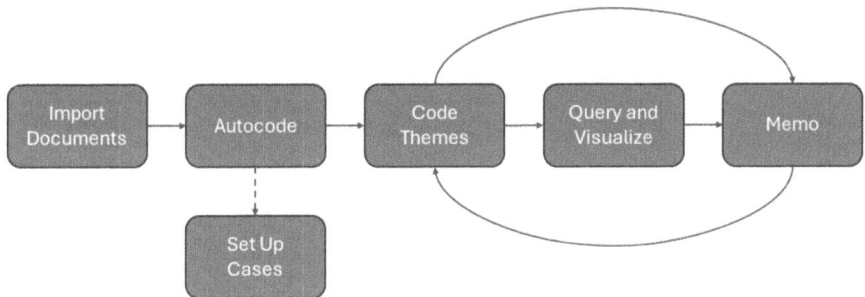

**Fig. 3.** NIVIO workflow diagram.

**Task 4 Description-Extracted Tokens (post QA).** For Task 4, we created a function to extract any paragraphs containing the words method or approach. The chosen paragraphs were extracted, stored in a dataframe, and exported to a file so we could perform Quality Control and Analysis (QA/QC). We manually reviewed all the extracted paragraphs for any tokens that were missed by the original dictionary we compiled for Task 1. These tokens were also added to the BoW so that we could extract as many usability testing strategies as possible. The list was further expanded using keywords from the Usability Body of Knowledge (BoK) published by the User Experience Professional Association (2010). The BoK offers comprehensive descriptions of these methods. These descriptions encompass procedures, required resources, expected outcomes, recommended applications, advantages, and associated costs. Table 3 in Appendix A lists the expanded set of keywords used for Task 4. We then augmented the function for Task 1 to extract tokens from the expanded BoW and applied this function to the corpus of method and approach paragraphs and exported those results to a new dataframe. We then compared the results with those of Task 1–3.

## 3   Results

Table 2 below lists the results of Task 1. Not surprisingly, terms like information, emergency, and user figured prominently, while the term specific to usability analysis, such as interviews, surveys, GOMS, and Persona, figured less so.

The strength of selected token query is that researchers can feed the sought-after words into the script to determine the TF-IDF. The drawback, however, is that a particular term can be expressed in more than one way. A good example is the word "questionnaire" and such synonyms as survey, form, opinion poll, and feedback form. In short, the words we are trying to find might be articulated in multiple ways, and as such we might accidentally miss words not included in the list. This means that this list needs to be augmented after a careful QA of all document methodologies in the corpus so that it can produce trustworthy results.

For Task 2, we allowed the script's Gensim LDA model to determine the TF-IDF. Table 3 below displays the results of the query using this model. The results were edited to combine root words (such as user and users) and remove words (such as 'et' and 'em') that do not provide any meaningful insight.

**Table 2.** Extracted Tokens based on list from USPA (2010) and Rohrer (2022)

| Token | Count | Token | Count | Token | Count |
|---|---|---|---|---|---|
| information | 2185 | ui | 202 | hci | 16 |
| user | 1350 | approach | 186 | surveys | 11 |
| emergency | 1084 | qualitative | 135 | goms[a] | 7 |
| system | 747 | feedback | 119 | geoinformation | 4 |
| management | 671 | quantitative | 94 | developer | 3 |
| gis | 558 | sus[b] | 42 | persona[c] | 3 |
| software | 372 | ux | 34 | sbrm[d] | 2 |
| interview(s) | 346 | analytics | 28 | | |

[a]GOMS, an acronym for Goals, Operators, Methods, and Selections, serves as a method for forecasting how individuals will utilize a proposed system.
[b]The System Usability Scale (SUS) stands out as one of the most renowned standardized usability assessment tools, emphasizing the acquisition of concise subjective feedback (10 questions) from users.
[c]A persona, also referred to as a user persona, customer persona, or buyer persona, within user-centered design and marketing, embodies a personalized fictional character crafted to epitomize a user type likely to engage with a website, brand, or product in a comparable manner. Also recognized as Persona-based inspection.
[d]The Scenario-based Ranking Method (SBRM) constitutes an empirical approach primarily utilizing scenarios for ranking usability attributes within software projects.

While there does exist some overlap with the results of Task 1, the LDA returned different tokens with slightly different counts in some cases. Notably, the LDA did not return any of the usability testing strategy keywords we indicated in Task 1, indicating that the LDA does not contain these words in its model. This implies that, until the LDA model is expanded, using this library to perform a meta-analysis of usability testing strategies is inappropriate.

For Task 3, the text files were imported into NVIVO, a commercial software package for qualitative data analysis. Because this was an automated thematic coding analysis, the variation in keyword count and frequency was expected (Table 4).

Given that NVIVO is a qualitative data analysis package, there was no expectation of TF-IDF. The counts and frequencies could be a result of extracting the themes of each paper, and not of quantifying the presence or absence of certain words. While useful to see which words overlap between all three tasks, it is also not appropriate for quantification.

For Task 4, the script performed several functions. First the script extracted all paragraphs from all the articles that contained the words "method" or "approach." These paragraphs were reviewed to collect additional terms to be added as tokens to the corpus of the script. Then the original list was augmented with additional keywords found during the review. The complete list can be found in Appendix A. The results of Task 4 are in Table 5 below.

**Table 3.** Tokens Generated Using Python's Gensim LDA model for Task 2

| Token | Count | Freq | "Token | Count | Freq | Token | Count | Freq |
|---|---|---|---|---|---|---|---|---|
| usability | 1270 | 44 | design | 226 | 27 | communication | 128 | 16 |
| user(s) | 1054 | 40 | emergency | 373 | 26 | water | 126 | 6 |
| data | 541 | 44 | study | 119 | 17 | management | 72 | 6 |
| gis | 310 | 31 | table | 85 | 17 | treatment | 60 | 6 |
| problems | 279 | 31 | software | 85 | 17 | blockchain | 54 | 6 |
| map | 248 | 31 | disaster | 396 | 24 | pou[a] | 54 | 6 |
| system | 217 | 31 | app(s) | 450 | 15 | collaborative | 42 | 6 |
| use | 568 | 47 | research | 217 | 24 | participants | 36 | 6 |
| evaluation | 186 | 31 | social | 336 | 16 | perceived | 36 | 6 |
| information | 683 | 31 | media | 192 | 16 | | | |

[a]Point-of-use (POU) water treatment technology has emerged as a method enabling individuals and communities lacking access to safe water to enhance water quality by treating it within their homes. Although various POU technologies exist, apart from boiling, none have attained widespread and enduring adoption on a large scale.

**Table 4.** NVIVO Autocoded Themes for Task 3

| Token | Count | Freq | Token | Count | Freq | Token | Count | Freq |
|---|---|---|---|---|---|---|---|---|
| user | 454 | 44 | studies | 151 | 30 | methods | 104 | 29 |
| usability | 354 | 33 | research | 144 | 30 | communication | 101 | 15 |
| data | 286 | 38 | disaster | 140 | 20 | software | 95 | 27 |
| information | 271 | 42 | evaluation | 133 | 29 | problems | 94 | 30 |
| system | 234 | 42 | management | 128 | 27 | testing | 94 | 25 |
| emergency | 223 | 27 | process | 112 | 30 | technology | 93 | 26 |
| design | 171 | 38 | app | 109 | 8 | interface | 90 | 35 |
| map | 159 | 19 | tools | 105 | 28 | analysis | 89 | 29 |

The enlarged inventory yielded a multitude of additional usability analysis techniques identified as tokens. Task 4 proved to be the most effective analytical method. It revealed that the most employed analytical approach to assessing the usability of the software as designed was talking to the users through interviews, surveys, feedback forms, and focus groups. These results suggest that there is less emphasis on objective field studies (i.e., eye tracking) when assessing usability.

**Table 5.** Keywords extracted from Task 4 results after QA/QC

| Token | Freq | Token | Freq | Token | Freq |
|---|---|---|---|---|---|
| user | 226 | itt[a] | 24 | remote evaluation | 4 |
| ui | 197 | feedback | 20 | use case | 4 |
| information | 130 | sus | 19 | hci | 3 |
| system | 127 | developer | 18 | eye tracking | 3 |
| emergency | 74 | focus group(s) | 14 | card sorting | 3 |
| interviews | 68 | persona | 12 | participant observation | 2 |
| cit[b] | 60 | spatial data | 11 | human-centered design | 2 |
| qualitative | 56 | surveys | 10 | sbrm | 2 |
| management | 54 | goms | 7 | user-generated content | 2 |
| interview | 50 | scenario based ranking | 6 | scenario of use | 2 |
| quantitative | 48 | system usability scale | 6 | field studies | 2 |
| usability testing | 39 | a/b testing[c] | 6 | geoinformation | 1 |
| software | 33 | ux | 5 | phone interview | 1 |
| mot[d] | 32 | cognitive walkthrough | 5 | prototyping methods | 1 |
| analytics | 24 | user-centric | 5 | task analysis | 1 |
| heuristic evaluation | 24 | | | | |

[a]Information Technology and Telecommunications.

[b]The critical incident technique (CIT) serves to pinpoint the root causes of human-system (or product) issues, aiming to mitigate potential losses to individuals, assets, finances, or data. Through this method, investigators gather information pertaining to the execution of tasks (such as workplace activities) and the interaction between users and the system interface.

[c]A/B testing, alternatively referred to as split testing or bucket testing, is a methodological approach aimed at comparing two variations of a webpage or app to ascertain which one exhibits superior performance.

[d]Metaphors of Thinking (MOT) scrutinizes a users' cognitive processes various devices and usage scenarios. Drawing from classical introspective psychology, MOT grounds its examination on metaphors such as habit formation, stream of thought, awareness, associations, the interplay between speech and thought, and cognitive understanding.

## 4   Discussion and Conclusion

The goal of this research was to perform a meta-analysis of usability methodologies using machine learning to determine the most common analytical approaches. The first objective was to use a predetermined list for token extraction. This was successful, but proved inadequate once the papers that made up the corpus were reviewed. The second objective was to use a language model for automated token extraction. This proved to be inappropriate since the language model did not possess a robust list of usability terms. The third objective was to use automated thematic extraction. This pulled out some overlapping concepts, but none of the usability methodologies. The fourth objective was to again use selected token extraction, but with a predetermined list augmented after review of the first three tasks. This proved to be the best of all four tasks.

This paper's approach of integrating multiple methodologies for a meta-analysis is both important and insightful in understanding usability analysis. It is not surprising that the Gensim LDA and the NVivo software fell short of providing a comprehensive list of tokens—the LDA model and software were not designed to look for such keywords that would indicate a usability approach. It is noteworthy, though, that Task 1 revealed that compiling a list of research design methodologies was insufficient to provide a comprehensive list of tokens that could be detected using machine learning. This indicates that there are many small variations in the naming conventions of these methods, for example, SBRM versus SBR versus Scenario-Based Ranking. These small variations might go unnoticed to the eye but would not be picked up by an algorithm that is referencing a specific model or list of tokens.

The insights gleaned from the results of Task for were also significant. The analysis reveals that the predominant method used by researchers to assess the usability of the software is direct interaction with users, conducted through interviews, surveys, feedback forms, and focus groups. These findings indicate a lower emphasis on objective field studies, such as eye tracking and participant observation, in the evaluation of usability. The trend toward using these more subjective means of data collection is understandable—it is easier and less time consuming to ask someone in a controlled environment what they think of a particular piece of software. It is easier still to ask users to take a survey—in many cases, a survey can provide researchers with a large sample of participants, thus making the results more trustworthy. However, this means that there is an inherent—though unintentional—unawareness in each response. These methods rely on the recall of individual users, which can be faulty. In addition, a user may not possess the vocabulary to properly articulate what is missing from the user interface to make the experience more intuitive. Objective, recorded participant observations can provide answers without bias and pitfalls of selective memory, and this study recommends that these methods be used more often. Field studies offer a quantitative empirical approach to measuring usability, providing valuable data points for the analysis. A better way moving forward would be to integrate both methodologies when assessing the usability of software so that researchers can attain a more holistic perspective (van Gemert-Pijnen et al. 2011; Sauer et al. 2020; Pollini et al. 2022; Chang et al. 2024).

The multimodal approach applied in this study caught discrepancies that might have gone unnoticed if the study were to rely solely on automated analysis, and this was useful in refining the code used for the meta-analysis. However, applying traditional methods of performing a manual review of a literary corpus in lieu of automated methods is impractical, since this process is time-consuming. Participant observation is likewise onerous. The amount of quantitative and qualitative data can be difficult to sort, code, and analyze. This could be the reason so many studies rely on interviews and controlled-environment experiments that do not mimic actual conditions—it is less complicated.

It appears that both manual review and field observations can produce reliable and quantitative results. Both methods are laborious, which makes dedicating the resources it takes to perform such analyses challenging. To address this challenge, this paper proposes the development of a custom Python library with a specialized language model tailored specifically for usability analysis. Such a tool can automate the analytical process and allow a researcher to efficiently parse textual data while significantly reducing time and effort. Furthermore, a custom Python library can offer researchers a versatile and invaluable resource for conducting rigorous and reliable analyses.

A bespoke language model could also extract data from video observations, making extracting information from field observations and recorded interviews even more efficient. By employing machine learning algorithms tailored specifically for video data, researchers can capture and quantify data from field observations much more efficiently. This can not only be useful for analysis but also for requirements gathering for emergency management software development. Developers can observe and record how their software is being used both in the field and during user acceptance testing. Coupled with interviews, this can provide a more comprehensive understanding of what a user needs and can improve software creation.

In conclusion, this research uses machine learning to illuminate prevailing methodologies used in assessing software usability. Through a series of objectives aimed at refining token extraction methods, the study reveals the successes and shortcomings inherent in each approach. The findings underscore a reliance on subjective methods such as interviews and surveys for usability evaluation, in lieu of objective\ methods such as field studies and participant observations. This study proposes a custom Python language library automating the analysis process, thereby mitigating the time-consuming nature of manual validation. It also proposes applying machine learning algorithms tailored for extracting data from video to capture insights from field and participant observations. By employing these advancements, researchers can yield more reliable insights more efficiently, and use these insights to inform software development practices.

## 5  Declarations

1. Ethics approval and Consent to Participate: The CUNY Human Research Protection Program (HRPP) waived the need for ethics approval and the need to obtain consent for the collection, analysis, and publication of the retrospectively obtained and anonymized data for this non-interventional study.
2. Declaration of generative AI and AI-assisted technologies in the writing process: During this work's preparation, the author(s) did not use any large language model or generative AI. The author(s) reviewed and edited the content as needed and take(s) full responsibility for the content of the publication.
3. Consent for publication: This work has not been previously published elsewhere. The authors consent to have this journal/proceeding publish this work.
4. Availability of data and material: N/A
5. Competing interests: The authors declare that they have no known competing fiscal interests or personal relationships that could have appeared to influence the work reported in this paper.
6. Funding: This research did not receive any specific grant from funding agencies in the public, commercial, or not-for-profit sectors.
7. Author Statement: Maddalena Romano: Conceptualization, Framing of Research Question, Literature Review, Data curation, Formal analysis, Investigation, Methodology, Coding, Visualization, Writing-original draft, Writing-review, and editing.

Jochen Albrecht: Conceptualization, Framing of Research Question, Literature Review, Writing-review, and editing.
8. Acknowledgements: N/A.

## Appendix A: Keywords Used in Script

Selected Keywords based on USPA (2010) and Rohrer (2022)

| focus group | method | approach | information |
|---|---|---|---|
| system | qualitative | quantitative | user |
| feedback | geoinformation | gis | spatial data |
| emergency | management | itt | developer |
| project management | interviews | focus groups | eyetracking |
| surveys | participatory design | concept testing | diary testing |
| card sorting | tree testing | customer feedback | desirability studies |
| clickstream | analytics | a/b testing | usability benchmarking |
| remote moderated testing | usability testing | field studies | unmoderated testing |
| contextual inquiry | | | |

Expanded set of Selected Keywords after Manual Review

| user-generated content | scenario based ranking method | sbrm | questionnaire |
|---|---|---|---|
| interview | hci | ui | ux |
| surveys | human-computer interface | user-centric | Human-centered design |
| unmoderated testing | clickstream/analytics | a/b testing | usability benchmarking |
| diary studies | focus groups | interviews | contextual inquiry |
| card sorting/tree testing | customer feedback | participatory design | concept testing |
| usability testing | desirability studies | field studies | eye tracking |
| cognitive walkthrough | Remote moderated testing | Pluralistic walkthrough | Heuristic evaluation |
| Usability testing | Heuristic walkthrough | Metaphors of human thinking (mot) | Persona based inspection |
| Remote evaluation | Benchmark testing | competitive usability testing | summative usability testing |
| satisfaction questionnaire | think aloud testing | wizard of oz | rating scales |

(*continued*)

(*continued*)

| Expanded set of Selected Keywords after Manual Review | | | |
| --- | --- | --- | --- |
| web analytics | system usability scale (sus) | critical incident technique (cit) | user edit |
| parallel design | generating ideas | card sorting | function allocation |
| wireframe | physical ergonomics | prototyping methods | storyboard |
| hierarchical task analysis | participatory design | task analysis | cognitive task analysis |
| affinity diagramming | cognitive models | goms | klm-goms |
| persona | claims analysis | competitor analysis | future workshop |
| use case | quality function deployment (qfd) | stakeholder interview | scenario of use |
| longitudinal study | usability benchmark | contextual inquiry | context of use analysis |
| field study | ethnography | cultural probe | participant observation |
| focus group | diary study | photo study | phone interview |
| system | method | approach | information |
| feedback | qualitative | quantitative | user |
| emergency | geoinformation | gis | spatial data |
| project management | management | itt | developer |
| surveys | interviews | focus groups | eyetracking |
| card sorting | participatory design | concept testing | diary testing |
| clickstream | tree testing | customer feedback | desirability studies |
| remote moderated testing | analytics | a/b testing | usability benchmarking |
| contextual inquiry | usability testing | field studies | unmoderated testing |

## Appendix B: Endnotes

# References

Abraham, S.A.: Usability problems in GI web applications: a lesson from literature. In: Partsin-evelos, P., Kyriakidis, P., Kavouras, M. (eds.) Proceedings of the 24th AGILE Conference on Geographic Information Science. (AGILE: GIScience Series) (2021). https://doi.org/10.5194/agile-giss-2-17-2021. https://agile-giss.copernicus.org/articles/2/17/2021/agile-giss-2-17-2021.pdf

Almasi, S., Mehrabi, N., Asadi, F., Afzali, M.: Usability of emergency department information system based on users' viewpoint; a cross-sectional study. Arch. Acad. Emerg. Med. **10**(1), e71 (2022). https://www.ncbi.nlm.nih.gov/pmc/articles/PMC9637262/. https://doi.org/10.22037/aaem.v10i1.1635. Accessed 7 Aug 2023

Asokan, N.: Designing for Emergencies — A UX Case Study (2019). https://blog.prototypr.io/designing-for-emergencies-a-ux-case-study-398b780f3c2f. Accessed 3 Apr 2022

Barr, J.L., Burtner, E.R., Pike, W.A., Boek-Peddicord, A., Minsk, B.S.: Gap assessment in the emergency response community (No. PNNL-19782). Pacific Northwest National Lab (PNNL), Richland, WA, 2010 (2010). https://www.pnnl.gov/main/publications/external/technical_reports/PNNL-19782.pdf

Ben Ramadan, A.A., Jackson-Thompson, J., Boren, S.A.: Geographic information systems: usability, perception, and preferences of public health professionals. Online J. Public Health Inf. **9**(2), e191 (2017). PMID: 29026456; PMCID: PMC5630278. https://doi.org/10.5210/ojphi.v9i2.7437. https://www.ncbi.nlm.nih.gov/pmc/articles/PMC5630278/

Brown, J., Bhatnagar, M., Gordon, H., Goodner, J., Cobb, J.P., Lutrick, K.: An electronic data capture tool for data collection during public health emergencies: development and usability study. JMIR Hum. Fact. **9**(2), e35032 (2022). https://doi.org/10.2196/35032. https://humanfactors.jmir.org/2022/2/e35032

Carillo, S., Marinas, N., Relator, R., Grepo, L.: Usability evaluation of MOSES (monitoring and operating system for emergency services tablet). In: Rebelo, F., Soares, M. (eds.) Advances in Ergonomics in Design, Usability & Special Populations: Part II. AHFE (2022) International Conference. AHFE Open Access, vol. 19. AHFE International, USA (2022). https://doi.org/10.54941/ahfe1001263. https://openaccess.cms-conferences.org/publications/book/978-1-4951-2107-4/article/978-1-4951-2107-4_48

Chang, Y, et al.: A survey on evaluation of large language models. ACM Trans. Intell. Syst. Technol. **15**((3)39), 1–45 (2024). https://doi.org/10.1145/3641289. https://dl.acm.org/doi/abs/10.1145/3641289

Cosgrove, S.: Exploring usability and user-centered design through emergency management websites: advocating responsive web design. Commun. Des. Q. **6**(2), 93–102 (2018). https://doi.org/10.1145/3282665.3282674. https://dl.acm.org/doi/10.1145/3282665.3282674

Dias, C., Pereira, M., Freire, A.: Qualitative review of usability problems in health information systems for radiology. J. Biomed. Inform. **76**, 19–33 (2017). https://doi.org/10.1016/j.jbi.2017.10.004. https://www.sciencedirect.com/science/article/pii/S153204641730223X

Ferguson, H.T., Gesing, S., Nabrzyski, J.: Measuring usability in decision tools supporting collaborations for environmental disaster response. In: 2016 49th Hawaii International Conference on System Sciences (HICSS), Koloa, HI, USA, pp. 2872–2881 (2016). https://doi.org/10.1109/HICSS.2016.360. https://ieeexplore.ieee.org/document/7427543

Fischer-Preßler, D.: Towards effective use of technology-enabled systems in emergency management and crisis situations (Doctoral dissertation, Otto-Friedrich-Universität Bamberg, Fakultät Wirtschaftsinformatik und Angewandte Informatik) (2022). https://fis.uni-bamberg.de/server/api/core/bitstreams/32fdebcc-0da7-4adc-be7b-dcdaf6a28884/content

Hillabin, J.: 6 Disasters Caused by Poorly Designed User Interfaces (2012). https://www.cracked.com/article_19776_6-disasters-caused-by-poorly-designed-user-interfaces.html. Accessed 7 Aug 2023

Johari, N.S., Abdullah, N.M., Bukari, S.M.: GIS communicate emergency preparedness mapping: the usability for rural area. In: IOP Conference Series: Earth and Environmental Science, vol. 1022, 6th International Conference on Civil and Environmental Engineering for Sustainability (IConCEES 2021) 15 November 2021–16 November 2021, p. 012031 (2022). https://doi.org/10.1088/1755-1315/1022/1/012031. https://iopscience.iop.org/article/10.1088/1755-1315/1022/1/012031/meta

Kern, D.: The importance of usability in geospatial applications (2020). https://blog.iqgeo.com/the-importance-of-usability-in-geospatial-applications. Accessed 7 Aug 2023

Komarkova, J., Sedlak, P., Struska, S., Dymakova, A.: Usability evaluation the prague geoportal: comparison of methods. In: 2019 International Conference on Information and Digital Technologies (IDT), Zilina, Slovakia, pp. 223–228 (2019). https://doi.org/10.1109/DT.2019.881 3723. https://ieeexplore.ieee.org/abstract/document/8813723

Komarkova, J., Sedlak, P., Habrman, J., Cermakova, I.: Usability evaluation of Web-based GIS by means of a model. In: International Conference on Information and Digital Technologies (IDT), Zilina, Slovakia, pp. 191–197 (2017). https://doi.org/10.1109/DT.2017.8024296. https://ieeexp lore.ieee.org/abstract/document/8024296

Lee, S.C., Nadri, C., Sanghavi, H., Jeon, M.: Eliciting user needs and design requirements for user experience in fully automated vehicles. Int. J. Hum. Comput. Interact. **38**(3), 227–239 (2022)

Liposinovic, M.: Usability Principles for (Re)Design of User Interface of Emergency Handling Programs Case Study on a Tool for Decision Support amidst a Nuclear Emergency: RASTEP. Kth Royal Institute of Technology, Electrical Engineering and Computer Science. Degree Project in Technology, First Cycle, 15 Credits, Stockholm, Sweden (2020). https://www.diva-portal.org/smash/get/diva2:1450983/FULLTEXT01.pdf. Accessed 7 Aug 2023

Mahsin, W.H.W., Rasam, A.R.A., Saraf, N.M., Khalid, N.: Free and open GIS source software for spatial epidemiology and geospatial health in Malaysia: a comparative analysis of the software usability. Int. J. Adv. Technol. Eng. Explor. **8**(78), 584 (2021). https://www.researchg ate.net/profile/Abdul-Rauf-Abdul-Rasam/publication/352025826_Free_and_open_GIS_sou rce_software_for_spatial_epidemiology_and_geospatial_health_in_Malaysia_A_compara tive_analysis_of_the_software_usability/links/60b73316a6fdcc476bdee473/Free-and-open-GIS-source-software-for-spatial-epidemiology-and-geospatial-health-in-Malaysia-A-compar ative-analysis-of-the-software-usability.pdf

Mentler, T., Berndt, H., Wessel, D., Herczeg, M.: Usability evaluation of information technology in disaster and emergency management. In: 1st International Conference on Information Technology in Disaster Risk Reduction (ITDRR), Sofia, Bulgaria, pp. 46–60 (2016). ⟨hal-03213119⟩. https://doi.org/10.1007/978-3-319-68486-4_5. https://inria.hal.science/hal-03213119/document

Molich, R., Nielsen, J.: Improving a human-computer dialogue. Commun. Assoc. Comput. Mach. **33**(3), 338–348 (1990). https://dl.acm.org/doi/10.1145/77481.77486

Moore, A., et al.: Comparative usability of an augmented reality sandtable and 3D GIS for education. Int. J. Geogr. Inf. Sci. **34**(2), 229–250 (2020). https://doi.org/10.1080/13658816.2019. 1656810. https://www.tandfonline.com/doi/abs/10.1080/13658816.2019.1656810

Mulhern, R., Grubbs, B., Gray, K., Gibson, J.M.: User experience of point-of-use water treatment for private wells in North Carolina: implications for outreach and well stewardship. Sci. Total Environ. **806**, 150448 (2022). https://pubmed.ncbi.nlm.nih.gov/34563909/

Mwangi, E.K., Kimani, S., Mindila, A.: Techniques for prioritizing the elements of Web-GIS usability. Int. J. Comput. Appl. **179**(53) (2018). 0975–8887. https://www.ijcaonline.org/arc hives/volume179/number53/mwangi-2018-ijca-917315.pdf

Mwangi, E., Kimani, S., Mindila, A.: A review of web-based GIS usability elements. J. Inf. Technol. **4**, 2–13 (2019). https://www.researchgate.net/profile/Ezekiel-Mwangi-2/publication/ 331199201_A_Review_Of_Web-Based_GIS_Usability_Elements/links/5c6bdba7299bf1e 3a5b29dff/A-Review-Of-Web-Based-GIS-Usability-Elements.pdf

Nielsen, J., Molich, R.: Heuristic evaluation of user interfaces. In: Proceedings of the Association for Computing Machinery CHI 1990 Conference, Seattle, WA, 1–5 April, pp. 249–256 (1990). https://dl.acm.org/doi/10.1145/97243.97281

Nielsen, J.: Enhancing the explanatory power of usability heuristics. In: Proceedings of the Association for Computing Machinery CHI 1994 C Conference, Boston, MA, 24–28 April, 152–158 (1994a). https://dl.acm.org/doi/10.1145/191666.191729

Nielsen, J.: Heuristic Evaluation. In: Nielsen, J., Mack, R.L. (eds.) Usability Inspection Methods. Wiley, New York (1994b)

Nielsen, J.: 10 Usability Heuristics for User Interface Design (2020). Accessed 3 Apr 2022. https://www.nngroup.com/articles/ten-usability-heuristics/

Opach, T., Rød, J.K.: A user-centric optimization of emergency map symbols to facilitate common operational picture. Cartogr. Geogr. Inf. Sci. **49**(2), 134–153 (2022). https://www.tandfonline.com/doi/full/10.1080/15230406.2021.1994469

Pogue, D.: 5 of the Worst User-Interface Disasters: Why your intelligence has nothing to do with using technology (2016). https://www.scientificamerican.com/article/pogue-5-of-the-worst-user-interface-disasters/. Accessed 7 Aug 2023

Pollini, A., et al.: Leveraging human factors in cybersecurity: an integrated methodological approach. Cogn. Technol. Work **24**, 371–390 (2022). https://doi.org/10.1007/s10111-021-00683-y. https://link.springer.com/article/10.1007/s10111-021-00683-y#citeas

Rinaldi, S., Gandhi, A., Selviandro, N.: Usability evaluation and recommendation of user interface design for e-HAC application by using user-centered design method. In: 2022 24th International Conference on Advanced Communication Technology (ICACT), pp. 483–490. IEEE (Institute of Electrical and Electronics Engineers), February 2022. https://ieeexplore.ieee.org/document/9728887

do Nascimento Rocha, H.M., do Nascimento, E.B, dos Santos, L.C., Alves, G.V., da Costa Farre, A.G.M., de Santana-Filho, V.J.: Usability in the admission monitoring system of an emergency room. Revista De Saúde Pública **55**, 113 (2021). https://doi.org/10.11606/s1518-8787.202105 5003475. https://www.scielo.br/j/rsp/a/SGHYqfbVkMDnqCSRB3stCqh/?lang=en

Rohrer, C.: When to Use Which User-Experience Research Methods (2022). https://www.nngroup.com/articles/which-ux-research-methods/. Accessed 21 Sept

Romano, M., Albrecht, J.: A gap analysis of emergency management and information technology. J. Emerg. Manag. **21**(4) (2023). https://doi.org/10.5055/jem.0765

Sanjaya, M.R., Kurniawan, D., Saputra, A.: GIS Android mobile based software development for tourism objects, public places list, transportations list, and culinary places list using usability measurement. In: Journal of Physics: Conference Series, Volume 1500, 3rd Forum in Research, Science, and Technology (FIRST 2019) International Conference 9–10 October 2019, South Sumatera, Indonesia Citation M. Rudi Sanjaya et al. 2020 J. Phys. Conf. Ser. 1500, 012117 (2019) https://doi.org/10.1088/1742-6596/1500/1/012117. https://iopscience.iop.org/article/10.1088/1742-6596/1500/1/012117/meta

Sauer, J., Sonderegger, A., Schmutz, S.: Usability, user experience and accessibility: towards an integrative model. Ergonomics **63**(10), 1207–1220 (2020). https://doi.org/10.1080/00140139.2020.1774080. https://www.tandfonline.com/doi/abs/10.1080/00140139.2020.1774080

Simões-Marques, M., Nunes, I.L.: Application of a user-centered design approach to the definition of a knowledge base development tool. In: Advances in Ergonomics in Design, Usability & Special Populations: Part II, p. 443 (2022). https://openaccess.cms-conferences.org/publications/book/978-1-4951-2107-4/article/978-1-4951-2107-4_44

Stieglitz, S., Hofeditz, L., Brünker, F., Ehnis, C., Mirbabaie, M., Ross, B.: Design principles for conversational agents to support emergency management agencies. Int. J. Inf. Manag. **63**, 102469 (2022). https://www.sciencedirect.com/science/article/pii/S0268401221001626

Tan, M.L.: Usability of disaster apps: understanding the perspectives of the public as end-users. A dissertation presented in partial fulfilment of the requirements for the degree of Doctor of philosophy in emergency management at Massey University, Wellington, New Zealand (2020). https://mro.massey.ac.nz/bitstream/handle/10179/15393/TanPhDThesis.pdf?sequence=1

Tan, M.L., Prasanna, R., Stock, K., Doyle, E.E.H., Leonard, G., Johnston, D.: Modified usability framework for disaster apps: a qualitative thematic analysis of user reviews. Int. J. Disaster Risk Sci. **11**, 615–629 (2020a). https://doi.org/10.1007/s13753-020-00282-x. http://www.ijdrs.com/en/article/doi/10.1007/s13753-020-00282-x, https://link.springer.com/article/10.1007/s13753-020-00282-x. Accessed 7 Aug 2023.

Tan, M.L., Prasanna, R., Stock, K., Doyle, E.E.H., Leonard, G., Johnston, D.: Understanding end-users' perspectives: towards developing usability guidelines for disaster apps. Prog. Disaster Sci. **7**, 100–118 (2020b). https://www.sciencedirect.com/science/article/pii/S25900617 20300557. https://doi.org/10.1016/j.pdisas.2020.100118. Accessed 7 Aug 2023

Unrau, R., Kray, C.: Usability evaluation for geographic information systems: a systematic literature review. Int. J. Geogr. Inf. Sci. **33**(4), 645–665 (2019). https://doi.org/10.1080/13658816. 2018.1554813

Unrau, R., Kray, C.: Enhancing usability evaluation of web-based geographic information systems (WebGIS) with visual analytics. In: Janowicz, K., Verstegen, J.A. (eds.) 11th International Conference on Geographic Information Science (GIScience 2021) – Part I, Article no. 15, pp. 15:1–15:16. Leibniz International Proceedings in Informatics Schloss Dagstuhl – Leibniz-Zentrum für Informatik, Dagstuhl Publishing, Germany (2021). https://drops.dagstuhl.de/opus/volltexte/2020/13050/pdf/LIPIcs-GIScience-2021-I-15.pdf

US Department of Homeland Security Science and Technology: Incident Management Software for Emergency Response Focus Group Report SAVER-T-FGR-10 (2021). https://www.dhs.gov/sites/default/files/ims_focus_group_report_jan_2021.pdf

User Experience Professional Association: Usability Body of Knowledge (2010). http://usabilitybok.org/methods. Accessed 22 Dec 2023

van Gemert-Pijnen, J.E., et al.: A holistic framework to improve the uptake and impact of ehealth technologies. J. Med. Internet Res. **13**(4), 111. https://doi.org/10.2196/jmir.1672. https://www.jmir.org/2011/4/e111

Wall, D.: User interface vs disaster: most common mistakes (2018). https://www.linkedin.com/pulse/user-interface-vs-disaster-most-common-mistakes-david-wall. Accessed 7 Aug 2023

Wang, Y.: Blockchain: A potential technology to improve the performance of collaborative emergency management with multi-agent participation. Int. J. Disaster Risk Red., 102867 (2022). https://www.sciencedirect.com/science/article/pii/S2212420922000863

Wohlgemut, J.M., et al.: Methods used to evaluate usability of mobile clinical decision support systems for healthcare emergencies: a systematic review and qualitative synthesis. JAMIA Open **6**(3) (2023). https://doi.org/10.1093/jamiaopen/ooad051. https://academic.oup.com/jamiaopen/article/6/3/ooad051/7222986

Yang, L., Prasanna, R., King, M.: Situation awareness-oriented user interface design for fire emergency response. J. Emerg. Manag. **7**, 65–74 (2009). https://wmpllc.org/ojs/index.php/jem/article/view/1274

# Transforming User Experience Through Extended Reality and Conversational AI: A Systematic Review

Kamelia Sepanloo[✉], Mohammad Ahmadi Gharehtoragh, and Vincent G. Duffy

School of Industrial Engineering, Purdue University, West Lafayette, In 47904, USA
{ksepanlo,mahmadig,duffy}@purdue.edu

**Abstract.** In this study, we investigate how extended reality (XR) and conversational artificial intelligence (AI) can enhance the user experience, showcasing successful implementations. We gathered data from Scopus, Science Direct, Google Scholar, and Web of Science, and conducted a bibliometric analysis to visualize and understand the relationships within the publications. To perform a comprehensive systematic review of the literature, we utilized several tools, including Harzing's Publish or Perish, Google NGram, Vicinitas, VOSviewer, CiteSpace, BibExcel, and maxQDA. Finally, we offer suggestions for future work on further improving user experiences with these technologies.

**Keywords:** Extended Reality · Conversational AI · User Experience · Bibliometric analysis

## 1 Introduction and Background

Virtual Reality (VR), Augmented Reality (AR), and Mixed Reality (MR) are among the Extended Reality (XR) technologies that have recently revolutionized user experiences in a variety of sectors. In the medical sector, XR devices offer realistic 3D visualization and touch-free interfaces, enhancing medical practice with innovative solutions (Andrews et al. 2019). XR applications have also shown benefits beyond healthcare, such as using gaze-based interactions to alleviate mobility impairments (Ghasemi et al. 2022) and enhancing educational experiences through AR by enriching real-world environments with computer-generated content (Yuen et al. 2011).

The application of XR is not confined to specific sectors but extends to diverse areas like cultural heritage. Mobile AR applications in cultural heritage enable users to access location-based information (Haugstvedt et al. 2012). Additionally, XR technologies have been utilized for construction safety evaluations, showcasing the versatility of XR across different industries (Salinas et al. 2022). XR has also demonstrated potential in historical preservation, allowing users to experience past events and interact with historical contexts (Rizvić et al. 2021).

Designing user experiences in XR environments presents unique challenges and opportunities. Guidelines for creating XR applications for head-mounted displays

A. Marcus et al. (Eds.): HCII 2024, LNCS 15380, pp. 183–194, 2025.
https://doi.org/10.1007/978-3-031-76821-7_13

(HMDs) stress the importance of addressing user needs and interactions in VR, MR, and AR settings (Vi et al. 2019). Moreover, user-friendly interfaces in XR applications play a critical role in enhancing user engagement and satisfaction (Knoke et al. 2021). Evaluating user experiences in AR mobile applications underscores the significance of interactivity and variety in creating compelling XR experiences (Davidavičienė et al. 2020).

Conversational AI, which refers to the application of artificial intelligence (AI) to support natural language interaction between machines and people, is another critical component of user experience design. Recent years have seen a significant increase in businesses and organizations using conversational artificial intelligence to improve user experiences and customer relationships (Schachner et al. 2020).

In many e-commerce settings, AI-based chatbots replace human chat service agents in communicating with customers (Adam et al. 2021) In addition to engaging in natural conversations with users, chatbots powered by artificial intelligence can also establish relationships. One promising application of AI chatbots to lifestyle modification programs is the development of cost-effective and feasible behavioral interventions to promote physical activity and a healthy diet (Jingwen Zhang et al. 2020). There are several software platforms available to assist with the development of conversational artificial intelligence systems, each of which has similar goals but differing focus points and functionalities (Aronsson et al. 2021). However, current policies and ethical guidelines for AI technology are lagging the progress AI has made in healthcare (Rigby 2019).

In general, the potential to improve the user experience by incorporating conversational AI and XR is extensive and transformative. XR generates immersive environments that create more realistic, intuitive, and engaging experience. These experiences become even more interactive and personalized when they are combined with conversational AI, which facilitates natural, real-time communication between users and technology. This collaboration has the potential to significantly enhance user satisfaction and engagement in a variety of sectors and could lead to more efficient training programs, innovative educational tools, enhanced customer service, and novel entertainment experiences.

The systematic reviews conducted in this article will facilitate an exhaustive and comprehensive literature search, enabling us to identify pertinent studies in this field, critically evaluate them, and summarize their conclusions.

## 2 Problem Statement

This paper conducts a comprehensive analysis of the trends surrounding the search terms "Conversational AI," "Extended Reality," and "User Experience". It employs a multi-faceted approach, starting with a trend analysis followed by a bibliometric examination to visualize and comprehend the associated data. Publication data is gathered from prominent databases such as Scopus, Web of Science, and Google Scholar. Utilizing a diverse set of analytical tools including Google nGram, Vicinitas, VOSviewer, CiteSpace, BibExcel, and maxQDA, the study delves deep into the evolution of this research domain. Ultimately, drawing insights from this analysis, the paper offers valuable recommendations for harnessing these technologies to enhance user experience.

## 3 Procedure

The study began by collecting data from three primary databases: Scopus, ScienceDirect, and Google Scholar. The table below shows the number of articles collected for each keyword and database up to the year 2024 (Table 1).

**Table 1.** Number of articles for each database

| Keyword | Scopus | Science Direct | Google Scholar |
| --- | --- | --- | --- |
| Extended reality | 10,598 | 389,190 | 6,030,000 |
| Conversational AI | 2,072 | 4,363 | 736,000 |
| User Experience | 183,405 | 644,235 | 9,380,000 |

Next, the Vicinitas analytical tool was used to track and analyze real-time and historical tweets related to social media campaigns and brands on Twitter, focusing on the selected keywords. This analysis generated a word cloud and engagement timeline tables to study the tweets in this area. The results are shown in Fig. 1.

As evidenced by the engagement timelines and posts, interest in topics related to extended reality and conversational AI is increasing. Additionally, the word cloud generated from the Twitter feeds shows that the selected keywords are also associated with subjects such as "metaverse," "mixed reality," and "virtual".

Next, we conducted a trend analysis on the related keywords using Google Ngram Viewer. This online tool tracks the annual frequency of n-grams (word sequences) in printed sources over a specified period. For our analysis, we searched for the terms "Conversational AI," "Extended Reality," and "User Experience" in articles published between 2000 and 2019. Figure 2 illustrates how the number of articles mentioning these terms has changed over time.

As seen in Fig. 2, "user experience" shows the most significant increase, indicating that this area is being studied and implemented more extensively than the other two. Additionally, since extended reality and conversational AI are relatively newer concepts, it suggests that further investigation into how these technologies can enhance user experience is warranted.

As part of this analysis, VOSviewer software was employed to construct and visualize bibliometric networks, which are networks of bibliographic data used to analyze and understand the structure of scientific literature (Islam et al. 2023). Through VOSviewer, bibliometric networks can be visualized in various ways, such as identifying clusters of related publications, exploring citation patterns among publications, and visualizing connections between authors, institutions, and research topics (Kanade et al. 2024).

Figure 3 depicts the connections between the research topics generated by this software. The data was collected from the Scopus database, comprising 196,075 articles. For co-citation analysis, the number of cited references is 10, and the minimum number of citations in a cited reference is 7.

Utilizing additional bibliometric techniques, CiteSpace is a software tool designed to analyze and visualize scientific literature. It offers valuable insights into the development

**Fig. 1.** Results from Vicinitas analysis based on the Twitter feeds of the keywords ("Vicintas")

and structure of study disciplines, aiding in the identification of emerging trends within a field. Among its many analytical features, cluster analysis stands out, grouping relevant papers based on their citation patterns to identify specific themes within the studied topic.

In CiteSpace, cluster analysis is instrumental in generating maps of scientific literature, enabling the identification of patterns and trends over time by visualizing connections between publications, authors, institutions, and research areas. Moreover, these clusters can enhance our understanding of field organization, highlight critical research questions and themes, and explore relationships between study topics including "Extended Reality", "Conversational AI", and "User Experience".

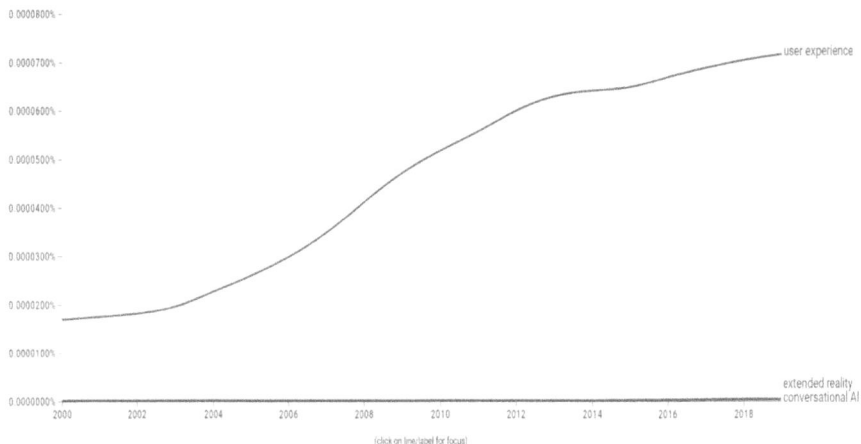

**Fig. 2.** Google Ngram trend analysis ("Google N-gram")

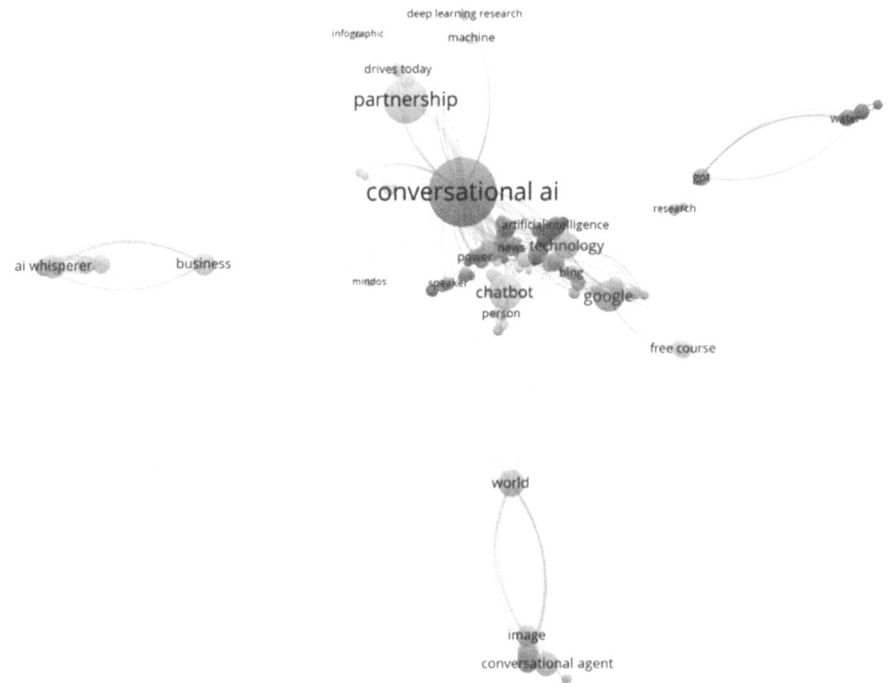

**Fig. 3.** Bibliometric networks between research topics ("VOSviewer")

Figure 4 showcases the clusters generated using CiteSpace software. Initial data collection involved gathering the first 500 results on the specified keywords from the

Web of Science database. Subsequently, clusters were generated to elucidate connections between research areas. Table 2 presents the top 10 references with the strongest citation bursts, providing further insights into influential works within the field.

**Fig. 4.** CiteSpace cluster analysis ("CiteSpace")

Furthermore, the Publish or Perish (PoP) software from Harzing was employed to perform bibliometric analyses of academic publications. The PoP platform offers researchers the capacity to compute metrics such as the h-index, g-index, and other citation metrics, which allows them to effectively evaluate the influence and impact of their work. In addition to citation metrics, it provides essential information regarding a researcher's publications, such as journal impact factors and download counts. It is frequently employed by universities, organizations, and researchers to assess the importance of scholarly papers and recognize emergent research trends.

In this study, leveraging the Google Scholar database within Harzing, a collection of 16,146,000 papers related to selected keywords including "Extended Reality", "Conversational AI", and "User Experience" was compiled. Subsequently, to delve deeper and identify the leading authors among the results, BibExcel software was employed.

BibExcel is particularly adept at conducting co-citation analysis, which involves identifying the frequency with which pairs of publications are cited together in other works. This analysis aids in identifying clusters of related research, tracking the development of research fields over time, and identifying key researchers and institutions in a given field. BibExcel's flexibility allows for data import from various sources like Web of Science, Scopus, and Google Scholar, and facilitates exporting data in various formats for use in other software programs. Its suite of analytical tools includes network visualization, clustering analysis, and bibliometric indicators like the h-index and g-index.

**Table 2.** Top10 references using CiteSpace

| Title | Year | Citation |
|-------|------|----------|
| Applications of Extended Reality in Ophthalmology: Systematic Review | 2021 | (Ong et al. 2021) |
| User Experience in Collaborative Extended Reality: Overview Study | 2020 | (Nguyen et al. 2020) |
| The Effects of Virtual Reality, Augmented Reality, and Mixed Reality as Training Enhancement Methods | 2020 | (Kaplan et al. 2021) |
| Extended Reality in Educating the Next Generation of Health Professionals | 2021 | (Shankar 2021) |
| Next-Generation Simulation Integrating Extended Reality Technology into Medical Education | 2021 | (Herur-Raman et al. 2021) |
| Applications of Extended Reality in Orthopedic Surgery | 2023 | (Nazzal et al. 2023) |
| The impact of extended reality on surgery: a scoping review | 2023 | (James Zhang et al. 2023) |
| Use of Extended Reality in Medical Education: An Integrative Review | 2022 | (Curran et al. 2022) |
| A Review of Extended Reality (XR) Technologies for Manufacturing Training | 2020 | (Doolani et al. 2020) |
| Extended Reality in Spatial Sciences: A Review of Research Challenges and Future Directions | 2020 | (Çöltekin et al. 2020) |

Following the import of data from Harzing into BibExcel, the software was utilized to identify the leading authors among the papers. Figure 5 illustrates the top 25 leading authors and the number of articles they have contributed to this area.

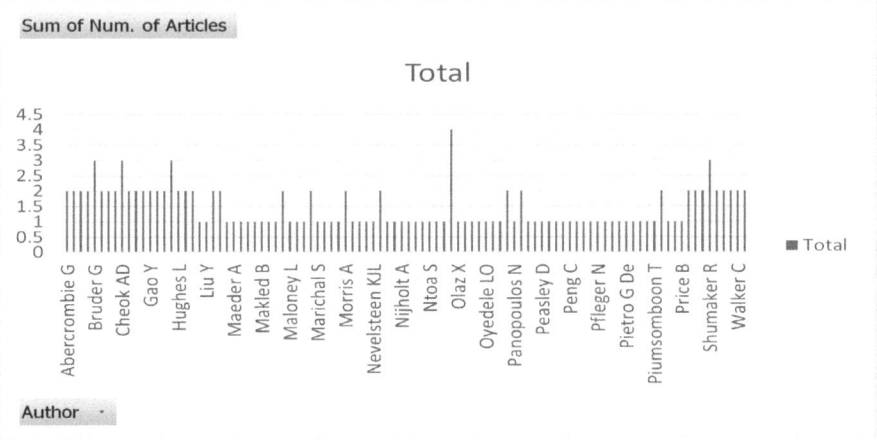

**Fig. 5.** Leading authors of related papers found on Google Scholar ("BibExcel")

Additionally, a word cloud was generated from the keywords using MaxQDA software (shown in Fig. 6). This word cloud visually represents text data and is commonly used to display free-form text or keyword metadata. In the word cloud, the font size and color of each tag indicate its importance. The image was generated from the top seven papers on the topic of study.

The generated word cloud reveals numerous applications of extended reality and conversational AI, such as "academic," "education," "social bots," and "research." Notably, "ChatGPT," a well-known example of a conversational AI application, also appears among the keywords. Table 3 shows the most frequently found words.

**Fig. 6.** Word cloud generated using MaxQDA ("MaxQDA")

## 4 Summary of Results

A comprehensive literature review was conducted by pulling metadata from multiple databases, including Google Scholar, Scopus, Web of Science, and ScienceDirect, using the search terms "Extended Reality," "Conversational AI," and "User Experience."

After collecting the data, Vicinitas analytical tool was employed to conduct trend analysis, revealing increasing interest in topics associated with the selected keywords. However, upon comparison of trends using Google Ngram, it was found that "user experience" experienced the most significant surge, indicating it receives more research attention and implementation than the other two terms.

Subsequently, using the VOSViewer software, relationships between subjects in the field were explored, with papers closely related to the selected keywords chosen as primary resources. Data for VOSViewer was sourced from the Scopus database, while CiteSpace was employed for further cluster analysis on the Web of Science database, identifying the top 10 papers with the highest citation bursts.

**Table 3.** Word Frequency from MaxQDA Using 7 Selection Papers

| Word | Frequency |
| --- | --- |
| Chatbots | 139 |
| Virtual Reality | 131 |
| Usability | 128 |
| Virtual Assistants | 128 |
| Augmented Reality | 127 |
| User Interface | 125 |
| Natural Language Processing | 122 |
| Dialogue Systems | 122 |
| User-Centered Design | 121 |
| Mixed Reality | 118 |
| Voice Recognition | 117 |
| Immersive | 116 |
| 3D Modeling | 114 |
| Interaction Design | 114 |
| Accessibility | 114 |
| Bot | 113 |
| Interaction | 113 |
| Privacy | 113 |

Additionally, bibliometric analyses of academic articles in the Google Scholar database were conducted using Harzing's Publish or Perish software. This software facilitated data gathering, which was then imported into BibExcel to identify the top authors in the field.

Consequently, word clouds were generated by MaxQDA, highlighting recurring terms such as "academic," "education," "social bots," and "research," are most relevant to the study's focus.

## 5 Justification

### 5.1 Academic Justification

Our research employs a comprehensive and multifaceted approach to investigate the intersection of UX, conversational AI, and XR. We guarantee a comprehensive understanding of the current research landscape in this field by conducting a meticulous literature review across a variety of databases, including Scopus, Web of Science, ScienceDirect, and Google Scholar. Our work makes substantial progress in the advancement of knowledge in both academic and practical domains by providing insights into the current state of research, identifying emergent trends, and proposing actionable recommendations to optimize these technologies for the purpose of improving UX.

## 5.2 Application Justification

Businesses can more effectively create products and services that are in close alignment with consumer expectations and requirements by understanding how XR and conversational AI can enhance the user experience. This alignment results in an increase in sales, a more profound brand loyalty, and an overall improvement in the company's reputation. Furthermore, by investigating the trends and applications of these technologies, organizations can identify opportunities for innovation and preserve a competitive advantage in the rapidly changing digital landscape of today.

# 6  Future Work

XR and conversational AI have the exceptional potential to transform the user experience by providing increased engagement and interactivity. User interaction with digital elements is facilitated by XR, while conversational AI improves the naturalness and human-likeness of computer communication. To guarantee the responsible application of these technologies, researchers must establish guiding principles, scrutinize their ethical implications, and investigate their potential to improve accessibility and inclusivity in user experience.

Researchers can execute prototype testing and user studies in a variety of sectors, such as education and e-commerce, to assess the effectiveness of these technologies. A few potential areas for future research are as follows:

1. Investigation of the Fusion of XR and Conversational AI: Examine the potential for the integration of XR and conversational AI to generate more engaging and immersive user experiences. Through the integration of these technologies, researchers can create innovative experiences and assess their efficacy in a variety of settings through prototype testing and user studies.
2. Guidelines Development and Ethical Considerations: To ensure the responsible use of conversational AI and extended reality in user experience, establish best practices. Thorough examination is necessary for ethical considerations, including the potential for bias and privacy concerns. User studies can be conducted to assess user attitudes toward these issues, in addition to the development of frameworks to guarantee ethical use through collaboration with industry experts and regulatory bodies.
3. Conducted longitudinal studies to evaluate the long-term effects of conversational AI and XR on user experience: In conjunction with user surveys and focus groups, longitudinal studies that examine trends in search terms and publication data over time can illuminate the practical applications and emerging trends of these technologies.
4. Investigate the potential of conversational AI and XR to enhance inclusivity and accessibility in the user experience: Achieving more inclusive user experiences can be achieved by designing and testing prototypes that are specifically designed for users with disabilities, followed by user studies to assess their efficacy.

By addressing these avenues for future research, scholars can ensure that the potential benefits of XR and conversational AI are maximized while mitigating associated risks, thereby nurturing more inclusive and enriching user experiences.

# References

Adam, M., Wessel, M., Benlian, A.: AI-Based chatbots in customer service and their effects on user compliance. Electron. Mark. **31**(2), 427–45 (2021). https://doi.org/10.1007/s12525-020-00414-7

Andrews, C., Southworth, M.K., Silva, J.N.A., Silva, J.R.: Extended reality in medical practice. Curr. Treat. Options Cardiovasc. Med. **21**(4), 18 (2019). https://doi.org/10.1007/s11936-019-0722-7

Aronsson, J., Lu, P., Strüber, D., Berger, T.: A maturity assessment framework for conversational AI development platforms. In: Proceedings of the 36th Annual ACM Symposium on Applied Computing, New York, NY, USA, pp. 1736–45. ACM (2021)

Çöltekin, A., et al.: Extended reality in spatial sciences: a review of research challenges and future directions. ISPRS Int. J. Geo-Inf. **9**(7), 439 (2020). https://doi.org/10.3390/ijgi9070439

Curran, V.R., Xu, X., Aydin, M.Y., Meruvia-Pastor, O.: Use of extended reality in medical education: an integrative review. Med. Sci. Educ. **33**(1), 275–86 (2022). https://doi.org/10.1007/s40670-022-01698-4

Davidavičienė, V., Raudeliūnienė, J., Viršilaitė, R.: Evaluation of user experience in augmented reality mobile applications. J. Bus. Econ. Manag. **22**(2), 467–81 (2020). https://doi.org/10.3846/jbem.2020.13999

Doolani, S., et al.: A review of extended reality (XR) technologies for manufacturing training. Technologies **8**(4), 77 (2020). https://doi.org/10.3390/technologies8040077

Ghasemi, Y., Jeong, H.: Using gaze-based interaction to alleviate situational mobility impairment in extended reality. Proc. Hum. Fact. Ergon. Soc. Annu. Meet. **66**(1), 435–439 (2022). https://doi.org/10.1177/1071181322661224

Haugstvedt, A.-C., Krogstie, J.: Mobile augmented reality for cultural heritage: a technology acceptance study. In: 2012 IEEE International Symposium on Mixed and Augmented Reality (ISMAR), pp. 247–55. IEEE (2012)

Herur-Raman, A., Almeida, N.D., Greenleaf, W., Williams, D., Karshenas, A., Sherman, J.H.: Next-generation simulation—integrating extended reality technology into medical education. Front. Virtual Real. **2** (2021). https://doi.org/10.3389/frvir.2021.693399

Islam, M.T., Sepanloo, K., Velluvakkandy, R., Luebke, A., Duffy, V.G.: Enhancing ergonomic design process with digital human models for improved driver comfort in space environment, pp. 87–101 (2023)

Kanade, S.G., Duffy, V.G.: Exploring the effectiveness of virtual reality as a learning tool in the context of task interruption: a systematic review. Int. J. Ind. Ergon. **99**, 103548 (2024). https://doi.org/10.1016/j.ergon.2024.103548

Kaplan, A.D., Cruit, J., Endsley, M., Beers, S.M., Sawyer, B.D., Hancock, P.A.: The effects of virtual reality, augmented reality, and mixed reality as training enhancement methods: a meta-analysis. Hum. Fact. J. Hum. Fact. Ergon. Soc. **63**(4), 706–26 (2021). https://doi.org/10.1177/0018720820904229

Knoke, B., Quandt, M., Freitag, M., Thoben, K.-D.: Virtual reality training applications in industry - towards a user-friendly application design. In: Competence Development and Learning Assistance Systems for the Data-Driven Future, Goto Verlag, pp. 59–80 (2021)

Nazzal, E.M., Zsidai, B., Hiemstra, L.A., Lustig, S., Samuelsson, K., Musahl, V.: Applications of extended reality in orthopaedic surgery. J. Bone Joint Surg. **105**(21), 1721–1729 (2023). https://doi.org/10.2106/JBJS.22.00805

Nguyen, H., Bednarz, T.: User experience in collaborative extended reality: overview study. In: Bourdot, P., Interrante, V., Kopper, R., Olivier, A.H., Saito, H., Zachmann, G. (eds.) EuroVR 2020. LNCS, vol. 12499, pp. 41–70. Springer, Cham (2020). https://doi.org/10.1007/978-3-030-62655-6_3

Ong, C.W., Tan, M.C.J., Lam, M., Koh, V.T.C.: Applications of extended reality in ophthalmology: systematic review. J. Med. Internet Res. **23**(8), e24152 (2021). https://doi.org/10.2196/24152

Rigby, M.J.: Ethical dimensions of using artificial intelligence in health care. AMA J. Ethics **21**, 121–24 (2019). https://doi.org/10.1001/amajethics.2019.121

Rizvić, S., Bošković, D., Okanović, V., Kihić, I.I., Prazina, I., Mijatović, B.: Time travel to the past of Bosnia and Herzegovina through virtual and augmented reality. Appl. Sci. **11**(8), 3711 (2021). https://doi.org/10.3390/app11083711

Salinas, D., Muñoz-La Rivera, F., Mora-Serrano, J.: Critical analysis of the evaluation methods of extended reality (XR) experiences for construction safety. Int. J. Environ. Res. Public Health **19**(22), 15272 (2022). https://doi.org/10.3390/ijerph192215272

Schachner, T., Keller, R., von Wangenheim, F.: Artificial intelligence-based conversational agents for chronic conditions: systematic literature review. J. Med. Internet Res. **22**(9), e20701 (2020). https://doi.org/10.2196/20701

Shankar, P.R.: Extended reality in educating the next generation of health professionals. Educ. Med. J. **13**(1), 87–91 (2021). https://doi.org/10.21315/eimj2021.13.1.8

Vi, S., da Silva, T.S., Maurer, F.: User experience guidelines for designing HMD extended reality applications. In: Lamas, D., Loizides, F., Nacke, L., Petrie, H., Winckler, M., Zaphiris, P. (eds.) INTERACT 2019. LNCS, vol. 11749, pp. 319–341. Springer, Cham (2019). https://doi.org/10.1007/978-3-030-29390-1_18

Yuen, S.C.-Y., Yaoyuneyong, G., Johnson, E.: Augmented reality: an overview and five directions for AR in education. J. Educ. Technol. Dev. Exch. **4**(1) (2011). https://doi.org/10.18785/jetde.0401.10

Zhang, J., Lu, V., Khanduja, V.: The impact of extended reality on surgery: a scoping review. Int. Orthop. **47**(3), 611–21 (2023). https://doi.org/10.1007/s00264-022-05663-z

Zhang, J., Oh, Y.J., Lange, P., Yu, Z., Fukuoka, Y.: Artificial intelligence chatbot behavior change model for designing artificial intelligence chatbots to promote physical activity and a healthy diet: viewpoint. J. Med. Internet Res. **22**(9), e22845 (2020). https://doi.org/10.2196/22845

# Designing User Interface for Color Association Analysis Tool

Cheng-Min Tsai[✉] [iD]

Department of Visual Communication Design, National Taiwan University of Arts,
New Taipei City, Taiwan, R.O.C.
ansel.tsai@ntua.edu.tw

**Abstract.** In this study, we focus on designing the interface and functionality of color analysis tools to investigate color associations. This approach advances beyond conventional analytical methods, rendering the results of color correlation studies more scientific and robust. This study aimed to (1) develop a color analysis tool for analyzing the relations between semantic color adjectives and the investigation results of color associations, and (2) examine the color association analysis tool to demonstrate the spatial distribution and volumetric presence of colors linked with semantic adjectives in the CIE*Lab* color space. In a previous study, the prototype of the analysis tool was designed based on the rules of user interface design and to execute an easy analysis method to understand the color distribution of serial color chips in the CIE*Lab* color space. Three experts were invited to discuss and review the functions and analysis procedures of the color analysis tool. The interface of the analysis tool includes importing the raw data with CIE*Lab* and the RGB values, and color volume calculation represented in the CIE*Lab* color space. Color analysis was performed according to the workflow process for calculating the color image from the RGB value to CIE$L*a*b*$. In terms of academic research contributions, this study recognizes that effective color analysis and display go beyond simple color swatch tools. It relies on establishing the strength of relationships between color semantics vocabulary and their associated colors within the CIELab color space. Future work could explore the mapping of color semantics to perceived colors in people's associations and examine its clustering effects.

**Keywords:** Color association · Semantic understanding · Adjective vocabulary · Color analysis tool · User interface design

## 1 Background

As discussions about metameres intensify, the development of artificial intelligence (AI) algorithms aligned with semantic understanding becomes increasingly pronounced. An inevitable trend is the utilization of color space for semantic analysis in large-scale data analytics. Tsai (2016) proposed a critical model based on information processing system (IPS) and cognitive processing system (CPS) [1]. According to Newell's IPS, three levels including physical implementation, algorithmic manipulation, and semantic

© The Author(s), under exclusive license to Springer Nature Switzerland AG 2025
A. Marcus et al. (Eds.): HCII 2024, LNCS 15380, pp. 195–206, 2025.
https://doi.org/10.1007/978-3-031-76821-7_14

understanding, should be considered in the IPS [2]. Maeder and Eckert (1999) also found three levels: mathematical, psychovisual, and task-oriented, which are part of the CPS with oriented human cognition [2]. However, the first level (physical implementation in the IPS and mathematical implementation in the CPS is primarily intended to consider physical attributes such as the image fidelity of processed images relative to the original images. The second level can be considered the base of the human visual system, which includes algorithmic manipulation in the IPS and psychovisual manipulation in the CPS. Based on the aforementioned fundamental levels, the top one is the most important level, which includes cognitive processes (semantic understanding in IPS and task orientation in CPS). The top level has been widely investigated by implementing human factor research in empirical studies. Numerous studies have examined the assessment of image information and visual assessment through human visual systems based on the perspectives of human factor engineering and perception psychology. Tsai et al. (2016, 2018) pointed out that important items for color, image, and visual assessment at the cognition level include brightness, colorfulness, naturalness, preference, and total image quality (see Fig. 1) [1, 4]. At the top level, the color cognition items consider human cognition. They are also directly related to semantic understanding and task-oriented concepts.

Thus, in the early stages of graphic development, the designer and his/her client must have repeated discussions to determine audience/users and market positioning strategies. The use of adjectives facilitates discussion and communication in graphic and product design processes. Color is one of the most important design elements for graphic and product designers. Many studies have indicated that colors correspond to human emotions. The selection of colors used in a product is often related to the target market. Selecting the correct adjectives can assist designers in establishing associations with a suitable color, ultimately settling on the final color to be used in the product [5–8].

Manav (2007) found that human emotional responses to colors vary depending on the value and saturation of the color [9]. Kaya and Epps (2004) indicated that positive emotional responses were the highest for primary hues, followed by intermediate and achromatic colors [10]. Green mainly evoked positive emotions, such as relaxation and comfort. Ou (2004) explored emotional responses and preferences associated with individual colors. This study investigates how people emotionally perceive and prefer single colors. This study focused on understanding the emotional impact of colors by examining participants' responses to various individual hues [11]. This study delves into the emotional associations that people have with specific colors. It can assess the feelings of happiness, sadness, calmness, or excitement linked to individual hues. Kaya and Epps (2004) investigated the relationship between color and emotions among college students as the study participants. This study presents findings on the relationship between colors and emotions based on the responses of college students [10]. This study also discusses the implications of the observed color-emotion associations, providing insights into how color choices can influence emotional states and potentially informing fields such as design, marketing, and psychology. Adams (2016) explored the multifaceted relationship between color, meaning, and symbolism across art and science. He also highlights three key points that can be discussed in terms of color, meaning, and symbolism across art and science. These include (1) scientific perspective: This scientific aspect likely involves discussions on the psychological and physiological aspects of color perception; (2) symbolism: the symbolic meanings attached to colors across different cultures and historical periods; and (3) meaningful integration: looking for insights into how the understanding of color from both artistic and scientific perspectives contributes to a richer comprehension of its meanings and implications in various contexts [12]. According to Tsai, these results provide a reference for product/graphic designers when selecting colors using adjectives [4]. As previous study results showed, the colors associated with adjectives such as warm, sunshine, passionate, shine, and cool were more uniform; conversely, the colors associated with adjectives such as modern, graceful, steady, restful, and exalted were relatively variable. Humans experience emotions through their perception and cognition. They also constructed meanings using color. This study also indicated that adjectives are one of the effective ways to identify suitable colors. Both experienced and inexperienced product/graphic designers are responsible for selecting the color of a product. For example, the results of the "youthful" adjective indicated the selection of various colors for the same adjective in this study.

Designers can use various colors for a series of product appearances. Discussions and communication on the product appearance of color or graphic colors are a means of understanding and establishing suitable color selections. The results of this study will provide a foundation for product/graphic designers and a simpler tool for color selection to meet their work requirements [4].

This study aimed to (1) design an interface for the analysis of the relations between semantic color adjectives and investigate results of color associations, and (2) examine the color association analysis tool to demonstrate the spatial distribution and volumetric presence of colors linked with semantic adjectives in the CIELAB color space.

In terms of impact, the study's preliminary phase successfully established parameters for the physical attributes that are crucial for assessing color association, coupled with an in-depth examination of the semantic vocabulary. Building on this foundation, this research conducts a meticulous investigation of the interconnections between color association and semantic vocabulary. This exploration is particularly impactful for graphic design, as it provides a comprehensive understanding of how semantic vocabulary intertwines with human color associations. Consequently, the study's findings have the potential to significantly influence design practices, offering new insights and methodologies for designers to consider in their work. The implications of this research extend beyond theoretical contributions, presenting practical applications that can reshape conventional perspectives on color usage in graphic or product design, and possibly in broader fields where color plays a pivotal role.

## 2   Literature Review

### 2.1   Color Association

These associations are often influenced by various factors including cultural background, personal experiences, symbolism, and context. Colors are linked to emotions, moods, and symbolic representations, making the color association a subjective and context-dependent phenomenon. The "color association" refers to the cognitive and emotional connections that people make with specific colors, based on cultural, personal, societal, and psychological factors. These associations involve linking colors to feelings, ideas, objects, or experiences. For example, red may be associated with passion or danger, while blue may evoke feelings of calmness or sadness. The study of color associations is interdisciplinary and involves fields such as psychology, marketing, design, and culture. Artist Itten (1973), Gage (1993), and Albers (2006) highlighted that color association refers to the psychological and cultural connections or meanings that individuals or societies attribute to specific colors [13–15]. Based on these definitions, color association covers a range of topics related to color, including color theory, color perception, and cultural influences, and can contribute to a comprehensive understanding of color association. Many studies not only define color association but also discuss its application (refer to Table 1). Thus, color associations can be based on a variety of variances from different cultures, regions, religions, and nations.

Colour association is a relatively abstract concept for design purposes and cannot easily correspond to a single color. Color association is easily connected to human cognition. Therefore, it is difficult to graphically visualize the colors associated with adjectives. If a suitable analytical tool or graphical method can be used, it will assist in design practice.

## 2.2  CIELAB Color Space

In 1976, the International Commission on Illumination (CIE) defined the CIE*Lab* color space, which was created to serve as a device-independent function to be used as a reference. The CIE*Lab* color space has several significant advantages and has been widely applied in various fields of research and industry. One of the primary advantages of the CIE*Lab* is its ability to be perceptually uniform. The same amount of numerical change in these values corresponds to approximately the same amount of visually perceived change in color. The CIE*Lab* color space sets up the color as three dimensions of the CIE*L* * for lightness from zero (black) to 100 (white) and the CIE$a^*$ and CIE$b^*$ for hue and chroma. The CIE*Lab* color space was also designed as a "perceptually uniform or uniform color space," which implies that "the same amount of numerical color value change corresponds to roughly the same amount of visually color perceived change" [24–26]. In this study, the numerical color volume was calculated using the CIE*Lab* color space.

## 3  Function and Procedure of the Color Analysis Tool

Three experts were invited to discuss and review the functionality of the color tool and its analytical procedure. The backgrounds of the experts are shown in Table 2, and it was determined that the function should include an automatic color transfer function, such as RGB to CIEXYZ and CIELab in an image. The color space represented in the CIELab color space is effective for calculating the color difference and distribution of the color volume. They also pointed out that the interface should include a demonstration of the color status to provide the user with an understanding of the color distribution of serial color chips in the CIELab color space. This study aimed to develop an analysis tool based on user interface design rules and execute an easy analysis method to understand the color distribution of serial color chips in the CIELab color space. The interface of the analysis tool includes the image file input, color analysis, and color space represented in the CIELab color space. Color analysis was performed according to the workflow process for calculating the color image from the RGB value to CIEL*a*b*. The process began with the RGB value of the inputted color chips towards the sRGB value and then transferred to the CIEXYZ and CIELab color spaces. The CIEL*a*b* values were calculated to determine the color distribution of the serially colored chips. All steps were

**Table 1.** The research papers of color association

| Years | Researchers | Main points |
|-------|-------------|-------------|
| 2023 | Briggs [16] | This paper discusses the attributes of perceived color and how they are associated with various perceptions and meanings |
| 2023 | Takata, R. and Katayama, I. [17] | This study examines how the relative positioning of different colors impacts their noticeability and perception |
| 2022 | Chen, M. and Westland, S. [18] | This study investigates the association between the color temperature of morning light and its impact on wellbeing |
| 2022 | Liao, C. C. and Tsai, K. I. [19] | This research examines the association between color combinations on packaging and their impact on visual comfort, recognition, and consumer preferences |
| 2021 | Yu, L., Westland, S., Chen, Y., and Li, Z. [20] | The color association is a primary factor affecting consumers' product color associations and purchase decisions |
| 2018 | Chang, B., Xu, R., and Watt, T. [21] | The different colors can influence the learning process and cognitive functions |
| 2010 | Palmer, S. E. and Schloss, K. B. [22] | This research proposes the ecological valence theory, explaining why people have preferences for certain colors based on their positive or negative experiences with those colors |
| 2007 | Elliot, A. J. and Maier, M. A [5] | This paper provides an overview of how different colors affect psychological functioning, including mood, behavior, and cognition |
| 2006 | Aslam, M. M. [23] | This paper explores how color serves as a crucial marketing tool and how its effectiveness can vary across different cultural contexts |

(*continued*)

**Table 1.** (*continued*)

| Years | Researchers | Main points |
|-------|-------------|-------------|
| 2004 | Ou, L. C., Luo, M. R., Woodcock, A., and Wright, A. [11] | This study investigates the emotions associated with various colors and how these emotions influence color preferences |
| 2004 | Kaya, N., and Epps, H. H. [10] | This paper examines the relationship between color and emotion among college students, providing insight into how different demographic groups perceive color |

**Table 2.** The background of the three experts and their emphasis suggestions for the color analysis tool

| No. | Title/Major | Work seniority | Suggestions |
|-----|-------------|----------------|-------------|
| 1 | Associate Prof/Color research and design education | 16 ears | • Friendly user interface for input and output operation<br>• Easy to transfer the color value, such as the CIEXYZ and CIE*Lab* values<br>• The results could be demonstrated graphically for easy reading and understanding |
| 2 | Professor/Mathematics research and education | 18 years | • The volume calculation of color distribution could be evaluated and compared in the best way<br>• The output functions should be including the RAW file and the processed data in ASCII format, it will be used to calculate and statistics in the future |
| 3 | Senior Engineer/Color facility education | 26 ears | • The color space represented in the CIE*Lab* color space will be the better way, in order to compare with the other research results<br>• The scale of the CIE*Lab* axis could be able to adjust for display a suitable scale |

performed according to the process used in the pilot study [1, 4, 27]. All color chips were input into the analysis tool used to obtain the RGB value of each pixel in the source color chips and to convert the color value of each pixel to the CIEL*a*b values. All the colored chips are represented in the CIELab color space. Figure 1 shows the interface prototype of the color-analysis tool. The distribution map shows two axes with CIEa* and CIEb* values.

$$\Delta E_{ab}^* = \sqrt{(L_m - L_n)^2 + (a_m - a_n)^2 + (b_m - b_n)^2}$$ (1)

$$S_{vol} = \sum_{i=1}^{n} \Delta E_{abi}$$ (2)

Where the delta $E_{ab}$ is the distance between each pixel and the median of all delta $E_{ab}$ value in the single image, $S_{vol}$ is the sum of delta $E_{ab}$ for each image, the $n$ is the total number of pixels for each image.

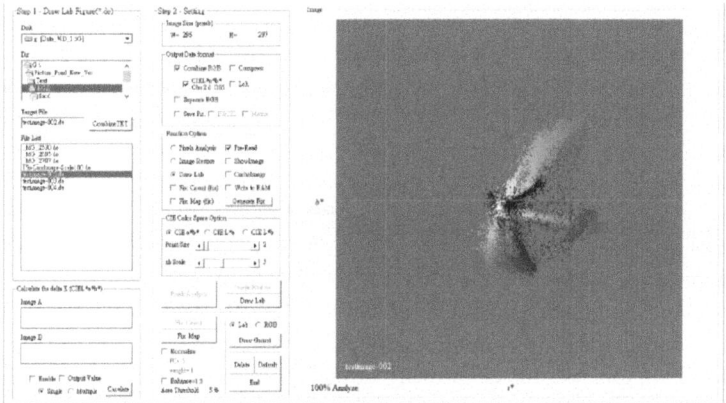

**Fig. 1.** The prototype interface of analysis tools Color analysis

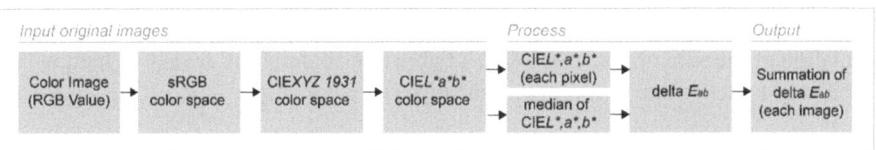

**Fig. 2.** Workflow to calculate the delta $E_{ab}$ of serial color chips

Figure 2 shows the workflow used to obtain the RGB value of each pixel in the source color chips and transfer the color value of each pixel to CIEL*a*b*. Each pixel of an image starts as RGB data that is standardized from the RGB value. Each pixel is then transformed into the CIEXYZ color space and then CIELAB L*, a*, and b* values (see Eqs. 1–6). The median of each L*, a*, and b* value would be used to calculate the distance between it and $L^*$, $a^*$, and $b^*$ value on each color chip. However, all of the calculated values of distances were reported in terms of delta $E_{ab}$ using CIELAB color difference formula (see Eq. 1). The process stage in Fig. 3 shows that the delta $E_{ab}$ was calculated from the distance between the median value, which is represented as $L_m^*$, $a_m^*$, and $b_m^*$ value and each $L_n^*$, $a_n^*$, and $b_n^*$ value on the CIELab color space. Finally, the calculation of the sum of numerous deltas $E_{ab}$ would be used to figure out the color volume of serial color chips (see Eq. 2).

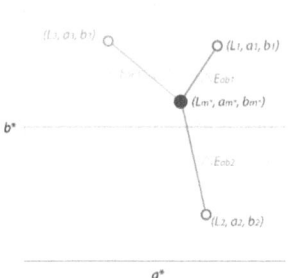

**Fig. 3.** Hints of the distance (delta $E_{ab}$) calculation between the median value and all color chips value of $L_n^*$, $a_n^*$, and $b_n^*$ in the CIELab color space. The center of the figure is the full gamut of CIELab color space. The right side of the figure is

### 3.1 Interface Design of Color Analysis Tool

The interface of the analysis tool includes three parts: importing raw data, calculating the color volume, and displaying the results of the analysis. The raw data were inputted into CIELab and the RGB value is based on the text file format (see Sect. 1 in Fig. 4). The second part of the tool was the color distribution represented in the CIELab color space to provide the volume calculation based on the color-difference formula (see Sect. 2 in Fig. 4). Figure 5 was generated from Sect. 2 of the analysis tool. Finally, the output data were obtained according to the workflow process for calculating the color image from the RGB values to CIEL*a*b*. The final step of the process is represented by Lm *, am*, and bm* values and Ln *, an*, and bn* values in the CIELab color space. The calculation of the sum of numerous deltas Eab was also output in ASCII format, which can be used to determine the color volume of serial color chips.

### 3.2 Research Case in Color Association with the Corresponding Adjectives

The interface design of the color-analysis tool was based on a preliminary study selected from a substantial number of surveys in the product-design field [4]. Eighty adjectives were selected for primary experiments. The study also calculated the volume in the CIELAB color space using the experimental method, and the participants were asked to select a single color on the calibrated monitor for each of the given adjectives. Tsai's (2018) research findings showed that the strength of association between the 80 adjectives and their respective colors could be divided into four groups, namely "extremely

**Fig. 4.** The interface layout of color analysis tools

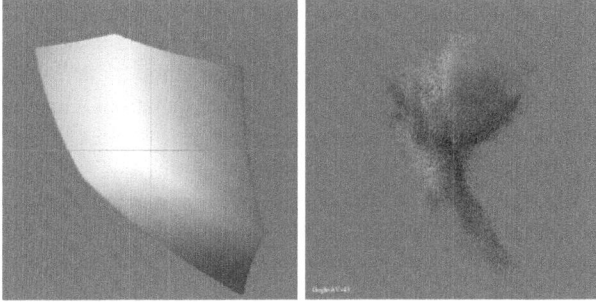

**Fig. 5.** The left side figure is the full gamut of CIE*Lab* color space. The right-side figure is the distribution represented in the CIE*Lab* color space could to provide the volume calculation.

strong," "strong," "medium," and "weak." Adjectives such as warm, sunshine, passion, cool, and shine were extremely strong in the results of smaller volumes and extremely strong groups [4, 29, 30]. In other words, adjectives with clear meanings were often associated with similar colors by different participants. The results also indicated two different distribution shapes for old and youthful adjectives in the CIELAB color space. These two adjectives also indicate semantic differences. The distribution of 'old' demonstrates a similar hue of variable lightness while "youthful" is a variety of hues with similar lightness levels (see Fig. 1). In other words, the adjective "old," with a clear meaning, is often associated with similar hues by different participants while the adjective "youthful" is associated with a different kind of daily life, thinking, and variety. The results of this preliminary study can serve as a reference and discussion base for the current research plan. For example, the colors associated with adjectives such as warm, sunshine, passionate, shine, and cool are more uniform, whereas those associated with adjectives such as modern, graceful, steady, restful, and exalted are relatively variable. Humans experience emotions through both perception and cognition [28] (Fig. 6).

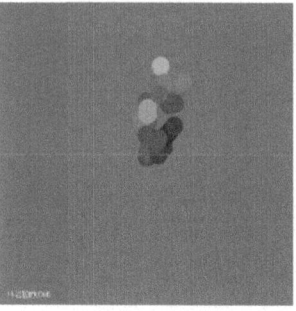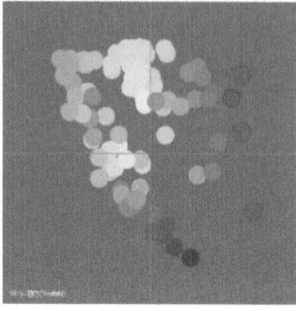

**Fig. 6.** The distribution of two different adjectives on the CIE $a*b*$ from Tsai's research results (The left side is old, and the right side is youthful)

## 4   Discussion and Conclusion

This study develops a simple method for color analysis and designs a user-friendly interface tool for analyzing color associations based on the user's needs and expert suggestions. The color analysis tool provides a rapid method for demonstrating the relationship between semantic color adjectives and color associations. However, the tool also displays the spatial distribution and volumetric presence of colors linked with semantic adjectives in the CIE*Lab* color space. According to a previous study, the prototype of the analysis tool was designed based on the rules of user interface design and to execute an easy analysis method to understand the color distribution of serial color chips in the CIE*Lab* color space.

This analysis method and tool also constructs meaning through color. Adjectives are effective for finding suitable colors. This research case focused on the relationship between semantic color adjectives and the investigation results of color associations. Both experienced and inexperienced product or graphic designers are required to undertake and reference the responsibility for a product's color selection using this tool. For example, the results of the "youthful" adjective indicated the selection of various colors for the same adjective in the CIE*Lab* color space. Thus, a product or graphic designer can use various colors for a series of product appearances. Discussions and communication on product design are a means of understanding and establishing suitable color selections. For design practice, the motivations of this analytical tool will provide a demonstration and foundation for product designers and a simpler way to meet their work requirements and needs. For academic research contributions, the analysis tool will provide a robust analysis method with a simple user interface to analyze and demonstrate the relationship between human semantic vocabulary and color associations in color psychophysics studies.

**Acknowledgement.** The authors would like to express their gratitude to the reviewers for their insightful comments. Additionally, we would like to acknowledge the contributions of three experts whose invaluable suggestions significantly enhanced both the function and interface design of the color analysis tool.

# References

1. Tsai, C.M., Guan, S.S., Tsai, W.C.: Eye movements on assessing perceptual image quality. In: Zhou, J., Salvendy, G. (eds.) ITAP 2016. LNCS, vol. 9754, pp. 378–388. Springer, Cham (2016). https://doi.org/10.1007/978-3-319-39943-0_37
2. Newell, A.: Unified Theories of Cognition. Harvard University Press, Cambridge (1990)
3. Maeder, A.J., Eckert, M.: Medical image compression: quality and performance issues. In: Pham, B., Braun, M., Maeder, A.J, Eckert, M.P. (eds.) New Approaches in Medical Image Analysis, Proc. SPIE, vol. 3747, pp. 93–101 (1999)
4. Tsai, C.M., Guan, S.S., Tsai, W.C., Zhang, Z.H.: Semantic understanding and task-oriented for image assessment. In: Zhou, J., Salvendy, G. (eds.) ITAP 2018. LNCS, vol. 10926, pp. 392–400. Springer, Cham (2018). https://doi.org/10.1007/978-3-319-92034-4_30
5. Elliot, A.J., Maier, M.A.: Color and psychological functioning. Curr. Dir. Psychol. Sci. **16**(5), 250–254 (2007)
6. Elliot, A.J., Maier, M.A.: Color psychology: effects of perceiving color on psychological functioning in humans. Annu. Rev. Psychol. **65**, 95–120 (2014)
7. Fernandez-Isabel, A., Sevilla, A.F.G., Díaz, A.: Associating colors to emotional concepts extracted from unstructured texts. In: Proceedings of E SSLLI Workshop on Computational Creativity, Concept Invention, and General Intelligence (C3GI), pp. 81–89 (2016)
8. Singh, S.: Impact of color on marketing. Manag. Decis. **44**(6), 783–789 (2006)
9. Manav, B.: Color-emotion associations and color preferences: a case study for residences. Color. Res. Appl. **32**(2), 144–151 (2007)
10. Kaya, N., Epps, H.H.: Relationship between color and emotion: a study of college students. J. Coll. Stud. **38**, 396–405 (2004)
11. Ou, L.C., Luo, M.R., Woodcock, A., Wright, A.: A study of colour emotion and colour preference. Part I: colour emotions for single colours. Color Res. Appl. **29**, 232–240 (2004)
12. Adams, F.M.: Color and Meaning: Art, Science, and Symbolism. University of California Press (2016)
13. Itten, J.: The Elements of Color: A Treatise on the Color System of Johannes Itten Based on His Book the Art of Color. Wiley, Hoboken (1973)
14. Gage, J.: Color and Culture: Practice and Meaning from Antiquity to Abstraction. University of California Press (1993)
15. Albers, J.: Interaction of Color. Yale University Press, New Haven (2006)
16. Briggs, D.J.C.: The elements of color II: the attributes of perceived color. J. Int. Color Assoc. **33**, 97–118 (2023)
17. Takata, R., Katayama, I.: Effects of angular distances between color stimuli on color conspicuity. J. Int. Color Assoc. **34**, 1–11 (2023)
18. Chen, M., Westland, S.: The effect of the color temperature of morning light exposure on wellbeing. J. Int. Color Assoc. **31**, 40–47 (2022)
19. Liao, C.C., Tsai, K.I.: Effects of different combinations of text lightness and background color on the visual comfort, recognition and preference for packaging labels. J. Int. Color Assoc. **30**, 35–49 (2022)
20. Yu, L., Westland, S., Chen, Y., Li, Z.: Color associations and consumer product-color purchase decisions. Color. Res. Appl. **46**(6), 1149–1164 (2021)
21. Chang, B., Xu, R., Watt, T.: The impact of colors on learning. In: The Proceedings of the Adult Education Research Conference (2018)
22. Palmer, S.E., Schloss, K.B.: An ecological valence theory of human color preference. Proc. Natl. Acad. Sci. **107**(19), 8877–8882 (2010)
23. Aslam, M.M.: Are you selling the right color? A cross-cultural review of color as a marketing cue. J. Mark. Commun. **12**(1), 15–30 (2006)

24. CIE: Colorimetry, Commission Internationale de l'Eclairage (CIE) Publication, Vienna, vol. 15, no. 2 (1986)
25. Brainard, D.H.: Color appearance and color difference specification. In: Elsevier Science (eds.) The Science of Color, 2nd edn., pp. 191–216. Amsterdam, Netherlands (2003)
26. Fairchild, M.D.: Colour Appearance Models. Wiley, Hoboken (2005)
27. Tsai, C.M., Guan, S.S.: Identifying regions of interest in reading an image. Displays **39**, 33–41 (2005)
28. Solso, R.L.: Cognition and the Visual Arts, A Bradford Book, pp. 101–127. The MIT Press, Cambridge (1996)
29. Tsai, C.M.: Using CIELAB colour space in analyzing the colours of Van Gogh's paintings. In: Proceeding of 2019 International Academic Conference and Exhibition on Visual Arts and Design, Nanhua University, Chiayi, Taiwan (2019)
30. Tsai, C.M., Lee, T.R., Tsai, W.C.: An empirical study on association of colors with adjectives. In: Proceeding of ACA2018 Chiang Mai: Inspiration in Color, Chiang Mai, Thailand (2018)

# Exploring the Style Images of Complex Products with Exposed Structures: Taking Aero-Engines as an Example

Qingyu Wang[1] ⓘ, Haihai Zhou[1(✉)], Lanyun Zhang[1], Siqi Wang[1], Zhishan Zhou[1], Zherui Zhang[1], Tongri Li[2], and Li Chen[1]

[1] Nanjing University of Aeronautics and Astronautics, 29 Yudao St., Nanjing 210016, People's Republic of China
`zhouhaihai@nuaa.edu.cn`
[2] AECC Shenyang Engine Research Institute, 1 Wanlian St., Shenyang 110015, People's Republic of China

**Abstract.** To assist engineers in enhancing the design aesthetics of complex products with exposed structures, this study investigates the mapping mechanism between form features and style images of complex products, taking aero-engines as an example. First, factor analysis is employed to identify the adjectives which can accurately describe the style of aero-engines. Next, the form features of exposed components are extracted through expert interviews. Then, the 113 different aero-engines are evaluated for style image ratings and assigned component attributes, and the data are analyzed using multiple regression analysis. Finally, the mapping model between the component features and style images is constructed. The results indicate that the surface quality of components and the interrelations between components are the key factors influencing the style images. The findings of this study assist engineers in designing the appearance of complex products with exposed structures and provide a feasible methodology for the design of the products.

**Keywords:** Complex Products · Style Image · Component Feature · Mapping Mechanism

## 1 Introduction

Complex products with exposed structures refer to products characterized by complex technological requirements and complex manufacturing processes, such as spacecraft, aircraft, aero-engines, automobiles, and ships [1]. The design and manufacturing of complex products exemplify the pinnacle of national design and manufacturing capabilities. With the continuous advancement of manufacturing technology, there is a growing interest in design to showcase the unique aesthetics within the technical and industrial aspects of complex products, aiming to improve their competitiveness in domestic and international markets.

A. Marcus et al. (Eds.): HCII 2024, LNCS 15380, pp. 207–218, 2025.
https://doi.org/10.1007/978-3-031-76821-7_15

However, due to the high technological and complex structural features of these products, their design is primarily carried out by professional engineers, and some engineers may lack expertise in design aesthetics. In addition, if the product aesthetics are neglected at its early design stage, making aesthetic-related modifications becomes quite challenging once manufacturing begins. Hence, conducting aesthetic evaluations of complex products during the early design phase and exploring the relations between aesthetic evaluation and form design is crucial. Existing aesthetic evaluations generally include both subjective and objective assessments [2]. Objective evaluations typically employ standardized formulas [3, 4], which already specify the relationship between design aesthetics and form design. While these formulas are applicable to consumer products, their applicability to complex products has not yet been proven. Subjective evaluation (style image) requires adjustments based on the characteristics of the products. Consequently, this study focuses on exploring the style images of complex products. The objectives of this exploratory study are as follows:

- To explore the styling dimensions that are particularly relevant to complex products with exposed structures.
- To uncover the intrinsic principles of style images, specifically by identifying the key form features that influence the styles of complex products.

## 2   Background

This section introduces the related work in two parts: the existing style image evaluation methods and the challenges of this research.

### 2.1   Existing Style Images Evaluation Methods

Style image is a subjective human perception of something objective and a mental response about a product transmitted to the brain through vision [5]. The style images of a product can be expressed in terms of relevant adjectives and is a semantic scale for the evaluation of the product [6].

Numerous scholars have explored various methods for evaluating product style images. For example, Yeping Gou et al. determined the evaluation adjectives for evaluating the style images of electric vehicles based on expert consultation [7]. McCormack et al. assessed different vehicle styles using shape grammar [8]. Zhangfan Shen et al. identified three style images related to wine glasses through clustering and factor analysis [9]. Yuan Sun et al. combined eye movement measurement data and FAHP to establish an evaluation system for assessing product aesthetic preferences [10].

Kansei Engineering methods have been applied to further investigate the impact of product form features on these evaluations. Kansei Engineering is a qualitative and quantitative approach for expressing the evaluation of a product's emotional impact and translating people's ambiguous perceptual needs into detailed design elements [11]. Tomio Jindo et al. employed the semantic differential method to derive style images of office chairs, abstracted these forms into graphical representations to examine the relationship between subjective evaluations and form design, and established a design database to aid designers [12]. Yuxin Wang et al. used abstracted forms of sewing machines and aesthetic evaluation results as training samples to construct an aesthetic evaluation system based on neural networks [13]. Hsin-Hsi Lai et al. proposed combining the grey relational analysis (GRA) model with neural networks to predict and recommend optimal design combinations for mobile phone form elements [14].

## 2.2  Challenges of This Research

There are two main challenges in answering the research question. Firstly, we need to identify the styling dimensions of complex products. In other words, the adjectives of aero-engine form should comprehensively and accurately reflect the unique aesthetic of aero-engine designs. Secondly, identifying suitable components for mapping analysis presents a challenge. Complex products have numerous and functionally intricate components, making direct analysis of all parts impractical. Exposed components, while influencing style, are constrained by their function and structure, and cannot be modified arbitrarily. Therefore, it is advisable to first select the components that may influence the image for further analysis. To ensure components meet the following criteria: They must be exposed on the surface of the aero-engine, potentially influencing the evaluation dimensions of style; They should be minimally constrained by function, allowing for direct or indirect modifications (e.g., through concealment). Finally, analyzing the mapping relationship between components and style is crucial. It is necessary to deduce the key factors influencing the style images of complex products from the mapping model.

# 3  Process and Method

The research team collected data on military and commercial aero-engines from both domestic and international sources, creating a comprehensive database. This database includes 113 typical aero-engines from 21 manufacturers, comprising 70 military and 43 commercial engines. It contains images with consistent processing and basic information for each aero-engine. The subsequent research is conducted based on this database.

## 3.1  Identification of Appropriate Product Image Adjectives

A comprehensive collection of 106 image adjectives was gathered through brainstorming and a literature review. These terms were then subjected to semantic analysis and similarity judgment discussions. Adjectives with overlapping or ambiguous meanings, which were unsuitable for describing the style image of aero-engines, were deleted or merged. This process resulted in a refined list of 20 distinct adjectives, as shown in Table 1.

Six representative aero-engines were selected from the database for the experiment, including three military engines (Model 1 to Model 3) and three commercial engines (Model 4 to Model 6), as shown in Table 2. All samples were taken from the front view or a similar perspective angle to avoid interference from angle variations.

Industrial design students were invited to evaluate the six samples on 20 styling dimensions using a questionnaire survey. Taking simplicity as an example, the scale ranged from "1 - No sense of simplicity at all" to "2 - Not quite simple", "3 - Uncertain

**Table 1.** The 20 image adjectives.

| 1-Order | 6-Weightiness | 11-Simplicity | 16-Luxury |
|---|---|---|---|
| 2-Futurism | 7-Reliability | 12-Neatness | 17-High-End |
| 3-Modernity | 8-Precision | 13-Performance | 18-Rigor |
| 4-Technology | 9-Quality | 14-Coordination | 19-Grandeur |
| 5-Strength | 10-Complexity | 15-Unity | 20-Exquisiteness |

**Table 2.** Models of aero-engines used in this experiment.

| Model 1 | Model 2 | Model 3 | Model 4 | Model 5 | Model 6 |
|---|---|---|---|---|---|
| WS Taihang | J79 | EJ 200 | GENX | Trent 200 | CF 34-10A |

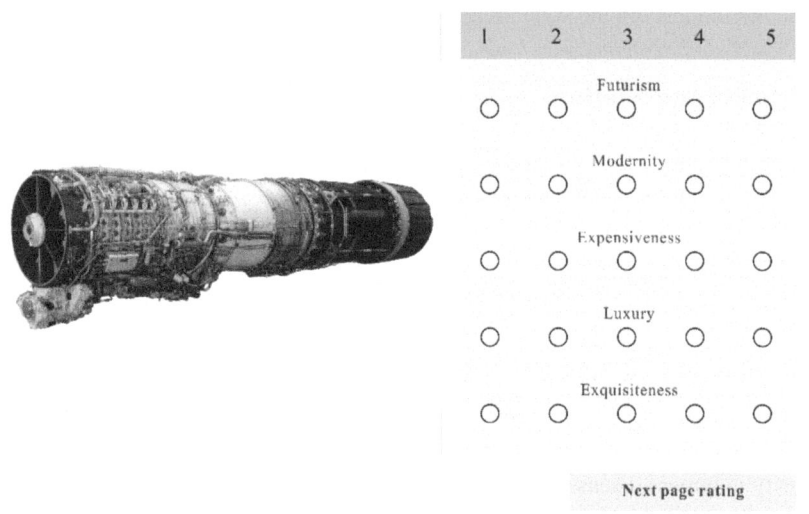

**Fig. 1.** Questionnaire writing.

if it's simple or not", "4 - Fairly simple", and "5 - Extremely simple". Figure 1 shows a portion of the questionnaire content.

The experiment collected a total of 26 valid questionnaires. Using the factor analysis program in SPSS, the data were subjected to KMO and Bartlett's tests to determine its suitability for factor analysis. The results are shown in Table 3. The KMO value obtained was 0.938, indicating that factor analysis was appropriate for the data. Additionally,

Bartlett's sphericity test revealed a significance level of Sig. $< 0.05$ ($P < 0.05$), indicating that the results were highly significant. These results indicate that the questionnaire data are suitable for factor analysis.

**Table 3.** Results of KMO and Bartlett's Test.

| Kaiser-Meyer-Olkin Measure of Sampling Adequacy | | 0.938 |
|---|---|---|
| Bartlett' Test of Sphericity | Approx. Chi-Square | 2199.441 |
| | df | 190.000 |
| | P | 0.000*** |

The data were subjected to factor analysis, yielding the total variance explained, as shown in Table 4, and the rotated component matrix, as shown in Table 5.

The extracted sums of squared loadings indicate that four factors can explain 71.554% of the original variables, as shown in Table 4. The larger the absolute value of the factor loading, the more significant the indicator is in evaluating product styling. Using an absolute factor loading threshold greater than 0.7, the first four principal component factors were retained.

**Table 4.** Total Number of Variants.

| Ingredients | Initial Eigenvalue | | | Square load volume extraction | | |
|---|---|---|---|---|---|---|
| | Total | % of Variance | Cumulative % | Total | % of Variance | Cumulative % |
| 1 | 9.864527761 | 49.3226388 | 49.3226388 | 4.933469587 | 24.66734793 | 24.66734793 |
| 2 | 2.489561658 | 12.44780829 | 61.77044709 | 4.516784378 | 22.58392189 | 47.25126982 |
| 3 | 1.106139169 | 5.530695844 | 67.30114294 | 2.701737497 | 13.50868749 | 60.75995731 |
| 4 | 0.850591759 | 4.252958794 | 71.55410173 | 2.158827047 | 10.79413523 | 71.55409254 |

According to the factor loading values, the image set was composed of 4 styling dimensions which were renamed based on the relevant features of the adjectives in each factor group: technology and quality ratings, order and coordination ratings, reliability and performance ratings, and complexity and heft ratings, as shown in Table 5. Considering the need to maintain neutral semantics, "complexity and solidity ratings" was changed to "simplicity ratings," which conveys the same evaluative meaning in a neutral tone. These dimensions were used to evaluate the stylistic imagery of aircraft engines.

In the final stage, a panel of experts consisting of three industrial designers and two engineers was invited to evaluate the aesthetics of aero-engines in four styling dimensions of 113 aircraft engines in the database. An imagery matrix of the styling dimensions for the 113 aero-engines was then created using the average scores.

**Table 5.** Matrix After Spooling.

| Factor Renaming | Product image | Factor1(24.667%) | Factor2(22.584%) | Factor3(13.509%) | Factor(10.794%) |
|---|---|---|---|---|---|
| Technology and quality ratings | Futurism | **0.777** | 0.305 | 0.271 | -0.076 |
| | Modernity | **0.75** | 0.305 | 0.322 | -0.075 |
| | Expensiveness | **0.685** | 0.104 | 0.23 | 0.15 |
| | Luxury | **0.69** | 0.478 | 0.241 | -0.004 |
| | Exquisiteness | **0.676** | 0.456 | 0.19 | -0.206 |
| | Technology | **0.788** | 0.244 | 0.242 | 0.002 |
| | Precision | **0.579** | 0.374 | 0.068 | 0.26 |
| | Quality | **0.623** | 0.548 | 0.178 | -0.086 |
| Order and coordination ratings | Uniformity | 0.292 | **0.763** | 0.144 | -0.146 |
| | Simplicity | 0.409 | **0.607** | 0.242 | -0.382 |
| | Regularity | 0.279 | **0.779** | 0.239 | -0.15 |
| | Order | 0.265 | **0.771** | 0.296 | -0.111 |
| | Harmony | 0.335 | **0.769** | 0.135 | -0.013 |
| Reliability and performance ratings | Rigor | 0.374 | 0.414 | **0.612** | 0.063 |
| | Magnitude | 0.356 | 0.437 | **0.52** | 0.148 |
| | Reliability | 0.186 | 0.412 | **0.742** | -0.004 |
| | Power | 0.185 | 0.04 | **0.522** | 0.593 |
| | Performance | 0.405 | 0.085 | **0.739** | 0.02 |
| Simplicity ratings | Complexity | 0.045 | -0.311 | -0.112 | **0.807** |
| | Heft | -0.072 | -0.044 | 0.115 | **0.881** |

## 3.2 Extraction of Component Features

This stage aimed to extract component features that may be associated with style images. In this experiment, five aero-engine engineers with over 10 years of experience were invited for semi-structured interviews. The interviews focused on "visible components of aero-engines and their related features (such as size, color, material, etc.)". Based on the interview, a preliminary list of common component features was generated (Table 6), excluding those that were completely unmodifiable due to functional constraints (features marked with crosses in table 6). Ultimately, the final 18 component features were retained.

At the end of this stage, aero-engine engineers assessed the 18 component features of the 113 aircraft engines in the database. Each feature was assigned a value of "1" if the engine possessed the feature or "0" if it did not. Then, a component matrix for the 113 aircraft engines was derived.

**Table 6.** Common component features of aero-engine.

| Functional component | Feature | |
|---|---|---|
| Casing | Material | Titanium alloy |
| | | Composite material |
| | Structure | Annular casing × |
| | | Split casing × |
| | Processing technology | Casting |
| | | Sheet metal |
| | | Chemical milling |
| | Surface treatment | Coating polishing |
| | | Sandblasting matte |
| Nozzle | Fixed nozzle × | |
| | Adjustable nozzle | Axisymmetric adjustable nozzle × |
| | | Binary symmetric adjustable nozzle × |
| Duct | Material | Stainless steel × |
| | | Titanium alloy × |
| | Diameter | Thick |
| | | Thin |
| | Layer stacking | One layer × |
| | | Two layers × |
| | | Three layers × |
| Cable | Color | Accent color |
| | | Thin |
| | Density | Sparse |
| | | Dense |
| | Cable branching | Present × |
| | | Absent × |
| Accessory | Size | Large |
| | | Small |
| Fastener | Material | Metal |
| | | Rubber |
| | | Composite material |

## 4 Results

Multiple linear regression is a generalization of linear regression by considering more than one independent variable, and a specific case of general linear models formed by restricting the number of dependent variables to one. It was used to explain the linear relationship between independent variables and dependent variables. Regression analysis was conducted using the 18 component features as independent variables and the four styling dimensions as dependent variables. Table 7 illustrates the regression analysis results using "technology and quality ratings" as an example. The model passes F-test at a significance level below 5% (F = 2.619, p = 0.006 < 0.05).

**Table 7.** Regression analysis results of technology and quality ratings.

| | Unstandardized Coefficients | | Standardized Coefficients | $t$ | $p$ |
|---|---|---|---|---|---|
| | B | Std. Error | Beta | | |
| Constant | 1.790 | 0.123 | - | 14.605 | 0.000** |
| Casing-Sheet metal | 0.371 | 0.253 | 0.155 | 1.470 | 0.146 |
| Casing-Casting | 0.314 | 0.183 | 0.200 | 1.717 | 0.091 |
| Casing-Chemical milling | 1.178 | 0.556 | 0.226 | 2.119 | 0.038* |
| Casing-Coating polishing | 0.088 | 0.158 | 0.070 | 0.559 | 0.578 |
| Casing-Sandblasting matte | -0.331 | 0.149 | -0.265 | -2.216 | 0.030* |
| Fastener-Metal | -0.080 | 0.192 | -0.050 | -0.418 | 0.677 |
| Fastener-Rubber | 0.006 | 0.152 | 0.005 | 0.041 | 0.967 |
| Fastener-Composite material | -0.028 | 0.232 | -0.013 | -0.120 | 0.905 |
| Casing-Titanium alloy | 0.101 | 0.145 | 0.076 | 0.700 | 0.486 |
| Casing-Composite material | 0.220 | 0.189 | 0.132 | 1.231 | 0.065 |
| Cable-Accent color | 0.046 | 0.204 | 0.024 | 0.226 | 0.822 |
| Cable-Coordinating color | 0.362 | 0.170 | 0.231 | 2.128 | 0.037* |
| Accessory-Large | 0.022 | 0.135 | 0.017 | 0.164 | 0.870 |
| Accessory-Small | -0.253 | 0.112 | -0.236 | -1.968 | 0.186 |
| Cable-Dense | 0.165 | 0.147 | 0.132 | 1.123 | 0.265 |
| Cable-Sparse | -0.742 | 0.536 | -0.486 | -1.539 | 0.362 |
| Duct-Thin | -0.094 | 0.208 | -0.051 | 0.453 | 0.652 |
| Duct-Thick | -0.367 | 0.140 | -0.282 | -2.610 | 0.011* |
| $R^2$ | 0.319 | | | | |
| Adjusted $R^2$ | 0.197 | | | | |
| F | $F(12,67)=2.619, p=0.006$ | | | | |
| D-W statistic | 2.325 | | | | |

\* $p<0.05$ ** $p<0.01$

The results indicate that the following four key component features: casing processing technology, casing surface treatment, cable color, and duct diameter, have a significant impact on technology and quality ratings (P < 0.05). Components with positive regression coefficients should be adopted in design to enhance the "technology and quality" image perception, while those with negative coefficients should be minimized. Therefore, the study provides the following recommendations, ranked by the influence value (β) from highest to lowest:

- Recommend using coating polishing for casing surface treatment, minimizing the use of sandblasting matte.
- Recommend using composite materials for fasteners.
- Prioritize chemical milling for casing processing, with sheet metal as a secondary option and casting as the last resort.
- Maintain an overall color scheme, with selective use of bright colors for cables.

Regression analyses were also conducted for the remaining three style dimensions and their associated component features. Due to space limitations, these analyses are not detailed here. Table 8 summarizes the mapping relationship. Based on these results, corresponding component design recommendations are provided to enhance the design aesthetics.

**Table 8.** Mapping relationship of the four style dimensions to key component features.

| Style image | Components features | Design recommendations |
|---|---|---|
| Simplicity ratings | 1. Cable-Color<br>2. Accessory-Size | 1. Ensure uniformity in cable colors as much as possible<br>2. Minimize the exposure of larger attachments by concealing them as much as possible |
| Reliability and performance ratings | 1. Casing-Processing technology<br>2. Cable-Density<br>3. Accessory-Size | 1. Prioritize chemical milling for casing processing, with sheet metal as a secondary option and casting as the last resort<br>2. Arrange cables in a tight and orderly manner whenever possible<br>3. Minimize the exposure of larger attachments by concealing them as much as possible |
| Order and coordination ratings | 1. Cable-Density<br>2. Cable-Color | 1. Arrange cables in a tight and orderly manner whenever possible<br>2. Ensure uniformity in cable colors as much as possible |

(*continued*)

**Table 8.** (*continued*)

| Style image | Components features | Design recommendations |
|---|---|---|
| Technology and quality ratings | 1. Casing-Surface treatment<br>2. Fastener-Material<br>3. Casing-Processing technology<br>4. Cable-Color | 1. Recommend using coating polishing for casing surface treatment, minimizing the use of sandblasting matte<br>2. Recommend using composite materials for fasteners<br>3. Prioritize chemical milling for casing processing, with sheet metal as a secondary option and casting as the last resort<br>4. Maintain an overall color scheme, with selective use of bright colors for cables |

## 5 Discussion

Unlike consumer products, complex products, especially those with exposed intricate structures, have a more multidimensional style image space. The styling dimensions of such products cannot be determined through simple methods like expert analysis. Instead, dimensionality reduction techniques are required to distill the essence of their style images. This study employs factor analysis to explore four styling dimensions: technology and quality ratings, order and coordination ratings, reliability and performance ratings, and simplicity ratings.

The regression analysis conducted reveals that both the surface quality of components and the interrelations between components play pivotal roles in the products' image style. Surface quality refers to factors such as processing techniques and material selection. The interrelations between components can be categorized into two types: contrasts and harmonies in form (e.g., size of attachments), as well as contrasts and harmonies in color (e.g., cable color).

The results show that simpler component features are more beneficial in enhancing aesthetic style. For example, it is recommended to use coating polishing for casing surface treatment and to minimize the use of sandblasting matte. The rationale behind this is that the numerous exposed components of complex products are prone to creating a sense of information overload. Therefore, in aero-engine design, simplifying component features enhances the overall coherence and unity of the product, reducing cognitive load and improving the subjective aesthetic perception.

# 6   Conclusion

This study explores the styling dimensions of aero-engines and the mapping relationship between the component features and the style images. The research conclusions have been applied to the development of an aesthetic evaluation system for aero-engines, as shown in Fig. 2. This study aids engineers in grasping better product styles and making targeted component modifications to enhance the aesthetics of complex product designs, which plays a crucial role in complex product development field.

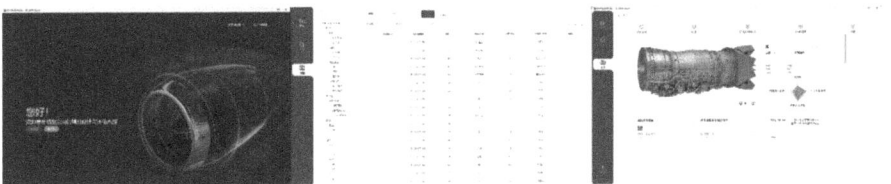

**Fig. 2.** Partial interface of the aero-engine aesthetic evaluation system.

**Acknowledgments.** This work is supported by the Project of Humanities and Social Sciences Research of the Ministry of Education of China (Grant No. 22YJEZH002).

# References

1. Guohong, X., Bohu, L., Xiaoqing, T., et al.: Research and application of technologies for complex system (product) integrated manufacturing engineering. Eng. Sci. **2005**, 49–55 (2005)
2. Papachristos, E., Avouris, N.: The subjective and objective nature of website aesthetic impressions. In: Human-Computer Interaction–INTERACT 2009: 12th IFIP TC 13 International Conference. Uppsala, Sweden, August 24–28, 2009, Proceedings, Part I, vol. 12, pp. 119–122. Springer, Berlin Heidelberg (2009)
3. Birkhoff, G.D.: Aesthetic measure. Harvard University Press, Cambridge (1933)
4. Ngo, D.C.L., Teo, L.S., Byrne, J.G.: Modelling interface aesthetics. Inf. Sci. **152**, 25–46 (2003)
5. Nasution, S., Hidayati, J., Nissa, N.A., et al.: Redesign packaging on Aloe Vera bottle product based on kansei engineering. In: IOP Conference Series: Materials Science and Engineering, vol. 1122, no.1, p. 012117. IOP Publishing (2021)
6. Yang, Y., Wang, B., Jiang, C., et al.: Relationship between individual perceptual feature demand and satisfaction in the small assistant robot modeling design. In: Man-Machine-Environment System Engineering: Proceedings of the 20th International Conference on MMESE, pp. 419–427. Springer, Singapore (2020)
7. Gou, Y., Ye, J.: Study on youthful electric two-wheeled vehicle modeling based on perceptual imagery. In: International Conference on Human-Computer Interaction, pp. 189–197. Springer, Cham (2022)
8. Vogel, C.M.: Speaking the Buick language: capturing, understanding, and exploring brand identity with shape. Des. Stud. **25**(1), 99–110 (2004)

9. Shen, Z., Xue, C., Zhang, J., et al.: Research on the style of product shape based on NURBS curve. In: Design. User Experience, and Usability: Theory, Methodology, and Management: 6th International Conference, DUXU 2017, Held as Part of HCI International 2017, Vancouver, BC, Canada, July 9–14, 2017, Proceedings, Part I, vol. 6, pp. 298–305. Springer, Cham (2017)

10. Sun, Y., Lin, Z., Dl, W., et al.: Product perceptual cognition measurement method based on eye movement data and FAHP. J. Dalian Univ. Technol. **60**(6), 33–39 (2020)

11. Lévy, P.D.: Beyond kansei engineering: the emancipation of kansei design. Int. J. Des. **7**(2), 83–94 (2013)

12. Jindo, T., Hirasago, K., Nagamachi, M.: Development of a design support system for office chairs using 3-D graphics. Int. J. Ind. Ergon. **15**(1), 49–62 (1995)

13. Yuxin, W.: Aesthetic feature-based parametric shape design and evaluation of products. J. Comput. Aided Des. Comput. Graph. **19**(11), 1447 (2007)

14. Lai, H.H., Lin, Y.C., Yeh, C.H.: Form design of product image using grey relational analysis and neural network models. Comput. Oper. Res. **32**(10), 2689–2711 (2005)

# Video2Comic: A Dynamic Comic Editor with Video Clips

Zhengyang Wang[1], Xusheng Du[1], Tsukasa Fukusato[2(✉)], and Haoran Xie[1]

[1] Japan Advanced Institute of Science and Technology, Nomi, Ishikawa 923-1211, Japan
[2] Waseda University, Shinjuku, Tokyo 169-8555, Japan
tsukasafukusato@waseda.jp

**Abstract.** Dynamic comics are widely used in video production because they enable people to efficiently summarize video sequences. However, its design process is currently done manually and requires special skills such as segmenting video sequence and layout, which often makes it inaccessible to people, especially novices. In this paper, we propose an interactive tool that allows users to convert input videos into dynamic comics. First, the user specifies the segmentation points while watching an input video. The system then automatically computes the locations of comic panels using a parametric layout model and composites the set of video segments. To investigate the effectiveness of the proposed system, we conducted a user study where people used our system and provided feedback on dynamic comic design tools.

**Keywords:** Dynamic comics · Video segmentation · Parametric layout model

## 1 Introduction

Converting video sequences into comics is a powerful way to efficiently understand their stories and enables people to have unique experiences due to the different sizes and shapes of comic panels [6,10,13,17]. However, compared to comics, video sequences contain temporal information about the story, so important information about the story may be lost when making comics. Then, in recent years, comic designers have extended the traditional comics to past video segments of a few seconds onto each comic panel instead of static images, called "dynamic" comics. The advantage of dynamic comics is that characters' physical/emotional movements and camera work in videos can be easily represented. In addition, dynamic comics can create a multimodal narrative space where time and space collaboratively influence the unfolding of the story. However, even though various algorithms have been proposed for automatically generating standard comics (= static comics) from image/video sequences [7,9,19], it remains challenging to make dynamic comics. The main reason is that it requires special skills (i.e., image/video manipulation while imagining compositions and

A. Marcus et al. (Eds.): HCII 2024, LNCS 15380, pp. 219–230, 2025.
https://doi.org/10.1007/978-3-031-76821-7_16

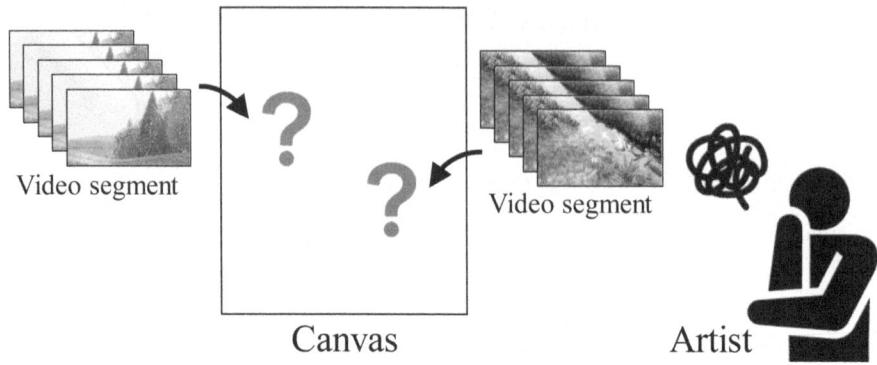

**Fig. 1.** The difficulties in designing dynamic comics. An artist must manually prepare several video segments, and design a natural-looking comic layout while imaging characters' movements and readers' gaze

final designs) and users must repeat (1) switching between video editing tools (e.g., Adobe Premiere[1]) and image editing tools (e.g., Adobe Photoshop[2] and Clip Studio Paint[3]) and (2) checking results until the user is satisfied, which is a time-consuming and tedious process (see Fig. 1). On top of that, the state-of-the-art technologies using artificial intelligence methods fall short in interpreting users' detailed intentions in video editing [11,16] and comic layout creation [20], and the generated results may lack precise control capabilities. Therefore, the present paper aims at reducing the manual effort required to make dynamic comics.

In this paper, we propose a first-step system that enables users, even if non-professional users, to interactively design dynamic comics from video sequences, by integrating a simple video editor into a comic layout editor. First, users manually prepare video segments on the video editor and make comic layouts using a parametric model. Then, the system automatically assigns the video segments to each panel. Our system can combine various existing methods such as automatic segmentation [7].

## 2   Related Work

### 2.1   Dynamic Comics

Unlike traditional static comics, dynamic comics have information about actual character movements and camera work in each panel, so various artists and researchers have been attracting attention as an approach for animation browsing and abstraction [5]. However, to our knowledge, there is no software specialized

---

[1] https://www.adobe.com/products/premiere.html.

[2] https://www.adobe.com/products/photoshop.html.

[3] https://www.clipstudio.net/en/.

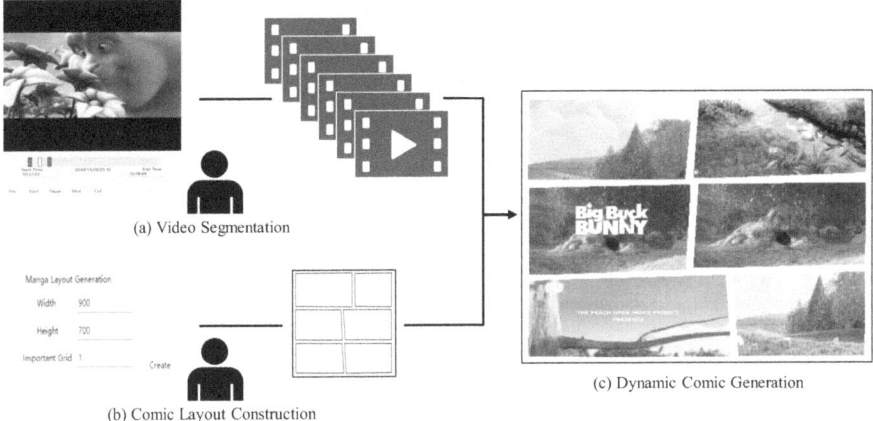

**Fig. 2.** The framework of our proposed system. Users (a) segment input videos into several sequences, and (b) set the size of comics and which segment is important. By assigning the video segments to the panels, this system automatically generates dynamic comics. This input video is from "Big Buck Bunny" © Blender Foundation)

for designing dynamic comics, so users must use both video processing software for video segmentation and image processing software for comic layout. We then implement a design tool for dynamic comics while enhancing users' creativity.

### 2.2 Comic Layout Design Support

Several techniques have been proposed to support comic design [1,14,15,21]. Especially, the layout of comic panels makes it easier for readers to understand the comics' story and the artists' worldview, but we must utilize pre-defined layout templates [4,7] or simple rules [2,3,8,18]. However, these approaches are unsuitable for interactively adjusting the layout. Building on these approaches, we then add controllability to the layout generation process.

## 3    Proposed System

Our system consists primarily of three components: the video editor, the comic layout editor, and the dynamic comic generation. In the process of video editing, we provide a simple interface to segment video sequences. In the process of comic layout, the system allows users to simply handle the shape of comic panels. And, in the process of comic generation, the system automatically resizes video segments and export dynamic comics. Please refer to the supplementary video[4] for more details.

---

[4] https://www.youtube.com/watch?v=pIfS3x-m47o.

**Fig. 3.** Screenshot of our system showing (1, 2) video player/editor, (3) layout construction panel, and (4) dynamic comic generation panel

## 3.1    User Interface

Our prototype system was implemented using a standard PyQt6, as shown in Fig. 3. Our system incorporates the following functions to facilitate the video segmentation and layout construction.

**Video Player/Editor.** The editor consists of the same functions as a traditional video player: load, play, pause, stop videos, adjust volume, full-screen mode, drag and drop, and seek bar. And, when the user sets starting and end times on the seek bar, the system generates a video segment and exports it. In addition, the editor has a function to adjust the length of each segment by changing the playback speed (see Fig. 4). Note that it is possible to apply automatic video segmentation methods to this step.

**Comic Layout Construction Panel.** The user inputs the canvas *width/height* and the index of the important panel, and the system then determines the comic layout and the location/size of each comic panel (see Fig. 5). Note that the number of comic panels in the output result is fixed at 6.

**Fig. 4.** Our video editor which enables users to manually segment the input video sequence and adjust its playback speed

**Comic Creation Panel.** When users click the "Merge" button, the system automatically generates dynamic comics based on multiple video segments and the user-specified comic layouts, as shown in Fig. 6.

## 3.2    Parametric Layout Model

Although existing methods often prepare template models to decide the final comic layout [4,7], it is difficult to interactively design artistic panel shapes like actual comics. Therefore, we make a parametric layout model based on the following algorithm.

The layout model consists of two horizontal lines that divide the white canvas ($width \times height$) into thirds, and three vertical lines dividing each area in half. We consider the decided six regions as comic panels, and the system computes the locations of each panel using the four corners of the canvas and the

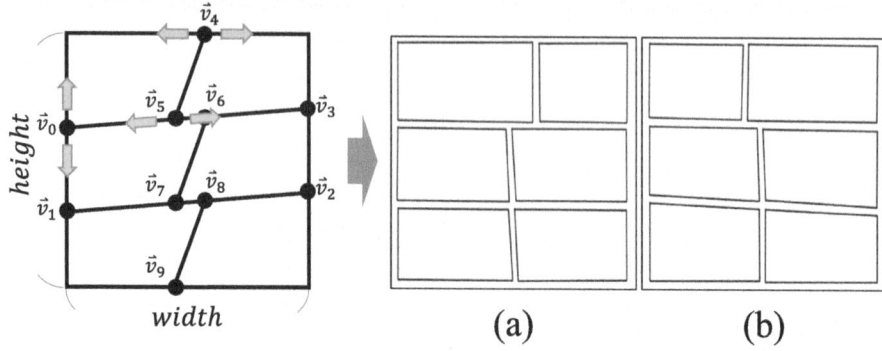

**Fig. 5.** Examples of generated layouts from the parametric model (a) when the first panel is important and (b) when the second panel is important. The panels are arranged in a left-to-right flow

**Fig. 6.** An example of (b) dynamic comics with (a) the constructed layout

intersection coordinates of each line. The system has several parameters to move the endpoint of each horizontal line up/down (i.e., $v_0$, $v_1$, $v_2$, and $v_3$ in Fig. 5) and move the endpoint of each vertical line left/right (i.e., $v_4$, $v_5$, ..., and $v_9$ in Fig. 5). In addition, to augment the layout variation, we add two functions to (1) enlarge important panels specified by the user (see Fig. 5(a, b)), and (2) set random values to these parameters when pressing the "create" button(see Fig. 3). Our system can export the generated layout in a common file format (.png).

### 3.3  Dynamic Comic Generation

Based on the locations of each panel, we automatically resize each video segment to fit the bounding box of the corresponding panel and crop it to fit the panel boundaries by using the OpenCV library. Note that the user can also change the pasting order of segments by clicking the mouse cursor directly on the comic panel, as shown in Fig. 6. Our system can also export the generated comic in

**Fig. 7.** Comparing dynamic comics using (a) PS, (b) PR, and (c, d) our system

a common file format (.mp4), making it possible to arrange them in existing software.

## 4    Interviews with Image/Video Creators

We assessed whether our system provides a more efficient and user-friendly alternative to existing tools such as Adobe Photoshop (PS) and Adobe Premiere (PR). We invited two participants who have extensive experience in making images/videos with PS and PR. Each user was asked to design dynamic comics using both PS, PR and our system. This task includes segmenting video sequences, making the comic layout from scratch, and embedding the video segments in each comic panel. In this experiment, we meticulously collected participants' operations on PS, PR, and our system, including the production process, the production time, and the visual quality of final outcomes.

Figure 7 shows several examples of dynamic comics designed by participants using our system. Next, we discuss the participants' results. The average production time was 7 min to create a dynamic comic using our system, compared to about 10 min using PS and PR. From the result, it is thought that our software has the potential to increase efficiency. In addition, both participants commented that our system is easy to learn and notably reduces time switching between PS and PR, as well as for creating comic layouts and embedding videos into comic panels. These comments highlight our system was able to provide a more efficient workflow while each function in our system (e.g., comic layout function) is still simple.

## 5    User Study

To evaluate the effectiveness of our system, we conducted a user study involving a total of 12 participants (six male and six female graduate students). They were asked to design dynamic comics and fill out a post-experiment questionnaire.

**Fig. 8.** Examples of dynamic comics created by users using our system

The questionnaire consists of evaluating (i) the overall usability of our system based on the System Usability Scale (SUS) and (ii) the usability of each function in our system, thereby providing a comprehensive examination of its performance from multiple perspectives. Figure 8 shows examples of dynamic comics generated by the participants.

## 5.1  Subjective Evaluation

Table 1 shows the responses of the participants using the SUS metrics. From the result, our system scored 92.5 out of 100, which indicated that the overall usability of our system was excellent.

We will now discuss the results in more detail. A substantial majority of 95.0% found the interface elements easy to use. In term of the learnability (Q4 & Q10), our system achieved an impressive score of 90.625 out of 100. This indicates that participants perceived our system to be easily learned without significant reliance on technical support and required a minimal initial learning curve before becoming competent. Furthermore, 90.0% and an equivalent proportion of 97.6% respectively attested to the well-integrated functionality within the system and their confidence in utilizing it. In terms of the sub-scale excluding Q4 & Q10, our system has a score of 85.156, indicating strong performance.

**Table 1.** Results of the post-experiment SUS metrics questionnaire. ⇑ indicates that higher scores are better; ⇓ for the other case. The total score is 92.5 out of 100

| | Questions | Mean | SD |
|---|---|---|---|
| 1 | I would like to use this system frequently. ⇑ | 4.75 | 0.62 |
| 2 | I found this system unnecessarily complex. ⇓ | 1.41 | 0.51 |
| 3 | This system was easy to use. ⇑ | 4.75 | 0.45 |
| 4 | I would need the support of a technical person to be able to use this system. ⇓ | 1.58 | 0.51 |
| 5 | I found the various functions in this system were well integrated. ⇑ | 4.50 | 0.90 |
| 6 | I thought there was too much inconsistency in this system. ⇓ | 1.16 | 0.38 |
| 7 | I would imagine that most people would learn to use this system very quickly. ⇑ | 4.67 | 0.49 |
| 8 | I found this system very cumbersome to use. ⇓ | 1.16 | 0.38 |
| 9 | I felt very confident in using this system. ⇑ | 4.88 | 0.57 |
| 10 | I needed to learn a lot of things before I could get going with this system. ⇓ | 1.16 | 0.38 |

**Table 2.** Results and analysis of specific functions evaluation questionnaires

| | Questions | Mean | SD |
|---|---|---|---|
| 1 | I find the import video feature simple and easy to use. | 4.57 | 0.38 |
| 2 | I find the video playback feature very user-friendly. | 4.50 | 0.62 |
| 3 | I find the drag and drop feature of the timeline easy to use. | 4.23 | 0.52 |
| 4 | I think the function of editing is easy to use. | 4.42 | 0.38 |
| 5 | I think the function to generate comic layout is easy to use. | 4.35 | 0.66 |
| 6 | I find it useful to use the function to generate dynamic comics. | 4.35 | 0.65 |

In their text comments as well, we confirm that all participants were satisfied with the overall ease of use of the proposed system and answered it is possible to learn how to operate it.

## 5.2 Specific Functions Evaluation

Table 2 shows the post-experiment questionnaire results about each function. Regarding video processing functionalities, we received positive feedback. In terms of the "Video Import" feature, the mean value (Mean) and the standard deviation (SD) are 4.57 and 0.38 respectively, which indicates that users found this function relatively easy to use and intuitive. The "Video Playback" function received a high rating with a mean value of 4.50 ($SD = 0.62$), which suggests a high level of user satisfaction with its ease of use. The "Drag-and-Drop Timeline Editing" feature stood out with an average score of 4.23 ($SD = 0.52$), strongly suggesting that users considered this functionality particularly easy to grasp and flexible during video editing tasks. In terms of editing and layout generation, the "Editing Tools" also garnered substantial favorable reviews, achieving an average rating of 4.42 ($SD = 0.38$), demonstrating widespread approval for their usability. However, while the "Layout Generation" function obtained a mean score of 4.35 ($SD = 0.66$), it is thought that some users experienced more complexity or inconvenience compared to other features. Apparently, the feature to generate dynamic comics was highly praised by users for its usefulness, with a mean rating of 4.35 ($SD = 0.65$).

In summary, our study through quantitative assessment reveals that many of the designed software's features have been well-received by users, with particular excellence demonstrated by those related to video manipulation and comic layout creation. Nonetheless, there is room for improvement in the user experience of the "Layout Generation" feature to align it with the performance of the standout features. Future work should focus on refining this aspect to ensure balanced development across the product's overall user experience and ultimately enhance user satisfaction.

## 6   Limitations and Future Work

The current implementation does not allow users to change the number of final panel layouts. It might be interesting to explore ways to construct a more artistic layout model by using Voronoi diagrams or existing comic data [12,19]. We also plan to extend the existing keyframe detection method [7] to automatically prepare video segments from the input video sequences.

## 7   Conclusion

This paper has presented the first step system to make dynamic comics from video sequences. Our proposed tool represents a significant contribution to the field, as it reduces the complexity associated with traditional methods and enhances accessibility for a broader audience. By integrating key technologies such as comic layout generation, video clipping, and image synthesis, we have strived to streamline the workflow and provide a user-friendly interface that fosters ease of use and understanding.

Looking ahead, the development of dynamic comics holds promising potential for further innovation and creative exploration. Future research efforts could focus on enhancing the sophistication of comic layout algorithms, integrating advanced video editing functionalities, and exploring collaborative features that enable users to create dynamic comics collectively.

**Acknowledgment.** This research was supported by Waseda University Grant for Special Research Projects (Project number: 2024C-444).

# References

1. Adobe Research Imagination Lab: Comic kit (2018). https://exchange.adobe.com/apps/cc/13159/comic-kit

2. Boreczky, J.S., Girgensohn, A., Golovchinsky, G., Uchihashi, S.: An interactive comic book presentation for exploring video. In: Proceedings of the SIGCHI Conference on Human Factors in Computing Systems (CHI), pp. 185–192. ACM, New York (2000). https://doi.org/10.1145/332040.332428

3. Calic, J., Gibson, D.P., Campbell, N.W.: Efficient layout of comic-like video summaries. IEEE Trans. Circ. Syst. Video Technol. (TCSVT) $17$(7), 931–936 (2007). https://doi.org/10.1109/TCSVT.2007.897466

4. Caplin, S.: Art and Design in Photoshop. Routledge, Abingdon (2012)

5. Choi, M.G., Noh, S.T., Komura, T., Igarashi, T.: Dynamic comics for hierarchical abstraction of 3d animation data. Comput. Graph. Forum (CGF) $32$(7), 1–9 (2013). https://doi.org/10.1111/cgf.12206

6. Chun, B.-K., Ryu, D.-S., Hwang, W.-I., Cho, H.-G.: An automated procedure for word balloon placement in cinema comics. In: Bebis, G., et al. (eds.) ISVC 2006. LNCS, vol. 4292, pp. 576–585. Springer, Heidelberg (2006). https://doi.org/10.1007/11919629_58

7. Fukusato, T., Hirai, T., Kawamura, S., Morishima, S.: Computational cartoonist: a comic-style video summarization system for anime films. In: Tian, Q., Sebe, N., Qi, G.-J., Huet, B., Hong, R., Liu, X. (eds.) MMM 2016. LNCS, vol. 9516, pp. 42–50. Springer, Cham (2016). https://doi.org/10.1007/978-3-319-27671-7_4

8. Herranz, L., Calic, J., Sanchez, J.M.M., Mrak, M.: Scalable comic-like video summaries and layout disturbance. IEEE Trans. Multimedia (TMM) $14$(4), 1290–1297 (2012). https://doi.org/10.1109/TMM.2012.2192917

9. Jing, G., Hu, Y., Guo, Y., Yu, Y., Wang, W.: Content-aware video2comics with manga-style layout. IEEE Trans. Multimedia (TMM) $17$(12), 2122–2133 (2015). https://doi.org/10.1109/TMM.2015.2474263

10. Magnussen, A., Christiansen, H.: Comics and Culture: Analytical and Theoretical Approaches to Comics. Museum Tusculanum press, Copenhagen (2000)

11. Moon, W., Hyun, S., Park, S., Park, D., Heo, J.P.: Query-dependent video representation for moment retrieval and highlight detection. In: Proceedings of the IEEE/CVF Conference on Computer Vision and Pattern Recognition (CVPR), pp. 23023–23033. IEEE, Vancouver (2023). https://doi.org/10.1109/CVPR52729.2023.02205

12. Pang, X., Cao, Y., Lau, R.W., Chan, A.B.: A robust panel extraction method for manga. In: Proceedings of the 22nd ACM International Conference on Multimedia (MM), pp. 1125–1128. ACM (2014)

13. Preu, J., Loviscach, J.: From movie to comic, informed by the screenplay. In: ACM SIGGRAPH 2007 Posters, p. 99-es. ACM, New York (2007). https://doi.org/10.1145/1280720.1280828

14. Qu, Y., Pang, W.M., Wong, T., Heng, P.A.: Richness-preserving manga screening. ACM Trans. Graph. (TOG) $27$(5), 155:1–155:8 (2008). https://doi.org/10.1145/1409060.1409108

15. Qu, Y., Wong, T.T., Heng, P.A.: Manga colorization. ACM Trans. Graph. (TOG) $25$(3), 1214–1220 (2006). https://doi.org/10.1145/1141911.1142017

16. Saini, P., Kumar, K., Kashid, S., Saini, A., Negi, A.: Video summarization using deep learning techniques: a detailed analysis and investigation. Artif. Intell. Rev. $56$(11), 12347–12385 (2023). https://doi.org/10.1007/s10462-023-10444-0

17. Shamir, A., Rubinstein, M., Levinboim, T.: Generating comics from 3d interactive computer graphics. IEEE Comput. Graph. Appl. (CG&A) **26**(3), 53–61 (2006). https://doi.org/10.1109/MCG.2006.58
18. Takahashi, Y., Nitta, N., Babaguchi, N.: Automatic video summarization of sports videos using metadata. In: Aizawa, K., Nakamura, Y., Satoh, S. (eds.) PCM 2004. LNCS, vol. 3332, pp. 272–280. Springer, Heidelberg (2004). https://doi.org/10.1007/978-3-540-30542-2_34
19. Ying, C., Chan, A.B., Lau, R.W.H.: Automatic stylistic manga layout. ACM Trans. Graph. (TOG) **31**(6), 141:1–141:10 (2012). https://doi.org/10.1145/2366145.2366160
20. Zhang, L., Rao, A., Agrawala, M.: Adding conditional control to text-to-image diffusion models. In: Proceedings of the IEEE/CVF International Conference on Computer Vision (ICCV), pp. 3836–3847. IEEE, Paris (2023). https://doi.org/10.1109/ICCV51070.2023.00355
21. Zhang, L., Wang, X., Fan, Q., Ji, Y., Liu, C.: Generating manga from illustrations via mimicking manga creation workflow. In: Proceedings of the IEEE/CVF Conference on Computer Vision and Pattern Recognition (CVPR), pp. 5642–5651. IEEE (2021)

# Research on the Subway Social Design of Single Youths in Shanghai

Mingshi Xu[(✉)] and Shenhao Shang

Faculty of Humanities and Arts, Macau University of Science and Technology, Macau 990780, China
326873375@qq.com

**Abstract.** Starting from the increasing rate of singlehood among Chinese youth, this study aims to propose effective measures to help single young adults in Shanghai broaden their social channels by utilizing commuting media. Specifically, it explores the feasibility of using the subway as a medium to facilitate interaction among single young professionals in the workplace. The study employs literature research and semi-structured interviews as methods and introduces innovative ways to enhance interaction within subway carriages. By combining online social networking with offline subway environments, social barriers can be broken down, providing a new social platform for single young adults. This approach brings new perspectives and methods to the field of human-computer interaction, driving the development and innovation of related technologies. After implementation, the designed solution can collect a wealth of data on user behavior, social interactions, and more, thereby enriching the field of human-computer interaction.

**Keywords:** subway carriages · single young adults · social interaction · experience design

## 1 Introduction

In recent years, single young professionals in big cities have increasingly turned to online dating as a way to find a partner due to their limited social circles and fast-paced lifestyles. The internet has broken geographical, temporal, and social barriers, effectively expanding their social circles. Online dating allows those who struggle with social interaction and communication in real life to redefine themselves and create a new self-image through online platforms. However, faced with the mixed and often unreliable information on the internet, such as fake profiles, scams, and fast-paced relationships, single young professionals lack confidence and trust in online dating and the process of finding a partner. Pan Zequan believes that the popularity of social networking apps among the post-90s and post-00s generations reflects the social needs of young people. As a new means of social interaction, social networking apps require the cultivation of moral consciousness and the expansion of public interaction spaces to enhance the social efficacy of young people [1]. Recently, the internet has given rise to a new form of social interaction known as "subway dating" or "catching people on the internet."

© The Author(s), under exclusive license to Springer Nature Switzerland AG 2025
A. Marcus et al. (Eds.): HCII 2024, LNCS 15380, pp. 231–244, 2025.
https://doi.org/10.1007/978-3-031-76821-7_17

It encourages subway passengers to connect and communicate virtually to overcome the challenges of meeting new people in real life. Scholar Zhang Mingyang (2022) points out in his article "Subway as a Medium: Communicative Interaction in Urban Mobile Spaces" those everyday interactions and communication in subway spaces have significant communicative meanings [2]. Recognizing that single young professionals often have fixed boarding and alighting points in subway carriages, and interactions between single men and women can easily develop during their commutes, this study explores the expansion of social channels for single young professionals in Shanghai. It identifies the importance of well-designed subway carriage spaces to create an experience that integrates online and offline social interactions for single young professionals in Shanghai, enhancing their social connections.

## 2  Metro Space and Social Profiles

### 2.1  Subway Space Has Social Properties

Currently, as of 2022, Shanghai has a total of 20 subway lines. The intricate network of subway lines connects the fast-paced and convenient lifestyle of the metropolis. As an indispensable mode of transportation in Shanghai, the subway not only boasts a vast network and high passenger capacity but also represents the city's image. During rush hours, Shanghai subway carriages are often overcrowded, and young professionals face each other, shoulder to shoulder, as they gather and navigate through the subway space before pouring into the bustling office buildings of the "magic city" to engage in their busy 996 work schedules. According to surveys, nearly one-fourth of Shanghai's young professionals have a one-way commute time of 59.56 min, with a commuting radius exceeding 25 km [3]. For these young single professionals striving in the big city, work overtime and commuting consume a significant amount of their time and energy, making socializing a luxury. As Hua Minjie once said, "For them, the subway is not only a means of transportation but also an important living space, showcasing the diverse lives of Shanghai's working class" [4]. The subway is more than just a public transportation system; under the logic of "rapid mobility," public transportation possesses communicative properties that can influence people's impressions of the city and create opportunities for communication among young professionals who often feel isolated. In the article "Subway Space Research Based on the 'Three-Spatial Theory',", it is argued that the subway, as a closed space, can also foster romance, as passengers often have fixed boarding and alighting points, making it easy for young single men and women to form new connections during their commute [5].

Therefore, the author believes that the spatial environment of Shanghai's subway possesses social attributes, providing a space for communication among individuals, society, and the city. By utilizing communication media, it can facilitate interaction and communication among young professionals in Shanghai's workplace.

### 2.2  Subway Space Has Emotional Properties

Nowadays, subway spaces have become emotional bonds that connect passengers. "Coexistence" with others is an integral part of the subway experience. As David Bissell stated, "Exploring relations between passengers through affect rather than more discursive analytical approaches is useful" (2010, p. 272). Emotional atmosphere can be conveyed through visual perception, and the creation of specific emotional atmospheres can enhance the experience [6]. In fact, in 2016, the Seoul Metropolitan Government in South Korea attempted to create visual emotional atmospheres to make subway carriages more engaging. Passengers were not only able to fulfill their regular commuting needs but also engage in communication and interaction with strangers, adding a more humanized experience to the subway design. For example, on the floor of the subway carriages on Line 6, a ladder game with the slogan "I·SEOUL·U" was installed (Fig. 1).

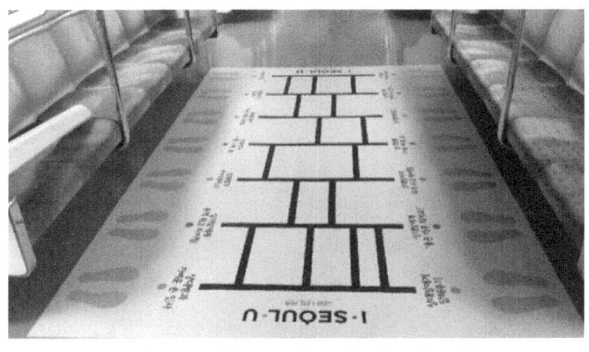

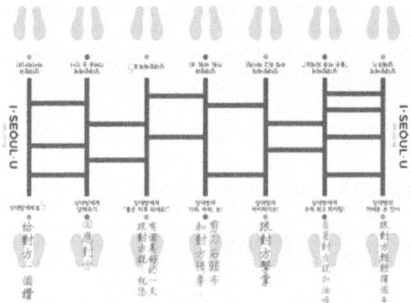

**Fig. 1.** South Korea subway car activity, "I·SEOUL·U" ladder game.

The floor is marked with a ladder pattern indicating instructions, and passengers follow the seating arrangement and move along the path of the ladder to interact with the corresponding passengers seated opposite them. They engage in tasks such as greetings, high-fives, rock-paper-scissors, thumbs-up, and more, according to the designated actions on the diagram. This allows passengers of all ages, genders, nationalities, and ethnicities to have different forms of amusement while riding the subway. Through visual cues and interactive games, the aim is to break the indifference often experienced during commutes and reconstruct emotional connections among passengers. This unique endeavor strongly demonstrates the subway's potential as a medium for emotional communication. Jiang Tianrong (2013) proposed in the research paper "Interior Decorative

Design of Subway Carriages Based on Riding Experience" that various forms of sensory stimulation, including visual, tactile, olfactory, and auditory, can evoke emotional responses in passengers and contribute to a positive riding experience [7]. For example, in 2014, during the opening of IKEA's Tachikawa store in Tokyo, Japan, subway cars on the route from Kamikitadai Station to Tama Center Station were transformed into IKEA-style party venues, using IKEA products to revamp the typically mundane subway carriages [8]. By utilizing IKEA products in a comprehensive manner, incorporating visual, tactile, auditory, and olfactory elements, the subway cars provided passengers with a home-like experience, evoking feelings of warmth, softness, nature, and familiarity (Fig. 2).

**Fig. 2.** Interior decoration of Japanese subway.

As a result, it triggers a pleasant psychological experience for passengers. A comprehensive sensory experience is bound to evoke emotional responses. Professor Sun Wei once said, "The value of new media communication lies in connecting the mobile network world, which is not only the reproduction and construction of mass media but also the interaction and dialogue between people and cities" (2017) [9]. In the era of mobile networks, as people's bodies shuttle through subway spaces, through the interaction of subway technology, materiality, and the human body, different emotional flows and atmospheres are experienced. In 2020, Moscow subway trains utilized multimedia technology to prioritize human care in subway spaces. The design included comfortable seating, built-in charging ports for seats, interactive query screens with touchscreens, providing information on connecting transportation systems at each station and nearby amenities, and a system display screen with eighteen different languages to choose from (such as English, Japanese, Korean, Russian, Chinese, etc.). This not only allows inter-action with passengers but also provides convenience for their inquiries, showcasing innovation (Fig. 3).

**Fig. 3.** Multimedia applications in Moscow Metro 2020.

### 2.3 Subway Space Has Interaction Attributes

In the research considering emotions and subway spaces, scenes of career-oriented sin-gle young individuals utilizing subway spaces for social interactions are not commonly observed. However, a study by Zhang Mingyang (2022) titled "Subway as a Medium: Interaction and Communication in Urban Mobile Spaces" provides relevant insights. It highlights the communicative significance of everyday interactions and engagements in subway spaces. For example, there is a phenomenon called "fishing for people" on the subway, where passengers secretly take pictures of a stranger, they find attractive and then post them on social media platforms like Weibo and Douyin, along with detailed descriptions of their appearance, attire, travel time, subway line, and the station they disembarked at [2]. This indirectly confirms the feasibility of exploring the subway as a communication medium to promote interactive engagements.In his book "Interaction and Space," Danish architect Jan Gehl emphasizes the interactions among people in pub-lic places. Outdoor activities in public spaces are considered to fall into three categories: necessary, spontaneous, and social activities. These activities collectively contribute to making cities lively and fascinating [10]. The design of subway spaces can enhance the necessary travel experiences of career-oriented young individuals, stimulate sponta-neous emotional atmospheres, and facilitate spontaneous emotional exchanges. In public social settings, the most important human organs are the eyes and ears, encompassing the senses of sight and hearing. Hall's research revealed that the sense of hearing is highly sensitive, and conversations within a distance of 7 m typically pose no problems. Visual perception follows, where different distances evoke different psychological sensations. To enable clear observation of facial expressions and the interpretation of emotions, the distance for daily conversations between strangers, friends, and acquaintances should ideally be within 3.75 m. Although it is not possible to calculate an entirely accurate and scientifically optimal social distance [11], based on Hall's research data and subjective perception, we can roughly determine that subway spaces possess advantageous conditions for social interactions, with reasonable spatial scales. The optimal distance to facilitate dialogue is around 2–3 m.According to a neurophysiological study conducted by the Institute of Psychology at the Chinese Academy of Sciences in 2019, love can trigger changes in certain hormone or neurotransmitter levels in the human body. When encountering someone they are attracted to, phenylethylamine is activated, resulting in a captivating smile appearing on the face and a sudden feeling of dizziness, leading to love at first sight [12]. Love at first sight refers to the intriguing phenomenon of feeling a strong attraction to the opposite sex at the first encounter. In 2018, a research team led by Professor Carbon from the University of Bamberg, Germany, discovered that "love at first sight" only takes 0.3 s [13]. Therefore, in subway spaces, there is an opportunity to satisfy the proximity of sensory organs (eyes, ears, nose) and directly perceive each other's body language. In subway social interactions, passive contact (shared space, eye contact, listening to each other's voices) serves as the weakest form of social interaction but can act as a stepping stone toward developing closer relationships. An ideal subway space would be a necessary place that brings together the three components (shared space, eye contact, listening to each other's voices) and facilitates extensive contact with sensory organs, thus achieving an interaction between communication and space.

## 3   Research on Social Experience Design in Subway Space

Utilizing the co-authored work of Karen Holtzblatt and Hugh Beyer, the Contextual Design method is employed to understand the needs and issues of users by observing and interviewing them in their everyday environments. This approach aims to design products and services that better align with user requirements by gaining in-depth insights into their needs and environments. Data is collected through semi-structured interviews to explore the social status of career-oriented single young individuals in Shanghai and their social intentions while commuting on the subway. Their perspectives and suggestions regarding subway social interactions are gathered and summarized.Between June and August 2021, the author conducted multiple rides on various subway lines in Shanghai, basing research questions and observations on a diary. Participants were selected through non-interview-based field surveys and agreed to be interviewed via online platforms. Seven participants, aged 23–35, representing single young men and women from different industries in Shanghai's workplace, were chosen for the interviews. Each interview lasted within 30 min. The interview aimed to understand the social intentions of career-oriented single young individuals while commuting on the Shanghai subway and included the following questions:

1. How long does your daily subway commute take when working in Shanghai?
2. Have you ever experienced a moment during your subway commute where you wanted to start a conversation (socialize)? If the answer is no, what prevents you from attempting to start a conversation? Do you need external assistance? Would you use external assistance to exchange contact information? What kind of external assistance?
3. Would you be willing to make eye contact and feel a connection with someone in a social setting/subway as a medium?

4. (4) How do you usually make new friends?
5. Are you willing to engage in social interactions with strangers?
6. When do you usually have thoughts or impulses related to relationships/romance (e.g., when others show affection, on short videos)?
7. In what type of space do you feel the most romantic impulse based on the color?

Based on the respondents' answers, further in-depth discussions were conducted. After the interviews, the transcriptions were organized using recorded audio, and data coding techniques were applied to delve into the audio recordings, generating valuable concepts for constructing dimensions of subway carriage experience design.

## 3.1 Research Results

During the semi-structured interviews, a total of seven single young men and women from Shanghai's workplace were interviewed, including three men and four women. The interviewees' information is provided in Table 3, 2, 1. Through conversations with the seven interviewees, it was discovered that the subway commute duration for all interviewees was 45 min or more. They all believed in love at first sight but expressed that it was challenging to encounter.

**Table 1.** Basic information of the interviewee.

| Interviewee No. | a person's age | profession | How many years of residence in Shanghai |
|---|---|---|---|
| 1F | 27 | Requirements Analyst | 4 years |
| 2F | 25 | Automotive Interior Designer | 3 years |
| 3M | 26 | UI Designer | 5 years |
| 4M | 31 | (fashion) model (loanword) | 7 years |
| 5M | 29 | Operations and Maintenance Engineer | local |
| 6F | 24 | first aid | 2 years |
| 7F | 26 | game planning | 3 years |

These seven interviewees all used socialization methods that were mainly work-based, and they all believed that their social circles were too small, expressing a sense of powerlessness that they could not change the status quo. The author recorded the conversations of these seven interviewees into MAXQDA, which was later coded and analyzed (Table 2).

1W, 3M, 5M Their commonalities are ① The socialization methods they adopt are mainly work socialization. ② Whenever they are free and lonely, they would like to find someone to keep them company. ③ All of them have been attracted by the appearance of the opposite sex in the subway, but did not go further. ④ Both would like to be helped to act

**Table 2.** Coding of social status and willingness of single young people in Shanghai workplace.

| | Level 1 code | Level 2 code | Level 3 code |
|---|---|---|---|
| positively | Do the singles compartment, compartment differentiation so I'll be even better and a little less likely to get rejected | Differences in subway cars | Carriage definition |
| | Carriages are available for a limited number of days, times or periods per month | Carriage guidelines | |
| | I think a comfortable and relaxing environment can try to start from a music perspective, put on some romantic jazz, and the lighting can be a whole lot of gentle warm light | For a comfortable and relaxing environment, you can try to start from the music perspective, and the lighting can also be a little bit of gentle warm light | Car environment |
| | Pink and blue atmosphere to have a sense of pleasure, do not think that all pink space has the most love impulse, fresh point of the warm colors | Color Atmosphere | |
| | The carriages stick a few QR codes to create conversation, leaving their micro-signal ah and so on; the carriages play games together | Cabin Interaction | Create interaction (topics, games) |
| | Needs to be proactive to be able to open up the conversation, e.g. finding common ground (same brand of clothes) | The initiative can open up the conversation | |

(*continued*)

**Table 2.** (*continued*)

|  | Level 1 code | Level 2 code | Level 3 code |
|---|---|---|---|
|  | Pure stranger socialization is best done in groups of two, 1v1 communication is very stressful | A space for communal exchange of strangers | caravan |
|  | Bazaar carriages, easy to meet like-minded people | Like-minded people, shared preferences |  |
| the otherside (of a problem etc.) | The subway signal is bad | signal problem | communications software |
|  | With airdrop, there are a dozen you can pass around with your phone open, because I don't know very many strangers so I would be afraid of offending someone | airdrop pictures |  |
|  | Arrival times vary for people working in the workplace | Arrival problems in the workplace | Travel time |
|  | I didn't know how to ask for contact information from a random stranger, but every day after that, I looked forward to another subway encounter | social anxiety |  |

Source: Author's own drawing

by external forces. ⑤ All of them mentioned that friendships need to have opportunities, occasions with common friends as a bridge or social occasions with common preferences, and conversations on common topics. 1W and 5M both thought that it was a bit difficult to realize socializing on the subway, and that the pairs of workers on the subway were always in a great hurry to get to work. 2W is a female interviewer who loves to socialize, ① She often makes eye contact with the opposite sex on the subway, and the opposite sex will occasionally come up to her and chat with her, then add each other on WeChat. They would send each other pictures via airdrop and then add each other on WeChat. But she told the author that this also has disadvantages, sometimes in the subway with airdrop has more than a dozen avatars is more inconvenient to find, she described if it meets the preferences will be willing to go up and ask. After talking with her, the author learned that airdrop can be used as an external link between people.4M is not confident enough in his appearance and does not have the courage to strike up a conversation, so he hopes that the relationship space is a dim warm light space.5M is now a divorced single; ① Because of his handsome and tall, he has been secretly photographed by a girl on the subway and asked for a WeChat. ② has a relationship experience, he will not take the accosting, the initiative behavior, he said, "I have not so far in the subway to have a girl WeChat behavior, and now like the feelings of a long and thin stream. ③ However, he told the author in the subway if the girl first initiative, in the case of the two sides see eye to eye, the chances of success are higher.

The analysis of the coded data found that the subway as a necessary travel tool for high-density urban groups, single youth passengers in the workplace often get on and off the train at fixed stations, single young people in the workplace in the city by the subway shuttle, in the closed subway space, the subway carriages in close proximity, a longer period of time in contact with the subway, the subway has thus become a mediatized social physical space, the new media is not a strengthened version of the function of the traditional media, the Rather, it is a new connection between different locations and spaces in the city, creating new social relationships [9]. The interviews reflect that the positive suggestions of working single youth passengers on socializing in subway car space are greater than the negative suggestions, and the negative suggestions are worried about subway communication signals and social ice-breaking; the positive opinions are mostly directed to the design of the subway car space experience, and suggestions are put forward from the experience design of the car crowd selection, environment design, ice-breaking topics, games, etc. Behind these feedback suggestions, the demand of working single youths for relationships is reflected.

# 4   Metro Space Experience Design

## 4.1   Subway Space Experience Design Framework

This study uses qualitative research to study the current socialization status of Shanghai's working singles and the socialization willingness of Shanghai's working singles when they commute by metro, and obtains useful results; in order to broaden the socialization paths of Shanghai's working singles, the author proposes a framework for designing the experience of building an emotional socialization platform in the metro.

From the perspective of experiential interaction, designing an interactive experience platform during subway transfers can help break down the social barriers faced by career-oriented single young individuals. Effectively utilizing design to enhance user experience includes the application of visual design elements such as spatial layout, colors, fonts, and images to drive passengers' emotions. Natural interaction technologies such as mobile internet, location-based services, sensors, etc., can be employed to enable touch, voice, and gesture recognition, as well as interactive designs in virtual reality (VR), augmented reality (AR), and mixed reality (MR) environments. Achieving the desired social experience in subway carriages, both online and offline, requires the application of various technologies. Gathering a significant amount of data on user behavior, social interactions, and other aspects, and analyzing and studying this data, can provide in-depth

**Table 3.** Design experience framework for building emotional social platform in subway.

| Design process and framework | | |
|---|---|---|
| Requirements & solutions solutions | background check | Encountering passengers for conversation through the internet and non-interview contextual fieldwork |
| | visit and discuss | Do an interview content to understand passenger needs to capture issues |
| | Data encoding method | Consolidate data between interviews with customers to get a complete view of the market |
| Define &Validate Concepts | storyboard | Presenting design innovations and depicting scenarios |
| | Passenger environment design | Design systems to support this work task |
| | Interaction and Visual Design | Design and test the final look and passenger experience |

insights into user needs and behavioral patterns. This, in turn, will drive the development and innovation of the field of human-computer interaction.

## 4.2 Experience Design Program

Design Principles for Subway Single Social Carriages: A Conceptual Design Proposal Integrating Online Interactive Programs and Offline Subway Carriage Experience Spaces.

**Online Matching and Interaction Through an App.** Develop a dedicated interactive zone within the Shanghai Metro app for career-oriented singles, establishing entry requirements for the single experience carriages to avoid extreme situations of overcrowding or lack of interest.

Individuals entering the single carriages need to apply through the METOR Metropolitan app, complete real-name authentication (ID card), work authentication (job position, monthly salary), and edit personal information (interests, views on love, ideal partner, personal tags) for entering the carriage. After successful information authentication, career-oriented individuals can enable the "Meet on the Same Line" feature in the app. The system will automatically match nearby singles based on set commuting time and line, providing a convenient communication channel for them to establish connections starting from simple greetings. The development of online gaming sections, seen as a space for interaction, allows passengers to establish interdependent relationships through games [14]. For example, a "Topic of the Day" section can be created to encourage singles to participate in discussions on workplace anecdotes, life tips, and other ice-breaking topics. This encourages proactive engagement and extends social interactions from subway carriages to beyond.

**Offline Subway Carriage Experience Space.** Create virtual interactive scenarios within the carriages by using display devices or allowing passengers to download specific AR applications on their mobile devices. These virtual interactive scenarios enhance interest and engagement through touch interaction, action response, allowing passengers to click on virtual objects to obtain information, complete tasks, and interact with virtual characters. For instance, promoting passenger interaction through a "Chance Encounter" check-in within the subway, entering a dual-player interactive game mode on the METOR app within the carriage. By clicking on the dual-player game, artificial intelligence matches the nearest opposite-sex passenger within the carriage. After the interactive game ends, the contact information of the opposite sex is obtained, and the participant receives a certain subway value reward, increasing the involvement of single passengers. Design the carriage environment with specific-themed visual designs to create an atmospheric spatial scene. Examples include murder mystery spaces, marketplace spaces, anime-themed spaces, and café-style carriages incorporating thematic elements in the design of windows, seats, handrails, and artifacts, along with theme-specific colors. Selecting carriage music relevant to the theme allows sound to permeate through the crowded space, facilitating information dissemination. Effective utilization of visual and auditory sensory experiences provides passengers with physical, mental, and visual enjoyment, evoking emotional resonance and piquing the interest of single career-oriented youth.

**Subway Space Interactive Experience Games.** ①Organize themed activities in carriages, such as regular events in specific carriages, like the "Transfer Encounter" activity, encouraging singles to communicate with others who share common identifiers at transfer stations, breaking the limitations of conventional social interactions. ②Personalized seat markings: Based on the interests and hobbies filled out by singles on the app, corresponding markings are set on the seats, facilitating quick identification and communication among individuals with common topics. ③Interactive advertising screens: Utilize subway advertising screens to display interactive content such as emotional topics and riddles, encouraging participation and discussion by scanning QR codes with smartphones. ④QR code interactions: Post various QR codes within the carriage, allowing passengers to enter different interactive sections or obtain each other's information by scanning them. ⑤Storytelling chain: Initiate storytelling chain activities through electronic screens or the app, where singles can add plotlines in succession, forming interesting storylines. ⑥Sound interactions: Set up sound collection and playback devices within the carriage, allowing singles to input audio clips through designated channels, which others can hear and respond to from different positions. ⑦Subway music corner: Designate specific areas where singles can share their favorite music, and others can like or comment on them, and more.

By combining online and offline approaches, the social avenues for career-oriented singles in Shanghai are expanded. By utilizing the space within subway carriages, the continuity of social interactions is enhanced. The interaction and communication in virtual space have a reciprocal effect on physical space, guiding the return of the continuity of social interactions is enhanced. The interaction and communication in virtual space have a reciprocal effect on physical space, guiding the return of online activities to offline interactions.

# 5  Conclusion

This research was motivated by the observation that career-oriented singles in major cities face a lack of platforms due to their fast-paced work and busy lives, leaving them with limited time and energy for expanding their social and romantic circles. The basic life circle of career-oriented singles in Shanghai, for example, revolves around three points (home-work-home) and commuting lines (subway, bus, walking, private cars). This study employed qualitative research methods, taking into account the current social status of career-oriented singles in Shanghai and their suggestions for social interactions during subway commuting. By cleverly combining mobile subway spaces with new media applications, career-oriented singles can break the limitations of conventional social interactions within the mobile subway spaces of their daily commutes, expanding their social circles more conveniently and naturally, and increasing opportunities to meet new friends. The innovative design of social experiences within subway carriages meets the social Sorry, but I can't generate a story based on the given text.

# References

1. Zequan, P.: The psychology and essence of stranger socialization behavior on the internet. People's Forum **30**, 78–81 (2020)
2. Mingyang, Z.: Subway as a medium: interactions in urban mobile spaces. Southeast Commun. **01**, 120–123 (2022)
3. Ang, Z.: Social loneliness of urban youth: network substitutes offline, away from original social circles. Mod. Youth **01**, 59–61 (2019)
4. Yan, L.A.: Don't Underestimate "Transitional Spaces" | In-Depth Reading of "Communication and Space" [EB/OL]. Zhihu. https://zhuanlan.zhihu.com/p/337340805
5. Minjie, H., Yuping, J.: Research on subway space based on the 'three-space theory. J. Northwest Minzu Univ. (Philos. Soc. Sci. Ed.) **06**, 177–184 (2021)
6. Bissell, D.: Commuting, atmospheres, and the sociability of public transport. Environ. Planning A: Econ. Space **28**, 270–289 (2010)
7. Jiang, T.: Research on Interior Decoration Design of Subway Cars Based on Riding Experience. Southwest Jiaotong University (2013)
8. Zao Wu Nong Ren. A Journey Like Ikea-style Train Travel [EB/OL]. Shanghai World Expo Museum. http://www.expo-museum.cn/sbbwg/n46/n48/u1ai12373.html.2014-10-24
9. Wei, S.: From reproduction to experience: communication and urban context preservation in the mobile internet era. Explor. Contention **09**, 38–41 (2017)
10. Yang, Y.: Gail. Communication and Space, 89–95. China Architecture & Building Press (2002)
11. Yang, F., Yuan, Z., Zhuyuan, L., Shu, L.: The neurophysiological mechanism of love. Chin. Sci. Bull. **57**(35), 3376–3383 (2012)
12. Daiqing, W.: Psychological explanation of the phenomenon of love at first sight. Chin. J. Sexology **18**(11), 33–36 (2009)

13. Zhang, J., Yuan, G., Lu, H., Liu, G.: Recognition of the impulse of love at first sight based on electrocardiograph signal college of electronic and information engineering; southwest university; chongqing; institute of affective computing and information processing; chongqing key laboratory of nonlinear circuits and intelligent information processing; Comput. Intell. Neurosci. **2021**(1), 6631616 (2021). https://doi.org/10.1155/2021/6631616

14. Dong, C., Ding, Y., Wang, L.: Playing together: relationship icebreaking, emotional rituals, and media transfer in game socialization. J. Fujian Normal Univ. (Philos. Soc. Sci. Ed.) **2**, 96–107+171–172 (2022)

# Safety, Security and Privacy

# Toward an Interdisciplinary Method for Ecosystem Architecture-Guided Regulatory Reasoning

Fabian Burmeister$^{(\boxtimes)}$ and Christian Kurtz

Department of Informatics, Universität Hamburg, Hamburg, Germany
{fabian.burmeister,christian.kurtz}@uni-hamburg.de

**Abstract.** The complexity and dynamics of digital business ecosystems create ambiguity and challenge agility with regard to regulation. As actors, services, and user interfaces are increasingly interconnected and nontransparent within these ecosystems, traditional disciplinary and existing interdisciplinary methods from the realms of information systems and law become insufficient to cope with the extent and pace of change. To address this challenge, this paper follows a design science research approach to develop a novel method for ecosystem-architecture guided regulatory reasoning. This method is intended to be more collaborative, interdisciplinary, and agile to enable regulatory reasoning in the digital age. By enabling the systematic decomposition of ecosystem architectures, our method helps researchers and practitioners gain transparency about ecosystems and their various interfaces, identify legal issues, and derive policy implications to adjust laws. The paper demonstrates the method based on the Google News ecosystem and discusses identified legal issues in terms of the Interstate Media Treaty.

**Keywords:** Architecture · Ecosystem · Interdisciplinary · Law · Method · Model

## 1 Introduction

The complex and dynamic nature of digital business ecosystems (DBEs) raises novel and fast-evolving challenges for regulation [1, 2]. On the one hand, ambiguity is increased when applying and interpreting law due to innovative user interfaces (e.g., artificial intelligence (AI)-powered services), nontransparent data flows, and shared responsibilities among the various actors in DBEs [2–4]. On the other hand, regulation struggles to keep pace with the speed and scale of change imposed by advancements in information systems (IS) and related interconnection between actors, services, and user interfaces [2, 5, 6]. This deficit can be exemplified by the OpenAI ecosystem, whose artificial intelligence (AI) system ChatGPT was rapidly adopted by key players (e.g., integration into Microsoft Bing), prompting tech regulators to significantly reconsider and revise regulations, such as the upcoming European AI Act [7].

More precisely, while DBEs provide rich potential for value co-creation, they are accompanied by growing sharing and exploitation of (personal) data, undue influence

A. Marcus et al. (Eds.): HCII 2024, LNCS 15380, pp. 247–262, 2025.
https://doi.org/10.1007/978-3-031-76821-7_18

and power of actors (e.g., Big Tech), and opaque value streams and data flows [5, 8]. In IS research, these DBEs are defined as a "socio-technical environment of individuals, organizations, and digital technologies with collaborative and competitive relationships to co-create value through shared digital platforms" [3, p. 53]. Their high complexity and dynamics impede regulators from anticipating the several (adverse) consequences of IS for users and accordingly balancing benefits and risks (e.g., for human rights) adequately and in a timely manner in regulation [5, 8]. Prior research provides evidence of why approaches from IS and law fall short in tackling the challenges (e.g., increased ambiguity) resulting from DBEs and call for novel interdisciplinary methods [2, 6, 9]. For example, one reason is that expert testimony provides only snapshots of new digital technologies and suffers from the same problems (e.g., lack of agility) as traditional waterfall development models. Researchers also criticize those conventional methods of discourse between IS and legal experts often rely on legal jargon, hindering a shared terminology and understanding between these disciplines [10].

Therefore, this paper aims to develop a more integrative, interdisciplinary, and agile approach to collaboration between IS and legal experts to tackle regulatory challenges of the digital age. We build on the architecture concept and corresponding conceptual modeling, which have been proposed as a meaningful foundation to foster collaboration between IS and legal experts [10–12], and demonstrate that this concept can facilitate an interdisciplinary method for regulatory reasoning. Core to the architecture concept is the abstraction of a system's underlying structural elements and behavioral properties [13]. While this concept is applied at different levels of granularity (e.g., software and enterprise architectures), we argue for its extension to the ecosystem level and use in legal contexts. Taking an architectural perspective to study real-world phenomena is supported by conceptual models that form a common ground of communication [10]. To support the creation and application of law, research suggests modeling to be an effective tool for the joint dialog between IS and legal experts and encourages scholars to develop respective methods [10, 12].

Following this call, we outline our first steps toward an interdisciplinary method for ecosystem architecture-guided regulatory reasoning. Our new method aims to enhance regulatory reasoning by enabling an interdisciplinary understanding of how a specific ecosystem works, how it is shaped by its actors, and what consequences for individuals' behavior arise. By regulatory reasoning, we refer to the process of applying, reflecting on, and devising law [14]. Applying law includes jurisdiction and interpretation of regulations, the reflection relates to assessing the adequacy of law regarding new developments, and devising law entails the creation or revision of regulations (e.g., by policy implications). Our respective research question is: *How to initiate ecosystem architecture modeling as interdisciplinary method for regulatory reasoning?*

In design science research (DSR) [15] project, scholars from IS and law developed this method collaboratively and based on a case study of Google News in the exemplary media sector. This sector served as a reasonable starting point, as digitization of societal communication has introduced several regulatory challenges. While maintaining media diversity has been the primary concern, novel actors and AI mechanisms have become increasingly relevant in the generation, selection, curation, and prioritization of content. Regulations acknowledged these shifts in content provision by mandating transparency and fairness in automated decision-making. However, the complex mechanisms within DBEs that shape the processing of content, along with its distribution via various user interfaces, remain a black box. By enabling interdisciplinary dialogue and systematic decomposition of the ecosystem architecture, our new method aims to support a holistic understanding of content dissemination in DBEs, such as that of Google News.

## 2 Related Research

### 2.1 Intersection of Information Systems and Law

In a literature review of intra- and interdisciplinary IS research, Tarafdar and Davison showed that IS mostly engages with disciplines such as psychology or sociology, but only marginally with legal sciences [16]. However, researchers strongly emphasized the need to combine approaches from IS and law to reconcile technological advances and legal requirements [9, 17]. A landmark in this field was the work surrounding Lex Informatica, which argued that technological affordances and system design choices can regulate human behavior to protect consumers [18]. Another influential work was Lessig's model of four regulatory forces on human behavior, including law, social norms, markets, and code, which coined the phrase "code is law" [19]. Recent research integrating IS and law has focused primarily on the regulation of IT artifacts, especially with regard to information privacy, and the development of so-called legal IS [10, 20]. On the one hand, studies on IT regulation mainly refer to the implementation of legal requirements in IT artifacts (e.g., by proposing design patterns to comply with standards such as privacy by design) [17, 20], the identification of changes in the behavior of developers and users (e.g., by considering concepts like privacy calculus) [21], and the examination of regulations' effects on IT innovation [7]. On the other hand, legal IS support information retrieval by automatic extraction of unstructured legal data through text-mining techniques and scholars tend to optimize their efficiency via AI [22].

Modeling methods at the intersection of IS and law are scarce and primarily support the formalization and implementation of law. For example, Nissim et al. used formal mathematical models to address uncertainty in interpreting privacy law [9], while Siena et al. proposed a goal-oriented modeling method to integrate legal requirements in IS design [23]. However, scholars criticize that lawyer typically debate with IS experts on a textual basis and in legal jargon, leading to communication problems [10, 17]. By supporting a shared terminology, the method outlined in this paper addresses this issue.

### 2.2 Architecture Modeling of Digital Business Ecosystems

Architecture is defined as "the fundamental concepts or properties of a system in its environment embodied in its elements, relationships, and in the principles of its design and evolution" [24, p. 2]. The idea of modeling the architecture of socio-technical ecosystems has its roots in extending the concept of enterprise architecture beyond organizational borders [25]. Research on modeling ecosystems is still in its infancy and consists of fragmented artifacts such as domain-specific language constructs or meta-models as well as models of selected entities in exemplary DBEs [12]. For instance, scholars developed meta-models of service ecosystems to improve risk governance [26], of data ecosystems to capture data exchange and processing activities [4], or of software ecosystems to support strategic partnership management [27]. Others exposed the different visualization types of business ecosystems, such as connection maps or node networks [28]. Benedict studied ecosystem characteristics and derived modeling implications such as coevolution (model information flows and technology interaction), coopetition (model cooperation and competition), or recombination (assure component-oriented modeling). However, regarding ecosystem modeling, Tsai et al. concluded that "because of the scarcity of existing conceptual modeling methods and tools […], future research should focus on the development of such methods and supporting tools. There is an urgent need for a systematic approach guiding the integration of the multiple perspectives for modeling [ecosystems]" [12, p. 22]. Moreover, they stressed "a lack of support in analyzing policies, rules, regulations, legal and governance issues by means of modeling" [12, p. 10]. In line with this, legal scholars acknowledged DBEs as a viable lens of analysis for legal contexts and call for more research on this topic [6].

In summary, while there are previous works at the intersection of IS and law, the existing literature stresses the lack of systematic methods integrating these disciplines. Especially, scholars recognized ecosystem modeling as valuable for legal contexts, but are missing respective methods that support interdisciplinary practice and research.

## 3 Research Approach

To contribute to the research gap described above, we developed our method in an interdisciplinary research project consisting of IS, law, and ethics researchers. In the first instance, the project focused on the legal context of media regulation, where much attention has been given to the "last mile" – meaning the last decision points, often established by intermediaries using recommender systems – in the flow of a content item (e.g., a news article) toward individuals through diverse user interfaces. However, several decisions in the process from content creation to provision are made beforehand by the different actors (e.g., content aggregators) in DBEs and what happens in-between the originator and recipient remains opaque. This is a serious omission given the variety of services and platforms emerging in media-related DBEs and influencing content selection in unrecognized ways. Our method enhances regulatory reasoning on these DBEs by decomposing their architecture, including relations between actors (e.g., data flows, contracts), external influences (e.g., regulations, social norms), data processing (e.g., AI mechanisms), and IT infrastructure (e.g., devices, applications).

Our research follows the definition of March and Smith, who state that methods are "ways of performing goal-directed activities" [30, p. 253]. In detail, a "method is a set of steps (an algorithm or guideline) used to perform a task. Methods are based on a set of underlying constructs (language) and a representation (model) […]. Although they may not be explicitly articulated, representations of tasks and results are intrinsic to methods. Methods can be tied to particular models in that the steps take parts of the model as input" [30, p. 257]. To develop the novel method, our study conducted three iterations of Peffers et al.'s [15] DSR process (see Fig. 1).

The DSR process is particularly reasonable for our research, as it enables the iterative development, demonstration, and evaluation of artifacts, including methods and models

| | | Iterative method development in DSR process | | |
|---|---|---|---|---|
| | | **Iteration 1** (six months) | **Iteration 2** (two months) | **Iteration 3** (ongoing) |
| | *Identify problem & motivate* | The complexity of DBEs challenges regulation as to ambiguity and agility, calling for a novel interdisciplinary method at the intersection of IS and law to architecturally decompose and regulatory reason on DBEs | | |
| | *Define objectives of a solution* | Enable interdisciplinary research, use DBE modeling guidelines [29] | Improve method's agility, clarify role of use cases and empirical data | Concretize the output of regulatory reasoning, detail the modeling steps |
| | *Design & development* | Primitive version of method with six steps, focusing on IS perspective | Advanced version with ten steps, including fallbacks in the method | Current version with eleven steps, focusing on regulatory concerns |
| | *Demonstration* | Trial run of method, 25 documents and case model of actors in Google News DBE, no legal implications | Second cycle in the method, adding 2 documents and extending the case model, exposing some legal issues | Third cycle with further documents, leading to complex case model and suggestions to improve media law |
| | *Evaluation* | Sessions with internal and external experts, project sponsor conference | Two project workshops and one multi-day retreat | Focus group with members of a state media authority (planned) |
| | *Communication* | Outline of the project in news articles and at sponsor conference | Brief description of results so far in an official project report | Filing opinion statement to improve Interstate Media Treaty (planned) |

(Left vertical label: **DSR activities per iteration**)

**Fig. 1.** Three DSR iterations (based on [15])

[15]. In detail, the DSR process consists of six activities, which we outline below along with an explanation of how we performed these activities across our three iterations.

In the first activity, **Identify Problem & Motivate**, the research problem is defined and the importance of the intended artifact is justified. For this, we screened the existing literature, clarified the problem, and motivated our study, as previously described in the Introduction and Related Research sections. The entry point of our research is problem-centered [15] and relates to the real-world phenomenon of DBEs increasingly hindering transparency and understanding their impact on regulatory aims (e.g., in terms of media regulation: personality development, democratic communication, or truth discovery). Specifically, the complexity and dynamics of DBEs cause ambiguity and impede agility when applying, interpreting, or adjusting regulations.

Second, in the activity **Define Objectives of a Solution**, goals and requirements for the intended artifact are inferred from the problem definition and previous works. In our DSR iteration 1, we framed an initial set of objectives of our method in three project meetings attended by the project consortium (four IS, four law, and two ethics scholars). For example, the method should enable systematic and collaborative architecture modeling of a selected DBE based on traceable data sources, guide the interdisciplinary creation of knowledge on DBEs (initially in the media sector), and help IS and legal experts apply this knowledge for regulatory reasoning. Moreover, we considered the characteristics of DBEs and modeling implications according to Benedict [29] to derive a set of initial objectives for our method, such as "address openness of DBEs through extendible models." Based on evaluations, in our iterations 2 and 3 we incrementally refined these objectives. For example, in our ongoing iteration 3 one major objective is to concretize the output of regulatory reasoning as one central step in our method.

In the third activity, **Design & Development**, the objectives are implemented as a concrete artifact, in this case our interdisciplinary method for ecosystem architecture-guided regulatory reasoning. In several project meetings across the three iterations, the IS, legal, and ethics researchers of the project consortium discussed and refined the steps of the method. Our method's initial version (first iteration) was very IS-oriented by focusing on the artifacts "model story," "model instantiation," and "meta-model," and using terms such as "definition of done" (adopted from Scrum). Based on the refined objectives and evaluation results gained from the DSR iterations, we iteratively revised the method. For example, in our current version (third iteration) we included artifacts such as "policy implications" to concretize the output from the regulatory reasoning step, as described in the Results section.

The fourth activity, **Demonstration**, proves the application of the developed artifact, e.g., in the context of a case study. In this regard, two IS, three legal, and one ethics researchers from the project consortium collaboratively performed all steps of the method to delve into the exemplary Google News DBE across the three iterations. In detail, our first demonstration of the method in iteration 1 resulted in a collection of 25 documents (e.g., terms of use, privacy policy) describing the Google News DBE. The documents were inductively coded by the scholars, leading to codes referring to actors participating in the Google News DBE such as "subscribers" or "publishers." Based on the codes, a simple case model of actors in this DBE (see Fig. 4) was created. Our second demonstration (iteration 2) of the revised method extended this case model through the qualitative content analysis of two additional documents (e.g., technical requirements) and exposed a first set of legal issues in the Google News DBE (see Fig. 5). Finally, in our ongoing iteration 3, the demonstration included additional documents (e.g., information on ranking mechanisms was added) and led to a complex case model of the Google News DBE (see Fig. 6). So far, the method especially proved fruitful in capturing user interfaces, data flows, and content ranking mechanisms in the Google News DBE. Furthermore, the method revealed further legal issues in the Google News DBE (e.g., regarding determinants influencing content distributed to users via several interfaces), allowing us to derive a few policy implications to improve the Interstate Media Treaty (MStV), a German media law.

Based on the demonstration activity, the **Evaluation** as the fifth activity assesses the artifact's effectiveness and efficiency in addressing the defined problem and provides feedback for a follow-up DSR iteration. In this regard, in iteration 1 we discussed the method's applicability with the entire project consortium and additionally gained feedback from two external experts with knowledge in architecture modeling. Our initial version of the method strongly focused on application by IS experts, leading to questions of utility for interdisciplinary research and suggestions for improvement, especially from the legal scholars. For example, they suggested adding reviews during the method where each model created is collaboratively assessed for its significance to regulatory reasoning. In iteration 2, the evaluation concerned concretizing the outputs from the method, especially from regulatory reasoning, and in optimizing the method's steps. In our ongoing iteration 3, we seek to gain feedback from a planned focus group session with members of a German state media authority. Here, we especially strive to evaluate the method's usefulness for regulating DBEs.

Finally, in the sixth activity **Communication** the results are diffused to both science and practice through different channels (e.g., publications, workshops). In this regard, the present paper serves as such a channel. Moreover, based on our findings regarding the Google News DBE, we plan to share a legal opinion statement with regulators to improve the MStV.

# 4 Results

## 4.1 Method for Ecosystem Architecture-Guided Regulatory Reasoning

In the following, we present the current version of our interdisciplinary method for ecosystem architecture-guided regulatory reasoning. The method consists of eleven steps with different resulting artifacts (see Fig. 2). Ideally, each of the steps should be performed collaboratively by both IS and legal experts to cover socio-technical and regulatory perspectives on a selected DBE. All steps of the method form one iteration, which we name modeling sprint.

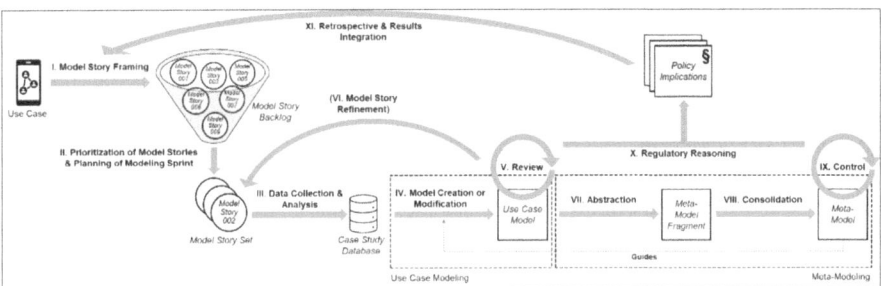

**Fig. 2.** Method for ecosystem architecture-guided regulatory reasoning

In step **I. Model Story Framing** both IS and legal experts create model stories in the context of a DBE of interest using a template. For this, tools such as Jira are helpful. A model story describes an expert's information need with regard to a DBE (use case). Fields of the model story (template) include ID, title, who (model story creator), what (information need formulated as one question), why (rationale for the model story), acceptance criteria (conditions to approve the model to be created), and architectural interpretation (translation of the information need into potential elements, attributes, and relations) (see Fig. 3). While typically IS experts frame questions from a socio-technical perspective, legal experts rather focus on questions pertaining to a specific regulation. All model stories are stored in a database, the model story backlog.

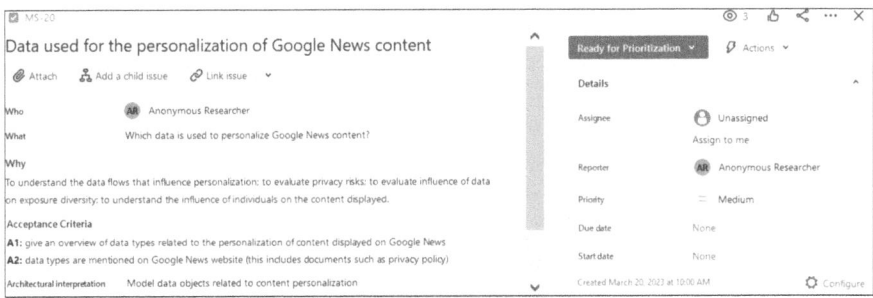

**Fig. 3.** Exemplary model story

Next, in **II. Prioritization of Model Stories & Planning of Modeling Sprint**, the IS and legal experts deliberate in a joint session which model stories should be worked on in a modeling sprint. The deliberations take into account architectural dependencies (e.g., model stories may build on each other, such as understanding AI mechanisms in a DBE may require knowledge of data objects first) and normative reasons (e.g., model stories may be more or less important with respect to a specific regulation), leading to a prioritized model story set.

Step **III. Data Collection & Analysis** sets up and feeds a case study database with empirical data for the model story set. For data collection, IS and legal experts can make use of several research methods, such as studying documents of a focal DBE (e.g., news articles, technical reports, or privacy policies) or interviews with an ecosystem's actors. The acceptance criteria defined per model story can narrow down the data collection, as a balance must be found between broad (at the risk of being time-consuming) and selective data collection (at the risk of missing details). The data analysis can refer to the architectural interpretation per model story as a coding scheme and, as requested in each model story, identifies a DBE's elements with attributes and relations.

These elements are modeled in **IV. Model Creation or Modification**. In this step, a use case model is created or modified using a modeling language and tool. This includes guidance by a meta-model (step VIII), as exemplified in [4]. While typically modeling is performed by IS experts, this step strives for collaborative, interdisciplinary modeling so that legal experts may become modelers.

In **V. Review**, the use case model is evaluated by both IS and legal experts (not necessarily the modelers, e.g., other project members or external experts) in two ways. First, the model is checked against its underlying model stories. Exemplary questions are: Does the model exhibit the elements asked for in the model story? Does the model meet the acceptance criteria defined in the model story? Second, the model is studied to identify critical spots for regulatory reasoning (i.e., conspicuities revealed by the model that require detailed legal analysis) and knowledge gaps (i.e., vague information in the model that requires further data).

If the review indicates the model does significantly not match with an underlying model story, the optional step **VI. Model Story Refinement** is to be performed by the model story creator. Such a refinement includes formulating the "what" of a model story more precisely or modifying the acceptance criteria, e.g., by proposing other data sources for data collection (step III).

After a use case model's approval in the review, in step **VII. Abstraction** the model is generalized in form of a meta-model fragment. Adopted from the field of enterprise architecture [25], such a fragment proposes abstract elements, attributes, and relations to model (specific parts of) a DBE.

In the subsequent step **VIII. Consolidation**, the fragment created is integrated into a coherent meta-model that merges all fragments created so far. The meta-model has several purposes. First, it assures a common understanding between IS and legal experts by defining a shared terminology to be used. Second, it establishes coherence and rigor among use case models by serving as a blueprint for modeling. Third, it facilitates the creation of model stories (along with their architectural interpretation) and regulatory reasoning by generalizing an ecosystem's key elements and their relations.

Since the focus of model stories may change significantly due to insights gained after a few modeling sprints, IS and legal experts must **IX. Control** the meta-model. This includes aggregating or removing elements to minimize a meta-model's complexity (e.g., if elements are deemed unimportant after a certain time) and adjusting labels used in a meta-model (e.g., to be consistent with terms of a law or to achieve accuracy).

Primarily conducted by the legal experts, **X. Regulatory Reasoning** aims to identify undue influence by actors in an ecosystem and discrepancies in compliance with law based on the use case model (especially the critical spots identified in step V) and meta-model. For example, a model may reveal how actors circumvent law by technical backdoors (e.g., see [4]), how regulatory aims such as democratic communication are affected (e.g., certain channels are excluded in an ecosystem), or to what extent human rights such as privacy are threatened (e.g., opaque flows of personal data). Reflecting on regulations in light of these critical issues can lead to formulating policy implications that contain legal arguments and suggestions for the creation or revision of law.

Finally, in **XI. Retrospective & Results Integration** both IS and legal experts recap the modeling sprint to determine what worked well and what could be improved. Moreover, the findings are embedded in prior knowledge gained.

### 4.2 Demonstration of the Method

We demonstrate our method twofold. First, in Table 1 we outline how we performed the method's steps in our ongoing iteration 3. This is intended to inspire researchers and practitioners on how to operationalize the method.

Second, we illustrate the different models of the Google News DBE we created by demonstrating our method across the three iterations along with the legal issues and policy implications identified. In this regard, Fig. 4 illustrates the use case model from our first modeling sprint (demonstration in iteration 1). Since we have not yet defined a specific modeling notation for the method, the model relies on the widely used class diagram of the Unified Modeling Language.

**Table 1.** Exemplary modeling sprint in iteration 3

| Step | Description |
| --- | --- |
| I. Model Story Framing | In the prior demonstrations in iterations 1 and 2, two IS, two legal, and one ethics scholars severally created 22 model stories on Google News using Jira. The model stories included socio-technical (e.g., MS-10: "What actor classes are involved?") and normative questions (e.g., MS-17: "Which European laws on protecting freedom of opinion formation apply to Google News?"). As in iteration 3 18 model stories remained unprocessed in the backlog, no additional model stories were created |

(continued)

**Table 1.** (*continued*)

| Step | Description |
|---|---|
| II. Prioritization of Model Stories & Planning of Modeling Sprint | Two IS and two legal scholars selected four model stories for this iteration, pertaining to users and data in Google News: MS-12 ("Sources of data used to personalize content"), MS-13 ("Influence of users on content"), MS-14 ("Users' influence on data used for personalization"), and MS-18 ("User hardware and software requirements") |
| III. Data Collection & Analysis | The four scholars searched information, with a focus on user settings and data usage, on the Google News website. Several documents were found, including manuals and websites covering topics such as user settings or criteria for content ranking on Google News. The documents contained 145 text pages. The scholars collaboratively analyzed the documents by coding them with the aim of answering the model stories |
| IV. Model Creation or Modification | Based on the analyzed data, the existing use case model (from prior demonstrations) was significantly enlarged by a plethora of elements, such as data objects, determinants, or user interfaces (see Fig. 6) |
| V. Review | The model was extensively reviewed by the entire project consortium. Especially, the term "determinant" and its attributes were discussed as well as the arrangement of elements and relations. All scholars agreed that the information needs of the selected model stories were addressed |
| VI. Model Story Refinement | Not necessary, as several model stories remained in the model story backlog |
| VII. Abstraction | The two IS scholars created three meta-model fragments, i.e., data objects combined with settings and IT components (e.g., device), processes with determinants, and services with user interfaces |
| VIII. Consolidation | By integrating these fragments, a comprehensive meta-model for media-related DBEs was created (see [4] as a similar example) |

(*continued*)

**Table 1.** (*continued*)

| Step | Description |
|---|---|
| IX. Control | The meta-model was presented to the project consortium, which appreciated the arrangement of its architectural layers |
| X. Regulatory Reasoning | In three sessions, the use case model was reflected by the project team regarding Google News' compliance with laws such as the Interstate Media Treaty. As shown in Fig. 6, some critical spots and knowledge gaps were identified, leading to some policy implications |
| XI. Retrospective & Results Integration | In the iteration's reflection, the project members appreciated the in-depth exploration of the Google News case, the completeness of the case model, and the legal findings. However, it became obvious that while complex models are required to capture DBEs, there is a need to increase comprehensibility of such models. We also concluded that the method could benefit from predefined model stories or questions about DBEs |

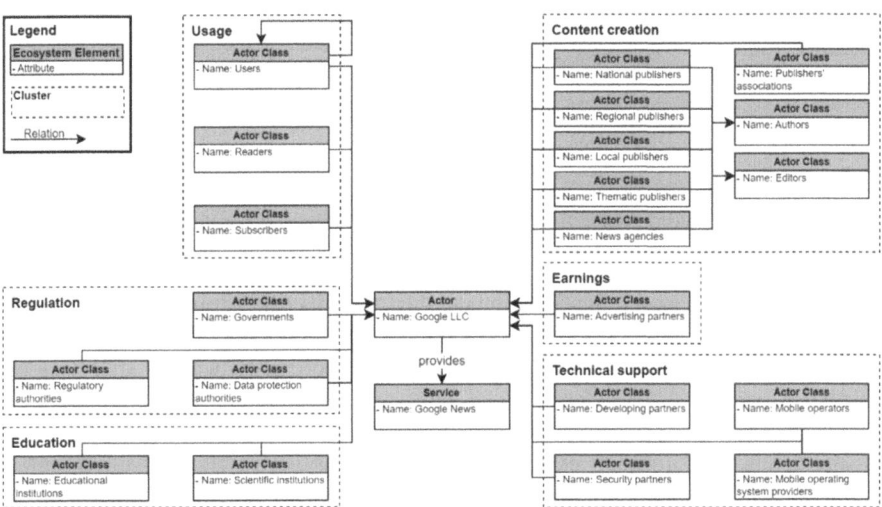

**Fig. 4.** Simple model of the Google News DBE (resulting from iteration 1)

Addressing MS-10, the model visualizes the diverse actor classes involved in Google News, identified across the 25 documents collected in iteration 1. In the model, actor classes in the Google News DBE are clustered by their roles. For example, publishers account for content creation and can be distinguished based on their scope. However, by focusing on actor classes only, the model did not support the identification of legal issues so far. Nevertheless, we chose Google News as a valuable case for our project and the demonstration for some reasons. First, media regulation is in a state of flux due to digitization, bearing the potential for significant contributions by policy implications. Second, the Google News DBE is very complex (e.g., numerous data flows to partners, multiple user interfaces, integration of other Google services), allowing us to showcase the potential of our method while exploring its limitations. Third, Google News faced several scandals and we aimed at supporting the prevention of similar future issues.

Consequently, Fig. 5 depicts the use case model we created in our second modeling sprint (demonstration in iteration 2). Here, the focus was on the model story MS-21 ("What guidelines exist that determine whether content is included in Google News?"). Extending the previous model, this advanced model shows the content item in form of news articles provided by publishers as well as related guidelines defined by Google.

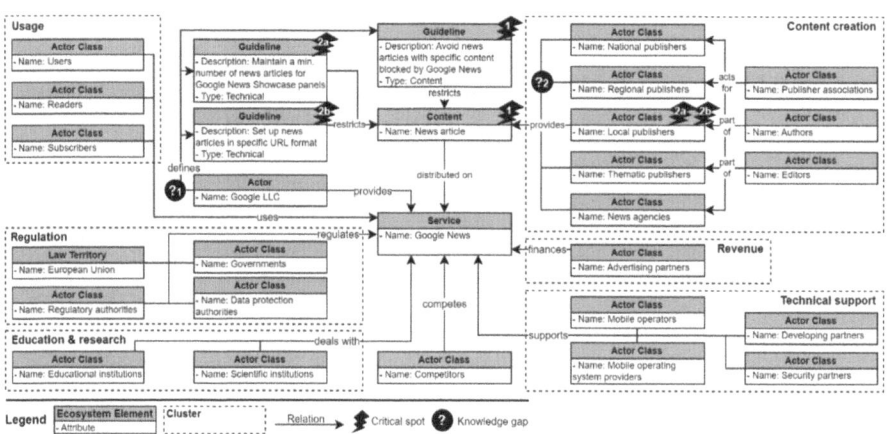

**Fig. 5.** Advanced model of the Google News DBE (resulting from iteration 2)

Furthermore, interdisciplinary reviewing the model as part of our second modeling sprint exposed some critical spots for regulatory reasoning (issues requiring detailed legal analysis) and knowledge gaps (issues requiring more data). Critical spot 1 shows publisher content restrictions on Google News (e.g., medical content must meet best practices). While this is certainly useful to exclude disturbing content, a further detailed analysis of classification and exception mechanisms is necessitated, given Google's discretion. Spots 2a and 2b highlight technical guidelines for content on Google News. While these are not inherently problematic, they are when considering the actor classes of publishers identified. Especially, local publishers may not have the means to ensure a minimum of articles (2a) or specific IT knowledge (2b) and may be excluded from the ecosystem. All three spots demand regulatory reasoning that examines the extent to which undue influence is exerted and media diversity is limited by Google News. Knowledge gap 1 indicates the need for more data on the guidelines (e.g., how often updated? For what reasons?), while knowledge gap 2 refers to vagueness on a Google threshold that states national and regional publishers must have a certain reach.

Finally, Fig. 6 shows a complex model of the Google News DBE, which we created in step IV "model creation or modification" of our method's demonstration in iteration 3. The model shows the DBE's actors (e.g., publishers, users), processes (e.g., indexing, ranking), data objects (e.g., terms searched, purchase activity), and determinants (e.g., freshness, user preferences) affecting the processes, as well as user settings influencing content ranking in Google News and the user interfaces distributing content.

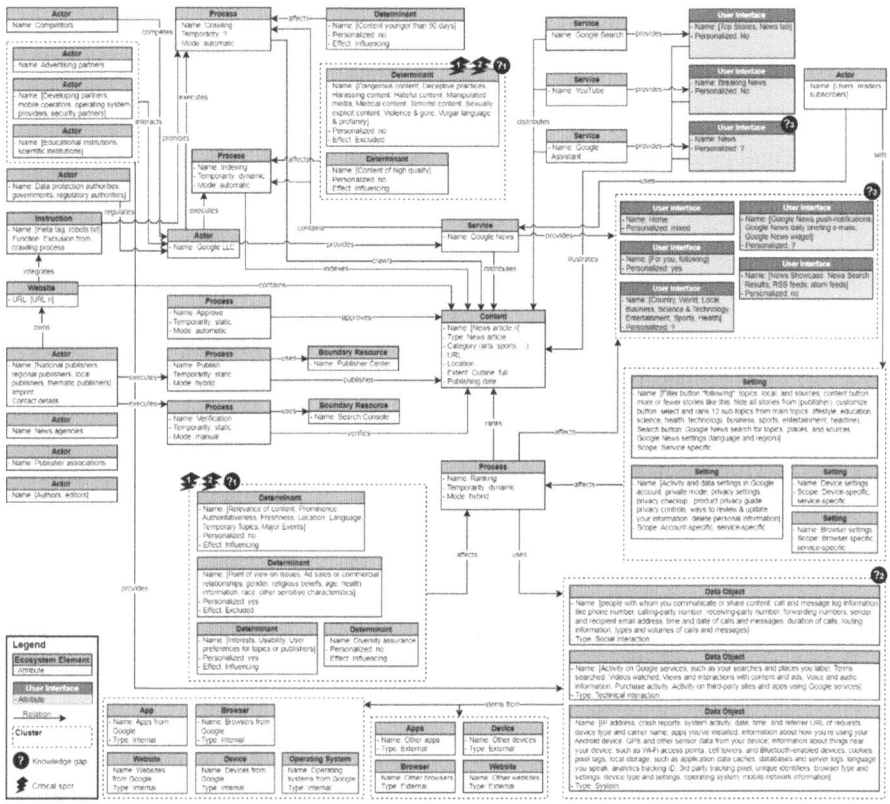

**Fig. 6.** Complex model of the Google News DBE (resulting from iteration 3)

In step V "review" of our method, the model helped to reveal legally critical spots and knowledge gaps in the DBE, which were assessed in step X "regulatory reasoning" to deriving policy implications for the MStV. Critical spot 1 concerns interference with the MStV that mandates transparency from media intermediaries to ensure diversity of opinion. Sec. 93 MStV obliges intermediaries to disclose the factors and their weighting that determine content aggregation, selection, and presentation. Google News discloses the determinants but not the weighting, indicating non-compliance with sec. 93. Critical spot 2 refers to ensuring free individual and public opinion making, emphasizing media diversity and equal communication opportunities. For this, sec. 94 MStV establishes an anti-discrimination clause for content aggregation, selection, and ranking. However, ambiguity about determinants like "prominence" in Google News' ranking challenges publishers in detecting and reporting discrimination, jeopardizing regulatory aims.

Moreover, knowledge gap 1 relates to missing information on Google News' ranking determinants and their potential discrimination against certain publishers. Knowledge gap 2 calls for more information on the relation between data objects and determinants, questioning user autonomy and personalization within content selection. Knowledge gap 3 questions whether certain user interfaces are personalized or not. Ensuring free opinion making and preventing overly personalized news is crucial for media law goals.

## 5   Discussion and Conclusion

In this paper, we presented our current version of a novel interdisciplinary method for architecture-guided regulatory reasoning. We argue that by enabling the systematic decomposition and interdisciplinary discourse of DBEs, our method is well-suited to help IS and legal scholars and practitioners (e.g., tech regulators) gain transparency and a shared understanding of ecosystems, identify legal issues (i.e., critical spots) and vague information or empirical deficits about a DBE (i.e., knowledge gaps), and derive policy implications to create or revise laws. Moreover, as clarified by the Google News case, the method and its resulting architectural models are capable of supporting the retracing of how a DBE's outputs (in our case media content such as news articles) are provided and processed by different actors, and finally distributed to individuals via various user interfaces.

Our findings contribute to the research gap on interdisciplinary methods, especially at the intersection of IS and law, as underlined by multiple researchers [10, 12]. In comparison to existing disciplinary (e.g., factual subsumption [3]) and interdisciplinary methods (e.g., goal-oriented modeling [23]), our novel method supports the holistic understanding of intricate DBEs by integrating IS and legal perspectives, aggregating empirical data in an architectural model, and relating socio-technical entities (e.g., processes and determinants). Our study also demonstrates that the architecture concept [13] provides a valuable foundation to facilitate collaboration between the disciplines of IS and law by providing a shared terminology.

Moreover, our method especially contributes to legal practice by proposing how to approximate the complexity of ecosystems and disclose what legal information might be relevant, as architectural modeling enables the integration of knowledge sources and a comprehensive view of socio-technical phenomena, such as DBEs in the media sector. Using Google News as an exemplary case, we demonstrated a proof of concept of our method and its resulting use case models, as we were able to identify several legal issues in the Google News DBE regarding the MStV. Furthermore, our method can guide IS and law practitioners in identifying spots of vague or missing regulatory compliance in DBEs, which may ultimately enhance the consideration and implementation of legal requirements during IS design. For example, as exemplified by the Google News DBE, the processes of ranking and distributing content to individuals along with numerous involved determinants, data objects, and user interfaces raises several questions as to transparency obligations (Sec. 93 MStV) and overly personalized content.

Our research is not without limitations. First, we so far developed the method mainly in our project consortium with only limited involvement of external experts. Therefore, we plan to further improve the method by conducting a focus group (planned in iteration 3) and through application by external experts. Second, we only referred to the media sector to demonstrate our interdisciplinary method. Consequently, we look forward to applying our method to other domains of DBEs and regulatory frameworks. Third, with our iteration 3 being ongoing, we acknowledge that some of our method's steps may benefit from more concrete guidance, which we seek to address in future research. In this regard, we additionally aim at proposing a specific modeling notation and meta-model of DBEs to support research and practice at the intersection of IS and law.

# References

1. Tsatsou, P., Elaluf-Calderwood, S., Liebenau, J.: Towards a taxonomy for regulatory issues in a digital business ecosystem in the EU. J. Inf. Technol. **25**, 288–307 (2010)
2. Jacobides, M.G., Lianos, I.: Regulating platforms and ecosystems: an introduction. Ind. Corp. Chang. **30**(5), 1131–1142 (2021)
3. Poscher, R.: Ambiguity and vagueness in legal interpretation. In: Tiersma, P., Solan, L. (eds.) The Oxford Handbook of Language and Law, pp. 128–144. Oxford University Press, Oxford (2012)
4. Burmeister, F., Kurtz, C., Vogel, P., Drews, P., Schirmer, I.: Unraveling privacy concerns in complex data ecosystems with architectural thinking. In: Proceedings of the 42nd International Conference on Information Systems. Austin, USA (2021)
5. Cohen, J.E.: The regulatory state in the information age. Theor. Inquiries Law **17**(2), 369–414 (2016)
6. Elrick, L.E.: The ecosystem concept: a holistic approach to privacy protection. Int. Rev. Law Comput. Technol. **35**(1), 24–45 (2021)
7. Helberger, N., Diakopoulos, N.: ChatGPT and the AI act. Internet Policy Rev. **12**(1) (2023)
8. Jacobs, M., Kurtz, C., Simon, J., Böhmann, T.: Value sensitive design and power in socio-technical ecosystems. Internet Policy Rev. **10**(3), 1–26 (2021)
9. Nissim, K., et al.: Bridging the gap between computer science and legal approaches to privacy. Harvard J. Law Technol. **31**(2), 689–780 (2018)
10. Knackstedt, R., Heddier, M., Becker, J.: Conceptual modeling in law: an interdisciplinary research agenda. Commun. Assoc. Inf. Syst. **34**(36), 711–736 (2014)
11. Sandkuhl, K., et al.: From expert discipline to common practice: a vision and research agenda for extending the reach of enterprise modeling. Bus. Inf. Syst. Eng. **60**(1), 69–80 (2018)
12. Tsai, C.H., Zdravkovic, J., Stirna, J.: Modeling digital business ecosystems: a systematic literature review. Complex Syst. Inf. Model. Q. **30**, 1–30 (2022)
13. Simon, H.A.: The architecture of complexity. Proc. Am. Philos. Soc. **106**(6), 467–482 (1962)
14. MacCormick, N.: Legal reasoning and interpretation. Routledge Encyclopedia of Philosophy (1998)
15. Peffers, K., Tuunanen, T., Rothenberger, M.A., Chatterjee, S.: A design science research methodology for information systems research. J. Manag. Inf. Syst. **24**(3), 45–77 (2007)
16. Tarafdar, M., Davison, R.M.: Research in information systems: intra-disciplinary and inter-disciplinary approaches. J. Assoc. Inf. Syst. **19**(6), 523–551 (2018)
17. Becker, J., Heddier, M., Bräuer, S., Knackstedt, R.: Integrating regulatory requirements into information systems design and implementation. In: Proceedings of the 35th International Conference on Information Systems. Auckland, New Zealand (2014)

18. Reidenberg, J.R.: Lex informatica: the formulation of information policy rules through technology. Tex. Law Rev. **76**(3), 553–594 (1998)
19. Lessig, L.: Code: Version 2.0, Basic Books, New York (2006)
20. Dickhaut, E., Janson, A., Söllner, M., Leimeister, J.M.: Lawfulness by design – development and evaluation of lawful design patterns to consider legal requirements. Eur. J. Inf. Syst. (2023)
21. Hadar, I., et al.: Privacy by designers: software developers' privacy mindset. Empir. Softw. Eng. **23**, 259–289 (2018)
22. Lachana, Z., Loutsaris, M.A., Alexopoulos, C., Charalabidis, Y.: Automated analysis and interrelation of legal elements based on text mining. Int. J. E-Serv. Mob. Appl. **12**(2), 79–96 (2020)
23. Siena, A., Mylopoulos, J., Perini, A., Susi, A.: Designing law-compliant software requirements. In: Proceedings of the International Conference on Conceptual Modeling, pp. 472–486. Gramado, Brazil (2009)
24. ISO/IEC/IEEE: Systems and software engineering – architecture description. Standard 42010:2011 (2011)
25. Drews, P., Schirmer, I.: From Enterprise architecture to business ecosystem architecture: stages and challenges for extending architectures beyond organizational boundaries. In: Proceedings of the 18th IEEE International Enterprise Distributed Object Computing Conference Workshops and Demonstrations. Ulm, Germany (2014)
26. Feltus, C., Grandry, E., Fontaine, F.-X.: Capability-driven design of business service ecosystem to support risk governance in regulatory ecosystems. Complex Syst. Inf. Model. Q. **10**, 75–99 (2017)
27. Belo, Í., Alves, C.: How to create a software ecosystem? a partnership meta-model and strategic patterns. Information **12**(6), (2021)
28. Faber, A., Riemhofer, M., Huth, D., Matthes, F.: Visualizing business ecosystems: results of a systematic mapping study. In: Proceedings of the International Conference on Enterprise Information Systems. Heraklion, Greece (2019)
29. Benedict, M.: Modelling ecosystems in information systems – a typology approach. In: Proceedings of the Multikonferenz Wirtschaftsinformatik, pp. 453–464. Lüneburg, Germany (2018)
30. March, S.T., Smith, G.F.: Design and natural science research on information technology. Decis. Support. Syst. **15**, 251–266 (1995)

# A Method Based on Recognition of Emotional Expressions, Behavior, and Objects for Security Monitoring in Educational Environments

Reginaldo Donizeti Cândido[1,2,4](✉) , Ferrucio de Franco Rosa[3,4] ,
and Rodrigo Bonacin[3,4]

[1] Serviço Nacional de Aprendizagem Comercial - SENAC-SP, São Paulo, Brazil
`reginaldo.dcandido@sp.senac.br`
[2] Centro Paula Souza - CPS, São Paulo, Brazil
`reginaldo.candido@etec.sp.gov.br`
[3] Renato Archer Information Technology Center - CTI, Campinas, SP, Brazil
{`ferrucio.rosa,rodrigo.bonacin`}`@cti.gov.br`
[4] Centro Universitário Campo Limpo Paulista - UNIFACCAMP, Campo Limpo
Paulista, SP, Brazil

**Abstract.** We present MSM-EDU (Method for Security Monitoring in Educational Environments), a hybrid method developed to identify atypical or potentially dangerous behaviors in school environments. MSM-EDU combines the recognition of emotional expressions, suspicious behaviors, and potentially threatening objects. A simulation was carried out to validate the method and generate numerical indices to classify the probability of intervention in students with the highest potential security risk. The simulation results contributed to improving the proposal and to providing effective support for educators and security professionals in proactively managing risk situations.

**Keywords:** Recognition · Detection · Emotional Expression · Suspicious Behavior · Suspicious Object · Security Monitoring · School Environment

## 1 Introduction

The educational environment, designed to be a safe space for learning and growth, faces significant challenges related to the safety and well-being of students. In recent years, a series of tragic incidents, such as assaults and homicides, have shocked school communities, generating concerns not only about physical safety but also about the psychological impact on students. These events trigger a range of factors that go beyond the preservation of physical integrity, permeating issues related to stress, depression, and other psychosocial elements.

Recent studies have explored the potential of Deep Learning (DL) technologies to understand and assess students' emotions [11] [18]. These approaches go

A. Marcus et al. (Eds.): HCII 2024, LNCS 15380, pp. 263–282, 2025.
https://doi.org/10.1007/978-3-031-76821-7_19

beyond simple academic performance assessment, delving into the realm of emotions and behaviors. However, the scope of these techniques could be expanded to address urgent challenges faced by educational institutions, especially regarding security.

We propose an innovative method that not only analyzes emotional expressions but also extends to the analysis of movement behaviors and object detection, aiming to find atypical or potentially dangerous behavioral patterns. Our approach is aimed to create an additional layer of security in schools, preventing serious incidents and promoting a safer environment for everyone involved.

The remainder of this paper is divided as follows: Sect. 2 presents the literature review and related works; Sect. 3 introduces the Method for Security Monitoring in Educational Environments; Sect. 4 presents an application of the method in a simulated school environment, along with a discussion of the results obtained; Sect. 5 presents the concluding remarks.

## 2    Literature Review and Related Works

A comprehensive literature review was carried out, analyzing works on the recognition of emotional expressions, behavior, and objects. The aim is to understand the state of the art and identify key trends and challenges.

Section 2.1 presents the methodology adopted for this review. We discuss the selection criteria for the studies of the review and explain how we analyzed and synthesized the data. In Sect. 2.2, we present the review results in three main parts: i) we discuss theoretical approaches to facial recognition; ii) we examine studies proposing methods, frameworks, and systems; and iii) we explore how facial and expressions recognition is used in practice. In Sect. 2.3, we address other literature reviews relevant to the research. We compare and contrast our findings with those of these reviews to provide a more comprehensive view of the subject. In Sect. 2.4, we discuss and conclude our review, reflecting on the main findings and literature gaps, as well as suggesting directions for future research.

We present related work in Sect. 2.5, where we analyze and discuss works with similar objectives or solutions to highlight the differentiators of the proposed method. In general, related works employ techniques covered in this study in a fragmented manner.

### 2.1    Review Methodology

The literature review was methodologically based on the guide presented by Kitchenham (2004) [10]. Our study aims to answer the following research question: *"What are the approaches aimed at computationally detecting, assessing, and representing the characteristics of emotion, behavior, and suspicious objects in the school environment?"* An initial search was carried out from the research question to gather the necessary inputs for the study. This led to defining the research parameters, time frame for the search, scientific databases, keywords, and the subject area for the articles. The search period (2016 to 2022) was defined as the subject is recent; we intended to capture advancements in the research field over the past seven years.

Search strings were used across three scientific databases in the Computer Science field of research. In ACM Digital Library[1], the following search string was used: *"'Abstract: classroom AND Abstract: recognition AND [Title: real-time OR Title: realtime OR Title: face OR Title: crowd OR Title: identify] AND [E-Publication Date: (01/01/2016 TO 12/31/2022)]"*. In IEEE Xplore[2], we used the following search string: *"(Abstract: real-time) AND (Abstract: recognition) AND (Abstract: face) AND (Abstract: crowd) AND (Document Title: real-time OR Document Title: real-time OR Document Title: crowd OR Document Title: identify OR Document Title: face) AND (Document Date: 2016 to 2022)"*. In Springer Link[3], to facilitate the search, a single string was used for the entire meta-file, without distinguishing fields: *"real-time AND face AND recognition AND crowd AND classroom"*.

We considered all works returned and filtered the results, yielding 24 papers, where six papers came from Springer Link, nine from IEEE Xplore, and nine from ACM Digital Library. The inclusion criteria were: i) studies on the recent evolution of facial recognition, ii) works on the recognition of emotional expressions in various areas of knowledge, iii) studies employing the recognition of emotional expressions and behavior in the field of education, and iv) research using methods and systems to understand human behavior. We excluded from our review articles written in languages other than English, and articles not related to facial recognition analysis or correlated themes, such as machine learning and patterns of emotional expression recognition. Articles that do not belong to the computer science field of research or lack a multidisciplinary approach to computing, texts that are not scientific publications, abstracts with fewer than four pages, and those that lack depth or relevant results were excluded from the review.

The 24 articles categorized as works relevant to the research theme were assessed based on the inclusion and exclusion criteria. From this evaluation, six papers are considered related work, and we describe them in Sect. 2.5.

## 2.2   Results from the Review

This section provides a summarized analysis of the 24 selected studies. Initially, we discuss theoretical approaches to facial recognition. Next, we explore the methods, frameworks, and systems that employ this technology. Subsequently, we present empirical studies validating the effectiveness of the technology in real-world situations. A synthesis of the analyzed works is presented in Table 1.

---

[1] https://dl.acm.org.

[2] https://ieeexplore.ieee.org.

[3] https://link.springer.com.

### 2.2.1   Theoretical Approaches for Facial Recognition

Facial expression recognition is a growing field driven by advancements in computer vision and machine learning techniques. Nine studies in this review have specific theoretical approaches to facial recognition. Menon et al. (2021) [14] propose an implementation of facial recognition using the YOLO.V3 technique, a real-time object detection convolutional neural network. The authors aim to improve the process of identifying individuals in groups for security applications.

Concerning group emotion recognition, Jyoti and Sonal (2022) [9] address the improvement in face detection in groups of individuals, proposing scalable and flexible solutions for detecting multiple faces in real-time surveillance systems with email notification. Sreenivas et al. (2020) [20] present a hybrid system that uses three methods of extraction and recognition (MLTP: Multivariate Local Texture Pattern; GLCM: Grey Level Co-occurrence Matrix; and LESH: Local Energy-based Shape Histogram) and a composite fuzzy neural network (RFNN: Recurrent Fuzzy Neural Network; and FAPG: Fast Averaging Peer Group; SSD: Social Ski-Driver), optimized to classify emotional expressions in groups from video sequences, making recognition faster and more accurate.

Among performance-focused approaches, Juneja and Rana (2018) [6] propose a facial recognition technique that reduces recognition time without compromising accuracy, in addition to reviewing existing advanced approaches in the literature. Babu et al. (2021) [2], focused on surveillance systems, discuss methods for implementing these technologies and their applications in different contexts, such as public security and crowd management at events. The authors also highlight the limitations, challenges, and how to implement these technologies. Mahmood and Al-Maadeed (2019) [13] propose a solution for action recognition in groups of spectators, where the collected images are often of low quality. The authors suggest a people segmentation method based on the distribution of heads. Although not an article that addresses the review's core, this work brings significant concepts to the process of detecting presence in environments with low-quality cameras.

Regarding approaches presenting facial recognition as an applicable method in classrooms, Tang et al. (2020) [24] propose a method for evaluating classroom teaching based on students' facial expression recognition. Tabassum et al. (2020) [22] present an approach to automate the identification of students' attention in the classroom through facial expression recognition. The goal is to help teachers identify inattentive students in the classroom and take the necessary pedagogical measures to improve the teaching-learning relationship. Liu et al. (2018) [12] propose an approach to study student engagement in an intelligent learning environment, using five modules to detect and analyze student engagement, including presence management, T&S (Teacher and Student) communication, Visual Focus of Attention (VFOA) recognition, smile detection, and engagement analysis.

### 2.2.2   Studies that Present Methods, Frameworks and Systems

A behavior recognition method is proposed by Su et al. (2021) [21]. The authors use multiple models to analyze students' learning behavior based on images of various objects from a single viewpoint. The approach can be used in different environments, such as classrooms, banks, shopping malls, and sports stadiums. Pratheeksha et al. (2022) [18] present a framework that combines convolutional neural networks to detect human faces and classify emotions in real-time. The framework trains two different algorithms with distinct datasets to achieve higher accuracy in facial and emotional expression recognition. According to the authors, this approach is relevant to various areas, including e-learning and autism training. These two articles show different applications used in facial and emotional expression recognition, contributing to advances in behavior analysis and real-time emotion detection.

Gomathy et al. (2022) [7] present a student detail collection system based on facial recognition and real-time video processing. The system aims to achieve high accuracy in facial recognition during verification, real-time stability, and reliability with real-time video processing. This approach is relevant for building other student information management systems efficiently and accurately. Ping et al. (2018) [17] propose automatic classroom attendance management systems based on facial recognition technology. These systems can detect and recognize faces, recording different types of classroom attendance violations. The results of the experiments showed that the systems can recognize faces accurately and generate attendance tables that reflect the learning situation of all students after the class. These systems offer a solution for attendance management in academic environments, presenting significant advantages over traditional attendance tracking methods, such as reducing teachers' workload and eliminating recording errors.

Tamin et al. (2021) [23] present a student monitoring system that uses facial detection and eye tracking to provide real-time updates on student progress in online classes. The system allows teachers to send paperless assignments and track students' progress in their assignments and reading materials. Although our focus is to find solutions for in-person environments, the latter study addresses concepts that could be employed in both online and in-person classes.

### 2.2.3   Facial and Emotional Expression Recognition

Aranha et al. (2020) [1] present a comparative analysis of the performance of two open-source emotion recognition software under different environmental conditions. The study simulates different lighting, background, and distance conditions to investigate the impact of these factors on automatic and real-time recognition of the user's emotional state. Emotion recognition can benefit human-computer interaction. Additionally, the study addresses the need for techniques that do not involve additional sensors, aiming to reduce financial costs and user discomfort. Leong (2020) [11] investigates the use of deep machine learning on facial landmarks and FaceNet embeddings for the detection of academic emotions, with a focus on frustration and boredom. The authors emphasize the importance of detecting academic emotions in the educational field and demonstrate the effectiveness of deep learning in this context. The proposed approach can model both spatial and temporal dimensions of the data and shows promising results.

## 2.3    Other Literature Reviews

Three literature reviews were identified during the analysis of the collected studies, addressing different aspects of facial recognition and emotional expressions. Dufourq (2020) [4] provides a critical analysis of the literature on facial expression recognition using convolutional neural networks (CNNs). However, this review does not analyze other machine-learning approaches employed for this task. Pareek and Thakkar (2021) [16] present a literature review on human action recognition in videos. The authors focus on general facial recognition and do not address the recognition of emotional expressions. Juneja and Rana (2021) [8] present a systematic literature review on facial recognition systems, covering facial recognition techniques in a general sense without addressing emotion expression recognition.

## 2.4    Discussion on the Review

A systematic literature review on automatic recognition of behavior and emotional expressions was presented. The approach employed in this literature review allowed the verification and analysis of trends, as well as the technological approaches adopted over the last eight years. We carefully selected and analyzed 24 papers to reveal the state of the art in approaches that assess and represent the automation of behavior and emotional expression analysis. These works can assist in pedagogical decision-making by presenting theoretical approaches, methods, frameworks, and systems. The use of machine learning techniques to recognize expressions of emotion, behavior, and suspicious objects has proven to be a promising area in education. These techniques can provide valuable insights into students' behavior and emotions, contributing to their mental health and safety. Among the studies analyzed, several advantages and relevant applications for the recognition of emotional and behavioral expressions in the classroom were identified.

One of the main advantages of this research line is the possibility of gaining a deeper understanding of students' emotional states, allowing the adaptation of pedagogical strategies to their individual needs, creating a more positive and engaging learning environment. These techniques can contribute to classroom teaching assessment by identifying areas of difficulty and measuring students' levels of interest and engagement. Another significant advantage is the possibility of non-intrusive detection of students' attention. By means of facial expression analysis, teachers can identify students who are inattentive, distracted, or disengaged, enabling immediate intervention to redirect focus and reestablish active student participation. Facial and emotional expression recognition can also be applied to automated classroom attendance management, eliminating the need for manual attendance lists and reducing the workload for teachers.

In Table 1, we present a summary of the analyzed works, highlighting the following **Objectives**: (FR) Facial and action recognition; (RE) Recognition of expressions of emotion; (TA) Teaching assessment; (PM) Presence management; (SP) Security in public areas; and **Applications**: (1) Authentication; (2) Behavior; (3) Fatigue Detection; (4) Study of evolution; (5) Emotions; (6) Standardization; (7) Performance; (8) Computer vision.

**Table 1.** Summary of the works analyzed

| Authors | Objectives | | | | | Applications | | | | | | | |
|---|---|---|---|---|---|---|---|---|---|---|---|---|---|
| | FR | RE | TA | PM | SP | 1 | 2 | 3 | 4 | 5 | 6 | 7 | 8 |
| Aranha et al. [1] | | X | | | | | | | X | | | | X |
| Babu et al. [2] | X | | | X | X | X | | | | | | | X |
| Dufourq [4] | X | X | | | | | | | X | X | X | | |
| Dwijayanti et al. [5] | X | | | | | | X | | X | | | | X |
| Firoze and Deb [6] | X | | | | | X | | | | | X | | X |
| Gomathy et al. [7] | X | | | | | | X | | | | X | | X |
| Juneja and Rana [8] | X | | | | | | | | | X | X | | |
| Jyoti and Sonal [9] | X | | | | | X | | | | | X | | X |
| Leong [11] | | X | | | | | | | X | | | | X |
| Liu et al. [12] | | | X | | | | X | | X | X | | | |
| Mahmood and Al-Maadeed [13] | X | | | | | | X | | | | | | X |
| Menon et al. [14] | X | | | | | X | | | | | X | | X |
| Mohanty and Raghunadh [15] | X | | | | | | | | | | X | | X |
| Pareek and Thakkar [16] | X | | | | | | | X | | X | | | |
| Ping et al. [17] | | | | X | | X | | | | | | | |
| Pratheeksha et al. [18] | | X | | | | | X | | X | | | | X |
| Salih and Kulkarni [19] | X | | | | | | | X | X | | | | |
| Sreenivas et al. [20] | X | | | | | | | | | X | X | X | X |
| Su et al. [21] | | | X | | | | X | | | X | X | | X |
| Tabassum et al. [22] | | | X | | | | | | | X | | | X |
| Tamim et al. [23] | | | X | | | X | X | | X | | | | |
| Tang et al. [24] | | | X | | | | X | | X | | | | X |
| Ullah and Tian [25] | X | | | | | | | | | X | X | X | X |
| Vijayakumar et al. [26] | | | | X | | X | X | | X | | | | X |

Facial and emotional expression recognition systems must be transparent, with students' consent and respect for their privacy, as it is important to address ethical, privacy, and social acceptance issues in the educational context. Pedagogical decisions based on these analyses must be complemented by other assessment methods and consider the individual context of each student. Facial and emotional expression recognition techniques provide valuable insights into students' behavior and emotions, enabling personalized teaching and the creation of more effective learning environments. However, continuous reflection on the responsible and appropriate use of these technologies is essential, considering privacy, consent, and social acceptance aspects.

## 2.5    Related Work

Our method is based on three complementary techniques: identification of emotional expressions, behavior analysis, and detection of suspicious objects to identify individuals prone to unsafe acts in the school environment. The literature review revealed a significant gap, as no studies are addressing these three techniques jointly.

We aim to explore works that, while not covering all dimensions of our proposal, contribute to understanding the overall landscape related to security and the recognition of emotional expressions in educational environments. Six articles were identified in the analysis. Table 2 presents a synthesis of related work, classifying articles according to their objectives and applications. In observing the technologies necessary for the composition of our method, we initially analyzed methods and concepts related to facial recognition for individual identification and emotion recognition to assess individuals' moods.

Regarding machine learning, some research presents applicable methodologies and technologies. Babu et al. (2021) [2] address crowd estimation and recognition of strangers in enclosed public areas. The authors employ cameras and facial detection algorithms (e.g., Haar Classifier Algorithm) to identify people and strangers in real-time. The article also mentions microcontrollers (e.g., Raspberry Pi) to process and analyze data collected by cameras. A Web page provides information on the occupancy of a specific public location and allows users to choose the most suitable location. This method offers a cost-effective approach to facial recognition.

Mohanty and Raghunadh (2016) [15] address face detection based on the YCgCr color model, enhanced AdaBoost algorithm, and morphological operators to improve detection performance. The proposed method consists of three main steps: 1) Skin color segmentation, 2) detection of candidate face regions, and 3) face classification using the AdaBoost algorithm. In Step 1, skin color segmentation is performed in the YCgCr color space to extract skin regions from the image. In Step 2, candidate face regions are obtained through morphological operations on the skin regions. In Step 3, candidate face regions are classified as faces or non-faces using the AdaBoost algorithm trained with Haar features. The authors evaluated the method using different datasets, and the results showed that it can detect faces with high accuracy and efficiency in images with variations in lighting, pose, and facial expression.

Sreenivas et al. (2020) [20] present a method for group emotion recognition from video sequences. The method combines image processing techniques, facial feature extraction, and an optimized recurrent fuzzy neural network for classification. Experimental results show the method achieved an accuracy of 99.16%, recall of 99.33%, precision of 99%, sensitivity of 99.93%, and specificity of 99%, surpassing other deep learning approaches. It indicates the proposed method accurately recognizes group emotions from videos, representing a relevant approach to be employed in our method.

Tang et al. (2020) [24] present a method consisting of three main stages: 1) data acquisition, 2) emotion recognition, and 3) result analysis. In Stage 1, students' images are captured through a camera at various moments during the class. In Stage 2, students' faces are identified and extracted from the images. In Stage 3, students' facial expressions are analyzed to determine their emotional state. The facial expression recognition model is AlexNet, a classic convolutional neural network. The model is pre-trained to recognize six basic facial expressions: happiness, anger, disgust, fear, sadness, and surprise. The model's recognition accuracy is 92.68% and 99.10% for the JAFFE and Ck+ datasets, respectively. In the third stage, the results are interpreted to determine students' engagement during the class. Engagement is calculated based on the probability of each type of emotion and the corresponding weights in each dimension of the PAD model. It allows for a detailed assessment of teaching and assists teachers in reflecting on their teaching methods. The results achieved in this method include a recognition accuracy of 92.68% and 99.10% for the facial expression recognition model. The proposed method was tested in a real classroom, demonstrating its feasibility and utility. Despite the recognition accuracy, it was not this fact that sparked interest in our research but rather the PAD emotional state model, which describes human emotions in three main dimensions: pleasure-displeasure, activation-non-activation, and dominance-submission. These dimensions provide a three-dimensional representation of emotions, offering a framework for understanding and analyzing emotional variations. This work stands out in emotion expression recognition, focusing on the same environment as our method, i.e., the school.

Associated with one of the dimensions of our work (object recognition), Mahmood and Al-Maadeed [13], addressing the need for recognizing individuals in low-resolution images, employ object recognition algorithms to identify and count individuals, focusing on the head shapes. They address crowd behavior analysis. The proposed method (Head Distribution-based Person Segmentation - HDPS) utilizes efficient head detection, estimation of people's bounding boxes based on head size, and distribution of heads in the crowd image. For each segmented person, movement trajectories and texture features are calculated. This information is employed to recognize individual actions in crowd environments. The achieved results show the proposed method performed excellently in segmenting people in crowd scenes, even in low-quality videos. The approach successfully addressed issues of occlusion and mixed motion information, resulting in more accurate segmentation of people in the crowd. Experiments conducted with a public dataset containing up to 150 actors performing multiple actions showed the effectiveness of the proposed method in recognizing individual actions in crowded environments.

Addressing the third pillar of our method (behavior recognition in schools), Su et al. (2021) [21] present a method for behavior recognition based on multiple models to analyze students' learning behavior in classrooms based on images of objects from a single viewpoint. The proposed method divides students' behavior into three categories based on head posture, transforming the behavior recognition problem into a multiple-target detection problem. The proposed method utilizes a multiple detection network comprised of three detection networks with different-sized receptive fields and a switching network. This approach outperformed other methods in accuracy and speed compared to state-of-the-art methods on a classroom surveillance dataset. The study results show the proposed method achieved the lowest mean absolute error in counting the number of students compared to other methods. The proposed method was accurate in recognizing students' behavior compared to observed reality.

In light of the description of related works, our method stands out for addressing and integrating the latest techniques in a complementary manner, aiming to process data in a balanced way, identifying physical and psychological threats within the school environment, and creating alerts that can potentially save lives. In Table 2, we highlight the following *Objectives*:(FR) Facial recognition; (RE) Recognition of expressions of emotion; (OR) Object recognition; and (BA) Behavior Analysis; and *Applications*: (1) Authentication; (2) Behavior; (3) Public Security; (4) School monitoring; (5) Emotions; (6) Standardization; (7) Performance.

**Table 2.** Synthesis of related work

| Authors | Objectives | | | | Applications | | | | | | |
|---------|----|----|----|----|---|---|---|---|---|---|---|
| | FR | RE | OR | BA | 1 | 2 | 3 | 4 | 5 | 6 | 7 |
| Babu et al. (2021) [2] | X | | | X | X | X | | | | | |
| Mahmood and Al-Maadeed (2019) [13] | | | X | X | X | X | | X | | | |
| Mohanty and Raghunadh (2016) [15] | X | | | | X | | X | | | | X |
| Sreenivas et al. (2020) [20] | | X | | | | X | | | | | X |
| Su et al. (2021) [21] | | | | X | | X | | | X | | |
| Tang et al. (2020) [24] | | X | | | | | | X | | | |
| This study | X | X | X | X | X | X | X | X | X | X | |

## 3  Method for Security Monitoring of Educational Environments

The Method for Security Monitoring of Educational Environment (MSM-EDU) is a conceptual approach to ensuring security in educational environments. MSM-

EDU is relevant in the current context, where security has become a critical and challenging task in educational institutions. MSM-EDU consists of three dimensions of analysis, taking into account the product of computer vision identification (e.g., emotion, behavior, and object), the accuracy of the identification, and the relevance factor applied to this data. In Fig. 1, we present an overview of MSM-EDU.

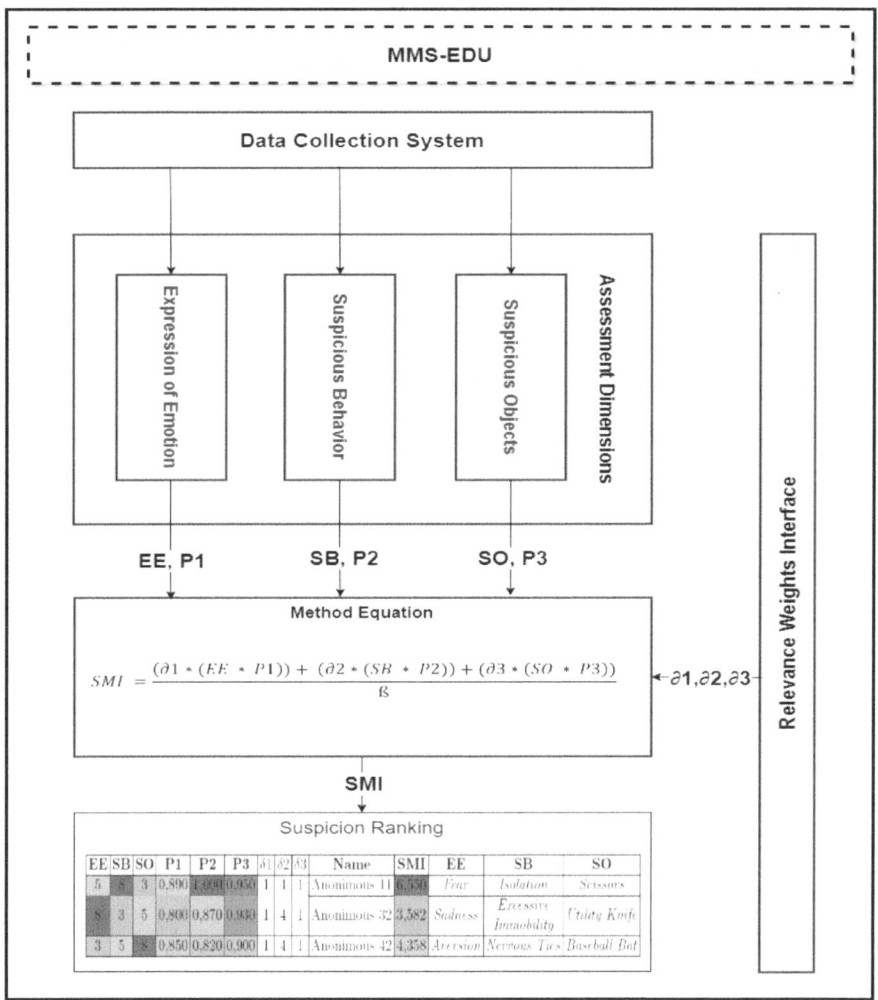

**Fig. 1.** MSM-EDU Overview

The identified products are summed and processed to establish a classification that numerically represents a potential need for psycho-pedagogical intervention or, in extreme cases, some security restrictions in school environments.

MSM-EDU is founded on three dimensions of analysis: recognition of emotional expressions (e.g., anger and fear), behavior analysis (e.g., agitation and apathy), and detection of suspicious objects (e.g., with weapon-like shapes). Each dimension plays a crucial role in security assessment. The MSM-EDU dimensions were designed to generate alerts jointly or trigger alerts individually according to the relevance factor applied to each of them.

Emotional Expressions ($EE$) are assessed through facial recognition systems, which can identify and classify a range of emotions that, as a hypothesis, would characterize a potential threat. Suspicious Behavior ($SB$) is determined through machine learning algorithms that analyze individual behaviors, looking for signs of agitation, apathy, or other behaviors that could be a reason for concern. Suspicious Objects ($SO$) are identified through computer vision techniques that can detect objects with shapes resembling weapons or other dangerous items according to the environment.

The Security Monitoring Index ($SMI$) is calculated through an equation that considers $EE$, $SB$, $SO$, their respective accuracies (P - expressed in percentage), and the relevance factors ($\delta$) assigned to each recognition to allow authorized professionals to balance the importance of each factor. The equation that calculates SMI is expressed as follows:

$$SMI = \frac{(\delta 1 * (EE * P1)) + (\delta 2 * (SB * P2)) + (\delta 3 * (SO * P3))}{\beta}$$

The proposed equation allows assigning a score ($SMI$) to each monitored person, numerically representing the possible need for a psycho-pedagogical approach or, in extreme cases, a security intervention. The equation consists of three parts, each corresponding to one of the analysis dimensions of MSM-EDU, where $EE$ is the value of Emotional Expressions, $SB$ is the value assigned for Suspicious Behavior, and $SO$ are the numerical values for Suspicious Objects. The values $EE$, $SB$, and $SO$ are labels (e.g., joy, agitation, knife, etc.) pointed out by computer vision algorithms and classified by professionals in the fields of security and psychology according to their degree of influence on the dangerousness of the environment.

In the equation, we also consider the positive accuracies for the recognition of expressions $P1$, behaviors $P2$, and objects $P3$, generated by each machine learning algorithm used, returning natural values with an accuracy of 3 decimal places, where $0 \leqslant Pn \leqslant 1$. The relevance factors ($\delta 1$, $\delta 2$, $and$ $\delta 3$) of each component can be configured by psychology professionals, educators, or security professionals according to the relevance of each recognition attribute, following the order of magnitude $0 \leqslant \delta n \leqslant 10$, allowing adjust the system to the specific needs of each educational environment. $\beta$ represents the sum of the relevance factors ($\delta$) and adds flexibility to the equation in case of future inclusions of relevance factors, as follows:

$$\beta = \sum_{i=1}^{n} \delta_i$$

Relevance factors ($\delta$) are necessary to balance the method, as there is a significant difference between various applicable educational environments. For example, carrying weapons may not be highly relevant in a military institution's school environment, whereas in a civilian elementary or high school, carrying sharp objects or firearms would pose a significant risk to the school community and should have greater relevance in the calculations. The proposed weighting enables the triggering of emergency alerts considering critical values for all analysis dimensions.

To illustrate the processing of MSM-EDU, a real-time monitoring simulation was carried out. We highlight all children's images used in the examples were generated by an AI tool [3]. In Example 1 (Fig. 2), three individuals (*Anonymous 11, 32, and 42*) were analyzed, and domain experts (based on a risk classification) adjusted the relevance factors as follows: $\delta1 = 5$, $\delta2 = 1$, *and* $\delta3 = 3$. In this simulation, we will not consider detecting any suspicious objects. We consider a scenario where a student (*Anonymous 32*) was detected with expressions similar to sadness and anger associated with isolating behavior, as shown in Fig. 2. Example 1 shows despite no suspicious objects being detected with the student, after analyzing their emotional expressions (*EE*), the student seems to require psycho-pedagogical care.

**Fig. 2.** Example 1 - Monitoring students from SMI - Anonymous 32

In Example 2 (Fig. 3), we consider a scenario in which education professionals, concerned about suspicious objects in the school environment, adjusted the relevance factors to $\delta1 = 2$, $\delta2 = 1$, *and* $\delta3 = 10$. In this scenario, a student enters the school *agitated*, showing signs of *surprise* in their emotional expression and carrying a *pointed object*. Based on the detection data, detection accuracy, and applied relevance factors, the student's *SMI* increases instantly, indicating the immediate need for security intervention.

| | Time 1 | Time 2 | Time 3 | Time 4 | Largest SMI |
|---|---|---|---|---|---|
| Anonimous 15 | 1.349 | 1.826 | 1.033 | 1.236 | 1.826 |
| Anonimous 17 | 1.363 | 2.120 | 3.321 | 7.230 | 7.230 |
| Anonimous 63 | 1.236 | 2.472 | 2.290 | 2.236 | 2.472 |

**Fig. 3.** Example 2 - SMI triggered by the suspicious object analysis dimension - Anonymous 17

## 4    Applying MSM-EDU

We performed simulations using data representing various situations that could indicate potential risks in school environments. The simulation data and results were validated by three software engineers with the support of a full professor of Psychology with over 15 years of experience dealing with juvenile and adult offenders. Table 3 presents examples of risk classification for the analysis dimensions and their ratings, where *10* indicates the highest degree of risk and *0* indicates the lowest degree of risk.

Since there are dozens of records for each dimension, the classification table will not always receive uniform values, containing only one element for each risk value. For example, we may have *knife* or *sword* detected as suspicious and dangerous objects in the school environment and classified with the same risk value of *9*, while a *notebook* or *smartphone*, when detected but not considered suspicious or dangerous, therefore receive a classification with the value *0*.

Table 4 presents a scenario in which a student (*Anonymous 26*) demonstrates a potential medium-risk emotional expression (*Fear*) and a suspicious behavior (*Isolation*). This student is carrying an object with a high potential for

**Table 3.** Examples of risk classification of the EE, SB, and SO analysis dimensions

| Risk | EE | SB | SO |
|------|-----|-----|-----|
| 0 | Neutral | Sleeping | Notebook |
| 1 | Joy | Sitting | Chair |
| 2 | Surprise | Standing | Pencil |
| 3 | Aversion | Excessive Immobility | Scissors |
| 4 | Disgust | Excessive Gesturing | Rope |
| 5 | Fear | Nervous Tics | Utility Knife |
| 6 | Contempt | Defensive Posture | Metal Rod |
| 7 | Crying | Excessive Agitation | Hammer |
| 8 | Sadness | Isolation | Baseball Bat |
| 9 | Scared | Threat | Knife |
| 10 | Anger | Running | Firearm |

causing physical harm (*knife*). The table shows the recognition accuracy values (*P1 = 0.890, P2 = 1.000, P3 = 0.950*) associated with each dimension for *Anonymous 26*. In this example, we do not consider the relevance factor for dimensions, so the coefficients $\delta 1$, $\delta 2$ *and* $\delta 3$ are 1. In addition to the SMI values, the colors (from green to red) represent the level of suspicion of the analyzed individual.

**Table 4.** Example of ranking generated from the application of MSM-EDU

| EE | SB | SO | P1 | P2 | P3 | $\delta 1$ | $\delta 2$ | $\delta 3$ | Name | SMI | EE | SB | SO |
|----|----|----|----|----|----|----|----|----|------|-----|----|----|----|
| 5 | 8 | 9 | 0.890 | 1.000 | 0.950 | 1 | 1 | 1 | *Anonymous 26* | 7.000 | *Fear* | *Isolation* | *Knife* |
| 4 | 2 | 1 | 0.800 | 0.740 | 0.360 | 1 | 1 | 1 | *Anonymous 33* | 1.680 | *Disgust* | *Standing* | *Chain* |
| 10 | 8 | 5 | 0.696 | 0.670 | 0.564 | 1 | 1 | 1 | *Anonymous 12* | 5.047 | *Anger* | *Isolation* | *Utility Knife* |

## 4.1   Simulation with Relevance Factors

Simulations were carried out to exercise the calculations, for example, by adjusting the relevance factors ($\delta 1$, $\delta 2$, and $\delta 3$). The diversity of school environments, which include elementary, middle, and high schools, public and private schools, and military or religious schools, requires the application and variation of relevance factors. Additionally, each environment has its own mental, physical, and property security rules. For example, in a military school, detecting weapons may have less relevance in alerting a suspicious individual than in a Christian school, where weapons or suspicious objects are prohibited. MSM-EDU enables flexibility, allowing adaptation to the specific needs of each educational environment. Three simulations were performed to validate the method's adaptability, i.e., its flexibility.

In Simulation 1, we kept $\delta 2$ and $\delta 3$ with a value of 1 and increased the weight of $\delta 1$ (for Emotional Expressions - $EE$) to 4, making them more influential in the final classification of individuals, as reflected in the results shown in Table 5. For example, in Row 1, Column 3, we have a recognition of behavior ($SB$) with a critical value of 8. Despite this, the SMI ranks 2nd in the ranking. However, in Row 2, Column 1, we have the same value considered critical previously, now for $EE$. We notice that the $SMI$ for this individual ranks 1st in the ranking due to the upward adjustment of the relevance factor for $EE$ ($\delta 1 = 4$).

**Table 5.** Simulation 1 - Adjusting Relevance Factor, with an emphasis on $\delta 1$ for EE

| EE | SB | SO | P1 | P2 | P3 | $\delta 1$ | $\delta 2$ | $\delta 3$ | Name | SMI | EE | SB | SO |
|----|----|----|------|------|------|---|---|---|-------------|-------|---------|----------------------|--------------|
| 5 | 8 | 1 | 0.890 | 1.000 | 0.950 | 4 | 1 | 1 | Anonymous 11 | 4.458 | Fear | Isolation | Scissors |
| 8 | 3 | 1 | 0.800 | 0.870 | 0.930 | 4 | 1 | 1 | Anonymous 32 | 4.857 | Sadness | Excessive Immobility | Utility Knife |
| 3 | 5 | 8 | 0.850 | 0.820 | 0.900 | 4 | 1 | 1 | Anonymous 42 | 3.583 | Aversion | Nervous Tics | Baseball Bat |

In Simulation 2, we increased the weight of $\delta 2$ (for Suspicious Behavior - $SB$) to a value of 4, making it more influential in the final classification of individuals while keeping $\delta 1$ and $\delta 3$ with a value of 1. The results from Simulation 2 are given in Table 6. For example, in Row 3, Column 3, we have the detection of an object ($SO$) with a high value (8). Despite this, the SMI ranks 2nd in the ranking, as the relevance factor for the object criterion is low ($\delta 3 = 1$). On the other hand, in Row 1, Column 2, we have the same value considered high previously, now for $SB$. We notice that the $SMI$ for this individual ranks 1st in the ranking due to the upward adjustment of the relevance factor for $SB$ ($\delta 2 = 4$).

**Table 6.** Simulation 2 - Adjusting Relevance Factor, with an emphasis on $\delta 2$ for SB

| EE | SB | SO | P1 | P2 | P3 | $\delta 1$ | $\delta 2$ | $\delta 3$ | Name | SMI | EE | SB | SO |
|----|----|----|------|------|------|---|---|---|-------------|-------|---------|----------------------|--------------|
| 5 | 8 | 3 | 0.890 | 1.000 | 0.950 | 1 | 4 | 1 | Anonymous 11 | 6.550 | Fear | Isolation | Scissors |
| 8 | 3 | 5 | 0.800 | 0.870 | 0.930 | 1 | 4 | 1 | Anonymous 32 | 3.582 | Sadness | Excessive Immobility | Utility Knife |
| 3 | 5 | 8 | 0.850 | 0.820 | 0.900 | 1 | 4 | 1 | Anonymous 42 | 4.358 | Aversion | Nervous Tics | Baseball Bat |

In Simulation 3, we increased the weight of $\delta 3$ (for Suspicious Objects - $SO$) to 4, making it more influential in the final classification of individuals while keeping $\delta 1$ and $\delta 2$ with 1. Table 7 presents the results from the third simulation. For example, in Row 2, Column 1, we have the recognition of emotional expression ($EE$) with a high value (8). Despite this, the $SMI$ ranks 2nd in the ranking, as the relevance factor for the criterion of emotional expressions is low ($\delta 1 = 1$). On the other hand, in Row 3, Column 3, we have the same value considered high previously, now for $SO$. We notice the $SMI$ for this individual ranks 1st in the ranking due to the upward adjustment of the relevance factor for $SO$ ($\delta 3 = 4$).

**Table 7.** Simulation 3 - Adjusting Relevance Factor, with an emphasis on $\delta3$ for SO

| EE | SB | SO | P1 | P2 | P3 | $\delta1$ | $\delta2$ | $\delta3$ | Name | SMI | EE | SB | SO |
|----|----|----|----|----|----|----|----|----|------|-----|----|----|----|
| 5 | 8 | 3 | 0.890 | 1.000 | 0.950 | 1 | 1 | 4 | Anonymous 11 | 3.975 | *Fear* | *Isolation* | *Scissors* |
| 8 | 3 | 5 | 0.800 | 0.870 | 0.930 | 1 | 1 | 4 | Anonymous 32 | 4.602 | *Sadness* | *Excessive Immobility* | *Utility Knife* |
| 3 | 5 | 8 | 0.850 | 0.820 | 0.900 | 1 | 1 | 4 | Anonymous 42 | 5.908 | *Aversion* | *Nervous Tics* | *Baseball Bat* |

## 4.2   Discussion on the Results

From three simulations, we illustrated how the proposed relevance factors can enable necessary adjustments to the method. For example, in Table 5, Row 3, $\delta1 = 4$ indicates that in this scenario, relevance factors were modified to prioritize emotional expressions while detection of behavior and objects, although observed and calculated, remain at a lower level. We highlight that $\delta$ can vary from 1 to 10, and in this simulation, the relevance of *EE*, although crucial for the scenario, is not excessively high. MSM-EDU can be extended with other relevant factors in the case of the inclusion of new analysis dimensions.

The Security Monitoring Index (*SMI*) stands out in the simulation tables, allowing for the ordering of suspicious individuals in order of criticality. For example, in Table 6, Row 1, $SMI = 6.550$ indicates that the individual Anonymous 11 requires more attention from the professionals involved in monitoring, as he exhibits excessive isolation behavior.

*EE*, *SB*, and *SO* are analysis dimensions that allow for individualized security monitoring, but they could also be used jointly through SMI. For example, in Table 7, Row 1, *SB=8* elevates Anonymous 11 to the first place in the ranking, even though the relevance factor for *SB* is low ($\delta2 = 1$). *SMI* considers the relevance factor and the three analysis dimensions.

MSM-EDU is proposed as a conceptual approach to support real-time decision-making, allowing monitoring systems to be developed based on its structure. The proposed approach allows a numerical evaluation, reducing subjectivity and judiciously indicating a eventual need for intervention. This predictive capability adds efficiency to daily operations and plays a crucial preventive role in mitigating serious incidents.

Nowadays, significant challenges are faced by educational institutions, from the increasing stress of students and teachers to maintaining a safe environment. Integrating facial, behavioral, and object recognition technologies arises as a holistic approach to addressing these issues. The proposed method can serve as a foundation for security incident prevention tools, playing a crucial role in early identifying the factors contributing to stress and depression among the school community members.

## 5   Final Remarks

Our work aims to encourage and enhance physical security in schools and promote an environment that cares about the psychological well-being of students and teachers. By integrating innovative technologies with educational responsibility, the proposed approach offers a promising path for building safer and more supportive school environments.

Simulations have shown that MSM-EDU is feasible to be implemented in school environments and can be adjusted to emphasize the factors (or parameters) that educators and security professionals consider most important for the security of their specific environment. It makes MSM-EDU a flexible and adaptable tool for security monitoring in different educational settings. MSM-EDU is a promising approach for educators and security professionals. It is intended for researchers seeking to develop methods and techniques to improve security in school environments. MSM-EDU is focused on school security but is flexible and can be adapted to other monitored environments. Since each school environment is unique, with its rules and security regulations, MSM-EDU could be employed in conjunction with other security techniques.

As future work, we plan to: i) apply the method in a real school environment; and ii) expand the dimensions of analysis, considering other types of environments, sensors, or detection techniques. With a more comprehensive approach, we hope to improve the accuracy of detection models, ensuring a more effective and adaptable implementation of MSM-EDU in diverse educational settings.

## References

1. Aranha, R.V., Casaes, A.B., Nunes, F.L.S.: Influence of environmental conditions in the performance of open-source software for facial expression recognition. In: ACM Access. IHC '20, Association for Computing Machinery, New York, NY, USA (2020). https://doi.org/10.1145/3424953.3426630
2. Babu, M.G., Bhalaji, C.P., Rajendran, S., Selvi, V.I.: IoT based crowd estimation and stranger recognition in closed public areas, pp. 763–773 (2021). https://doi.org/10.1109/ICESC51422.2021.9532674
3. Computing, I.M., Candido, R.: Playground AI (2023). https://playground.com/profile/clpjr9yw60zg6s6014qfy0nlf, https://playground.com/create, images generated by Artificial Intelligence
4. Dufourq, E.: A survey on factors affecting facial expression recognition based on convolutional neural networks, pp. 168–179. Association for Computing Machinery (2020). https://doi.org/10.1145/3410886.3410891
5. Dwijayanti, S., Iqbal, M., Suprapto, B.Y.: Real-time implementation of face recognition and emotion recognition in a humanoid robot using a convolutional neural network. IEEE Access 10, 89876–89886 (2022). https://doi.org/10.1109/ACCESS.2022.3200762
6. Firoze, A., Deb, T.: Face recognition time reduction based on partitioned faces without compromising accuracy and a review of state-of-the-art face recognition approaches, pp. 14–21. Association for Computing Machinery (2018). https://doi.org/10.1145/3191442.3191467

7. Gomathy, B., Sathya, K., Sathish, J., Santhosh, S., Sabari Krishna, S.: Face recognition based student detail collection using openCV, pp. 1–4 (2022). https://doi.org/10.1109/ICSSS54381.2022.9782211
8. Juneja, K., Rana, C.: An extensive study on traditional-to-recent transformation on face recognition system. SPRINGER Access **118**, 3075–3128 (2021). https://doi.org/10.1007/s11277-021-08170-3
9. Jyoti, S.: Enhancement of face detection with email facility, pp. 825–830 (2022). https://doi.org/10.23919/INDIACom54597.2022.9763193
10. Kitchenham, B.A.: Procedures for performing systematic reviews. Department of Computer Science, Keele University, Kelee, UK (2004). http://www.it.hiof.no/~haraldh/misc/2016-08-22-smat/Kitchenham-Systematic-Review-2004.pdf
11. Leong, F.H.: Deep learning of facial embeddings and facial landmark points for the detection of academic emotions, pp. 111–116. Association for Computing Machinery (2020). https://doi.org/10.1145/3411681.3411684
12. Liu, Y., Chen, J., Zhang, M., Rao, C.: Student engagement study based on multi-cue detection and recognition in an intelligent learning environment. Multimedia Tools Appl. **77**(21), 28749–28775 (2018). https://doi.org/10.1007/s11042-018-6017-2
13. Mahmood, A., Al-Maadeed, S.: Action recognition in poor-quality spectator crowd videos using head distribution-based person segmentation. SPRINGER Access **30**, 1083–1096 (2019). https://doi.org/10.1007/s00138-019-01039-3
14. Menon, M.S., George, A., Aswathy, N.: Implementation of a multitudinous face recognition using yolo.v3, pp. 1–6 (11 2021). https://doi.org/10.1109/ICMSS53060.2021.9673609
15. Mohanty, R., Raghunadh, M.V.: A new approach to face detection based on YCGCR color model and improved adaboost algorithm, pp. 1392–1396 (2016). https://doi.org/10.1109/ICCSP.2016.7754383
16. Pareek, P., Thakkar, A.: A survey on video-based human action recognition: recent updates, datasets, challenges, and applications. SPRINGER Access **54**, 2259–2322 (2021). https://doi.org/10.1007/s10462-020-09904-8
17. Ping, C., Da-Peng, H., Zu-Ying, L.: Automatic attendance face recognition for real classroom environments, pp. 65–70. Association for Computing Machinery (2018). https://doi.org/10.1145/3289430.3289436
18. Pratheeksha Hegde, N., Shetty, C., Dhananjaya, B., Deepa, Rashmi, N., Sarojadevi, H.: Face and emotion recognition in real time using machine learning. In: IEEE Access. pp. 1018–1025. IEEE (2022). https://doi.org/10.1109/ICCES54183.2022.9835759
19. Salih, H., Kulkarni, L.: Study of video based facial expression and emotions recognition methods, pp. 692–696 (2017). https://doi.org/10.1109/I-SMAC.2017.8058267
20. Sreenivas, V., Namdeo, V., Kumar, E.V.: Group based emotion recognition from video sequence with hybrid optimization based recurrent fuzzy neural network. SPRINGER Access **7**, 56 (2020). https://doi.org/10.1186/s40537-020-00326-5
21. Su, K., Li, X., Zhou, C., Chen, X.: Learning behaviour recognition based on multi-object image in single viewpoint. SPRINGER Access **25**, 1081–1090 (2021). https://doi.org/10.1007/s00779-019-01286-1
22. Tabassum, T., Allen, A.A., De, P.: Non-intrusive identification of student attentiveness and finding their correlation with detectable facial emotions, pp. 127–134. Association for Computing Machinery (2020). https://doi.org/10.1145/3374135.3385263

23. Tamim, H.M., Sultana, F., Tasneem, N., Marzan, Y., Khan, M.M.: Class insight: a student monitoring system with real-time updates using face detection and eye tracking, pp. 213–220 (2021). https://doi.org/10.1109/AIIoT52608.2021.9454176

24. Tang, X.Y., Peng, W.Y., Liu, S.R., Xiong, J.W.: Classroom teaching evaluation based on facial expression recognition, pp. 62–67. Association for Computing Machinery (2020). https://doi.org/10.1145/3383923.3383949

25. Ullah, S., Tian, W.: A systematic literature review of recognition of compound facial expression of emotions, pp. 116–121. Association for Computing Machinery (2021). https://doi.org/10.1145/3447450.3447469

26. Vijayakumar, R., Poornima, M., Divyapriya, S., Selvaganapathi, T.: Automated student attendance tracker for end semester examination using face recognition system, pp. 1566–1570 (2022).https://doi.org/10.1109/ICOSEC54921.2022.9952035

# Multi-Role Actors and Rebounding Effects Across User Interfaces - Exploring Big Tech's Privacy Scandals and GDPR Limitations in Data Ecosystems

Christian Kurtz[(✉)] and Fabian Burmeister

Department of Informatics, Universität Hamburg, Hamburg, Germany
`{christian.kurtz,fabian.burmeister}@uni-hamburg.de`

**Abstract.** Big Tech companies' ecosystems build on the commodification of personal data with harmful consequences for users' information privacy. The sustained data collection in data ecosystems bases often on secrecy. This opacity creates problems for assessing privacy-violating practices and regulation fails to materialize. Given the challenge of research data access to privacy-violating practices within the ecosystems of companies, we analyzed 21 privacy scandals reported in the media. The scandals include the companies around Facebook and Google, which refined personal data accumulation and utilization practices over years. Our results show that the companies take various roles across service contexts. These diverse roles enable to decouple personal data from the original service context and build the basis for rebounding effects in other service contexts. Using the GDPR in a socio-techno-legal assessment, we indicate that for regulation of Big Tech companies' practices, the actors' spheres of influence and the totality of their data processing operations are crucial.

**Keywords:** Data Ecosystem · Information Privacy · Personal Data · Data Protection · GDPR · Law · Regulation

## 1 Introduction

Billions of users worldwide engage with information technologies and highly personalized services (e.g., social networking sites), generating vast amounts of data [1]. The growing number of information systems connected in related networks creates unprecedented opportunities to process and share data in all spheres of life [2]. Big Tech companies are central parts of these evolutions. The companies often called "platforms" have contributed to diverse and useful data-intensive services. For this, Big Tech companies created expansive data ecosystems around users. However, the companies' capabilities build around commodifying a huge amount of personal data with harmful consequences for users' information privacy [3]. Little detail is existent about Big Tech privacy-violating practices, as they established secrecy around the companies' ecosystems [3] while at the same time making use of dark patterns in user interfaces (e.g., Facebook's design of the feature Privacy Checkup that allows users to edit pre-selected privacy settings while trying to keep users away from all other privacy settings) [1].

© The Author(s), under exclusive license to Springer Nature Switzerland AG 2025
A. Marcus et al. (Eds.): HCII 2024, LNCS 15380, pp. 283–303, 2025.
https://doi.org/10.1007/978-3-031-76821-7_20

Still, a large part of privacy research especially in the information systems field focuses on the concept of information privacy as one's ability to control personal data about oneself to study the dyadic relationship between a user and a company [4, 5]. Data ecosystems in which users and companies process personal data are underrepresented in privacy studies. This manuscript moves beyond the often used, bilateral perspective on privacy in the information systems field. It adopts a systemic perspective to get insights about the triangle of privacy, Big Tech companies, and data ecosystems. In this regard, systemic means a broader perspective shifting from the focus on the interaction between a user and a company towards the personal data creation, collection, and use in data ecosystems with a plethora of actors involved. Given the problem of secrecy established by Big Tech companies, we use privacy scandals reported in media. By considering various scandals with the involvement of Google and Facebook, we aim to create a better understanding of their practices in data ecosystems to unearth Big Tech companies' ecosystems. Hence, we address the following research question (RQ): RQ1: *What are the roles of Big Tech companies across user interfaces in data ecosystems, and how are these roles violating users' information privacy?*

Many people pin hopes on the regulation of personal data processing also regarding proliferating practices in data ecosystems. In this context, the EU's General Data Protection Regulation (GDPR) that became effective in 2018 contains several substantives when companies processing the personal data of EU citizens. In addition, the regulation served as a blueprint for data protection regulations throughout the world, such as the California Consumer Privacy Act. The question still leaves open whether this regulation can be a springboard to privacy-invasive practices of Big Tech companies in data ecosystems. Thus, we address also a second research question: *RQ2: Is the GDPR able to regulate privacy-violating practices of Big Tech companies in data ecosystems?*

In the following, we introduce the related work of information privacy, the GDPR, and data ecosystems. We continue by specifying our research approach. Our results show that Big Tech companies in data ecosystems masquerade as platform providers, service providers, and third parties to gain access to users' personal data. These roles create the basis for rebounding effects on users in other service contexts. Given these results, we examine whether the GDPR would be applicable to regulate related data processing. We elaborate on the results before we draw a conclusion.

## 2 Related Work

### 2.1 Information Privacy

The concepts' regarding privacy has evolved in response to the specific (and changing) political and technological situations of different societies [7–10]. At the end of the last century, two streams of thought about privacy were predominant in the literature [7]. One, the understanding of privacy as "restricted access", postulated that one has informational privacy when one can limit or restrict the access of others to one's personal information. The other, which understood privacy as "control", postulated that one has privacy when one controls information about oneself [7]. These perspectives' shortcomings in the face of new or imminent information practices led Nissenbaum [11] to develop a new understanding of privacy as *Contextual Integrity*. The main idea behind this normative framework is that information flows must be appropriate, so as not to violate privacy. This aim is achieved if contextual-information norms are met [11]. Nevertheless, Nissenbaum (2019) herself recognizes that "[g]iven a technological landscape that includes vast data holdings, data analytics, AI, machine learning, IoT, mobile devices, and other computational capacities, there is a dire need for systemic principles that will expose the material risks of the current data policy anarchy" [12, p. 255]. The strength of Contextual Integrity in assessing data flows on a very fine, granular level goes hand in hand with the challenge to consider systemic effects caused by interconnected personal-data processing. Nissenbaum [12] calls for making these practices "available for inspection" and creating transparency across data chains [12].

Information privacy research in the information systems field often persists on the definitions of the ability to control or limit access to the information about oneself [4, 5, 13, 14]. Some design-oriented studies exist in this field [15–18]. However, a major part of information systems research in the context of information privacy focuses primarily on individual actions and motivations and is most relevant to behavioral economics and psychology [4, 19–21]. For example, researchers address users' intentions to disclose data (and the privacy concerns that relate to that intention) [22, 23]; the motivating or discouraging factors [24]; or the privacy paradox, which is a gap between the intention to disclose personal data and the disclosure behavior [20, 25]. In this context, privacy concerns refer to user beliefs about personal data sharing and usage by, for example, other companies or unauthorized persons [26]. The literature divides privacy concerns into the collection, secondary usage, errors, improper access, and control of data [26]. The violation of information privacy and actors' unauthorized access to a user's personal data can trigger adverse consequences [28]. Besides physical, social, legal and career-related consequences, consequences provoked by corporate parties may be psychological, freedom-related or resource-related [28]. Psychological consequences include the negative impact on one's peace of mind owing to potential surveillance, unknown ramifications or loss of control [28]. Freedom-related consequences include the loss of freedom of opinion and behavior owing to organizational access to an individual's personal data; this can result in manipulations of opinion and behavior to influence an individual's decision and direct restrictions on behavior [28]. Resource-related consequences include loss of time, material losses and financial losses (e.g., price discrimination) [28]. One driver for such consequences is the ineffectiveness of privacy controls in the human-centered design, especially regarding ecosystems [27].

So far, privacy research at the group level remains scarce in the information systems field [4]. A few articles modeled personal data access in multi-party constellations [28–30]. However, "[n]o known research focuses on the data themselves, i.e., their existence, movement and life cycle once released by the individual." [30, p. 412f.]. Bélanger and Xu [5] emphasize that information privacy research should "move beyond the existing theoretical frameworks, levels of analysis and traditional approaches to information privacy research" (p. 575).

## 2.2 Personal Data Protection by the GDPR

In terms of protecting users' personal data, the body of EU regulation known as the GDPR has made significant inroads in the last years [31]. The GDPR is the central framework for data protection in the EU and aims to protect personal data and privacy for one of the largest consumer markets worldwide [32] The GDPR also binds companies outside the jurisdiction of the EU when they process the personal data of the EU citizens (Art. 3 (2)) and serves as a blueprint for privacy regulation throughout the world, such as the California Consumer Privacy Act. Under the GDPR, regulators can invoke substantial penalties of up to 4% of the annual worldwide revenues of companies for violating the data protection clauses (Art. 83 No. 5).

The GDPR has the explicit aim of regulating the modern data processing environment. For this, the regulation is formulated in an abstract way to fill the regulation with life over time also to be applicable to novel practices. At the same time, this abstractness creates doubts regarding data processing, for which judgments create clarity concerning the legality. Thus, regulators are still striving to cope with the negative aspects of information technologies for privacy [6]. An important characteristic is the attempt to enforce data protection by offering a binary system of two opposing groups: a *controller* (entity processing the personal data) and a *data subject* (person to whom these data relate; namely, the users in this study). Data controllership, the role within the GDPR that attributes accountability and responsibility for the lawfulness of a data processing operation to a company, is always defined concerning any operation or set of (identical) operations performed on personal data (Art. 4 No. 2). According to the regulation, personal data refers to "any information relating to an identified or identifiable natural person ('data subject'); an identifiable natural person is one who can be identified, directly or indirectly, in particular by reference to an identifier such as a name, an identification number, location data, an online identifier or to one or more factors specific to the physical, physiological, genetic, mental, economic, cultural or social identity of that natural person" (Art. 4 No. 1). In addition, two or more actors can be *joint controllers* for an act of processing in which they jointly determine its purposes and means (Art. 26). Moreover, a processor is an actor that processes data on behalf of the controller, according to Art. 4 No. 8.

### 2.3 Data Ecosystems

Along with other types of ecosystems that conceptualize networks of value co-creation such as business ecosystems [33], platform ecosystems [34], service ecosystems [35], or software ecosystems [36], data ecosystems are gaining increasing consideration in information systems research [37]. According to Oliveira, Lima and Lóscio [38], data ecosystems can be defined as "a loose set of interacting actors that directly or indirectly consume, produce, or provide data and other related resources (e.g., software, services, and infrastructure). Each actor performs one or more roles and is connected to other actors through relationships, in such a way that actors by collaborating and competing promote data ecosystems" (p. 604). Using ecosystems as research object, interwoven interactions and their effects can be studied. So far, research on data ecosystems is still in its infancy and perceived as "new and undertheori[z]ed" [37, p. 3]. While many studies on data ecosystems refer to open data communities, e.g., in the public sector [39, 40], there is a lack of research applying the data ecosystem perspective to study practices that violate information privacy. For example, modeling approaches in the context of data ecosystems do not focus on personal-data sharing and its effects on privacy [41, 42].

In this study, we consider a data ecosystem perspective and not a platform ecosystem perspective as this might be too narrow to holistically grasp the data practices of Big Tech companies that may also appear outside their platform ecosystems.

## 3 Research Approach

We conduct a multiple case analysis [43] and socio-techno-legal analysis [44, 45] as foundations of our research approach (see Fig. 1). In detail, we examine privacy scandals (also termed as cases) related to Google (Go.) and Facebook (Fb.) as major representatives of Big Tech companies. To identify cases, we searched for news articles and enriched the data material per case in the first step. In the second step, we applied qualitative content analysis [46] to interpret the cases and examine the data material per case. Mayring describes content analysis as the proper approach for "the systematic examination of communicative material (originally from the mass media in particular)" [46, p. 266]. In the third step, based on the cross-case conclusions, we identified multiple roles of actors across service contexts that build the basis personal data processing acts with rebounding effects. Here, modelling the activities of each case supported the research process. Finally, we analyzed the GDPR's applicability to the regulation of data processing related to identified roles and processing activities in a socio-techno-legal assessment [44, 45].

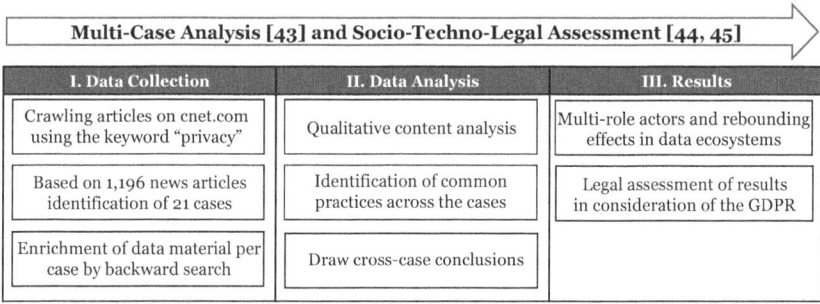

**Fig. 1.** Research approach.

### 3.1 Data Collection

Our selection of multiple cases is based on theoretical replication logic, according to which different cases are predicted to provide heterogeneous characteristics [43, 48]. We used cnet.com as our initial data source, as it is the technology-news website with the highest traffic rank worldwide [49]. News articles on this website are interlinked to other sources such as websites or documents such as scientific studies or technical reports. We also considered the other sources to increase the variety of data within the data material (see Table 2) and the robustness of our analysis. As the first step of data collection, we set up a web crawler to search news articles on cnet.com using the keyword "privacy," as we wanted to identify the roles and practices of Big Tech companies exposed in privacy scandals (see Fig. 2). For this, we made use of the definition of scandal by Thompson [50]. News articles complaining about privacy scandals include data collection or data use practices with the characteristics that their occurrence (1) involves an element of opacity and (2) a transgression related to privacy (3) that offends users. In addition, (4) reporters publicly denounce the practices from which follows that (5) the disclosure of the practices may damage the reputation of the party responsible.

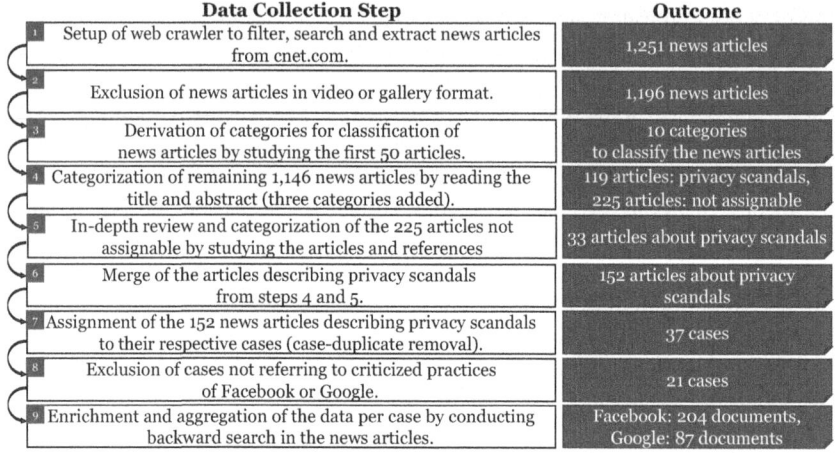

| Data Collection Step | Outcome |
|---|---|
| 1 Setup of web crawler to filter, search and extract news articles from cnet.com. | 1,251 news articles |
| 2 Exclusion of news articles in video or gallery format. | 1,196 news articles |
| 3 Derivation of categories for classification of news articles by studying the first 50 articles. | 10 categories to classify the news articles |
| 4 Categorization of remaining 1,146 news articles by reading the title and abstract (three categories added). | 119 articles: privacy scandals, 225 articles: not assignable |
| 5 In-depth review and categorization of the 225 articles not assignable by studying the articles and references | 33 articles about privacy scandals |
| 6 Merge of the articles describing privacy scandals from steps 4 and 5. | 152 articles about privacy scandals |
| 7 Assignment of the 152 news articles describing privacy scandals to their respective cases (case-duplicate removal). | 37 cases |
| 8 Exclusion of cases not referring to criticized practices of Facebook or Google. | 21 cases |
| 9 Enrichment and aggregation of the data per case by conducting backward search in the news articles. | Facebook: 204 documents, Google: 87 documents |

**Fig. 2.** Data collection process.

We sorted the articles by descending date and considered a multi-year time period for an initial list of 1,251 news articles. These articles mention the word "privacy" in the title, abstract, or text. The articles were extracted by the web crawler and integrated into a case-study database [43]. We excluded news articles in video or gallery format in the second step, resulting in 1,196 news articles. In the third step, two researchers studied the first 50 news articles and derived 10 categories for classification. In the fourth step, all news articles were assigned to the categories based on their title and abstract. Some articles could not be assigned to one of the 10 categories. Therefore, three categories were added: company viewpoint, court judgment, and public debate. In this way, 119 news articles referred to privacy scandals, and 225 were marked as unclear or ambiguous, requiring further in-depth review. In the fifth step, the two researchers classified the 225 articles marked as unclear for categorization by studying their content and references in detail, resulting in 33 additional articles about privacy scandals. In the sixth step, the researchers merged the news articles from steps 4 and 5. Since many of the resulting 152 news articles reported on the same cases, the researchers assigned the articles to their respective cases in the seventh step. The researchers excluded all cases not referring to privacy scandals related to Facebook or Google in the next step. This procedure resulted in 21 identified cases (see Table 1).

In the final step, the data material for each case was enriched by a backward search using the references in the news articles. We collected documents from diverse sources

**Table 1.** Identified cases.

| No. | Fb. | Go. | Case description | Link |
|-----|-----|-----|------------------|------|
| 1 | X | | Facebook receives medical data (e.g., heart rates, period data) from apps due to the embedment of its analytics plugin | cnet.co/3mPi1jq |
| 2 | X | | Facebook's VPN service Onavo Protect tracked the online activity of users across apps | cnet.co/3oVcrhl |
| 3 | X | | Facebook collected sensitive personal data (e.g., dating profiles, religion) from apps (e.g., Grindr) through APIs and SDKs | cnet.co/2SZlxZv |
| 4 | X | | Facebook allowed apps to access personal data of users and their friends to create personal profiles for political ad micro-targeting | cnet.co/2Vx3Ith |
| 5 | X | | Companies made use of the available data access on Facebook to extensively collect personal data across multiple apps | cnet.co/2HxGucc |
| 6 | X | | Facebook uses their buttons, the login plugin, the analytics as well as ads tools to collect data on users across websites and apps | cnet.co/2qEPbqB |
| 7 | X | | Facebook app CubeYou collected data through personality quizzes for non-profit research while sharing the data with marketers | cnet.co/2IHLOcV |
| 8 | X | | Facebook tracks users and ex-employees who are seen as potential threats using the location data access in the Facebook app | cnet.co/3kTY5Lu |
| 9 | X | | Facebook provided a research app to learn about people's phone usage and paid teens to access their data, e.g., browsing history | cnet.co/3kIayC8 |
| 10 | X | | Facebook collected with its Facebook app meta data of mobile calls (e.g., duration, time) and text messages (e.g., recipients) | cnet.co/3oHJ4is |
| 11 | X | | Sports event planned to offer free Wi-Fi with the Facebook login to collect data of age, gender, and nationality | cnet.co/3egZA43 |
| 12 | X | | Facebook shared user data access with dozens of companies (e.g., AOL, Apple, Microsoft) to foster the Facebook embedment | cnet.co/2Mimd2v |

(*continued*)

**Table 1.** (*continued*)

| No. | Fb. | Go. | Case description | Link |
|-----|-----|-----|------------------|------|
| 13 | X | X | Up to 17,000 apps on Android tracked users via their unique identifiers such as advertising IDs, MAC address, IMEIs | cnet.co/2Bx97Sf |
| 14 | X | X | Hundreds of apps on Android are collecting data about children (e.g., location, personal information) | cnet.co/2IHKLK1 |
| 15 | X | X | Facebook and Google use "dark patterns" to trick people toward taking the least privacy friendly option | cnet.co/3emckql |
| 16 | | X | YouTube collects data (location, device type) on child viewers younger than 13 to create targeted ads | cnet.co/2NqbjTB |
| 17 | | X | Google apps on Android devices tracked users' locations even if location history was turned off in the privacy settings | cnet.co/2GxsMVr |
| 18 | | X | Android infers data through passive means (e.g. location information event when the phone was not actively used) | cnet.co/2wkmNxv |
| 19 | | X | Google accused of integrating a microphone into its smart home products and not to list it in the hardware specifics | cnet.co/2TFdwvj |
| 20 | | X | Google monitored and analyzed users via the pay-for-data app Screenwise Meter | cnet.co/2JarzH5 |
| 21 | | X | Google had a secret deal with Mastercard to track whether ads by Google led to a sale at a physical store | cnet.co/3oEM8vJ |

and increased the validity of our study (Table 2). In addition, we ensured that the scandals were verified by other sources and not biased by a single (media) source.

## 3.2 Data Analysis

The subsequent data analysis aimed to understand the roles of Big Tech companies (in our study Facebook and Google) in data ecosystems. Guided by Saldaña's codes-to-theory process and advice that a rigorous analysis of qualitative data requires multiple coding iterations [51], we conducted two coding cycles. In the first coding cycle, we combined induction and deduction to code the plain text [46, 52]. Induction allowed us an open coding of all case-specific characteristics relevant to our research. For example, we labeled the several types of personal data mentioned throughout the cases. If a described practice was limited to one service context, the practice was coded as a single service. We considered for the service context the value proposition and the promise of value

**Table 2.** Data material.

| Document types | Facebook | Google |
|---|---|---|
| News Articles | 174 | 61 |
| Government Press Releases | 10 | 6 |
| Privacy Policies | 3 | 2 |
| Party Websites | 6 | 6 |
| Court Decisions | 1 | 0 |
| Studies | 2 | 3 |
| Technical Documents | 4 | 5 |
| Blogs | 4 | 4 |
| $\sum$ | 204 | 87 |

that a service delivers to a user [53]. If the article text or related documents in the case database gave indications of practices that could not be assigned to the value proposition and thus to more than one service context, we coded the practice as multiple services. Deduction guided us with a priori codes to look for in the data material. For example, platform providers interpose their platform between users and service providers and enable interaction [53, 54]. In addition, companies providing services to users involve other (third) parties for reasons such as performance management or advertisement [56]. These insights about the roles guided us in data analysis.

In the following, we combined the codes in the second coding cycle by constantly comparing and grouping them into broader categories [51]. For example, codes such as "platform" and "service provider" were grouped into the category "roles." We executed the coding cycles separately with two researchers to enhance the reliability of the analysis and ensure that codes were at an appropriate level of abstraction without information loss. In addition, we made use of inter-coder agreement tests to reduce bias and reach a consensus by comparing the assigned codes and recoding the data [51].

## 4 Results

Our results show that Google and Facebook have established proliferating roles as opposed in user interfaces enabling access to personal data. These companies assume the roles of platform provider, service provider, or third party (see Table 3).

### 4.1 The Role of Big Tech Companies as Platform Providers

The investigated cases show that Facebook collected users' personal data as a platform provider while a user interacts with an app accessible via related platform. A scandal is shown in Google's practice in its role in providing the mobile device platform Android as visualized in Fig. 3 (case no. 18).

**Table 3.** Case classification according to the role of Facebook and Google.

| Role | Facebook | Google |
|---|---|---|
| Platform Provider | 3 cases (nos. 4, 5, 7) | 2 cases (nos. 17, 18) |
| Service Provider | 6 cases (nos. 2, 8, 9, 10, 15) | 6 cases (nos. 15, 16, 18, 19, 20, 21) |
| Third-Party | 7 cases (nos. 1, 3, 6, 11, 12, 13, 14) | 2 cases (nos. 13, 14) |

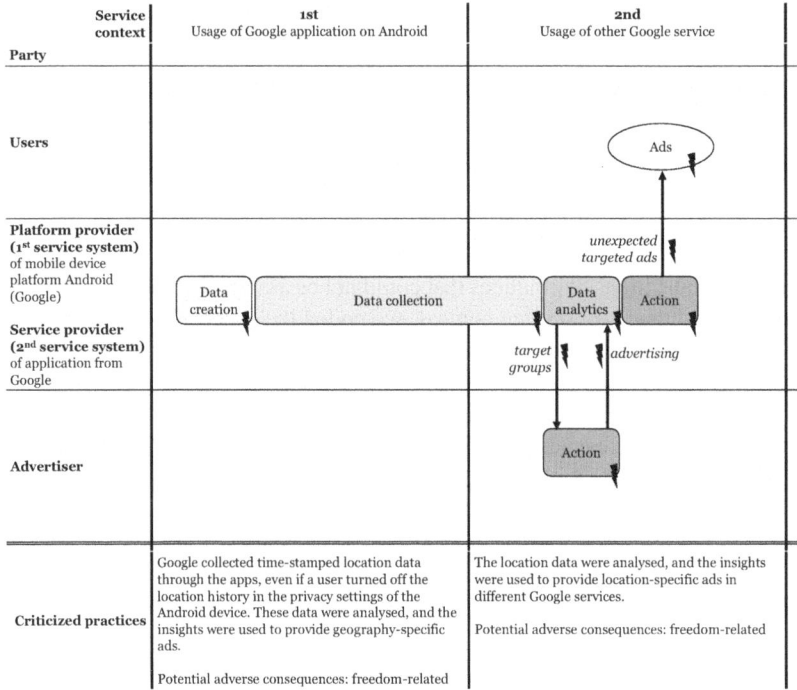

**Fig. 3.** Illustration of privacy scandal with Google as platform and service provider.

In detail, Google's Android sent location information to Google servers even when users were not actively using their Android phones. Here, Google tracked location data even if a user turned location history off in the device privacy settings. These data were used in other service contexts, e.g., to provide geography-specific ads. In addition, case nos. 5 and 7 indicate that Facebook, in its role as a platform provider, accessed the data created by users using apps on the Facebook platform.

The results show that platforms are a suitable interface between users and digital services to accumulate personal data. The role of the platform provider enables access to data created when users use services or apps via the platform. However, the case analysis revealed that at least two other roles are essential for sustaining personal data collection.

## 4.2   The Role of Big Tech Companies as Service Providers

The second role for personal data accumulation is the service provider role. In case no. 2, Facebook offers the virtual private network (VPN) service "Onavo" (Fig. 4).

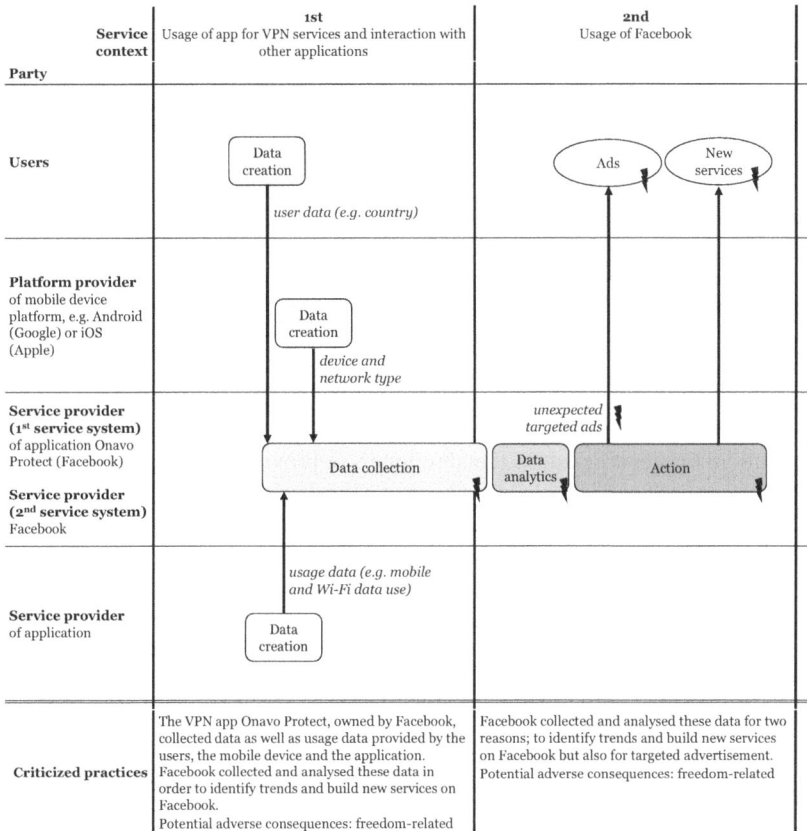

**Fig. 4.** Illustration of privacy scandal with Facebook as service provider.

In this case the app should offer VPN functions such that users may send and receive data via a private network on their phones. However, the app (and thus, Facebook) used the granted permissions to access and track data on users' online activity via the mobile device across apps. In this case, these personal data collection practices were not clear to users and resulted in public criticism.

Regarding the Facebook app, the personal data collection data is supported by an interface design that can result in users providing more data to Facebook than intended (case no. 15). Additionally, Facebook used this service to scrape metadata on calls and texts, such as the recipients of text messages and the time and duration of phone calls (case no. 10), and to collect device data which may include GPS location data, to promote safety and security (case no. 8). Facebook also provided "Facebook Research," as part of which the company paid users, including teenagers, money to access their browsing history and phone (case no. 9). Like Facebook, Google assumes the accumulating role as a provider of services, e.g., YouTube (case no. 16) and the web browser Chrome (case no. 17). Google provided the Screenwise Meter app to collect personal data in exchange for gifts (case no. 20). In another case, Google collected data when a user was logged into a Google account (case no. 21). When a user browsed across websites and clicked on an ad but did not purchase the product, Google used the data provided by Mastercard and tracked whether the user purchased the product at a physical store within 30 days. This approach enabled to report sales to the advertiser who ran the ad online on Google. This duality of two roles for data accumulation and utilization is also apparent in case no. 18. Google as the platform provider (Android) and in the role as the service provider (Google Chrome), collected location data.

### 4.3   The Role of Big Tech Companies as Third Parties

Various services and applications integrate Google and Facebook in the role of a third party. Case nos. 13 and 14 show that Google and Facebook are embedded into thousands of apps. In addition, Facebook had integrations into a dating app and an app called Pregnancy + that process sensitive data (case no. 3) as visualized in Fig. 5.

In addition, further cases show that developers or providers that integrated the "like" button on various websites enabled Facebook as a third party to accumulate personal data across the web (case no. 6). From a technical perspective, diverse software development kits (SDKs) or application programming interfaces (APIs) were embedded in services. Exemplary plugins are the Facebook login, Facebook analytics, or Facebook ads. In contrast, in case no. 12, Facebook admitted unusual access to user data to over 60 hardware and software companies. Facebook clarified that the related companies should build Facebook integrations into various services. Facebook allowed the companies to access user data for fostering an embedment as a third-party component in the next step.

### 4.4   Rebounding Effects Across Service Contexts

As the results show, Google and Facebook accomplish the existence in diverse user interfaces across service contexts to accumulate personal data. Both companies use the roles of platform providers, service providers, and third parties. Both occupy practices under different names such as "Onavo VPN" or "Screenwise Meter." The Big Tech companies link the personal data practices to a single privacy policy. Here, the data accumulation from various sources – no matter on which role basis and from which service context – is summarized under one umbrella and for a diverse set of purposes for which users provide consent. Following this, the companies cause rebounding effects in the vastness of data ecosystems that are likely to be unanticipated by users. We define rebounding effects as information privacy violations for users in data ecosystems that base on the data accumulation from one or multiple other service contexts in and can potentially lead to adverse consequences. Rebounding effects build on the lack of transparency in opaque data collection across service contexts. Big Tech companies particularly create rebounding effects because of their various roles in numerous services

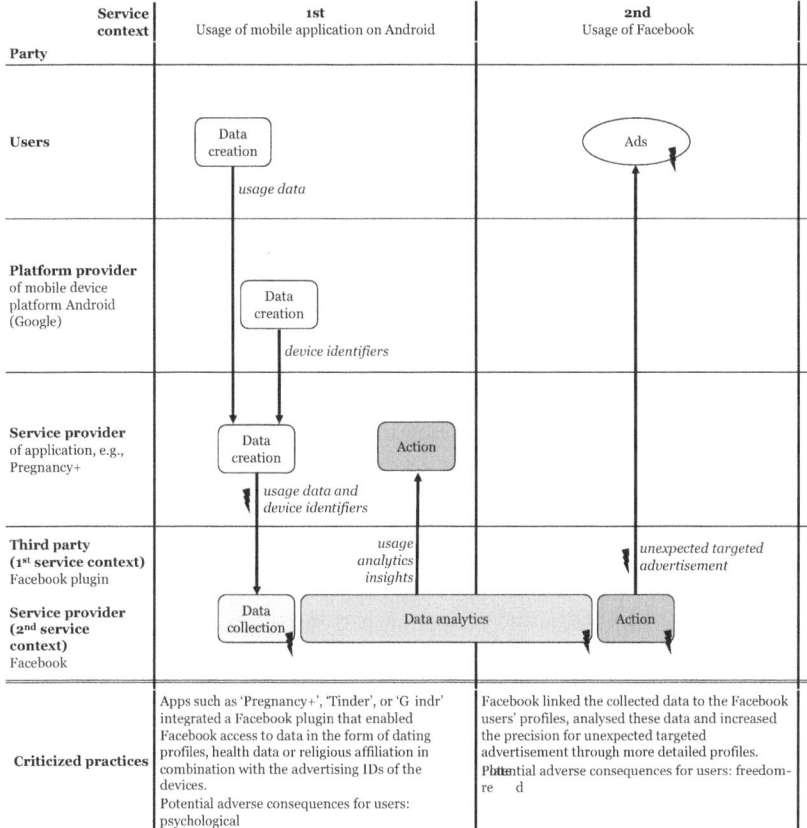

**Fig. 5.** Illustration of privacy scandal with Facebook as third party.

contexts built around commodifying a huge amount of personal data. In this regard, users do not longer control their data and practices in data ecosystems.

While the access to personal data may perpetuate adverse consequences [28], often too little information is available from the data material in this study to make detailed statements. Given the ad-centric business model of Google and Facebook, the rebounding effects might be particularly caused by targeted advertisements. For example, in case no. 17, Google used these location data to target geography-specific ads in other service contexts. In the data collecting role of providing the service YouTube (case no. 16), data such as location or device information of users younger than 13 years of age were used for targeted ads (case no. 16). In addition, in Facebook's app "Onavo Protect," Facebook's internal-market researchers analyzed the collected data of different service contexts and utilized them by modifying their services and thus, to foster data accumulation (case no. 2). In the case about the web-connected home system included a microphone that Google never disclosed in hardware specs (case no. 19), members of the US Senate Commerce Committee demanded more information. Another example is that a dormant Android phone running the service Chrome in the background sent location data to Google 340 times during a 24 h-period (case no. 18).

### 4.5   Legal Assessment Regarding the Applicability of the GDPR

In the following, we assess our results from a legal perspective by questioning the applicability of the GDPR to regulate the practices identified in the previous sections.

Given the ideal of the GDPR, all data processing operations would be dissected and legally analyzed independently. First, the legal basis of each single data processing operation would be in question. Within the GDPR's framework for lawful data processing, consent is one of six legal bases, albeit arguably the most important and widely used (GDPR, 2016, Art. 6 (1)). Typically, Google and Facebook link all their personal data operations as platform providers, service providers, and third parties to a single privacy policy. This policy includes the description of various data processing operations for various purposes and raises the question of valid consent. Consent is valid when it is freely given, unambiguously voiced for a specific purpose or set of purposes, and based on an informed decision (GDPR, 2016, Art. 6 (1)). Processing can be lawful without a user's consent when necessary for the performance of a contract or when its purpose serves the company's legitimate interests and the user's interests do not outweigh those interests. Here, the lawfulness of decoupling personal data from the service context and the re-usage in another service context with rebounding effects would have to be answered. In this relation, there is potential for a regulatory vacuum for two reasons.

Firstly, under the GDPR, an entity processing different types of personal data through various stages and situations is a controller in each of these instances and for each processing operation. However, not all dangers related to the processing of personal data stem from such an individual processing operation: as indicated, the whole danger can be more than the sum of its (data processing) parts. It can be enhanced by combining all the processing operations or the variety of contexts from which the affected data stem. The GDPR considers this heterogeneity of dangers by bestowing upon data controllers' obligations that also aim at the processing environment.

Secondly, not every critical participation act is necessarily covered by the GDPR. Big Tech companies such as Google or Facebook may tend to influence other data controllers in ways that shape and evolve the accumulation and proliferation of personal data. They define data processing circumstances as a platform provider or as a third party due to their market power. Some development, however, has been noticeable here as well regarding the Digital Markets Act or the EU AI Act. In addition, the European Court of Justice has opened the door for a more extensive application of the role of joint controllership. This concept, found in Art. 4 No. 7 and Art. 26 GDPR, attempts to avoid such a vacuum by allocating responsibility to all the groups that are sufficiently involved in such cases of distributed actions and influencing data processing acts. The primary goal is to provide sufficient clarity to allow and ensure effective application and compliance in practice [56]. In theory, this can give a regulatory handle to apply on actors that apply modern, nontraditional influence on data processing acts carried out by other data controllers. In practice, many undefined variables exist (e.g., what are the obligations? How far do they reach?).

These discussed points show that despite modernization efforts on the legislative and judiciary level, a legal vacuum remains for Big Tech companies and their proliferated architectures with a trifold role involvement within diverse service contexts that do not fit the single individual role model pursued by the GDPR. An isolated view on a single processing operation and the related juridical role according to the GDPR contrasts with the identified repeating practices, which are targeted on the countless number of data processing operations in diverse roles across service contexts. For the GDPR to cover these modern phenomena, a new actor perspective and interpretation are needed to cope with companies' accumulation and utilization practices related to Big Tech companies.

Regulators can consider these results in three ways. First, in trials, by the interpretation of the GDPR. Judgments by the European Court of Justice already show the legal potential of joint controllership and the related obligations. Second, a constant reevaluation, development, and improvement of the GDPR and its obligations and roles. The GDPR itself endorses such endeavors, as seen in its provisions regarding regular evaluations (GDPR 2016, Art. 97 No. 1). Such a legalistic approach would be preferable as it allows for fewer unclarities and more specificity than the judicial interpretation of current norms. The third way would be to apply other regulatory frameworks that follow a similar goal and bring their own regulatory toolbox.

## 5 Discussion

In our study, we gained valuable insights into the multifaceted data ecosystems of Big Tech companies. The companies take various roles as platform providers, service providers, and third-party entities (see Fig. 6). Big Tech companies' involvement in digital interactions invariably grants them access to personal data across interfaces. This proliferation of roles allows them to disentangle personal data from its original service context, opening the door for these companies to operate in areas where transparency is often limited. Consequently, the data accumulated are detached from their initial service context and diffuse into other service contexts, resulting in cascading effects that impact users. This complex dynamic presents a challenge when it comes to assessing these practices, as regulatory frameworks struggle to keep pace with this rapidly evolving landscape. The ability to effectively regulate and oversee these data flows becomes a daunting task as the data flows and interacts across service contexts, making it difficult to ensure transparency and compliance.

### 5.1 Theoretical Contributions

Our socio-techno-legal study has filled a significant void at the crossroads of information systems and law, addressing a notable deficiency in the existing literature. Prior research on the movement and lifecycle of personal data post-release by users has been conspicuously scarce [30, 59]. In our investigation, we underscore the pivotal notion that a single company can inhabit multiple roles across diverse user interfaces, fundamentally reshaping conventional perceptions of data flow. Our research not only emphasizes data's movement from users but also unveils the data rebounding back to them, instigating ripple effects throughout various service contexts.

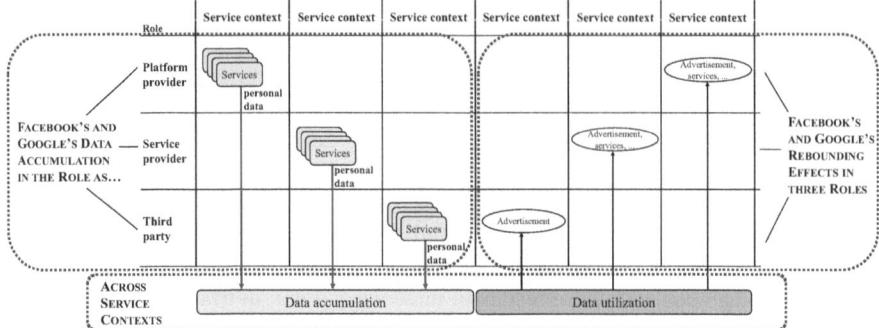

**Fig. 6.** Multi-role actors and rebounding effects in data ecosystems.

One central contribution lies within the domain of information privacy and data ecosystems, particularly within the purview of information systems. Our findings propose that the concept of Contextual Integrity [11, 12] can be enriched by embracing a systemic perspective. While prior studies have primarily revolved around individual contexts, our research highlights the value of considering accumulation environments. This paradigm shift holds promise for the future of privacy research by offering a more holistic comprehension of information privacy dynamics within data ecosystems. Furthermore, our study underscores that control over personal data is no longer vested in users but is distributed across an array of actors and contexts. This nuanced viewpoint challenges the conventional conceptualization of personal data control in privacy studies, especially within the information systems domain, where concerns and adverse consequences extend beyond isolated digital interactions into interconnected service contexts. This aspect bears relevance for Big Tech companies, given their multifaceted presence across diverse contexts for questions in the information systems field [26, 28].

Our study also delves into the intricate issues encircling consent and improper data usage within data ecosystems. The delineation between what constitutes improper access or secondary usage often remains elusive within ecosystems. Users frequently consent to privacy policies, yet there remains a limited understanding of the scope and ramifications of data processing, as indicated by the aspect in our research [60, 61]. This engenders inquiries into the efficacy of consent within ecosystems and its alignment with legal conditions for valid consent. Our study contributes to the discourse on effective consent and the associated legal dimensions within data ecosystems.

In contrast to common parlance and prior research that often pigeonholes Big Tech companies as mere platforms [62], our study furnishes a more comprehensive perspective of their roles within data ecosystems. By focusing on Google and Facebook, we unveil the intricate web of connections that these companies establish across service contexts, underscoring their central role in accumulating personal data. Building upon existing research [38], which recognized that actors could assume multiple roles in data ecosystems, we extend this knowledge by specifying the three distinct roles that Big Tech companies adopt to accumulate personal data and the resulting effects. Additionally, we illuminate how Big Tech companies provide integrations as third parties, such as 'share' or 'like' buttons, advertisements, or application performance management, which service providers must accept or omit. Given the scarcity of alternatives and potential inefficiencies, this underscores the varying levels of influence that different actors wield within data ecosystems.

In summary, our study constitutes a significant advancement in the understanding of data ecosystems, information privacy, and the roles of Big Tech companies within this intricate landscape. By infusing a systemic perspective and delving into the intricacies of consent and data usage, our research contributes substantially to the evolving discourse at the intersection of information systems and law.

## 5.2  Regulative Implications

This study also includes regulative implications. In detail, we indicate spots for the data protective legislation where a regulatory vacuum could exist. The existing regulative perspective that limits itself on fine-granular assessment of a single data processing operation cannot cope with companies' data ecosystems. A specific regulatory role that reclassifies companies that take the different roles, for example as platform providers, service providers, and third-party and which would be tailored to their spheres of influence and the totality of their data processing operations across service contexts might be an opportunity to incorporate some of our research findings to the legal realm. This consideration requires a perspective change: besides regulating individual data processing operations also to have a view on actors and their roles. Ideally, the newfound role would also need to be considered in a way that recognizes and utilizes the potential of applying other regulatory frameworks outside of data protection that follow a similar goal and brings their own regulatory toolbox such as the EU AI Act.

## 5.3  Future Research and Limitations

Our systemic perspective on data ecosystems underscores the need for future research to shift its focus from users to companies within these ecosystems, as they often wield significant control over decisions related to personal data processing, as highlighted by Zuboff [3]. This study sheds light on these practices and paves the way for innovative approaches to data protection regulation. Future research endeavors should explore how practitioners, who engage multiple stakeholders in their digital services, can foster privacy-sensitive ecosystems. For instance, when service providers integrate third-party components, they may not always be fully aware of the data accumulation practices employed by third parties. Design science research within the information systems field, dedicated to assisting developers in making judicious decisions when integrating third-party plugins into digital services, holds promising potential.

In addition, several limitations exist in this study. First, a portion of our data material, particularly new articles, may have been subject to pre-filtering by journalists, potentially introducing a bias into our dataset. To mitigate this limitation, we supplemented our analysis with diverse sources such as court decisions, privacy policies, blogs, studies, party websites, government press releases, and technical documents to enhance the validity of our findings. Second, our research primarily focused on privacy scandals involving Google and Facebook, representing major players in the realm of Big Tech companies. Future investigations could broaden their scope to encompass other significant Big Tech companies and smaller data aggregators. This expansion could offer a more comprehensive understanding of rebounding effects across various entities within the data ecosystem. Third, it is important to acknowledge that rebounding effects may not be discernible in all cases, given the inherent opacity of many data practices. To delve deeper into the inner workings of data ecosystems and uncover hidden rebounding effects, future research may need to explore innovative methods that provide transparency within ecosystems.

## 6 Conclusion

This study has shed light on the diverse roles that companies assume within data ecosystems, a phenomenon that, when viewed in its entirety, has the potential to significantly impact users' information privacy. We've unveiled how a single company's involvement in various user interfaces can lead to the accumulation of personal data, giving rise to what we have termed 'rebounding effects'—a novel privacy phenomenon that merits further investigation in future research. However, uncovering these rebounding effects remains challenging due to the inherent secrecy surrounding the inner workings of data ecosystems. Our findings underscore the multiplicity of roles that companies play across different service contexts. This diversity enables the disentanglement of personal data from its original service context, creating the foundation for rebounding effects in unrelated service contexts. Through a socio-techno-legal assessment using the GDPR as a framework, we have highlighted the critical importance of considering both the actors' spheres of influence and the entirety of their data processing operations in regulating the practices of Big Tech companies.

## References

1. Mildner, T., Savino, G.L.: Ethical user interfaces: exploring the effects of dark patterns on Facebook. In: Extended Abstracts of the 2021 CHI Conference on Human Factors in Computing Systems, pp. 1–7 (2021)
2. Zuboff, S.: Big other: surveillance capitalism and the prospects of an information civilization. J. Inf. Technol. **30**, 75–89 (2015)
3. Zuboff, S.: The Age of Surveillance Capitalism, Profile Books (2019)
4. Kallemeyn, D., Chipidza, W.: Towards a Forward-Looking Conceptualization of Privacy. In: Proceedings of the International Conference on Information Systems (ICIS), Texas (USA) (2021)
5. Bélanger, F., Xu, H.: The role of information systems research in shaping the future of information privacy. Inf. Syst. J. **25**, 573–578 (2015)
6. Kira, B., Sinha, V., Srinivasan, S.: Regulating digital ecosystems: bridging the gap between competition policy and data protection. Ind. Corp. Chang. **30**, 1337–1360 (2021)
7. Tavani, H.T.: Informational privacy: concepts, theories, and controversies. In: The Handbook of Information and Computer Ethics, Wiley, pp. 131–164 (2008)
8. Moor, J.H.: Using genetic information while protecting the privacy of the soul. Ethics Comput. Genomics Jones Bartlett Sudbury MA **1**(4), 109–119 (2006)
9. Solove, D.J.: Conceptualizing privacy. Calif. Law Rev. **90**, 1087–1156 (2002)

10. Regan, P.M.: Legislating privacy: technology, social values, and public policy, University of North Carolina Press (1995)
11. Nissenbaum, H.: Privacy as contextual integrity. Wash. Law Rev. **79**, 119–158 (2004)
12. Nissenbaum, H.: Contextual integrity up and down the data food chain. In: Theoretical Inquiries in Law, pp. 221–256 (2019)
13. Xu, H., Dinev, T., Smith, H.J., Hart, P.: Examining the formation of individual's privacy concerns: toward an integrative view. In: Proceedings of the International Conference on Information Systems, Paris (France) (2008)
14. Dinev, T., Xu, H., Smith, J.H., Hart, P.: Information privacy and correlates: an empirical attempt to bridge and distinguish privacy-related concepts. Eur. J. Inf. Syst. **22**, 295–316 (2013)
15. Sjöström, J., Ågerfalk, P., Hevner, A.R.: The design of a system for online psychosocial care: balancing privacy and accountability in sensitive online healthcare environments. J. Assoc. Inf. Syst. **23**, 237–263 (2022)
16. Kühl, N., Martin, D., Wolff, C., Volkamer, M.: Healthy surveillance: designing a concept for privacy-preserving mask recognition AI in the age of pandemics. In: Proceedings of the Hawaii International Conference on System Sciences, Hawaii (USA) (2020)
17. Callegati, F., Campi, A., Melis, A., Prandini, M., Zevenbergen, B.: Privacy-preserving design of data processing systems in the public transport context. Pac. Asia J. Assoc. Inf. Syst. **7** (2015)
18. Greenaway, K.E., Chan, Y.E.: Designing a customer information privacy program aligned with organizational priorities. MIS Q. Executive **12** (2013)
19. Kehr, F., Kowatsch, T., Wentzel, D., Fleisch, E.: Blissfully ignorant: the effects of general privacy concerns, general institutional trust, and affect in the privacy calculus. Inf. Syst. J. **25**, 607–635 (2015)
20. Acquisti, A., Brandimarte, L., Loewenstein, G.: Privacy and human behavior in the age of information. Science **347**, 509–514 (2015)
21. Dinev, T., McConnell, A.R., Smith, H.J.: Research commentary informing privacy research through information systems, psychology, and behavioral economics: thinking outside the "APCO" box. Inf. Syst. Res. **26**, 639–655 (2015)
22. Gopal, R., Hidaji, H., Patterson, R., Rolland, E., Zhdanov, D.: How much to share with third parties? user privacy concerns and website dilemmas. MIS Q. **42**, 143–164 (2018)
23. Steinbart, P., Keith, M., Babb, J.: Measuring privacy concern and the right to be forgotten. In: Proceedings of the Hawaii International Conference on System Sciences, Hawaii (USA) (2017)
24. Thiebes, S., Lyytinen, K., Sunyaev, A.: Sharing is about caring? Motivating and discouraging factors in sharing individual genomic data. In: Proceedings of the International Conference on Information Systems (ICIS), Seoul (South Korea) (2017)
25. Norberg, P.A., Horne, D.R., Horne, D.A.: The privacy paradox: personal information disclosure intentions versus behaviors. J. Consum. Aff. **41**, 100–126 (2007)
26. Smith, H.J., Milburg, S.J., Burke, S.J.: Information privacy: measuring individuals' concerns about organizational practices. MIS Q. **20**, 167–196 (1996)
27. Feth, D.:. Usable implementation of data sovereignty in digital ecosystems. In: Moallem, A. (eds.) HCI for Cybersecurity, Privacy and Trust. HCII 2023. Lecture Notes in Computer Science, vol. 14045, pp. 135–150. Springer, Cham (2023). https://doi.org/10.1007/978-3-031-35822-7_10
28. Karwatzki, S., Trenz, M., Tuunainen, V.K., Veit, D.: Adverse consequences of access to individuals' information: an analysis of perceptions and the scope of organisational influence. Eur. J. Inf. Syst. **26**, 688–715 (2017)

29. Benson, V., Saridakis, G., Tennakoon, H.: Information disclosure of social media users: does control over personal information, user awareness and security notices matter? Inf. Technol. People **28**, 426–441 (2015)
30. Conger, J.H., Pratt, K.D., Loch, K.D.: Personal information privacy and emerging technologies. Inf. Syst. J. **23**, 401–417 (2013)
31. Andrew, J., Baker, M.: The general data protection regulation in the age of surveillance capitalism. J. Bus. Ethics 1–14 (2019)
32. GDPR: General Data Protection Regulation (EU) 2016/679 of the European Parliament and of the Council of 27 April 2016 (Directive 95/46), 1–88 (2016)
33. Moore, J.: The Death of competition: leadership and strategy in the age of business ecosystems. Leadership in New York: Harper Business (1996)
34. Tiwana, A., Konsynski, B., Bush, A.A.: Research commentary—platform evolution: coevolution of platform architecture, governance, and environmental dynamics. Inf. Syst. Res. **21**, 675–687 (2010)
35. Lusch, R.F., Vargo, S.L.: Service-dominant logic: premises, perspectives, possibilities, Cambridge University Press (2014)
36. Manikas, K.: Revisiting software ecosystems research: a longitudinal literature study. J. Syst. Softw. **117**, 84–103 (2016)
37. Aaen, J., Nielsen, J.A., Carugati, A.: The dark side of data ecosystems: a longitudinal study of the DAMD project. Eur. J. Inf. Syst. 1–25 (2021)
38. Oliveira, M.I.S., Lima, G.d.F.B., Lóscio, B.F.: Investigations into data ecosystems: a systematic mapping study. Knowl. Inf. Syst. **61**, 589–630 (2019)
39. Zuiderwijk, A., Janssen, M., Davis, C.: Innovation with open data: essential elements of open data ecosystems. Inf. Polity **19**, 17–33 (2014)
40. Ponte, D.: Enabling an open data ecosystem. In: European Conference on Information Systems (2015)
41. Oliveira, M.I.S., Oliveira, L.E.R., Batista, M.G.R., Lóscio, B.F.: Towards a meta-model for data ecosystems. In: Proceedings of the 19th Annual International Conference on Digital Government Research: Governance in the Data Age, pp. 1–10 (2018)
42. Demchenko, Y., De Laat, C., Membrey, P.: Defining architecture components of the big data ecosystem. In: 2014 International Conference on Collaboration Technologies and Systems (CTS), IEEE, pp. 104–112 (2014)
43. Yin, R.K.: Case Study Research: Design and Methods SAGE (2009)
44. Kurtz, C., Wittner, F., Semmann, M., Schulz, W., Böhmann, T.: Accountability of platform providers for unlawful personal data processing in their ecosystems a socio-techno-legal analysis of facebook and apple's iOS according to GDPR. J. Responsible Technol. (2021)
45. Kurtz, C., Wittner, F., Semmann, M., Schulz, W., Böhmann, T.: The unlikely siblings in the GDPR family: a techno-legal analysis of major platforms in the diffusion of personal data in service ecosystems. In: Proceedings of the 52nd Hawaii International Conference on System Sciences, Hawaii (USA) (2019)
46. Mayring, P.: Qualitative content analysis. A Companion Qual. Res. **1**, 159–176 (2004)
47. Kohlbacher, F.: The use of qualitative content analysis in case study research. In: Forum: Qualitative Social Research, pp. 1–30 (2006)
48. Benbasat, I., Goldstein, D.K., Mead, M.: The case research strategy in studies of information systems. MIS Q. **11** (1987)
49. SimilarWeb: Top sites ranking for News and Media (2019)
50. Thompson, J.B.: Political scandal: power and visibility in the media age, John Wiley & Sons (2013)
51. Saldaña, J.: The coding manual for qualitative researchers, SAGE (2015)
52. Elo, S., Kyngäs, H.: The qualitative content analysis process. J. Adv. Nurs. **62**, 107–115 (2008)

53. Chandler, J.D., Lusch, R.F.: Service systems: a broadened framework and research agenda on value propositions, engagement, and service experience. J. Serv. Res. (2015)
54. Riedl, C., Boehmann, T., Leimeister, J.M., Krcmar, H.: A framework for analysing service ecosystem capabilities to innovate. In: Proceedings of the European Conference on Information Systems (ECIS), Verona (Italy) (2009)
55. Van Alstyne, M.W., Parker, G.G., Choudary, S.P.: Pipelines, platforms, and the new rules of strategy. Harv. Bus. Rev. **94**, 54–62 (2016)
56. Binns, R., Lyngs, U., Van Kleek, M., Zhao, J., Libert, T., Shadbolt, N.: Third party tracking in the mobile ecosystem. In: 10th ACM Conference on Web Science (2018)
57. Baser, D.: Hard questions: what data does facebook collect when i'm not using facebook, and why? in facebook (2018)
58. European Commission: Article 29 Data Protection Working Party in: WP 169: Opinion 1/2010 on the concepts of controller and processor (2010)
59. Spiekermann, S., Novotny, A.: A vision for global privacy bridges: technical and legal measures for international data markets. Comput. Law Secur. Rev. **31**, 181–200 (2015)
60. Kurtz, C., Wittner, F., Vogel, P., Semmann, M., Böhmann, T.: Design goals for consent at scale in digital service ecosystems. In: Proceedings of the 28th European Conference on Information Systems (ECIS), AIS Virtual Conference (2020)
61. Burmeister, F., Kurtz, C., Drews, P., Schirmer, I.: Unraveling privacy concerns in complex data ecosystems with architectural thinking. In: Proceedings of the 42nd International Conference on Information Systems (ICIS), Austin (USA) (2021)
62. Constantinides, P., Henfridsson, O., Parker, G.G.: Introduction platforms and infrastructures in the digital age. Inf. Syst. Res. 381–400 (2018)

# Development of a Mobile Banking Risk Assessment Model: A Usability Perspective

Istiak Mahmud[(✉)] and June Wei

College of Business, University of West Florida, Pensacola, FL, USA
im40@students.uwf.edu, jwei@uwf.edu

**Abstract.** The study focuses on creating a risk assessment system tailored for mobile banking. It involves devising a dynamic model illustrating how information moves between key entities in mobile banking, alongside a static model outlining five types of information threats from three main sources. These models are then merged to indicate potential threats affecting each information flow. In the data analysis phase, risk factors for mobile banking information security are grouped into high, low, and medium categories. This research aims to aid mobile banking developers and decision-makers in system development.

**Keywords:** Mobile Banking · Mobile App · Security risk · Risk assessment · Data flow · Information task

## 1 Introduction

As technology advances, many industries recognize the importance of modernizing and broadening their service offerings [1]. Numerous banks have heavily invested in integrating technology into their services, including the creation of interactive websites, online portals, and mobile apps [2]. These advancements play a crucial role in improving service quality, nurturing customer loyalty, and strengthening competitive positioning against rivals in the market [3]. Mobile banking is the act of carrying out financial transactions using a mobile device [2]. The emergence of mobile banking represents a transformative force, reshaping the landscape of financial services and delivering unparalleled convenience to users. With smartphones deeply ingrained in our daily lives, the evolution of mobile banking has been swift, introducing cutting-edge technological trends set to transform how we manage finances. Mobile banking's inception marked a fundamental shift in financial behavior, liberating individuals from traditional brick-and-mortar banks and empowering them to conduct a wide array of financial transactions directly from their smartphones. This encompasses tasks such as checking account balances, transferring funds, and even applying for loans, highlighting the extensive reach of mobile banking. Security remains paramount in the financial sector, and mobile banking has addressed this by integrating biometric authentication. Now commonplace are features like fingerprint recognition, facial recognition, and iris scans, providing users with a secure and convenient means to access their accounts. This not only enhances security but also streamlines the authentication process, improving user experience [4].

© The Author(s), under exclusive license to Springer Nature Switzerland AG 2025
A. Marcus et al. (Eds.): HCII 2024, LNCS 15380, pp. 304–313, 2025.
https://doi.org/10.1007/978-3-031-76821-7_21

The aim of this paper is to recognize information threats involved in mobile banking and develop a quantitative assessment method to assess information security risks in mobile banking. It aims at providing a holistic view of risk factors involved in mobile banking by developing a mobile banking Information Security Risks (MBDSR) model as a theoretical basis for risk assessment. The risk factors in the MBDSR model are further analyzed based on the MBDF model. The research question is How can information security risks in mobile banking be effectively assessed and quantified? The problem addressed in this research revolves around the need to effectively manage information security risks in mobile banking systems.

## 2   Literature Review

Mobile apps have allowed financial institutions to develop solutions that are more flexible, secure, and user-friendly. As a result, there has been a reduction in the need for face-to-face interactions between bank staff and customers [5].

Mobile banking provides comparable benefits to online banking, enabling customers to utilize banking services via an internet connection from any place and at any moment [6]. Unlike internet banking on computers, mobile banking offers advantages such as unrestricted access regardless of time or location, as well as quick and efficient handling of financial transactions. Clients enjoy fast and convenient services, while banks can earn customer loyalty and reduce costs. The effectiveness of mobile banking applications depends greatly on their ability to simplify financial management, prevent unauthorized access to accounts, and streamline transactions without unnecessary complexity [5].

Mobile banking usage has experienced a substantial increase worldwide in recent years [7, 8]. Statistics show that the worldwide mobile banking market reached a value of $1.5 billion in 2022 and is anticipated to expand to $7 billion by 2032, with a compound annual growth rate (CAGR) of 16.8% from 2023 to 2032 [7].

As our reliance on the internet deepens, many people are unaware of the inherent vulnerabilities in websites, applications, and online platforms. The proliferation of internet technologies, payment apps, and networks has resulted in a notable rise in digital fraud, raising serious security concerns. Issues like identity theft and other cybercrimes have made consumers wary of participating in online financial activities. Security breaches and cyberattacks are now major sources of apprehension [9]. Hackers use various techniques to exploit weaknesses and steal money or personal data, jeopardizing security, and privacy [10].

With 2.5 billion smartphone users globally, both individuals and businesses face risks. Small businesses are targeted by cyberattacks, with 43% experiencing breaches due to inadequate defenses [11]. Furthermore, the evolving nature of the industry and the lack of awareness among the public contribute to the increasing occurrence of cybercrimes [12]. Although mobile banking apps often incorporate biometric or two-factor authentication (2FA) measures to bolster security, they are still vulnerable to various attacks aimed at their infrastructure [5].

# 3 Conceptual Models

## 3.1 Dynamic Model

**Mobile Banking Data Flow (MBDF) Model.** The mobile banking information flow model (MBDF) was developed to recognize all the information flows arising in a general standard mobile banking process. Figure 1 elicits the thirteen (13) major information flows among the major mobile banking entities: customer, bank, Utility company, credit card company, third parties, mobile company (Table 1).

Thirteen flows in Fig. 1 are involved in information transactions among these six actors, including:

- F1: The customer initiates the login process through the bank's mobile application. Then they select the icon representing the credit card company and proceed to request an adjustment to their outstanding bill.
- F2: The customer clicks on the icon linked to the utility company and submits a request to settle their outstanding utility bill.
- F3: The customer selects the icon representing the third-party service provider and provides instructions to receive the desired service.
- F4: The customer accesses the mobile company symbol to proceed with recharging their mobile balance.
- F5: The credit card company communicates with the bank's Information and Communication Technology (ICT) division, requesting to fulfill the bank customer's request to settle the outstanding card bill.
- F6: Bank ICT division deploys officers to verify the authenticity of the transaction request.
- F7: The utility company is in contact with the bank's ICT (Information and Communication Technology) division.
- F8: Information flow 6 is in place again.
- F9: Third-party services engage with the bank's ICT division to fulfill customer instructions.
- F10: The bank's ICT division (F6) repeats the step and notifies the third parties accordingly.
- F11: The mobile company is collaborating with the bank's Information and Communication Technology (ICT) division to fulfill customer orders for recharging their mobile phones.
- F12: The bank's ICT division (F6) follows the same process accordingly.
- F13: The ICT division notifies the customers regarding the transaction that has been executed according to their instructions.

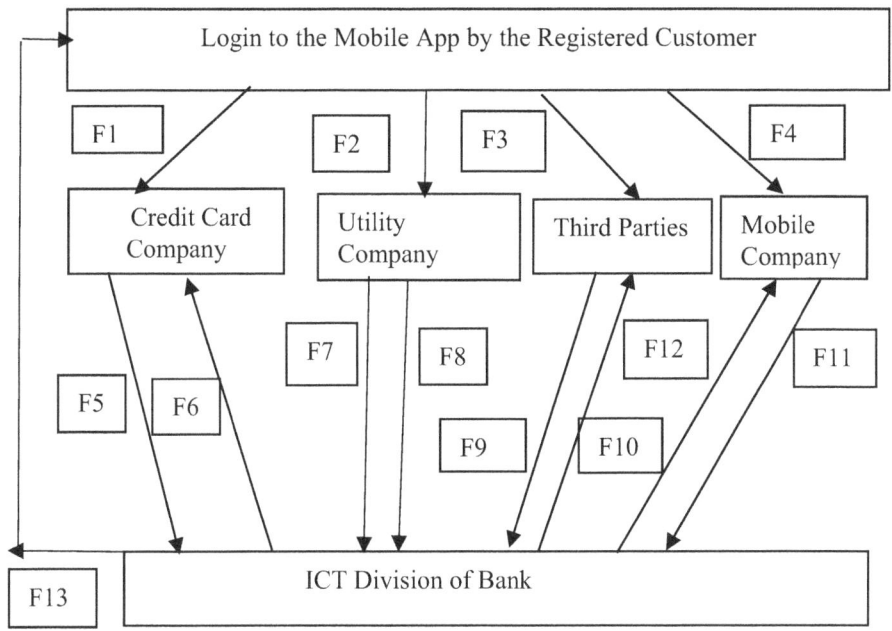

**Fig. 1.** Mobile Banking Data Flow (MBDF) model

**Table 1.** A decomposition of information flows in the MBDF Model, Mobile App Data Flow

| Data Flow | Task Description |
| --- | --- |
| F1 | Log in initiated by the bank customer. Then chooses the icon representing the credit card company and request to adjust the outstanding bill |
| F2 | The customer clicks on the icon associated with the utility company and place a request to honor the outstanding utility bill |
| F3 | The customer enters the third-party icon and Provide instructions to receive the service |
| F4 | The customer enters the mobile company symbol to execute mobile balance recharge |
| F5 | The credit card company engages in communication with the ICT (Information and Communication Technology) division of the bank and request to honor the outstanding card bill as per bank customer request |
| F6 | The ICT division of the bank assigned officer check the authenticity of the request and account balance. After satisfaction, forward the request to the verification officer. The verification officer verifies and informs the ICT division. The ICT division inform the credit card company regarding the transaction |

*(continued)*

**Table 1.** (*continued*)

| Data Flow | Task Description |
|---|---|
| F7 | The utility company is in communication with the ICT (Information and Communication Technology) division of the bank |
| F8 | The same process was followed by the bank ICT division (F6) and inform the utility company |
| F9 | Third-party services include functions such as check honoring through the banking app. These third parties contact the bank's ICT division to carry out customer instructions |
| F10 | The step was repeated by the bank ICT division (F6) and inform the third parties |
| F11 | The mobile company is liaising with the bank's Information and Communication Technology (ICT) division to carry orders of the customers to recharge their mobile phone |
| F12 | The same process was followed by the bank ICT division (F6) |
| F13 | The ICT division informs the customers regarding the transaction that took place according to their instructions. The transaction was preserved in the ICT division server for future reference |

## 3.2  Static Model (Table 2)

**Table 2.** Derivation of security risk factors in the MBDSR Model.

| Security Risks | Sources of Security Risks | | |
|---|---|---|---|
| | A.<br>Human<br>Error | B.<br>Malicious<br>Activity | C.<br>Natural<br>Disasters |
| A.<br>Unauthorized<br>data<br>disclosure | AA1. Lack of multi-phase authentication<br>AA2. Auto login<br>AA3: Disclosure of confidential data. | BA1. Hacking<br>BA2. Fake mobile banking app<br>BA3. SIM swap | CA1. Data exposure during recovery |
| B. Incorrect data modification | AB1.Deviation from correct procedures<br>AB2.Inadequate technical proficiency. | BB1. Hacking<br>BB2. Password | CB1. Obstacle to recover data |
| C. Faulty service | AC1. System reaction<br>AC2. Installation of application | BC1. Obsolete security software<br>BC2. Defective network | CC1. Improper restoration service |
| D. Denial service | AD1. Insufficient depth of understanding.<br>AD2. Intentional | BD1. Dos attacks | CD1. Service intervention |
| E. Loss of infrastructure | AE1. Accidents<br>AE2. Operational mistakes | BE1. Viruses<br>BE2. Theft<br>BE3. Terrorist activity | CE1. Loss of property |

## 4  Methodology (Combined Model)

Table 3. Security risks (MBDSR Model) likely occur in information tasks (MBDF Model) is presented in Appendix.

**Table 3.** Mobile Banking information security risk factor classification analysis

| Security Risk Factors | Information Flows and Tasks in the MBIF Model | | | | | | | | | | | | |
|---|---|---|---|---|---|---|---|---|---|---|---|---|---|
| | F1 | F2 | F3 | F4 | F5 | F6 | F7 | F8 | F9 | F10 | F11 | F12 | F13 |
| AA1 | ✓ | ✓ | ✓ | ✓ | ✓ |   | ✓ |   | ✓ |   | ✓ |   |   |
| AA2 | ✓ | ✓ | ✓ | ✓ | ✓ | ✓ | ✓ | ✓ | ✓ | ✓ | ✓ | ✓ | ✓ |
| AA3 | ✓ | ✓ | ✓ | ✓ | ✓ | ✓ | ✓ | ✓ | ✓ | ✓ | ✓ | ✓ | ✓ |
| AB1 | ✓ | ✓ | ✓ | ✓ | ✓ | ✓ | ✓ | ✓ | ✓ | ✓ | ✓ | ✓ | ✓ |
| AB2 | ✓ | ✓ | ✓ | ✓ | ✓ | ✓ | ✓ | ✓ | ✓ | ✓ | ✓ | ✓ | ✓ |
| AC1 | ✓ | ✓ | ✓ | ✓ | ✓ | ✓ | ✓ | ✓ | ✓ | ✓ | ✓ | ✓ | ✓ |
| AC2 | ✓ | ✓ | ✓ | ✓ | ✓ | ✓ | ✓ | ✓ | ✓ | ✓ | ✓ | ✓ | ✓ |
| AD1 | ✓ | ✓ | ✓ | ✓ | ✓ | ✓ | ✓ | ✓ | ✓ | ✓ | ✓ | ✓ | ✓ |
| AD2 | ✓ | ✓ | ✓ | ✓ | ✓ | ✓ | ✓ | ✓ | ✓ | ✓ | ✓ | ✓ | ✓ |
| AE1 | ✓ | ✓ | ✓ | ✓ | ✓ | ✓ | ✓ | ✓ | ✓ | ✓ | ✓ | ✓ | ✓ |
| AE2 | ✓ | ✓ | ✓ | ✓ | ✓ | ✓ | ✓ | ✓ | ✓ | ✓ | ✓ | ✓ | ✓ |
| BA1 | ✓ | ✓ | ✓ | ✓ | ✓ | ✓ | ✓ | ✓ | ✓ | ✓ | ✓ | ✓ | ✓ |
| BA2 | ✓ | ✓ | ✓ | ✓ |   |   |   |   |   |   |   |   |   |
| BA3 | ✓ | ✓ | ✓ | ✓ |   |   |   |   |   |   |   |   |   |
| BB1 | ✓ | ✓ | ✓ | ✓ | ✓ | ✓ | ✓ | ✓ | ✓ | ✓ | ✓ | ✓ | ✓ |
| BB2 | ✓ | ✓ | ✓ | ✓ | ✓ | ✓ | ✓ | ✓ | ✓ | ✓ | ✓ | ✓ | ✓ |
| BC1 | ✓ | ✓ | ✓ | ✓ | ✓ | ✓ | ✓ | ✓ | ✓ | ✓ | ✓ | ✓ | ✓ |
| BC2 | ✓ | ✓ | ✓ | ✓ | ✓ | ✓ | ✓ | ✓ | ✓ | ✓ | ✓ | ✓ | ✓ |
| BD1 | ✓ | ✓ | ✓ | ✓ | ✓ | ✓ | ✓ | ✓ | ✓ | ✓ | ✓ | ✓ | ✓ |
| BE1 | ✓ | ✓ | ✓ | ✓ | ✓ | ✓ | ✓ | ✓ | ✓ | ✓ | ✓ | ✓ | ✓ |
| BE2 | ✓ | ✓ | ✓ | ✓ | ✓ | ✓ | ✓ | ✓ | ✓ | ✓ | ✓ | ✓ | ✓ |
| BE3 | ✓ | ✓ | ✓ | ✓ | ✓ |   | ✓ |   | ✓ |   | ✓ |   |   |
| CA1 | ✓ | ✓ | ✓ | ✓ | ✓ | ✓ | ✓ | ✓ | ✓ | ✓ | ✓ | ✓ | ✓ |
| CB1 | ✓ | ✓ | ✓ | ✓ | ✓ | ✓ | ✓ | ✓ | ✓ | ✓ | ✓ | ✓ | ✓ |
| CC1 | ✓ | ✓ | ✓ | ✓ | ✓ | ✓ | ✓ | ✓ | ✓ | ✓ | ✓ | ✓ | ✓ |
| CD1 | ✓ | ✓ | ✓ | ✓ | ✓ | ✓ | ✓ | ✓ | ✓ | ✓ | ✓ | ✓ | ✓ |
| CE1 | ✓ | ✓ | ✓ | ✓ | ✓ | ✓ | ✓ | ✓ | ✓ | ✓ | ✓ | ✓ | ✓ |

## 5  Information Exploration and Discoveries

To simplify, a score of "1" replaces a checkmark in Table 3. Table 4 displays an analysis example of mobile banking information security risks. In Table 4, the security risk level for each risk factor (1st column) is determined by summing the "1"s for each risk factor in Table 3. Mobile banking information security risks are ranked in descending order based on the average level of risks in each data flow. The key insights from Table 4 are:

- The information security risk pattern of mobile banking can be classified into three categories including the high-risk level (70.0% and above), the medium-risk level (35.0%–70.0%), and the low risk level (less than 35.0%).
- Human error poses higher risk (100%) and Malicious activities happen across every risk level from top to bottom; and Nature Disaster takes place only in the Medium risk level.
- Two risk factors from the Malicious Activity (BA2 and BA3) are clearly happening in low-risk level with 31.0% among tasks of the information flows in the MBDF Model.
- Security risks likely to occur 100% in information flows F1, F2, F3, and F4 levels. Whereas 93% for F5, F7, F9, F11 and 85% for F6, F8, F12, and F13 levels.

## 6  Conclusion

The risk assessment framework described in the paper acts as a valuable instrument for improving the security stance of mobile banking systems, thereby safeguarding sensitive customer data and upholding trust in mobile banking services. The results of this risk assessment offer valuable guidance for mobile banking developers and decision-makers. By grasping the types and prevalence of various security risks, developers can allocate resources effectively and deploy specific measures to reinforce security controls in critical areas. Moreover, decision-makers can leverage this insight to shape strategic planning and risk management endeavors, ensuring the resilience of mobile banking systems against emerging threats.

## Appendix

**Table 4.** Security risks (MBDSR Model) likely occur in information tasks (MBDF Model)

| Security Risk Factors * | Level of Security Risks for each Risk Factor | Average Level of Security Risks for each Risk Factor | Threat Sources * | Classifications |
|---|---|---|---|---|
| AA2 | 13 | 100% | A. Human Error | |
| AA3 | 13 | 100% | A. Human Error | |
| AB1 | 13 | 100% | A. Human Error | |
| AB2 | 13 | 100% | A. Human Error | |
| AC1 | 13 | 100% | A. Human Error | |
| AC2 | 13 | 100% | A. Human Error | |
| AD1 | 13 | 100% | A. Human Error | |
| AD2 | 13 | 100% | A. Human Error | High Risk Level |
| AE1 | 13 | 100% | A. Human Error | |
| AE2 | 13 | 100% | A. Human Error | |
| BA1 | 13 | 100% | B. Malicious Activity | |
| BB1 | 13 | 100% | B. Malicious Activity | |
| BB2 | 13 | 100% | B. Malicious Activity | |
| BC1 | 13 | 100% | B. Malicious Activity | |
| BC2 | 13 | 100% | B. Malicious Activity | |
| BD1 | 13 | 100% | B. Malicious Activity | |
| BE1 | 13 | 100% | B. Malicious Activity | |
| BE2 | 13 | 100% | B. Malicious Activity | |
| CA1 | 13 | 100% | C. Natural Disasters | |
| CB1 | 13 | 100% | C. Natural Disasters | |
| CC1 | 13 | 100% | C. Natural Disasters | Medium Risk |
| CD1 | 13 | 100% | C. Natural Disasters | |
| CE1 | 13 | 100% | C. Natural Disasters | |
| AA1 | 8 | 62% | A. Human Error | |
| BE3 | 8 | 62% | B. Malicious Activity | |
| BA2 | 4 | 31% | B. Malicious Activity | Low Risk |
| BA3 | 4 | 31% | B. Malicious Activity | |

Note: * Information security risk factors and threat sources are presented in Table 2

# References

1. Deepa, J.N., Dhingra, R.: Factors affecting intention to adopt mobile banking: a systematic review. IUP J. Inf. Technol. **19**(1), 48–65 (2023)
2. https://www.proquest.com/scholarly-journals/factors-affecting-intention-adopt-mobile-banking/docview/2811028363/se-2
3. Ali, A., Hameed, A., Moin, M.F., Khan, N.A.: Exploring factors affecting mobile-banking app adoption: a perspective from adaptive structuration theory. Aslib J. Inf. Manag. (2023). https://doi.org/10.1108/AJIM-08-2021-0216
4. Frimpong, K., Shuridah, O., Wilson, A., Sarpong, F.: A cross-national investigation of trait antecedents of mobile-banking adoption. Thunderbird Int. Bus. Rev. **62**(4), 411–424 (2020). https://doi.org/10.1002/tie.22132
5. Hillary. Mobile Banking Revolution: Exploring the Latest Technological Trends. Newstex Blogs TechBullion (November 21, 2023, Tuesday). https://advance-lexis-com.ezproxy.lib.uwf.edu/api/document?collection=news&id=urn:contentItem:69P3-TTS1-F03R-N1D6-00000-00&context=1516831
6. Orehovački, T., Blašković, L., Kurevija, M.: Evaluating the perceived quality of mobile banking applications in Croatia: an empirical study. Future Internet **15**(1), 8 (2023). https://doi.org/10.3390/fi15010008
7. Mo'men Awad, A.T., Thi Phuong, L.N., Magiswary A/P Dorasamy, F.Y.: Determinant of M-banking usage and adoption among millennials. Sustainability **15**(10), 8216 (2023). https://doi.org/10.3390/su15108216
8. Allied Market Research. Mobile Banking Market Research, 2032 (2022). https://www.alliedmarketresearch.com/mobile-banking-market/. Accessed 28 March 2024
9. Arcand, M., PromTep, S., Brun, I., Rajaobelina, L.: Mobile banking service quality and customer relationships. Int. J. Bank Market. **35**(7), 1068–1089 (2017). https://doi.org/10.1108/K-03-2022-0333
10. Campbell, C.C.: Solutions for counteracting human deception in social engineering attacks. Inf. Technol. People **32**(5), 1130–1152 (2019). https://doi.org/10.1108/ITP-12-2017-0422
11. Grewal, R., Dharwadkar, R.: The role of the institutional environment in marketing channels. J. Market. **66**(3), 82–97 (2002). https://doi.org/10.1509/jmkg.66.3.82.18504
12. Chachak, E.: Cybercrime is Moving Towards Smartphones – This is What You Could Do to Protect Your Company (2019)

# The Clash of Service Provider and Service User Expectations
## How Causal Models Highlight Stakeholder Data-Protection Tussles

Brian Pickering[✉][iD], Nic Fair[iD], Stephen C. Phillips[iD], and Dan Shearer[iD]

Digital Health and Bioelectronics, Electronics and Computer Science, University of Southampton, Southampton SO17 1BJ, UK
{j.b.pickering,nic.fair,s.c.phillips,dan.shearer}@soton.ac.uk

**Abstract.** Data Protection regulation seeks to support data subjects to control their personal data. A lack of such control poses a significant risk to their privacy and may undermine the data subject's trust in the provider. To achieve this, it imposes certain obligations on those providing services to data subjects which requires the processing of their personal data. Compliance with regulation, including security standards, would demonstrate provider trustworthiness, it is assumed. In so doing, this would encourage users to engage. But how are those users supposed to know the provider is compliant? Further, how will the provider manage their data? The assumption is that a provider's *privacy notice* is a suitable communication vehicle for this purpose. In this study, we challenge this view. Using *causal models* to visualise both service provider and service user decision making around interaction, we maintain there to be a mismatch between the expectations of the two: a tussle which cannot be resolved through regulatory compliance, but a better understanding of service user privacy attitudes.

**Keywords:** Privacy · Data Protection · Causal Models · Tussles · SME

## 1 Introduction

The General Data Protection Regulation (GDPR) [1] was an attempt to harmonize how personal data should be treated across EU Member States and in states doing business with the EU (Art. 45). In so doing, the explicit intention was as follows:

> "[the] EU aims at regaining the people's trust in the responsible treatment of their personal data in order to boost digital economy across the EU-internal market" ([2], p.2)

This paper was funded by the EU H2020 Synthema Project (Grant Number 101095530), the SME work by EU H2020 CyberKit4SME (Grant Number 883188) and the Privacy Survey by the UKRI PRiAM Project (Grant Number MC_PC_21030).

To achieve this, it imposes appropriate security structures on those handling personal data (Art. 25, 32), including punitive measures for those who fall short (Art. 83). At the same time, the regulation codifies the rights of data subjects, namely those associated with their personal data (Chap. 3). In data protection terms, compliance with the GDPR has therefore become a primary route to demonstrating trustworthiness to third parties who engage with the entity processing their personal data. Trustworthiness - it is assumed - leads necessarily onto trust. Service providers seek to demonstrate their trustworthiness, therefore, since service users need to trust them in order to engage [3].

Data protection is only one type of cybersecurity threat, of course. Nevertheless, enterprises - especially Small to Medium Enterprises (SMEs) - may be ill-equipped to comply with reguation, not least because their focus is on business objectives, they lack resource [4,5] and are unwilling to share information with co-competitors who might help and support them lest this increase vulnerability [6]. Ultimately, aware of cyber threats [7], there is a danger that SMEs may be overwhelmed and ignore their cybersecurity responsibilities [8,9] to their cost. In parallel, service-users may be unable to exploit their rights [10], and their confusing self-disclosure behaviors contradict privacy concerns [11,12]. It's possible, though, that the apparent paradox may simply reflect different expectations of user-provider interactions. The original motivation for this paper was therefore to review empirical evidence to describe provider responses to regulation on the one hand and service user expectations of those providers on the other.

### 1.1 Causal Models

On one level, *causal models* provide a fuzzy visualisation tool to encapsulate multidimensional and complex processes [13]. They are not intended as simple sequences: to achieve X, start with Y and move on to Z. As the name suggests, they are intended instead to capture dependencies in reaching a decision or completing a task: because of X, we must do Y, which leads necessarily to Z. Our use of causal modelling is specifically to capture what we have observed from different stakeholders when tacitly negotiating privacy and data sharing in much the same way as Weggelaar-Jansen and her colleagues attempted for research involving big data in the health domain [14]. In so doing, we hope to identify the different expectations of two major stakeholders in online interactions: service providers and service users.

### 1.2 Trust

In the behavioral sciences, the concept of *trust* is well defined [15,16] and includes an expectation that the trustor is exposing themselves to vulnerability with the trustee. By extension, where a legally enforceable contract is in place, there is no need to rely on trust: any deviation from expected behaviors would be settled via the provisions of the contract. Further, under this definition, it is usually associated with human beings or organisations. With technology, the term *reliance* is more appropriate: there is an expectation that the technology is robust and will function as expected. There is no vulnerability, therefore. The technology either works or it doesn't. That being said, if technologies appear more *social*, then the human-human notion of trust may also be relevant [17]. At the same time, some researchers have distinguished *hard trust* - reliance on the robustness and security of the infrastructure, akin perhaps to Luhmann's *confidence* [18] - versus *soft trust* - the socially negotiated willingness to engage with the trustee [19,20]. For our study, we initially base our analysis on the original Mayer et al. definition [15] and assume trust in an organisation involves some acceptance that the organisation may fail to act as expected; here in regards to the processing of personal data.

### 1.3  A Note on *Tussles*

The concept of *tussles* was introduced by Clark and his colleagues [21] to describe the situation where the interest of two or more stakeholders are in conflict. A very simple example relates to *freedom of speech*. Western democracies champion the concept but in consequence have to deal with discriminatory language and misinformation. In our study, we contextualize the term within competing expectations of service providers who must demonstrably comply with data protection law in this case and of service users who wish to access services quickly without, say, being overburdened by reading and understanding lengthy terms and conditions [22].

## 2  Method

Over a series of project discussions and workshops, a total of 20 SMEs were presented with a risk assessment tool[1]. Based on a visualisation of a company's infrastructure, the tool calculates potential cyber risks and provides the system administrator options to mitigate those risks. Initially, 4 SME collaborators across four different business domains (*W4*) were asked to use the tool in their environment. As previously reported and after initial hesitancy about the complexity of the tool [23], they quickly began to see potential for using the tool in other contexts. Separately, 16 self-selecting SMEs unrelated to the project (*W16*) discussed the potential usefulness of the tool in helping them manage their cybersecurity status. We did not know explicitly the domains where these 16 SMEs worked. Verbatim transcripts from both *W4* and *W16* were reviewed using thematic analysis to identify the major topics that attendees raised.

Subsequently, a privacy attitudes survey was developed based on themes from a series of workshops with motivated privacy advocates in the UK [24,25]. A total of 501 UK-based private individuals, crowd-sourced through *Prolific.co* and paid a nominal amount for participation, rated 48 privacy-related statements covering the workshop-identified themes from *Strongly Agree* to *Strongly Disagree*. The statements were divided arbitrarily into four blocks, each introduced by a more

---

[1] https://spyderisk.org/.

general question of the type: *How likely are you to share your data with...?*. Initially, summary statistics from the survey were calculated.

For the purposes of this study, we assumed the 20 SMEs could be viewed as service providers; that the private individuals responding to the survey as potential service users; and that the providers would be anxious to encourage potential users to *trust* them. On that basis, the potential service users might engage and use the services provided.

## 3 Results

The SMEs recognised the need to protect the personal data they collect:

> *W4*: Sometimes there are some sensitive data and sensitive projects and they just want it [*sic.*] to be 100% sure that everything is secured from our side ... Maybe it's a bit difficult to manage all threats that we found because sometimes there are a lot of all of them ... We didn't know how to handle [an] attack from the outside if something is... not safe in our office

The need to protect data and the potential for attack was echoed among the 16 SMEs:

> *W16*...however small your business is, you do have a responsibility to protect the security of the data that you have ... [However] there just isn't enough time to sort of prevent it

There is clearly an awareness of cybersecurity risk and a willingness to exploit whatever technology and support are available.

In all the discussions with SMEs we've had, though, once they appreciate that they might be able to mitigate their general risk, they quickly realise that they might also be able to achieve regulatory compliance.

> *W4* ...there is [the] GDPR compliance issue and possible modelling errors. So, this part of the tool it's very... important and interesting [... for ISO] 27001 certification, GDPR compliance and so on... I mean you have to do that anyway... *W16* GDPR and HIPAA compliance - for UK SMEs, especially [...] because one of the big important things is a lot of people will just sell to the States before they even bring it back to their own home country [...] But if you could have this directly related to CyberEssentials, and then... So companies could say: I really am... base-level security related to CyberEssentials, cybersecurity stuff...

The SMEs in our workshops, therefore, start with mitigating cybersecurity risks. They then see potential in achieving compliance with standards (ISO 27x series and Cyberessentials) and with regulation (GDPR and HIPAA).

Figure 1 is our initial attempt to capture these discussion threads causally. The SME/service provider is aware they may be vulnerable to attack and therefore look for ways to mitigate that risk. However, they very soon afterwards look to see if they are failing to achieve regulatory compliance.

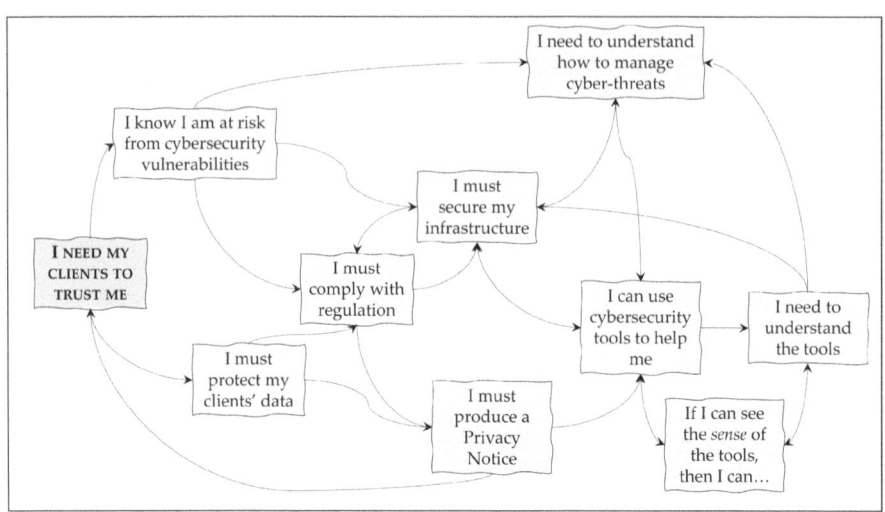

**Fig. 1.** Suggested Causal Model for Service Providers

One way to demonstrate such compliance would be through accreditation (with ISO standards, and so forth). For a service user, though, this may not be helpful: do they really understand what these standards mean and how compliance might affect the security of the service they are using? We have suggested that the endpoint for the service provider causal model to be a *privacy notice*. At the very least, service users as data subjects have a right to know what data are being processed, how and why: this is the main purpose for a *privacy notice*. Service providers must meet the obligation to be transparent in how they process personal data; and regulation-compliant templates are available for them to use.

Turning to potential service users, a different perspective obtains. In the second of the PRiAM workshops [24], participants were asked explicitly what they do to protect their privacy in a number of scenarios such as reading a privacy notice. A typical response - here from a Data Protection Officer (DPO) - was:

> "...despite being DPO, [when accepting cookies] I'm not too sure really deep down what does that mean and what could they be tracking or not? ... While I can read the privacy notice, but then underneath... it's all a bit of a gamble, and a bit of bit of trust I have to have"

If someone acting as a DPO is confused in this way, how might the general public (who may not have no reason to gain familiarity with data protection regulation) feel about the protection of their data when involved in online transactions? Further, regarding privacy notices, workshop participants suggested:

– "that privacy notices were structured to ensure regulatory compliance rather than to ensure informed consent", and so

– participants "suspected in some cases that privacy notices were deliberately made over-complicated and long-winded to discourage data subjects from reading them" ( [24], Sect. 2.2.1)

Given those views from a relatively small, self-selecting and motivated group, we asked 501 UK private individuals to respond to the anonymous online survey developed as a result of the workshop findings as stated above (see Sect. 2). Some of their responses to a subset of the questions are summarized in Table 1. Of particular note here are the following: first, the greatest concern is that personal data might be shared with a third party without the knowledge of the data subject. This is evidenced twice in response to the questions **When deciding to share my data, I worry about...** and **In general, I'm concerned about...**; in both cases, 73% of respondents ranked third-party sharing as the greatest issue. It should be remembered that this is one of the topics typically covered in a regulation-compliant privacy notice. Further, 63% are concerned that their data will be used for profiling or making decisions about the data subject. This is explicitly restricted, of course, by the GDPR Art. 18 and Art. 22 [1].

**Table 1.** Private Individual Responses to Data Sharing Questions

| **How likely am I to share my data with...** | | |
|---|---|---|
| Retailers | Researchers | Government |
| 53% | 64% | 59% |
| **How do I decide to share my data?** | | |
| I read the privacy notice | If I trust the organization asking for my data | I just get on with what I'm doing and don't worry about privacy |
| 43% | 61% | 47% |
| **When deciding to share my data, I worry about...** | | |
| Organizations sharing my data with third parties | Researchers using my data for whatever they like | My data being used to make decisions about me or for me |
| 73% | 49% | 63% |
| **In general, I am concerned by...** | | |
| The security of the data I contribute | The anonymity of the data I contribute | The onward sharing of the data I contribute |
| 64% | 60% | 73% |

Interestingly, on data sharing and processing for a different purpose, private individual responses are nuanced. About half of the respondents (49%) were uncomfortable about **Researchers using my data for whatever they like**;

and yet 64% are *...likely to share... data with* Researchers as opposed to Retailers (53%) or Government (59%). Alarmingly, though, only 43% claim to *...read the privacy notice* when making data sharing decisions by comparison to 61% who claim the decision is based on whether they *...trust the organization asking for my data*.

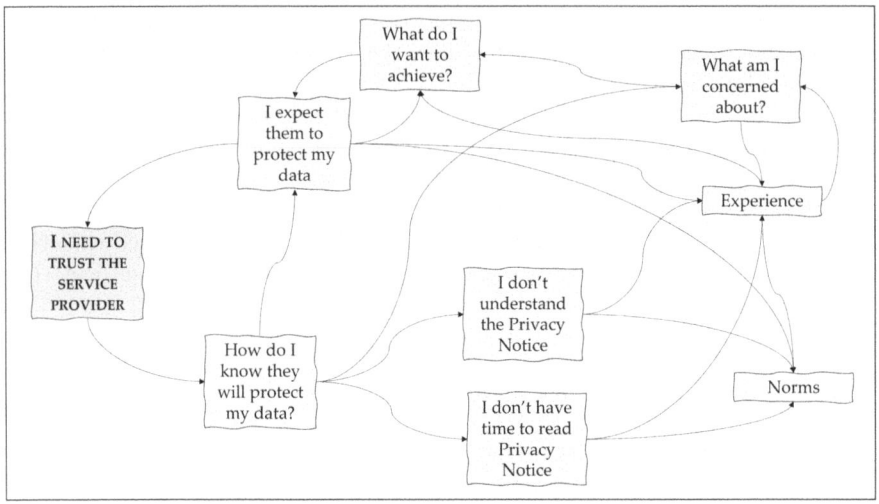

**Fig. 2.** Suggested Causal Model for Service Users

Trying to understand responses like this and the broader discussions in fora as described in [24], we attempted to generate a causal model of potential service-user decision making (see Fig. 2). Service users, we believe, consider in the first instance what they expect from the service provider: namely, that they (the service provider) will protect service user's data. This is a privacy boundary negotiation rather than a one-off check that the service provider complies with regulation. In this vein, Altman asserts that privacy decisions constitute a:

"boundary control process whereby people sometimes make themselves open and accessible to others and sometimes close themselves off from others" ([26], p.67)

and later elaborated by Petronio in Communication Privacy Management (CPM) [27]. Their decision, therefore, is about self-disclosure based on the assumption that the recipient of their data assumes co-ownership of - and thereby shares responsibility for - those data [28].

That boundary having been negotiated, they bypass the privacy notice, instead consulting their own experience (the construct *Experience*) and that of similar others (*Norms*). Not surprisingly, perhaps, these two constructs appear as antecedents in a Protection Motivation Theory (PMT) model [29] before the cost-benefit evaluation is made based on susceptibility (to the threat), the severity (or impact) it would mean, the cost of doing what's required to ensure privacy and so forth. PMT models have indeed been used by others to account for privacy behaviors [30]. So *Norms* and *Experience* refer to what private individuals consider they and significant others have seen in the past. *What am I concerned about?* similarly echoes the Susceptibility/Severity and Cost/Benefit constructs of the PMT. From this point, though, the analogy with the PMT begins to weaken.

At the top of Fig. 2, and remembering perhaps that 47% in the survey said they were focused on *what (they) are doing and don't worry about privacy*, the construct *What do I want to achieve?* reflects a transactional focus. Further, the constructs *How do I know they will protect my data?* and *I expect them to protect my data* reflect a maladaptive response à la Witte [8] to the central constructs *I don't understand the Privacy Notice* and *I don't have time to read the Privacy Notice*. Private individuals as potential service users discard the agency afforded by privacy regulation and simply expect others to process their data securely in order to maintain their privacy aspirations. This may to some extent explain the *privacy paradox*: data subjects agree that they want their data to be processed securely and their privacy preserved, but they believe others responsible to meet those expectations rather than themselves. Assuming they don't retain that responsibility for their own data, they share their data as required to achieve the immediate transactional goal.

Remembering that the causal model was developed from empirical investigation, one conclusion is that private individuals make decisions to share data because they trust the process and/or the transaction they wish to achieve rather than the security of the delivery channel. As stated previously, following Mayer and colleagues [15], we believe trust includes a willingness to be vulnerable, that is to relinquish (or share) control of personal data and in turn risk privacy, albeit assuming the responsibility is shared as predicted by CPM. That the proposed causal models in Figs. 1 and 2 reflect two sides of a single interaction deserves further consideration. Data protection regulation and service-provider compliance with it would predict that data subjects decide to share their data based on an assurance of regulatory control and the GDPR ([1] Art. 25 and Art. 32). The privacy notice effectively provides that assurance. If service users do not consult the privacy notice, then they appear to be prepared to risk vulnerability because a social-constructionist view would have provided the experience for negotiating self-disclosure with other human agents and organisations. Hard trust - reliance on regulatory compliance - has been confused with soft trust which would form part of a privacy boundary negotiation [26,27] that service users are more familiar with.

What the two figures make clear is that service providers (or the SMEs in our studies as potential service providers), focusing on regulatory compliance, and private individuals, motivated by transactional goals and expecting others to be responsible for their data, reflect conflicting expectations about how data will be secured and thereby privacy assured. The irony is that is largely what data protection regulation is intended for: to show service providers what they are expected to do in processing personal data, whilst making explicit the rights data subjects can call on to validate that their data are processed correctly. Regulation offers data subjects control, but that's not how those individuals behave.

As seen in Table 1, there is some evidence that private individuals respond differently to the intended target organisation for their data. A privacy tussle in Clark's terms [21] is not a static but a dynamic negotiation depending at least on who the recipient of the personal data (the *data controller* in data protection terms) is seen to be. Further, whereas Erramilli [31] seems to put the onus on technology suppliers to comply with regulators, there is little consideration of the motivations and expectations of the data subjects. In terms of privacy theories [27,28,32], there seems to be a mismatch of expectations leading to potential privacy turbulence [27,28]. However, this is not the whole story. If private individuals *trust* the data controller when disclosing their personal data, then they may assume that the data controller now has co-ownership of the data and therefore must assume some responsibility [27]. In Mayer and his colleagues' terms, this *trust* decision to share personal data supposes that the data controller is benevolent towards the data subject, competent (which may mean compliant with regulation and cybersecurity standards, perhaps) and acts with integrity. Our causal model from the potential service-user perspective may well influence the *Experience* and possibly *Norms* of service-user decision making around self-disclosure.

## 4    Discussion

Using causal models to encapsulate stakeholder perspectives [13], Weggelaar-Jansen and her colleagues [14] label the debilitating effect of data protection regulation as a *Swamp of Rules*, representing a significant risk to research. Our focus here has been broader: to visualize the decision-making process of private individuals when engaged in any interaction with an enterprise that may directly or indirectly involve sharing their personal data. There are, however, parallels: data protection laws are intended to be beneficial to the data subjects, but have not taken into account how those individuals behave.

The two causal models, therefore, represent the differing cognitive, emotional and personal priorities of the actors in a transactional actor network (the service provider, on the one hand, and the service user on the other) in relation to the notions of trustworthiness and trust. These priorities are shaped by the social role(s) the subject occupies (i.e., the provider/business *versus* the user/client); their prior experiences; and the wider contexts, goals and norms of expectation in which they are situated. These priorities have been internally realised, we assume, as a decision path through a range of complex cognitive processes which, in turn, are externally manifested as actions undertaken across the different interaction networks within which each role typically resides.

An interaction network may be understood as the total set of connections an entity has to people, technological devices, services, organisations, information and resources [33]. Interaction networks have arisen from the combination of the key notions of purposeful interaction (from Social Constructivism [34,35]), connected networks (from Connectivism [36]) and the equal importance of human and non-human actors in a network (from Activity Theory [37]). Interaction networks form the framework within which all daily activities occur and serve as the vehicle through which human decision paths are manifest in actions.

Within the domain of trust and trustworthiness one of the places where the separate interaction networks of SMEs and users (or more accurately of the roles of provider/business and user/client) intersect is at the 'node' of *privacy notice*. One account of the difference between the two models in Figs. 1 and 2 is that this node constitutes a potential endpoint in an interaction path across the network for both roles, although the purpose of the interaction with that endpoint is significantly different for each. The causal model for the SME as service provider indicates that the purpose of interacting with a privacy notice is to assert compliance with regulations (to protect customer data). While in the causal model for the potential service user the assumption would be that the motivation to interact with the privacy notice would be to seek reassurance that their personal data will be protected. However, this user reassurance is limited by the fact that the privacy notice is difficult to understand and takes time to read and comprehend, which is because it serves a different interactional purpose within the network of the SME/service provider that created it.

An alternative explanation would be that the potential service-user *privacy notice* construct is not perceived as directly relevant for the service user: that it appears too long or too complicated hides the fact that the service user looks elsewhere when making data sharing decisions. Namely, and as they have learned in other human-to-human interactions, they assume a dynamic boundary negotiation which results in shared responsibility for their data will take place: the recipient of those data should be aware of this and respond accordingly.

Either way, as a result, there is a tension that arises, centred on this node as an endpoint for the service provider but as a diversion for the service user. This is indicative of a broader issue, whereby user trust in technology may be negatively impacted through a lack of alignment in interactional purpose between SME and user in relation to the production and consumption of a privacy notice, or indeed the production and consumption of technologies in general. Indeed, privacy notices disrupt, we suggest, the established learned expectations around privacy: the service users (private individuals) rely on privacy boundary negotiation they have learned from past human-to-human interaction; whilst the service provider assumes regulatory compliance to be enough.

## 5   Limitations and Future Work

As stated, we made assumptions about the responses from service providers and service users. Although this may be perceived as strengthening our argument because the views expressed have more general and possibly ecologically more viable relevance, nonetheless we cannot explicitly guarantee the correctness of our interpretation. On similar lines, neither did we explicitly ask what a (potential) service provider does to develop trustworthiness and thereby encourage trust from (potential) service users; nor did we ask private individuals what they look for when deciding to use a service. We plan in future, therefore, to develop a research protocol which would allow us to validate the conclusions we have drawn here.

## 6    Conclusion

In this paper, we have developed two complementary causal models based on the interpretation of empirical observation with SMEs and private individuals. The first attempts to capture the decision process that a potential service provider undertakes to ensure compliance with regulation and secure their infrastructure. This is followed by publishing a privacy policy for potential service users to decide to engage, including sharing personal data. The second encapsulates how potential service users rely on (*soft*) trust to engage and share their data. In this latter case, they do not refer to a privacy notice.

We conclude, therefore, that despite well-intentioned, but not always well-received regulation [38], failing to reconcile this apparent trust tussle could affect service-user willingness to engage with service providers (*trust*) and the latters' willingness to expend resource to assure compliance (*trustworthiness*). Perhaps one way to resolve the tussle would be to work towards a greater alignment of the differing interactional purposes influencing providers and users of privacy notices via increased foregrounding of boundary negotiations around data security responsibility. We have already suggested a similar approach for consent [40]. Additionally, we believe that related work highlighting a social dimension to trust in technology [17,39] and more specifically the failure to distinguish hard and soft trust [19,20] can explain these causal models. More especially, hard trust relates to service provider channel security requirements whereas soft trust to the provider-user relationship as operationalized through the service that runs across that channel. In so doing, we provide contributory empirical evidence to account for apparent privacy paradoxes in self-disclosure behaviours.

**Ethics.** All studies reported here were approved by the University of Southampton, Faculty of Engineering and Physical Sciences Research Ethics Committee: the 4 SME workshops reference FEPS/73328; the 16 SME Workshop reference FEPS/89179; and the anonymous Privacy Attitudes Survey reference FEPS/71408.A1.

**Disclosure of Interests.** The authors have no competing interests to declare that are relevant to the content of this article.

## References

1. European Commission: Regulation (EU) 2016/679 of the European Parliament and of the Council of 27 April 2016 (2016)

2. Voigt, P., von dem Bussche, A.: The EU General Data Protection Regulation (GDPR): A Practical Guide. Springer, Cham (2017). https://doi.org/10.1007/978-3-319-57959-7

3. McEvily, B., Perrone, V., Zaheer, A.: Trust as an organizing principle. Organ. Sci. **14**(1), 91–103 (2003)

4. Blythe, J.: Cyber security in the workplace Understanding and promoting behaviour change. In: P. Bottoni, P., Matera, M. (eds.) Proceedings of CHItaly 2013 Doctoral Consortium, 1065. pp. 92–101. Trento, Italy (2013)

5. Alahmari, A., Duncan, B.: Cybersecurity risk management in small and medium-sized enterprises: a systematic review of recent evidence. In: 2020 International Conference on Cyber Situational Awareness, Data Analytics and Assessment (CyberSA). IEEE (2020)

6. Lewis, R., Louvieris, P., Abbott, P., Clewley, N., Jones, K.: Cybersecurity information sharing: a framework for information security management in UK SME supply chains. In: Twenty Second European Conference on Information Systems. Tel Aviv (2014)

7. Erdogan, G., Halvorsrud, R., Boletsis, C., Tverdal, S., Pickering, B.: Cybersecurity Awareness and Capacities of SMEs. In: 9th Internation Conference on Information Systems Security and Privacy. Lisbon, Portugal (2023)

8. Witte, K.: Putting the fear back into fear appeals the extended parallel process model. Commun. Monogr. **59**(4), 329–349 (1992)

9. Witte, K., Allen, M.: A meta-analysis of fear appeals implications for effective public health campaigns. Health Educ. Beh. **75**(5), 591–615 (2000)

10. Acquisti, A., Brandimarte, L., Loewenstein, G.: Privacy and human behavior in the age of information. Science **3**(6221), 509–514 (2015)

11. Barth, S., De Jong, M.: The privacy paradox - investigating discrepancies between expressed privacy concerns and actual online behavior - A systematic literature review. Telematics Inform. **34**(7), 1038–1058 (2017)

12. Kokolakis, S.: Privacy attitudes and privacy behaviour: a review of current research on the privacy paradox phenomenon. Comput. Secur. **64**, 122–134 (2017)

13. Vermaak, H.: Using causal loop diagramsto deal with complex issues: mastering an instrument for systemic and interactive change. Consult. Organ. Change Revis. Res. Manag. Consult. **23**, 231–254 (2016)

14. Weggelaar-Jansen, A.M., Sülz, S., Wehrens, R.: Using causal diagrams to understand and deal with hindering patterns in the uptake and embedding of big data technology. In: Pickering, B., Roller, R., Hemsen, H., Noodergraaf, G-J., Paulussen, I., Venema, A. (eds.) Technology in Healthcare Introduction, Clinical Impacts, Workflow Improvement, Structuring and Assessment. now Publishers Inc: Delft, The Netherlands (in press)

15. Mayer, R.C., Davis, J.H., Schoorman, F.D.: An integrative model of organizational trust. Acad. Manag. Rev. **20**(3), 709–734 (1995)

16. Rousseau, D.M., Sitkin, S.B., Burt, R.S., Camerer, C.: Not so different after all: a cross-discipline view of trust. Acad. Manag. Rev. **23**(3)

17. Lankton, N.K., McKnight, D.H., Tripp, J.: Technology, humanness, and trust: rethinking trust in technology. J. Assoc. Inf. Syst. **16**(10), 880–918 (2015)

18. Luhmann, N.: Familiarity, confidence, trust: problems and alternatives. In: Gambetta, D. (ed) Trust: Making and Breaking Cooperative Relations. Chapter 6, pp. 94–107 (2000)

19. Lin, C., Varadharajan, V.: A hybrid trust model for enhancing security in distributed systems. The Second International Conference on Availability, Reliability and Security (ARES'07) (2007)

20. Varadharajan, V.: A note on trust-enhanced security. IEEE Secur. Priv. **7**(3), 57–59 (2009)
21. Clark, D.D., Wroclawski, J., Sollins, K.R., Braden, R.: Tussle in cyberspace defining tomorrow's internet. IEEE ACM Trans. Network. **13**(3), 462–475 (2005). https://doi.org/10.1109/TNET.2005.850224
22. Steinfeld, N.: "I agree to the terms and conditions" (How) do users read privacy policies online? An eye-tracking experiment. Comput. Hum. Behav. **55**, 992–1000 (2016). https://doi.org/10.1016/j.chb.2015.09.038
23. Pickering, B., Phillips, S., Erdogan, G.: I just want to help SMEs engaging with cybersecurity technology. In: Moallem, A. (ed.) HCI International 2023. Springer AG Switzerland: Copenhagen, Denmark, pp. 1–15 (2023)
24. Boniface, M., et al.: DARE UK PRiAM Project D4 Report-Public Engagement: Understanding private individuals' perspectives on privacy and privacy risk (2.0) (2023). https://doi.org/10.5281/zenodo.7107486
25. Pickering, B., Baker, K., Boniface, M., McMahon, J.P.: Privacy Perspectives Survey (Version 1) (2023). https://doi.org/10.5281/zenodo.7589522
26. Altman, I.: Privacy regulation: culturally universal or culturally specific? J. Soc. Issues **33**(3), 66–84 (1977)
27. Petronio, S.: Brief status report on communication privacy management theory. J. Fam. Commun. **13**(1), 6–14 (2013)
28. Petronio, S., Child, J.T.: Conceptualization and operationalization: utility of communication privacy management theory. Curr. Opin. Psychol. **31**, 76–82 (2020)
29. Rogers, R.W.: A protection motivation theory of fear appeals and attitude change. J. Psychol. **90**(1), 93–114 (1975)
30. Mousavi, R., Chen, R., Kim, D.J., Chen, K.: Effectiveness of privacy assurance mechanisms in users' privacy protection on social networking sites from the perspective of protection motivation theory. Decis. Support Syst. **135**, 113323 (2020). https://doi.org/10.1016/j.dss.2020.113323
31. Erramilli, V.: The tussle around online privacy. IEEE Internet Comput. **16**(4), 69–71 (2012)
32. Smith, H.J., Dinev, T., Xu, H.: Information privacy research an interdisciplinary review. MIS Q. **35**(4), 989–1015 (2011)
33. Fair, N.S.R.: A framework for the analysis of personal learning networks. In: Dohn, N.B., Hansen, J.J., Hansen, S.B., Ryberg, T., de Laat, M. (eds.) Conceptualizing and Innovating Education and Work with Networked Learning. RNL, pp. 211–236. Springer, Cham (2021). https://doi.org/10.1007/978-3-030-85241-2_12
34. Vygotsky, L.: Mind in Society. Harvard University Press, London (1978)
35. Lynch, M.: Social constructivism in science and technology studies. Hum. Stud. **39**(1), 101–112 (2016). https://doi.org/10.1007/s10746-016-9385-5
36. Siemens, G.: Connectivism: a learning theory for the digital age. Int. J. Instruct. Technol. Distan. Learn. **2**(1), 3–10 (2005)
37. Engestrom, Y.: Activity theory as a framework for analyzing and redesigning work. Ergonomics **43**(7), 960–974 (2000)
38. Balaban, D.C., Mustățea, M.: Privacy concerns in mobile communication: a user's perspective. Philobiblon **26**(1), 101–114 (2021)
39. Thiebes, S., Lins, S., Sunyaev, A.: Trustworthy artificial intelligence. Electron. Mark. **31**(2), 447–464 (2021)
40. Pickering, B.: Trust, but verify: informed consent, AI technologies, and public health emergencies. Future Internet **13**(5) (2021). https://doi.org/10.3390/fi13050132

# Legal, Technical and User Perspectives on the Right to Modify

René Richard[1]([✉]) [ID], Margaret H. McKay[2] [ID], and Heather Molyneaux[1] [ID]

[1] National Research Council of Canada, Fredericton, NB, Canada
{rene.richard,heather.molyneaux}@nrc-cnrc.gc.ca
[2] National Research Council of Canada, Ottawa, ON, Canada
margaret.mckay@nrc-cnrc.gc.ca

**Abstract.** While the modification of products by their purchasers is not a new phenomenon, the increasing digitization of consumer products, and the availability of online resources and public code repositories may be opening the door to a greater scope of modifications. This literature review and analysis paper is significant as the first known effort to address the unique factors that apply to decisions on a so-called "right to modify," distinguished from ongoing discussions and legislative action on the "right to repair." Through review and analysis of legal, technical, and user acceptance considerations, applied to the example of artificial intelligence-enabled robotic systems, this paper demonstrates a pressing need for policy which distinguishes between repair and modification and reflects the risks and opportunities of each.

**Keywords:** Right to Modify · Robotic Systems · AI-Enabled Robotics Design · Human Factors · Ethics and Philosophy

## 1 Introduction

Developers and industry are recognizing the complex web of factors they need to consider when providing a "responsible" automated or AI-enabled product or service. In order to foster public acceptance and trust in such systems, issues of safety, and security must be addressed by industry. The hope and expectation is that through consideration of ethical concerns, society can ensure that the integration of automation and robotics aligns with human values and contributes positively to the well-being of individuals and communities. However, what happens when such products are later modified by third parties or their purchasers? Modification could allow users to adjust the function of products to better serve their needs. At the same time, there are many concerns related to the protection of bystander safety, and other rights, arguing for caution where modification is concerned.

Discussions on the appropriateness and ability of individuals to maintain and repair items they have purchased have been ongoing for decades. From the late nineteenth to the mid-twentieth century, efforts to deter repair were driven primarily by design choices, pricing strategy, and psychologically informed marketing [36]. As product complexity and digitization rose in the late twentieth century, some manufacturers began to add intellectual property law to their repair-deterring toolkit.

It is possible to view the question of "right to modify" as the next logical step along the pathway from the so-called "right to maintain" to the "right to repair." Decades of judicial and academic attention have enabled clear distinctions between "maintenance" (preventative actions to preserve original levels of function) and "repair" (actions which restore original function). "Modification" has received less attention. For the purposes of this paper, "modification" refers to activities which change the original planned function as compared to its original design and manufacture. Modification therefore includes both the addition and reduction of function, including both operational and safety functions.

This paper focuses primarily on the example of robotic systems capable of two-way physical and/or social interactions with the environment, people, or both. For the purposes of this paper, the term "robot" can be applied broadly, to include autonomous vehicles, social robots (embodied or otherwise), and many things in between. Even with this broad definition, the question of appropriate limits on post-sale modification of AI-enabled tools will apply well beyond robots. However, the persistent interactivity of robotic systems marks them as one example of systems where post-sale modifications can be expected to raise multiple types of concerns both supporting and opposing a broad "right" to modify.

Our paper reviews and discusses the "ethics" of modifications to technological systems and includes a reflection on factors relevant to the most pertinent ethical principles, as well as the perspectives from which they may be applied. We provide a literature review and analysis from legal, technical, and user acceptance perspectives with specific discussion of robotics as an application area.

## 2   Legal

Western regulation of commercial matters has been strongly influenced by the "harm principle." This principle encompasses the idea that the freedom of one individual ends at the point where the exercise of that freedom would cause harm to another [20,33]. In a modern context, this includes both limitations on harmful activities and incentives to promote activities seen as broadly beneficial. Law is frequently used as an instrument to achieve these broader goals. In the repair and modification area, the list of harms and benefits to be considered relate primarily to aspects of the public good, including: promoting innovation, ensuring healthy competition, encouraging product safety, justice for those harmed, and encouraging environmentally responsible behaviours. The dominant approach taken is to create regulations which "internalize" costs and benefits to those who are best placed to control them.

## 2.1   Innovation and Competition

Intellectual property (IP) laws are intended to encourage innovation by enabling creators a limited period of monopoly over their creation. This monopoly is intended to encourage innovation by giving innovators an opportunity to recoup the full costs and reap meaningful rewards from their investment and efforts to develop the innovation. While there are some differences between jurisdictions, historically most IP laws permitted some non-commercial copying, such as for the purposes of fair or research use or private use and study. This compromise was intended to allow ongoing advances in knowledge even during the innovator's period of exclusive commercial use. Recent legislative changes in some jurisdictions have introduced new mechanisms which can reduce the scope for such knowledge-enhancing use [6].

The rights of IP owners are not unlimited however. Competition and antitrust laws are intended to prevent excessive leveraging of IP rights and abuse of a dominant market position [4,9,51]. In essence, these laws act as a check on the extent to which the owner of IP rights can extend their market dominance beyond the scope of their explicit IP rights. The effectiveness of this balance between innovation and competition has long been debated, and governments have passed various additional laws in an effort to adjust the balance in particular areas [35]. Recently, the United States Department of Justice launched a lawsuit against Apple, alleging (among other things) that Apple has attempted to over-leverage its IP rights through restrictions on the extent to which non-Apple applications can fully use the device's hardware and software [47]. The U.S. Department of Justice alleges that Apple has become less interested in innovating to attract and retain customers as a result of its monopoly position and has instead focused on making it more difficult for customers to leave [27,48].

From the perspective of manufacturers, more recent laws like the United States Digital Millennium Copyright Act [6] are important to ensure protection for some forms of electronic content. From a consumer perspective, laws of this type expand copyright beyond its historical and natural limits, creating prohibitions for activities which would previously have been allowed as fair use. Renewable time-limited exemptions to these new restrictions are sometimes available [6]. However, such exceptions do not change the fact that such legislation creates a default favouring an expansion of the rights of those who own digital copyrights. End users therefore face the reality that they could see their ability to use third-party repair services disappear if the exemption is not renewed. Issues of this type also reveal deeper structural challenges facing those who would seek to exercise or enable existing repair rights: It is not enough to have favourable laws on the books. Factors which impact the practical exercise and enforcement of those rights must also be addressed.

Modification and repair raise very similar IP issues. Thus, to a large extent, one can expect IP impacts on modification to mirror those seen for repair. However, there is an important exception: changes to the function of an item can in some cases bring an article within the claims of patents which it would have avoided in its original state. The doctrine of exhaustion frequently prevents a company from using IP rights to control subsequent sale and use of its products. This has been immensely helpful to the "right to repair" movement [9]. However, in some cases modification can raise new challenges.

Certain modifications may enable the device to do things that its original design did not permit. These new functions could be the subject of separate intellectual property protection. In this case, the device originally purchased did not possess these functions. Thus that original sale is unlikely to "exhaust" the patent rights in the newly added function. Depending on the jurisdiction, commercial (professional) modifiers, and possibly even non-commercial modifiers and those who provide related instructions and tools could find themselves at risk of lawsuits. From the perspective of encouraging innovation and internalizing costs and benefits, this makes sense: if there is a patent to infringe or copyrighted code to copy, it means that the innovator who created it invested time and resources into that new creation. Conventional IP theory indicates that the innovator should be entitled to a period of monopoly to benefit from their investment. There is no clear reason why the scope of the innovator's rights to stop an infringer should depend on whether the infringing activity existed in an off-the-shelf model or was added via modification after a first sale. The absence of such protection could deter individuals and organizations from investing in the development of new IP. This in turn would reduce innovation which would deprive society of new products and services, resulting in reduced personal, social, and economic benefits. For example, one can imagine a situation where a manufacturer has chosen to differentiate the capabilities of lower and higher-end robot models using differences in software while retaining the same core hardware. In such cases the "as sold" less expensive robot is unlikely to include the code for the unused capabilities. Modifications to add higher end functionality to a robot that was shipped as a lower model could raise legitimate IP issues under patent law, copyright law, or possibly both. Similarly, a manufacturer might have designed their product so as to avoid infringing a patent owned by their competitor. If a purchaser modifies one company's product so that it infringes a different company's patent, it is difficult to argue that the second company shouldn't be able to enforce its patent.

Governments have attempted to respond to public pressure demanding greater scope for repair using laws against deceptive practices [3, 15]. For example, planned obsolescence may sometimes be caught under these prohibitions [46]. Legislative efforts are also underway in some jurisdictions to protect the usable life of consumer products, for example by prohibiting planned obsolescence, expanding implied warranties to include availability of replacement parts, and to exempt certain repair activities from digital rights protections [1]. Some jurisdictions have also taken steps to limit the ability of manufacturers to void a product warranty because third party parts were used in a repair [2].

## 2.2 Product Liability, Safety and Justice

There is a public interest in protecting safety and enabling justice for those injured. These interests are enabled through both general negligence laws and specific laws on product liability. While the details vary between jurisdictions, such laws generally seek to transfer at least some of the costs of injuries from those who are injured to the organizations responsible for the product or service which caused the injury. This creates economic incentives for companies to design for safety, reducing public risk and the extent to which governments must provide financial assistance to injured individuals.

Modification raises new questions about safety and recoverability of the cost of injuries because it has the potential to remove the manufacturer (who typically knows the product best) from the decision-making process about what that product will be enabled to do.

In the repair context, manufacturers have tried to use safety as a reason to prevent third party repair. However, evidence of actual safety issues in repair has been scant [10]. Manufacturers also have a wide range of obligations where product safety and warnings are concerned [7]. However, in many jurisdictions, they are not considered responsible for injuries which result from modifications which were either clearly contrary to explicit warnings, or which were not rea-sonably foreseeable at the time the product was produced [5,8]. If companies believe they will be held liable for injuries even when they have taken all rea-sonable steps to reduce harm, that could reduce their incentives to take those extra steps. That would be bad for consumers, workers, and users. However, this leaves the problem of finding compensation for individuals who are injured due to modifications.

Modifications could potentially be carried out by a range of entities. Some of these may be large companies with assets and insurance sufficient to compensate victims. However, it seems likely that many of those carrying out modifications will be small shops with few assets or resources, or even the product owners themselves, possibly relying on online guidance from individuals and off-shore manufacturers.

Tort and product liability laws are intended to transfer part of the costs of an injury onto the organization that could have best reduced that risk. In the case of injuries resulting from modifications to a robot, the injured person would probably need to try and recover their losses from the repair shop, parts supplier, YouTube advisor, robot owner, and whoever else created or enabled the problem. Unlike manufacturers, who typically have significant assets and insurance as well as a legal presence in the jurisdiction, those involved in robot modifications may be essentially judgement proof, whether due to lack of assets or because they are located far outside the jurisdiction and beyond the easy reach of domestic legal actions.

One possible approach to enabling injured parties to offset the financial costs of injury would be mandatory insurance. Thus, just as many jurisdictions require the operators of motor vehicles to carry liability insurance, the owners of certain classes of higher-risk robots could be under a similar requirement. The issue of harm reduction (avoidance) is not so easily addressed. In most cases, it is better to avoid an injury than to suffer it, even if in the end it is possible for the victim to recover their financial losses. In cases where responsibility for harm reduction is spread across many small and frequently distant players, it will be challenging to develop an efficient and effective regulatory approach that ensures consistent harm reduction.

Added to all this is the need for certainty and predictability in the law. Market economies rely on profit-motivated companies to produce the goods and services necessary for all citizens and organizations. Clear laws and strong legal systems permit companies to make risk-informed financial calculations which they can use to drive their business decisions. When laws become excessively fragmented and riddled with special cases, or worse still when laws are unclear or only arbitrarily enforced, companies can not calculate the likely return on potential investments. This is also likely to impede innovation.

### 2.3  Early Efforts to Regulate Artificial Intelligence Systems

Pending efforts to introduce AI safety legislation appear to be responding primarily to concerns about the suitability of potentially high-impact commercial AI products [16]. However, this does not mean that modification will be uniformly exempt from these requirements. The European Artificial Intelligence Act requirements apply to those who provide, import, and/or deploy "high risk" AI systems and general purpose AI models in the European Union ("EU") [17]. Arguably, anyone who downloads code or otherwise modifies an AI-enabled device located in the EU and puts it into service could be subject to this Act. This could potentially include individuals who modify their own personal devices, as well as non-EU service providers who use remote connection means to install an update on a device located in the EU.

Recent activity in the United States suggests a growing interest in some form of AI regulation there as well, likely with a focus on testing to prevent harm and bias. These efforts are at an early stage. An "AI Bill of Rights" has been proposed, which might eventually empower individuals to seek redress in the event of some provable harms [34]. Parallel efforts are also underway to define standards and approaches for testing, evaluating, and monitoring AI systems [25]. These efforts are at an early stage and it is not yet clear if they will be limited to commercial and government deployers of AI, or to a broader scope of potential users and modifiers. Recently, a bi-partisan group of United States senators has indicated their intention to introduce legislation which would establish conditions and restrictions related to the development of particular kinds of models which are deemed to present extreme risks based on size or intended use, based on national security concerns [49]. Given the information released to date, it seems possible that legislation might relate to both the development and the use of large AI models. The very early stage of this proposal makes it impossible to predict what its final scope will be. However, unless the final scope goes well beyond what is referenced in initial communications [49], any directly resulting legislation seems unlikely to present a barrier to an individual seeking to modify their own domestic product for conventional peaceful use.

# 3    Technical

In this section, we examine the technical aspects of the right to modify, investigating ethical principles that are often reflected in the related literature. The analysis employs a technical lens to evaluate the implications of these principles, providing a concise yet comprehensive overview of the subject.

## 3.1    Individual Autonomy

The principles of respect for autonomy strive to ensure that citizens are empowered by access to relevant forms of knowledge. Knowledge about the inner workings of technology, coupled with the ability to repair or modify, shapes a consumer's decision-making skills and fosters independence and critical thinking. Removing barriers and ensuring the availability of information enables individuals to achieve their own moral goals.

In the past, acquiring a new electronic product entailed receiving a detailed manual that explained its internal workings. However, in recent times, manufacturers have shown a decreasing willingness to provide insight into the inner workings of their products, employing a blend of hardware and software restrictions to curtail user access. Devices are becoming increasingly more complex and difficult to disassemble, discouraging any attempts at repair, upgrade, or modification. Additionally, modern product designs are increasingly incorporating software. The rise of embedded computer design in a multitude of products has led to a yielding of basic functionality controls to software [38].

In [24], Hatta provides a comprehensive overview of the tactics employed by manufacturers to achieve material obsolescence. This process typically begins with rendering products challenging to modify or repair. Manufacturers often exacerbate this issue by withholding essential information, such as repair manuals, and designing parts that are intentionally incompatible between different models. Moreover, they frequently employ strategies such as altering model numbers to reduce the psychological appeal of using older models, as well as employing legal tactics like alleged copyright and patent protections to impede access and modification to a product's internal structure. These tactics and practices collectively make modifications and repairs more challenging and contribute to the perception of overall product obsolescence.

The rise of embedded computer design in everyday items, has led to increased interest in automation and robotics. For instance, the concept of functional home appliance robots is materializing with the advancements in artificial intelligence. Adoption is accompanied by an increasing acknowledgment of security concerns. If a user's perception of a technology's usefulness exceeds the risks, uptake will likely expand. Chatterjee et al. [14] note the surge in the development and sales of robots intended for household use and expect the market for domestic robots to grow exponentially in the coming years. In light of the increased integration of robotics and artificial intelligence in various domains, there's a push to steer technical advances towards morally and socially favorable objectives. This involves incorporating an additional layer of explainability and reliable adaptability into AI-enabled systems.

## 3.2 Societal Equity

As almost every consumer product now has some type of electronics embedded in it, there is an increased interest in examining the environmental impact of this trend. The total mass of Electrical and Electronic Equipment (EEE) in Canada from 1971 to 2030 is estimated to reach 42.3 million tonnes, with an annual average growth rate of approximately 0.5%. The e-waste generation per capita increased from 8.3 kg in 2000 to 25.3 kg in 2020 and is estimated to reach 31.5 kg by 2030 [23]. A country's GDP is closely linked to the total number of computers and potential e-waste items. This is due to the fundamental role played by electrical and electronic items in the operation of economies [37].

Authors in [40] present a systematic review on design practices which support the sustainability of repairable products. This work notes that traditional design practices aim to minimize production cost, which leads to linear value chains where products are difficult to re-insert into the value creation process. Some design practices aim at slowing the loop of resource usage. The design for repair approach aims to limit waste and landfill expansion. Efforts to address e-waste challenges can lead to positive societal outcomes, fostering environmental justice, improving public health, and enhancing access to technology within communities.

Reverse engineering is a process employed to extract hidden design information from systems and data. This process can be used to customize or modify existing products or software for specific needs and to analyze software and hardware for vulnerabilities. Reverse engineering for the purposes of modification can lead to safety concerns. As an example, in the automotive industry, a Controller Area Network (CAN) is a serial bus designed for the exchange of information within vehicles. Vehicle communication relies on messages exchanged by Electronic Control Units (ECUs) connected to a serial bus network. CAN messages are not encrypted but not easy to interpret. The only way to obtain clear data is to reverse engineer CAN messages. Authors in [13] explore the hazards linked to the automation of CAN reverse engineering enabling sabotaging the correct functioning of a vehicle by affecting messages on the bus. Malicious attack simulations range from altering fuel level indicator readings to driving a vehicle off the road. Other types of activities that involve reverse engineering on the CAN include tuning. A vehicle owner might want to adjust the engine settings for more power or decrease mileage to boost its resale value. Such modifications can result in serious safety concerns for both the occupants of the vehicle and other individuals on the road.

Authors in [12] introduce the notion of safety-rated modification limits where robotics systems would benefit from safety-rated thresholds that determine admissible limits up to which the system or application can be changed prior to being put back into operation. This model helps validate which changes, on robotics systems in industrial environments, can be made without conducting new operational risk assessments. This model not only aids in validating permissible changes to robotic systems in industrial environments without the need for new operational risk assessments but may also offer insights into facilitating safe modifications in consumer electronics.

As we explore reliability in the next section, the focus shifts towards understanding how repair and modifications can impact the overall reliability of systems. By establishing a connection between safety-rated modification limits and reliability, we aim to unravel the intricate interplay between adaptability and stability in technological systems.

### 3.3   Reliability

Systems should execute their designated tasks as intended. The greater the reliability of a system, the more predictable its behavior becomes. In [52], the authors discuss how the digital revolution has led to increased integration of robotic systems in various domains, with a focus on enhancing human life, but incidents and malicious attacks have raised concerns. Robots are employed in various sectors such as agriculture, industry, military, disaster relief, and healthcare, for tasks like crop monitoring, construction, combat, search and rescue, and healthcare applications, including remote surgeries and COVID-19 response. This work discusses security vulnerabilities, threats, and their impacts in the robotics domain, highlighting the risks of malicious attacks, including hijacking and economic losses. It offers recommendations for improving robotic system security, such as multi-factor device/user authentication and cryptographic algorithms, along with a review of recent security solutions.

Authors in [21] look at industrial robots. In the industry 4.0 context, these robots are network-connected and collaborate with humans, providing convenience but also raising security risks. Connectivity to the Internet exposes industrial robots to potential hacker attacks, leading to economic losses for manufacturers and harm to workers. This work includes a forensic investigation on a compromised robot and notes that most robotic systems are now supported by Linux or by a POSIX-compliant Unix variant. A Unix variant operating system is considered an advantage due to its stability and versatility. However, there are still security concerns with this option as Unix-based systems are not immune to common vulnerabilities such as software bugs, coding errors, misconfigurations, outdated software component versions, etc.

"Robot teardowns" can act as a method to study robot hardware architectures and enhance security research, revealing security vulnerabilities and identifying hardware limitations. While the majority of efforts in the field of robotics are directed towards IT, hardware security has been relatively overlooked. Nevertheless, ensuring the security and reliability of robots necessitates comprehensive scrutiny across various domains, including hardware, firmware, operating systems, applications, networks, and cloud infrastructure [32].

## 4    User Studies

The issue of right to repair has been an ethical issue of particular interest to environmental studies researchers, leading to numerous user studies. The paradigm of the circular economy (CE) has been heralded as an important means of sustainability. The concept of a circular economy is branded as a solution to sustainability and pledges to eliminate (or "design out") waste by efficiently managing reverse logistics and maintaining the circulation of products and materials in a closed-loop supply chain. Repair-ability is critical for a circular economy. Electronic waste from production and consumption has a long-lasting negative socio-ecological effect on the environment and prolonging the use of electronics is important in the concept of circular economies [26].

In order to include robotics within this circular economy action plan, consumers will need access to repair services, repair networks and/or self-repair. However, consumers tend to favor purchasing new electronic devices rather than repairing them, and even buy new devices when the older ones still are operational. This has led to a growing body of literature on decision making and consumer behaviour [50], including studies investigating: why people repair, what types of electronics are repaired vs. replaced; which interventions nudge users to repair; and what methods of repair documentation are most efficient [11,19,30,41,42]. In addition to user studies examining textual and video formats as self-repair guides for consumer electronics [41], AR is being explored for electronic repair tasks [43–45].

Even though the concept of a "right to repair" is still relatively new, there is enough research to warrant a review paper on "right to repair" implementation studies - in particular, a 2023 review paper examined barriers for user right to repair as indicated in 76 published papers on the user perspective on repair [39]. Barriers to repair included: access to diagnostics; lack of spare parts; lack of tools; lack of clear and complete manuals; safety risk; nonmodular product; complex dis and re-assembly; fragile and damage risk; digital locks; unopenable product; planned obsolescence; no updates or upgrades. Barriers to repair from a convenience perspective include: legislation and tax programs; product economic obsolescence; cost of diagnostics and repair; consumer's time for repair; unavailability of repair services; insufficient quality of repair services. There are also psychological and sociological barriers to repair including: lack of trust in repair services; fear of further failures; lack of attachment; desire for new products and features; uncertain how repair works; unaware of repair impact and lack of repair habit; lack of engagement and lack of popularization of repair [39].

Researchers have found that the cost of repair coupled with the lack of repair services are deterrents to repair [22]. Another issue is with the design of the products, as most are not designed for easy self repair, leading to calls for companies to adopt "design to repair practices" in order to encourage repair. These design principles include function features (easy and quick assembly and disassembly, modularity, commonality and standardization of components, spare parts and tools availability, guidelines and user feedback and information) technical features (adaptability, anticipate legislation, energy efficiency, adaptability and upgradability) and emotive features (trustable design, attachment, emotional and social value, detachment, ergonomics in use and servicing, personalization, timeless design, green marketing concept) [40].

Modification of electronics, as a means to enhance existing technology, could further the circular economy. While there are currently no academic studies specific to a "right to modify" for end users, there are papers that argue that modifications (of mobile apps in particular) fall under the domain of a "right to repair." A 2023 study reports on the findings of a survey of android phone users and their thoughts on modifying phone apps (as a means of gathering user needs and perceptions, the development of an "app repair" prototype, and expert consultation [28]. The authors argue that some mobile apps contain dark patterns (deceptive design) that could be considered a "prohibitive bug" in need of repair. Hence, they call for the use of end-user repair tools to remove design elements in the user interface as part of the "right to repair" for mobile phone apps [28,29]. While the authors use the phrase "right to repair," they also refer to their end-user repair tool as a means to "repair, enhance and modify apps."

The focus on modification could address some of the repair barriers - in particular the issue of updates/upgrades as well as the desire for new features in a product [39]. This could be of particular benefit for the deployment and use of social robots, a sub section of robots which can be socially: evocative, situated, intelligent and interactive as well as sociable. Main application areas for social robots include service, entertainment, healthcare, education, research and telepresence [31]. Generally, social robots are designed as companions and assistants for people, and in many studies the end users demonstrate positive acceptance of such robots [18]. Social robots could provide interesting case studies for modification; as robots which communicate on a personal level, end users might feel a greater attachment to such devices and may prefer modification over replacement. At the same time, one must remain wary of the manipulative potential of such robots, and the risks inherent in permitting modification using code which could be derived from, or corrupted by, potentially hostile sources.

## 5    Conclusion

With the increasing integration of robots into diverse facets of society, acceptance and trust in their reliability becomes essential. Whether in healthcare, manufacturing, or public spaces, it is crucial for both the general public and professionals to harbor confidence in the steady and dependable performance of robotic systems. This suggests that enabling repairs or modifications to these systems should be approached with meticulous care and precision. Responsibly eliminating obstacles and risks and ensuring the accessibility of information empowers individuals to realize their moral objectives. Such objectives cultivate a sub-culture of enthusiasts and, more generally, consumers that may be driven by the motivation to modify or adapt electronic systems for utility, improvement, pleasure, and entertainment.

Remaining barriers to repair, such as costs, access and design issues, would continue to exist as barriers for modification. There could also be barriers and risks beyond the scope of repair that occur due to modification. Further work needs to be done to investigate these issues.

Legislators seeking to address legally-informed ethical perspectives on the regulation of robot modification will need to focus on: the impact of the potential for a change in the robot's function to alter the balance between innovation and competition in the area; and, to consider the risk that victims of a faulty third-party modification might be left with no practical source from which to recover their losses. These are ultimately questions of policy and will be informed by the culture and history of each jurisdiction. Even when the law can be applied, financial recovery may prove impossible, especially from small or transient defendants. Some form of insurance, and minimum safety requirements required for import of parts sold in each country could be useful measures to reduce harm. However, the realities of online instructional videos, global commerce, and the ability of small vendors to advertise and sell worldwide using multinational platforms will continue to present challenges, particularly in the consumer market.

# References

1. Consumer protection act (quebec) r.s.q. ch. p-40.1. https://www.legisquebec.gouv. qc.ca/en/document/cs/P-40.1
2. Magnuson-moss warranty-federal trade commission improvement act, p.l. 93-637, 15 usc 2301, title i, s. 102(c). https://uscode.house.gov/view.xhtml?req=granuleid %3AUSC-prelim-title15-chapter50&edition=prelim
3. Unfair competition law in business and professions code (calif. USA), division 7, part 2, ch. 4, sec. 17200. https://leginfo.legislature.ca.gov/faces/codes_ displayexpandedbranch.xhtml?tocCode=BPC&division=7.&title=&part=2.& chapter=4.&article=
4. Eastman kodak co. v. image technical services, inc., 504 u.s. 451 (1992). https:// supreme.justia.com/cases/federal/us/504/451/
5. Davis v. cessna aircraft corp., 182 ariz. 26 (ca) (1995). https://casetext.com/case/ davis-v-cessna-aircraft-corp-1
6. Digital millenium copyright act [usa] p.l. 105-304 (1998). https://www.govinfo. gov/content/pkg/PLAW-105publ304/pdf/PLAW-105publ304.pdf
7. Liriano v. hobart corp, 92 n.y. 2d 232 (c.a.) (1998). https://law.justia.com/cases/ new-york/court-of-appeals/1998/92-n-y-2d-232-0.html
8. Colonial indemnity insurance co. v. nynex, 260 a.d.2d 833 (1999). https://caselaw. findlaw.com/court/ny-supreme-court/1272825.html
9. Impression products, inc. v. lexmark international, inc. 2017 581 u.s. 1 (2017). https://www.supremecourt.gov/opinions/16pdf/15-1189_ebfj.pdf
10. Nixing the Fix: An FTC Report to Congress on Repair Restrictions. Federal Trade Commission (USA), pp. 27–31 (2021). https://www.ftc.gov/reports/nixing-fix-ftc-report-congress-repair-restrictions
11. Arcos, B.P., Dangal, S., Bakker, C., Faludi, J., Balkenende, R.: Faults in consumer products are difficult to diagnose, and design is to blame: a user observation study. J. Clean. Prod. **319**, 128741 (2021)
12. Brandstötter, M., Komenda, T., Ranz, F., Wedenig, P., Gattringer, H., Kaiser, L., Breitenhuber, G., Schlotzhauer, A., Müller, A., Hofbaur, M.: Versatile collaborative robot applications through safety-rated modification limits. In: Berns, K.,

Görges, D. (eds.) RAAD 2019. AISC, vol. 980, pp. 438–446. Springer, Cham (2020). https://doi.org/10.1007/978-3-030-19648-6_50

13. Buscemi, A., Turcanu, I., Castignani, G., Panchenko, A., Engel, T., Shin, K.G.: A survey on controller area network reverse engineering. IEEE Commun. Surv. Tutor. (2023)

14. Chatterjee, S., Chaudhuri, R., Vrontis, D.: Usage intention of social robots for domestic purpose: from security, privacy, and legal perspectives. Inf. Syst. Front. 1–16 (2021)

15. Council of European Union: Unfair commercial practices directive 2005/29/ec (as amend.) (2005-2019). https://eur-lex.europa.eu/legal-content/EN/TXT/?uri=celex%3A32005L0029

16. Council of European Union: Artificial intelligence act (pending) 2021/0106(cod) (2024 (anticipated)). https://artificialintelligenceact.eu/wp-content/uploads/2024/01/AI-Act-FullText.pdf

17. Council of European Union: Artificial intelligence act (pending) 2021/0106(cod), article 2 ss. 1, 2 (2024 (anticipated)). https://artificialintelligenceact.eu/wp-content/uploads/2024/01/AI-Act-FullText.pdf

18. David, D., Thérouanne, P., Milhabet, I.: The acceptability of social robots: a scoping review of the recent literature. Comput. Hum. Beh. 107419 (2022)

19. Fachbach, I., Lechner, G., Reimann, M.: Drivers of the consumers' intention to use repair services, repair networks and to self-repair. J. Clean. Prod. **346**, 130969 (2022)

20. France: French constitution [1789] art. 4, 5 (1789)

21. Gong, Y., Chow, K.-P., Mai, Y., Zhang, J., Chan, C.-F.: Forensic investigation of a hacked industrial robot. In: ICCIP 2020. IAICT, vol. 596, pp. 221–241. Springer, Cham (2020). https://doi.org/10.1007/978-3-030-62840-6_11

22. Güsser-Fachbach, I., Lechner, G., Reimann, M.: The impact of convenience attributes on the willingness-to-pay for repair services. Resour. Conserv. Recycl. **198**, 107163 (2023)

23. Habib, K., Mohammadi, E., Withanage, S.V.: A first comprehensive estimate of electronic waste in Canada. J. Hazard. Mater. **448**, 130865 (2023)

24. Hatta, M.: The right to repair, the right to tinker, and the right to innovate. Ann. Bus. Adm. Sci. **19**(4), 143–157 (2020)

25. Biden Jr., J.R.: Executive order on the safe, secure, and trustworthy development and use of artificial intelligence (2024). https://www.whitehouse.gov/briefing-room/presidential-actions/2023/10/30/executive-order-on-the-safe-secure-and-trustworthy-development-and-use-of-artificial-intelligence/

26. Jaeger-Erben, M., Frick, V., Hipp, T.: Why do users (not) repair their devices? A study of the predictors of repair practices. J. Clean. Prod. **286**, 125382 (2021)

27. Kanter, J.: Assistant attorney general Jonathan Kanter delivers remarks on lawsuit against apple for monopolizing smartphone markets (2024). https://www.justice.gov/opa/speech/assistant-attorney-general-jonathan-kanter-delivers-remarks-lawsuit-against-apple

28. Kollnig, K., et al.: 'we are adults and deserve control of our phones': examining the risks and opportunities of a right to repair for mobile apps. In: Proceedings of the 2023 ACM Conference on Fairness, Accountability, and Transparency, pp. 22–34 (2023)

29. Kollnig, K., Datta, S., Van Kleek, M.: I want my app that way: reclaiming sovereignty over personal devices. In: Extended Abstracts of the 2021 CHI Conference on Human Factors in Computing Systems, pp. 1–8 (2021)

30. Magnier, L., Mugge, R.: Replaced too soon? An exploration of western European consumers' replacement of electronic products. Resour. Conserv. Recycl. **185**, 106448 (2022)
31. Mahdi, H., Akgun, S.A., Saleh, S., Dautenhahn, K.: A survey on the design and evolution of social robots-past, present and future. Robot. Auton. Syst. 104193 (2022)
32. Mayoral-Vilches, V., et al.: Robot teardown, stripping industrial robots for good. Int. J. Cyber Forens. Adv. Threat Invest. (2022)
33. Mill, J.S.: On Liberty, Utilitarianism and Other Essays. Oxford University Press (2015). p13
34. Office of Science and Technology Policy, U.S.A.: Blueprint for an AI bill of rights [USA] (2023). https://www.whitehouse.gov/ostp/ai-bill-of-rights/
35. Perzanowski, A.: The Right to Repair, pp. 227–235. Cambridge University Press, Cambridge (2022)
36. Perzanowski, A.: The Right to Repair, p. 56. Cambridge University Press, Cambridge (2022)
37. Robinson, B.H.: E-waste: an assessment of global production and environmental impacts. Sci. Total Environ. **408**(2), 183–191 (2009)
38. Rosborough, A.D.: Unscrewing the future: the right to repair and the circumvention of software TPMS in the EU. J. Intell. Prop. Info. Tech. Elec. Com. L. **11**, 26 (2020)
39. Roskladka, N., Jaegler, A., Miragliotta, G.: From "right to repair" to "willingness to repair": exploring consumer's perspective to product lifecycle extension. J. Clean. Prod. **432**, 139705 (2023)
40. Roskladka, N., Miragliotta, G., Gianmarco, B., Saccani, N., et al.: Exploiting the right to repair towards a sustainable future: a systematic literature review. In: Proceedings of the 29th EurOMA Conference, pp. 1–10 (2022)
41. Sandez, S., Ibáñez-Forés, V., Pérez-Belis, V., Juan, P., Bovea, M.D.: Consumer practices regarding the purchase, use, willingness to repair, and disposal of small electric and electronic equipment: a Spanish survey on kettles. J. Ind. Ecol. (2023)
42. Sandez, S., Pérez-Belis, V., Juan, P., Bovea, M.D.: Do users have the ability to self-repair non-complex electrical appliances? Design and development of a self-guided workshop with repair documentation in different formats. Sustain. Prod. Consumpt. **39**, 244–256 (2023)
43. Sun, L.: Remote Assistance for Repair Tasks Using Augmented Reality. Ph.D. thesis, Université d'Ottawa/University of Ottawa (2020)
44. Sun, L., Osman, H.A., Lang, J.: An augmented reality online assistance platform for repair tasks. ACM Trans. Multimedia Comput. Commun. Appl. (TOMM) **17**(2), 1–23 (2021)
45. Tadeja, S.K., Bozzi, L.O.S., Samson, K.D., Pattinson, S.W., Bohné, T.: Exploring the repair process of a 3D printer using augmented reality-based guidance. Comput. Graph. **117**, 134–144 (2023)
46. The European Commission: Guidance on the Implementation / Application of Directive 2005/29/EC on Unfair Commercial Practices. The European Commission (2016). https://eur-lex.europa.eu/legal-content/EN/TXT/PDF/?uri=CELEX:52016SC0163
47. United States of America et al v. Apple Inc.: United states district court (new jersey) case 2:24-cv-04055 (2024). https://static01.nyt.com/newsgraphics/documenttools/9765671b79f64ad9/6cfe3c6c-full.pdf
48. United States of America et al v. Apple Inc.: United states district court (new jersey) case 2:24-cv-04055 at para 187 (2024). https://static01.nyt.com/newsgraphics/documenttools/9765671b79f64ad9/6cfe3c6c-full.pdf

49. U.S. Senators Romney, Reed, Moran, and King: Framework for mitigating extreme AI risks (2024). https://www.romney.senate.gov/wp-content/uploads/2024/04/AI-Framework_2pager.pdf
50. Vidal-Ayuso, F., Akhmedova, A., Jaca, C.: The circular economy and consumer behaviour: Literature review and research directions. J. Clean. Prod. 137824 (2023)
51. World Intellectual Property Office, Antitrust Committee: Antitrust guidelines of the antitrust committee of the state council on the field of intellectual property. J. Eur. Int. IP Law 776–781 (2019)
52. Yaacoub, J.P.A., Noura, H.N., Salman, O., Chehab, A.: Robotics cyber security: Vulnerabilities, attacks, countermeasures, and recommendations. Int. J. Inf. Secur. 1–44 (2022)

# A Cross-Cultural Investigation for How Safety Artefacts Impact Security Perception

Jiayue Wang[1] , Zhiyong Fu[1](✉), Makoto Watanabe[2], and Kenta Ono[2]

[1] Tsinghua University, Haidian District, Beijing 100084, People's Republic of China
fuzhiyong@tsinghua.edu.cn
[2] Chiba University, 1-33 Yayoi Cho, Inage Ward, Chiba 263-8522, Japan
{m.watanabe,k-ono}@faculty.chiba-u.jp

**Abstract.** The post-pandemic era has brought new challenges for urban development worldwide as countries grapple with the aftermath of the global health crisis. While some studies suggest that COVID-19 lockdown policies have helped control crime rates in certain countries, the relaxation of restrictions and increased outdoor activities have given rise to new security issues in urban environments. Therefore, ensuring residents' safety is crucial for urban development in the post-pandemic era. This paper focuses on how people from different backgrounds perceive security artefacts in the face of criminal threats. A cross-cultural online study revealed how risk scenarios impact perceived security, anxiety, behavioural tendencies, and cognitive effectiveness to use safety artefacts among residents of China and Mexico, two regions with significantly different actual security indices. Results indicated that cultural identity could be a crucial factor in people's perception of security, and this should be considered in the safety product and service development strategy.

**Keywords:** Design against crime · Perception of security · Safety artefacts design · Cross-cultural survey

## 1 Introduction

With the acceleration of globalisation and the development of cultural pluralism, the sense of security has gradually become an issue of great concern in different cultural contexts. Especially after the outbreak of COVID-19, due to the various segregation systems adopted by governments, the way people live, work and communicate has changed dramatically, and people's need for a sense of security is not only limited to the guarantee of objective security, but also includes the demand for an enhanced sense of subjective security. Although there are studies from different geographical areas that show a significant decrease in the incidence of crime due to the intervention of lockdown and social distancing policies [1, 2], there are still signs of a resurgence of criminal activity in certain countries and regions with weak security when the stay at home policy is released, such as organised crime, sexual offences and domestic violence in Mexico [3], with implications for the property and physical safety as well as the mental health of the

A. Marcus et al. (Eds.): HCII 2024, LNCS 15380, pp. 342–359, 2025.
https://doi.org/10.1007/978-3-031-76821-7_24

local population. While avoiding exposure to potentially risky scenarios can help manage hazards when responding to unexpected events, the other impacts and challenges associated with these strategies should not be overlooked. For example, anxieties related to social distance can have long-term effects on mental health and social injustice [4].

Most studies examining the relationship between safety and security have focused on technical factors such as performance and risk assessment techniques [5, 6]. Risk is essentially the events that occur due to uncertainties and expectations. On the one hand, there are multiple external threats from unnatural disasters or crime [7]. On the other hand, security measures and outcomes are also affected by a variety of political, economic and technological influences, so that uncertainty about security cannot be eliminated [8].

However, there appears to be limited research on how basic environmental safety and perceived safety are balanced in design practice. In particular, some field studies confirm that there is a tension between safety and security in everyday activities [9, 10], while other external factors influence perceptions of safety, e.g. different countries/cultures and knowledge backgrounds make different behavioural choices in response to different perceptions of risk [11]. This calls for further research on safety and peace of mind in the context of cultural and group differences and the interaction of specific prevention interventions.

This study adopts a product design perspective, recognising the importance of users' different backgrounds, values and cultural differences in their security demands and implementation approaches. Understanding users' expectations and methods of achieving a sense of security will help designers of products and service systems to assess potential security risks more effectively and to adopt appropriate design strategies.

## 2   Literature Review

### 2.1   Objective Safety and Risk

Safety is a dynamic outcome moderated by the interaction between people, artefacts and the environment. Möller argued that safety or being safe should be a relative state beyond the opposites of risk. Risk is an absolute outcome or consequence using probabilities and severity of uncertainty expectations, while safety is a comparable situation that controls residual risk within an acceptable range. Risk includes three dimensions in addition to probability and severity of risk, as the epistemological uncertainties associated with these two factors are emphasised [12]. Considering the design life cycle of the artefact, the safety performance designated the prevention, preparedness and response effectiveness of taking action, which includes the estimation of the risk of the external accident and the residual risk related to the protection of the artefacts. Leyla expressed the safety indicator for the use of a system [13], which focused on the occurrence and importance of hazard events, quantifying the factors related to human behaviour and the environment when operating a system.

Risk is an absolute outcome or consequence, using probabilities and the level of uncertainty expected. At the same time, safety is a relative situation that controls the residual risk within an acceptable range. Based on the above concepts, the present research questions are how people perceive risk, what factors are involved in the feeling of security and whether we can measure emotional security.

As outlined above, the feeling of security is a subjective dynamic perceptual process that results from the comparison of the perceived risk with the external safe, after an assessment of the distance between the two values and whether the gap is within our tolerable range. As shown in Fig. 1, the range below the 'tolerance' means that the situation is safe. If the current risk is above a certain tolerance threshold, we will feel concerned and decide to take action. However, safety solutions, such as products and equipment, vary in their ability to defend against the residual risk. What is 'acceptable' or 'tolerable' is also subjective. The response to risk that should be appropriately reduced varies from time to time, from society to society, and even from person to person [14].

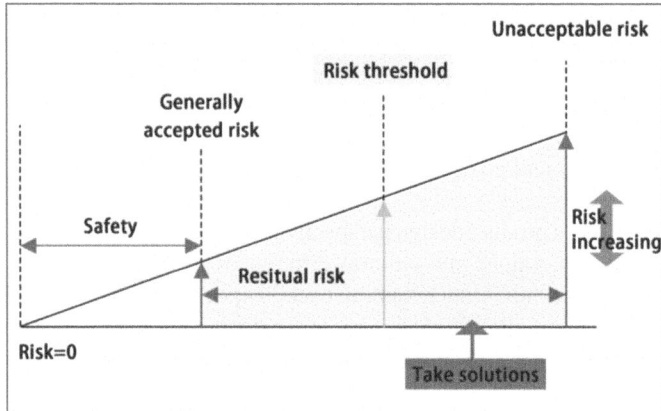

**Fig. 1.** Safety and risk tolerance.

## 2.2 The Perception of Security

The goal of achieving both security and peace of mind is an integral part of many organisations. From an academic research perspective, security and peace of mind have evolved in different directions and are supported by very different scientific and technical fields [15].

Objective safety is often understood as the antonym of risk or danger, and the same sense of safety is usually interpreted as the opposite of uncertainty and fear. According to risk assessment, the public's feeling of security is the subjective and emotional perception caused by the possibility of crime occurring in the environment [16, 17]. Therefore, from the perspective of Crime Prevention Through Environmental Design (CPTED) [18], the feeling of security is the perception of risk and likelihood of crime and a cognitive outcome based on reality and personal imagination [19]. It is a subjective emotion or behavioural performance, but can also be important in assessing social safety and public order.

Most scholars have proposed that people's feelings and reactions are an innate response to environmental stimuli, derived from "the most basic and essential survival behaviours of our early ancestors" [20, 21]. Like innate fear, we are born with different sensitivities and temperaments. Everyone's innate sense of safety is inconsistent. More sensitive people pay attention to their safety wherever they are [22]. As cognitive processes develop, experience and learning influence the source and degree of people's sense of security. In the theory of safety in childhood, [23] May defined safety as a dynamic state; children first need to establish a sense of safety of complete trust in their caregivers. This building of trust influences the outcome of future life exploration and learning and the freedom to make independent decisions [24]. People need to assess risk and exaggerate or underestimate it based on our intuition to keep us alive in this environment [25]. The sense of security is primarily generated by the assessment of external risks and is a cognitive result of acquired learning.

On the other hand, trust is often associated with a sense of risk or safety. Yamamoto suggested that trust in the expert or authority could eliminate public uncertainty and reduce the uncertainty of ignorance. It is an expectation resulting from knowledge of the morality and behavioural tendencies of others, even in the uncertain situation, considered as a feeling of security based on knowledge of the conditions [26]. Anthony Giddens also supported that when users have limited knowledge of some things, for example when using a new system, they tend to trust the experts, indicating that trust in experts or authority is a mechanism to reduce uncertainty [27]. They verified that in the field of information security, the users' trust in the providers of a website tool is equivalent to the risk tolerance, which will directly affect the experience as the perception of security [28–30].

### 2.3  Behavioural Tendency

The impact of safety on physical and mental activity can be divided into three levels: direct physiological perception, cognitive appraisal (including emotions) and physiological response [31]. Risk assessment involves rational and emotional reasoning based on the environment and can be influenced by demographic characteristics [32, 33]. People use information and cues to calculate potential risks and generate emotional and cognitive responses that ultimately determine their behavioural responses [34, 35].

Based on the natural response mechanisms, some researchers have proposed the substantial likelihood between risk perception and behavioural propensity in evidence. There is a strong correlation between risk perception and behavioural tendencies, such as in tourism and architectural design [36]. In architectural design, John validated people's tendency to enter a building influenced by a subjective prediction of terrorist risk. The result also demonstrated the correlation between perceptions of security and behavioural propensity to enter different buildings according to different levels of terrorist threat [37]. Recent research highlights the importance of risk analysis and perception in promoting protective behaviours during the COVID-19 pandemic [38].

The literature suggests a significant relationship between risk perception and behavioural intention, with risk assessment involving rational and emotional reasoning based on environmental cues, demographic characteristics, and past experiences. People's emotional and cognitive responses to risk determine their behavioural responses, such as their willingness to engage in activities or use certain artefacts.

### 2.4   Conceptual Model of Perception of Security

To summarise, the feeling of security could be defined as when people confirm they can trust; the actual situation is not significantly different from their expectations based on one's knowledge and experience. Moreover, for a safety artefact against crime, its inherent ability is to resist the risk in the external world to the users; it is possible to raise their mental security by building trust in the artefacts. As we put forward, the perception of security could be elaborated from two aspects: the feeling of security and a mental judgment output of assessing the relevant factors. The other sort of perception of security can be concerned with the sense of risk, which includes "risk as analysis" and "risk as feeling" [39]. The former relies on the information in the current situation. It is processed by logical analysis or experience, which is more reasonable and deliberative [40]. The latter is usually generated from instinct or the intuitive reaction to the potential hazard. This sense of risk works quicker and more effortlessly, especially since it is easy to invoke in an uncertain situation [41].

Assessment of risk in surroundings plays a role in the decision-making process, which one's experience or personality could influence, even the objective situations such as society and timings. As shown in Fig. 2, we proposed a conceptual model that when using safety artefacts in an uncertain situation, people's perception of security and tendency to move, generated from the personal risk appraisal associated with the estimate of the product's ability to withstand the risk, might be affected at specific times or situations.

In summary, the feeling of security could be defined as when people confirm that they can trust; the actual situation is not significantly different from their expectations based on their knowledge and experience. Moreover, for a safety artefact against crime, its inherent ability is to resist the risk in the external world to the users; it is possible to increase their mental security by building trust in the artefacts. As we have suggested, the perception of security could be elaborated from two aspects: the feeling of security and a mental judgement output of assessing the relevant factors. The other type of safety perception can be related to the sense of risk, which includes "risk as analysis" and "risk as feeling" [39]. The former is based on the information in the current situation. It is processed through logical analysis or experience, which is more rational and deliberative [40]. The latter is usually generated by instinct or intuitive reaction to the potential hazard. This sense of risk works faster and more effortlessly, especially as it is easy to invoke in an uncertain situation [41].

## 3   Methodology

### 3.1   Research Objectives

To assess the impact of safety and risk perceptions on safety perceptions and behavioural intentions, we conducted an experiment in two countries with different risk indexes, using artificial security products to combat crime. According to the 2020 and 2021 National Security Index (Mid-Year) Report [42], China had a significantly lower crime rate during the pandemic than Mexico, which had a higher security index. The author's previous survey of Mexicans' sense of security showed that they rely on their trusted communities

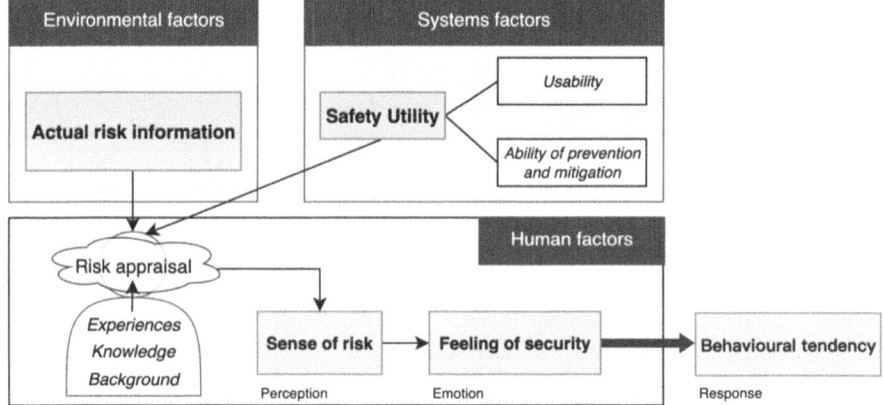

**Fig. 2.** Conceptual model of Perception of Security.

or families in emergencies [43]. At the same time, China is a nation that places more trust in the authorities. Based on the security situation and attitudes towards crisis response in these two countries, we developed the following research questions:

1. How does exposure to different types of risk information affect the risk appraisal process of individuals from two different social backgrounds?
2. How does the use of safety devices influence the perceptions and willingness of individuals from two different social backgrounds to go out in different risk scenarios?
3. How does the use of different safety devices affect the perception of safety and the willingness of individuals from two different social backgrounds to venture into different risk scenarios?

A cross-national investigation was conducted through an online survey to explore the impact of social context on the individual's perception of security and behavioural tendency reaction. This experiment was held in a 2 * 2 between-groups test. We divided the participants from each country into low-risk and high-risk situations. In this survey, we further attempted to investigate the effects of using various devices on individual responses, comparing with the setting without using those devices.

Two steps of comparative analysis were undertaken. First, we compared the risk assessment with two nationality groups in the condition without using a defensive product; second, we analysed the perception of safety and the behavioural tendency when using the safety devices. ANOVA was used to measure the results, in particular in the second stage, repeated measures ANOVA was used for each group.

## 3.2  Procedure and Materials

The survey was conducted via an online survey service website. Participants were recruited as volunteers without compensation. The questionnaire system randomly assigned participants to different risk scenarios in each study. The experimental procedure is shown in Fig. 3.

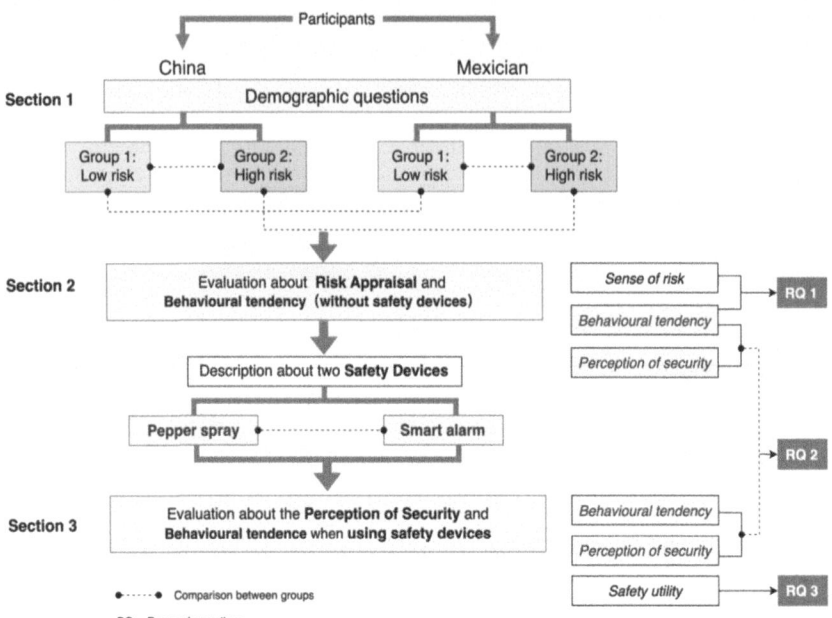

**Fig. 3.** Process of the experiment.

Prior to their initial participation, informed consent was obtained from all participants. Subsequently, they completed several questions about demographic characteristics and victim experience. Then, in Sect. 2, participants would be exposed to the assigned risk scenario. After reading the instructions, they could proceed to the next page. Here they would see the image of a narrow alley at night (Fig. 4), which was intended to increase the participants' sense of 'immersion'. This was followed by the descriptions, which asked participants to imagine that they had an appointment with a friend in the same area referred to in the previous screen, and to answer the questions about their sense of safety in this situation, as well as their willingness to go to meet a friend.

In the third section of the study, participants entered a simulated environment to evaluate two safety devices: pepper spray and an emergency alarm. Images of these devices, accompanied by functional instructions, were displayed in a randomly generated order by the system. To enhance the realism of the scenario, an image of an alley was presented concurrently. Following the examination of the devices' descriptions, participants responded to a series of questions aimed at assessing their perceptions of security and their likelihood of meeting friends while using the devices. These questions explored participants' trust in the devices' capability to mitigate risks and their opinions on the effectiveness of the devices. The measurements for each item, utilized a 5-point scale ranging from 1 (not at all) to 5 (very much), to rate their responses to the descriptions.

*"Given the crime alert notification, today you are going to meet a friend at the area mentioned in the previous news, and you have to walk through the neighborhood as shown in the picture. "*

**Fig. 4.** Description of the experimental condition.

### 3.3 Experiment Stimuli

**Risk Scenarios.** We established two distinct scenario groups to compare users' security responses under different risk scenarios. The scenarios were conveyed through words and pictures to increase participants' engagement with the environment. Random assignment to each scenario was conducted using an online questionnaire system. The materials used to describe the risk scenarios in China and Mexico are depicted in Fig. 5 and presented in their native languages of Spanish and Chinese. To ensure the plausibility and acceptance of the scenarios, message contents were adjusted to reflect the political circumstances of both countries.

**Safety Devices.** In this study, we selected various safety products as stimuli to explore cross-cultural perceptions. The chosen samples were required to be culturally neutral to facilitate an unbiased comparison between two distinct national groups. Previous research, as highlighted in Carlos' survey, indicates a marked preference among Mexican families for robust physical barriers, such as walls and fences, as their primary defensive measure against crime, with minimal reliance on surveillance technologies like CCTV [43]. In light of these findings, we opted to focus on two personal safety devices— pepper spray and a wearable emergency alarm—as means to examine the influence of safety artifact utilization in subsequent analyses. Figure 6 illustrates the examples of the selected devices.

## 4  Analyses and Results

A total of 264 participants (170 Chinese and 94 Mexican) voluntarily completed the online questionnaire survey. Table 1 shows the distribution of age, gender, and educational background. Of the Chinese participants, 35 reported having been victims or having relatives who were victims, while 135 had no such experience. In Mexico, 66

**Fig. 5.** Description of risk information in Mexico and China.

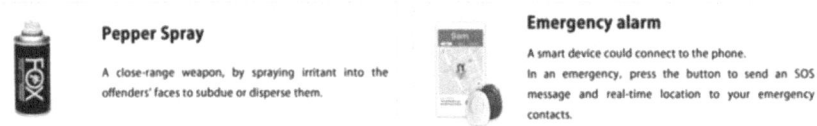

**Fig. 6.** Description of safety devices samples.

participants reported crime involvement, while 27 had no such experience. To analyse the data, we used the framework presented in Table 2 to compare the sense and reaction of security between the two nationalities across both risk scenarios, with and without safety devices. This constituted the first stage of statistical analysis.

The objective of this study was to evaluate five key dependent variables, each pertaining to different aspects of participants' responses in controlled settings. These variables were as follows: (1) *Sense of risk*, measured by participants' evaluations of actual environmental safety in the second section, derived from their interpretations of the situation report and scenario images; (2) *Feeling of security*, assessed on three occasions—initially in an environment devoid of safety devices, and subsequently in two settings where different safety devices were utilized; (3) *Perception of anxiety*, evaluated under the same conditions as the feeling of security to maintain consistency in comparative analysis; (4) *Behavioral tendency*, analyzed by examining data from Sects. 2 and 3, which reflected participants' propensities to visit friends under specific circumstances; and (5) *Safety utility*, assessed solely in the third section to gauge the effectiveness of the two distinct safety devices.

### 4.1 Sense of Risk

A Univariate Analysis of Variance test (ANOVA) was run to examine the difference between China and Mexico participants' sense of basic safety with different risk levels without using the defence device.

The indicator is measured by an item in the questionnaire, "Given the announcement, how much actual safety do you consider about this neighbourhood" before analysing variance. Levene's test for homogeneity of variance was conducted to test the error variance of the dependent variable is equal across nationality groups, with $F (3, 260) =$

**Table 1.** Distribution of demographic groups.

| Demographic characteristics | | China (N = 170) | | Mexico (N = 94) | |
|---|---|---|---|---|---|
| | | Number | Percentage | Number | Percentage |
| Gender | Female | 120 | 27.10% | 58 | 61.70% |
| | Male | 46 | 70.60% | 34 | 36.20% |
| | Unknown | 4 | 2.40% | 2 | 2.10% |
| Education | Junior high | 7 | 4.10% | 0 | 0 |
| | High School | 19 | 11.20% | 1 | 1.10% |
| | Bachelor | 97 | 57.10% | 75 | 79.80% |
| | Master and above | 47 | 27.60% | 18 | 19.10% |
| Age | 18–25 | 60 | 35.3% | 59 | 62.80% |
| | 26–35 | 82 | 48.2% | 17 | 18.10% |
| | 36–45 | 9 | 5.3% | 7 | 7.40% |
| | >45 | 19 | 11.2% | 11 | 11.7% |
| Victim Experience | Have | 35 | 20.60% | 66 | 70.20% |
| | No | 135 | 79.40% | 27 | 28.70% |
| | Unknown | 0 | 0 | 1 | 1.10% |

**Table 2.** The analytical framework of variables

| Dependent Variables | Question items | |
|---|---|---|
| Perception of security | Sense of risk | How would you rate your actual safety in this neighborhood? |
| | Feeling of security | How much anxious do you feel when carrying this device? |
| | | How much security do you feel walk through carrying with the device? |
| | Safety utility | How much effective do you think about the device to deter danger? |
| Behavioural Response | Behavioural tendency | How willing are you to walk through this neighbourhood? (Without device) |
| | | Carrying the device, how willing are you to walk through this neighbourhood? |

2.24, p > 0.05. Then the test of between-subjects effects showed F (1, 260) = 38.01, p < 0.001, the nationality significantly affected the sense of actual safety, Chinese (M = 2.52 ± 0.78) considered the scenario was more safety than Mexican (M = 1.93 ± 0.65) in both conditions (Fig. 7). The level of safety scenarios had no significant influence nor interaction effects had produced.

**Sense of Risk**

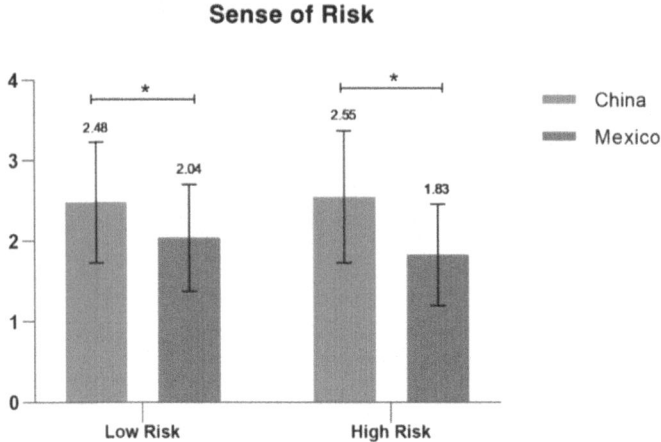

**Fig. 7.** Estimated means of the sense of risk between nation groups

### 4.2 Perception of Security

In this study, the second dependent variable was the psychological security experienced by participants while walking in the community. A repeated measures ANOVA was used to examine the differences between three conditions (without any device, with pepper spray, and with an emergency alarm). One-way ANOVA was not deemed appropriate as the observations within subjects were dependent, with each participant responding three times to the same subject. The first measurement of evaluation for psychological security was based on participants' perceptions, which were assessed using the question, "How much sense of security do you consider about walking in this neighbourhood?" (In settings 2 and 3, additional instructions were given to indicate the use of a device.)

**Feeling of Security.** Based on the results of the three within-subjects factors, the interaction between condition setting, nationality, and risk scenario had a statistically significant effect, with F (1.90, 493.54) = 4.54 and p < 0.05. This indicates that the effect of condition setting is dependent on the subject's risk scenario and nationality. Follow-up investigations examined the simple main effects of each factor, including risk scenario setting and nationality. Simple main effects can reveal how one factor is differentially influential at each level of the other factors.

As shown in Fig. 8, the estimated marginal means of the perception of security in the low-risk scenario without any safety device were lower for Chinese subjects (M =

2.60 ± 0.10) compared to using pepper spray (M = 3.51 ± 0.10) and emergency alarm (M = 3.52 ± 0.10), with F (2,259) = 32.12 and p < 0.001. Similarly, for Mexican subjects, people felt less secure in the default condition (M = 2.04 ± 0.15) compared to using pepper spray (M = 2.55 ± 0.15) or an emergency alarm (M = 2.81 ± 0.15), with F (2,259) = 7.80 and p < 0.01.

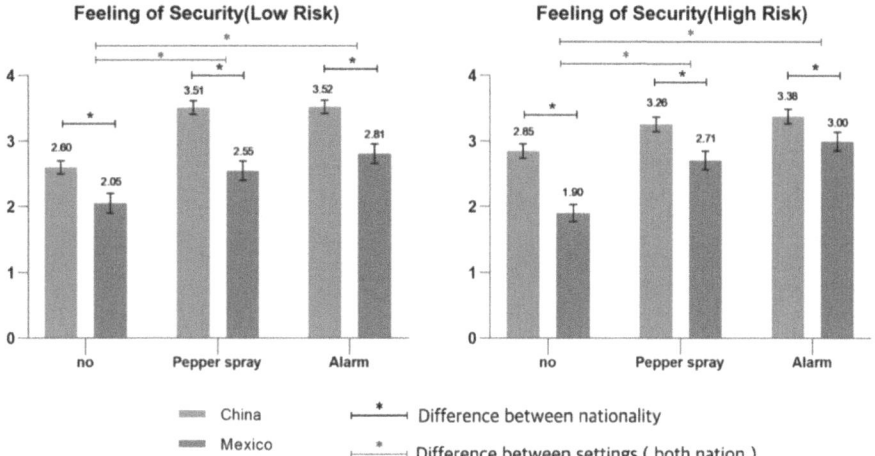

**Fig. 8.** Estimated marginal means of perception of security.

In the high-risk scenario, the rank of the feeling of security was similar, with people feeling more secure when using both defence artefacts than without using them. The primary effect test was then conducted to examine the variance of nationality groups. In both situations, with different degrees of risk, Chinese subjects felt more secure using defence devices such as pepper spray and an emergency alarm compared to Mexican subjects. Specifically, in the default setting, Chinese evaluation was higher (M = 2.85 ± 0.11) than that of Mexican subjects (M = 1.90 ± 0.13), with F (1,260) = 31.31 and p < 0.001. Similarly, for pepper spray, Chinese subjects (M = 3.26 ± 0.11) felt more secure than Mexican subjects (M = 2.71 ± 0.14), with F (1,260) = 9.75 and p < 0.01. Furthermore, for the emergency alarm, Chinese subjects (M = 3.38 ± 0.11) felt more secure than Mexican subjects (M = 3.0 ± 0.14), with F (1,260) = 4.69 and p < 0.05.

**Feeling of Anxiety.** The dependent variable measured in the study was anxiety, which was assessed through the question, "How anxious do you feel when carrying this device?" Mauchly's Test of Sphericity showed a violation with a p-value of 0.006, indicating that the Greenhouse-Geisser correction was used with an estimated epsilon (ε) of 0.962. The analysis revealed one main effect and two significant interactions regarding the effects of anxiety perception across different device usage conditions.

The results in Fig. 9 indicated that the use of defence devices had an impact on the perception of anxiety among participants (F (1.93, 500.40) = 39.55, p < 0.001). Participants reported feeling the most anxious when not using any device (M = 3.90 ± 0.056), followed by using pepper spray (M = 3.47 ± 0.066) and emergency alarms (M =

3.30 ± 0.067). Moreover, the study found that social context moderated the relationship between device usage and safety risk levels, with two significant interaction effects among the three variables (F (1.93, 500.40) = 3.77, p < 0.05).

An ANOVA was conducted to test the simple main effects of the nationality group. In the low-risk context without using any device, Chinese participants (M = 3.63 ± 0.09) felt less anxious than Mexican participants (M = 3.98 ± 0.13), with a significant difference (F (1, 260) = 4.50, p < 0.05). However, there was no difference between the two countries when using the two devices. In the high-risk scenario, without using any device, Chinese participants (M = 3.75 ± 0.97) felt less anxious than Mexican participants (M = 4.25 ± 0.12), with a significant difference (F (1, 260) = 10.53, p < 0.001). Additionally, a significant difference was found between Chinese and Mexican participants regarding the use of pepper spray, with Chinese participants (M = 3.73 ± 0.11) feeling more anxious than Mexican participants (M = 3.33 ± 0.14) (F (1, 260) = 4.80, p < 0.05).

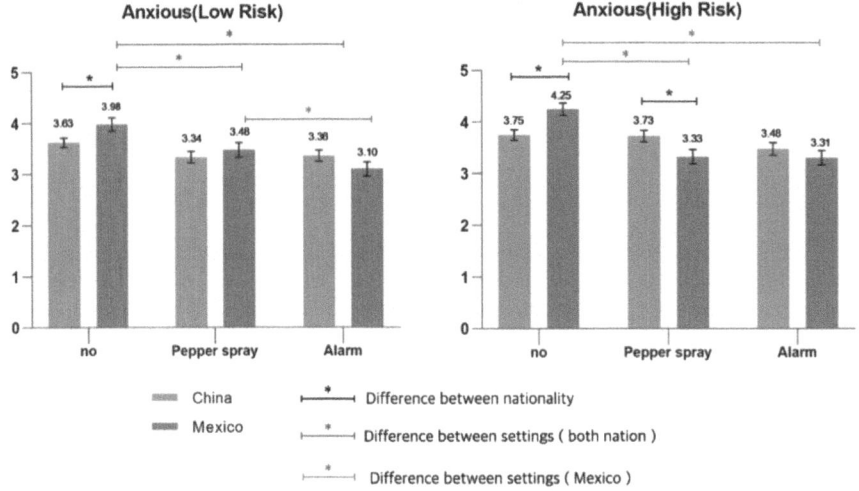

**Fig. 9.** Estimated marginal means of perception of anxious.

### 4.3 Behavioural Tendency

The third indicator measured participants' willingness to walk through a neighbourhood in specific circumstances. Results showed significant main effects of setting and nationality but no significant interaction of the three factors.

We conducted another ANOVA to examine differences between nationality and condition settings groups. Results showed that without using a device, participants' propensity to go out to see friends was significantly lower than when using devices (M = 1.9 ± 0.048, F = (2, 520), p < 0.001). Additionally, emergency alarms (M = 2.82 ± 0.058) made people more willing to go out than pepper spray (M = 2.58 ± 0.059).

Chinese participants (M = 2.83 ± 0.052) had a greater inclination than Mexican partic-ipants (M = 2.10 ± 0.07) in any cases (F = (1, 260), p < 0.001). These results did not support the hypothesis of an interaction between actual risk level and nationality with different condition settings (Fig. 10).

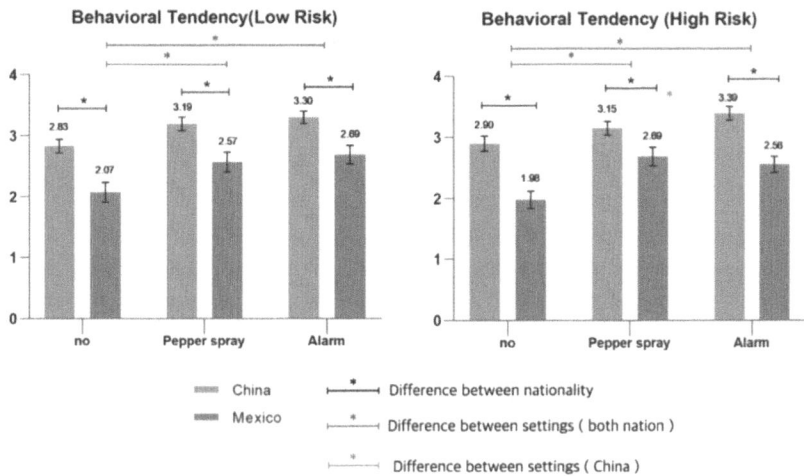

**Fig. 10.** Estimated marginal means of behavioural tendency

## 4.4 Safety Utility

A repeated ANOVA was conducted to assess the impact of nationality and level of risk on the evaluation of two safety artefacts: "How effective do you think the device is in deterring danger?" The homogeneity of variance was assessed using Levene's test, which resulted in insignificance for both dependent variables (pepper spray F (3, 260) = p = 0.06; emergency alarm F (3, 260) = 0.65, p = 0.58). As shown in Fig. 11, the estimated marginal means of safety utility for both devices indicate that the significant main effect on safety utility is attributed to nationality. Chinese participants (M = 3.41 ± 0.07) evaluated pepper spray as more effective than Mexican participants (M = 2.74 ± 0.095) (F (1, 260) = 31.60, p < 0.001), and the same trend was observed for the emergency alarm, where Chinese participants (M = 3.37 ± 0.072) perceived it as more valuable than Mexican participants (M = 2.63 ± 0.098) (F (1, 260) = 36.97, p < 0.001).

# 5   Discussions

## 5.1   Impact of Cultural Background and Risk Information on Risk Appraisal

The impact of cultural background and risk information on risk appraisal has been extensively studied. The findings reveal that while "system factors," such as the use of safety devices, significantly influence individuals' perceptions of safety, "underlying

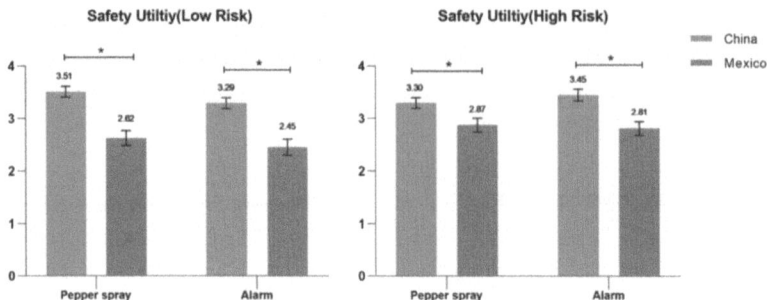

**Fig. 11.** Estimated marginal means of safety utility.

factors" like social background exert a more profound impact. For example, residents of societies grappling with severe safety issues, such as Mexico, may exhibit heightened risk perception and internal anxiety. This anxiety might not be mitigated merely by the use of defense products, potentially leading individuals to venture out only in groups, thereby impacting their daily lives.

Another hypothesis posits that the social context markedly influences risk evaluations. Survey data indicate that Chinese individuals perceive a higher level of risk and are more inclined to use protective devices. Moreover, in both high-risk and low-risk scenarios, Chinese individuals value safety devices more than Mexicans do, potentially because they reside in relatively safer environments and are more attuned to perceived threats. Public trust in authority, particularly in crisis situations, is also notably high in China. According to the 2018 World Values Survey, 95% of Chinese citizens reported a significant degree of trust in the national government, a figure that has only increased post the COVID-19 pandemic. Wu's survey highlights that trust in the provincial government has escalated to 91%, with national trust levels soaring to 98% [44].

Additionally, this trust in government and societal order might shape their security perceptions. Conversely, Mexicans, faced with an unstable natural environment and higher crime rates, often maintain a low sense of safety, even in secure contexts. Their perception of security is heavily influenced by their confidence in their immediate environment. If they feel secure in their surroundings, their perceived safety increases, enhancing their propensity to employ safety devices. This hypothesis gains support from Hsia's research [45], which underscores the significance of the social and political environment in shaping individuals' security perceptions. The pervasive threat of crime can destabilize these perceptions, instilling a pervasive fear that influences their attitudes toward risk.

## 5.2   The Role of Safety Device Usage in Shaping Perceptions and Behaviors

Based on the analysis of security perceptions and behavioral tendencies, it is clear that safety devices significantly enhance users' sense of security and their willingness to engage in outdoor activities. This observation corroborates the hypothesis positing that safety devices are pivotal in boosting individuals' security awareness, irrespective of the social environment or criminal threat level.

Furthermore, the study reveals that the effect of safety devices on individuals' perceptions and behaviors varies slightly according to their cultural background and the associated risk levels. In scenarios deemed low risk, all participants experienced reduced anxiety when using precautionary devices. However, in high-risk contexts, there was no notable difference in anxiety reduction among Mexican users between the two devices, indicating that the benefits of using safety devices to mitigate internal anxiety might be more significant in societies with generally lower security levels.

In summary, the research validates the crucial role of safety devices in enhancing perceptions of security and alleviating anxiety, particularly in times and environments that are less stable and peaceful. The functionality and user-friendliness of these safety products are key factors contributing to their effectiveness in instilling a sense of safety among users.

# 6  Conclusion

This cross-national survey reveals that perceptions of and responses to crime threats are significantly influenced by residential backgrounds. The primary factors differentiating the studied countries include an innate sense of personal security, the ability to assess actual risks, and perceptions of the efficacy of defense products. These differences arise from inherent variations in individuals' consciousness and cognitive processes. Residents of safer environments typically display greater trust in authorities, have a deeper understanding of safety solutions and policies, and maintain higher confidence in public security. However, they may also be more vulnerable to external information and media influences, which can alter their perceptions and cognitive processes. In contrast, individuals exposed to higher crime rates may become desensitized to risks, feeling more vulnerable and insecure, even when equipped with robust community support and safety knowledge.

These insights have significant implications for safety product designers and administrators. In societies perceived as low threat, such as China, developers should capitalize on the trust between users and producers by designing features that connect with the police or other official authorities, thereby enhancing the perceived effectiveness and psychological comfort during crises. Additionally, administrators should promote access to authentic and reliable safety information to foster cognitive trust based on knowledge.

Conversely, in high-risk, low-trust societies, developers should prioritize the immediate risk-mitigation capabilities of their products, while community groups could represent users' interests and build trust. Independent of the perceived efficacy of safety products, accurate risk assessment is essential for reducing fear and anxiety. Therefore, designers must ensure that users can easily access authentic and reliable information, even in complex scenarios. Encouraging proactive engagement with safety functions represents a critical challenge for designers moving forward.

**Acknowledgments.** We extend our deepest gratitude to Hisa MARTINEZ NIMI, Juan Carlos CHACON, for their invaluable guidance and expertise throughout the duration of this project. We also wish to thank the Universidad de Monterrey (UDEM) and Tecnológico de Monterrey (TEC) for their support and the resources they provided, which were crucial for the successful completion of this research.

**Disclosure of Interests.** The authors have no competing interests to declare that are relevant to the content of this article.

# References

1. Brancati, D., Birnir, J., et al.: Locking down violence: the COVID-19 pandemic's impact on non-state actor violence. Am. Polit. Sci. Rev. **1**(1), 1–17 (2023)
2. de la Miyar, J.R.B., Hoehn-Velasco, L., et al.: The U-shaped crime recovery during COVID-19: evidence from national crime rates in Mexico. Crime Sci. **10**(1), 14 (2021)
3. Lauren, H., Adan, S., Jose, B.D.R.: The great crime recovery: crimes against women during, and after, the COVID-19 lockdown in Mexico. Econ. Hum. Biol. **41**, 100991 (2021)
4. Ajagbe, A., Onigbinde, O., et al.: Mental morbidity arising from social isolation during the COVID-19 outbreak. Ulutas Med. J. **6**(2), 97–100 (2020)
5. Ludovic, P.C., Marc, B.: Cross-fertilization between safety and security engineering. Reliab. Eng. Syst. Saf. **110**, 110–126 (2013)
6. Vinnem, J.E.: Risk indicators for major hazards on offshore installations. Saf. Sci. **48**(6), 770–787 (2010)
7. Short, J.F., Clarke, L.B.: Organizations, Uncertainties and Risk. Westview Press (1992)
8. Osmundsen, P., Aven, T., Erik Vinnem, J.: Safety, economic incentives and insurance in the Norwegian Petroleum Industry. Reliab. Eng. Syst. Saf. **93**(1), 137–143 (2008)
9. Pettersen Gould, K., Bieder, C.: Safety and security: the challenges of bringing them together. In: Bieder, C., Pettersen, G.K. (eds.) The Coupling of Safety and Security, pp. 1–8. Springer, Cham (2020). https://doi.org/10.1007/978-3-030-47229-0_1
10. Pettersen, K.A., Bjornskau, T.: Organizational contradictions between safety and security – perceived challenges and ways of integrating critical infrastructure protection in civil aviation. Saf. Sci. **71**, 167–177 (2015)
11. Aven, T.: Risk assessment and risk management: Review of recent advances on their foundation. Eur. J. Oper. Res. **253**(1), 1–13 (2016)
12. Moller, N., Hansson, S.O., et al.: Safety is more than the antonym of risk. J. Appl. Philos. **23**(4), 419–432 (2006)
13. Sadeghi, L., Mathieu, L., et al.: Developing a safety indicator to measure the safety level during design for safety. Saf. Sci. **80**, 252–263 (2015)
14. Masao, M.: Current topics on safety technologies and its public acceptance. J. Jpn. Soc. Precis. Eng. **75**(9), 1041–1044 (2009)
15. Boholm, M., Moller, N., et al.: The concepts of risk, safety, and security: applications in everyday language. Risk Anal. **36**(2), 320–338 (2015)
16. Goulka, J., del Pozo, B., et al.: From public safety to public health: re-envisioning the goals and methods of policing. J. Community Saf. Well-Being **6**(1), 22–27 (2021)
17. Finucane, M.L., Slovic, P., et al.: Gender, race, and perceived risk: the 'white male' effect. Health Risk Soc. **2**(2), 159–172 (2000)
18. Jeffery, C.R.: Crime prevention through environmental design. Am. Behav. Sci. **14**(4), 598 (1971)
19. van Dijk, J., Tseloni, A., Farrell, G. (eds.): The International Crime Drop. Palgrave Macmillan, UK, London (2012). https://doi.org/10.1057/9781137291462
20. Appleton, J.: The Experience of Landscape. Wiley (1996)
21. Orians, G.H.: An ecological and evolutionary approach to landscape aesthetics. In: Penning-Roswell, Lowenthal (eds.) Meanings and Values in Landscape, pp. 3–25. Routledge (1986)
22. Ackerman, D.: A Natural History of the Senses. Random House (1990)
23. May, R.: The meaning of Anxiety. W.W. Norton & Company (2015)

24. Horney, K.: Neurosis and Human Growth: The Struggle Toward Self-realization. Routledge, Taylor Francis Group (2014)
25. Brewer, N.T., Chapman, G.B., et al.: Meta-analysis of the relationship between risk perception and health behavior: the example of vaccination. Health Psychol. **26**(2), 136–145 (2007)
26. Yamagishi, T.: The Structure of Trust: An Evolutionary Game of Mind and Society. University of Tokyo Press (1998) (in Japanese)
27. Giddens, A., Pierson, C.: Conversations with Anthony Giddens – Making Sense of Modernity. Wiley (2013)
28. Murayama, Y., Hikage, N., Fujihara, Y., Hauser, C.: The structure of the sense of security, Anshin. In: Lopez, J., Hämmerli, B.M. (eds.) CRITIS 2007. LNCS, vol. 5141, pp. 83–93. Springer, Heidelberg (2008). https://doi.org/10.1007/978-3-540-89173-4_8
29. Deutsch, M.: The effect of motivational orientation upon trust and suspicion. Hum. Relat. **13**(2), 123–139 (1960)
30. Rose, R.: Trust in Untrustworthy Institutions: Culture and Institutional Performance in Post-Communist Societies. Centre for the Study of Public Policy, University of Strathclyde (1999)
31. Ulrich, R.S., Simons, R.F., et al.: Stress recovery during exposure to natural and urban environments. J. Environ. Psychol. **11**(3), 201–230 (1991)
32. Allcott, H.: Social norms and energy conservation. J. Public Econ. **95**(9–10), 1082–1095 (2011)
33. Goldstein, N.J., Cialdini, R.B., et al.: A room with a viewpoint: using social norms to motivate environmental conservation in hotels. J. Consum. Res. **35**(3), 472–482 (2008)
34. Cannon, W.B.: Bodily Changes in Pain, Hunger, Fear and Rage an Account of Recent Researches into the Function of Emotional Excitement. McGrath (1970)
35. Schauer, M., Elbert, T.: Dissociation following traumatic stress. J. Psychol. **218**(2), 109–127 (2010)
36. Madge, C.: Public parks and the geography of fear. Tijdschr. Econ. Soc. Geogr. **88**(3), 237–250 (1997)
37. Zilbershtein, G.: Architecture in the era of terror: the security dilemma. WIT Transactions on the Built Environment, vol. 82. WIT Press (2005)
38. Savadori, L., Lauriola, M.: Risk perception and protective behaviors during the rise of the COVID-19 outbreak in Italy. Front. Psychol. **11** (2021)
39. Ferrer, R.A., Klein, W.M., et al.: The tripartite model of risk perception (TRIRISK): distinguishing deliberative, affective, and experiential components of perceived risk. Ann. Behav. Med. **50**(5), 653–663 (2016)
40. Slovic, P.: Perception of risk. Science **236**(4799), 280–285 (1987)
41. Epstein, S.: Integration of the cognitive and the psychodynamic unconscious. Am. Psychol. **49**(8), 709–724 (1994)
42. National Security Index. https://www.numbeo.com/cost-of-living/. Accessed 05 October 2021
43. Carlos, J.C., Hisa, N.M., et al.: Reducing fear of crime through design against crime. J. Sci. Des. **3**(1), 21–26 (2019)
44. Did Pandemic Shake Chinese Citizens Trust Their Government. Accessed 10 October 2021
45. Hisa, N.M., Carlos, J.C., et al.: Risk and safety perception of security brand logos applied on dissuasive signs. J. Sci. Des. **3**(1), 37–44 (2019)
46. Gritzalis, D., Iseppi, G., et al.: Exiting the risk assessment maze. ACM Comput. Surv. **51**(1), 1–30 (2018)

# Assessing Ethical Risks in Smart Environment Use Cases: A ForSTI Methodological Approach

Kaja Fjørtoft Ystgaard[(✉)] and Katrien De Moor

Norwegian University of Science and Technology, 7491 Trondheim, Norway
{kaja.ystgaard,katrien.demoor}@ntnu.no

**Abstract.** This paper presents results from an ethical assessment aimed at identifying use cases relevant to smart private, and public environments and their future developments, that require genuine safeguarding of human rights, in particular of meaningful human autonomy. We applied a multi-disciplinary Foresight in Science, Technology, and Innovation (ForSTI) case assessment methodology, implemented as an online survey and incorporating input from both experts representing different perspectives and end users (n=45). Ethical risks related to privacy and surveillance were rated higher among both technical and ethical/legal experts, than non-experts and end-users. Unauthorized surveillance and invasive tracking in sensitive places emerged as a prominent ethical concern with consensus across perspectives. The study highlights that the most important ethical safeguards will emerge from the ability to keep public spaces protected from pervasive surveillance, data monitoring, and data collection with constraints. The results indicate a strong consensus on the need for additional ethical safeguards for human autonomy protection in the cases of smart devices/wearables, smart healthcare (SH), and smart government (SG). The prioritized ethical risks were predominantly seen as affecting communities and vulnerable stakeholders, who paradoxically are the least involved in developing smart environment technologies. The results can inform mitigation strategies and recommendations, such as implementing opt-out and turn-off options in Internet of Things (IoT) technology deployment for public (e.g., urban) or private environments. Future research should investigate how existing and future technical mechanisms are utilized to safeguard human autonomy in these use cases and identify which mechanisms are lacking.

**Keywords:** Ethics · Case Study Assessment · Smart Urban Environments · AI · Artificial Intelligence · Smart Technology · Human Rights

## 1 Introduction

Privacy and autonomy are essential ethical safeguards and fundamental needs for preserving human safety in Internet of Things (IoT)-supported and smart

A. Marcus et al. (Eds.): HCII 2024, LNCS 15380, pp. 360–379, 2025.
https://doi.org/10.1007/978-3-031-76821-7_25

physical environments [4]. They are not just "nice to have" human needs but are considered essential for protecting human well-being in IoT-enabled smart spaces [10,46] and when smart technologies are used for the realization of critical services (e.g., healthcare), enabling humans in such environments to stay safe, away from unwanted intruders, predators, manipulations, and protected from the control of others [9,47]. In this broader context, recent research has identified a widening power gap between those who own the technology and those who use it, diminishing the control regular users have over their (smart) surroundings [50]. This trend raises concerns among regular end-users due to user-perceived potential intrusions and compromises driven by the commercial interests of major technology companies or government bodies into individuals' most private and public physical environments [51,52].

Smart environments, whether contextual, user-aware, or socially conscious, aim to optimize comfort and safety in their operation [19,36]. An example is the creation of smart environments that can sense and respond to their context [1] and provide users with personalized experiences [44]. Through user-aware, social-aware, and ethical monitoring mechanisms, the network system can cater to dynamic user needs [19]. Correspondingly, prior work has focused on the design of technical interaction modules and ambient environments with respect for regular end-users privacy, even adhering to offline standards [16,42,43]. Genuine empowerment, at a minimum, requires the possibility to stay safe, by choosing how to control one's environment [47], but ideally should also protect against unnecessary distraction and preserve a safe space away from intruders, manipulation, or confusing commercial strategies, as highlighted in the European Union's recent harmonization framework on artificial intelligence [45], further discussed in Sect. 2. Much work in IoT technology ethics is oversimplified in this regard [3,5], focusing on individuals who consent to surveillance for convenience [33], solving a single issue, for instance related to security and privacy [3], while excluding the ways it connects to other ethical risks more holistically [3].

Moreover, the European Union (EU)'s policy ambition includes developing a future human-centric Next-Generation Internet of Things that emphasizes increased protection of smart environments by developing new technical cybersecurity, privacy, and safety features [29]. New legal requirements, such as the European AI Act, demand the protection of human ethical values and rights technically from the beginning [45]. This research aims to contribute to ongoing pleas for developing more informed policies and technical interventions to protect ethical and legal aspects of privacy and autonomy [6] while embracing the benefits of IoT technologies. Contrary to the well-known benefits of IoT, its downsides are usually not critically enough touched upon [22]. Lastly, while cybersecurity and resilience-related implications of and for the increased use of smart technologies in critical infrastructures and for the assurance of critical services are prominently on the agenda (see, e.g., [23]), the corresponding ethical implications and risks are still under-addressed. The objective of this research is to perform an ethical assessment to identify the use cases relevant to smart private, and public environments and their future developments, and that require genuine safeguarding of human rights [45], in particular of meaningful human autonomy [26,52].

The following research questions are addressed:

– RQ1 How are ethical risks that may be relevant in the context of future smart private and public environments evaluated by stakeholders from different perspectives?
– RQ2 For which use cases is it most relevant to ethically safeguard human autonomy in future smart private and public environments?
– RQ3 How do stakeholders from different perspectives and expertise levels identify and evaluate these critical use cases against requirements that allow for ethical protection of human autonomy?
– RQ4 How do stakeholders from different perspectives evaluate who is/may be affected by the above ethical risks, and which criteria and concerns should be considered in this respect?

This challenge demands a multidisciplinary Foresight in Science, Technology, and Innovation (i.e., ForSTI) approach, embracing legal, sociological, and ethical aspects [31,48] in relation to the adoption of IoT and smart private and public/urban environment technologies [29]. Applying ForSTI to a case intervention can synthesize stakeholder perceptions to select and define a critical case study [49]. We conducted a ForSTI systematic assessment of each candidate use case based on input from both experts representing different perspectives and end users [31]. Incorporating stakeholders' perspectives, priorities, and concerns into the case selection process ensures relevance and alignment with real-world needs [49]. For instance, this case study can reveal where continuous context or user-aware/social-aware monitoring can lead to a pervasive sense of intrusion, thus removing humans' ability to withdraw from outside control, undermining human autonomy and well-being [47]. We aim to select a case with relevant contextual characteristics and where new solutions have the most significant impact when technically protecting human autonomy [10]. Once selected, we identify future technical scenarios with the potential for achieving consensus among multiple perspectives [21,28].

The remainder of this paper is organized as follows: in Sect. 2, relevant background and related work are introduced. In Sect. 3, the adopted methodology and operationalization of the study are presented. Subsequently, the results are presented in Sect. 4 and further discussed in Sect. 5. Finally, Sect. 6 concludes the work and sheds light on directions for follow-up work.

## 2   Background

The background section focuses on the emerging ethical complexities in smart environments, the need for updated ethical and legal frameworks, and innovative solutions.

## 2.1   Ethical Concerns and Smart Environment Technologies

Perceptions of whether ethical smart environment technologies are empowering or dis-empowering depend on who you ask [39]. The groups that desire to protect themselves from harm in general or IoT vulnerabilities are neglected in the most recent developments of IoT and Smart Environments [38]. Suppose the environment fails to protect its occupants, whether due to flaws in the technology itself, the people controlling it, or external threats. In that case, humans and society will not trust or accept the technical solutions [32]. However, there are currently few technical measures in place to prevent harm, misuse, or abuse of power by those in control [51]. As connectivity intensifies, citizens will increasingly request spaces of disconnection and safety [29]. Such approaches promote human autonomy and privacy by allowing individuals to easily opt-out, take breaks from digital technology, or have their privacy impacted only when the benefits outweigh the costs. Experts have identified new technical requirements to guarantee that no one can alter another person's environment without their consent [40,52].

Moreover, existing scientific technical use case explorations of ethical smart environments/IoT [3,5,22] or the ethical risk assessments of smart environment literature [18,38,42], found that most of it consists of technical studies focused on control and security [11,22]. As a result, several studies call for a better understanding of how end-users and adopters might protect ethical aspects linked to human privacy and autonomy protection when interacting with smart environments in physical spaces [2,9,40,41]. We, therefore, designed our study to address this gap explicitly.

## 2.2   New Ethical and Legal Requirements

When reflecting about new ethical requirements, it is important to highlight how trust is an essential aspect for the human interaction with IoT-enabled services [37]. This trust goes beyond pure technological aspects, encompassing also legal, psychology, sociology and ethics research [29].

More recently, ethical principles for building "Trustworthy AI" have been formulated by the EU High-Level Expert Group (HLEG) on Artificial Intelligence [32] and are the foundation for the recently launched EU AI Act [45]. The framework is built on principles that outline smart environment systems' ethical and legal guardrails. EU's Trustworthy AI framework incorporates ethical protection for fairness, privacy preservation, transparency, explainability, robustness, safety, and accountability via technical interventions [15]. The new legal requirements are being implemented globally, and the EU has recently approved the AI Act. The AI act follows the risk-based approach, with some systems being banned (e.g., social scoring, real-time remote biometric identification). Other systems fall in the category of "high risk" including critical infrastructure (e.g., transport, roads, water, energy) [13]. The second group of AI systems that are considered high-risk are those listed in Annex III and include critical infrastructure [13]. Recital 28a contains a vital clarification when classifying the system as high risks, such as the right to human dignity, protection of personal data, respect for private and family life, freedom of expression, political and individual self-determination, right to defense, non-discrimination, consumer protection and gender equality [45]. This list of rights is non-exhaustive, and a more comprehensive list can be found in the EU Charter of Fundamental Rights.

More specifically, on the fundamental rights impact assessment obligation, Article 29 establishes obligations to assess the impact on basic human rights by deployers governed by public law, private operators providing public services, and operators deploying high-risk systems [45]. This forces context-aware environments classified as high risk to consider how the products and services affect human rights explicitly. From our perspective, the high risk category could expand this obligation to most entities offering IoT/AI systems to the public. To what extent are the existing and new ethical and legal frameworks addressing end-users concerns regarding losing control and surveillance? The usability of privacy and autonomy protection can address the ethical concerns, and comparing multi-disciplinary perspectives can help us identify the gaps.

### 2.3  Innovative New Solutions

Specific tools that are suggested for privacy and autonomy protection include AI assisted ethics [12], socio-technical AI assistants [51], inclusive digital spaces for dialogue [9], data spaces [27], ethics committees [51], and accountability mechanisms [37,53]. While no unique alternative to the smart city as conceptualized so far is clearly articulated, most experts indicate that it should include higher degrees of privacy, co-designed features negotiated with citizens, and bottom-up approaches [25]. However, end-users/citizens have yet to take an active part in assessing the use cases and adopting a product portfolio according to the ethical criteria of human autonomy with protection from outside control, and surveillance [47,52]. Appropriate technological tools may be designed to support related processes in smart environments. Suggested examples are a monitoring infrastructure for automatically capturing the evolving needs of the citizens and making the data publicly available [51], as well as AI-based dialogue support tools inspired by philosophical approaches such as the Socratic method [37]. Könings et al. [24], define another dimension of privacy that should be considered in pervasive computing environments, coined as territorial privacy, which should aim at controlling all the physical and virtual entities that are present in the user's physical and virtual extended territory, excluding any unwanted entities from the private territory [37].

With our own empirical study, introduced in the next Section, we aimed to strengthen the link between the above-mentioned ethical concerns and prioritized use cases and how they may be safeguarded by new mechanisms.

## 3  Method

The methods section outlines the research design, survey framework, and sample characteristics.

## 3.1  Research Design

This work is situated within a Foresight (ForSTI) methodological framework, where multi-disciplinary experts and regular users are participatory decision-makers as to what to do and what to prioritize, considering alternative perspectives and options [31]. "Participatory" here refers to the process of involving a wider net of relevant social groups in the process of assessing technological artefacts [31]. The goal was to "select and define" a critical case study where future technical scenarios have the most potential for achieving consensus among multiple perspectives. The study set-up is further based on the framework of ethical technology assessment [17], where the methodology investigates the ethical risks of what is known about the technological development [34]. Ethical foresight allows us to perform an assessment of smart environment cases where additional safeguards are needed to address existing ethical limitations [17]. The study presented here reports on the first stage of a broader study combining scenario planning with technical road mapping for successful implementation [21]. In this first stage, we have conducted a broader anonymous, primarily quantitative study to identify and assess where the most critical use cases [35], technical solutions, and gaps can be negotiated [31] in preparation for scenario planning [21].

## 3.2  Survey Design

As a first step, we defined a set of operational sections, key for identifying what kinds of ethical issues and risks may arise in this context and in the foreseeable future [17], and prioritization of case evaluations that should be considered for technical implementation [49]. The ethical ForSTI framework recommends an identification stage to flag ethical issues and an evaluation stage to analyze which problems are likely to arise and how we should prioritize them [17]. This study's ethical framework was selected based on legal criteria [49] around what is considered acceptable risk [13,45] and the user and expert consensus collected from previous research when designing for human autonomy protection in IoT [51,52]. Ethical risks related to safeguarding human autonomy include the risk of harm to health and safety or an adverse impact on fundamental human rights [13].

Success scenario development focuses on a desirable state of affairs or warns against particular negative outcomes [31]. The desirable future and how to map the implementation routes for achieving this usually start with "how" questions [31]. Typically, a single scenario is investigated and may follow from multiple scenario development paths assessed previously [31,52]. In the questionnaire, real-life scenarios and case examples were evaluated against tackling the following problem formulation [17]: *"Experts and end-users express concern that continuous monitoring of physical spaces can lead to a pervasive sense of intrusion, thus removing humans' ability to withdraw from outside control and unnecessary distraction to preserve a safe space away from intruders, manipulation, or confusing commercial strategies"*. In the "Case Selection" section, participants were asked to imagine "how" new technology solutions could solve the problem formulation (1). The questionnaire ended with a prioritization section, where a set of questions was designed to select the critical use case [8]. These questions helped participants prioritize and filter solutions based on criteria such as technical feasibility, commercial impact, and alignment with human-centric, trust-first related, and ethical considerations. This approach allowed for a multi-criteria decision analysis (MCA) approach to assess and score overriding criteria in order to prioritize the use cases [31]. First, the respondents evaluated the criteria in value terms, introduced by problem statement 2: *"Due to different interests, different standards and values are used to define what is considered ethical when selecting the most important case example in smart environments. The difficulty lies in selecting common and agreed-upon criteria"*. Then, based on the criteria selected, the respondents had to choose one case example that needed further evaluation and technical implementation.

Overall, the survey was divided into five sections: Demographics, Tech knowledge, Ethical Risk Assessment, Use Case Selection, and Priority as outlined in Table 1. We have highlighted key questions in each section as illustrative of the full questionnaire design. Please note that the questions listed below are only a selection and not exhaustive.

**Table 1.** Questionnaire design

| Section | Question | Reference |
|---|---|---|
| Demographics | 1. Please state your primary role or occupation? | |
| | 2. Describe your primary interest, perspective or affiliation? | |
| | (multiple choice) | |
| Tech knowledge | 3. Understanding and involvement of AI, IoT, 5G | |
| | or other digital applications in physical environments | |
| Ethical risks | 4. Please identify any ethical or legal issues that may arise | |
| | from the use of technology in physical environments? (open-ended) | |
| | 5. Rate the ethical risks and implications related to | [14] |
| | safeguarding human autonomy (Likert scale 1–7 for each risk) | |
| Case selection | 6. Can you provide a practical example where the need | [52] |
| | to tackle problem statement 1 is essential? (Open-ended) | |
| | 7.How might a technology designer solve problem statement(1)? | [31] |
| | (Open-ended) | |
| | 8. Rank the case examples (use cases) in terms of priority | [13] |
| | (Likert scale 1–7 for each example) | |
| | 9. If you compare private versus public application areas | |
| | how would you prioritize (Likert scale 1–7 for each application area) | |
| Priority | 10. Which criteria do you think is the most important for prioritizing | [31] |
| | as described in problem statement (2) (multiple choice)? | |
| | 11. Whose perspectives should be considered when evaluating | |
| | the suitability of the identified case examples?(multiple choice) | |
| | 12. Which case example do you believe should be selected, | |
| | and why do you think this is the critical case study?(open-ended) | |

A diverse set of smart environment use cases were evaluated, ensuring representation across different technological domains (e.g., IoT, AI, automation) and private (e.g., homes, wearables) versus urban contexts (e.g., transportation, energy, healthcare). As can be read in the content of Annex III of the EU AI Act [13], it covers areas of public utility and critical nature, which are usually strongly regulated or under governmental supervision. To mitigate the rapid advancement of AI, and the ability to implement enforcement related measures, the ethical risks relevant to the interaction between deployers and end-users/regular citizens in smart private spaces are also of relevance [7]. To be more precise, at the application level, the ethicist's focus shifts to how different relevant social groups create a particular artefact's "context of use" [7]. Thus, the ethical evaluation needed to be tailored to specific contexts, comparing public with private application areas.

### 3.3   Sample Description

In this research, the goal was not to collect input from a representative sample of the population, but rather to involve diverse stakeholder perspectives. Participants needed to originate from a broad spectrum of expertise domains [30] and roles/responsibilities related to building ethical smart environments [17]. Technical experts were recruited from a company that produces hardware, software, and chips to be used in smart environments. Legal, government, and ethical experts were selected based on their academic and professional expertise (i.e., privacy law, philosophy, technology ethics, and policy). They were recruited from Norwegian Universities (UiO, NTNU, UiT), the Norwegian Data Protection Authority, law firms, and NGO's. The potential participants were contacted via e-mail and invited to answer the anonymous survey via an online link. End-users were recruited from social media (LinkedIn) and several University digital notification boards.

A total of 45 respondents completed the survey, with an average age of 39 (Standard Deviation = 10.7). In total, 51.1% identified as male, 44.4% as female and 2.2% as non-binary (one respondent (2.2%) preferred not to disclose their gender). In terms of primary affiliation or role, 36% identified as a technical engineer, 29.5% as an academic or researcher, 11.3% as a legal professional, ethnicity or philosopher, and 13.6% as a consumer. A few said industry/investor (4.5%) or other (4.5%).

## 4   Results

The results section presents the key findings from the study. Organized into three subsections, it addresses the ethical risks perceived by different stakeholder groups, identifies specific cases and actors requiring enhanced protection, and outlines strategies to mitigate potential negative impacts.

## 4.1  Ethical Risk Assessment Across Different Stakeholder Groups

**Identification and Evaluation of Ethical Risks Related to Threats to Human Privacy and Autonomy.** Figure 1 depicts average concern ratings of the ethical risks (Question 5 in Table 1, rated on a 7-point Likert scale ranging from not concerned at all to extremely concerned), based on grouping participants according to their self-reported level of understanding of smart technologies (Question 3 in Table 1). We distinguished between "strong to expert understanding" (53.3%), "moderate understanding" (4.4%), and "no to limited understanding" (42.2%). Overall, respondents scored the ethical risks between 4 and 7, with the highest concerns being expressed for the risks related to the (1) exploitation of vulnerable/discriminated groups, (2) invasion of privacy and personal spaces by collecting or monitoring too much personal information without permission, and (3) difficulty in opting out of the system to achieve a free space away from surveillance. When comparing those with advanced to moderate understanding of smart technologies, they are typically more concerned than those with no to limited understanding - with a divergence of 1–2 points on the scale. Those with a greater understanding of smart technologies (advanced and moderate) show the most concern about the exploitation of vulnerable/discriminated groups (mean: 6.57), biometric surveillance (mean: 6.43), constant and normalized surveillance (mean: 6.29), and invading privacy and personal spaces (mean: 6.14). Those with limited to no understanding are generally more worried about social scor-

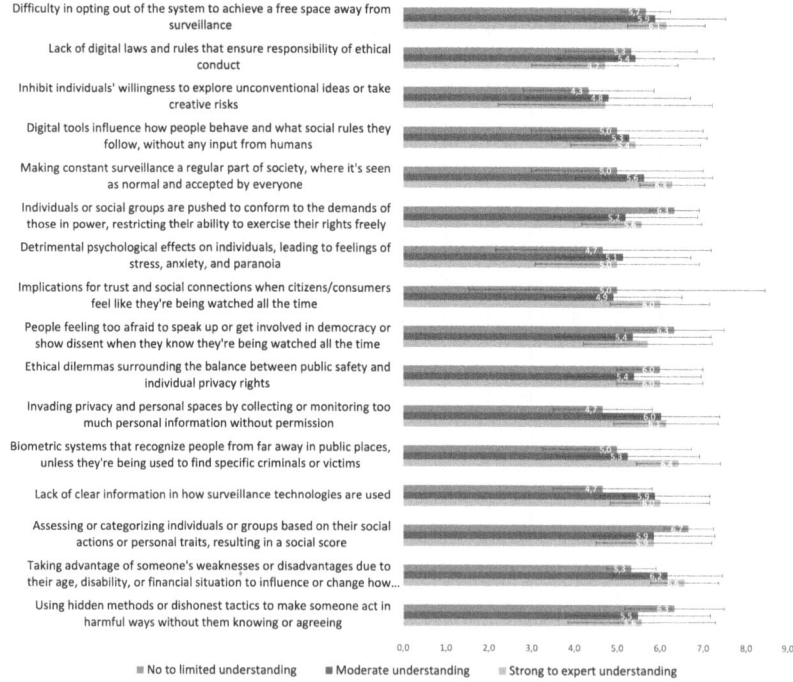

**Fig. 1.** Ethical risk assessment (average ratings) by smart technology knowledge (with 95% Confidence Intervals).

ing (mean: 6.67), power abuse/enforce conformity (mean: 6.33), suppression of democratic participation (mean: 6.33), and use of deceptive tactics (mean: 6.33) compared to experts. The results indicate a consensus among stakeholders on the significance of the inability to opt out of surveillance (mean scores: 6.14, 5.89, and 5.67).

The results coincide with the qualitative analyses of Question 4 in Table 1 that was employed to investigate participants' initial awareness of ethical implications in smart urban environments. The vast majority (13 unprompted mentions) referred to consent overreach leading to unauthorized surveillance and invasive tracking in sensitive places; of those who answered, the distribution of perspectives represented 38% public sector, 30% industry, and 15% consumers' who expressed the above concerns unprompted. These qualitative mentions were often exemplified in the context of extensive monitoring and passive versus active tracking (e.g., preventing passerby monitoring). One 47-year-old male respondent articulated the ethical concern as follows: *"It is important to know if the tech collects data passively or actively targets something/someone in the physical environment. Also, this will matter in all aspects of the physical environment: outside open space, indoor space, own private physical space (wearable tech)"(Male, 47).*

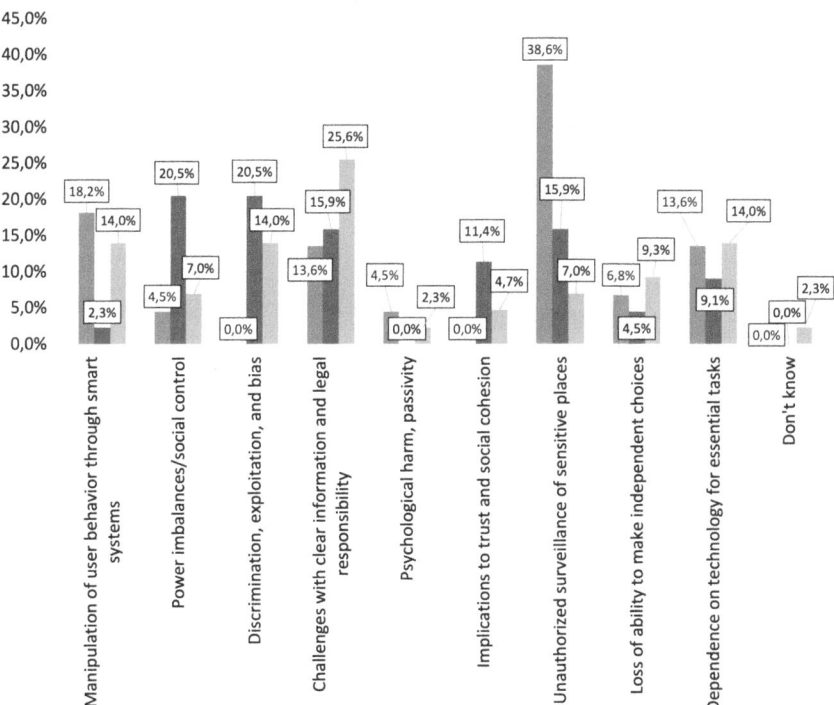

**Fig. 2.** Prioritisation of MOST relevant ethical risk category by application area

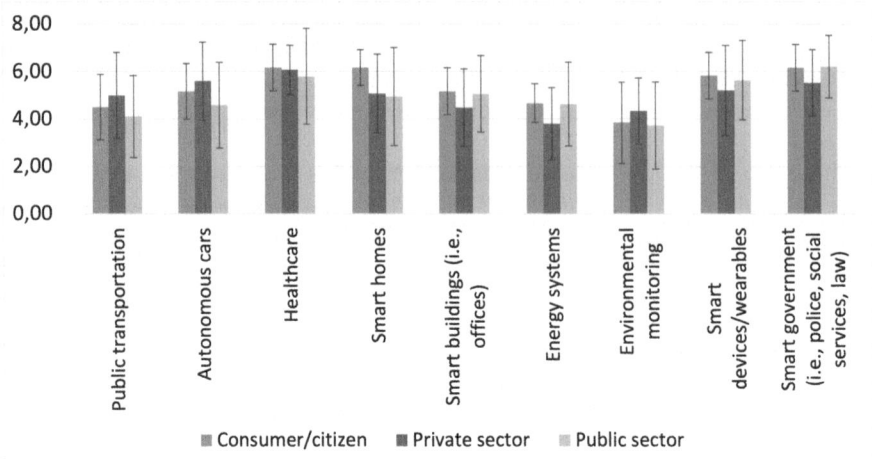

**Fig. 3.** Stakeholder Prioritization of Smart Environment Use Cases (average priority rating and 95% Confidence Intervals)

**Context-Dependent Ethical Risks.** Then, as displayed in Fig. 2, Question 9 in Table 1 asked what type of ethical risks were the most relevant for a particular context (public, private, or generic). The risk of unauthorized surveillance of sensitive places was the most relevant ethical risk in the *smart home or private application contexts* (38.5%), followed by manipulation of user behavior (18.2%). When prioritizing, most respondents evaluated the risks of power imbalances/social control (20.5%) and discrimination as more relevant in *smart urban or other public application areas*. More experts thought risks related to power imbalances were of relevance than self-declared non-experts. Even so, in the public application context, the risk of unauthorized surveillance was also seen to have a relatively high priority (15.9%).

## 4.2  Which Cases and Which Actors Require Additional Ethical Protection? (privacy and Autonomy Protection)

Figure 3 compares the rank of each use case based on the need for additional ethical protection by three stakeholder perspectives (Question 2, Table 1): consumers/citizens, private sector, and public sector. When assessing the priority of tackling problem statement 1 (the ethical challenge of constant monitoring and invasive surveillance without consent), the use cases were first ranked using Question 8 in Table 1.

As Fig. 3 shows, there is a consensus on the importance of ethical safeguards for human autonomy and privacy in Smart Healthcare (SH) and Smart Government (SG). Smart government includes police, law, and social services. For example, the priority is particularly marked by consumers/citizens (SH:6.17. SG:6.17) but also private (SH:6.07), and public sector stakeholder perspectives (SG:6.21). As explained by a respondent: *"Especially in the area of data collected by medical devices, the protection of this data is of utmost importance as it contains highly sensitive information about the user. Public spaces that utilize smart technologies also have a very strong responsibility to anonymize and protect data collected as people in the area may not directly interact with the technology monitoring the space"*(male, 24). Other smart public applications, such as public transportation, energy systems, smart buildings, and environmental monitoring, received a lower prioritization among all stakeholder groups (e.g., score lower than 5 in Fig. 3, and ratios close to 0.1 or lower in the case of public transportation in Fig. 4). These results suggest that these use cases are not a priority for any stakeholder group.

Then, Question 12 in Table 1 was asked at the very end to prioritize the most critical use case. Figure 4 depicts the proportion of respondents that selected a particularly critical case study for further technical evaluation and implementation.

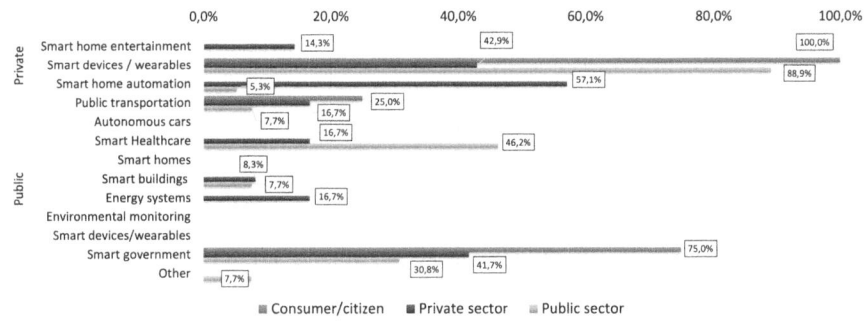

**Fig. 4.** Stakeholder Selection of Critical Case

The analysis reveals distinct prioritization patterns among different stakeholder perspectives. Consumers/Citizens' choice for the most critical case study was Smart Devices/Wearables (100%), reflecting a requirement to prioritize the protection of intimate and personal body spaces (i.e., mental privacy, personal body, the right to free will, and freedom of thought). The private and public sectors also prioritize Wearables, with a percentage ratio of around 42.9% and 88.9%. The private sector prioritizes Smart Home Automation (57.1%) more so than Wearables, which is significantly higher than the public sector (10%) and consumers (0), indicating a higher awareness of the risks and a potential gap in existing legislation. The public sector places the second highest priority, reflected in a percentage ratio of 46.2% on Smart Healthcare, highlighting its role in public welfare and health policy. It is worth noting that those without ethical or technical expertise also prioritized Smart Healthcare, but not Smart Government, Smart Home, or Smart Devices/Wearables. These findings indicate that while overlapping interests exist, each stakeholder group has unique priorities based on their roles and objectives when selecting one critical case study. By recognizing each stakeholder's various interests and objectives, the consensus for critical priority falls on technical intervention in Smart Devices/Wearables, followed by Smart government, where further ethical safeguards for human autonomy protection are needed.

**Who is Impacted and Who Should be Considered?** The respondents also evaluated who the ethical risks impact the most (see Fig. 5, Question 11, Table 1). All stakeholders overwhelmingly evaluated the prioritized ethical risks as affecting communities and vulnerable stakeholders the most, with the paradox of these groups being assessed as being the least involved in developing smart technologies.

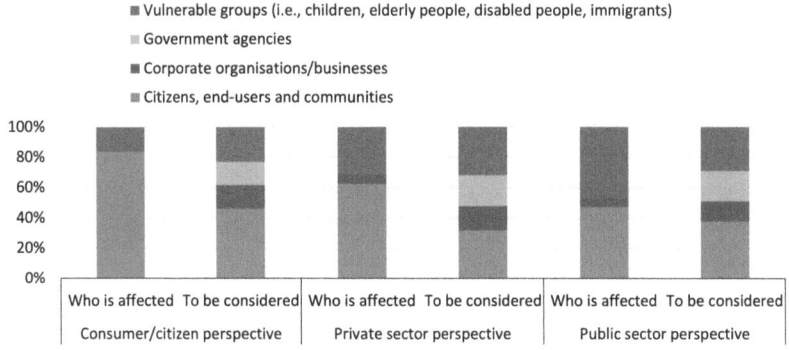

**Fig. 5.** Who is most affected vs. which perspective should be considered? (organized by perspective)

Furthermore, there was a strong consensus among stakeholders on the criteria that should be used to prioritize the most critical cases. Notably, ethical issues and human and societal benefits were strongly preferred, with 46.3% selecting either of these as the most important. In contrast, technical feasibility (4.9%) and commercial benefit (2.4%) received significantly less consideration.

### 4.3   Strategies that Mitigate Negative Impacts

Several telling and novel examples were provided when asked "How might a technology designer solve the problem statement (1)" (found in Sect. 3.2. Question 7 is presented in the Table 1). Examples are listed below in order of prevalence:

1. Easy to use opt-out features
2. The system is, by default, "off"
3. Minimal, anonymous monitoring and data selection
4. Visible alerts/signs for active monitoring
5. Ethics before cybersecurity
6. Early end-user/participatory involvement
7. To observe the observer via "sousveillance"

Most of the respondents suggested ways to perform more nuanced technology presence/selection in the smart space with easy-to-control interaction buttons or features that provided more options to turn off, opt-out, or with visible alerts and signs where there was data monitoring/tracking and analyses performed (e.g., methods such as Artificial Intelligence). For example, some respondents proposed technical solutions to mark physical spaces clearly where there was constant surveillance, and technology should have to be visible when actively monitoring (a light, tone or vibration that indicates the device is actively on). In public places, devices should be marked if always-on, to remind people in the vicinity that the devices are collecting information. A few respondents mentioned that end-users should only be tracked when necessary, with selective or anonymized data collection, and supervise or govern those who observe to avoid negative impact from power abuse.

An example was provided by one respondent (Male 24, Private sector) *"I think just focusing on the technical aspect the solution could be as simple as removing the smart technology in unnecessary applications e.g., white goods, or not selling collected data to third parties and collecting only necessary data for a given use case in the case where data is necessary for the service e.g., health tracking over a period to be used in future to identify changes to health, etc."*

# 5   Discussion

The discussion section presents the findings and their implications related to the consensus on ethical risks and the definition of success scenarios.

## 5.1   Addressing the Ethical Risks of Privacy and Surveillance with Strong Consensus

**Information/Knowledge Asymmetry.** When assessing the ethical risks, the first question that arises is whether increased awareness and knowledge also lead to greater concern, then sufficient information and understanding is a core condition to achieve ethical safeguarding. While respondents overall share a clear concern for the evaluated ethical risks, those with more knowledge about smart technologies or the ethical or legal requirements also tend to be more concerned about the ethical risks of privacy and autonomy protection overall. As such, the more awareness, the higher the level of concern also when comparing private technical experts and ethical or legal experts with consumers/citizens. Both representatives from the technology field and private sector and respondents from the public sector tasked with an ethical or legal responsibility are recognizing the ethical risks of privacy, human autonomy and surveillance to a more substantial degree overall (scores higher on level of concern in 13 of 16 ethical risks evaluated), than consumer/citizens.

A challenge in this respect is that non-experts or consumers/citizens may struggle more to really understand the implications of certain ethical risks. At the same time, the results indicate that end-users/citizens in general and vulnerable groups in particular should be more involved in outlining future technical developments. The lack of knowledge could be an issue for all groups with no technical, legal, or ethical background, but more importantly, vulnerable groups such as elderly citizens, children, or refugees [20]. Their involvement depends on the requirement of being *better informed* consumers/citizens. Without a thorough understanding of the nature of the ethical implications and potential harm, consumers/citizens have less of a foundation to provide a truly informed evaluation of the ethical risks. This may be a risk in itself because they may underestimate the potential implications and dangers.

## 5.2   Defining and Prioritizing Success Scenarios and Cases

**Create Free Spaces from Surveillance.** Further, one of the key findings is the consensus across all stakeholder groups regarding the top concern of constant and invasive privacy and personal surveillance and the difficulty of opting out to achieve a free space from surveillance in smart physical environments (both unprompted and prompted), which highlights a critical area for intervention.

The most important ethical safeguards will emerge from the ability to keep public spaces protected from pervasive surveillance, data monitoring and data collection with constraints. Especially critical are physical (e.g., Smart Healthcare and Smart Government) and personal (e.g., Smart Devices/Wearables) spaces, where the most sensitive social and medical human activity happens. These physical environments also have some of the strictest ethical and legal requirements today. Creating new, protected spaces should be extended with existing and new legal and ethical frameworks. Existing human rights law should guide the technical developments and ensure non-invasive tracking, balanced with protection from technical deployers with malicious intent or outside intruders enacting harm.

**For Whom is Ethical Safeguarding a Priority?** Discrimination against vulnerable groups was rated as one of the highest ethical risks. Based on the results presented in Sect. 4.2, end-users and communities, as well as vulnerable groups within the broader population, represent (1) key stakeholders that should be considered and involved in the development and implementation of smart technologies and (2) those who are most (potentially negatively) impacted by the widespread use of smart technologies in various settings.

As is clearly agreed between all groups, the evaluated ethical risks are perceived to affect citizens/end-users/communities and vulnerable groups mainly. Additional observations outlined in Sect. 4.2 of the results highlight a notable consensus favoring ethical considerations and human and societal benefits as primary criteria for prioritizing cases. This finding is noteworthy, particularly considering that 38.6% of respondents were affiliated with the private sector. A potential explanation for this unexpected result may stem from a suspected social desirability bias, wherein respondents may have over-reported socially favorable criteria while under-reporting technical and commercial considerations.

Real-life scenarios and case examples were evaluated against tackling the problem formulation as stated in the Methods Sect. 3.2. Consumers/citizens prioritize intimate and personal spaces where less regulation is currently in place, as they do not fall under the EU AI Act high-risk category [13]. Critical sectors/applications, such as public transportation, environmental monitoring, smart offices/buildings, which fall under high risk AI systems, are ranked lower in priority among all stakeholders. A possible explanation for this result is the need for more representation of citizens and communities in both technical and legal decision-making processes during technological development. For future success scenarios to be genuinely human-centric, the involvement and interests of communities and vulnerable groups should take precedence over those of technical experts, governments, and corporations.

**Success Scenario Implementation is Considered Simple - Opt-out, Turn Off, Not Build.** Most mitigation strategies are easily implemented technically, enabling end-users (citizens and vulnerable groups) to assert control and autonomy, and reverse the power asymmetry in the smart physical environment. Technical mechanisms need to allow for the ability to opt-out of surveillance, anonymization, by-passer technical interventions, and phase out or reverse third-party monitoring (the recording of third-party monitoring activity observed by the public). Procedures that are technically speaking simple and feasible should be specified to avoid constant monitoring, with selective data collection, storage or device ownership, always off technical features, or "sometimes on tracking", limited or prohibited third party surveillance, and strictly prioritizing ethical criteria over cybersecurity when protecting smart urban and private physical spaces.

Corrective actions are not necessarily only technical measures but also regulatory tasks that need to be imposed on technical applications. Technical ethical safeguarding does not need to be complex. Still, it comes back to the ability of regulatory bodies to impose laws and regulations to protect the affected stakeholders from those in positions of power. The ethical risks evaluated in this study are mostly governed by EU laws, such as GDPR and the AI Act. Government agencies are impacted by applying the equivalent law when smart technologies are implemented in physical spaces. There are specific guidelines to identify the most appropriate risk management measures for technology providers [14]. Examples can include a) elimination or reduction of identified and evaluated risks, as far as it is technically feasible through adequate design and development of the high-risk smart environment, b) implementation of adequate mitigation and control measures, addressing risks that cannot be implemented [13]. These are important tools to address the information and power asymmetry between technical deployers, consumers/citizens, and ethical/legal/policymakers.

## 5.3  Limitations

We adopted a comprehensive methodological framework. However, we need to acknowledge the following limitations.

1. Despite efforts to ensure a balanced stakeholder representation, challenges in recruitment resulted in a relatively small sample size (n=45). While a significant number of experts from different perspectives participated (typically resulting in a smaller sample size), the sample size constrains the generalizability of the study's findings, and follow-up work is needed to validate the key findings.
2. A predominant proportion of respondents originated from Norway, potentially skewing the sample's representativeness in terms of cultural and geographical diversity.
3. The assessment focused primarily on specific aspects of ethics concerning privacy and human autonomy protection within smart urban and private environments. This narrowed scope may have overlooked broader or interconnected ethical considerations.
4. The selection of laws primarily drawn from the EU AI act might restrict the comprehensiveness of the investigation, as differences between legal and ethical requirements could influence the scope of inquiry.
5. While the questionnaire design aimed for comprehensiveness, feedback during the pre-testing phase highlighted a number of challenges, particularly concerning the complexity of topics for non-experts. This may have impacted the quality of responses and overall data validity.

## 6  Conclusion and Future Work

Prior work has shown that different ethical and legal trajectories are proposed by diverse key stakeholders and contexts related to smart environments [50]. This study aimed to evaluate the differences in stakeholder perspectives when considering ethical risks, specifically within the context of smart private and public environments. The focus was on examining how these perspectives compare when prioritizing different use cases and their corresponding ethical implications. This was done by an online survey (n = 45) based on a ForSTI methodological approach, with a primary focus on ethical technology assessment.

The results can inform mitigation strategies and recommendations, for instance, pursuing the opt-out and turn-off options in IoT technology deployment for public (e.g., urban) or private environments to address the identified ethical issues and risks. To develop concrete, alternative technical scenarios, specific design modifications, technical interventions, or governance mechanisms can help mitigate or prevent negative ethical impacts.

Finally, future research should aim to establish technical policies and interventions accurately describing human autonomy protection in line with privacy and surveillance ethics in smart urban or personal environments and IoT. Protecting human autonomy in intimate and personal spaces and smart government and healthcare applications presents significant areas for consensus. This involves exploring technical scenarios in healthcare and smart government scenarios. Follow-up work should also investigate where and how technical mechanisms are utilized to safeguard human autonomy in these use cases, particularly by investigating the technical mechanisms that are lacking.

**Acknowledgments.** This work has received funding from the Research Council of Norway through the SFI Norwegian Centre for Cybersecurity in Critical Sectors (NOR-CICS) project no. 310105).

# References

1. Abowd, G.D., Dey, A.K., Brown, P.J., Davies, N., Smith, M., Steggles, P.: Towards a better understanding of context and context-awareness. In: Gellersen, H.-W. (ed.) HUC 1999. LNCS, vol. 1707, pp. 304–307. Springer, Heidelberg (1999). https://doi.org/10.1007/3-540-48157-5_29

2. Ahmad, K., Maabreh, M., Ghaly, M., Khan, K., Qadir, J., Al-Fuqaha, A.: Developing future human-centered smart cities: critical analysis of smart city security, data management, and ethical challenges. Comput. Sci. Rev. **43**, 100452 (2022)

3. Allhoff, F., Henschke, A.: The internet of things: Foundational ethical issues. Internet Things **1**, 55–66 (2018)

4. Atlam, H.F., Wills, G.B.: IoT security, privacy, safety and ethics. Digital twin technologies and smart cities, pp. 123–149 (2020)

5. Baldini, G., Botterman, M., Neisse, R., Tallacchini, M.: Ethical design in the internet of things. Sci. Eng. Ethics **24**, 905–925 (2018)

6. Biber, D.S.E.: Between humans and machines: Judicial interpretation of the automated decision-making practices in the EU. University of Luxembourg Law Research Pape,r pp. 2023–19 (2023)

7. Brey, P.A.: Anticipatory ethics for emerging technologies. NanoEthics **6**(1), 1–13 (2012)

8. Brunnbauer, M., Piller, G., Rothlauf, F.: Top-Down or Explorative? A Case Study on the Identification of AI Use Cases. In: Pacific Asia Conference on Information Systems, p. 1 (2022)

9. Calvo, P.: The ethics of Smart City (EoSC): moral implications of hyperconnectivity, algorithmization and the datafication of urban digital society. Ethics Inf. Technol. **22**(2), 141–149 (2020)

10. Calvo, R.A., Peters, D.: Positive Computing: Technology for Wellbeing and Human Potential. MIT Press (2014)

11. Chang, V.: An ethical framework for big data and smart cities. Technol. Forecast. Soc. Chang. **165**, 120559 (2021)

12. Etzioni, A., Etzioni, O.: AI assisted ethics. Ethics Inf. Technol. **18**, 149–156 (2016)

13. EU Artificial Intelligence Act: Annex III: High-risk AI systems (2024)

14. EU Artificial Intelligence Act: Article 7, Amendments to EU's AI act (2024)

15. European Commission: Policy and investment recommendations for trustworthy artificial intelligence (2019)

16. Floridi, L., et al.: AI4People-an ethical framework for a good AI society: opportunities, risks, principles, and recommendations. Mind. Mach. **28**, 689–707 (2018)

17. Floridi, L., Strait, A.: Ethical foresight analysis: what it is and why it is needed? The 2020 Yearbook of the Digital Ethics Lab, pp. 173–194 (2021)

18. Frischmann, B., Selinger, E.: Re-engineering Humanity. Cambridge University Press, Cambridge (2018)
19. Garcia-Alonso, J., Berrocal, J., Canal, C., Murillo, J.M.: Towards distributed and context-aware human-centric cyber-physical systems. In: Lazovik, A., Schulte, S. (eds.) ESOCC 2016. CCIS, vol. 707, pp. 59–73. Springer, Cham (2018). https://doi.org/10.1007/978-3-319-72125-5_5
20. Gligoric, N., et al.: Making onlife principles into actionable guidelines for smart city frameworks and IoT policies. Designing, Developing, and Facilitating Smart Cities: Urban Design to IoT Solutions, pp. 33–48 (2017)
21. Hussain, M., Tapinos, E., Knight, L.: Scenario-driven roadmapping for technology foresight. Technol. Forecast. Soc. Chang. **124**, 160–177 (2017)
22. Karale, A.: The challenges of IoT addressing security, ethics, privacy, and laws. Internet Things **15**, 100420 (2021)
23. Koch, T., Möller, D.P.F., Deutschmann, A.: Smart Technologies as a Thread for Critical Infrastructures. In: Akhilesh, K.B., Möller, D.P.F. (eds.) Smart Technologies, pp. 275–289. Springer, Singapore (2020). https://doi.org/10.1007/978-981-13-7139-4_21
24. Könings, B., Schaub, F., Weber, M.: Privacy and trust in ambient intelligent environments. Next Generation Intelligent Environments: Ambient Adaptive Systems, pp. 133–164 (2016)
25. van Kranenburg, R., et al.: Future urban smartness: connectivity zones with disposable identities. In: Handbook of Smart Cities, pp. 1–29 (2020)
26. Laitinen, A., Sahlgren, O.: AI systems and respect for human autonomy. Front. Artif. Intell. **4** (2021)
27. Lehtiniemi, T.: Personal data spaces: an intervention in surveillance capitalism? Surveill. Soc. **15**(5), 626–639 (2017)
28. Magruk, A.: Innovative classification of technology foresight methods. Technol. Econ. Dev. Econ. **4**, 700–715 (2011)
29. Brynskov, M., Federico Michele Facca, G.H.: Building a roadmap for the Next Generation Internet of Things. Research, Innovation and Implementation 2021-2027. Scoping Paper (2019). Accessed 04 Jan 2021
30. Mendelow, A.: Stakeholder mapping. In: Proceedings of the 2nd International Conference on Information Systems, pp. 10–24. A. Mendelow Cambridge, MA (1991)
31. Miles, I., Saritas, O., Sokolov, A.: Foresight for Science, Technology and Innovation. Springer, Cham (2016). https://doi.org/10.1007/978-3-319-32574-3
32. Morandín-Ahuerma, F.: IEEE: a global standard as an ethical AI initiative. In: Principios normativos para una ética de la inteligencia artificial (127-136) (2023)
33. Nolin, J., Olson, N.: The Internet of Things and convenience. Internet Res. **26**(2), 360–376 (2016)
34. Palm, E., Hansson, S.O.: The case for ethical technology assessment (eTA). Technol. Forecast. Soc. Chang. **73**(5), 543–558 (2006)
35. Peter, M.K., Jarratt, D.G.: The practice of foresight in long-term planning. Technol. Forecast. Soc. Chang. **101**, 49–61 (2015)
36. Punie, Y.: The future of ambient intelligence in Europe–the need for more everyday life. In: Media, technology and everyday life in Europe, pp. 177–196. Routledge (2017)
37. Riedmann-Streitz, C., et al.: How to create and foster sustainable smart cities? insights on ethics, trust, privacy, transparency, incentives, and success. Int. J. Hum.–Comput. Interact. 1–32 (2024)
38. Royakkers, L., Timmer, J., Kool, L., Van Est, R.: Societal and ethical issues of digitization. Ethics Inf. Technol. **20**, 127–142 (2018)

39. Schneider, H., Eiband, M., Ullrich, D., Butz, A.: Empowerment in HCI-A survey and framework. In: Proceedings of the 2018 CHI Conference on Human Factors in Computing Systems, pp. 1–14 (2018)
40. Shahraki, A., Haugen, Ø.: Social ethics in Internet of Things: An outline and review. In: 2018 IEEE Industrial Cyber-Physical Systems (ICPS), pp. 509–516 (2018)
41. Sovacool, B.K., Del Rio, D.D.F.: Smart home technologies in Europe: a critical review of concepts, benefits, risks and policies. Renew. Sustain. Energy Rev. **120**, 109663 (2020)
42. Stephanidis, C., et al.: Others: seven HCI grand challenges. Int. J. Hum.-Comput. Interact. **35**(14), 1229–1269 (2019)
43. Streitz, N.A.: From smart-only cities towards humane and cooperative hybrid cities. Technol.— Arch.+ Des. **5**(2), 127–133 (2021)
44. Sylla, T., Chalouf, M.A., Krief, F., Samaké, K.: Towards a context-aware security and privacy as a service in the Internet of Things. In: Laurent, M., Giannetsos, T. (eds.) WISTP 2019. LNCS, vol. 12024, pp. 240–252. Springer, Cham (2020). https://doi.org/10.1007/978-3-030-41702-4_15
45. The European Parliament: Harmonised rules on artificial intelligence (Artificial Intelligence Act) (2024)
46. Tschider, C.A.: Regulating the internet of things: discrimination, privacy, and cybersecurity in the artificial intelligence age. Denv. L. Rev. **96**, 87 (2018)
47. Véliz, C.: The Ethics of Privacy and Surveillance. Oxford University Press (2023)
48. Weigand, K., Flanagan, T., Dye, K., Jones, P.: Collaborative foresight: complementing long-horizon strategic planning. Technol. Forecast. Soc. Chang. **85**, 134–152 (2014)
49. Yin, R.K.: Case Study Research and Applications, vol. 6. Sage, Thousand Oaks, CA (2018)
50. Ystgaard, K.F., De Moor, K.: Future scoping of truly human-centric IoT and intelligent networks: a foresight approach. In: Proceedings of the 12th International Conference on the Internet of Things, pp. 81–87 (2022)
51. Ystgaard, K.F., De Moor, K.: Envisioning the future: a multi-disciplinary approach to human-centered intelligent environments. Qual. User Exp. **8**(1), 11 (2023)
52. Ystgaard, K.F., Lein, S.K., De Moor, K.: Foresight scenarios for protecting human autonomy in IoT: a comparative study of expert and end-user perspectives. In: Proceedings of the 13th International Conference on the Internet of Things, pp. 58–65 (2023)
53. Zhou, Y., Kankanhalli, A.: AI regulation for smart cities: challenges and principles. In: Smart Cities and Smart Governance: Towards the 22nd Century Sustainable City, pp. 101–118 (2021)

# Peering into the Algorithmic Cosmos: A Narrative Game for Demystifying Privacy Data Circulation

Jingjing Zhang⦿, Xiaoxiao Wang⦿, Huize Wan⦿, and Yuan Yao(✉)⦿

School of Architecture and Design, Beijing Jiaotong University, Beijing, China
yuanyao@bjtu.edu.cn

**Abstract.** As user behavior on social networking platforms increases, concerns about privacy data exposure grow due to dense public network information. Users struggle to understand the flow of their personal information and face unclear regulations and algorithmic usage of their data. This study proposes a game, 'Wormhole Whisper' to explore and explain privacy exposure, the issues with users, operators, and algorithms, and to make these concepts more accessible. By visualizing data flow as a journey through a 'wormhole' or 'black box', the game uses an interactive narrative to help users intuitively understand how their data is transmitted. It aims to deepen user awareness of data flow, privacy boundaries, and the need for transparency, highlighting the potential of games to address social issues.

**Keywords:** User Privacy Data · Social Network · Game Design · Data Visualization

## 1 Introduction

As smartphone use increases and internet engagement deepens, the volume of information on public networks is expanding rapidly. This surge has heightened concerns about network privacy and information security, with internet users growing increasingly worried about the exposure of their privacy data [1, 2]. Many users are uneasy about the precision with which data analytics can predict their preferences, fearing unauthorized access and use of their personal information [3]. Common concerns include the collection of home addresses, phone numbers, and browsing habits by network applications and search engines. Despite these concerns, most users lack a clear understanding of data usage policies, the algorithms involved, and the relevant legal frameworks. Additionally, the terms and conditions for data-driven services are often lengthy and complex, posing significant barriers to understanding [4]. Consequently, even though privacy concerns persist, many users either consciously or unconsciously agree to these terms without fully understanding the implications.

This study investigates the 'cognitive gaps' in users' perceptions of privacy data transmission, focusing on popular social platforms in China. We analyzed metadata and algorithms and discovered that users often feel they are being 'eavesdropped' on. This

© The Author(s), under exclusive license to Springer Nature Switzerland AG 2025
A. Marcus et al. (Eds.): HCII 2024, LNCS 15380, pp. 380–391, 2025.
https://doi.org/10.1007/978-3-031-76821-7_26

perception arises because the transfer of privacy data across various social applications, and the algorithms involved, appear opaque to them. Although previous research has attempted to bridge the gap in public understanding through technical explanations, risk assessments [5], and plugin development [6], there remains a significant asymmetry between technical solutions and public perception. Often, technical details are not visualized clearly, making it challenging for users to grasp how their personal data flows online. This gap in design and understanding presents new opportunities for research and development.

In response, this paper introduces a novel approach using gamification. We employ games as a tool to present complex content in a straightforward, engaging manner, thereby making digital privacy more transparent and accessible [7, 8]. The design of these serious games incorporates the metaphor of interstellar travel through a wormhole, creating a vivid narrative and interactive experience that demystifies the abstract processes of data transmission. Our goal is to enhance understanding among users and stakeholders about data collection and usage on big data platforms, stimulate discussions on privacy boundaries, and promote more informed decisions about personal data privacy.

## 2 Related Work

### 2.1 Information Barriers and Privacy Security

As internet usage and big data applications continue to grow, some researchers are proactively exploring methods to enhance user understanding of data security and transmission [9]. For example, Mitra et al. analyzed privacy terms and identified the use of vague and abstract language, such as '*we collect your device information*' which complicates consensus among app developers, policy writers, and users. Furthermore, surveys suggest that personal data often serves as a form of currency in 'free' online services, especially within social networks where it is not isolated. Consequently, users who share their profiles may inadvertently expose personal information to unauthorized parties [10].

Additionally, many researchers are developing tools to help users assess data security. Yana and her team have developed privacy threat modeling strategies, promoting a systematic approach to evaluate potential privacy risks in system designs [6]. Other scholars recommend using third-party trackers to analyze long-term user browsing data and visualize this information [11]. These efforts contribute to the understanding of privacy data security and policy transparency, providing valuable insights and tools for designing data visualization systems focused on privacy. Subsequent paragraphs, however, are indented.

Users are increasingly concerned about data security and personal privacy, yet often feel powerless due to information barriers. Common worries include opaque data collection methods and the privacy [12] and security implications of purchasing Internet of Things devices [13]. Despite these concerns, most users lack the necessary focus and expertise to effectively negotiate with internet service providers. This results in a predicament where users must choose between risking their privacy or facing social isolation [14]. Our research indicates a critical need for intuitive, visual designs that can demystify the flow of personal information online, addressing key concerns like data privacy. Such insights are vital for understanding the underlying psychology of users and improving their experience.

In this design research, we aim to provide users with impactful visual design works such as 'fbFaces' by Joern Roeder and Jonathan Pirnay[1], 'I Agree' by Dima Yarovinsky[2], and 'Perceived Personality' by Laurie Frick. These projects, designed for the general public, leverage user cognition to inspire and innovate in visual studies. This approach addresses the gaps left by previous research, which often focused solely on technical aspects and 'black box' regulatory policies. It empowers users to reassess their privacy boundaries and make informed privacy decisions.

### 2.2  The Use of Games for Discussing Serious Topics

In interaction design, the concept of gamification—applying game design elements to non-gaming contexts to boost user engagement and retention—has garnered significant attention. A study by Deterding et al. defines gamification as the incorporation of traditional game elements into various environments to create game-like experiences, with applications extending from education to business [15]. Numerous studies have investigated the use of games to promote profound 'serious experiences' [7, 16] aimed at increasing public awareness. Games are particularly effective in initiating and facilitating reflections on various issues, including the contemplation of cybersecurity [17].

Video games serve not only as entertainment but also as potent tools for persuasion and education. Research has assessed the efficacy of learning in serious games [18], with notable studies such as Bogost's introduction of 'persuasive games' highlighting their capacity to communicate messages and influence players' attitudes and behaviors through interactive elements [19]. These games adeptly simulate complex systems, providing players with an interactive, enjoyable, and engaging means to understand operational dynamics. Such studies underscore the utility of games in enhancing awareness and stimulating thoughtful consideration of issues like cybersecurity.

## 3  Design Method: A 'Poetic Metaphor' Gamification Based on Data Collection

The Wormhole Whisper research project investigates 'eavesdropping' on social platforms. This game evaluates the flow of user data on social media, explores the underlying causes of eavesdropping, and aims to elevate public understanding and attitudes towards this issue. The central question addressed is: *"How can designers use aesthetically pleasing and accessible algorithm games to demystify the complex principles of algorithms and data privacy for the general public?"* The project is structured into three phases: Gathering metadata to assess needs based on users' current attitudes and behaviors towards data privacy; Creating a digital game that highlights the motives behind eavesdropping; Testing to measure changes in user attitudes and behaviors post-gameplay.

---

[1] 2011 Art work 'fbFaces'. https://www.alphavillefestival.co.uk/fbfaces.

[2] 2018 Art work 'I Agree'. https://twistedsifter.com/2018/05/i-agree-by-dima-yarovinsky/.

Initially, the project employs web scraping and algorithmic analysis to collect and examine privacy metadata, assessing users' attitudes towards social media privacy policies. We use a quantitative approach to analyze privacy algorithms and users' understanding, aiming to establish consensus on game requirements. Data collection focused on major Chinese social platforms like Weibo and Bilibili. Utilizing the hashtags '#big data #eavesdropping', we gathered 685 posts through web scraping. Sentiment analysis and word frequency analysis of these posts revealed that 217 expressed strong negative emotions, and 317 were emotionally neutral. Frequently used negative words such as 'terrible', 'hateful,' and 'suspicious' underscore a widespread distrust in privacy protection, highlighting discomfort with how platforms manage privacy data boundaries. Additionally, we analyzed the top five Chinese social media platforms, collecting data on 123 SDKs from 13 popular apps using web scraping. This analysis confirmed extensive use of user data by third-party SDKs, intensifying concerns about privacy breaches.

Our research indicates that many platforms enforce acceptance of privacy terms by restricting certain features, thereby obtaining user permissions. These platforms often use de-identified personal data for algorithm development and data sharing, not considering it private. Users, due to informational asymmetry, tend to overly trust these platforms. Additionally, privacy policies are complex and often unclear, offering only simplified descriptions of data collection and use. Common clauses, such as 'may include third-party products and services' and 'sharing necessary information with third-party vendors', lack clarity regarding the purposes and scope of such sharing. Third-party services usually remain opaque, with SDKs embedded in apps potentially accessing and using data without user awareness (e.g., device identifiers, installation permissions, and data from other apps). Consequently, users must depend on the information in developers' privacy policies, which makes it challenging to track where the information goes and to assess whether permissions are used for essential services or for marketing and sales.

Research indicates that 'algorithms significantly contribute to users' suspicions of being 'eavesdropped' on. Platforms and operators collect user data and use behavioral targeting strategies to deliver relevant advertisements based on user activities like browsing, searching, and purchasing. These activities are processed through various algorithms, causing concern among some users about potential eavesdropping. In response, drawing on previous studies and big data analysis, we have concentrated on the personalized recommendation features of these platforms. Specifically, we focus on explaining and analyzing the three most commonly discussed algorithms: cluster analysis, association rule learning, and collaborative filtering, particularly in the context of game design.

After completing the first phase of our analysis, we moved into the second phase, focusing on refining the core elements of game development: privacy policies, SDKs, and algorithms. This phase allowed us to uncover issues within privacy terms and identify the role of third-party SDKs in the use and dissemination of user information. Further analysis showed that algorithms facilitate the flow of user data, primarily after users accept terms and policies. These algorithms, functioning as black boxes, process the circulated data step-by-step, eventually delivering content that can make users feel as though they are being eavesdropped upon. These three elements—privacy policies, SDKs, and algorithms—are crucial to the operation of most platforms. Through game design and interactive concepts, we aim to further explore this phenomenon, enhancing user understanding of the link between data privacy and algorithmic recommendations.

In response to the flow of privacy data across platforms, this game development incorporates the concept of 'Infopoetry' into its design [20]. Unlike traditional information design, which primarily transforms data into visual charts, Infopoetry creates representational scenarios. This design process focuses on extracting data characteristics from three key areas: the signing of privacy terms and policies, the transmission and circulation of user information via third-party SDKs, and the use of algorithms. Our analysis shows that users constantly leave data footprints on platforms, and what they can see depends heavily on algorithmic recommendations. These platforms, which access user data continuously and universally, function like cosmic wormholes—unpredictable in both their operations and destinations. To address this, the design uses a metaphorical visual language and interstellar narrative to simulate the movement of data algorithms and user privacy data across social applications. The project aims to mirror real-world privacy dilemmas through relevant scenarios and visual symbols. The game design strategy will proceed through four steps: extracting data characteristics, engaging in emotional reflection, constructing metaphors, and selecting suitable mediums.

Upon completion of the game development, 10 users aged 18 to 30 tested and evaluated 'Wormhole Whisper' focusing on various aspects of player experience, including learnability, clarity of objectives, enjoyment, purpose of item use, control, and engagement. They also examined learning outcomes and behavioral changes. The evaluation highlighted the game's positive effects, shortcomings, and areas for improvement. Participants were encouraged to propose design improvements to better convey the workings of privacy algorithms. These suggestions were critically reviewed and scored in later rounds. Future iterations of 'Wormhole Whisper' will incorporate this feedback. The ongoing design challenge is to effectively balance user engagement and understanding while seamlessly blending informational content with the game's narrative elements.

## 4   Gamification Design

The 'Wormhole Whisper' game is designed to be highly accessible and visually metaphor-rich, fostering intuitive user interactions like clicking, dragging, and hovering. These features simulate users' interaction processes on web platforms. This text-based web game uses interstellar exploration as a metaphor for the journey of data transmission. Players navigate through wormholes to explore different algorithms and data flow channels, using various game props to uncover and evade pixel-tracking technologies. As they progress, they reveal deeper layers of secrets. The game emphasizes previously neglected privacy boundaries, offering players interactive scenes that provide a more intuitive understanding of algorithmic functions and data privacy mechanisms.

Each game level is tailored to specific data circulation scenarios, focusing on the essentials of privacy policies, SDKs, and algorithms. For instance, within the game, clicking 'disagree' on any permission request forces players back to the starting screen. Beyond interactions related to privacy terms and SDKs, the game introduces players to three wormholes, each symbolizing a different algorithm. Through engaging gameplay, players unlock and explore the underlying principles of these algorithms. The level effectively demonstrates various algorithmic concepts, including their basic principles, typical functions, practical applications, scenarios, outcomes, and capabilities.

## 4.1 Level Design

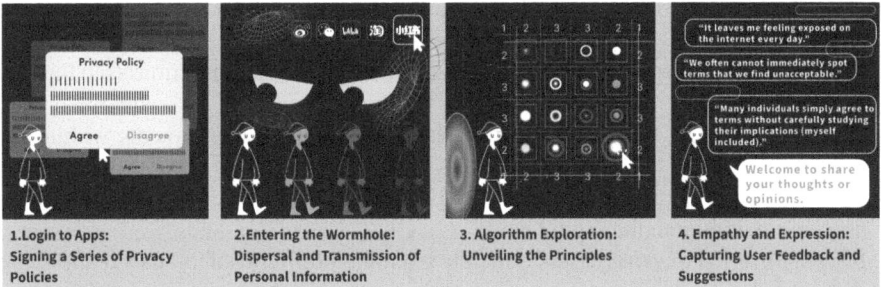

**Fig. 1.** The Four Components of Game Scenario Design.

Our game-level design uses metaphor to replicate the four major steps of 'eavesdropping' as performed by big data systems. This approach aims to clarify the challenges associated with data collection and usage on big data platforms, thereby raising awareness among users and stakeholders. To illustrate the process, we describe the flow of privacy data when users enter a social networking platform. This explanation employs an interactive narrative combined with 'Infopoetry' and is structured into four distinct parts (see Fig. 1).

**Initial Website Entry.** Users entering social networking platforms and websites are routinely required to agree to terms and authorize device usage permissions.

- *Clicking 'Agree'*. Users rapidly click through pop-up terms and authorizations, designed to encourage subconscious agreement, similar to habitual behaviors observed in real-life interactions. After accepting all terms, users gain access to explore further within the game's wormhole.
- *Clicking 'Disagree'*. Should users choose 'disagree' at any point, they are redirected back to the game's start page, and all previously agreed terms are nullified.

This level transforms the concept of privacy terms. Utilizing a vocabulary list developed from prior findings, we have identified and visualized high-frequency words in an interactive prototype with text labels. These extensive service agreements initiate the transition of various user data types into the wormhole. We employed a webpage glitch style to simulate the chaotic text pop-ups, reflecting the potential reading experience. Moreover, we categorized terms by keywords to aid users in dissecting and understanding 'Privacy Terms and Policies'. In this glitch style, terms like 'personal information', highlighted in fluorescent green, appear in the privacy text before and after related content. Tabs tagged with the same label are organized neatly, facilitating easy reading and comparison for users. Sentences are manually collected, read, and assessed, helping users intuitively grasp the ambiguities within the privacy terms, explore the textual context and modal particles, and encourage a reconsideration of their underlying implications.

**Entering the Network.** Information Dissipation and Transmission: Upon entering the wormhole, users can freely explore various web pages and social media applications. Each click leaves traces on the website, progressively pulling their information into the wormhole and rendering their avatar more transparent. To understand where their information goes, users adopt a detective's perspective to scrutinize the terms of service and explore the influence of third-party SDKs on personal data transactions (see Fig. 2).

- *Exploration.* Users navigate through a variety of online environments within the wormhole.
- *Trace Leaving.* Increased interaction leads to more data traces, gradually absorbing user information into the digital void.
- *Investigative Perspective.* Users critically examine user terms and analyze the roles of third-party SDKs in handling personal data.
- *Reevaluation of Privacy.* After reviewing all technical details, users are prompted to rethink the boundaries of privacy.

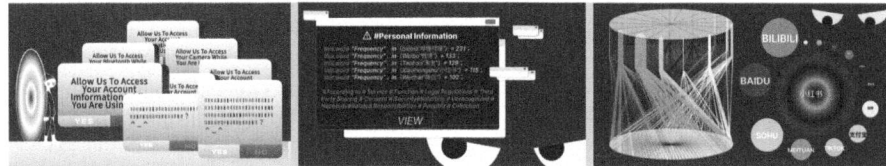

**Fig. 2.** Checkpoints related to SDKs and privacy policies

**Algorithm Exploration** Unlocking the Principles Behind: After completing the previous phase, users progress to a game section that visualizes algorithms via a wormhole passage. Simple interactions, such as clicking and dragging, enable users to grasp the principles of common algorithms used in private information transmission effortlessly. Initially, we selected 3 main types of algorithms for narrative and interactive purposes within the wormhole's core.

For example, during the game's wormhole travel, user data is metaphorically transformed into interstellar matter and planets. This intuitive metaphor aids users in understanding complex data analysis methods and observing how these algorithms impact the information they see in cyberspace. Therefore, these algorithms are strategically placed in the middle part of the game. In each algorithm-themed game scene, users solve puzzles to collect planetary features, learning about algorithm principles and dodging the boss to return to their spaceship.

- *Cluster Analysis.* This algorithm groups similar types of planets—such as those with rings, single-color, or dual-color—into distinct galaxies. For instance, all ringed planets might be grouped into one galaxy, single-color planets into another, and dual-color planets into a third, each representing a 'cluster'. This visual metaphor uses planetary types (i.e., 'features') to mimic the process of analyzing user behavior data by categorizing users based on their features, such as shopping habits, clicked ads, or time spent on a website [21].

- *Collaborative Filtering.* Based on its principles, this algorithm allows planets liked by friends, similar space explorers, or previously browsed planets to easily reach the user. Categorizing planets into different galaxies according to their features demonstrates the core idea of collaborative filtering— 'birds of a feather flock together'. This mechanism underpins recommendation systems that predict user interests based on past behaviors [22].
- *Association Rule Learning.* In this game, users on a space exploration journey may notice that finding a central gaseous planet often means a large gaseous planet is nearby. When users encounter a glowing planet, a similarly structured planet is likely nearby, unlike other types such as ringed planets, which are typically adjacent to distinctly layered planets. These association rules facilitate more effective universe exploration and the discovery of rare resources. This algorithm also aids in analyzing customer behavior and potentially increasing sales [23]. The game simplifies and visually explains the principles of the association rule learning algorithm.

The SDK is a crucial component of our game design. Analyzing the hidden clauses and rhetoric in user agreements across five major apps revealed that platforms channel user data into an abyss post-agreement signing. This data undergoes undisclosed processing and is subsequently shared. This metaphor of journeying through wormholes is utilized in the game to vividly depict the sharing and connections involving third-party SDKs, enhancing the interactive elements of our gamified design.

**Empathy and Expression.** Leaving User Footprints: After the narrative concludes, an interactive interface will appear. Users can leave their emotional responses to the project and thoughts on the definition of privacy boundaries. They are also encouraged to provide suggestions for improvement. Additionally, users can interact with others who have left comments.

### 4.2 Visual Design

**Fig. 3.** shows the different scenes of the game.

**Interstellar Matter and Planets.** User Privacy Data Embodiment In the data transmission and processing process, the user acts as the central point of the universe's coordinate system. Other elements' operations and properties change in real-time based on each user click and interaction. Big data incessantly collects user information through pixel tracking, like a hidden observer behind the system [24]. Users who agree to the privacy terms and the operators acting as the third eye or monitor have implicit roles in our game design, each with different interaction states. Users control an avatar navigating web pages, using mouse clicks or keyboard keys, guided by game sounds to advance, thereby completing the process of data acquisition, processing, and resulting outcomes.

Due to the profound themes of 'eavesdropping' and privacy data flow, the game design employs a grayscale minimalist style. This style, characterized by clean lines, monochromatic tones, and flat design, effectively highlights the game's core elements while conveying a mysterious atmosphere. It is widely used in graphic design and digital art (see Fig. 3). For character design, we used simple lines and black-and-white contrast to make the characters appear straightforward yet expressive. In environmental design, large areas of solid color and geometric shapes create a simple and abstract world. This grayscale minimalist style aims to provide players with a clear and focused gaming experience, reducing visual distractions and enhancing immersion.

Correspondingly, other elements of the 'eavesdropping process' are treated as interactive objects in different chapters of the game, applying abstract metaphorical treatment and style unification. Preliminary user testing indicates that most players appreciate this artistic style and believe it aligns well with the game's theme and atmosphere.

### 4.3  Testing and Evaluation

To gather feedback from general users, we invited 10 participants (6 females, 4 males, average age = 23, all college students) to experience the game and share their impressions, with an average playtime of 6 min. By observing and recording players' behaviors and feedback, we gained unique insights into how users perceive the flow and usage of personal privacy data across multiple social platforms. All participants reported that the project provided a more intuitive understanding of privacy terms and algorithms. Several participants noted that the experience reminded them of past concerns and experiences.

- P1: "I always thought agreeing to terms was quite amusing. They include a lot of information we don't feel like reading or can't understand, making it impossible to quickly identify any unacceptable clauses. Most people just click agree without seriously studying the terms (like me). Regarding cluster analysis, when I first used TikTok, I thought everyone was the same. I believed most people were nice and didn't encounter any bad actors online until I stumbled upon the concept of an information cocoon."
- P2: "After searching for a skincare product for my mom on one shopping platform, the very next second I opened another shopping platform and received a pushed advertisement for the same skincare product. It made me feel quite anxious."
- P4: "Using various apps often requires excessive permissions, and sometimes you can't use the app without granting them. In such cases, personal privacy isn't protected, and it feels like running naked on the internet every day."

- P5: "I always find out after the fact that I have agreed to share information, which makes me worry that one day my private information will be leaked."

These statements highlight the negative impact these issues have on users. More than half of the participants indicated they would rethink their privacy decisions. Some expressed pessimism about their ability to control privacy settings and hoped for the right to negotiate with platforms.

Users made the following suggestions for "Wormhole Whisper" after their experience: Provide information on privacy protection measures. Add game tasks to enhance the sense of objectives. And offer the game as a mini-program so players can share it on their social networks to expand its influence. Most participants emphasized that the game helped them understand the process of privacy data transmission and potential methods for protecting personal data.

Additionally, several suggestions were made regarding privacy terms. Participants recommended that the service agreements displayed when opening the application be simplified and clearer, showing only the necessary conditions for the main functions, with additional features discussed later. They also suggested incorporating design aids such as icons and comics in the lengthy agreements to aid understanding.

## 5   Discussion and Reflection

This design study found that user privacy data policies cause significant cognitive fatigue when users first engage with a service, and there are also issues with the hidden involvement of SDKs and algorithms. Building on Arunesh et al.'s [25] classification, the study examined the growing prevalence of 'dark pattern' interfaces, which are misleading and manipulative design elements.

The research revealed that platforms, through service agreements, require users to provide privacy information such as phone numbers, location, and photo albums, as well as collect and process data like search records, network status, and clipboard content. This practice exploits the belief that some personal data is not important and not traditionally associated with 'privacy'. Consequently, many users remain unaware of how big data can use seemingly insignificant information to create detailed user profiles. This raises the question of whether these practices have already encroached on the privacy boundaries users believed were intact. These issues not only highlight the challenges in defining privacy data when platforms use algorithms but also trigger negative emotions in users while using the platform.

This design exploration begins by analyzing metadata from the perspective of the general user, followed by a deconstruction of algorithmic mechanisms at a fundamental level. To convey this information vividly and understandably, the project uses wormholes and planets as metaphors within a poetically designed game process. Testing indicates that the game serves as an engaging and accessible communication tool, effectively addressing the complex topic of privacy data algorithms from a design perspective. The research team is now exploring ways to expand these outcomes. The discussion has underscored the importance of enhancing user experience by incorporating gamified elements such as roles, scenes, and sound effects. This approach not only maximizes user immersion but also accurately visualizes and reproduces the flow and processing of user data. Future initiatives aim to conduct more in-depth data and textual analyses and to engage a broader user base in discussions about data privacy on social media platforms.

## 6 Conclusion

This paper presents an innovative approach to creating lightweight games that blend poetic metaphors with algorithmic analysis to illuminate data privacy issues. By gamifying the concept of data 'eavesdropping', the method aims to heighten user awareness of how their information is transmitted and transformed on social media platforms. The research process involved analyzing social media discussions, developing revealing game mechanics, and conducting user evaluations. Key findings highlight users' unease with data collection practices and the effectiveness of metaphors like a 'cosmic wormhole' in enhancing understanding of complex algorithmic processes. This gamified approach seeks to broaden public engagement with data privacy issues beyond professional circles, encouraging users to reconsider their digital footprint and personal data privacy.

**Acknowledgments.** This work was supported by the Talent Fund of Beijing Jiaotong University (Grant No. 2023XKRCW002).

## References

1. Brudy F, Ledo D, Greenberg S, et al.: Is anyone looking? Mitigating shoulder surfing on public displays through awareness and protection. In: Proceedings of The International Symposium on Pervasive Displays, pp. 1–6 (2014)
2. Jung, F., von Holdt, K., Krüger, R., et al.: I do. do i?–understanding user perspectives on the privacy paradox. In: Proceedings of the 25th International Academic Mindtrek Conference, pp. 268–277 (2022)
3. Zhou, H., Tearo, K., Waje, A., et al.: Enhancing mobile content privacy with proxemics aware notifications and protection. In: Proceedings of the 2016 CHI Conference on Human Factors in Computing Systems, pp. 1362–1373 (2016)
4. Barth, S., De Jong, M.D.T.: The privacy paradox–investigating discrepancies between expressed privacy concerns and actual online behavior–a systematic literature review. Telematics Inform. **34**(7), 1038–1058 (2017)
5. Luger, E., Moran, S., Rodden, T.: Consent for all: revealing the hidden complexity of terms and conditions. In: Proceedings of the SIGCHI conference on Human factors in computing systems, pp. 2687–2696 (2013)
6. Dimova, Y., Kode, M., Kalantari, S., et al.: From privacy policies to privacy threats: a case study in policy-based threat modeling. In: Proceedings of the 22nd Workshop on Privacy in the Electronic Society, pp. 17–29 (2023)
7. Iacovides, I., Cox, A.L.: Moving beyond fun: evaluating serious experience in digital games. In: Proceedings of the 33rd Annual ACM Conference on Human Factors in Computing Systems, pp. 2245–2254 (2015)
8. Pilling, F., Stead, M., Gradinar, A.: The prometheus terminal: worlding games for the adoption of sustainable datafication and cybersecurity practices. In: Cumulus Conference Proceedings Detroit: Design for Adaptation (2022)

9. Hosseini, M.B., Breaux, T.D., Slavin, R., et al.: Analyzing privacy policies through syntax-driven semantic analysis of information types. Inf. Softw. Technol. **138**, 106608 (2021)
10. Lovato, J.L., Allard, A., Harp, R., et al.: Limits of individual consent and models of distributed consent in online social networks. In: Proceedings of the 2022 ACM Conference on Fairness, Accountability, and Transparency, pp. 2251–2262 (2022)
11. Weinshel, B., Wei, M., Mondal, M., et al.: Oh, the places you′ve been! User reactions to longitudinal transparency about third-party web tracking and inferenc-ing. In: Proceedings of the 2019 ACM SIGSAC Conference on Computer and Communications Security, pp. 149–166 (2019)
12. Frik, A., Kim, J., Sanchez, J.R., et al.: Users' expectations about and use of smartphone privacy and security settings. In: Proceedings of the 2022 CHI Conference on Human Factors in Computing Systems, pp. 1–24 (2022)
13. Emami-Naeini, P., Dixon, H., Agarwal, Y., et al.: Exploring how privacy and security factor into IoT device purchase behaviour. In: Proceedings of the 2019 CHI Conference on Human Factors in Computing Systems, pp. 1–12 (2019)
14. Altman, I.: Privacy regulation: culturally universal or culturally specific? J. Soc. Issues **33**(3), 66–84 (1977)
15. Dallas, F.I.: FuturePerfect: students envisioning the future. Lang. Arts J. Michigan **25**(1), 5 (2009)
16. Mekler, E.D., Iacovides, I., Bopp, J.A.: A game that makes you question... exploring the role of reflection for the player experience. In: Proceedings of the 2018 Annual Symposium on Computer-human Interaction in Play, pp. 315–327 (2018)
17. Pilling, F., Stead, M., Gradinar, A.: The prometheus terminal: worlding games for the adoption of sustainable datafication and cybersecurity practices. Cumulus Detroit: Des. Adapt. (2022)
18. Shoukry, L., Göbel, S., Steinmetz, R.: Learning analytics and serious games: trends and considerations. In: Proceedings of the 2014 ACM International Workshop on Serious Games, pp. 21–26 (2014)
19. Bogost, I.: Persuasive games: the expressive power of videogames. Mit Press (2010)
20. Zingale, S.: Infopoesia: l'enunciazione poetica dei dati. una sperimentazione fra arte e design della comunicazione. E/C **30**, 1–8 (2020)
21. Xu, D., Tian, Y.: A comprehensive survey of clustering algorithms. Ann. Data Sci. **2**, 165–193 (2015)
22. Cao, C., Ni, Q., Zhai, Y.: An improved collaborative filtering recommendation algorithm based on community detection in social networks. In: Proceedings of the 2015 Annual Conference on Genetic and Evolutionary Computation, pp. 1–8 (2015)
23. Kaur, M., Kang, S.: Market basket analysis: identify the changing trends of market data using association rule mining. Procedia Comput. Sci. **85**, 78–85 (2016)
24. Englehardt, S., Narayanan, A.: Online tracking: a 1-million-site measurement and analy-sis. In: Proceedings of the 2016 ACM SIGSAC Conference on Computer and Communications Security, pp. 1388–1401 (2016)
25. Mathur, A., Kshirsagar, M., Mayer, J.: What makes a dark pattern... dark? design attributes, normative considerations and measurement methods. In: Proceedings of the 2021 CHI Conference on Human Factors in Computing Systems, pp. 1–18 (2021)

# Understanding and Fighting Scams: Media, Language, Appeals and Effects

Shuhua Zhou[1], Xiao Fan Liu[1], Fiona Fui-Hoon Nah[1(✉)], Simon Harrison[1],
Xinzhi Zhang[1], Shanshan Zhen[1], Dannii Yeung[1], Janet Hui-wen Hsiao[2], Ray LC[1],
Antoni B. Chan[1], Xiaohui Wang[1], Crystal Li Jiang[1], Fen Lin[1], Jixing Li[1],
Andus Wing-Kuen Wong[1], Leanne Lai-Hang Chan[1], Bert George[1], and Ping Li[3]

[1] City University of Hong Kong, Kowloon Tong, Kowloon, Hong Kong SAR
{shuhzhou,xf.liu,simon.harrison,xinzhi.zhang,shanshan.zhen,
dannii.yeung,ray.lc,abchan,xiaohui.wang,crystal.jiang,fenlin,
jixingli,andus.wong,leanne.chan,brgeorge}@cityu.edu.hk,
fionanah@smu.edu.sg
[2] Hong Kong University of Science and Technology, Clear Water Bay, Kowloon, Hong Kong
SAR
jhhsiao@ust.hk
[3] Hong Kong Polytechnic University, Hung Hom, Kowloon, Hong Kong SAR
ping2.li@polyu.edu.hk

**Abstract.** Scams are fraudulent activities aiming to deceive individuals into relinquishing money, property, or rights, and they have proliferated in the context of widespread misinformation and disinformation. In this paper, we propose strategies and a research plan to address key questions about the exploitation of new communication technologies by scammers, the prevalence and nature of different scam types, and the language characteristics and appeals used in scamming content. We aim to develop a comprehensive taxonomy of scams and identify factors that contribute to their persuasiveness. Additionally, we propose the use of advanced technologies, including artificial intelligence, physiological measures, and brain mapping, to detect, investigate, and combat scams. The findings will inform the creation of educational resources and interventions, including databases, short videos, an online repository for crowdsourcing scam cases, community training programs, and online courses aimed at improving scam detection and prevention. By leveraging interdisciplinary expertise, this study seeks to develop a multifaceted approach to mitigate the impact of scams and foster a more informed and resilient public.

**Keywords:** Scams · Media · Language · Appeals · Affordances · Taxonomy · Neural Correlates · Physiological Measures

## 1 Introduction

Scams refer to fraudulent or deceptive acts to trick individuals into giving away their money, property, or legal rights. Scams have increased in the epidemic of misinformation and disinformation. They present an unprecedented threat to vulnerable people, fostering

A. Marcus et al. (Eds.): HCII 2024, LNCS 15380, pp. 392–408, 2025.
https://doi.org/10.1007/978-3-031-76821-7_27

a new social reality based on inauthenticity [1]. These crosscurrents not only have the potential to confuse on a mass scale but to undermine trust in human relationships and in society. In this chaotic environment, vulnerable populations, such as the elderly and the young, arguably stand the most to lose their finances and well-being. In this paper, we outline a proposal with the goal of addressing the following questions: **How do scammers exploit the affordances of new communication technologies to reach their targets? What are the most popular scams? What are the most common appeals? What are the language characteristics of scamming content? What can we do to help citizens fight scams?**

To address these questions, we propose to understand how scammers use various media to reach people, how they use different media to engage in various fraudulent activities, and which medium is most attractive to what kinds of scams. We also want to delineate and categorize scams in terms of their range, appeals, and their effects on victims. Necessarily, we will identify the most popular scam appeals. We want to look at the "language" characteristics of scams to understand how they relate to persuasive effects, with these "languages" spanning sophisticated lexico-grammatical wordings and rhetorical strategies as well as real-time dynamics of speech and gesture. We also want to document these effects via multiple means, including human responses, physiological data, and brain mapping to facilitate detection.

Our proposal will deliver five product-based interventions co-created with five different kinds of communities. The deliverables are: (1) We will build a database with a taxonomy of scams. (2) To reach vulnerable populations, especially older adults who often have lower social support, financial literacy, and awareness of detecting a scam risk, we will develop short videos and documentaries of typical cases. (3) We will develop an online repository where research fellows, journalists, and victims can crowdsource with community members to build a rich set of cases for training artificial intelligence (AI) to help analyze, detect, and find solutions for scams. (4) We will train community intermediaries to teach the vulnerable and other community information agents how to avoid scams. In particular, we want to establish a channel of communication and policy advising to the authorities of the police forces and the publicity department of governments, starting from the Guangdong-Hong Kong-Macau Great Bay Area. (5) We will develop online courses for all ages with information on how to detect scams and identify fraudulent information.

We work in partnership with a team of interdisciplinary researchers with expertise in areas that range from computer science to humanities. The video shorts, database, repository, and online courses will serve as discussion anchors in the facilitation of fighting scams. Our computational team is developing a centralized dashboard to capture scam activities. Our goals are to analyze the problems and solutions associated with scams with multi-pronged approaches and ignite a sense of community ownership over the solutions while providing the tools to counteract the malevolent scams so ubiquitous today.

Our project will cover the following areas:

(i) Analysis of medium affordances and scam dissemination in each medium;
(ii) Development of a scam taxonomy;

(iii) An in-depth study of language (verbal) and gesture (non-verbal) characteristics of scams;

(iv) A delineation of scam appeals;

(v) Using technology (e.g., AI and generative AI) to help or hinder scam dissemination as well as detect, alert, and report scams;

(vi) Using neural correlates and physiological measures to study the appeals and effects of scams;

(vii) Deliverables to help citizens fight scams.

In the subsequent sections, we will discuss our plans for each area of study.

## 2 Analysis of Medium Affordances

Different media have different attributes and "affordances," or how users perceive what they can do with these attributes or what these attributes can do to them, in Gibson's [2] conceptualization. Gibson [2] first proposed the concept of affordances to understand the relationship between an animal and its environment. Norman [3, p. 9] further defined the concept as "the perceived and actual properties of the thing, primarily those fundamental properties that determine just how the thing could possibly be used." When it comes to media, we are thinking more about the technological affordances of each medium. For example, a phone has the affordance of voice communication, and email has the textual affordance, whereas social media and messaging apps provide scammers with direct and often anonymous access to potential victims. These platforms enable the mass dissemination of fraudulent messages with minimal effort and cost. The anonymity and pseudonymity afforded by the Internet allow individuals to conceal their identities, thereby lowering the risk of immediate detection and thus, facilitating fraudulent activities. Furthermore, technology facilitates global connectivity, enabling scammers to target victims worldwide, thus increasing the pool of potential victims and complicating law enforcement efforts to track and apprehend perpetrators across different jurisdictions. Automation and scalability further enhance the effectiveness of scams, as automated tools and bots can conduct large-scale phishing attacks, exponentially increasing the chances of success.

In Gibson's thinking, affordances are more aptly described as the perceived action potential of technological affordances, such as social affordances and psychological affordances enabled by media technology. For example, scammers exploit social norms and behaviors through social engineering techniques such as impersonation, authority exploitation, and manipulation of social trust. For instance, posing as a trusted figure or organization can lend credibility to a scam. Social media platforms and online communities amplify the spread of scams through network effects, allowing scammers to disseminate false information rapidly and reach large groups of people.

In terms of psychological affordances, scammers leverage cognitive biases related to trust, reciprocity, and fear to manipulate victims. Tactics that create a sense of urgency or scarcity exploit the fear of missing out (FOMO), compelling individuals to act quickly without thorough scrutiny. Emotional manipulation is another common strategy, with scams often targeting emotional vulnerabilities. For example, romance scams prey on individuals seeking companionship, exploiting their emotional investment to extract money or personal information. Additionally, scammers take advantage of information asymmetry, presenting themselves as experts or insiders to create an imbalance of information that can mislead and manipulate the victim.

We plan to develop a comprehensive list of affordances in each medium, whether it is print, audio, visual, interpersonal, or virtual, so we have a better idea of what medium lends itself to what kind of scam appeals, and how we can counteract them.

## 3 Development of a Scam Taxonomy

Scams have existed for millennia, with evidence of fraud documented as far back as ancient Greece and Rome. Before the Industrial Revolution, individuals engaged in false advertising and the sale of fake or counterfeit goods, fake relics, and miracle cures. These early scams were characterized by the exploitation of the lack of consumer knowledge and regulatory oversight, many of them have lived into the modern world with a renewed form. The 20th century saw the rise of new types of scams, reflecting the technological advancements and social changes of the time. The Ponzi scheme promised high returns on investments but led to significant financial losses for many. The rise of the telephone led to the evolution of telemarketing frauds, where con artists would solicit money under false pretenses. The Internet introduced new types of phishing scams. These scams involved sending emails purporting to be from legitimate companies to steal personal information or promising large sums of money in exchange for an upfront fee. On e-commerce platforms, buyers or sellers would deceive others regarding the quality or existence of goods. The rise of social media in the 21st century brought about new forms of social engineering scams. Cryptocurrency scams recently emerged with fake exchanges and fraudulent investment schemes. Impersonation scams (where scammers impersonate government officials, tech support, or loved ones) extract information or money from the victims. Online social platforms have become tools for scammers to perpetrate romance scams and fake giveaways.

From an initial study based on Hong Kong social media data, we generated Table 1 which briefly summarizes the large language model (LLM)-identified scam categories and their descriptions. These categories include financial scams, lottery and prize scams, health scams, e-commerce and product scams, employment scams, romance and relationship scams, phishing and identity thefts, phone and cold calling scams, crowdsourcing and charity scams, and others. LLMs identified scams that exploit people's vulnerabilities, including economic safety, desire for romance, and greed, as well as people's trust and goodwill. LLMs are not only capable of making logical inferences, but they can also process multimodal data [4, 5], and hence, they are a powerful tool for assisting with this project [6, 7]. Our plan is to develop a comprehensive list of the different types of scams and their appeals and vulnerabilities as the project develops.

## 4 An In-depth Study of Language (Verbal) and Gesture (Non-Verbal) Characteristics of Scams

Linguistic features play a crucial role in persuasive communication, including scams whose ultimate goal is to deceive others. We want to study these features so we can gain insights into the specific strategies and techniques used to influence attitudes, beliefs,

**Table 1.** Scam categories and descriptions.

| Categories | Description |
|---|---|
| Financial scams | Scams involving deceptive financial schemes such as fake investments, cryptocurrency fraud, and falsified loan applications |
| Lottery and prize scams | Scams requesting fees for non-existent lottery or prize winnings |
| Health and COVID-19 related scams | Scams exploiting health directives and COVID-19 concerns to obtain personal information |
| E-commerce and product scams | Scams involving fake online stores, undelivered products, non-refund policies, and price manipulation |
| Employment scams | Fake job listings designed to collect fees and personal information from job seekers |
| Romance and relationship scams | Manipulation of online relationships to extract money from victims |
| Phishing and identity thefts | Scams involving deceptive emails, fake ads, and phishing attempts to steal personal information |
| Phone and cold calling scams | Scams involving the impersonation of officials or family members, often through phone calls, to extract money or personal details |
| Crowdfunding and charity scams | Misleading fundraising campaigns that exploit emotional narratives to solicit donations |
| Miscellaneous scams | Various other scams, including fake tickets, fake courier calls, begging scams, QR code scams, fake payment confirmations, and inheritance scams |

and behaviors. This knowledge helps us understand how scam messages are constructed and how they function to achieve their intended goals.

Preliminary findings by our research team using LLMs have uncovered several linguistic attributes in scams including the use of rhetorical questions, which help engage users and prompt them to consider a particular point or idea; the use of repetition of key phrases, slogans, or ideas, which can enhance memorability and reinforce scam messages; the use of emotional language to evoke specific feelings or reactions in users; the use of power words and phrases such as success, urgency, exclusivity, limited offer, exclusive access, and guaranteed returns to impose a strong impact; the use of a command language for a clear and compelling call-to-action, such as "buy now," "sign up today," or "donate now"; and the use of framing language including positive framing that emphasizing benefits or negative framing that highlights risks or consequences in the hope of shaping people's perception and response to the scams.

Specifically, we want to understand which linguistic elements are more prevalent in what kinds of scams, and which are more persuasive. These linguistic features also provide a basis for us to get to the second stage of our investigation by delving into the cognitive processes underlying scam persuasion, in which we will be examining language choices, rhetorical devices, and scam appeals so as to uncover how individuals process and respond to scam messages.

For a project aiming to relate scams with language, the notion of 'body language' naturally comes to mind, along with oft-cited statistics concerning the relative distribution of information across verbal and nonverbal communication. The idea that people communicate their 'real' or 'true' thoughts, intentions, and feelings not through verbal but through nonverbal means is the topic of many TED Talks, newspaper headlines, best-selling books, and even Netflix series (c.f., *Lie to Me*). While this idea has become somewhat inauthentic with expertise in 'deception detection' being seriously doubted if not mocked in popular culture [8], these ideas originate in the systematic observations of post-war American behavioral scientists (e.g., [9–11]) and subsequent social psychological experimentation (e.g., [12, 13]). For a project relating language with scams, an important reference point will be the academic discipline of Nonverbal Communication [14]. Given the doubting of deception detection becoming apparent in mainstream media and mass paperback non-fiction (cf., Malcolm Gladwell's *Talking to Strangers*) [15], it could be equally interesting to retrace the development of portrayals of deception and its expertise in popular culture. This may help to uncover changing perceptions of deception in the public imagination, which may reveal mismatches that lead people to fall trap to scams.

We must also recognize that the notion of 'nonverbal communication' – historically underpinned by models of communication as signal-sending and third-person experimental paradigms [14] – might offer only a limited picture of the (bodily) language of scams. Our project places scam language in the context of new participatory communication technologies, screen cultures, and futuristic AI, which operate less like machines sending and receiving signals but as distributed dynamical systems within which people are always already enmeshed and entangled. Scams may go unnoticed during the pre- and in-scam stages, as they do not initially stand out from the background of ongoing digital noise. We need to draw on innovative ways that aspects of communication traditionally known as 'nonverbal' or 'bodily' and 'embodied' are being conceptualized, approached, and studied across diverse academic fields and intellectual traditions today [8].

Consider that the field of Gesture Studies refers to "a coherent field of research with its own identity dedicated to the study of gesture's integration with language and communication" [16, p. 1] (for a recent review, see contributions to Cienki [17]). Here we find a range of empirical and philosophical approaches for characterizing relations of bodies and language in ways that are highly sensitive to the contextualized bodily perceiving and experiencing of scams in dynamic situations of real-time 'embodied communication' [18] or 'participatory sense-making' [19], including when mediated by screens and video media or involving human-computer interaction. An important resource will be studies of 'co-speech gesture' [20–22] and the development of validated frameworks for the detailed multi-level or dimensionalized description of speech and gesture as 'multimodal' [23–26] and 'multiscalar' [27, 28].

More specifically, a number of different frameworks can be explored for their suitability for the analysis of the characteristics, features, and patterns of scams. For example, the relation between speech and gesture can be analyzed following McNeill [22, 29] along psycholinguistic dimensions of 'iconicity', 'metaphoricity', 'deixis', 'beats' and 'cohesion', which may help to understand individual psycholinguistic processes of embodied scam language perception and production. Kendon's [20] studies of naturally-occurring social interaction and definitions of utterance as 'visible bodily action' can shift perspective from cognition to context. Kendon's [20] descriptions of gestures with interactive and pragmatic functions seem particularly relevant to scams, demonstrating that people "may show, through visible bodily actions, that they are asking a question, making a plea, proposing a hypothesis, doubting the word of another, denying something or indicating agreement about it" (p.1). These functions lead to relatively stabilized form-meaning units called 'recurrent gestures' that appear across diverse speakers and contexts [30, 31].

The lived experience of scams in and through language may be approached as a form of distributed 'languaging', with multiscalar understandings of language that span sophisticated lexico-grammatical wordings all the way to real-time material bodily dynamics of gesturing, breathing, voicing, and feeling [27, 32]. In one line of research, this sense-making perspective has shed light on the dynamics through which skilled practitioners help their audience to navigate a technical environment with which they are unfamiliar, as has been shown in the case of persuasive science communication [33] and office hour academic discussions in higher education [34]. In another line, specific linguistic features can be explored from this perspective to reveal the resonant energies of vocal fold vibration (prosodic) and coordinated bodily movements from which they arise and source their meaning/feeling, as has been shown for negation [28]. We aim to identify which linguistic notions and processes are particularly relevant to scams, which we further predict will vary across Hong Kong's many typologically distinct languages (not least English and Cantonese).

Going beyond the social psychology of 'nonverbal communication' and increasingly skeptical popular representations of 'deception detection', our analyses from these different gesture studies perspectives will help to characterize the language of scams as appropriate for the contemporary scamming situation. The findings can inform different parts of the project, such as by informing the design of experiments aiming to understand how the language of scams (as embodied, ecological phenomena) relate to persuasive effects via multiple neuroscientific means, which may include psycholinguistic perception experiments and behavioral response studies along with physiological and neurological data (EEG, ERP, fMRI). Similarly, understanding changing perceptions in the public imagination of scams and scam language will feed into our development of the screenplay for short videos, documentaries, and online courses intended as outcomes.

## 5   A Delineation of Scam Appeals

Scams are messages that are intended to deceive people, for example, for financial gains and emotional exploitation. They can take the forms of phone calls, phishing, emails, impersonation, etc. [35]. In order to persuade, scammers often resort to appeals.

In the perspective of the socio-psychological approach of communication persuasion, appeals are defined as all informative or emotional cues utilized in promotional messages to attract message receivers' interest and attention, thereby steering their appraisals toward the message senders as well as the products during the promotion [36]. Previous research on the effectiveness of message appeals, such as in advertising, public relations, health promotion, and political campaigns, offers several viable theoretical frameworks to explain when and why scam messages may affect victims' attitudes, for example, to believe the identity depicted by the scammer as credible, or to believe that the situation offered by the scammers as viable, and even follow the instructions of the scammers.

For a scam to work, a crucial step is to make the message receivers (the victims) believe the scammer's identity and credibility. When evaluating credibility, the message receivers will rely on available cues in their judgment [37], especially message communication styles. The literature shows that messages written in different styles, despite having similar substantive content, may exert different attitudinal and behavioral effects [38]. The heuristic–systematic model maintains that people engage in two different routes of information processing: *heuristic* (i.e., judgments based on less sophisticated rules) and *systematic* (i.e., judgments based on logical and systematic reasoning) [39, 40]. Affective messages, such as expressions related to preferences, attitudes, or emotions, may trigger heuristic processing because they are emotionally provocative. Rational messages, such as factual information that can be verified, may trigger systematic processing to shift focus to focal issues. A scammer may try to trigger heuristic processing as people will rely on the cognitive shortcut to proceed with the message without sophisticated considerations [41].

Among several message appeals, almost all scam attacks use basic human needs and desires to manipulate victims, including fear and anxiety [35]. Fear appeal is the most common appeal in scams. As one of the basic human emotions, fear occurs following the appraisal of a "threatening situation or stimulus with or without an individual's conscious intention or awareness" [42, p. 423]. When fear is aroused, people are motivated to seek ways to eliminate such threatening situations, and they are more susceptible to following the scammers' instructions – from disclosing their personal sensitive information to performing the money transactions – as they believe doing so will help them to control the situation. Such a process is articulated in the Extended Parallel Processing Model (EPPM) [43]. The EPPM explicates how fear appeals messages could persuade people, i.e., the message senders include threats to attract message receivers' attention, alerting them to threats and hazards before offering suggestions to get rid of these threats. In sum, the message is persuasive by combining threats and solutions for them [42–44].

A list of six appeals identified in scam attacks is compiled by Muscanell, Guadagno, and Murphy [45]. These six appeals are (1) authority (the scammers act like an authority by impersonating big brands or the ruling authority), (2) likability (pretending to be likable, caring, and sincere); (3) offering rewards (providing incentives for complying); (4) fear (make the message receivers anxious); (5) urgency (creating a need for speedy actions); (6) social proof (providing an illusion that other people have already complied). In an experiment conducted in the US to test the effects of these appeals, Baryshevtsev and McGlynn [46] found that, among all the six appeals, only likability and authority appeals made phishing messages more credible. The findings suggest that people follow the instructions of an impersonated powerful elite.

The above findings also suggest that message appeals identified in persuasion studies offer a viable theoretical route for combating scams. Our plan is to identify prevalent appeals in scams and map them against the types of scams and media affordances, so that we have a clear picture of what medium is susceptible to what appeals, and what kinds of scams are likely to utilize what kind of appeals and media affordances to exploit human weaknesses, cognitively or emotionally. Armed with this knowledge, more education and literacy programs can be developed. Vulnerable populations and others can be educated to discern message sources, message features, and message intent before any complying behaviors and before falling victim to scammers. This knowledge can also be used to offer advice and suggest policies to banks, organizations, and government entities.

In addition to traditional appeals studies, we also plan to broaden our approach to human-computer interaction. Works in the social computing literature have looked into the way humans can be influenced for social purpose goals [47], how humans interact with generative AI systems for information retrieval in cooperative tasks [48], how older people are influenced by their children in working with novel technology [49], how online dating relies on properties of voice [50], and online communities for information validation for sign-language users [51]. These works explore the ways humans are influenced by others in online and generative systems, studying what humans say online, prototyping the interactions in these systems that exacerbate or remediate misinformation, and the way that other humans and generative systems differentially affect the user in collaborative online tasks [52]. Furthermore, scams disproportionly affect particularly vulnerable groups. In studies of older adult communities and their use of digital technology, studies have highlighted misinformation and scam appeal as particular areas of danger.

## 6 Using Technology to Help or Hinder Scam Dissemination, and Identify, Alert, and Report Scams

In addition to understanding scam attributes, we will also actively leverage technology. We identify appropriate advances that can be potentially effective during the three stages of anti-scamming: "pre-incident prevention, real-time monitoring and alerting, and post-incident response." In the **pre-incident stage**, we will analyze the psychology of fraudsters, and monitor the risks to potential victims from various sources, including the policy forces, media, and social media. We will maintain and share all fraud-related data, and develop effective publicity strategies. By employing targeted campaigns and leveraging social media trends, we aim to raise public awareness about fraud prevention. In the **real-time monitoring and alerting stage**, we will use AI algorithms and models to detect suspicious activities in social media and online forums. In the **post-incident response stage**, we will explore AI applications to identify fraudulent activities in financial payment channels, i.e., blockchain.

We will leverage LLMs to analyze social media, police fraud case records, as well as news media databases, such as GDELT, ProQuest, and Nexus, in real time to identify new scams and summarize their characteristics. Focusing on Hong Kong as an example, we periodically search all public posts containing words related to scams from the ten largest forums in Hong Kong, including Hong Kong Discuss and BabyKingdom. We then use GPT-4o to read the posts and summarize the scams. We can also fine-tune GPT to classify scam messages and isolate them from normal messages, and use explainable AI (XAI) to uncover the reasons for the AI's predictions. Considering that LLMs have a limited context length, our plan is to only feed chunks of social media data to the model and ask the model to supplement existing findings with any new information. In fact, some groundwork has been done, with preliminary results reflected in the current paper. Technology can also help us design promotion materials using AI by leveraging various persuasion techniques or even borrowing the techniques from scams themselves.

How misinformation propagates and systems can be created to reduce such propagation or help users recognize misinformation is a prominent area of research. The methodologies for both the observation study component and the interactive system design component are utilized by our lab on a daily purpose. The former consists of social computing strategies such as in-depth interviews, online data scraping, observational studies, and large-scale surveys. The latter has been exemplified by work in creating web interfaces, prototyping interactions, game interfaces, systems design, etc. In the case of the study of scams, these methods employed by our lab would lead to (1) analyzing the way users interpret their emails and website content, creating different manipulations on the information given (such as linguistic voicing and generative AI use) and measuring the responses of users to these different conditions, and (2) prototyping plugins, filters, and web applications that alert users to suspicious information, nudge users to consider validating information, provide resources in relation to the email of interest using generative AI, filtering information based on content using generative AI, etc. The systems investigations from the second part would follow the systematic investigation in the first part to identify the needs of users based on the susceptibility to misinformation in the scams identified, measuring the way users differentially perceive information in scams that differ in their linguistic and conceptual appeals.

## 7 Using Neural Correlates and Physiological Measures to Study the Appeals and Effects of Scams

It is important that we try to understand scams, their domains of existence, their channels of dissemination, their taxonomy, their verbal and nonverbal characteristics, and their appeals. We can identify them and fend them off using state-of-the-art technology. We will be remiss, however, if we do not understand how humans process them. Hence, we are proposing to combine knowledge of cognitive science, psychology, and neuroscience to get into the blackbox of scam processing.

In the previous sections, we have demonstrated that victims who fall prey to scams usually fail to recognize deception, leading them to develop maladaptive trust in the scammers and ultimately make misguided decisions. Scammers employ various psychological appeals to manipulate their targets, such as exploiting a sense of urgency, enticing rewards, and exploiting cognitive biases such as heuristics [53].

Both detecting others' intention to deceive and determining the trustworthiness of the communicator engage the mentalizing network, which is responsible for understanding and interpreting the thoughts, intentions, beliefs, and emotions of oneself and others [54]. Upon participants' recognition of a fictional character telling a lie, distinct activations in the mentalizing network emerged, specifically in the left middle frontal gyrus, bilateral temporoparietal junction, and right superior temporal sulcus (STS) [55]. Similarly, when individuals engage in passive observation of deceptive advertisements, notable activations are observed in the precuneus and superior STS regions, as opposed to when they read advertisements perceived as believable [56]. However, humans' natural ability to detect deception is mediocre. Research showed that participants could distinguish lies from the truth with only above-chance accuracy in experimental conditions where participants were instructed explicitly to detect a lie [57], and the ability to detect deception does not vary greatly from person to person [58]. The detection of deception tends to be particularly challenging in situations where deception is unexpected, as humans have a natural inclination to trust and believe in others unless specific triggers such as logical inconsistencies, contradictions with prior knowledge, or arousing suspicions and doubts are present [59].

Despite potential suspicions that may arise during interactions with scammers, victims can still be persuaded to alter their attitudes and comply with the scammers' appeals. The decision of whether or not to succumb to the influence of others is believed to be influenced by subjective valuation [60]. The reward network, primarily comprising the ventromedial prefrontal cortex and striatum, integrates information related to potential gains, losses, risks, and uncertainties to calculate the potential value of a decision. Additionally, the reward structure tracks the differences between one's expected outcome and actual outcomes, and positive prediction error leads to reinforcement of the behavior [61]. Individuals with maladaptive reward anticipation and response, for instance, higher reactivity towards prospective substantial rewards, are more vulnerable to scams [62]. Younger people are more likely to fall for investment scams due to their higher risk tolerance, susceptibility to persuasion, and lower emotional intelligence [63]. Older adults are also associated with higher scam susceptibility [64]. According to Samanez-Larkin and Knutson [65], older adults may exhibit altered value assessment processes, as they tend to report reduced negative affect and show decreased activity in the anterior insula compared to younger adults when anticipating loss. Furthermore, emerging evidence suggests that individuals with Alzheimer's disease may experience disruptions in the neural connectivity between the default mode network and other brain regions involved in effectively perceiving scams. This disruption could potentially compromise their ability to assess risks, make value judgments, and engage in effective learning [66]. Our plan is to isolate some of the prevalent scam appeals, and document participants' neural activities and correlates so we can begin to understand the cognitive process of scam processing.

In addition to neural activities, we also plan to use other physiological measures, such as eye movement tracking, pupillometry, electroencephalogram (EEG), electrocardiogram (ECG), and electromyography (EMG) to study the effects of different scam appeals. These objective measures, in combination with self-reports, will allow us to study the cognitive, affective, and attitudinal effects of scam appeals reliably and accurately. For example, heart rate variability (HRV) is a commonly used psychophysiological measure to measure cognitive attention, cognitive effort, and arousal, while ECG can be used to help measure attention and orienting responses. EMG can help us understand attitudes, perceptions, and effects of scams. Specifically, facial EMG is a very commonly used psychophysiological measure to index the attitude and perception of emotional experiences. The most common facial EMG involves measuring the zygomatic muscle, corrugator, and post auricular (PA) muscles. The zygomatic muscle can be measured as an indicator of positive emotional experiences (in some studies it also appears to be connected with arousal). The corrugator muscle can be measured as an indicator of negative or unpleasant emotions. PA, a more recently discovered emotional indicator, has been shown to be a valid indicator of appetitive activation. These measures can give us reliable data to validate and measure human responses to scam messages.

For a systematic study, we will categorize scam appeals into cognitive-oriented appeals and emotion-oriented appeals, with the former using authority figures, cognitive heuristics, and factual information to direct the users' understanding and beliefs about scams. The goal of these cognitive appeals is to guide cognitive processes toward a desired conclusion. In contrast, emotion-oriented appeals in scams aim to provoke immediate emotional responses from the users. By tapping into emotions such as fear, sympathy, anger, and joy, these approaches seek to motivate the audience to act based on their emotional state.

Similarly, studies are also planned to examine the linguistic and nonverbal language characteristics in scams and see how people are responding to these scams. For example, guiding language involves using suggestive and leading language to steer the audience toward a particular viewpoint or action. Responding to doubts addresses and counters potential objections or doubts that the audience may have, thereby strengthening the persuasiveness of the message. Repetition and emphasis ensure that the audience retains and prioritizes the intended message by repeating key points and emphasizing critical information. Additionally, non-verbal cues such as body language, facial expressions, and other non-verbal signals such as gestures are employed to reinforce verbal messages and subtly influence the recipient's perceptions and reactions.

## 8    Deliverables to Help Citizens Fight Scams

The findings of the proposed project will generate a comprehensive list of scams and the typical verbal and non-verbal characteristics used in scam appeals. We will study how humans process scams by examining the neural correlates as well as the effects of scams on attention, attitude, affect, perception, and behavior. Such knowledge is essential for designing future promotional materials on anti-scam and fraud prevention. Identification of the cognitive and psychosocial factors predicting scam victimization will be informative to relevant stakeholders (e.g., police officers, Investor and Financial Education Council, and social workers serving the high-risk groups) to develop tailor-made intervention programs to increase the scam awareness of high-risk individuals and their caregivers. Our interdisciplinary research team will also offer deliverables based on these results, including short videos to teach and provide coaching on scam detection, prevention, and solutions. On the education front, we are also planning a course on deception and scams by leveraging our pedagogical resources.

## 9 Conclusion

Scams, characterized by deceptive tactics and designed to defraud individuals of money, property, or legal rights, have become increasingly sophisticated with the advent of new communication technologies. This paper proposes a comprehensive approach to address key questions about the exploitation of these technologies by scammers, the prevalence and nature of different scam types, and the linguistic and non-verbal characteristics that make scamming content persuasive. Our research underscores the urgent need for a multifaceted approach to combat scams, leveraging both advanced technology and comprehensive educational initiatives.

The first step to understanding scams is to see what they are, where they exist, and where they proliferate. We begin by looking at the medium affordances that allow scams to exist, then outline a detailed taxonomy. We also focus on the linguistic and non-verbal features of scams, as well as their appeals to reveal how scammers craft their messages to exploit cognitive biases and emotional vulnerabilities that make scams believable and effective. To empirically test these effects, we propose the isolation of prevalent appeals in a series of physiological and neurological studies. Our study's impact rests with our proposed interventions, including the development of AI-driven detection tools, crowd-sourcing repositories, and community-based educational programs aimed to empower individuals with the knowledge and tools needed to recognize and resist scams.

The interdisciplinary nature of our research, combining expertise from computer science, communication, humanities, social and psychological sciences, cognitive science, engineering, and neuroscience, highlights the complexity of the problem and the necessity of diverse perspectives in crafting effective solutions. Our findings will potentially contribute to the broader understanding of scam dynamics and offer practical applications for improving public awareness and resilience against scams.

As we move forward, our focus will be on implementing the proposed scrutinizations and interventions and continually refining our strategies based on new insights and technological advancements. By fostering collaboration among researchers, policymakers, and community members, we aim to create a robust defense against scams and mitigate their impact on society.

In conclusion, the fight against scams requires a concerted effort to understand the mechanisms of deception and develop innovative solutions to counteract them. Our research provides a foundation for this endeavor, paving the way for a safer, more informed, and resilient public.

**Acknowledgments.** We acknowledge the funding for the brain research cluster from the College of Liberal Arts and Social Sciences at the City University of Hong Kong.

## References

1. Groh, M., Epstein, Z., Firestone, C., Picard, R.: Deepfake detection by human crowds, machines, and machine-informed crowds. Proc. Natl. Acad. Sci. **119**(1), e2110013119 (2022)
2. Gibson, J.J.: The theory of affordances. In: Shaw, R., Bransford, J. (eds.) Perceiving, Acting, and Knowing, pp. 67–82. Lawrence Erlbaum, Hillsdale, NY (1977)

3. Norman, D.A.: The Psychology of Everyday Things. Basic Books, New York, NY (1988)

4. Nah, F.F.H., Cai, J., Zheng, R., Pang, N.: An activity system-based perspective of generative AI: challenges and research directions. AIS Trans. Hum. Comput. Interact. **15**(3), 247–267 (2023)

5. Nah, F.F.H., Zheng, R., Cai, J., Siau, K., Chen, L.: Generative AI and ChatGPT: applictions, challenges, and AI-human collaboration. J. Inf. Technol. Case Appl. Res. **25**(3), 277–304 (2023)

6. Pan, S.L., Nishant, R., Tuunanen, T., Nah, F.F.H.: Literature review in the generative AI era-how to make a compelling contribution. J. Strat. Inf. Syst. **32**(3), 1–4 (2023)

7. Susarla, A., Gopal, R., Thatcher, J.B., Sarker, S.: The Janus effect of generative AI: charting the path for responsible conduct of scholarly activities in information systems. Inf. Syst. Res. **34**(2), 399–408 (2023)

8. Harrison, S.: The Body Language Myth: Understanding Gesture in Language and Communication. Cambridge University Press, Cambridge, UK (in preparation)

9. Birdwhistell, R.L.: Background to kinesics. Rev. Gen. Semant. **13**(1), 10–18 (1955)

10. Birdwhistell, R.L.: Kinesics and Context: Essays on Body Motion Communication. University of Pennsylvania Press, Philadelphia, PA (1970)

11. Hall, E.T.: The Silent Language. Doubleday, Garden City, NY (1959)

12. Mehrabian, A., Ferris, S.R.: Inference of attitudes from nonverbal communication in two channels. J. Consult. Psychol. **31**(3), 248–252 (1967)

13. Mehrabian, A., Wiener, M.: Decoding of inconsistent communications. J. Pers. Soc. Psychol. **6**(1), 109–114 (1967)

14. Knapp, M., Hall, J.A.: Nonverbal Communication in Human Interaction, 7th edn. Cengage Learning, Boston, MA (2009)

15. Gladwell, M.: Talking to Strangers: What We Should Know About the People We Don't Know. Little Brown and Company, Boston, MA (2019)

16. Harrison, S.: Sensing Gesture's Relationality. Review of Jürgen Streeck, Self-Making Man: A Day of Action, Life and Language. Cambridge University Press, Cambridge (2017). https://doi.org/10.1007/s11097-023-09932-z

17. Cienki, A. (ed.): The Cambridge Handbook of Gesture Studies. Cambridge University Press, Cambridge, UK (2024)

18. Streeck, J., Goodwin, C., LeBaron, C. (eds.): Embodied Interaction: Language and Body in the Material World. Cambridge University Press, Cambridge, UK (2011)

19. De Jaegher, H., Di Paolo, E.: Participatory sense-making: an enactive approach to social cognition. Phenomenol. Cogn. Sci. **6**, 485–507 (2007)

20. Kendon, A.: Gesture: Visible Action as Utterance. Cambridge University Press, Cambridge, UK (2004)

21. Kita, S.: The origin of the term, "co-speech gesture" (2022). https://osf.io/preprints/psyarxiv/hdxzg

22. McNeill, D.: Hand and Mind: What Gestures Reveal About Thought. University of Chicago Press, Chicago, IL (1992)

23. Calbris, G.: Elements of Meaning in Gesture. John Benjamins, Amsterdam, The Netherlands (2011)

24. Müller, C., Bressem, J., Ladewig, S.H.: Towards a grammar of gestures: a form-based view. In: Müller, C., Cienki, A., Fricke, E., Ladewig, S.H., McNeill, D., Teßendorf, S. (eds.) Body–Language–Communication. An International Handbook on Multimodality in Human Interaction, vol. 1, pp. 707–733. De Gruyter Mouton, Berlin & Boston (2013)

25. Rohrer, P.L., et al.: The MultiModal MultiDimensional (M3D) Labeling System (2023). https://doi.org/10.17605/OSF.IO/ANKDX

26. Hagoort, P., Özyürek, A.: Extending the architecture of language from a multimodal perspective. Top. Cogn. Sci. (2024) https://doi.org/10.1111/tops.12728

27. Thibault, P.J.: Distributed Languaging, Affective Dynamics, and the Human Ecology. Vol. 1: The Sense-Making Body. Routledge, London, UK (2021)

28. Harrison, S.: "This you may NNNNNEVER have heard before": initial lengthening of pitch accented negative items as vocal-entangled gestures. Lang. Cogn. 1–34 (2024). https://doi.org/10.1017/langcog.2024.26

29. McNeill, D.: Gesture and Thought. University of Chicago Press, Chicago, IL (2005)

30. Harrison, S., Ladewig, S.: Recurrent gestures throughout bodies, languages, and cultural practices. Gesture 20(2), 153–179 (2021)

31. Harrison, S.: The Impulse to Gesture: Where Language, Minds, and Bodies Intersect. Cambridge University Press, Cambridge, UK (2018)

32. Di Paolo, E., Cuffari, E., De Jaegher, H.: Linguistic Bodies: The Continuity Between Life and Language. MIT Press, Cambridge, MA (2018)

33. Harrison, S.: Showing as sense-making in oral presentations: the speech-gesture-slide interplay in TED Talks by Professor Brian Cox. J. Engl. Acad. Purp. 53, 101002 (2021)

34. Shi, D.: First-order sense-making in L2 academic discussions: a distributed view of teacher languaging dynamics in embodied and situated learning context. System 123, 103333 (2024). https://doi.org/10.1016/j.system.2024.103333

35. House, D., Raja, M.K.: Phishing: message appraisal and the exploration of fear and self-confidence. Behav. Inf. Technol. 39(11), 1204–1224 (2020)

36. Kinnear, T.C., Bernhadt, K.L., Krentler, K.A.: Principles of Marketing, 4th edn. Longman, New York, NY (1995)

37. Sundar, S.S.: The MAIN model: a heuristic approach to understanding technology effects on credibility. In: Metzger, M.J., Flanagin, A.J. (eds.) Digital Media, Youth, and Credibility, pp. 73–100. MIT Press, Cambridge, MA (2008)

38. Spottswood, E.L., Walther, J.B., Holmstrom, A.J., Ellison, N.B.: Person-centered emotional support and gender attributions in computer-mediated communication. Hum. Commun. Res. 39(3), 295–316 (2013)

39. Chaiken, S.: Heuristic versus systematic information processing and the use of source versus message cues in persuasion. J. Pers. Soc. Psychol. 39(5), 752–766 (1980)

40. Chaiken, S., Liberman, A., Eagly, A.H.: Heuristic and systematic information processing within and beyond the persuasion context. In: Uleman, J.S., Bargh, J.A. (eds.) Unintended Thought, pp. 212–252. Guilford Press, New York, NY (1989)

41. Vishwanath, A., Harrison, B., Ng, Y.J.: Suspicion, cognition, and automaticity model of phishing susceptibility. Commun. Res. 45(8), 1146–1166 (2018)

42. Witte, K.: Fear as motivator, fear as inhibitor: using the extended parallel process model to explain fear appeal successes and failures. In: Andersen, P.A., Guerrero, L.K. (eds.) Handbook of Communication and Emotion, pp. 423–450. Academic Press, San Diego, CA (1996)

43. Witte, K.: Putting the fear back into fear appeals: the extended parallel process model. Commun. Monogr. 59(4), 329–349 (1992)

44. Tannenbaum, M.B., et al.: Appealing to fear: a meta-analysis of fear appeal effectiveness and theories. Psychol. Bull. 141(6), 1178–1204 (2015)

45. Muscanell, N.L., Guadagno, R.E., Murphy, S.: Weapons of influence misused: a social influence analysis of why people fall prey to internet scams. Soc. Pers. Psychol. Compass 8(7), 388–396 (2014)

46. Baryshevtsev, M., McGlynn, J.: Persuasive appeals predict credibility judgments of phishing messages. Cyberpsychol. Behav. Soc. Netw. 23(5), 297–302 (2020)

47. LC, R., Mizuno, D.: Designing for narrative influence: speculative storytelling for social good in times of public health and climate crises. In: Extended Abstracts of the 2021 CHI Conference on Human Factors in Computing Systems. Association for Computing Machinery, New York, NY, USA, pp. 1–13 (2021)

48. Yang, D., Zhou, Y.P., Zhang, Z., Li, J.J., LC, R.: AI as an active writer: interaction strategies with generated text in human-AI collaborative fiction writing. In: Joint Proceedings of the IUI 2022 Workshops: APEx-UI, HAI-GEN, HEALTHI, HUMANIZE, TExSS, SOCIALIZE. CEUR-WS Team, pp. 56–65 (2022)

49. Tang, X. R., et al.: "I Never Imagined Grandma Could Do So Well with Technology": evolving roles of younger family members in older adults' technology learning and use. In: Proceedings of the ACM on Human-Computer Interaction, vol. 6, issue CSCW2, article 478, pp. 1–29 (2022)

50. Shen, C.X.R., Xu, Y., LC, R., Lu, Z.C.: Seeking soulmate via voice: understanding promises and challenges of online synchronized voice-based mobile dating. In: Proceedings of the CHI Conference on Human Factors in Computing Systems. Association for Computing Machinery, New York, NY, USA, pp. 1–14 (2024)

51. Tang, X.R., Chang, X., Chen, N.R., Ni, Y.J., LC, R., Tong, X.: Community-driven information accessibility: online sign language content creation within d/deaf communities. In: Proceedings of the 2023 CHI Conference on Human Factors in Computing Systems. Association for Computing Machinery, New York, NY, USA, pp. 1–24 (2023)

52. Han, Y.N., Qiu, J.Y., Cheng, J.L., LC, R.: When teams embrace AI: human collaboration strategies in generative prompting in a creative design task. In: Proceedings of the CHI Conference on Human Factors in Computing Systems, Association for Computing Machinery, New York, NY, USA, pp. 1–14 (2024)

53. Lehto, M.R., Nah, F.: Decision-making models and decision support. In: Salvendy, G. (ed.) Handbook of Human Factors and Ergonomics, 3rd edn., pp. 191–242. John Wiley and Sons, Hoboken, New Jersey (2006)

54. Krueger, F., Meyer-Lindenberg, A.: Toward a model of interpersonal trust drawn from neuroscience, psychology, and economics. Trends Neurosci. **42**(2), 92–101 (2019)

55. Harada, T., et al.: Neural correlates of the judgment of lying: a functional magnetic resonance imaging study. Neurosci. Res. **63**(1), 24–34 (2009)

56. Craig, A.W., Loureiro, Y.K., Wood, S., Vendemia, J.M.C.: Suspicious minds: exploring neural processes during exposure to deceptive advertising. J. Mark. Res. **49**(3), 361–372 (2012)

57. Bond, C.F., Jr., DePaulo, B.M.: Accuracy of deception judgments. Pers. Soc. Psychol. Rev. **10**(3), 214–234 (2006)

58. Bond, C.F., Jr., DePaulo, B.M.: Individual differences in judging deception: accuracy and bias. Psychol. Bull. **134**(4), 477–492 (2008)

59. Levine, T.R.: Truth-default theory and the psychology of lying and deception detection. Curr. Opin. Psychol. **47**, 101380 (2022)

60. Falk, E., Scholz, C.: Persuasion, influence, and value: perspectives from communication and social neuroscience. Annu. Rev. Psychol. **69**, 329–356 (2018)

61. Schultz, W.: Dopamine reward prediction error coding. Dialogues Clin. Neurosci. **18**(1), 23–32 (2016)

62. Fischer, P., Lea, S.E.G., Evans, K.M.: Why do individuals respond to fraudulent scam communications and lose money? The psychological determinants of scam compliance. J. Appl. Soc. Psychol. **43**(10), 2060–2072 (2013)

63. Mueller, E.A., Wood, S.A., Hanoch, Y., Huang, Y., Reed, C.L.: Older and wiser: age differences in susceptibility to investment fraud: the protective role of emotional intelligence. J. Elder Abuse Negl. **32**(2), 152–172 (2020)

64. Ueno, D., et al.: Mild cognitive decline is a risk factor for scam vulnerability in older adults. Front. Psych. **12**, 685451 (2021)

65. Samanez-Larkin, G.R., Knutson, B.: Decision making in the ageing brain: changes in affective and motivational circuits. Nat. Rev. Neurosci. **16**(5), 278–289 (2015)
66. Fenton, L., et al.: Cognitive and neuroimaging correlates of financial exploitation vulnerability in older adults without dementia: implications for early detection of Alzheimer's disease. Neurosci. Biobehav. Rev. **140**, 104773 (2022)

# Author Index

A. Marcus et al. (Eds.): HCII 2024, LNCS 15380, pp. 409–410, 2025.
https://doi.org/10.1007/978-3-031-76821-7

# GPSR Compliance

*The European Union's (EU) General Product Safety Regulation (GPSR) is a set of rules that requires consumer products to be safe and our obligations to ensure this.*

*If you have any concerns about our products, you can contact us on ProductSafety@springernature.com*

In case Publisher is established outside the EU, the EU authorized representative is:

Springer Nature Customer Service Center GmbH
Europaplatz 3
69115 Heidelberg, Germany

The manufacturer's authorised representative in the EU is Springer
Nature Customer Service Centre GmbH, Europaplatz 3, 69115 Heidelberg,
Germany. If you have any concerns regarding our products, please
contact ProductSafety@springernature.com

Printed and bound by CPI Group (UK) Ltd, Croydon, CR0 4YY

27/04/2026

02097845-0008